Margaret Brewer

HEATH SOCIAL RELATIONS SERIES
JEROME DAVIS, *General Editor*

AN INTRODUCTION TO SOCIOLOGY. By JEROME DAVIS, Yale University, and HARRY ELMER BARNES, New School for Social Research (with L. L. BERNARD, Washington University, SEBA ELDRIDGE, University of Kansas, FRANK H. HANKINS, Smith College, ELLSWORTH HUNTINGTON, Yale University, and MALCOLM WILLEY, University of Minnesota).

READINGS IN SOCIOLOGY. Selected by the Authors of *An Introduction to Sociology* to supplement that volume.

IMMIGRATION AND RACE ATTITUDES. By EMORY S. BOGARDUS, Chairman of the Department of Sociology and Director of the School of Social Welfare, University of Southern California.

INTRODUCTION TO SOCIAL PSYCHOLOGY: MIND IN SOCIETY. By RADHAKAMAL MUKERJEE, Head of the Department of Economics and Sociology, Lucknow University, and NARENDRA NATH SEN-GUPTA, Head of the Department of Experimental Psychology, Calcutta University.

ECONOMICS AND ETHICS. By JOHN A. HOBSON, Formerly Lecturer on Economics, Oxford University.

CRIMINOLOGY. By ROBERT H. GAULT, Professor of Psychology, Northwestern University, Editor of the *Journal of Criminal Law and Criminology*.

THE CONCEPTS OF SOCIOLOGY. By EARLE EDWARD EUBANK, Head of the Department of Sociology, University of Cincinnati.

THE BEGINNINGS OF TO-MORROW: AN INTRODUCTION TO THE SOCIOLOGY OF THE GREAT SOCIETY. By HERBERT ADOLPHUS MILLER, Lecturer on Social Economy, Bryn Mawr.

IMMIGRATION AND ASSIMILATION. By HANNIBAL GERALD DUNCAN, Department of Economics, Political Science, and Sociology, University of Colorado.

AN INTRODUCTION TO EDUCATIONAL SOCIOLOGY. By Ross L. FINNEY, Late Associate Professor of Educational Sociology, University of Minnesota, and LESLIE D. ZELENY, Professor of Sociology, State Teachers College, St. Cloud, Minnesota.

RACE RELATIONS: ADJUSTMENT OF WHITES AND NEGROES IN THE UNITED STATES. By WILLIS D. WEATHERFORD, President and Professor of Applied Anthropology, Y.M.C.A. Graduate School, and CHARLES S. JOHNSON, Professor of Sociology, Fisk University.

In Press or in Preparation

HISTORY OF SOCIAL THOUGHT. By HARRY ELMER BARNES, New School for Social Research, and HOWARD BECKER, Smith College.

THE FAMILY. By HORNELL HART, Professor of Social Ethics, Hartford Theological Seminary.

INTRODUCTION TO THE STUDY OF SOCIAL STATISTICS. By ROBERT MORSE WOODBURY.

COMMUNITY ORGANIZATION. By E. C. LINDEMAN, Chairman of the Department of Sociology, New York School of Social Work, and Lecturer, New School for Social Research.

MENTAL HYGIENE. By FRANKWOOD E. WILLIAMS.

RACE RELATIONS

Adjustment of Whites and Negroes in the United States

BY

WILLIS D. WEATHERFORD, Ph.D.

President and Professor of Applied Anthropology
Y. M. C. A. Graduate School

AUTHOR OF

Negro Life in the South, Present Forces in Negro Progress,
The Negro from Africa to America

AND

CHARLES S. JOHNSON, Litt.D.

Professor of Sociology
Fisk University

AUTHOR OF

The Negro in American Civilization

D. C. HEATH AND COMPANY

BOSTON   NEW YORK   CHICAGO
ATLANTA   SAN FRANCISCO   DALLAS
LONDON

COPYRIGHT, 1934, BY
WILLIS D. WEATHERFORD AND CHARLES S. JOHNSON

No part of the material covered by this copyright may be reproduced in any form without written permission of the publisher.

3 F 5

301.451
W362r

PRINTED IN THE UNITED STATES OF AMERICA

INTRODUCTION

By JEROME DAVIS

Yale University

ONE of the most complex and difficult problems confronting American democracy is that of race relations between whites and Negroes. Under slavery, when the number of free Negroes was negligible and the vast majority of the race were in a position of complete subordination, the problem of race adjustment, though often troublesome, was comparatively simple, and the infrequency of slave uprisings affords evidence that an adjustment was reached and maintained. With emancipation, serious complications — social, economic, and political — were introduced. Propertyless, for the most part unskilled, and with the habit of depending on their "white folks" strongly established, the Negroes were the easy victims of unscrupulous Carpetbaggers and Scalawags who exploited them for political purposes, and by their activities did much to intensify if not create the bitterness that marked relations between North and South, and between southern whites and Negroes, during the Reconstruction era. Until recent years the problem of race relations between whites and Negroes has presented itself acutely only in the South. For decades after emancipation the Negroes remained in the rural areas of the southern states. But the industrial emergency created by the World War and the reduction of immigration caused a vast migration of Negroes to the North, where they have remained in large numbers; with the decline of agriculture and the increasing urbanization of American life, it seems unlikely that they can ever be returned to their former economic status. Their future is linked in a larger measure than before with that of American industry and business generally. Relations between whites and Negroes, no longer a sectional matter, are assuming increasing importance in our national life, both in the North and in the South. Race relations has thus become a field which demands the intelligent attention of every educated citizen.

The authors of this book are leaders in the attempt to work out a basis for intelligent and mutually tolerant relations between the two races. One is a white man, the other a Negro. To them, much of the maladjustment that unquestionably exists appears to be due to mutual lack of knowledge of the fundamental aspects of the problem. Whites and Negroes, though living side by side, have only superficial acquaintance with each other. Proceeding on the theory that knowledge begets sympathy, they analyze and discuss factually and candidly various aspects of the problem of race relations between whites and Negroes in the United States, relying on the historical, sociological, and statistical data which they adduce, to prove their contention that "sweeping generalizations about either race are apt to be largely false." They do not minimize the difficulties confronting both the whites and Negroes in their relationships, and they propose no easy solutions; they do, however, explode many popular fallacies, and it is safe to say that if every community could approach the problem in the spirit of the authors of this volume, much of the problem itself would be well on the way to adjustment.

PREFACE

THE United States is not the only spot in the world where race friction is found. Wherever two races of differing economic status, of differing culture, or of differing characteristics are set side by side in anything like equal numbers, there are apt to arise conflict and antagonism. The more closely these differing groups are thrown together the more severe is apt to be the shock. The very fact that the size of the world has been greatly decreased, through developments in means of communication and the consequent ease of contact between areas once isolated and remote, has raised a world problem of race relations. The world has become a neighborhood, and if neighborliness does not characterize all the groups, there will of necessity be unfriendliness and friction. It is this fact of juxtaposition of all races that has given rise to much anxiety whether the world can become a brotherhood. "Never has there been any period of the world's history," says Putnam Weale, "in which racial problems were invested with such consummate interest as they now are." [1] Speaking of the desire of the white man to dominate the world, Basil Mathews says it has created many problems and "of these world problems, the first, the greatest, the most momentous on every ground is the very one that is created by the white man's expansion, which has caused him to 'farm the world.' It is the race problem." [2] In facing this intermingling of the races, Lothrop Stoddard says: "A better reading of history must bring home the truth that the basic factor in human affairs is not politics but race." [3] Weale thinks: "There exists a widespread racial antipathy founded on color — an animal-like instinct, if you will, but an instinct which must remain in existence until the world becomes utopia. It is this instinct which seems to forbid really frank intercourse and equal treatment." [4]

That there is widespread race friction no one who knows the facts would dare deny, but that it is as hopeless as some of these writers would claim seems quite beyond the belief of many who know the

[1] *The Conflict of Colour*, p. 85.
[2] *The Clash of Color*, pp. 17–18.
[3] *The Rising Tide of Color against White World-Supremacy*, p. 5.
[4] *The Conflict of Colour*, p. 110.

facts intimately. But the friction which does exist is serious enough that all those who are hoping for a better world must reckon honestly with this problem. A better understanding between the races is undoubtedly the central issue if we are to have peace, harmony, and good will.

To have this better understanding certainly two things are necessary: namely, knowledge and sympathy. Comparatively few persons know the life of other peoples. This knowledge is not easy to acquire. Our prejudice, our differing background, our diverse interests, stand as barriers against such knowledge. Dr. Cuthbert Hall, who was many years ago Barrows lecturer to India, called attention to the fact that few Occidentals ever knew or understood Orientals. Our long background of thinking makes us almost incapable of understanding these people who seem to approach life from an angle opposite to that from which we approach it.

Nor is this strange when we think of the difficulty one person has in understanding another person. Across that chasm of personal distinctness it is not easy to throw a bridge of understanding. If to the fact of personal distinctness we add difference of sex, the difficulty is greater. If then we add difference of customs peculiar to various nations, and then difference of racial background, it is no wonder that people do not understand persons of another race. Facts just do not cross these barriers easily.

Furthermore, many seem not to want to understand. There is lack of sympathy, lack of trust. The first law of human friendship, according to Dr. Henry Churchill King, is mutual self-revelation and answering trust.[1] The two responses are reciprocal. I cannot reveal myself to you unless you trust me. No man has ever yet revealed his best self in the presence of criticism or suspicion. But on the other hand one cannot be trusted until he has so revealed himself as to prove worthy of trust. The more I reveal myself to you the more can you trust me if I am true, and the more you trust me the more can I reveal my soul to you. If this law holds for mutual understanding and good will between individuals, equally does it hold between races. Here perhaps has been the greatest failure on the part of those who would understand another people. We do not look down to those whom we trust. We do not condescend to those whom we really desire to understand. One reason why white men have so rarely understood colored men is that they have not trusted

[1] *The Laws of Friendship, Human and Divine*, p. 55 ff.

them sufficiently. They have expected other races to reveal themselves without self-manifestation on the part of the white man and without trust or real appreciation.

It is the attempt to meet just these problems that has called forth this volume. The authors feel that few persons have either the opportunity or the time to know the facts about the other race beside which they live. White people do not know the Negro, though many of them assume they do. There is no commoner word in the South than the statement of a southerner that he has been reared in the midst of Negroes, and hence he knows them. But a little probing will prove that neither from the standpoint of facts nor from the standpoint of sympathy can he make good his statement. Nor is it much more likely that the Negro knows the white man simply because he has met members of the white group every day of his life. The conditions have been against the two races coming to know each other. All too frequently the white man knows the ignorance or poverty or crime of the Negro without knowing his better life, and conversely the Negro is apt to see the domineering, the selfishness, the arrogance of the white man, while failing to see his virtues. The authors of this book believe that sweeping generalizations about either race are apt to be largely false — that there are so many facts that should be known, and so much of emotional background that is not usually seen, that understanding has been most difficult. They believe that present customs and patterns of thinking root themselves in the past; hence the past needs to be seen in its relation to the present. They frankly recognize that they themselves have a traditional background, which in spite of every honest effort may color their thought of other races. It has seemed to them highly desirable, therefore, to have a white man and a Negro collaborate in this study. Conference together has proven to them that their sympathies and motives are virtually identical, even if their interpretation of facts has not always been the same. They have been rather agreeably surprised to find how closely their interpretations have agreed. But they have believed it wise to let such honest differences as do exist stand. That decision at least will give those who read the volume a chance to see how one member from each of the two races views the problem. Each writer has been the sole arbiter as to what he would say. His initials appear in the table of contents after each chapter he wrote. He therefore does not place responsibility on the co-author for any of his own interpretations.

PREFACE

So far as the writers know, no textbook in sociology has heretofore been undertaken by a white man and a Negro as joint authors. It is their hope that others may try a similar task. What we need at present is more opportunities for white and colored to undertake common tasks, for the final desideration of understanding is coöperation. They therefore send this book out as a concrete expression of racial coöperation and, they believe, of racial good will and understanding.

W. D. WEATHERFORD
CHARLES S. JOHNSON

CONTENTS

PART I. THE PHILOSOPHY OF RACE RELATIONS

CHAPTER			PAGE
I.	The Origin of Race and Theories of Race	(C. S. J.)	3
II.	Negro Culture	(W. D. W.)	22
III.	The Basis of Racial Antagonisms	(C. S. J.)	50
IV.	Principles of Race Adjustment	(W. D. W.)	65

PART II. AMERICAN NEGRO SLAVERY

V.	The African Background of the American Negro	(C. S. J.)	83
VI.	The Origin of Negro Slavery	(C. S. J.)	99
VII.	Rise and Fall of Slavery in the New World	(W. D. W.)	113
VIII.	Economic Aspects of Slavery	(C. S. J.)	146
IX.	Life on the Southern Plantation	(W. D. W.)	164
X.	The Attitude of the Churches toward the Negro during Slavery	(W. D. W.)	183
XI.	Social Dogmas in Race Relations	(C. S. J.)	216
XII.	The Free Negro	(C. S. J.)	238
XIII.	Slave Laws and Insurrection among the Slaves	(W. D. W.)	260
XIV.	The Effect of Slavery on the Negro	(C. S. J.)	274
XV.	The Effect of Slavery on the White People	(W. D. W.)	290

PART III. THE PRESENT STATUS OF THE NEGRO AND RACE RELATIONS

XVI.	Present Economic Relations	(C. S. J.)	309
XVII.	Negro Migrations	(C. S. J.)	331
XVIII.	Problems of Education	(W. D. W.)	349
XIX.	Health of the Negro	(C. S. J.)	368
XX.	Home Life of the Negro	(C. S. J.)	384
XXI.	Civic and Political Status of the Negro	(W. D. W.)	403
XXII.	Negro Crime and the Treatment of Criminals	(W. D. W.)	424

CONTENTS

CHAPTER		PAGE
XXIII.	The Cultural Development of the Negro (C. S. J.)	442
XXIV.	Negro Literature . . . . (W. D. W.)	459
XXV.	Negro Leadership and the Growth of Race Pride . . . . (W. D. W.)	488
XXVI.	Changing Attitudes of White People . . (W. D. W.)	507
XXVII.	Programs Looking toward Solution or Amelioration of Race Relations . . . (W. D. W.)	519
XXVIII.	The Changing Attitude of the Negro. . (C. S. J.)	534
XXIX.	Can There Be a Separate Negro Culture? (C. S. J.)	543
	Bibliography	556
	Index	577

PART I
THE PHILOSOPHY OF RACE RELATIONS

CHAPTER I

THE ORIGIN OF RACE AND THEORIES OF RACE

The term "race" has a factual content; but it also has an emotional content which persistently obscures its meaning. This curious dualism marks an important division between what is scientifically known about race and what is uncritically believed about it. The meaning of race is no mystery to the ordinary man on the street; it is to him obvious in many ways, and he can defend his certitude and his definition through simple appeal to common sense. The older anthropologists, as late as twenty-five or thirty years ago, were almost as positive as the layman, and committed themselves to a considerable array of definitions of race and classification of races. Most of these definitions and classifications are interesting today largely as curious phases of the early history of anthropology. For they have been not only numerous but, in most important respects, mutually contradictory.

Present-day scientists, despite the layman's reliance upon observation and common sense, are by no means so certain as the earlier anthropologists. The more "race" is analyzed scientifically, the more difficult it becomes to define. Says Melville J. Herskovits, "One characteristic of race is that if you analyze it sufficiently you analyze it out of existence." Another anthropologist, in urging scientific caution on the matter, declares that there is nothing so misleading as that which is supposed to be self-evident.[1] For thousands of years it was "self-evident" that the sun revolved around the earth.

Strangely enough, it is usually on matters the investigation of which is regarded as unnecessary or undesirable or wicked that one finds the most resolute and aggressive certitude. Many religious dogmas, which for various reasons do not lend themselves to verification by scientific test, may be and frequently are held with the same unchallengeable conviction. Although race and religion may be quite different values, the behavior patterns in relation to them are essentially the same.

[1] Alfred L. Kroeber, *Anthropology*, p. 59.

Strictly speaking, race is a biological term and has to do with physical characters based on blood relationship. In dealing with race, therefore, it is necessary to keep in mind the distinction between biological and social phenomena. For what is usually meant by the term has more to do with cultural and social questions than with biological differentiation. In one sense it may be said, despite its paradoxical sound, that a truly scientific study of race has little, if anything, to do with race relations. It is not strange in a world of different peoples, who are unlike in many physical as well as cultural traits, that both layman and scientist should seek explanation of these differences, and attempt, for their own convenience at least, some classification of them. But races, even as we know these classifications now, are scarcely more than "a convenient way of grouping these types for reference."

It is customary to think of race as an age-old concept. According to Jean Finot,[1] the first writer to use it in the modern sense was François Taut, who derived it from *radix*, a root, and Taut thought of it as "the extraction of man, dog, or horse." The scholar who introduced it to science was Georges Buffon, and he described it merely as a variety caused and fixed by climatic influences and habits. The fact that the term originally referred to man and the lower animals alike may explain the early assumption that specie differences existed in man as well as in the lower animals and in plants. Geoffroy Saint-Hilaire defined race as comprising "a succession of individuals born of one another, and distinguished by certain characteristics which have become permanent." James C. Prichard, a little later, amended the definition to read "the collected individuals forming a race present certain characteristics more or less common to all, and transmissible by heredity whilst the origin of these characteristics is left on one side and held back." According to Félix Pouchet, who believed in polygenesis, "race" meant simply "the different natural groups of the human family." Johann Friedrich Blumenbach, "the father of anthropology," was one of the first to note that "the innumerable varieties of mankind run into one another by insensible degrees." Paul Topinard, a generation later, held that "race, in the present state of things, is an abstract conception, a notion of continuity in discontinuity, of unity in diversity." Modern anthropologists accept the term cautiously and somewhat broadly as denoting a subdivision of the species which inherits its

[1] *Race Prejudice*, pp. 51–52.

characteristics. Living creatures are reckoned to belong to the same species, Friedrich O. Hertz[1] declares, if they breed successfully when crossed, and if their offspring possess the same capacity without limits.

Classifications can only be rough generalizations, and generalizations are easily misleading. Types are drawn from what appear to be the most frequently occurring traits and are more or less an abstraction.[2] They tell nothing of the hereditary composition or range of variation of a population. If as many as ten independent traits are taken for a thousand people, not ten persons can be found who correspond to type. There is, indeed, so little clarity in the term "race" that Dr. Franz Boas has preferred to substitute the less questionable term "populations."

In spite of a surface obviousness of difference there is no single satisfactory criterion for establishing a reliable test of the physical varieties of mankind.[3] A definition to be exact should "state those attributes which distinguish a particular thing and which pertain to it to the exclusion of everything else." Being unable to define race, it is not strange that scholars have been unable to classify races. Lamarck pointed out many years ago that "divisions are only artificial names, for, in truth, nature has formed neither classes nor orders, neither families nor sorts, nor species." Linnæus, who was the first to attempt a scientific classification in the field of natural science, divided men into three sections: sapiens, ferus, and monstruosus. He subdivided sapiens into Europus, Asiaticus, and Africus. Cuvier followed with a classification and divided mankind into three races; Saint-Hilaire, Leibnitz, and Kant divided mankind into four; Blumenbach, into five; Buffon, into six; Prichard, into seven; Agassiz, into eight; Pickering, Haeckel, and Muller, into eleven; Bory St. Vincent, into fifteen; Topinard, into eighteen; Morton, into thirty-two; and Crawford, into sixty-two.[4] Certain anthropological congresses established as many as one hundred twenty races,[5] and Dr. George R. Gliddon, an early American anthropologist, accumulated the enormous total of one hundred fifty. It is evident that, although all of these were reputable scholars, there existed serious misunderstanding about race and races.

[1] *Race and Civilization*, p. 20.
[2] Franz Boas, *Anthropology and Modern Life*, p. 22.
[3] Alfred M. Tozzer, *Social Origins and Social Continuities*, p. 63.
[4] Friedrich O. Hertz, *Race and Civilization*, p. 20.
[5] Jean Finot, *Race Prejudice*, p. 55.

The structural criteria of race most commonly used have not proved satisfactory. Some of the more familiar of these criteria are color, texture of hair, stature, brain size, and head form. There are scores of others. The most careful students of comparative anatomy employ as many as seventy structural traits.

Color is, perhaps, the most obvious criterion of race difference, and has been, accordingly, the one most frequently used. However, all races are pigmented, some more deeply than others. Only albinos are without pigment. The many varieties of pigmentation in the human race are the result of accumulation and distribution of different quantities of exactly the same pigment. The chemical base is the same, but research so far has failed to reveal the origin of pigment. What is perhaps most significant is the extent of racial overlapping in deep pigmentation. The color of Caucasoid whites varies from bluish or pinkish white to tan, brown, and even near black, while that of the Negroid blacks varies from yellowish brown to various shades of brown to full shiny black.[1] The dark whites are darker than the light Negroes.

Texture of hair is regarded by Kroeber as one of the most important criteria because it is unusually stable in racial inheritance. Caucasoid types vary from straight to wavy to curly hair; Negroid types from medium to coarse, thick curls to scattered spirals. Difference in hair texture is explained by the shape of the hair in cross section, and the angle of the root of the hair in the skin.[2] There is likewise overlapping in stature. All variations within the Caucasoid and Mongoloid groups fall within the range of the Negroid, from very short to very tall. Some of the shortest (Pygmies) and some of the tallest peoples (Zulus) are Negroes.

In cephalic index both the Negro and the North European are dolichocephalic. Brain size is related to stature and body size, and differences between sexes of the same race are greater than the differences observed among the three racial classifications. This significant degree of overlapping thus very largely reduces the question of physical differences between races to a matter of statistics. Although in a scientific sense the question of race is greatly confused, at least the three major classifications of white, yellow, and black races can be distinguished.

[1] See Aleš Hrdlička, "Human Races," in *Human Biology and Racial Welfare*, edited by Edmund V. Cowdry, p. 160, and Carl J. Warden, *The Evolution of Human Behavior*, p. 195.   [2] Carl J. Warden, *The Evolution of Human Behavior*, p. 197.

Since Darwin it has been the custom to think in terms of the evolutionary development of structure in man, and to relate this development to a hierarchy of the racial stocks. Here again, as Dr. Boas has shown, there is such striking confusion as to make hazardous as yet any generalizations about the quality of races in this respect.[1] The basis upon which any comparison of anatomical traits in evolution can be built is the anatomical form of the ape. Certain individual traits can be placed in an ascending series. However, each of the principal racial classifications shows a different arrangement of these independent traits. The Mongoloid and Caucasoid types are farthest removed from animal forms in shape of the nose and in length of arm, while the Negroid type is farthest removed in shape of lips, in loss of heavy eyebrow ridges, and, along with the Mongoloid, in loss of hairiness of face and body. It may be assumed that each group developed certain specializations of form. The hair texture of the Caucasoids and of the Mongoloids is nearer than the hair texture of the Negroids to that of the lower animals; the short head hair of the Negroid seems to be a unique specialization.

The important fact about races, so far established, seems to be that, despite a degree of general overlapping in practically all physical traits, and despite the statistical stresses of common traits sufficient to recognize different populations, no single trait or known combination of traits appears to have any particular biological significance. With respect to structure, it is not certain that variation between groups in all physical traits is due to heredity. Stature, for example, may respond to variation in nutrition. The studies of Boas show that head form within the same racial group may change under different environment. Other studies indicate that body forms may be influenced by occupation, and the shape and length of the legs and arms may be influenced by posture and use. We have racial heredity only when all individuals share certain characteristic anatomical features. The important fact is not the large classificatory differences, says Dr. Boas, but the capabilities of family lines. There are many different family lines in each of our present race classifications. To the scientist personal heredity is more important than racial classifications.

The question of function is closely related to that of structure, for it is, presumably, upon function that social behavior rests. So far as anyone knows at present, no racial differences of any importance

[1] *Anthropology and Modern Life*, p. 38.

exist in basic bodily activities. There are variations within racial groups, between individuals, and within the same individual at different times. The variations are greater within than between groups. The normal temperature, pulse rate, and respiration are the same for adults in all groups under the same environment.[1] Even in the matter of adjustment to climate, as Dr. Ellsworth Huntington's studies indicate, the best climate for human energy output is about the same for all races. The sensory and motor capacities of mankind seem to be independent of race.[2] Differences in susceptibility to diseases, in most cases, appear to be less racial than regional, except where a new disease is introduced to a people before an immunity has been built up.[3]

With the matter of the functioning of the brain there has been greatest concern, because of its bearing upon the question of racial mentality. All that can be said by anthropologists at the present time is that there may be racial differences in mentality but they have not yet been satisfactorily established by any scientific test. There have been psychological tests which tend to show that the Negroes score lower than the whites, but it has been made evident that differential environmental factors entered to an undetermined degree. However, the more careful the test the smaller the differences found. In no test, however inadequate, has overlapping been absent. It is impossible, according to these scientists, to say whether one group has a larger number of original minds than another, because of the differences in cultures. Generally considered, function appears to be less hereditary than structural. The student of race, to the extent that he desires his work to have scientific value, would perhaps do well to heed the caution of Dr. Aleš Hrdlička, of the Smithsonian Institution, given at the end of his summary of the studies of the anthropology of the American Negro. He says that this scientific anthropology "is still barely above its beginnings. Almost everything remains to be done, or done over, and better or more fully, according to present standards and requirements." [4]

The question of race and culture has been an important one in the evaluation of races. Because some races have had unique cultural

[1] Carl J. Warden, *The Evolution of Human Behavior*, p. 202.
[2] Thomas R. Garth, *Race Psychology*, p. 208.
[3] Carl J. Warden, *The Evolution of Human Behavior*, p. 202.
[4] "Anthropology of the American Negro," *American Journal of Physical Anthropology*, April–June, 1927, pp. 205–235.

traits it has frequently and naturally been assumed that culture depends upon race. "This is a point in the discussion of culture," Dr. Clark Wissler warns, "where everyone should watch his step, for it seems that no one can handle the question of race in cold blood."[1] Though much has been written about the question, and this largely of a political nature, it has not yet been seriously investigated. Dr. Wissler mentions, on the one hand, the mutual fitness of different hereditary groups to participate in cultures other than their own, and on the other hand, the reasonableness of assuming that, although culture traits are not innate, the chief producing mechanism of culture is innate. Thus, the issue is carried back to the familiar question of differences in racial mentality.

The theory of the interdependence of race and culture is commonly based upon the assumption that the evolution of culture and the evolution of man go along together. As Dr. Wissler points out, if this were so, for every important advance in culture there must be a corresponding change in the nervous system. But changes in culture have been too frequent and too erratic to be correlated with morphological changes, which occur only over hundreds of thousands of years, and Dr. Jacob R. Kantor has added to this scepticism the further declaration that "no organic basis for culture, either as things, processes, ideas, beliefs, or as statistical or group conduct, is discoverable, for such a basis is lacking even for complex individual psychological activities."[2] Instead of a particular culture being dependent upon the innate mental endowment of the members of that group, it is perhaps just as reasonable a possibility that the mentality of the group depends upon "the kind of objects they find in their group or take away from other groups." Culture, it is known, depends upon many factors other than race, and in evidence of an actual independence of race and culture is the fact that they vary independently from time to time, and that the distribution of similar culture traits does not follow racial lines.

It must be obvious that when considerations of race are detached from social problems the issue becomes fairly academic and remote. The origin of races takes on an added temporal remoteness. The first differentiation of races occurred so long ago that scholars can only speculate on racial origins, and leave to time and chance dis-

---

[1] *Man and Culture*, p. 285.
[2] "Anthropology, Race, Psychology, and Culture," *American Anthropologist*, April, 1925, p. 279.

covery such fragments of verification of these hypotheses as may come. It can be said that there is more evidence that all races derive from a common stem than that they have different origins. Practically all reputable scholars have now discarded the theory of polygenesis. Although there is a traditional belief, deduced through some Scriptural implication, that man was created in the year 4004 B.C., the scientific evidence points to the age of man as being somewhere between 500,000 and 1,000,000 years, and there is evidence that definitely human types were widely distributed over the eastern hemisphere 50,000 years ago and possibly earlier.

The point of origin of man is unknown. Darwin gave reasons for his belief that Africa was the cradle of mankind. The discovery of important human skeletal remains in Asia, and the observation that there are still distributed about the edge of Asia some of the most primitive peoples of the world, have suggested Asia as the original home of man. But there have also been discovered remains of primitive human types of vast antiquity in South Africa, Europe, China, and America.

It is reckoned that the original racial differentiation occurred some time before the end of the Pleistocene period, allowing, by various estimates, from 200,000 to 500,000 years for this process of raciation.[1] In the subsequent migrations which are presumed to have occurred, the branch of the original stock which moved southward (assuming that Asia was the point of origin) into Africa became distinguished as Negroid; the ancestors of the Caucasoids moved southward also but stopped in Europe, southern Asia, and northern Africa; while the ancestors of the Mongoloids remained principally in Asia.

This separation, however, does not explain the different physical specializations which developed. Various theories have been advanced to account for the differences in color and various features. One of these is the Darwinian notion of variation through natural selection in the struggle for existence and in isolation. More recent students have advanced the theory of mutations to explain this racial differentiation. By this is meant merely some sudden and inexplicable change in the form of the organs. But how or why these mutations occurred is one of the profoundest mysteries of the evolutionary process. To these theories has been added still another speculation by Sir Arthur Keith, which gives importance to the influence of certain glandular factors in raciation. He regards the pituitary gland as

[1] Carl J. Warden, *The Evolution of Human Behavior*, p. 136.

"one of the principal pinions in the machinery" which regulates certain recognizable marks of race.

There are other factors, less remote and less obscured by the primordial processes, which merit attention in any consideration of the physical fact of races. The migrations of all races of man from the earliest period have brought them into contact with other groups, with the inevitable result of race crossing. All races can interbreed and have interbred. Kroeber says: "The lines of demarcation between races have time and again been obliterated by interbreeding."[1] There is no known case in history of two races in contact in which racial intermixture did not result. For this reason there are no pure races or subdivisions of the races existing today, except, perhaps, the Pygmy.

The social aspects of race lie not so much in the differences themselves as in the attempts to give them meaning. Theories of race and of race differences are of much more recent origin than race, and have been responsible for more conflict, arrogance, and persecution. These theories have in many cases not even pretended to be scientific. Being political and social in both character and inspiration, the dominating motive has more often been action than the quest for truth.

Race theories have a natural history, and this history is of great importance to the study of race relations. For the origins of these theories we must look, not to anthropology, but to those events and complex currents of social thought which began to take full expression in the eighteenth century.[2] This period witnessed the conflict of the new and liberal ideas regarding the rights of man with the older doctrines of the divine right of classes. The arguments, philosophic and scientific, in defense of the rights of remnant feudal classes were articulated bluntly, perhaps, for the first time, with the expansion of knowledge concerning the different peoples of the world. Following the Age of Discovery and the further explorations of science into language and culture, these arguments tended to crystallize around race. These cross currents of thought are of so great importance in the history of race theories that they should be given more than passing reference.

Slavery as well as feudalism had long existed in medieval Europe,

[1] *Anthropology*, p. 36.
[2] For an illuminating and extended discussion of social and philosophical theories of European scholars of this period see: Théophile Simar, *Étude Critique sur la Formation de la Doctrine des Races Au XVIIIe Siècle et Son Expansion Au XIXe Siècle*. This work has been translated by A. A. Goldenweiser as *Race Myth, A Study of the Notion of Race*.

but both of these had involved class and culture rather than race. The progress of the natural sciences during the Renaissance had helped to shake off the ancient domination of the medieval church, and to turn attention from otherworldliness to man's humanity. Scientific knowledge, significantly, was extended to the field of geography, which led to exploration and discovery and the first consciousness of new people and, more important still, new wealth. The doctrine of the rights of man was a normal outgrowth of the earlier emphasis of the Renaissance on the good life and the perfectibility of human personality, an ideal brought to classic maturity of expression by Rousseau and Montesquieu. The French philosophical writers of the period reveal a constant contest of ideas between the new rights of the masses and the remnant prerogatives of the nobles.

Throughout the Middle Ages the nobility had looked with scorn upon the common people. There is, indeed, a familiar pattern from this period in the claim of the nobility that the peasants, who of course were not Negroes, were descended from Ham and condemned by Noah to slavery. Before the notion of race was introduced as an explanation, the nobles, seeking some justification for their class position, had referred their origin to certain legendary heroes. Hertz [1] cites instances of French scholars, as late as the seventeenth century, tracing the ruling class of France back to Françoin, a son of Hector. A battle of theories, almost entirely political in significance, was waged on the question of the origin of the French.

Savants argued, for example, that the French were divided into (a) the nobles, who descended from German conquerers, and (b) the masses, who were descended from the Celts and Romans. Count de Boulainvilliers could thus prove the legitimacy of the claim of the nobler stock to sovereignty. The freeing of the serfs with the collapse of feudalism, he thought, was merely a social incident that had upset the natural order of things. The issue was made increasingly sharp with each new assertion of the rights of the people to power. Supported by a growing democratic sentiment, the sovereignty of the third estate, the people, was finally and forcefully proclaimed, in an impassioned assertion of Abbé Sieyès, just preceding the Revolution, that it is a nation of itself.

The amazing concourse of physical discoveries and the quickened intelligence of European scholars virtually changed social attitudes

[1] *Race and Civilization*, p. 5.

and human nature as profoundly as they altered the trend of history. The extension of the art of printing, for example, helped to shift the center of control from the clergy and nobility to those with a burning message for the people. By no other means could Voltaire's devastating attacks, first upon the Roman church and eventually upon all religion, have so dominated European thought. Nor could Rousseau's tremendous doctrine of the sovereignty of the people have reached them. It was in Montesquieu's *The Spirit of Laws* that there appeared that happy combination of words, "Liberty, Equality, and Fraternity," which became the battle cry of the French Revolution. Along with the generation of democratic sentiment there was, inevitably, the resistance of the nobility to such vulgar doctrines. They were fortunate in having on their side a persistent tradition of class division ordinarily difficult to break, scholars who could defend their contentions in learned terminology, property, and some political power. Thus, their resistance manifested itself in learned rationalizations of their status and, as a means of insuring national unity, in nationalistic programs.

The vagaries of religion during the Reformation had resulted in the divorce of spiritual and theological life from the common business of life. This separation was, no doubt, aided by the new spirit of materialism which had been generated as a result of the discovery of new countries, new peoples, and new wealth. There was evident a shift of emphasis from the idea of "spiritual power over everything to economic expediency in the struggle for wealth." It is not an accident that the secularization of political thought should be accompanied by the secularization of religious thought as manifest in the slave trade, which one writer has called the "first really Big Business in the world." [1]

During the early part of the nineteenth century in France, interest centered in retaining the gains of democracy. In England, the industrial revolution was gaining headway. Carlyle was one of the chief spokesmen in the intellectual sphere who tried to lay the ghost of democracy. The great initiator of human action to him was battle, and force the law. He railed at democracy. To him the man of force, the aristocrat, was ideal. In this glorification of diversity and predominance of action over speculation he helped prepare the ground for Anglo-Saxon imperialism. It is not strange that he came to be the favorite philosopher of the American slaveholders.

[1] Charles Duff, *This Human Nature*, p. 297.

In Germany, the chief spokesmen were concerned with establishing national unity. Herder, influenced by Rousseau, headed the cult of humanitarianism and cosmopolitanism. But Fichte, following the dictates of nationalism, became the prophet of the new state. To him there were only two kinds of Germans: pure and impure. It was not a matter of race but of cultural influence. Hegel, following Kant, synthesized the dreams of the rationalists for a universal society dominated by reason and the insistence of the Romanticists upon life and sentiment as over against reason. As Simar points out, there is a doctrine of predestination in Hegel: peoples rise, discharge their preordained mission, and fall before a younger people better armed for the struggle. Again, force was seen as the essential element of the state as well as the individual. The Romanticists stressed tradition as an historical power. They resisted revolutionary change, and glorified political quietude. Nationalistic feeling was stirred by such writers as Friedrich Schlegel and List. The historical philosophy of Pan-Germanism was here foreshadowed. The notion of race and nationality was an article of faith: "All people who speak the same language must form the same nation, because they belong to the same race!"

It was into this complex of ideas that the Aryan issue came. Philological and linguistic studies, which had both encouraged and been encouraged by the ideals of Pan-Germanism, Pan-Slavism, and Pan-Latinism, led to the discovery of the Sanscrit, the sacred language of Hindustan. Biblical tradition had suggested Asia as the cradle of the human race, and the Hindus, it could now be observed, lived nearest this source of civilization. There was rich romance in the hymns of the Rig-Veda and in the epics in which the Aryan conquest of the dark-skinned people was recorded. These mighty Aryans had one fixed social principle: they were sternly opposed to unions of any sort with the conquered peoples; they were conscious of the power and value of race, and of the purity of blood.

Scholars could embody in Aryanism the tri-logic of race, language, and nation advanced by Fichte. Out of this philological adventure there developed a confusion of race and caste. There was the problem of reconciling Aryan unity with racial and national diversity in Europe. It was this problem that created the opportunity for Count de Gobineau, who is regarded as the first enunciator of the doctrine of the inequality of the human races. In 1855 he gathered the scattered ideas of his period and systematized them in the now famous *Essay on the Inequality of the Human Races*. The solution suggested by Gobineau was that there was only one stock which was more or less pure, and that was the Germanic race. They were the inheritors of the torch of light and culture from the Aryans. The Latin races were impure because, although white, they were corrupted with Semitic and inferior Negro blood.

It is interesting that, although French, he made the Germanic peoples the chosen ones. He drew heavily and admittedly upon the old feudal theory as expressed in the earlier ideas of Counts Boulainvilliers and Montlosier; he admitted his hatred of democracy and of the new liberal ideas which had triumphed in France. His ideas were, however, tremendously popular in Germany and in America. Although lacking in science, his doctrine provided a convincing explanation of history, in the existence of some mysterious forces deriving their energy from nature; it regarded races as of different species; it attempted to found the principle of authority on biological heredity rather than on any personal merit. He succeeded in drawing to himself a considerable list of supporters. It was to be expected that his doctrine would win the support of the group indicated by him as the chosen people. There was, however, the further fact that the middle classes or bourgeoisie, who, in France at least, had supported the Revolution, were now beginning to feel their own power and becoming fearful of the aspirations of the proletariat. They also welcomed the opportunity to be incorporated into a great race that had been foreordained to rule.

Aryanism was accepted by hosts of scholars as well as less erudite laymen, despite the strikingly inconclusive results of virtually every attempt to investigate scientifically the existence of such a race. Beginning in a confusion of language with race, these scholars could not agree on where the Aryans came from, what they were like, how they lived, or what kind of culture they had. As a result of the persistent lure of this false light, the work of virtually every anthropologist of the period was vitiated, as present scientific judgment on the literature of the Aryan and the psychological attitudes supporting it reveals.

It is possible to trace the thread of this racial theory, in its effects upon mass attitudes toward Semitics and Negroes, from Gobineau almost in a family line. One of the most powerful advocates of Gobinism was Richard Wagner, the great German composer. He was not only a great musician but a nationalist through his own artistic medium. It was he who popularized the German myths and created for Germany the music which expressed its mood of imperialistic expansion. Wagner was anti-Semitic, although the stepson of a Jew. Dr. H. A. Miller traces his anti-Semitism to artistic pique over the first unfavorable reception of his music in 1850. This pique he registered in an article entitled "The Jew and His Music," which was in turn ridiculed by Jewish editors. His prejudice was reinforced; and as he gained in popularity, he was able to make it increasingly effective. He met Gobineau and directed the full current of his genius and popularity to the support of his doctrines. He "made" Gobineau. It is of no little significance that the next great popularizer of the Gobineau school was Houston S. Chamberlain, an Englishman in Germany, and that Chamberlain married Wagner's daughter. His book, *The Foundations of the Nineteenth Century*, was an exaltation of the Teutonic peoples. It laid the ground for a new theory of races which championed the strong and noble German people, with consequences which could be seen in the late World War. It was the direct progenitor of a still later theory of Nordicism promulgated with extraordinary effectiveness in America by Madison Grant and Lothrop Stoddard.

Chamberlain was, of course, not alone in the promotion of the theory of Teutonism. Historians, sociologists, economists, and military writers were at work under a common inspiration. It was characteristic of most of these writers to regard doctrines as stimulation to action, and as a means of glorification of imperialistic Germany. Said Chamberlain: "Pure science is a noble plaything. . . . The very fact that we are living beings gives us an infinitely rich and unfailing capacity of hitting upon the right thing even without learning wherever it is necessary."

The importance of Chamberlain's book to German nationalism and imperialism may be drawn from the fact that the German Emperor had it distributed among all the officers of the German army; and a substantial grant made possible free distribution to public and private libraries. The ex-Kaiser, Wilhelm II, sadly observes in his *Memories of My Life:* "The glory of Teutonism was first revealed and preached to an amazed Germany by Chamberlain's *Foundations of the Nineteenth Century*, but all in vain, as the collapse of the German people proves."

The racial theory most popular in England and America was, of course, Anglo-Saxonism, and it originated in a manner not very different from the others. The superior elect were in this case the English people. The theory is mentioned here primarily because it helps to illustrate the tendency of groups, under one guise or another, to postulate their own superiority over all other and different groups. The Anglo-Saxons, by this theory, were the born rulers of men — the world's great pioneers and adventurers, with an unsurpassed genius for political organization; the only true and pure descendants of the Aryans. Americans, as descendants of the Anglo-Saxons, shared the nobility of this race. Henry J. Ford [1] has traced this theory, which he refers to as "the Anglo-Saxon myth," to a papal suggestion going back to the year 731 A.D.

As Bede, a British monk, reports it: Gregory, an abbot of St. Andrew's Monastery in Rome and later Pope, observed some handsome slaves being offered for sale in the Forum and asked their nationality. They were described as "Angles." He promised to carry religion to them and later did actually send a missionary, who, however, went to the wrong place. Augustine went to the Saxon shore and he restored Christianity in Britain by Saxon aid alone. "None of the people," says Ford, "who invaded Britain as the Roman power declined were less entitled, indeed, to give their name to the country than the 'Angles.'" They soon disappeared as a distinct tribe, but in Rome the notion persisted that it was to the Angles that Augustine went, and so Angle-land remains its name.

Neither "England" nor "Anglo-Saxon" has any real descriptive value; they illustrate the futility of trying to trace racial antecedents by means of tribal names supplied by ancient chroniclers. It appears that the English stock was really Celtic, and that this group and the Teutonic group were about the same, and both of them language rather than racial groups. With respect to its purity, there is no more interesting record than that cited by Harry Elmer Barnes[2] of the ancestry of Darwin, which includes known strains from at least twenty-nine different lines of European stock, and no one has better claim to be called Anglo-Saxon than Darwin.

Within this people, according to the accounts of such scholars as Professor E. A. Freeman and Bishop Stubbs, were born "the germs out of which every free institution in the world has grown." The notion was based upon the ancient institution of the Mark, of which,

[1] "The Anglo-Saxon Myth," in *Readings from the American Mercury* (1926), edited by Grant C. Knight.
[2] *History and Social Intelligence*, p. 225.

according to Ford, the most assiduous scholars have been unable as yet to find a trace. Huxley declares that the myth has worked great "scientific and practical mischief." But it has been a cogent theory in bolstering the right of Anglo-Saxons and their descendants in America to rule, explore, and exploit.

Nordicism had its origin also in Germany, and very largely at the hands of scholars. It spoke a scientific language which was, however, given reckless handling by the popularizers of the theory. The great achievements of history were attributed to Nordics, as over against the Alpine and Mediterranean races. Eventually the theory, on such an obviously speculative and political basis, easily expanded to ridiculous extremes. Otto Hauser, for example, in his *Genie und Rasse* and *Der Blonde Mensch*, claimed that Jesus, a universally admitted Jew, was a Nordic because Mary was a blonde.[1] In America, as Peter Odegarde notes, the theory was incorporated by innuendo into our immigration laws. It constituted the "scientific" basis for the anti-Jewish, anti-South European, anti-Negro policy of the new Ku Klux Klan. Anthropologists today move warily around the theory or denounce it bluntly as myth and nonsense.

Despite the complex of theories, the phenomena observed in connection with race are likely to be as often social and cultural as racial, and race prejudice, as such, a particular class of social attitudes. The same phenomena which we call racial may be observed in relation to differences in religion and even differences in sex. It is only recently that men have ceased to justify their superiority over women by the same arguments of divine right employed in race. So close have these sentiments been at times that they have often been confused. Hegel, for example, less than a hundred years ago, pointed out that women are like plants, men like animals; the thinking of men is strong, vigorous, original; that of women goes on, one hardly knows how. R. N. Bradley in his *Racial Origins of English Character* actually tried to dismiss women from the superior Nordic race in one strange example of his reasoning. He says: "The purely Nordic women are probably rare, for in the nature of things they could not have been very numerous. . . . The Nordics were a male race."[2] Schopenhauer turned the force of his great intellect against women as well as Jews. The anti-racial manifestations in Germany under Chancellor Adolf Hitler relegate woman to her traditional rôle of subject sex.

[1] Frank H. Hankins, *The Racial Basis of Civilization*, p. 87, footnote.   [2] P. 119.

The situation of the Negro in America, says Dr. H. A. Miller, is one of the most common in human history. There is a parallel in the experience of practically every other conquered people. The expansion of the Roman Empire was supported by slaves. These slaves were of the same basic race as their masters, and are, interestingly enough, the present rulers of Europe who base their right to rule upon the divine right of race. One thing that race can do is furnish an identification of an economic group. It is not unlikely that, as long as we have groups even approximately separate in our civilization, there will be group and race consciousness; there will be demands for group or race purity, and theories to explain these group or race differences. Boas has observed analogous situations in animal societies in the tendency of some animals to live in open and others in closed societies. "The principles that hold societies together," he says, "vary enormously, but common to all of them is the feeling of antagonism against other parallel groups." [1]

One of the most common revelations of history is that wherever various peoples come into contact, either as a result of conquest, migration, or economic exploitation, the first condition is one of conflict between the two groups. There is disorganization of the culture of one or the other or both. The conflicts may be peaceful or violent, involving an immense array of elements. They involve language, family organization, economic organization, in fact the whole range of culture. But, as Dr. E. B. Reuter points out, conflict does not last forever. Some sort of adjustment eventually comes. This adjustment may or may not be the adjustment planned or hoped for by one race or the other as the only one acceptable to its principles. The struggle is long, and human attitudes become altered in the process. In this period of adjustment, race problems and race prejudice appear as the natural and inevitable accompaniment of the process.

The question of race relations is thus a complex of problems in the fields of biology and the social sciences — problems which, to the present, have been only partially investigated. Despite the fact that this is a sphere little known scientifically, there exist about most of the issues involved the greatest cocksureness in popular opinions, and the deepest and most persistent emotions. Any approach to these questions, then, must be made from a deliberately detached position. Like the question of race itself, the more race relations are

[1] *Anthropology and Modern Life*, p. 69.

dispassionately analyzed, the less formidable they become in the sense of being inherent and immutable phenomena. Since both are so largely social and cultural in content and effect, it becomes necessary to study these relations as a phase of our cultural and social process. To understand the process is, at least, a step in the direction of control.

PROBLEMS FOR STUDY

1. A distinction is made between biological and social factors in observed racial differences. What significance has this distinction for race relations?
2. In America any known degree of Negro blood classifies a person as a member of the Negro race. Does this situation hold for other races? If not, what factors, biological or social, account for this difference in the basis of racial classification?
3. Herskovits suggests that there has been developed in this country an American Negro type different in features and less variable among themselves than are many groups of less obvious and diverse mixture. Has this biological or social significance?
4. List the functional peculiarities of Negroes as a race which are not shared by other non-Negro groups.
5. Can the thesis of a racial temperament be sustained?
6. Race prejudice is sometimes justified on the grounds of the necessity for preserving the sanctity of the group and its cultural standards. Does this consideration justify race prejudice in Negro-white relations in America? Would the absence of race prejudice lower cultural standards?
7. Would the repudiation of the questionable data on the essential inequality of races improve race relations or increase race antagonisms?

BIBLIOGRAPHY

Harry E. Barnes, *History and Social Intelligence* (1926).
Franz Boas, *Anthropology and Modern Life* (1932).
Robert N. Bradley, *Racial Origins of English Character* (1926).
Charles Duff, *This Human Nature* (1930).
Jean Finot, *Race Prejudice* (1907).
Henry J. Ford, "The Anglo-Saxon Myth," in *Readings from the American Mercury* (1926), edited by Grant C. Knight.
Thomas R. Garth, *Race Psychology* (1931).
Frank H. Hankins, *The Racial Basis of Civilization* (1926).
Friedrich O. Hertz, *Race and Civilization* (1928).
Aleš Hrdlička, "Anthropology of the American Negro," *American Journal of Physical Anthropology*, April–June, 1927, pp. 205–235.

Aleš Hrdlička, "Human Races," in *Human Biology and Racial Welfare* (1930), edited by Edmund V. Cowdry.
Jacob R. Kantor, "Anthropology, Race, Psychology, and Culture," *American Anthropologist*, April, 1925, pp. 267–283.
Alfred L. Kroeber, *Anthropology* (1923).
Théophile Simar, *Etude Critique sur la Formation de la Doctrine des Races, Au XVIIIe Siècle et Son Expansion Au XIXe Siècle* (1922).
Alfred M. Tozzer, *Social Origins and Social Continuities* (1925).
Carl J. Warden, *The Evolution of Human Behavior* (1932).
Clark Wissler, *Man and Culture* (1923).

CHAPTER II

NEGRO CULTURE

The culture of a people is nothing less than the sum total of the modes of life of that people. It therefore includes "knowledge, beliefs, art, morals, law, custom and any other capabilities and habits acquired by man as a member of society."[1] All peoples have established modes of life and hence have cultures. If one studies the activities of two different peoples he will see a great many contrasts between the ways in which life functions with these two groups. The points of contrast are the elements that make each culture distinctive. The more primitive or the more isolated a people is, the more likely will it be that its culture will be distinctive, because there has been less opportunity to adopt the modes of life of others by imitation. Since the Eskimo is completely isolated, we should expect him to have fewer culture traits in common with Americans than would the English people; hence, the Eskimo culture would be called distinctive.

In some such degree the Negro culture of Africa would be expected to be distinctive because the people of that continent have been much more isolated than most other peoples of the world.

Although one of the oldest civilizations in history was found in Egypt, and some think Africa was the cradle of the human race,[2] this continent has been almost entirely separated from the rest of the world up to the present century. Although Africa is three times as large as the continent of Europe, its coast line is only 15,000 miles as compared with the 19,000 miles of European coast line. There are no bays, inlets, or estuaries, no capes, peninsulas, or promontories, but rather a straight, severe coast which reduces the coast line to the minimum. The African coast has at almost every point been forbidding to the seagoing vessel. It has seemed uninviting to all travelers through all the centuries.

Africa's rivers are no more inviting to the mariner than is its coast. The Congo, which is Africa's largest river, and easily one of

[1] Edward B. Tylor, *Primitive Culture*, Vol. I, p. 1.   [2] Cf. Elliott Smith.

the greatest water systems of the entire world, rises in the lake region toward the east coast, flows in a great curve toward the north, and then plunges from its highlands to the western sea, through a long series of cataracts and waterfalls which has made it the despair of all travelers. By superhuman effort Henry M. Stanley journeyed up this river and past these waterfalls in his search for Livingstone, and the world still marvels at his success. Ocean steamers can proceed up the river only 110 miles to Matadi.

Following up the west coast into the Bight of Benin, one can enter any one of eighteen or twenty mouths of the sluggish waters of the Niger. But one cannot go far inland on the waters of any of these numerous outlets, for the largest of these, the Nun, the Bonny, the Forcadas, and the Cross, are all choked with the heavy silt swept down from the slopes of Futa-Jallon — a highland 10,000 feet in elevation where the Niger takes its rise. For multiplied centuries the natives living in the interior have dared the perils of the desert in carrying their ivory to the coast rather than attempt to follow the slimy channel of this river to the sea. Skirting around the great headland of the continent, one finds the Senegal, the mouth of which is guarded by immense sandbars, which formed secure hiding places for the slave ships during the long period of the slave trade, but which forever effectually bar any free navigation of this river. From the mouth of the Senegal around the coast to the mouth of the Nile is a distance of 4,800 miles, with not a single river of any importance to break the monotony of the sea line. The Nile, more navigable than any of the other rivers, has given some access to the interior of the country, and here one of the greatest cultures of ancient times had its rise. But the upper reaches of the Nile were filled with cataracts; the desert hugged it close on one side, and the mountains guarded it on the other. Undoubtedly there was some commerce between the interior and the valley of the Nile, for some of the Pharaohs, if not all, possessed African slaves. But the lower Nile and the lake region from which it took its rise seemed almost as completely separate as the two poles. After leaving the Nile it is 2,400 miles to the next great river which empties into the sea. The whole east coast is rough and precipitous. The Zambesi is the most important river of that coast. It rises in the far western highlands of southern Angola, sweeps across the central table-lands, swerves suddenly southward, and then plows its way through the solid rock to the sea. Two hundred miles from the coast it drops several hundred feet over the sheer wall of Victoria Falls, which has been called the grandest natural sight of South Africa. This fall stops all navigation and renders this great river useless as an entrance way into the interior. The Orange and the Limpopo are practically useless for entering the interior. "All the great rivers," to quote Élisée Reclus, "Nile, Congo, Niger, are interrupted by cataracts and rapids which cut off from outward intercourse populous regions, whose fluvial systems ramify over many hundred millions of acres." [1]

Not only did Nature give no access to Africa through rivers and harbors, but she seemed to take malicious delight in piling up other barriers about the interior of this continent. The whole east coast is guarded by a long, high stretch of table-land which comes to a culmination in Mount Kenia and Kilimanjaro, each rising 18,000 feet above the sea. The west coast has a high table-land north of the Gulf of Guinea which culminates in the Futa-Jallon, 10,000 feet in elevation. Sweeping southward around the gulf one comes to the Kamerun mountains, whose giant peaks, the "Three Sisters," attain an altitude of 14,000 feet — peaks which, because they are so high and so constantly covered with snow, are called by the natives the "mountains of the gods." [2] Across the great northern section of the continent, extending almost from the mountains of the east to those of the west, is the great Sahara desert, which through all the centuries has struck terror to the heart of the would-be explorer of this continent. And as if to make the isolation complete, across the southern horn of the continent the Kalahari desert stands guard against any unwelcome intruder. Like the maiden of Norse mythology who was condemned to sleep surrounded by a ring of fire until some heroic lover should dare the dangers of the fire to awaken her, interior Africa, surrounded by mountains and deserts, for untold centuries lay asleep waiting the time when men with bold hearts would break through her barriers and arouse her.

Thus from time immemorial the great mass of the African peoples living in the interior have been effectually cut off from contact with the outside world. But this is not the whole of the story of isolation. Inside the continent itself the people are broken up into small groups with no means of communication. The great northern section of the continent lies across the equator; hence it has a very hot climate with very heavy rainfall. The forests and all vegetation are the most

[1] *The Earth and Its Inhabitants*, "Africa," Vol. I, p. 6.
[2] *Ibid.*, "Africa," Vol. III, p. 371.

luxuriant in the world. To make one's way through such a tangle is a task which only the resolute will undertake. If a road is cleared it cannot be neglected for a month lest it be overgrown again, so rapid is the springing of vegetation. It is reported that in the eastern highlands, where a tall cane-like grass takes the place of heavy forestry, every native carries a bush knife to cut his way along. Under such conditions the normal situation for primitive peoples would be to remain satisfied with the fellowship of their own tribe and not spend the energy necessary to travel into the country of far distant groups. One more real barrier to intercommunication is the presence of a deadly pest, the tsetse fly, the bite of which kills horses and cattle. This fly is found in all the central section of Africa, and is particularly deadly on the west coast. In that section, therefore, there are no beasts of burden, and man must carry all his own loads. Every journey must be made on foot unless a friendly stream flows in the proper direction, and all goods for transfer must be carried on the backs of men.

Under such conditions of isolation a culture tends to become static. It is generally agreed among anthropologists that there are three, and only three, ways in which a culture may develop. The first of these ways is by independent invention. When man faces a certain problem, he casts about to find a solution. Some anthropologists have felt that men in various parts of the world facing similar problems were apt to invent common means of solution. For example, in making a pottery vessel which will hold water, a glazing process was used both in the Old World and in widely scattered sections of the New World. But many anthropologists believe that the invention of so simple an expedient as pottery glaze was very difficult. If invented separately by different groups it could not have been purely accidental with primitive man, and while it would not be impossible that groups working at the common problem of a vessel to hold water might hit upon this common device, it seems very unlikely. In fact many students of the subject go so far as to say that there is almost never a duplication in inventions.

The second way in which people may come into possession of a culture trait is by borrowing. Thus a culture trait may travel long distances by diffusion. Under normal conditions a trait will diffuse in a circle around its center of origin, just as the waves travel outward from a point where a stone is dropped into a pond. It is even possible to measure the length of time a culture trait has taken in traveling a given distance from its center of origin. Thus Nelson, in the study of pottery, found that in the stratified deposits at its center of origin the lower strata, which were the oldest, had also diffused further than those later traits to be found in more recent stratification. On the other hand barriers encountered in the natural spread of a culture trait may entirely distort this circular diffusion. Thus Wissler points out that the Kayak culture trait of the Eskimo has spread in a long, wide belt and not in a circular area.[1] This distortion is due primarily to difficulty of travel which has restricted the natural passing of the traits inward from the sea, as well as the comparative lack of use of the Kayak except for hunting purposes at the coast. Distortion may have been further emphasized in this Eskimo culture by the fact that most of their culture complexes are built up around the hunting of seal on the coast and of caribou inland.

Where a culture is built up around a certain type of animal hunted for food, such as the buffalo among the plains Indians, naturally the culture traits so developed will not spread beyond the range of the animal concerned. Method of transportation may limit the spread of a culture. Thus the ancient Minoan culture hung tenaciously to the fringes of the Mediterranean. Political boundaries may be no barrier against the spread of a culture trait, but mountains, the sea, the desert, or other natural obstructions to travel may completely stop distribution and thus distort culture areas.

Wissler in his *Man and Culture*[2] discusses a third method of culture origin: namely, convergence, by which he means that culture traits which may have completely independent invention may, through a long process of adjustment to environmental needs, come to be almost identical. This is, so to speak, a questioning of the fact that a single culture trait can be invented in only one place and hence must diffuse from that center if found in other parts of the world. In other words, it is a theory built around the idea of independent invention of culture traits.

Whatever emphasis one wishes to put on one or other of these methods, it is clear that the overwhelming mass of our culture is not strictly original. The white man, particularly that section of the white race now popularly known as the Nordic, often assumes that his culture is all his own; hence he arrogates to himself a superior capacity, which he proves from the fact of what he thinks is his superior culture. But he probably has failed to take into consideration the fact that much of his culture is borrowed. Thus our alphabet

[1] *Man and Culture*, p. 129.　　[2] P. 105 ff.

we trace back to Semitic origin; the Semitics in turn perhaps got it from the Phœnicians; and these in turn, many ethnologists think, borrowed it from the Minoans or from the early Egyptians.[1] Certainly we did not invent it ourselves. Our numbers we borrowed from the Arabs, our art is a heritage from Greece, our religion in the main comes from the Hebrews, and many of our governmental ideas derive from the Romans. If the Nordics have any special superiority it is in their ability to borrow from all the culture of the world. At least a part of that ability to borrow was certainly developed out of the environmental conditions in which we found ourselves. Our strategic location on the shores of the Mediterranean before the westward waves of migration took place enabled us to gather up from all the then existing civilizations the elements of culture which were in possession of the human race. To our fortunate point of origin we probably owe more than we are aware.

As remarked before, a culture will probably be more distinctive if it is little influenced from without. A culture which is very simple may represent an almost perfect adjustment to its environment. Alexander A. Goldenweiser[2] finds the culture of the Eskimo almost a perfect adjustment to the environment, by which a real civilization was brought into existence, though the variety of culture traits, as compared with modern America, would be painfully limited. The Eskimo, unlike the American, has had scant opportunity to borrow any culture traits from other peoples of the world, though even here the borrowing process has gone on.

In the light of the comparative isolation of Africa, one would not expect to find there a culture which had absorbed a great variety of culture traits or complexes common to Europe and America. It was only a little more than a hundred years ago, in 1825, that the first white man, Major Laing, penetrated far enough into the interior of Africa to visit the city of Timbuctu, which had been known to story and fable for generations. Other travelers had often touched the coast of Africa and undoubtedly had introduced the natives to some of their culture ideas, but the great mass of the African population were until very recently completely untouched by the culture of the European world. Since the culture of Africa therefore is quite different from our own, we are apt to conclude it is inferior. For have we not felled the forest, dug up the ores from the earth, fashioned powerful

---

[1] Cf. *Encyclopedia Britannica* (14th ed.), article by B. C. F. Atkinson in Vol. I, p. 677 ff.   [2] *Early Civilization*, Part I, chap. 1.

machines, annihilated space, subdued nature to our bidding? The African has done none of these things in such marked degree as have we; hence we are inclined to say his culture is inferior and the Africans as a people are inferior. But so hasty a conclusion may be far from scientific. Aptitudes of people may be proven far more by ability to adapt their culture to the environment in which they live than by ability to borrow culture from all the rest of the world, and on this basis we may find upon further study that the African peoples have much to commend them to our respect.[1] Indeed it is a serious question whether culture can be arranged at all in ascending scales. Each group of people has adjusted its life to its peculiar environment, and who can say that a proper adjustment so made is not far better than conformity to any particular set pattern which might be arbitrarily applied? Goldenweiser has made a careful study of five types of primitive culture — the Eskimo, the Northwest Indian, the Iroquois, the Uganda, and the culture of Central Australia. After trying to classify these cultures as advanced or retarded by way of total cultures and then by way of individual aspects of culture, he remarks: "There seems to be no way in which the civilization of the five tribes could be arranged in an ascending series. No sooner is this attempted than the civilizations tend to break up into their constituent elements, each of which has undergone a distinctive development in each instance, both in degree and in kind."[2] The Uganda tribes seem to excel in political organization, though the Iroquois would be a close second, the Eskimo has made the most perfect economic adjustment to its environment, and each other group has some field of seeming superiority. It is obviously very hazardous to claim that any one culture is in all respects or even in most respects superior to any other culture. All cultures throughout the world have certain elements in common, based perhaps on the very nature of man himself. Thus all men are religious, all men have some type of family organization, and all men have some type of political organization. There are other elements which seem to grow out of the geographic conditions, such as the food habits of various continents; while still other elements of culture seem to be purely local, growing out of individual inventions and responses.[3]

[1] Cf. Franz Boas, *The Mind of Primitive Man*, chap. 1.
[2] *Early Civilization*, pp. 125–126.
[3] For full discussion of this point see: Alexander A. Goldenweiser, *Early Civilization*, chap. 6.

Augustus H. Keane divided the inhabitants of Africa into two great anthropological classes, the Sudanese and the Bantu.[1] The Sudanese are all those tribes living north of a line drawn from the mouth of the Senegal river, east by north to Timbuctu on the great bend of the Niger, thence east by south to Lake Chad, thence almost due east to Khartum at the confluence of the White Nile and the Blue Nile, and thence south to Lake Victoria and eastward to the ocean, near the equator. This whole group of peoples, again divided into tribes of western, central, and eastern Sudan, has been thoroughly infiltrated with Hamitic and Semitic migrants. In Keane's opinion it is due to the introduction of new ideas that this portion of Africa has "attained a much higher level of culture" than have the peoples south of this line.

The Bantus are all those tribes living in the great central section of Africa, south of the line thus described, and north of the Kalahari desert. South of the Kalahari lies the land of the Hottentots and the Bushmen.

For convenience we may discuss the cultures of Africa under four main heads: namely, economic life, political life, family life, and religious life, contrasting where possible the Sudanese and the Bantu.

Generally speaking, the economic life of the Sudanese is more strenuous than is the economic life of the Bantu of equatorial Africa. Nature is more penurious and the quality of frugality is engendered. In the cattle zone, horses, sheep, and goats appear in great abundance. The Dinkas, among the Eastern Sudanese, are said to love their cattle more than their wives and children. They even use cattle as their standard of values and medium of exchange. In all this section the cattle kraal is the center of life. Here a great pavilion sometimes three stories high is erected, and sentinels for guarding the cattle are posted day and night. Around this cattle industry there clusters a great culture complex, which includes methods of milking, uses of the milk, caring for the vessels, the use or not of cow's meat for food, the herding customs, which have social significance and in many cases moral significance, the problems of tribal relationships which involve stealing of cattle, tribal wars, and other tribal relations.

Agriculture is fairly well developed, and millet, yams, sweet potatoes, pumpkins, and ground nuts are grown. Interestingly enough, cotton, indigo, and tobacco are grown in commercial quantities.

Industrial arts are practiced throughout the region. In the west,

[1] *Man, Past and Present,* chaps. 3 and 4.

Timbuctu, Sokoto, and Kuka are great centers of manufacturing. Goat skins are said to be tanned in various colors, and boots, shoes, saddles, and fancy bags are made from them. Kuka cloth is said to be of a high quality, and iron and copper wares are made in beautiful designs and of good quality. Keane says the Eastern Sudanese "cultivate some of the useful industries, such as iron and copper smelting and casting, weaving, pottery, and wood carving with great success. The form and ornamental design of these utensils display real artistic taste, while the temper of their iron implements is often superior to that of imported European hardware." [1]

In the great northern section of the Bantu land, which lies across the equator, there are neither horses nor cattle, because of the tsetse fly, the bite of which is deadly to both. Neither is agriculture highly developed, because nature provides fruit and vegetables in abundance and man does not need to work carefully for his food. Industrial arts are not so well developed as among the Sudanese. Rough basketry is manufactured, the pottery is not so highly developed, the bark cloth is not of as fine texture as the Kuka cloth. Iron implements are made, and some of them have a remarkable design and temper. Near the western coast the industries of the natives were completely demoralized during the days of the slave trade, for the natives found it was easier to capture slaves and swap them for manufactured articles than it was to submit to the drudgery necessary in all hand manufacturing processes. Perhaps the gaudiness of the cheap articles of western manufacture also appealed to them. Mungo Park found that most coast tribes had in 1796 ceased to manufacture iron implements and depended on European traders to supply them. The Bantus near the coast gathered some gold from the streams, and gathered palm olives from the groves that grew on every hand. Ivory was also an item of barter with them. In the far interior, manufacturing was much better developed. Division of labor has not progressed very far, and the women are the chief laborers. Little capital has been accumulated, since the ready supply of food gives little incentive for saving.

All this is decidedly changed when we pass to the southern portion of Bantuland. Here again we come to high rolling grasslands, and cattle again become the center of the culture complexes. Zulus, Kafirs, Makalolo, Matabele, Bechuana, Mashona, Basuto, and Ova-Herero are some of the leading tribes of this region. The Zulus,

[1] *Man, Past and Present,* p. 82.

Kafirs, and Herero are among the most capable peoples of Africa. Here not only every family, but every person owns his or her cattle. Among the Herero, the child at birth inherits cattle and lives not from the income of the family, but from the income of its own property. The land is privately owned, and the uncultivated sections may be held in common by the tribe and assigned annually to various families.

Agriculture is not at a high stage of efficiency, but Kafir corn, millet, rice, pumpkins, hemp, and tobacco are raised. The corn and millet when gathered are stored in baskets or clay jars of native manufacture. Most of the work of agriculture is done by the women, while the men tend the cattle and do the milking. Milk is used mostly in a sour state. Cattle are rarely eaten for food. A singular fact about the Herero is that neither he nor his cattle like salt.[1]

These tribes have been little influenced until recently by the white man, or any invasion from the outside; hence their native industries have been held intact. They manufacture hoes, axes, lances, and knives from iron, and the temper of their cutlery is said to compare favorably with that of cutlery made in England. They also manufacture baskets, mats, and pottery, and their woodcarving is of a high order. Until 1870 there was no outside trade, and hence almost no means of transporting goods. There were few boats or canoes, and roads were almost unknown. Of late years the coming of the white man has introduced roads and even railroads.

Roland B. Dixon[2] reminds us that the environment in which people live may exert both a positive and a negative influence on their material culture. On no continent is this more finely illustrated than in Africa, where the presence of the tsetse fly makes cattle raising or pastoral life impossible in great equatorial sections, and in the southern cattle zone the high arid plains, with small rainfall, make agriculture unrewarding. The great heat of the equatorial region, with the abundance of fruits, has tended to reduce life to its simplest forms, and has made the motive for laying up capital much less pressing, while the struggle for existence both in the northern cattle zone and in the southern cattle zone has fostered the development of great herds, and the accumulation of material wealth. These conditions in turn have had a decided influence on the social and religious culture of these various peoples.

[1] Augustus H. Keane, *Man, Past and Present*, p. 110.
[2] *The Building of Cultures*, p. 10 ff.

When we turn from the material culture of Africa to its social culture, we find that environment has fully as marked an effect on this latter form of culture as it has been seen to have on the former. Among the Sudanese tribes, three environmental conditions have made for strong organized states. First, the country is open and offers opportunity for travel and for the movement of armed forces. Second, its openness also calls for defense, since every settlement is liable to attack from bands of marauders who can easily move from place to place. Third, the presence of the horse, which is due to pastoral conditions, makes it possible to develop a large swift-moving army and thus facilitates organization on a big scale. Since wealth in the form of cattle and agricultural products may be accumulated it is possible to sustain an army in the field for a considerable length of time. The population of this area is also much denser than in other sections, so that large states could more easily be formed. Opposed to centralization in government may be noted the independence of the people and the desire on the part of each village to govern itself.

One of the most ancient of the kingdoms of this region was that of Bornu. Its first capital was located at Birni, a city situated midway between Lake Chad and the ancient city of Timbuctu. According to Reclus, "Birni, although its wall was only six miles in circumference, at one time had as many as 200,000 inhabitants." [1]

The Bornu kingdom was probably founded in 900 A.D.[2] and its capital Birni lasted down to the years 1809 and 1810, when it was overrun by the Fulah tribes. It was an elective monarchy, the privilege of choosing a successor among the sons of the deceased king, without priority of birth, being conferred by the nation on three of the most distinguished men of the country.[3] Barth believed that the three distinguished men were probably chosen from the courtiers. After these three men had decided upon the future sovereign, he was conducted to the chambers in which his unburied father lay. There he took an oath binding himself to respect the ancient institutions and to uphold the glory of the country. While the government was theocratic in form it was not absolute. The authority of the sovereign was limited by a council of assistants.

[1] *The Earth and Its Inhabitants,* "Africa," Vol. III, p. 362.
[2] Henry Barth, *Travels and Discoveries in North and Central Africa,* Vol. II, p. 21.
[3] *Ibid.,* p. 27.

Most of the high offices were held by slaves.¹ The Sultan of Bornu once had a standing army of 30,000 soldiers, and the nation carried on a flourishing trade for centuries in slaves, ivory, and ostrich feathers. When the country was overrun in 1809 the capital was moved to Kuka, which Reclus described as a city of 60,000 inhabitants.²

The city of Kano was a tributary of Bornu and was itself a place of no mean population. Its wall was fifteen miles in circumference, enclosing sufficient territory to support a large population during a protracted siege. When Barth visited it in 1850 there were 30,000 inhabitants, and at the busiest time of the year the markets swelled the population to at least 60,000. Cotton cloth was manufactured in almost every household.³ Barth estimated that at the time of his visit this city exported annually this cloth alone to an amount valued at 300,000,000 Kurdi.⁴ Because of this great wealth, the city had during all the centuries been a coveted prize of marauding bands. Katsena, another tributary of Bornu, was surrounded by a wall thirty feet thick, forty feet high, and thirteen miles in circumference.⁵ Barth estimated that the population had at times reached at least one hundred thousand souls. Its wealth was fabulous for a city of central Africa. More than thirty-six hundred camel loads of salt were sent as export from this city in 1850, valued at probably $50,000.

Although Kano and Katsena often paid tribute to the Bornu kingdom, they were in reality a part of the great Hausa kingdom, which Barth says consisted of Biram, Daura, Gober, Kano, Rono, Katsena, and Zegzeg. These were called the Seven Hausa States. These various regions were supposed to be named after the seven sons of the original Hausa family which came from the north. Sokoto, located on the Sokoto river, where the roads branch eastward to Kano, Katsena and Lake Chad, was another of the flourishing towns of the Hausa kingdom. Barth ⁶ thought it contained at the height of its power 120,000 people. It was this city in which the great explorer Clapperton died in 1827, and near which he was buried. Yauri, on

---

¹ Élisée Reclus, *The Earth and Its Inhabitants,* "Africa," Vol. III, p. 364.

² *Ibid.,* p. 362.

³ Henry Barth, *Travels and Discoveries in North and Central Africa,* Vol. I, p. 511.

⁴ 12,000 Kurdi equaled one English pound.

⁵ Henry Barth, *Travels and Discoveries in North and Central Africa,* Vol. I, p. 458 ff. *passim.*

⁶ *Ibid.,* Vol. I, p. 453.

the Niger, was once a very populous city with an enclosure which was said to be 30 miles in circumference.[1]

The royal authority in the Hausa kingdom was limited by a ministry composed of a prime minister, a chief of cavalry, a chief or commander of infantry, and a minister of finance. The various cities or petty states had a certain amount of autonomy, for which they paid an annual tribute. The kingdom held together for centuries and had as much stability as not a few of our European nations. Among the Boganda peoples there was a strong centralized government with a king, with thirty-six gentes presided over by a chief; each gens was divided into a number of siga, each with a petty chief. All of these chiefs paid tribute to the central government, and had special responsibilities for maintaining that government. Roads to all parts of the kingdom were maintained by the various chiefs, so that the kingdom was fairly well coördinated. The king was elected by the chiefs in council. It appears quite clear that the openness of the country and the accumulation of wealth had much to do with the development of strong political states in this part of Africa.

Further south and near the equator, political life was quite different from that of the more rugged people of the north. It is true that the Dahomans and Ashantis built up considerable kingdoms. Dahomi stretched from the Gold Coast northward, and drew together a very populous region. It had a large standing army, of which a division of Amazons numbering 3,000 were said to be very desperate and hard fighters. The Ashanti kingdom was not so large or so well organized as the Dahomi. The people lived in small scattered villages, which made concentration more difficult.

Barth says these kingdoms were despotisms in which the power of the king was very great, but in each there was some limitation of power. The towns and villages were under the direct control of local chiefs, who held their positions by paying tribute to the king. Joint responsibility for crime committed by a member or slave of a family, or by a member of a town, was a law of universal sway. Persons and property were treated alike, and theft and murder were of the same grade of criminality. Punishment was very severe and of the cruelest type. During the long slave-trade period the punishment in Dahomi underwent radical changes. Crimes formerly punishable by death or banishment were changed so as to be punishable by life slavery.

[1] *Travels and Discoveries in North and Central Africa*, Vol. I, p. 458 *passim*.

The ruling classes were not very good examples for the people. Dissipation, indolence, and cruelty marked their character. "Speaking generally," says Jerome Dowd, "it seems to be a fact that aristocracies in tropical countries always have a tendency to sink below the moral level of the commonalty, whereas those of temperate countries have a tendency to rise above the masses and to lift them to a higher level." [1] Besides these two kingdoms of Dahomi and Ashanti, there were other smaller kingdoms of Benin, Ibo, Bonny, with much more restricted power and territory. In the Congo region, according to Reclus, kingdoms of considerable size were to be found, such as Lunda in the Kassai valley, Musta Kazembe in the Lua-Pula valley, Msiri in the Lua-Laba valley, and on the Congo itself the great kingdom of Kossango. But "the political ties must necessarily be somewhat lax in these regions, where the communications are extremely difficult, and where the subject tribes may easily migrate from clearing to clearing. Hence these associations constitute rather a confederacy of petty autonomous republics than monarchical states in the strict sense of the term." [2]

R. H. Nassau points out that fetishism as a system of religious belief was used as a governmental force among all the tribes of the banana zone. Thus Ukuku was a secret society to which only men and mature boys could belong. Members were under strict oath to follow the commands of the society, and to keep its actions and laws absolutely secret. To break this law was certain death. The command of the society was given out by a person chosen as priest for that occasion, who was usually concealed and spoke with an air of mystery. The decision of this court was final and authoritative.

The Bantu tribes of the southern cattle zone are Zulus, Kafirs, Makalolo, Matabele, Bechuana, Mashona, Basuto, Ova-Herero, and others. Most of them are distinctly warlike, and of a very aggressive and commanding nature. They probably migrated from further north. Keane [3] quotes Johnson to the effect that these migrations took place as early as 300 B.C., and suggests that Stuhlman may have been right in placing the African peoples as far back as Mousterian times. But Keane himself thought they migrated to this region within the last thousand years.[4] They occupy practically all

[1] *The Negro Races*, Vol. I, p. 181.
[2] Élisée Reclus, *The Earth and Its Inhabitants*, "Africa," Vol. III, pp. 440–441.
[3] *Man, Past and Present*, p. 93.
[4] *Ibid.*, p. 101.

the territory south of the Zambesi river. Owing to the necessity of finding land for grazing their cattle, they originally lived in small villages varying in size from 500 to 2,000 inhabitants. For military purposes the young men were not permitted to marry, and even children born to them by concubines were killed. The Zulus in particular were very severe in the discipline of their soldiers.

Prior to the founding of the powerful military empire under Chaka (1793–1828) the political organization of the Zulus was a patriarchal monarchy controlled by a powerful aristocracy.[1] The small tribe was controlled by a feudal chief who had supreme authority in his own tribe. The nobles, however, exerted a powerful influence on his conduct, by their common councils establishing a kind of common law. This common law "held everyone accused of crime guilty until he could prove himself innocent." [2] The head of the family was responsible for the conduct of all members of the family, the village was responsible for the conduct of all its inhabitants, and the tribe was responsible for the conduct of all the villages.[3]

Dixon's point holds here, that the culture of a people is definitely influenced by the three elements of environment: climate, topography, raw material.[4] This is wonderfully illustrated in the political life of Africa. The humid climate of central Africa reduces men to a lethargic state and prevents or tends to prevent combinations of large groups of people into central governments. Again, the great topographical difficulties hindering communication prevent people from getting together. Furthermore, the fact that food consisting of native fruits cannot be preserved for long periods makes it difficult to maintain a fighting force in the field. On the other hand, all these conditions are changed in both the northern and the southern cattle zone, and hence in each of these regions Negroes have developed very powerful states.

William C. Willoughby says: "Bantu life is essentially religious. The relation of the individual to the family, the clan, and the tribe, — politics, ethics, law, war, status, social amenities, festivals, all that is good and much that is bad in Bantu life, — is grounded in Bantu religion." [5] Almost as sweeping a statement might be made of the

[1] Augustus H. Keane, *Man, Past and Present*, p. 104.
[2] *Ibid.*, p. 104.
[3] *Ibid.*, p. 104.
[4] *The Building of Cultures*, p. 13.
[5] *The Soul of the Bantu*, p. 1.

religion of all native African tribes. Animism, which culminates in fetishism and ancestor worship, dominates the life in Africa. Even in those parts of Africa where Mohammedanism has spread, the power of fetishism is still present. The constituent elements in this religion are a belief in a creator, Njambi; belief in spirits; the use of fetishism to control the spirits; and of course the ever present witch doctor.

The first element in the African religion [1] is that of God, called by various tribes Njambi, Anzam, Anyambie, Yemi, Nyssiva, meaning variously maker, creator, supreme being, great one, and even "Great Friend" and Father. The God who is maker has created his people and then gone off and left them to the mercies of the spirits, good or bad. Hence the natives feel that he is an absentee God, who knows little and perhaps cares less about their daily lives. The fact that the African natives think their God has gone away and left them has caused many travelers to think that their religion is one of pure superstition and has no definite idea of God in it. Those who know them best do not agree with this idea. Mary Kingsley calls R. H. Nassau the most competent authority on Bantu religions, because of his long residence among them, his thorough knowledge of the languages, and "his singularly clear, powerful and highly educated intelligence." [2] Dr. Nassau says of the Central Africans: "After more than forty years' residence among these tribes, fluently using their language, conversant with their customs, dwelling intimately in their huts, associating with them in the varied relations of teacher, pastor, friend, master, fellow-traveller, and guest, and in my special office as missionary, searching after their religious thought (and therefore being allowed a deeper entrance into the arcana of their souls than would be accorded to a passing explorer), I am able unhesitatingly to say that among all the multitude of degraded ones with whom I have met, I have seen or heard none whose religious thought was only a superstition.

"Standing in the village street, surrounded by a company whom their chief has courteously summoned at my request, when I say to him, 'I have come to speak to your people,' I do not need to begin by telling them that there is a God. Looking on that motley assemblage of villagers, — the bold, gaunt cannibal with his armament of gun,

---

[1] This section is quoted from the author's *The Negro from Africa to America*, pp. 43–46, 46–48, 48–51, 53–55.

[2] Mary H. Kingsley, *Travels in West Africa*, p. 299.

spear, and dagger; the artisan with rude adze in hand, or hands soiled at the antique bellows of the village smithy; women who have hasted from their kitchen fire with hands white with the manioc dough or still grasping the partly scaled fish; and children checked in their play with tiny bow and arrow or startled from their dusty street pursuit of dog or goat, — I have yet to be asked, 'Who is God?'"[1] "The belief in one Supreme Being is universal. Nor is this idea held imperfectly or obscurely developed in their minds. The impression is so deeply engraved upon their moral and mental nature that any system of atheism strikes them as too absurd and preposterous to require a denial."[2] In the Niger delta, ancestor worship is more accentuated and it was through this conception of religion, thinks A. G. Leonard, that the Negro "eventually arrived at a worship of the Supreme God, from whom the origin of all life was traced."[3] "Among Northern Bantu tribes there is a well developed system of polytheism. Thus Muhama is the creator, Gasani is the giver of children, Bijungo is the god of plagues, Semuganda is the god of death, Ingo is the god who attends to the ordinary wants of men."[4] But throughout Africa the creator is supposed to be absent and indifferent to his people, having left them to the spirits.

It thus arises that the second constituent element in African religion is spirits. These are of three kinds: First, spirits conterminous with God, having always existed, but never considered quite equal to God. Second, spirits created by God, but seemingly playing a very small part in the thinking or religion of the African. And third, spirits which are the souls of departed men. Speaking of these spirits, Mary Kingsley says: "Their number is infinite and their powers varied as human imagination can make them. Individual spirits of the same class vary in power; some are strong of their sort, some weak."[5]

Each human being has two spirits, one the soul spirit, the other the body spirit. The spirit which corresponds to our conception of the soul lives after death, but the body spirit dies with the body. Dr. Nassau thinks this false conception of a double spirit has caused not a few Africans to be buried before they are dead, for when the sick one becomes unconscious the natives think he is dead, and only

[1] *Fetichism in West Africa*, p. 36.
[2] John L. Wilson, *Western Africa: Its History, Condition, and Prospects*, p. 209.
[3] *The Lower Niger and Its Tribes*, Introduction, p. xi.
[4] John Roscoe, *The Northern Bantu*, chap. 23.
[5] *Travels in West Africa*, pp. 300–301.

the body spirit is there troubling the body. He tells of such supposedly dead persons coming to consciousness on the way to the grave, and others having roused themselves in their death struggle to sitting postures in their shallow graves where they have barely been covered by a thin layer of dirt.[1] There seems also to be a belief in a dream soul which can wander at will even while the person is alive.

When a man dies his spirit joins the innumerable company of the spirits which fill the world about us. The spirit needs food and care just as it did in its human incarnation, save that it now only consumes the essence of the food, leaving the visible or material food, which is eaten by the natives. A hut is built for the spirit of the departed man, and food is regularly taken and left by the relatives. "I have seen in these sacred huts a dish of boiled plantain or a plate of fish. This food is generally not removed until spoiled. Sometimes, where the gift is a very large one, a feast is made; people and spirit are supposed to join in the festival, and nothing is left to spoil. That it is of use to the spirit is fully believed."[2] "Among the Ibani it was formerly customary, and no doubt still is, on the death of a chief or big person, to pour a couple of casks of rum or palm wine on the ground or over his grave, the idea being to provide the departed soul with a sufficient supply of spirits for the entertainment of his ghostly visitors."[3] In Nigeria, "it is also customary to bury implements, weapons, insignia of office, ornaments, and other articles, such as cloth, wearing apparel, plates, furniture, powder, pottery, wooden or clay images, in addition to the sacrificial victims, human and animal. The reason given in explanation of this custom is, as has already been pointed out, that while the former are for the use of the departed soul in spirit-land, the latter are his personal attendants."[4] Among the Inaku of the Niger valley it is customary to bury the chiefs inside the village; a hut is built over the grave, "which is always swept and kept clean, and offerings of food and medicines are regularly placed in two holes which are made in front of the mound."[5]

Nassau, writing of the west coast, divides the spirits of departed men into five classes according to their habitat and functions.

[1] *Fetichism in West Africa*, p. 54.
[2] *Ibid.*, p. 92.
[3] Arthur G. Leonard, *The Lower Niger and Its Tribes*, p. 166.
[4] *Ibid.*, p. 177.
[5] *Ibid.*, p. 183.

Inina. First, the inina (plural anina) of the Mpongwe tribes, called nissim among the great Fang tribes of the interior. This is a kind of shadow spirit, or dim manifestation of the human personality. Indeed among the Fang, one's nissim, or shadow, may be stolen by an enemy or may be injured by someone through stealth, in which case the person is sure to sicken and die.

Ibambo. Second, the ibambo (plural abambo) which are vague beings corresponding to our idea of ghosts. They have the capacity to become visible, and this "epiphany is dreaded, not reverenced." [1] This class of spirits seems to be very numerous, and many ceremonies are performed to deliver the natives from their power. They inhabit cemeteries and may appear "on lonely paths in the forest by night." The highly wrought imagination of the West African can see these terrible apparitions at every turn of the road, and he lives in mental terror of them.

Ombwiri. The third class of spirits is ombwiri (plural awiri), which corresponds to the ancient dryads, each one living in a "local rock, tree, promontory, or point of land, trespass on which by human beings they resent." [2] "The traveller must go by silently or with some cabalistic invocation, with bowed or bared head, and with some offering, — anything, even a pebble. Such votive collections may be seen on many spots along the forest paths, deposited there by the natives as an invocation of a blessing on their journey." [3] "The awiri are generally favorably disposed, especially to their former human relatives." [4]

Nkinda. A fourth class of spirits is called nkinda (plural sinkinda). These are the souls of the common or ordinary people as contrasted with awiri, which are the souls of prominent men. "Almost all sinkinda are evilly disposed. They come to the villages on visits to warm themselves by the kitchen fires or out of curiosity to see what is going on, and sometimes, temporarily, to enter into the bodies of the living, especially of their own family. The entrance of a nkinda into a human body always sickens the person. It may enter any one, even a child. If many of them enter a man's body, he becomes crazy." [5] These spirits are never visible and hence are all the more feared by the people. They are the spirits of disease and sickness, and often bring word of an approaching epidemic.

---

[1] Robert H. Nassau, *Fetichism in West Africa*, p. 65.
[2] *Ibid.*, p. 67.   [3] *Ibid.*, p. 67.
[4] *Ibid.*, p. 68.   [5] *Ibid.*, p. 69.

Mondi. Fifth, there are the mondi. They are also spirits of sickness and of hindering human plans. It will readily be perceived that there are good and bad spirits, or that a particular spirit may be good or bad according to its disposition at any particular moment.

In Nigeria the distinction between good and bad spirits is accounted for more carefully. The Ibo (from whom we got many of our slaves) place great faith in the due and proper observance of the funeral ceremony, for they are of the opinion that it enables the soul to go to God, and to find its destination, and that without this sacred rite the soul is prevented by the other spirits from eating, or in any way associating with them, and so, from entering into the Creator's presence. Thus it becomes an outcast and a wanderer on the face of the earth, haunting houses and frequently burial grounds, or is forced perhaps to return to this world in the form or body of some animal.[1] Among the Ibo a ghost is always one of these wandering spirits. Such spirits are supposed to form a class of demons, though it is believed that other spirits may return to earth to do evil to human beings. Since proper funeral ceremonies determine the destiny and hence the character of the spirit as benevolent or malevolent, much emphasis is placed on these ceremonies. Many a family spends all its earthly fortune on making these rites elaborate, and not infrequently a period of mourning leaves a crushing debt upon the family.

The spirits may return in the form of animals to plague and harm their family or their enemies. Nassau tells us of a man whose banana grove was being destroyed by a bull elephant. When asked why he did not kill the intruder, the African said he feared to because he believed the spirit of his "grandfather had taken up his abode in that animal." It is, therefore, highly desirable that the spirits of the departed shall go away and leave the family unmolested. Consequently, when a person dies, horns are blown, bells are rung, pans are beaten, mourners shout aloud, pleading that the spirits go away and leave the relatives unmolested. Describing the death of a chief's brother, J. H. Weeks says: "The men fired off guns to frighten away evil spirits, to give expression to their sorrow, and to inform the spirits in the great mysterious forest town, whither all the spirits of the dead go, that a great man was coming to join them."[2] Leonard says that the Aboh people (a branch of the Ibo in the Niger delta) are sceptical about the efficacy of noise in driving away spirits,

---

[1] Arthur G. Leonard, *The Lower Niger and Its Tribes*, p. 142.
[2] *Congo Life and Jungle Stories*, p. 23.

but this he thinks is "more or less a solitary exception," "for go where we will all over the delta, the strongest evidence in favor of the existence of the contrary belief is to be seen in the very practical demonstration of it in almost every community." [1] "Of one tribe in the upper course of the Ogowe, I was told, who, in their intense fear of ghosts, and their dread of the possible evil influence of the spirits of their own dead relatives, sometimes adopt a horrible plan for preventing their return. With a very material idea of a spirit, they seek to disable it by beating the corpse until every bone is broken. The mangled mass is hung in a bag at the foot of a tree in the forest. Thus mutilated, the spirit is supposed to be unable to return to the village, to entice into its fellowship of death any of the survivors." [2]

Living thus in the presence of multitudes of spirits, which are disembodied and therefore ubiquitous, and which seem to retain their consciousness and memories of past experience, the Negro is in constant terror lest he may be harmed by some spirit, whom he may have injured while in embodied human form. This constant element of fear has wrought greatly upon the emotions of the Negro as we shall see later, and explains in part his highly emotional temperament.

The third constituent element in African religion is fetish.

If one's God is an absentee God, having left one to the mercy of the spirits; and if one is surrounded by multitudes of such spirits, good or bad, which may do one good or work one great harm, it would be the natural bent of the human mind to find a way to establish friendly relations with the good spirits and to ward off the power of evil spirits. This the African does through his system of fetish. A fetish is any rag, string, stick, tooth, piece of wood, shell, hair, or what not, in which a spirit has been coaxed to take up its abode. The material object may be entirely useless and worthless, for the spirit abiding there is the only item of importance, and indeed it is sometimes thought that the more insignificant the material object the greater will be the manifest power of the spirit. Every man, therefore, must provide himself with a fetish or fetishes, for he must have a separate spirit to help him in each particular undertaking. He must have a special fetish for hunting, usually made with some combination of the flesh and horns or hair of the animal which he desires to kill. He must have another fetish for

[1] *The Lower Niger and Its Tribes*, p. 148.
[2] Robert H. Nassau, *Fetichism in West Africa*, p. 234.

journeying, which is made in the light of the possible dangers that await him in travel, and the securing of the appropriate charm to meet such dangers. There is a fetish for war also, for victory does not depend on courage alone, but also on the power of one's fetish. In these charms the natives have absolute confidence, but if in the beginning of the battle many of their comrades are killed, they will retire at once, acknowledging that their medicine did not work. There are fetishes for trading, for sickness, for living, for fishing, and for every other activity of life. All of these fetishes have something of the element of sympathetic magic in them. Like produces like is the fundamental principle. If you want a fetish which will harm another man, get a hair from his head, or a nail paring, or anything else that belongs to him, and you are sure to have power over him. If a woman wants to make a man love her, she scrapes a bit of skin from the sole of her foot and puts it, together with certain other mixtures, into the food she cooks for him, believing it is sure to have the desired effect. Sympathetic magic is practiced by almost all primitive peoples everywhere.

If your project fails, it is because your fetish was not strong enough. Some other stronger spirit has overcome yours. If you failed in war, your enemy had the stronger fetish. You may cast yours away and get another in the hope that this time you will be fortunate enough to get the stronger one. If the spirit leaves the material object, then the wood or stone is useless. So long as the spirit remains, there is power in the fetish. The native "addresses his prayer to it, and extols its virtues; but should his enterprise not prosper, he will cast his deity aside as useless, and cease to worship it. He will address it with torrents of abuse, and will even beat it to make it serve him better. It is a deity at his disposal, to serve in the accomplishment of his desires; the individual keeps gods of his own to help him in his undertakings." [1]

"So long as these fetishes are used simply for protection, the owner is a practicer of white art, but when they are used to injure others or force others to do certain things pleasing to the owner of the fetish, their possessor is said to practice black art. It is this latter that keeps the African native in constant fear. At any hour his enemy may by witchcraft destroy his property, rob him of his friends, or take his life. All that an enemy has to do is to get some of his victim's hair, his nails, or water in which he has bathed, and have a witch

[1] Allan Menzies, *History of Religion*, p. 35.

doctor make a concoction which, buried in front of the victim's door or secretly hung in his room, will bring sure death. If the man dies, this black art has worked; if he fails to die, then he himself has a fetish stronger than the spirit that was trying to induce his death. In this murderous superstition the natives have absolute confidence."[1]

To ward off evil, an African child, on the day of its birth, has a string tied around its body with a fetish attachment of bones, teeth, or some other appropriate object.

The fourth element in religion among the Africans is the witch doctor or medicine man, so called because he concocts the fetish which is used to cure sickness and drive away evil spirits which cause disease. He is almost as powerful as the chief himself since he has the power of life or death over every member of the tribe — except only the chief. Through their ceremonies the witch doctors decide all question of guilt, by their ordeal they may murder whom they will; they charge large fees for their services, and woe to anyone who fails to pay or in any way incurs their enmity. Describing the witch finder, Weeks says:

> I noticed that he was a small, active man with keen piercing eyes that seemed to jump from face to face and read the very thoughts of those who stood around. He was dressed in the soft skins of monkeys and bush-cats; around his neck was a necklace of rat's teeth mixed with the teeth of crocodiles and leopards. His body was decorated with pigments of different colors; thick circles of white surrounded the eyes, a patch of red ran across the forehead, broad stripes of yellow chased each other down the cheeks, bands of red and yellow went up the arms and across the chest, and spots of blue promiscuously filled in the vacant spaces. At the different points of his curious dress were bells that tinkled at every movement. The boys looked at him in deep awe, the girls and women cowered away from him, and the men, though they feared him, greeted him with a simulated friendliness that ill-accorded with their nervousness.[2]

These monsters thus hold the entire community in constant fear of them and according to their superstitious wisdom measure out life or death. They undoubtedly believe in their own work, or at least are self-deceived, though they do not scruple to use their office to their own advantage.

These then are the constituent elements of African religion: an absentee God, who created men and then left them; innumerable

[1] Willis D. Weatherford, *Negro Life in the South*, pp. 123–124.
[2] *Congo Life and Jungle Stories*, pp. 49–50.

spirits that must be placated; fetishes which are used to ward off evil and work harm to enemies; and the witch doctor, partly honest, partly selfish, who holds the destiny of human life in his keeping. Such a religion has little or no moral power. Lying seems to be very common, petty stealing is constantly practiced, sex immorality is disgustingly common. Cruelty to man and animal is so brutal and unvarnished that it sickens one. Witchcraft murder is a daily occurrence. All these and more are the outgrowth of the terrible fetish system, which paralyzes all ideals, and releases in every man something of the wild beast which fights to preserve its life. An absentee God is not calculated to produce strenuous moral life. If God has gone away into the corner of the universe, of what avail are moral standards? To outwit the spirits is the final goal of life; and if one outwits a few of his neighbors in passing, so much the greater his victory.

Absentee landlordism is no better in religion than in farming, and he who has an absentee God is sure to have a loose standard of morals and a religion without much moral content. It is from absenteeism that much of the Negro religion of today is suffering, and one has seen more than one white man who prayed on his knees on Sunday and preyed on his neighbors on Monday, all because his religion had no present or immanent God in it.

There is of course great variation in the forms of religion practiced or held in various sections of Africa. Thus in northern Africa the native fetish customs have been veneered with teachings of the Koran, and in many places the Christian missionaries have had considerable influence in changing the more superstitious beliefs. But on the whole the forms of religion described above are fairly accurate all over Africa.

Wife purchase seems to be almost a universal practice among African tribes. The price paid for a wife and the purely commercial aspect of the transaction vary greatly from tribe to tribe and from zone to zone. Among the Bantu tribes of central Africa women are much more numerous than men, owing partly at least to incessant intertribal war which kills off many men. Furthermore, since agriculture is not very highly developed, there is less productive work for women to do. For both of these reasons women are cheap. A young man can purchase a bride for a few ornaments and a goat and a few fowls. In certain sections where the girls are more scarce the men may have to pay a number of slaves with many ornaments.

R. H. Milligan found certain West African tribes where the price became quite exorbitant, including foreign goods, sheep, goats, and tobacco.[1] A young man in the agricultural region does not have to accumulate much goods before marriage. Food is cheap and plentiful, clothing almost unnecessary, and a house can be easily constructed. Hence marriage takes place at a very early age. Usually a girl marries as soon as she has passed puberty, between ten and thirteen, and she may be a grandmother at thirty. Girls who arrive at marriageable age make their début into society by painting their faces and bedecking themselves with finery, and exhibiting themselves in the streets. The groom goes to the home of the father of the girl with his purchase price — sometimes considered as a gift — and gets his bride in exchange. In this section of Africa the girl has nothing to say about the transaction. Women are considered as property, and if one dies or proves to be barren, the husband may demand another girl in her place, or may demand back the purchase price. If a man does not have the money to purchase a wife, he will often sell his sister for the necessary amount. Milligan reports, "I have heard Fang boys boasting that they were rich because they had several sisters." [2] Nassau says, "For a debt a man may give away a daughter or a wife, but he may not give away a son or a brother." [3] "If a man dies his brother may marry (that is inherit) any or all of his widows, or if there is no brother, a son inherits and may marry any or all of the wives except his own mother. It is preferred that widows shall be kept in the family circle, because of the dowry money which was paid for them, which is considered as a permanent investment." [4] Furthermore, the whole family has often contributed to the purchase of a wife or wives, and they have "claims on her for various services and work, which neither he nor she could refuse." [5] Marriage is usually not permitted between members of the same tribe or the same gens.[6] Capture of women from other tribes often supplies women for the wives of a particular tribe.

Polygamy is practiced among most of the tribes. Mary Kingsley thinks that it is economically necessary, because of the fact that no African woman can do all the work required in the household, for she must not only cook the food, but raise it, besides having all the

---

[1] *The Jungle Folk of Africa*, p. 227.   [2] *Ibid.*, p. 226.
[3] *Fetichism in West Africa*, p. 5.   [4] *Ibid.*, p. 6.   [5] *Ibid.*, p. 157.
[6] For a full discussion of this subject see: Alexander A. Goldenweiser, *Early Civilization*, chap. 4.

care of the house and the children. Miss Kingsley further thinks it suits the convenience of the head wife to have additional wives to help out, since a "whole African village of women will not do the work in a week"[1] that one English or Irish woman would do. Affection between husband and wife is usually very feeble, though Nassau and others who have known these people intimately report many notable exceptions. Chastity is certainly not highly regarded and a man will lend his wife to another man; or if she is enticed by another man, he will often exact not more than a fine.

When one turns from the central part of Africa to the northern and southern sections one finds a decidedly different family pattern. Both in the northern and the southern cattle zone, women have more independence, they share in the herding of the cattle, they have higher social status. While women are still to some extent considered as property, the money or cattle given to parents is not considered as a purchase price, but as a pledge of good conduct on the part of the husband. But if the wife proves unfaithful or barren, the man may demand the return of his cattle. In these zones love-making is fairly common, though parents have still a very large share in determining the future home life of both girls and young men. Since women in these zones are larger economic assets in the homes, parents are prone to demand much higher dowry fees for their daughters. Often Zulu young men made long journeys and underwent great hardships to secure the large amount necessary to pay such dowry.

Women even in these zones bear a heavy burden of family support. While polygamy is still practiced, the high dowry price prevents all but the wealthy having more than one wife. Concubinage therefore flourishes. Among the Zulus of the southern cattle zone, since the young men are forced to serve in the army and are not allowed to marry until later, concubinage has been very common. There seems to have been no social or political objection to any warrior having all the concubines he could command, but the children were all killed at birth.

Family ties seem to be stronger in these two zones than is usually the case in the banana zone. This would be normal since many more marriages take place as the result of mutual attraction. Most of the more powerful tribes, such as the Zulus, Kafirs, and Matabele, marry only within the tribe, but not within the same clan. Among

[1] *Travels in West Africa*, p. 492.

the Uganda of the northern cattle zone, Goldenweiser says, there are thirty-six gentes, each with two totems. These gentes have economic and political importance. They also definitely prescribe the marital selection. No marriage within any gens is permitted.[1] If a man takes a second wife she is supposed to come from the clan of his paternal grandmother.[2]

Marriage in both the northern and southern cattle zones takes place at a more mature age than in equatorial sections because the man must have accumulated considerable wealth before he can marry. He must have a house, he must have cattle, he must have wealth to pay a large dowry.

Defective children, albinos, and twins are put to death among many of the southern tribes such as the Matabele, Buhona, and Zulus. Descent is usually in the male line, the oldest son inheriting not only his father's property but also his wives.

As it was pointed out that environment has a large determining influence on the form of political organization, so here again in the family life the environmental influence on the culture pattern of the family is great. The fullest discussion of the influence of environment on racial culture is to be found in the writings of Ellsworth Huntington. Professor Huntington claims that climate not only has an influence on the cultural life of a people but also has a distinct effect on the destruction or preservation of definite types, and that this selection "is apparently one of the chief ways in which the character of races is altered." [3] After discussing the influence of climate on health, and the importance of the place of food, bacteria, and other factors in determining civilization, Huntington summarizes by saying: "All these results of the climatic environment must be put into due relation, not only with the results of other factors of physical environment, but with the opposite side of the shield — that is, with the purely human factors, such as institutions, customs, ideas, and all man's passions, ideals, and aspirations. Then it will be possible to form a true philosophy of History." [4] Although one often feels that Professor Huntington has overstated the case for the influence of

[1] Cf. Alexander A. Goldenweiser, *Early Civilization*, chap. 4.

[2] Augustus H. Keane, *Man, Past and Present*, p. 97.

[3] *Civilization and Climate* (3rd ed.), p. 6. For full discussion of this problem see: Ellsworth Huntington, *Civilization and Climate, The Character of Races as Influenced by Physical Environment, Natural Selection, and Historical Development*, and *The Pulse of Progress*.

[4] *Civilization and Climate*, p. 29.

environment — particularly climatic environment — on civilization in general, it would be hard to overstate the influence of this element in Africa. Of all the continents Africa perhaps has more handicaps than any other, with its severe seashore, its deserts, its dense forests, and with the great mass of its land area lying across the equator. One wonders not that the African people have not developed as varied a culture as the Europeans; but rather one marvels at the variety and richness of the culture which one finds.

PROBLEMS FOR STUDY

1. The peoples of northern Georgia, eastern Tennessee, eastern Kentucky, southwestern Virginia, and western North Carolina still speak a language having eighteenth-century characteristics. Account for this.
2. A bridge has been called a civilizer. Why?
3. While the Eskimo has made an almost perfect adjustment to his environment, he has few culture traits as compared with some African tribes. Can you suggest reasons for this?
4. Can you suggest reasons why ceremonials are more highly developed in central Africa than in either the northern or the southern portion of that continent?
5. Can you suggest reasons why the northern African states, such as Uganda and the Bornu kingdom, should have developed more highly than those of central Africa?
6. Are there cultural reasons why the Negroes of central Africa were much more numerously represented among the American slaves than were those from other sections?

BIBLIOGRAPHY

Franz Boas, *The Mind of Primitive Man* (1911).
Daniel Crawford, *Thinking Black* (1914).
John H. Denison, *Emotion as the Basis of Civilization* (1928).
Roland B. Dixon, *The Building of Cultures* (1928).
Jerome Dowd, *The Negro Races* (1907).
Alexander A. Goldenweiser, *Early Civilization* (1922).
Ellsworth Huntington, *The Character of Races as Influenced by Physical Environment, Natural Selection, and Historical Development* (1924).
Ellsworth Huntington, *Civilization and Climate* (1924).
Mary H. Kingsley, *Travels in West Africa* (1897).
Arthur G. Leonard, *The Lower Niger and Its Tribes* (1906).
Robert H. Lowie, *Primitive Society* (1920).
Robert H. Nassau, *Fetichism in West Africa* (1907).
Edward B. Tylor, *Primitive Culture* (1903).
Clark Wissler, *Man and Culture* (1923).

CHAPTER III

THE BASIS OF RACIAL ANTAGONISMS

Contrary to the traditional notion, group antagonisms based upon race are of comparatively recent origin. In ancient times there were, frequently enough, clashes of peoples and of states, but these were not felt as race antagonisms. There was, as one of the early manifestations of this special trait, the classic distinction between Greek and barbarian, but this was a matter neither of color nor of race, but of culture. And as the Hellenistic culture was taken on, the distinction tended to fade.[1] Feudalism helped to organize social divisions into fixed social classes against which the church and even the crusades were at one time opposed. Out of the subsequent religious wars and strife, there emerged distinctions of groups outside the pale: the Jew, the Turk, the heathen. These were aliens, but not yet races.

John L. Myers, in discussing the influence of anthropology on the course of political science, notes that until the latter part of the eighteenth century no one had doubted "that man so far as he could be regarded as animal at all, formed a single indivisible species." The Oxford English Dictionary quotes no occurrence of the word "race" in the present-day sense from any writer earlier than Goldsmith in 1774. It may be assumed that the distinction between civilized and preliterate peoples, begun in the seventeenth century, paved the way for the later distinctions based on race, but the prerogatives were attributed to the divine right of class or nation rather than race. Moreover, the exploitation was considered a matter of economic expediency rather than the high calling of superior blood. Sir Sidney Olivier traces the rise of race antagonisms, based on color, to the period of the rise of the British slave trade, and observes that it is now a complex of many reactions of Negro slaveholding. Viscount Bryce points out that "down to the days of the French Revolution there had been very little in any country at any time, of self-conscious racial feeling." One reason why these antagonisms were

[1] Frederick G. Detweiler, "The Rise of Modern Race Antagonisms," *American Journal of Sociology*, March, 1932, pp. 738–747.

not classified as racial was, as pointed out in an earlier chapter, that race itself was an undetermined classification.

The development of antagonisms based upon race can be observed in the interesting course of Negro-white relations in America. The first reaction of the colonists to the Negro appears not to have been one of racial repugnance. There were distinct feelings of righteous superiority directed at the heathenism of unbaptized individuals. The colonists were probably interested in the different color and culture of the Africans, but no racial considerations were at first given great importance. The Negroes were indentured or free; they held servants and intermarried or otherwise interbred. Material conditions changed, however, and a shift of sentiment accompanied the material change.

The rationalizations of the status of Negroes as slaves, in support of the profitable institution of slavery, served to place a stamp upon the Negroes as a race which remains today, only slightly changed in its main features. The scientific literature and other formal arguments required in proof of the presumed inferior qualities of the black race went to lengths scarcely contemplated at the inception of these relations. The stereotypes hang on, and have become a part of the culture of the common people as well as of that class originally concerned. And although anthropology itself has now repudiated practically every dogma of essential inequality which it once supported, the old emotional definitions remain.

Racial antagonisms, like racial prejudices, may have a wide variety of motives; even conflicting ones. The action patterns may be faint or intense; they may change, or even disappear entirely. However, it is seldom nowadays that such antagonisms do not appear, in one form or another, when two races are juxtaposed. This does not mean that these reactions are instinctive, since they have not always existed; rather it suggests that they are now customary.

Antagonisms do not appear where there is accommodation between two racial groups upon a plane acceptable or understood by both. Such a situation of accommodation appears in the class divisions between servants and masters in England, and between Negroes and whites under the fixed spheres of the institution of slavery. Antagonisms tend to develop wherever there is some form of conflict. Moreover, racial antagonisms are often not racial at all; for they frequently occur between groups which erroneously assume themselves to be racially different.

From the very nature of this phenomenon, its basic motives are rarely given. The causes frequently cited are most often rationalizations, arising from the need which men feel to be logical and reasonable. The fact is that antagonisms, as such, are sentimental rather than rational, and for the root of these we look to the emotions rather than to reason. It is expected, therefore, that motives as well as causes will be irrational, and not infrequently unworthy.

The causes of racial antagonisms may be grouped under two heads: (a) There are the immediate causes, which include those conspicuous factors and incidents such as color and hair, which give focus and collective significance to antagonistic group attitudes. (b) There are the remote causes, which include those more fundamental considerations of personal and group interest, and involve significantly group fear of loss of status, of loss of prestige, of loss of security, or all of these together. Some such classification as physical and psychological would serve quite as well, but the distinction is clear.

Such a simple classification of causes does not ignore such frequently cited questions as differences in racial temperaments, or in standards of living, or the familiar issue of superior and inferior peoples. With respect to these it might be mentioned in passing that the same race does not show the same characteristic temperament under different conditions. It has been noted, for example, that the English in South Africa and in China are entirely different from the English in New Zealand, although the factors of native complexion and civilization are about the same.[1] Again, the American attitude toward the Japanese has differed widely from the American attitude toward the Chinese at the same time, while the factor of complexion and strangeness remained the same. When an antagonistic attitude developed, it was first directed not against the lower living standard of the Chinese but against the higher living standard of the Japanese. Even in the matter of differences in culture there have been such widely different reactions as to minimize the purely racial character of the behavior. The American attitude toward the Indian has varied curiously from one of hostility based upon physical competition to one of tolerance, in which antagonism has been virtually suspended, while the factors of color and culture have remained constant. It could scarcely be said that there was racial antagonism

[1] Ellsworth Faris, "The Natural History of Race Prejudice," in *Ebony and Topaz*, edited by Charles S. Johnson; and "Racial Attitudes and Sentiments," *Southwestern Political and Social Science Quarterly*, March, 1929, pp. 479–490.

between white master and black slave during the period of slavery, despite the recognition of racial difference in color, civilization, and general social level. Other factors than mere difference in feature and condition are at the base of antagonisms.

Mr. J. H. Oldham appears to be essentially sound in his analysis of this phenomenon when he says that "the fundamental causes of racial dislike and hostility, where these exist, are similar to those which give rise to a dislike and hostility within communities of the same race. They are moral rather than racial. There is no necessity to postulate the existence of a specific and universal instinct of racial antipathy; while on the other hand there is strong, positive evidence that such an instinct does not exist. An adequate explanation of racial antagonism can be found in impulses and motives that are independent of race. These impulses and motives, however, though not racial in their origin, may *become racial* through being connected in the mind with the thought of another race. When this association takes place the feelings may be aroused by contact with any member of that race, and operate with all the force of an instinctive antipathy."[1]

Where different cultures are brought into contact we may expect to find conflict of interest. The differences between French and German cultures are in some respects so small that we more often think of them together as reflecting the same culture. However, factors of group and self-interest may express themselves in economic rivalries and political manipulations which are concerned with national security. These may take on an emotional coloring as when, for example, the element of fear is introduced. How these emotional elements may be aggravated and fired into conflict was well illustrated in the recent World War. The elements selected for exploitation as deliberate propaganda often provide a clue to the fundamental factors involved in group conflict. These are rarely the professed causes, but shrewd appeals to fear or personal or group interest.

Europe in Africa offers an example of one type of racial contact situation. The parceling out of Africa was not a casual accident. It came as the logic of economic forces: the need of new markets, the need of new sources of raw materials, the need of new fields for capital. These very largely determined the fate of millions of natives of Africa. First came the well-intentioned missionary, then the curious traveler, then the trader; and there followed later a zeal for

[1] *Christianity and the Race Problem*, p. 43.

souls and civilization for backward peoples hard to be distinguished from a need of their land, their labor, and their products. The latter part of the nineteenth century was one of imperialism which became so fierce in its zeal as to threaten international conflict and prompt some of the most shameful lapses of national ethics in treaty-making with the natives. There was inaugurated an age of reckless and heartless land-grabbing, of subjugation of native peoples to alien law and labor demands; of brutalities, trickery, and shameless exploitation in the name of civilization, culminating in the notorious scandal of the Belgian rubber venture in the Congo Basin, which aroused the conscience of the world.

Out of this contact of cultures has arisen an African Negro problem, variously styled the "Native Problem," the "White Man's Burden." On the one hand it is, as Pitt-Rivers suggests, the problem of realizing the white man's interest in a black man's country; and on the Negro's side the problem of maintaining his own existence, identity, and welfare. The status of the Negro in this situation is represented in the race relationships under these too often conflicting aims.

There is no problem of race antagonism until there is native resistance and a real threat of loss of the exploiter's position of security. Such a relationship, for example, has been recently reached by Britain in India, with the persistent and growing demand of the Indians for autonomy. In territories where the relations of Europe to Africa are not dependent upon the country itself; where a position may be maintained with the strength of arms of the mother country; where the position of the European is one of exploiter only, there is no antagonism. In South Africa, however, the situation is very different. The white population has colonized and cast its fortunes there. There is actual competition between the white settlers, who must labor, and the natives, who can do the same work just as well, if not better. Direct racial antagonism and perhaps the most backward racial situations existing anywhere in the world are the result. The question in this instance becomes fundamentally one of the security of the white colonists. Where groups are widely dissimilar in external features and traditions, the differences are accentuated, and carry all of the emotional coloring demanded for the protection of the group.

The genesis of another pattern of racial antagonism may be observed in the relation of Americans with the Oriental, the Jew, and the new immigrant. When workers were needed in the West the Chinese were welcomed and imported in large numbers. Race rela-

THE BASIS OF RACIAL ANTAGONISMS 55

tions between the whites and the Chinese were characterized by great tolerance. Their different background was accepted for its difference, and admired. When, however, the economic emergency passed and the large numbers menaced the security of the native workers of the West, antagonisms developed and stereotypes were created, which eventually resulted in Chinese exclusion. The Japanese followed the Chinese. Their farming methods, evolved through centuries of intensive farming, supported an efficiency of production which won the admiration of the country. However, this very efficiency became a serious threat to their less accomplished white neighbors, who could not successfully compete with them. Moreover, the Japanese were rapidly changing as a nation to a basis of international rivalry, and the self-protective interest of the American group soon dictated exclusion. Here again racial "instincts" followed economics rather than the original nature of either race.

Between 1890 and 1914 South Europeans were encouraged to migrate to this country. They were needed as laborers for the rapidly expanding industries of the North. There was general praise of the "melting pot" as a crucible in which were blended all the rich cultures of Europe, and Americanization movements and programs were assiduously advanced. When the volume of work declined and their numbers became menacing to the older American workers, the immigration of South Europeans was drastically restricted. The arguments employed in securing the legislation were given rational foundation by basing the undesirability of South Europeans on their standing in the Army tests of intelligence. The group attitudes, fostered by pressure against the means of subsistence, shifted from one of tolerance and welcome to one of hostility. It is, indeed, doubtful if many of those persons who began to manifest distinct racial animosities could make a racial distinction between North and South Europeans, except, perhaps, on the basis of occupation and dress. The findings of the tests have been reinterpreted, since the exclusion of the South Europeans, as having slight relation to intelligence and character, but this discovery has little influence on the group judgment. The same process may be observed in the present shifting of group attitudes on the question of Mexican immigrants, who have never been on a quota basis. In the Southwest and in California in particular, as the saturation point is reached in the labor market, these group attitudes are being redefined in terms of race. There is some ethnological confusion in the labor policy of certain California industries, some of them deciding that Mexicans are white and some that they are colored.¹ Recently a Mexican official addressed the Chamber of Commerce in a Texas city, and to avoid offense on one side and prejudice on the other he was referred to as a Latin American. The term "Mexican" was recognized as being freighted with racial emotions.

The operation of these interesting forces can best be observed in the case of the contact of Negroes with the American culture. Here we may see fundamental group attitudes in process of development; how they are formed and fixed; how stereotypes are created. There is likewise observable the operation of protective dogma, rationalizations, taboos, orthodoxy, and ritual, all of which provide in themselves innumerable points of possible conflict.

A few years ago, Mr. Gerald T. Robinson contributed a discerning essay on "Racial Minorities" to the symposium *Civilization in the United States*. In this essay he said:

> The goods and opportunities of the material life, unlike those of the intellectual life, are frequently incapable of division without loss to the original possessor. On this account, competition is likely to be particularly keen and vindictive where material interests are given the foremost place. It is also perhaps safe to say that the long preoccupation of the American majority with the development of its material inheritance has brought to the majority a heavy heritage of materialism. One may hazard the statement that the prejudice of America's native white majority against the Negro, the Indians, the Jews, and the Asiatics, is now and has always been in the same sense attributable and proportional to the majority's fear of some action on the part of the minority which might injure the material interests of the majority; while the only race differences which have had any real importance are those superficial ones which serve to make the members of the minorities recognizable at sight.²

The influence of the factor of concern over material security may be noted in a wide variety of examples. It is an historical fact of considerable significance that the bitter racial enmities between Negroes and an element of the white population descending from the so-called "poor white" class had its beginning in the mass use of Negro labor under the institution of slavery, which resulted in virtual impoverishment of this class of whites. The leaders of these non-slaveholding whites and "poor whites," after the war, were the most

---

¹ See discussion of Negro and Mexican labor, Chapter XVI, pp. 320–321.
² *Civilization in the United States*, edited by Harold E. Stearns, p. 354.

rabid Negro haters because this appeal was most effective with their constituents.

It will be noted that the highest figures for lynchings of Negroes correspond closely with the period of most bitter struggle of this southern white working class for economic status and social security. This competition was reflected impressively in the changes which occurred in the census figures for white and Negro artisans. The Negroes around 1880 showed for the first time an absolute decline in numbers in those skilled and semi-skilled fields which they had held since slavery was at its height. In the rural areas this competition was reflected in the struggle for survival in the poorer counties, where census figures show sometimes whites, sometimes Negroes moving out, and further southward where "night-riding" and "white-capping" were means of discouraging some Negro farmers who were more successful than the others.

The race riots, which erupted in the North like an overripe carbuncle, around the time of the northward migration of the Negroes, had a similar economic fear at their origin. The first serious riot, which occurred in East St. Louis, Illinois, had attributed to it no other cogent reason than that of "ignorant Negroes from the South coming in and taking white men's jobs."

One finds familiar patterns established in race relations which are attributable to the same economic motivation. Dr. H. A. Miller on one occasion said: "I am convinced that practically all race concepts are not race concepts at all, but concepts derived from economic situations. There are certain economic advantages to be derived from having one group subordinated to another." The disposition to restrict Negroes to menial labor tasks is one such racial pattern which is economically determined. It is without doubt true that many Negroes are unprepared for higher grades of work. At the same time there are many who are denied this opportunity despite their preparation. The objection is not based upon mere contact, for this occurs whether the Negro is just above or just below the individual white man. More commonly, it is explained in terms of the necessity for maintaining the superiority of the white race, which is but another way of labeling security; for "superiority," where it is a quality and entity in itself, does not normally demand the support of force.

Closely related to the question of economic security is the question of social status as a basis of race antagonisms. Social position and prestige are as much to be striven for as economic security; and, conversely, the threat of their loss occasions as great a fear. Just as it is felt that division of material goods may bring loss to the original possessor, so it can be and frequently is felt that the change of status upward of a lower group changes downward the status of the group above. The segregation and "Jim Crow" laws are crystallized expressions of this issue of security; so also is the practice of withholding from Negroes the titles of Mr. and Mrs., and the indiscriminate insistence of many white persons upon assuming the rôle of master, paternalistic or otherwise, in the calling of all Negroes by their first names, or referring to them as "Auntie," "Uncle," or "Mammy."

The most bitter antagonisms manifested toward the Negro are shown most frequently by those elements of the white population nearest to the Negro in status. Racial antipathies are by no means as common between Negroes and socially secure whites as between Negroes and whites who are precariously situated socially. The bitter feeling against Negroes who "invade" white residence areas may be interpreted in terms of this fundamental concern. There is the implication of common social as well as common economic status of those persons living together, and this in turn carries the suggestion, not so much of the improvement of the status of the Negroes, as the loss of status of the whites. It was the question of status more than security during slavery that kept impoverished white men from taking "Negro jobs," and this fear persisted for more than a half century after the abolition of the institution. This concern explains much of the vehemence about "keeping the Negro in his place," and makes understandable the meaning to this class of a "too smart nigger."

There is perhaps some merit in the notion that where there is greatest lag in the dominant white group there may also be found heightened racial antagonisms. Where real superiority is doubted or can most readily be challenged in open contest, there is also danger of promptest recourse to violence to reassert effective superiority. Progress is a relative condition. Many southern communities, for example, will tolerate and encourage the building of Negro schools and churches and of Negro homes. The tolerance and encouragement are freest when there is greatest progress within the white community. Negroes who are practical psychologists in racial situations know very well that if interracial peace is to be maintained in their com-

THE BASIS OF RACIAL ANTAGONISMS 59

munity, their schools may be good, but not better than the rest; that, if one of them should build a fine home, or purchase a high-priced automobile in a community in which there are few of these luxuries, his chances for comfort and security from violence are not the same as the chances of other Negroes living more modestly; that if he makes the mistake of expecting certain privileges which go with an advanced occupation or status, something very unpleasant may occur. These are well grounded in the mores and are seldom questioned by Negroes. In this manner, often good race relations are preserved.

Resentment of the dominant group, particularly where the margin of dominance is shallow, may concern quite trivial incidents, and even suppositions, and burst forth suddenly with an unexplainable violence. When southern Negroes returned from the war, it was imagined that they would bring with them new ideas of "social equality" and new confidence in the power of firearms. The military uniform thus became an aggravating symbol of a new social status and new aspirations for Negroes, and in many communities they were forced to take them off. Insubordination and insults were more often imagined than real, but it was considered wise to give the Negroes a lesson. Again, following the Johnson-Jeffries prize fight in which the Negro, Jack Johnson, won over a white man in a test of physical strength, there were assaults upon Negroes in many communities. In the minds of many persons, and most likely those who as individuals felt least secure physically, this prowess had to be reasserted in order to keep the local Negroes from too much presumption on the significance of the victory.

Basic motivations to conflict are frequently obscured by surrounding the real causes with powerful, though irrelevant, clusters of emotion. Sex is always an explosive element. More than any other element, it can arouse the imagination, horrify, and stir to reckless vindictive violence. The factor of sex is, perhaps more than any other, responsible for the long sectional tolerance of lynching. The race riots which have been clearly economic in origin are known to have been deliberately fanned to brutal intensity by false rumors of acts of sexual violence.[1] The Washington and Tulsa riots were actually touched off by reports of a series of rape incidents which later proved to be unfounded in fact. The suggestion of sex, whether founded or

[1] *The Negro in Chicago* (Report of the Chicago Commission on Race Relations 1922), pp. 584-587.

not, can so readily lend lethal seriousness to incidents, in themselves trivial, that it has been known to be employed in cases in which a mere personal advantage is to be gained. Instances of this are found in cases of crimes committed by white men and their escape from the penalties by alleging the protection of white womanhood from Negro insult or violence. It is not yet possible, over a large area of the country, to overcome the blinding indignation over the suggestion to investigate such a charge dispassionately, or, in extreme cases, to investigate them at all.

The most conspicuous argument employed in the formal attempt of the American Expeditionary Forces to convey to the French army and nation an American point of view on the Negro question was that of a proclivity for sex crimes. The appeal of sex is direct and unquestioned, and countless sins are possible in its name. Its power to arouse prejudice, with or without a race situation, is manifest in the propaganda stressed in America regarding the Soviet system of marriage. Referred to as "free love," the new contractual basis for marriage in Russia provides the most effective argument against the entire Soviet program, which is largely an economic issue and, to the average individual removed from it, a pure abstraction. It is not often recognized that sex is in itself a source of widespread and powerful appeal generally. It makes possible community tolerance of the "unwritten law" in crimes which have no relation at all to race. The recent scientific investigation of its potency and implications, social as well as psychological, has provided the basis for new interpretations of many types and degrees of pathologic neuroticism. When such a force is introduced into racial issues, the result is almost certain to be serious.

Quite as important, however, as these motivating factors at the source of race antagonisms is the effect of the customs, taboos, and conventions which have grown up as a result of these conflicts. These customs often persist long after the original cause is forgotten. In this way, children may inherit fully developed the patterns of racial antagonisms from their parents without knowing why; and newcomers to America, who begin without race prejudices, may take them on.

Attention may be called, suggestively, to certain of the more obvious results of racial antagonism upon the fabric of American life. It has hindered, at points, the free development of science, and particularly of social science. Despite the final arrival of anthropology at the point of declaring that there are no sure evidences of real racial difference in mental traits, virtually every racial comparison of mental traits by our scientists between 1885 and 1925 found this difference, because the investigators were looking for it. The urge, conscious or unconscious, to conformity with tradition has led many scientists of otherwise excellent reputations to take liberties with the scientific method of inquiry and proof whenever the subject of race has been introduced. This tendency, particularly in its bearing upon the Negro and the immigrant, has been noted in studies making use of the "intelligence" tests. The field of eugenics until recently had confused its issues in a fog of politics over superior and inferior racial stocks rather than human or family stocks.

In the field of labor, race consciousness and competition have, in large measure, taken the place of labor policy and coöperation among those who labor. Under the race tradition, it has been necessary to exclude Negroes and some others from the full advantages of labor, and to establish them as competing forces. In so doing, the cause of labor has been seriously handicapped, and needless racial conflict created at the very source of the livelihood of all workers.

The tradition of racial antagonism has led to modification of certain principles in law and justice. A difference has been frequently pointed out between the criminal rates of England and the United States. The clear implication is that there is greater respect for law in England than in America, and frequent occurrences tend to bear out this implication. It is impossible, in the first place, to maintain with any ultimate self-respect a differential scale of justice, whether it bears down upon the defenseless poor in the North, or the defenseless Negro in the South. When an exception to the rule of justice is allowed the structure of the legal machinery is damaged, and may and does permit exceptions in cases which do not involve Negroes. Moreover, it may be urged that to expect less than one's just deserts for violation of law is as damaging to those who are favored as it is to those who habitually get more than they deserve. In the end there is loss of respect for law on the part of both. Nothing more clearly demonstrates this lack of respect than the practice of taking Negro prisoners, suspected of crime, away from the law and murdering them without trial.

Mr. Walter Lippmann[1] analyzes the growth of racketeering and of the underworld in terms applicable to the field of race relations, and

[1] "The Underworld, Our Secret Servant," *Forum*, January, 1931, pp. 1–4.

what he says about the Eighteenth Amendment is, if one wishes to carry the analogy that far, equally applicable to the Thirteenth and Fourteenth Amendments. He says that the criminal who breaks the law solely for his own profit, or because he is provoked by passion, or is degenerate, is one thing, but the issues that are most perplexing and ominous are those presented by the underworld which defies the law, establishes a reign of terror and violence, and draws profits for services performed from conventionally respectable members of society. These racketeers are the outlaw aids to nullification of the Eighteenth Amendment, but are socially tolerated, with all the danger to maintenance of the spirit of the law and order which they entail. Just as deliberately are discriminatory practices in law as well as in custom tolerated against Negroes by many respectable persons, without realization of the more serious danger to all law and justice. The Fourteenth Amendment has defended more corporations in difficulty than Negroes, whose liberties it was designed to secure. Tolerance of violence which affects only Negroes frequently encourages extension of violence to other groups. Lynchings began with Negroes, but the pattern has been extended to include whites. Of the 4,761 persons lynched up to 1930, 1,375 were white. Bombings were tolerated in Chicago, as a means of discouraging Negroes from moving into certain residence areas on the South Side, but the practice finally extended to the bombing of other homes not belonging to Negroes. One of these was the home of a judge and another the home of a city attorney.

The tradition of racial antagonism has led to abuses in literature and art. Most persons familiar with the wide cultural range of Negro life in America know that the stereotypes of Negroes in literature and on the stage are only a perpetuation of traditional concepts which have only partial faithfulness to life. It would be considered both unwise and unprofitable to disturb this old concept, however well founded in fact such a revision might be. It may be mentioned only as an interesting and pertinent fact that, of the thousands of motion pictures filmed during the past twenty years, the most persistently popular has been Griffith's *Birth of a Nation*, which more than any other such picture has served to keep alive issues which feed racial hatred and contempt, where it does not create this hatred afresh.

The tradition of antagonism has placed a severe strain both upon the practices of Christianity and upon social philosophy and ethics.

One of the most difficult struggles of the church in America has been against the tendency to give sanction to current conventions. Indeed, during slavery, there was strong defense of the institution, with arguments drawn from the Scriptures. Although the church has shared in the traditions to a considerable degree, there have been created within the institution certain forces aimed at the conciliation of these fundamental antagonisms. This has been a phase of liberal social Christianity.

While racial antagonisms have a natural history and are widespread, they are not instinctive and they can and do disappear. Not only may physical circumstances change, but human nature itself changes. Prejudices cannot be argued away, but an investigation of the fundamental processes involved can contribute to an understanding of them as simple social phenomena, and, perhaps, provide a rational basis and point of view for new experiences.

PROBLEMS FOR STUDY

1. Lord Bryce, Sir Sidney Olivier, E. B. Reuter, and many other writers assert that race consciousness is a comparatively recent phenomenon. These feelings of difference, however, are now regarded as instinctive despite the fact that instincts require ages to develop. How are the present strength and widespread extent of race consciousness feeling to be explained?
2. There was less race antagonism during slavery than after the emancipation of Negroes. What accounts for this?
3. A prominent sociologist holds that group antagonisms are most acute in situations of least difference and cites the greater bitterness of the fight between Communists and Socialists than between either the Communists and the Capitalists or the Socialists and the Capitalists.
4. Since the basis of race antagonism is most often emotional, what effect can rational argument have in influencing a change of attitude?
5. Does the decline in lynching indicate a corresponding decline in race antagonism?
6. Many Negroes assert that their racial progress is conditioned by the intelligence and energy of the local white population, and that the more backward the white population the more resentful they are of the success of individual Negroes. To what extent is this true?
7. Is the necessity for control and discipline of the Negro population sufficient justification for a differential code of justice for whites and Negroes in the law?

BIBLIOGRAPHY

Frederick G. Detweiler, "The Rise of Modern Race Antagonisms," *American Journal of Sociology*, March, 1932, pp. 738–747.

Ellsworth Faris, "The Natural History of Race Prejudice" in *Ebony and Topaz*, edited by Charles S. Johnson (1926).

Ellsworth Faris, "Race Attitudes and Sentiments," *Southwestern Political and Social Science Quarterly*, March, 1929, pp. 479–490.

Walter Lippmann, "The Underworld, Our Secret Servant," *Forum*, January, 1931, pp. 1–4.

The Negro in Chicago. Report of the Chicago Commission on Race Relations (1922).

Joseph H. Oldham, *Christianity and the Race Problem* (1924).

Gerald T. Robinson, "Racial Minorities," in *Civilization in the United States* (1922), edited by Harold E. Stearns.

CHAPTER IV

PRINCIPLES OF RACE ADJUSTMENT

All the evidence seems to show that children start life without race prejudice. The child which has been tended by a Negro nurse scarcely knows the difference between its nurse and its mother, for the first three or four years of its life. Many times it will run to the nurse for protection or sympathy or help, just as it would run to its mother. So far as one can discover, there is no consciousness that there is any marked difference between the two. Of course this same child suddenly faced by a strange Negro man might shrink away in fear, which action has led some persons to assume that the young child has an innate race prejudice. But it would in all probability likewise shrink from the presence of any other stranger, even though the stranger might be its mother's own brother. This is probably not due to race consciousness, but to unfamiliarity, or newness. Professor Franklin H. Giddings long since pointed out that among animals as well as among men, when two individuals come in contact with each other for the first time, there is a sense of shock due to difference.[1] The more marked the difference the greater will be the psychophysical disturbance. "If impressions of unlikeness were never converted into impressions of likeness, all the psychological phenomena of aggregations would be dispersive, and there could be no society." [2] Therefore the young child who suddenly meets a strange face will often be terrified, as many of us can readily testify from our experience in trying to fondle a child. Difference in race is apt to accentuate greatly this dissimilarity of appearance and hence cause greater disturbance. It would be only normal, therefore, that the casual observer should conclude that the child instinctively knew the difference of race or had an innate race consciousness. That this view is substantially correct is well brought out by a story which Bruno Lasker quotes in his *Race Attitudes in Children*.[3] In this incident Dr. Howard W. Thurman tells of spending a week-end in the home of a white minister, who had a four-year-old daughter.

[1] *Principles of Sociology, passim.*   [2] *Ibid.*, p. 105.   [3] P. 67 ff.

The child had evidently never seen a Negro before; so she rubbed her hands on Dr. Thurman's face and then looked at her hands to see if the black had rubbed off on to her hands. Discovering that the color did not rub off, she asked Dr. Thurman if he was black all over, and when assured that he was, she gradually forgot about the difference and became quite friendly. Here was a case of shyness and fear, due to difference, then a gradual recognition of common qualities, and finally the disappearance of any particular consciousness of difference, which is ultimately the socializing process.

However, owing to the social situation in which the child grows up, he often acquires racial prejudices at a very early age. Lasker found many children who bandied about epithets such as *dago, nigger, jew*, without knowing what they meant, save that they were somehow epithets derogatory to the character of the person about whom they were used. "A little colored boy, four years old, calls any child who makes him angry a 'nigger.' He thinks of the word as something to make one angry because he sees other children get angry at being called 'nigger.'"[1] This is of course entirely a matter of imitation. It has no basis whatever in race consciousness. It is not until a child becomes five or six years old that he begins to be conscious of real racial differences, and it is at this period that he begins to note the separation of groups in accordance with race. In cases where the home influence and the social atmosphere in which the child grows are free from race prejudice the child will continue to play with and treat as an equal children of other races. I have watched with genuine interest the attitude of my own boy toward Negro boys who live near us in one of the large parks of Nashville. He is now fourteen, but has been shielded so far as is possible from anything that would prejudice him toward members of other races. At Christmas time he delights to give some remembrance to these Negro boys, and does it with exactly the same attitude that he would give a remembrance to a white boy of the same economic status. So far as one can judge from his actions and words he has no particle of prejudice against them because they are black. In this particular case the colored boys belong to poor families and they are therefore poorly clad and often have the appearance of extreme untidiness. But this is credited by my boy, so far as I can judge, to economic status, for which he has deep sympathy, and is in no way charged to race. I am thoroughly convinced that, could we have shielded

[1] Bruno Lasker, *Race Attitudes in Children*, p. 4.

him from racial prejudice among his playmates, up to the present time, he would hardly be conscious of any racial difference.

It is not until the child begins to come into competition with children of other groups that he becomes antagonistic. When he meets in the classroom or on the athletic field a boy of another race who surpasses him, he is apt to assume an attitude of rivalry, which sets up an antagonism stimulus. As long as antagonism is aroused by another member of his own race it remains an individual matter, but when it is aroused by a member of another race it is apt to become generalized and spread to the whole race. Thus, if a white boy is in competition with another white boy he is competing with an individual, but if he comes into competition with a Negro boy he is apt to generalize and think of himself as in competition with the Negro race. It is the tendency to generalize, when dealing with a less fortunate race, that causes so many newspapers to emphasize the race of a criminal when the criminal belongs to a race other than that of the ruling class. While such procedure cannot be justified, it at least can be understood.

It is to be noted in this connection that racial antipathies are usually connected with unlovely or repulsive culture traits which are specially exemplified in some individuals of a race. Thus many people think of all Jews as penurious and grasping, partly because Shylock was a Jew, partly because they have met here or there a Jewish pawnbroker as a second-hand dealer who was hard and shrewd, but mostly because they have allowed themselves to generalize and impute to all Jews the unlovely qualities they have heard of or seen in an individual member of that race. Oddly enough, such persons may recognize that there are members of their own race who are as hard and grasping as any member of the Jewish race. The difference is that the members of their own race are treated as individuals, while the members of the other race are treated as typical of the whole race.

Propaganda has much to do with the growth of these antipathetic attitudes. During the World War, cruelty imputed to individual Germans stigmatized all Germans as cruel monsters. Men of German descent in this country who had been known in their communities as honest, loyal, and patriotic citizens suddenly found themselves objects of suspicion and derision, solely because they belonged to the German peoples. Because some atrocities actually did happen, a cruelty which was beast-like was imputed to all Germans. I personally knew highly educated people who allowed themselves to be swept into this attitude of generalization. I heard eminent ministers deliberately preach a gospel of hate against all Germans, because they believed individual Germans had been cruel to prisoners of war. No doubt the same psychology operated among the Germans in their attitude toward the Allies.

The attitude of antagonism between children of different races referred to above develops into a more settled antagonism when as men they come into economic competition. Fear that the Negro will underbid me and take away my livelihood has been at the basis of a great deal of racial prejudice. The statement that we like "Negroes in their place" means that we do not want them to infringe on our economic or social status. Status, according to Emory S. Bogardus,[1] is synonymous with standing, and refers to social or economic rating. An attack upon one's status by competition leads at once to race prejudice. Prejudice therefore becomes a defense mechanism, by which the individual undertakes to protect himself against a competition in which he fears he may be the loser. This has led some students to suppose that many conflicts have been purely economic and have no race elements in them. But this seems a superficial view, for although the invading of economic status may be the acute cause of prejudice, it is only the acute cause, while the primary cause is deeper and has grown into an antagonism of a race by a process of generalization.

This process of competition for economic status has had much to do with a growing sense of racial prejudice during the last half century. For long centuries the white man, with his more advanced civilization, his greater economic progress, and his superior implements of force, has forged his way into almost every country of the world in order that he might exploit the wealth of these countries, which so often have lain dormant at the feet of a less aggressive and less greedy people. Inch by inch the white man drove the red man back in America, and, it must be confessed, often with a red-handed cruelty and a rank injustice which will ever remain a blot on the pages of history. He has held sway for many decades over the three hundred million brown men of India; he almost completely controls the destinies of the one hundred forty or more millions of Africa. Even the teeming millions of eastern Asia are not free from his dominance. The white man is a world-conquering and world-dominating species,

[1] *Immigration and Race Attitudes*, p. 30.

restless of all barriers, and eager for new conquests always. His early ancestors came out of Asia [1] and soon overran and conquered all Europe; thence he has gone out to subjugate the whole world. Although the white races are outnumbered two to one by the colored races, the white man controls a large part of the world's area.[2] Of this domination the colored races are increasingly impatient, and either a new era of understanding must come or else the white races will ultimately find themselves overwhelmed. This is the deliberate conclusion of numerous students of the question.

Again, conflict of culture may superinduce race antipathy. Bogardus quotes a clear example of race antipathy based on difference in culture: "One of the races I would not admit to citizenship in the United States is the Hindus. When I was in high school, we visited a foreign vessel in R. It was manned with Hindu labor and white officers. The Hindus had such greasy hair. Isn't that an idiotic thing to remember? And their tribal customs were so hard and fast. Two tribes were represented on the boat, and neither would have anything to do with the other, as religious customs forbade. I remember too that the ship was foul smelling because the Hindus could only eat fresh killed mutton, and they therefore always carried a large supply of livestock. The animals had to be killed in a certain manner, and by a headman or priest. Such customs seem so crude and superstitious." [3] When children, all of us thought others who acted differently from the customs of our own homes were "funny." It never occurred to us that their customs might be better than ours. Where customs differ, even grown-ups are apt to mark down persons following the other customs as inferior. If one listens to the talk of ultra southerners as they return from the North, he is apt to detect a note of criticism of the inferior custom of that section; and if one rides on the through Florida trains as they carry northern people home, the same critical note is sure to be heard. Difference of custom means difference of standard, is the line of argument. All customs save our own must be a bit inferior. Americans laugh at Chinese because they write from right to left, and Chinese think Occidentals queer for the reverse reason. A friend of mine asked a Chinese why he wore his fingernails long, and the Chinese replied by asking my friend why he wore that white board around his neck. Custom has

---

[1] Henry F. Osborn, *Men of the Old Stone Age*, chap. 6.
[2] Cf. Putnam Weale, *The Conflict of Colour*, p. 111.
[3] *Immigration and Race Attitudes*, p. 63.

the atmosphere of the right, the superior way. All who do otherwise are inferior. "No creed, no moral code, and no scientific demonstration can ever win the same hold upon men and women as habits of action, with associated sentiments and states of minds, drilled in from childhood." [1]

The Greeks and Romans called all outsiders barbarians, certain Indians said they alone were people, and the Jews had no dealings with the Samaritans.

Difference of culture makes it difficult for people of wealth to understand people who have always lived in dire poverty; and white men and Negroes, of different levels of culture, find it difficult to understand each other.

This difficulty in understanding other people is made clear when we understand the way in which various persons respond to mental stimuli. If the same mental stimulus is applied to a dozen different persons we will get a dozen different responses. Each response is colored by the past experience of the person from whom the response comes. The greater the difference in past experiences of the group, the greater will be the variety of responses. "In all our thoughts," says Boas, "we think in terms of our own social environment. But the activities of the human mind exhibit an infinite variety of form among the peoples of the world. In order to understand these clearly, the student must endeavor to divest himself entirely of opinions and emotions based upon the peculiar social environment into which he is born. He must adapt his own mind, as far as feasible, to that of the people whom he is studying. The more successful he is in freeing himself from the bias based on the group of ideas that constitute the civilization in which he lives, the more successful will he be in interpreting the beliefs and actions of men." [2]

The traditional material or accumulated experience of the mental life colors all new mental stimuli offered to a mind, so that all interpretations are made in the light of past experience. Since racial groups have had varying elements of experience, although much experience is common, they will undoubtedly respond differently, just as two individuals of the same race will respond differently, but perhaps less differently than two persons of different races. The difference in interpretation is not due to difference in mental capacity or difference in mental process, but to difference in mental experience.

[1] William G. Sumner, *Folkways*, p. 61.
[2] *The Mind of Primitive Man*, pp. 97–98.

It follows therefore that it is no easy matter for persons coming from different environments to understand each other. And lack of understanding is the fertile soil from which race prejudice grows.

This leads us to say that one must know the mores of a people before he can know the people. The mores are the ways of doing things which have been so far developed that they seem to have a specific bearing on the welfare of society. They are, so to speak, the generalized philosophy or interpretation of experience, and as such they are sacred, inviolate. To break over these mores is to become an enemy of society, to become anti-social. Hence, these mores become tyrants of conservatism. Taboos grow up as a process of enforcing the mores, and thus measure the first forms of social responsibility. Every new idea presented is associated with the mores and interpreted in the light of these past ways of doing and thinking. Thus in almost every community there are definite ways of acting toward alien groups. If whites and Negroes eat together, each breaks caste because the mores prescribe that this must not be done. A University of California woman once told me that her sorority had a Japanese student for house boy, because custom decreed that white girls and Japanese had no social contacts. The mores were set and fixed; to break over them was unthinkable either by the boy or by the girls in the house. It is in the mores that we call our housemaids by their given names whether they be white or black, young or old, married or unmarried. I shall never forget how shocked I was the first time I visited a home in New York City and heard my host, a man of great culture, call a German servant of mature years by her given name. That was not in my mores. I had never known a mature white woman to be familiarly addressed by any save her own relatives. But had she been colored it would not have struck me as strange, for that was in my mores. In America a bride would resent the groom's offering her father a dowry; in Africa she would resent failure to do so. It is a matter of mores. Herodotus tells us the Egyptians thought the Greeks unclean because they ate cow's meat. The Gentiles think Jews queer because they do not eat hog meat. It is all a matter of mores. And yet racial hatred and antagonism will continue as long as mores differ, unless humanity comes to know that difference of mores does not mean difference in capacity, or inferiority of culture.

It is in the light of facts like these that folk lore becomes important as a study. Since the folk lore embodies the response of a people it helps us to understand their mores. It interprets life. Contrast the folk lore of the African Negro and the American Indian. The folk lore of the one clusters around the gazelle, which, in the folk stories of the transplanted slave, became "brer rabbit" in America. The folk lore of the Indian centers around the fighting animal — the buffalo among the plains Indians. The emotional responses of the two groups are as different as the two sets of animals. The Negro has always won his way by shrewdness — exemplified in "brer rabbit"; the Indian fought back and destroyed himself in the face of fearful odds. Infinite labor and patience has been expended by Boas, Goldenweiser, Wissler, and scores of others in discovering the folkways and compiling the folk lore of the American Indian, and American people are just now beginning to appreciate the worth of the American Indian. The folk life and literature of many other alien groups should be studied by American youth in order that we may come to have a fuller appreciation of these groups. Familiarity with the folk lore of another people often lessens the shock when we come into personal contact with members of that group. In this field the *National Geographic* has rendered no small service to world friendliness by letting Americans know how other people live. Books such as Heyward's *Porgy* and *Mamba's Daughters* and books like those written by Gonzales, which bare the inner life of a retarded group, help us to understand them better and hence lessen our emotional repulsion when we first come in contact with them.

Some day the real story of the old South will be written. It will reveal a strange combination — a kind of feudal society with its stately mansions and peasant huts, its courtly manners and crude lack of culture, its ruling class and its serfs, its rigid individualism and yet its sectional solidarity, its high emotionalism and yet its controlled reserve. All of this and much more entered into the warp and woof of the old South. It made the mores what they were. But perhaps more than any other one element the attitude toward the Negro influenced the mores of the people. As George W. Cable has so well said, the Negro during slavery was always an alien. He was brought as a crude savage from far distant shores. He was thought of much as was the faithful horse or the dog. Yes, he was loved, but often it was love that resembled that which was inspired by a faithful animal. Socially he had no standing and never could have. "Generations of American nativity made no difference; — his children and children's children were born in sight of our door, yet the old notion held. He accepted our dress, language, religion, all the fundamentals of our civilization, and became forever expatriated from his own land; still he remained to us an alien." [1] The old Black Code declared: "That free people of color ought never to . . . presume to conceive themselves equal to the white; but on the contrary, that they ought to yield to them in every occasion, and never speak or answer to them but with respect, under penalty of imprisonment according to the nature of the offence." The white child on the old southern plantation breathed an atmosphere of superiority. He was master and the black boys were expected to do his bidding. Superiority and inferiority complexes became thoroughly embedded in the mores. No lack of ability on the part of a white planter's sons, and no amount of ability on the part of one of the slaves, could ever make any difference in their status. The white man was always superior, the black man was always inferior. Dominance and mastery normally gave rise to arrogance, so that Thomas Dixon, Jr., could describe the old South as "cruel and cunning, when fighting a treacherous foe, with brief volcanic bursts of wrath and vengeance." But withal there was a romantic side. The old plantation bred a love of home into her children. It poured into their lives a pride of race, which expressed itself in a form of chivalry to women and a hospitality to guests which was the pride of the South and the wonder of the North. Society was medieval, almost baronial; a few thousand landed proprietors set the standards of thought and manners just as truly as any European court would do. Aristocracy and aristocratic feeling were in the air. Tradition of family — and hence tradition in general — was all-powerful. Feudal society has always fed upon the superiority of the few, the dependence and menial character of the many. A landed proprietor liked to have a number of slaves at hand to do his bidding; it gave him a sense of power. Caste became a fixed pattern of culture. Those who did not belong to the ruling class were either slaves or poor whites. Free blacks were classed along with slaves, both in social status and increasingly in legal treatment.

Out of this romantic and almost unreal life, there grew up a mutual understanding between whites and blacks. No black could pass over into the status of the white man; that was clearly recognized by both blacks and whites, and hence there grew up a fixed status. The fact of separation became a sacred element of the mores. To raise the

[1] *The Silent South*, p. 7.

question was considered improper. None but the impious would ever question the status meted out to the Negro. In one field alone the Negro took on real status — namely, in religion. Running through the deliberations of all the churches is a constant note of responsibility to Christianize — usually described as evangelize — the slaves. The Presbyterian Synod of North Carolina in 1846 passed the following resolution:

> Our servants are part and parcel with our children, of our household, strictly and emphatically minor members of our families and so regarded both by the civil and the moral law. Hence the laws of the country hold the heads of families, bound to feed and clothe, to treat humanly, to protect and defend both children and servants; thus making them both minors, the one class through life, the other until they arrive at a certain age. The term "household" in scriptures too, though variously used, is often so employed as to include with the children, the servants of the house whether bond or hired. Hence household servants we find to be a scripture phrase. The term servant moreover is very frequently if not generally, so used as necessarily to imply this relation. In the fourth commandment they, as well as the sons and daughters are especially enumerated in the prohibition. Thus not only does the whole framework of society, with the universal operation of social and domestic ties, but also the genius and spirit of the Bible, with all its implications touching the subject, bear us out in the conclusion that our servants are minors, members of our households, bearing a relation to their masters in many respects similar to that which children bear to their parents.
>
> Hence, we infer that there is a solemn obligation resting upon masters to care and provide for their servants, to say the least, as binding as that to provide for their children.[1]

Numerous quotations could be given from the Annals of other Presbyteries, and from the minutes of general assemblies, as well as from the Annals of the Methodist, Baptist, Episcopal, and other churches. But all of them would be to the same general effect. There was a general feeling in all the churches that slaves were human beings and as such must be given full access to the privileges of religion. Here there was less of caste than in any other sector of life. Slaves attended the same churches as their masters, being seated sometimes in a gallery specially provided, sometimes in a section of the main floor of the church. They went in a body to the commun-

---

[1] John Robinson, *The Testimony and Practice of the Presbyterian Church in Reference to American Slavery*, p. 133.

ion table after the master class had partaken, and were given the same elements out of the same vessels as were used for the whites. Religious worship came nearer having the democratic element of value of all persons than any other phase of life. This also was a part of the mores. It had the sanction of religion and no one questioned it. But this democracy was not transferred to other sections of life.

There grew up therefore in the South a spirit of servility on the part of the Negro people. It was the one way of survival. By way of compensation the Negro boasted of the standing of his own "white folks" and vied with other servants as to the relative magnificence of plantations. The seeming happiness of the Negro, and his genuine loyalty to his own master, particularly in the case of the better masters, led the white people to believe that the slaves were entirely content with their lot. In fact the white masters in many cases felt slavery was a real blessing to the Negro. A servile black class, a paternal quasi-benevolent white class, with a sense of loyalty of each to the other "in his place" — these were the dominating elements in the mores.

Then the Civil War came, and the whole temple of southern society tumbled to the ground. The Negroes were no longer slaves, but freemen. The whites were no longer masters, but fellow citizens. The Negroes did not have to work for the white man, and the white man did not have to protect and provide for the Negro. The plantations without Negroes to work them were worthless. The Negro with no land to work and without experience in self-control or power of self-direction was helpless. In the confusion of the reconstruction period the Negro and the North felt the southern whites were trying to reënslave the Negro. The South felt the Negro and the North wanted to dominate social and political life. The southern white man and the Negro were driven into opposing camps. They ceased to trust each other, they grew apart. The old mores were entirely broken. For years the two lived side by side with no basis of understanding. By legal enactment the white man attempted to reëstablish a method of coöperation — a new mores. The Negro was disfranchised by grandfather clauses and other like expedients, but legal enactments do not produce mores. As the Negroes have advanced they have desired more status, and where it has not been granted they have become bitter. A sense of oppression has grown up among the Negro people. Many of them have not only come to hate white people but they have lost all faith in the honesty and fair play of the whites. This in particular applies to the southern whites. In the presence of this feeling of discrimination the Negro has become sensitive, touchy, independent. The white man takes this for presumptuousness. He says the Negro is trying to demand too much, that he thinks of rights more than he thinks of obligations. The Negroes are in turn driven into unities — they segregate themselves in clubs and national organizations at the same time that they cry out against Jim Crowism in all forms. So the vicious circle continues.

The problem of the present hour is to develop new and adequate mores. We must develop in the mores a sense of value of all persons. They must carry a sense of fair play, of justice and of good will.

The question is how can this be done. It certainly cannot be done by working out elaborate codes. Men are not changed that way. It cannot be done by legislating on the status of all parties concerned. It cannot be done by educating both groups without helping them to see and know each other better. Knowledge must not be theoretical; it must be concrete, practical.

It is a well known fact of psychology that emotion succeeds action. As William James said, "I run not because I am scared, but I am scared because I run."[1] I hit a man in self-defense, and immediately anger and hatred rise within me. I do a service to a stranger and immediately I become interested in him. The strategy of the educational process therefore is to change actions; the emotions will take care of themselves. We must work out ways of common service of each group for the other.

I have for a number of years taught classes of graduate students in a course in Applied Anthropology and Racial Problems. We have tried to trace with some care the growth of cultures among various peoples, particularly the colored people of America. We have invited Negro professors from Fisk to come to our classroom to discuss with us phases of Negro life. We have set ourselves to plan practical programs of helpfulness which might be carried out by any Young Men's Christian Association, and more than all we have tried to have members of the class actually render some service to the colored people of Nashville. The results have been most gratifying. The students in these classes come from all parts of the South, including the lower South, where prejudice is apt to run high. Some have come from the atmosphere of Vardaman, and others from the atmosphere of

[1] William James, *Psychology, Briefer Course*, pp. 375–376.

Cole Blease and Ben Tillman, and yet I cannot remember a single student who has ever taken this course who has not gone away with a friendly attitude and a determination to do something about present injustices. One student, a graduate of a denominational college in Mississippi, said he didn't see how anyone could be more prejudiced than he had been; yet he ended the course eager to serve some Negro boys. He has been working hard at it ever since he left the Graduate School. Some years ago Fisk University had an important conference and invited members of my class to be present. I announced the invitation, but did not expect any of them to go, because the conditions of the invitation were such as to offer the acid test of friendliness and good will. When I arrived I was both amazed and pleased to find four of us there — two of us being native Texans, one a Mississippian, and one a South Carolinian — and yet I would say these are the very states of the South where racial feelings run highest.

It can hardly be doubted that the two races in the South are in a position to bring about a mutual understanding such as no other two races have yet attained. There is here a common language which makes communication easy. In most contacts between two races the complication of difference of language is a great barrier. There is here a common religion, and that the one religion which puts emphasis on the value of the individual, thus superinducing respect for all others. There is a common economic task of subsistence from the soil, for it is still true that the majority of the people, both white and black, live on the soil. Most of all there is a deep sympathy — one might almost use the strong word *love* — between individuals of the two races, inherited from their forefathers. Most of the best literature of the South gathers round the old associations of the plantation, where white and black mingled in mutual dependence and mutual helpfulness. Indeed, the opportunity to make a demonstration to the world of two races living side by side in mutual self-respect and mutual helpfulness can be worked out here in the South if it can be worked out anywhere. By such a demonstration — which is already on the way, compared with race relations in any other section of the world — the South would set the life of humanity forward by a greater advance than might otherwise be made in many hundreds of years.

This can be done only by helping each race to understand more fully the customs, the thoughts, and the aspirations of the other race. The mutual understanding can be secured ultimately by trust of each other, for the final desideratum of knowledge of persons is open-minded sympathy.

We must also open ways for helpful service. Not artificial ways, but normal everyday processes. The Y. M. C. A. Graduate School and Fisk University are developing in coöperation a great library on the Negro. We (the Graduate School) are collecting everything written on the relation between the races in America, and Fisk is collecting everything written about the Negro in other parts of the world. When Graduate School students need to trace some fact into the life of the Negro outside of America they go to the Fisk library, and when Fisk students want to trace a present problem of racial life back to the pre-Civil War days they come to our library. There is not a great deal of use of this interchange, but it is a normal way of helping each other. Students in both institutions know about it and it forms a basis of mutual understanding. The educational forces of America must find many more ways of promoting mutual helpfulness if we are ever to have the reign of good will between the white and colored races of America.

PROBLEMS FOR STUDY

1. If race prejudice is not innate, why is it so widespread?
2. Why do southern people usually resent the way people on the Pacific coast treat the Japanese, and Californians the way the South treats the Negro?
3. In a sociology class of Negro students there was bitter resentment of the word "nigger," but one young woman in the class referred to "dagoes." When corrected by the teacher she replied she had heard Italians call each other "dagoes." What is the full meaning of this incident?
4. Some of the great philanthropists of America have been Jews — e.g., Julius Rosenwald, Felix Warburg. Why do many people think of Jews as penurious?
5. Are stories about the stinginess of Scotchmen and the greediness of Jews based on facts? What facts?
6. Why are workingmen more apt than people of wealth and culture to hate Negroes?
7. Most Americans who visit Africa or China or even England are critical of the customs of these several peoples. Why is this so, and how do these visitors justify their attitudes?
8. Can one interpret the actions of people without knowing their mores?
9. Why is eating with persons of another race the crucial point of difficulty?

Why was there a storm of criticism when Booker T. Washington and Theodore Roosevelt dined together?
10. Can mores be changed? How?

BIBLIOGRAPHY

Franz Boas, *The Mind of Primitive Man* (1911).
Emory S. Bogardus, *Immigration and Race Attitudes* (1928).
Jean Finot, *Race Prejudice* (1907).
Thomas R. Garth, *Race Psychology* (1931).
Frank H. Hankins, *The Racial Basis of Civilization* (1926).
Bruno Lasker, *Race Attitudes in Children* (1929).
Henry S. Leiper, *Blind Spots* (1929).
Basil Mathews, *The Clash of Color* (1924).
National Conference on the Christian Way of Life, *And Who Is My Neighbor?* (1924).
William G. Sumner, *Folkways* (1906).
Willis D. Weatherford, *Negro Life in the South* (1915).

PART II
AMERICAN NEGRO SLAVERY

CHAPTER V

THE AFRICAN BACKGROUND OF THE AMERICAN NEGRO

Antam Gonçalvez, leader of one of the African caravels of that proselyting but somewhat predacious crusader, Prince Henry of Portugal, was young and impetuous but inexperienced in exploration. Instead of being sent on the high mission of seeking the gold for which the land of Guinea was known from fable and fact, Gonçalvez was restricted in his trading and plunder to the petty booty of skins and oils. "O how fair a thing it would be," he said, in exhorting his men to valor for so uninspiring a mission, "if we who have come to this land for a cargo of such petty merchandize, were to meet with the good luck to bring the first captives before the face of our Prince." [1] It was Gonçalvez who, to compensate for his trivial responsibility, captured the first two Moors who were in turn ransomed for ten blacks from Guinea. Thus was inaugurated for Prince Henry, for the nations of Europe, and for the New World just opening, that vast triumph of religion and trade, of which, as Azurara, the historian of the period, says, "the heavens felt the glory and the earth the benefit."

Within twelve years a traffic in Negroes of immense proportions sprang up and became "an acceptable and profitable part of European commerce, the privilege of carrying them being eagerly sought." [2] The Negroes who were carried first to Portugal and later to Spain were Christianized, some becoming servants, some slaves, some free; and finally they provided the first labor substitute for the unsuitable Indian labor in the New World. The conscience of the Spanish Crown restricted these new black slaves for the New World

---

[1] Gomes Eannes de Azurara, *The Chronicle of the Discovery and Conquest of Guinea* (tr. by C. Raymond Beazley and Edgar Prestage). Quoted from Elizabeth Donnan, *Documents Illustrative of the History of the Slave Trade to America*, Vol. I, p. 18.

[2] Elizabeth Donnan, *Documents Illustrative of the History of the Slave Trade to America*, Vol. I, pp. 1441–1447.

to those "born in the power of Christians." Thus, they were at first always carried to Europe before being sent to the Indies. They were numerous in Spain even when Columbus embarked upon his profitable western voyage, and there is evidence not only that some of these Negroes accompanied him but that one, in particular, was pilot of the *Nina*.[1]

Although "Guinea" is most commonly given as the point of origin of the slaves, the area has always been broadly defined. Benezet describes the area as extending along the coast as much as 4,000 miles, from the Senegal river at the 17th degree of north latitude (nearest point of Guinea to Europe and North America) to Angola. This territory included the Grain, Ivory, and Gold Coasts, the Slave Coast, Benin, the Kingdom of Congo, and Angola.[2] By the end of the period of the slave trade practically all of Africa seems to have been involved in one way or the other. The British, in attempting to suppress the traffic in the nineteenth century, concentrated several thousand captive slaves in Sierra Leone. These had been originally recruited in the usual manner, through interior trading, concentration, and reshipment from factories along the routes without regard for racial or tribal distinctions or groupings. A study of the languages of this comparatively small group revealed that they had come from practically all parts of the west coast, the upper Niger, the Sahara desert region, Senegal, the Lake Chad region, Southwest Africa, the Zambesi delta, and the southeastern coast.

Traders, least of all, were interested in the genealogies of their captives; and even if they had been interested, it is extremely doubtful if those who did the grading would have been capable of making accurate distinctions between tribes. The confusion of the traffic, the differential survival through the middle passage, the indifferent original classification of these captives, when taken with the long history of racial and tribal migrations, tend to enshroud the particular African background of American Negroes in the darkest obscurity.[3]

The custom is, usually, to think of all Africans as representing one homogeneous group and civilization, or lack of civilization. On

[1] Alonzo Pietro was accredited as being the pilot of the *Nina*. Pietro's name appears in the "Libretto" as Pietro Alonzo, il negro. *Peter Martyr's Decades.*

[2] Anthony Benezet, *Some Historical Account of Guinea* (new edition, 1788), p. 1. All subsequent references are to this edition.

[3] Melville J. Herskovits, on the basis of recent studies, suggests that most of the slaves in the New World came from an area about the west coast, and from communities with well established political and social organizations.

the basis of this assumption it is similarly believed that there can be observed not only biological but cultural continuities in the traits ascribed to American Negroes. The fact is that there are, and have been for centuries, many distinct Negro stocks in Africa, and that these stocks have differed strikingly among themselves. In physical characteristics, there are wide divergences. Sir Harry Johnston [1] has pointed out that the Negroes of Africa are not all black. Friedrich Ratzel observes that there are no pure Negro races in Africa and no quite black ones.[2] They are in general a dark brown. The northern Africans, showing the influence of contact with white races, are light brown in complexion, frequently with angular Caucasian features. The Bushman ranges in complexion from a brownish yellow to a light olive yellow; the Sudanese Negro is described by Johnston as a "sooty black." Intermixture of racial stocks with whites and with other Negro stocks, antedating historical records, accounts for some of this divergence, while differences in climate perhaps account for other divergences.

The "typical" African is described as black or brown, with coarse, frizzly (woolly) hair; tall in stature, dolichocephalic, prognathous, with flat nose, large thick lips turned outward, and with slight hairiness of body. The necessity for representing a general type has led frequently to absurdity. Leo Frobenius puts the new case for the ethnologists when he says: "Open an illustrated geography, and compare the *types of the African Negro*, — the bluish black fellow of the protuberant lips, the flattened nose, the stupid expression and short curly hair, with the tall bronze figures from Dark Africa, with which we have of late become familiar, their almost fine cut features, slightly arched nose, etc., and you have an example of the problems pressing for solution." [3] The problem, however, has been faced before by ethnologists, and resulted in an attempt to narrow the continent of Africa down to the home of the "true or genuine Negro" who gave reality to the type. The ethnologist Waite excluded from the pure Negro stock the Gallas, Nubians, Hottentots, Kafirs, Congo races, and Malagasies. Sweinfurth excluded the Shilloks and Bongos. The "true Negro" was eventually described as living in a narrow strip of country, extending from the mouth of the Senegal river to Timbuctu, and thence to the region about Senaar. Ratzel was led

---

[1] *A History of the Colonization of Africa by Alien Races*, pp. 6–19.
[2] *The History of Mankind*, Vol. II, p. 313.
[3] *The Origin of African Civilization*, pp. 637–639.

to assert that although "the name Negro originally embraces one of the most unmistakable conceptions of ethnology . . . it is one of the prodigious, nay amazing achievements of critical erudition to have latterly confined this (and that even in Africa, the genuine old Negro country) to a small district." Continuing, he says, "We find that the hideous Negro type, examples of which the fancy of observers once saw all over Africa . . . has, on closer inspection, evaporated from almost all parts of Africa to settle, no one knows how, in just this region." [1]

Not only are there notable differences in color, features, and hair among the Africans, but there is such a variety of cultures as to confound any attempt to regard them as a whole. There are, in the African background of the American Negro, civilizations of a high order, as well as cultures which are abhorrent to the European and American. With respect to the strangest of these African cultures, to which the surprise and horror of early missionaries and untrained observers gave exaggerated features, there are to be found the most extreme contradictions among themselves.

The difficulty of discovering consistency and continuity in the African background is no more clearly revealed than in an attempt made recently to discover basic racial factors in desertion by going back to the presumed cultural origins of American Negroes. The author, in explaining why Negroes living in New York, in 1927, as a race deserted their families, said:

> Life in Africa, along the coast where most of the slaves were captured, is a comparatively easy matter if one is left alone. Edible plants grow readily, the simplest form of shelter is sufficient, and clothing is decoration rather than a necessity. Companionship is sought for mutual defense and mutual enjoyment, not primarily for economic reasons. Women are pleasant to have about at times, and moderately useful for agriculture, weaving and cooking, but it is comparatively easy for men to get on without them after the love making period and vice versa. Where there are no free homes, home keepers and home makers naturally are infrequent.[2]

Search in the writings of several modern travelers in Africa offered passages of support. Herbert Ward had observed that among a tribe in the lower Congo "upon first signs of pregnancy women retire to a special part of the village which is kept apart from the

[1] *The History of Mankind*, Vol. II, p. 313.
[2] Corinne Sherman, "Racial Factors in Desertion," *The Family*, January, 1923, pp. 221–225.

male section of the population." Again, David Livingstone had noted in his voluminous work that among another tribe a wife "considers herself equally free to enter into a new relationship when the circumstances are favorable." These customs, therefore, were taken as an indication of native traits which have survived in the American Negro.

The extent of race crossing of the American Negro with a wide variety of white and Indian stocks, and the uncontrolled factors in their migration within this country, would lend a high degree of improbability, if not absurdity, to any speculations about origins of this character. If customs, taboos, ritual, peculiar sets of beliefs, or even institutions are to be taken as fundamentally racial, it would be expected that they would also manifest themselves in about the same way wherever the race exists alone. Otherwise there would be no racial significance. But nothing of the sort is true. Consider, for example, the customs regarding the birth of twins. Among the Yoruba, twins are regarded as an abhorrence, and this is felt to be an instinctive reaction. They are placed in a pot which is thrown away in the bush by a special iron. The Popo, on the other hand, of the same basic stock, welcome twins, celebrating the mother for her feat. This also is felt to be an instinctive response. Or, again, in the matter of adultery, among the Okpoto peoples nothing is expected of the aggrieved party, but the husband might fight the adulterer; among the Ikumunu the offended husband attempts revenge in kind; among the Yakaro the offended husband sets fire to the adulterer's home and orders him to court where he is fined. Among the Keake the fines imposed are so severe the adulterer is liable to be sold into slavery for non-payment; among the Onitsla the adulterer may be killed.

We may attribute to the untrained reporting of our early travelers and fledgling anthropologists in Africa most of the descriptions of native traits which are, even now, regarded as the important elements in the African background of the American Negro. The shock of new customs, of new and different modes of thinking and behavior, is foremost in the reaction of untrained and inexperienced persons to these differences in culture. The dress of the Africans, sensibly adapted to the climate, carried a profound implication of immodesty to many of our early missionaries and western moralists; polygamy, to a highly monogamic culture, was regarded as abhorrent. The worship by the Africans of any but the "true and living God" was a terrible form of human depravity. The Reverend J. L. Wilson, writing in one of the religious journals of the middle nineteenth century, offers a common example of the shocked reporter, whose theology and zeal may be said to have seriously hampered his insight:

> It is a common remark of the present day, that the heathen world is as depraved now as it was in the days of Paul. But this does not meet the case. There are but few modern missionaries who cannot testify to the existence of forms of human depravity among them, of which there is no mention in the Apostle's category. . . . The depth of infamy and pollution to which heathen tribes have already reduced themselves can scarcely be conceived. If it be true, as it undoubtedly is, that our moral character constantly assimilates to the character of the Being we worship, it follows, as a necessary consequence, that African character has been approximating for centuries to a model, the most hideously immoral and depraved the human imagination can conceive. And here is at once the secret cause of all that cunning duplicity that has ever characterized this people.
>
> The lineaments of the Divine image have been effectually effaced from their hearts, whilst those of the spirits of the infernal pit have been drawn with too bold a hand to be mistaken or misapprehended.[1]

The accounts of the customs of Africans by such writers as Mungo Park and David Livingstone have the virtue of much information in a desert of ignorance about these people, because they were among the most faithful of the chroniclers. The accounts and interpretations, however, of a long list of less discerning writers, regarding the meaning of cultures which they were incapable of understanding, are responsible for distortions which the ethnologists have only recently and partially succeeded in getting condemned.

It is unlikely that any traveler could acquire a sufficient grasp of the language and its nuances, of the speech of any of the groups or sub-groups, to presume to interpret such abstractions as a people's idea of God, morality, virtue, conceptions of right and wrong, as has so often been done. It is, indeed, doubtful if any individual of our own highly developed civilization could satisfactorily explain to an alien visitor bent upon study the meaning of our customs, religious observances, and concept of morality. Thus, much of the literature describing "Africans" has failed either to differentiate carefully between Africans, or to report accurately the culture of any of them.

[1] *Southern Presbyterian Review*, March, 1848.

An example of the literature is the following from the account of one explorer in central Africa:

He seems to belong to one of those childish races which, never rising to man's estate, fall like worn out links from the great chain of animated nature. He united the incapacity of infancy with the unpliancy of age; the futility of childhood and the credulity of youth with the scepticism of the adult and the stubbornness and bigotry of the old. . . . His mind, limited to the objects seen, heard and felt, will not, and apparently cannot escape from the circle of sense, nor will it occupy itself with aught but the present.[1]

He is at once very good-tempered and hard-hearted, combative and cautious; kind at one moment, cruel, pitiless and violent at another. Sociable and unaffectionate; superstitious and grossly irreverent; brave and cowardly, servile and oppressive; obstinate, yet fickle and fond of changes; with points of honor, but without a trace of honesty in word or deed; a lover of life, though addicted to suicide; covetous and parsimonious, yet thriftless and improvident; somewhat conscious of inferiority, withal unimprovable.[2]

The serious issue of the psychology of the African is treated thus:

It is almost impossible to draw his attention to anything serious, toys and trifles, diversified with diabolism engross his life. He is never in earnest except at play, mischief, or in pursuit of some infernal rapture. Next to destroying something himself he enjoys seeing them destroyed by others. He is afraid of the dark, peoples it with bugbears, therefore carouses all night, making a great noise to keep the devil off, and sleeps in the day; is subject to unaccountable gusts of passion, with cunning enough, however, to know when such humors may be safely indulged. Sulky or sociable by fits and starts, easily moved to tears or smiles, senseless and irrational in his pleasures, plans, passions, and brutalities; the sport of impulse, whim and exaggerated self conceit; you cannot rely upon him, do not know how to take him.[3]

One common practice has been that of treating temperamental differences between persons as if they were common racial traits. Invariably every temperamental type is found, and the only solution is to make the contradiction a temperamental trait. Thus, as one writer says, "the African is tractable or intractable, stubborn or pliable, kind or cruel, faithful or treacherous, as freak may dictate; stingy, grasping, avaricious, yet reckless, wasteful, improvident, without care, economy or foresight."

[1] Sir Richard Francis Burton, *The Lake Regions of Central Africa*, pp. 489–490.
[2] *Ibid.*, p. 490.
[3] Lindley Spring, *The Negro at Home.*

J. E. Alexander, a traveler in South Africa, reported that the African mind is "devoid of inquiry and suggestion . . . has no curiosity, no desire to learn, nothing in him craves moral or intellectual food."[1] Another student reported that the African "has no past; neither in history, traditions nor romances; no monuments, or other memorials; no moralists, legislators, heroes or other great names. Though loquacious and prone to exaggeration he has neither song nor eloquence; no written language, no letters. Such things are beyond his depth."[2]

Some of these early travelers have, indeed, been quite fantastic in their descriptions of the things they saw. Keeping claimed to have seen men with tails "resembling those of cats, but hairless and which they could move at will." Lord Momboddo gave credence to the existence of men with tails. In an edition of *Stray Voyage* (1681) it is maintained that he saw men with tails one foot long and covered with hair, at the south of Formosa and Mendora Islands.

Professor Ellsworth Faris has called attention to the prevailing conception of the mind of "primitive man" as representing a sort of link in the hierarchy from lower animals to highest types of mankind. The point of view was given authority by Herbert Spencer, and supported by sentences from the books of travelers and residents among Africans. Only during the last quarter century has the notion been seriously criticized by such scholars and anthropologists as John Dewey, James R. Angell, Franz Boas, W. I. Thomas, and others. The chief errors in the observations which have set the background picture, according to Faris, have been false assumptions regarding racial mentality, the unwarranted generalization of untrained observers, unwarranted but explicable "leaps of inference," the tendency of natives themselves to invent explanations of customs due to the unthinking adherence to the ways of former generations, and ignorance of the languages.

The Africans, according to the literature, are supposed to be "impetuous like children, noisy and excitable." Nevertheless, Africans are capable of engaging in contracts for years of labor and of keeping them. In the matter of inhibition of impulses, which is supposed to be one of the best indices to mentality, Africans are generally described as weak. Nevertheless the taboos of the life of most African peoples, which are many and complex, are habitually observed by them.

[1] Lindley Spring, *The Negro at Home*, p. 75.   [2] *Ibid.*, p. 72.

Modern ethnology is now reinterpreting many of the culture patterns of Africa. More discerning students are seeing less of evil than of local utility in certain customs, and a rational evolution of their rites and ceremonies, which, while odd and unfamiliar to alien cultures, are logical and moral in their own setting. Richard Thurnwald, one of the recent students of African cultures, makes a most forceful appeal to intelligence on these matters. In speaking of polygamy, he says:

> The economic background of the family organization . . . cannot be treated as moral aberration only. There are important considerations touching the nursing of the children, the health of the women, the mutual assistance in daily housework, the disproportion in the relative numbers of the sexes, the work on the plantations and the care of the children, and so on. These should be kept in mind in dealing with the problem of polygamy.[1]

The history of peoples and the history of civilization fall short of identity, Frobenius claims, only in the measure in which forms of civilization, more than peoples, are the creatures of their surroundings and the home soil. Along with the strange practices of various African peoples, the forms and ceremonies by which a family is founded, female preëminence, patriarchy, the rôle of the priest, of magic, barter, tolerance, the communal pattern of economic life, variously known about and just as variously interpreted, there are other manifestations of these cultures which can be better understood but are less known about. Dr. Bronislaw Malinowski of the University of London regards matrilinearism, or descent on the mother's side, so frequently encountered among the Africans, as almost in complete harmony with the biological course of development.[2] Attention might be called to the fact that the art of iron smelting was first developed among the Africans. Indeed, Von Luschan and Boas go further in suggesting that this knowledge was passed by the Africans to the Egyptians and Asia Minor, thence to Europe and the rest of the world. Trial by jury was an invention of the Africans. Copper was known in the Sudan in the fourteenth century. Brass work made West Africa famous at one period of history, the Hausa people referring to it as the "red iron." Alexander F. Chamberlain attributes to the African an important share in the

---

[1] "The Missionary's Concern in Sociology and Psychology," *Africa*, October, 1931, pp. 418–434.
[2] *Sex and Repression in Savage Society*, pp. 75–76.

domestication of animals, and in cattle milking which, while still old, is not even yet included in the range of culture of the Chinese or Japanese.[1]

In political and social organization there are notable instances of high development in a sense intelligible to the European. Archeological and ethnological investigations reveal a history of empires of astonishing organization and strength. The Empire of Ghana, told of by tradition and by the scholars of Timbuctu and various Arab historians, goes back to the fourth century of the Christian era. The Tarikh-es-Sudan (History of the Sudan), the great chronicle of the country of the Niger, tells of this kingdom, which stretched southward from the Senegal, encompassing the famous gold mines of Faleme and Hambuk. It reached its apogee under Negro rulers, and flourished, despite powerful assaults, for 900 years, until the drying up of the water supply. There was, likewise, the Songhoy Empire, second only to Ghana, which rose to power in the seventh century, one of whose kings in the fifteenth century actually set out to connect its capital with Timbuctu by a canal 250 kilometers long, for purposes of military defense.

The dynasty of Kano in the fifteenth century was a powerful state.[2] The Arab historian, Ibn Batuta, who visited the Mandingo Empire in 1352, described it as one whose organization and civilization could be compared with any of the Mussulman or Christian kingdoms of the same epoch.[3] The chroniclers of Timbuctu: Bekri, Cadamosto, de Barros, and Leo Africanus, describe its highly developed commerce which was maintained for centuries. What the Nile did for Egypt the Niger did for Timbuctu and the Sudan. Its library and university were far famed; there were learned scholars and teachers and men skilled in law. Towns kept representatives in Timbuctu. The Songhoy Kings posed these seven questions for solution by their learned men: How can communal transaction be regulated; how can fraud be suppressed; what is an equitable tax on land; what is a proper tithe on newly acquired territory; what are sound rules of inheritance; what are good measures for censuring morality, and for developing good manners among the

---

[1] "The Contribution of the Negro to Human Civilization," *Journal of Race Development*, April, 1911, pp. 482–502. See also: Alfred M. Tozzer, *Social Origins and Social Continuities*, p. 68.
[2] See Maurice Delafosse, *Negroes of Africa*, p. 105.
[3] *Ibid.*, p. 66.

Sudanese? These indicate a type of civilization which can be better understood in terms of our own.

Many Negroes brought to America in the slave cargoes actually came from the territory still marked by the influence of this culture. One of these, Job Solomon, son of a king of Bunda on the Gambia, versed in Arabic, and able to repeat the Koran from memory, was captured in 1730, brought to America, and sold into Maryland. He was in time purchased by a man sensitive to his accomplishments and sent to England, where he commanded great respect. Among his friends was Sir Hans Sloane, for whom he translated many Arabic manuscripts. He was received at the Court of St. James's.

Some African groups have developed the arts, both industrial and creative, to a high point, while others have not been at all distinguished for their skill or genius. Both Boas and Frobenius have pointed to the work of certain tribes as brilliant evidence of the capacity of Africans for art of a high order. Says Frobenius: "A stroll through the corridors of the Berlin Museum of Ethnology teaches that the real African need by no means resort to the rags and tatters of bygone European splendour. He has precious ornaments of his own of ivory and plumes, fine plaited willow ware, weapons of superior workmanship." [1] Sculpture of a high order flourished among certain tribes in the Congo, on the Ivory Coast and in Benin in particular. There are but few African peoples who do not have rich stores of philosophy in their proverbs. In one sense this is their "literature." Many of these proverbs have almost exact parallel in European and American proverbs.

In consideration of the African background of the American Negro a significant distinction forces itself between what is biological and what is cultural in the expected inheritance. The theory of evolution has crystallized certain widespread misunderstandings. Widely and uncritically accepted, "it confounds," as Clark Wissler remarks, "the principle of evolution with the mechanism of evolution." Culture is *an* evolution, not simply *the* evolution. "Here is where we all," continues Wissler, to the chagrin of the learned, "make the naïve assumption that it is all part of one process, for the average individual thinks of evolution as a sequence at the top of which stands the Euro-American culture and at the bottom mere protoplasm." [2] The evolution of the zoölogist is based upon in-

---

[1] *The Origin of African Civilization*, p. 368.
[2] *Man and Culture*, p. 297.

heritance and is a matter of germ plasm. Culture is not inherited and so cannot have the same kind of evolution. Even if there were any special significance in the biological equipment of the African Negro, it would now be hopelessly confused in the extensive intermixture of Negroes in America with various white and Indian stocks over the past two hundred years.

There is a further question regarding the influence of the African cultural background of the American Negro. The conditions attending the first coming to America of African slaves made it extremely difficult for any important numbers of them to remember the parts of Africa from which they came, and the policy of prompt distribution, both as a practical matter of sales and as assurance against insurrections, tended further to discourage the continuance of old customs in the new setting. Communication in the native tongue was forbidden, and even if it had been allowed, the mixture of tribal dialects and customs, in the chance assemblage of the slaves, would have made it well nigh impossible. Although students have occasionally pointed to what appear to be survivals of old customs in North American Negroes who have for one reason or another been isolated in this country,[1] the American Negro represents on the whole a cultural detachment as nearly complete as has occurred in the migration of any people.

So far as it is known at present, less than a dozen words of recognizable African origin survive in the speech of American Negroes, and these are as well part of common American speech. Professor George Philip Krapp of Columbia University has called attention to the fact that the dialect speech of the illiterate Negro, which is expected to be a most natural repository of the African pattern, is really not African in influence quite as much as it is Elizabethan and Chaucerian. Contact with the early American settlers first set the forms of speech which they in their social isolation have retained longer than all others, excepting perhaps some of the isolated mountain whites. Such recognized Negro expressions, for example, as "mought" for might, "oman" for woman, "holp" for help, "yerk"

[1] Melville J. Herskovits poses the question in a statement of a new anthropological problem in the *American Anthropologist*, January–March, 1930, p. 150. "What do the Africans do that the inhabitants of the Negro quarter of New York City also do? May we find, perhaps, on close examination that there are some subtle elements left of what was ancestrally possessed? May not the remnant, if present, consist of some slight intonation, some quirk of pronunciation? Are the revivals of the Christian Negro churches institutional carry-overs?"

for jerk, "ruinate" for ruin, "drap" for drop, are all good Shakespearean expressions. "Hit" for it, and "I is, you is, they is," are good thirteenth-century English dialect.[1]

Again, the folk tales and folk beliefs which have been associated with Negroes, frequently lending charm to their natures, are by no means recognized as a reflection of their African background. Dr. N. N. Puckett of Western Reserve University, after extensive cataloguing of these folk beliefs and comparison of them with the folk beliefs brought over to America from Europe, found it exceedingly difficult and hazardous to determine these origins.[2] He came to the conclusion that "the tendency is for the Negro to take over English practices in regard to the direct maintenance and perpetuation of life (that is, in folk cures, ghosts, witches, concepts of death, signs and omens, etc.) while in things relating to pleasure his customs seemingly have more of an African turn."[3] The spirituals of the American Negro are a new creation by Negroes in the American setting. Professor Erich M. von Hornbostel[4] recognizes them as new and ascribes the creation to some innate musical genius of the African. Herskovits, in considering the question of the persistence of this type of motor behavior, notes that the appearance of mixed Negroes and the pure ones when singing these songs is quite the same. The Seashore music tests, curiously enough, no more reveal innate Negro superiority in musical ability than the intelligence tests under properly controlled conditions reveal their inferior intellectual ability.

African art has been recently recognized as distinctive, and of high æsthetic quality and sophistication. It gave power and direction to European modernism in art. Nevertheless it is wholly unintelligible to most American Negroes, and there have been no

---

[1] "The English of the Negro," *American Mercury*, June, 1924, pp. 190-195.
[2] *Folk Beliefs of the Southern Negro*, p. 78.
[3] *Ibid.*, p. 2. "Of no less interest [than antiques and heirlooms taken over by Negroes] are the mental heirlooms of the old South. Here again choice items of folklore were handed down from the white master to the better class of slaves with whom he had more friendly contact. These European beliefs were later forgotten by the white man and relegated by the more advanced Negro to the garret of mental life, but in the more illiterate Negro sections, and especially in the rural sections — the very woodshed of Negro life — may be found many fragments of early European thought . . . this miscellany nevertheless shows the Negro to be, at least in part the custodian of former beliefs of the whites."
[4] "African Negro Music," *Africa*, January, 1928, pp. 30-62.

notable examples of creative expression by American Negroes fundamentally akin to these native African forms.

Professor Faris has contributed a further observation regarding the religious emotionalism of the Negro:

> It seems that the facts can be explained better without appealing to the native African endowment. The social situation in which the American Negro found himself, has, in all probability, furnished the pattern by means of which he was guided in his religious life. Extravagant as the reactions are they can all be matched by others just as remarkable in the white race that was the teacher of the black. In Cane Ridge, Kentucky, in 1803, 20,000 white people were gathered together for the great revival services, where they stayed till the provisions in the district were exhausted, and were then compelled to disperse. There were the most exciting manifestations of religious conversion. Some had "the jerks," and could not control their muscles. Others would take hold of the young trees and twist the bark off in their excitement.
>
> As late as twenty years ago one could be pretty sure of seeing someone "shout" at the revivals of the white people, but it has practically died out at present. . . . The American Negro is emotional in religion on account of the type of religion which his teachers possessed when he adopted the faith. He is rapidly changing this, owing to the corresponding change that has taken place in the superior social group. The Congo Africans would become as emotional as the slaves were before the war if the Holy Rollers were to go among them and establish congregations.[1]

The apparent persistence, in parts of South America and the West Indies, of such Africanisms as "day names"; certain speech idioms; and the prominence of the mother in the feeling tone of the Negro family in these parts, have suggested to Dr. Herskovits the inevitability of some elements of the culture in North America. Since, however, the historical circumstances under which they were introduced to the respective cultures of North and South America differ considerably, and since practically all of the North American Negro traits observed as possible persistence of African culture can be explained historically, Dr. Herskovits offers the further suggestion that the historical factors may have reinforced the original cultural drives. If there has been such persistence, there is a like possibility that both the American and African cultures have been mutually affected through this contact.

[1] "The Mental Capacity of Savages," *American Journal of Sociology*, March, 1918, pp. 603–609.

The African background, however, despite its elusive diversification and the uncertainty of any pronounced cultural continuity, has a sociological significance which is both real and acute. The concept of racial inheritance of culture, or the equipment for culture, controls much of the present-day thinking about races. Lack of prestige accompanies lack of historical background. There is an almost universal disposition to argue lack of capacity for civilization from differences in cultural forms. Again, the historical association of Negroes with slavery, and the rationalizations of Negro status in America in defense of their profitable use as slaves, the righteous and sincere contempt for "pagans and idolators" surviving from the first shock of proselyting missionaries, the devastating effects of the misguided observations of early travelers and naturalists, the peculiar situation and isolation of dark, mysterious Africa, the heavy silence of history — all these have contributed to the present appraisals and status of American Negroes.

While there have been notable modifications in attitudes toward American Negroes, with increased tolerance, on the basis of their presumed ancestral past, it is becoming increasingly clear that the real factors of importance lie in the present, and in what American Negroes are permitted to become in this the only culture that they know.

PROBLEMS FOR STUDY

1. What are the criteria by which cultures are judged as inferior and superior?
2. A Chinese placing a bowl of rice on a grave was asked by an American if he believed his dead would eat the rice. The Chinese inquired if the American believed his dead would smell the flowers he placed on a grave. Show how this illustrates the distortion of ethnocentrism.
3. Could an African culture pattern survive in the American culture?
4. How does the necessity for status and prestige require the adoption of the majority culture pattern, as illustrated in the case of immigrant European groups in America?
5. An African native observing an American missionary kneel down by the side of his bed before retiring noted that Americans worshiped inanimate objects of furniture. How does this illustrate the danger of misinterpreting alien religious conceptions from external behavior?
6. Accepting the view of some anthropologists that basic culture patterns persist, is it possible for the American white population in contact with African Negroes to have escaped being influenced by the African culture?

7. Negro emigrants to Liberia found themselves as alien to native cultures and as susceptible to African diseases as American whites. How is this explained in view of the African origin of these Negroes who migrated?

BIBLIOGRAPHY

Gomes Eannes de Azurara, *The Chronicle of the Discovery and Conquest of Guinea*. Tr. by C. Raymond Beazley and Edgar Prestage (1896–1897).

Anthony Benezet, *Some Historical Account of Guinea* (New edition, 1788).

Sir Richard F. Burton, *The Lake Regions of Central Africa* (1860).

Alexander F. Chamberlain, "The Contribution of the Negro to Human Civilization," *Journal of Race Development*, April, 1911, pp. 482–502.

Maurice Delafosse, *Negroes of Africa* (1931).

Elizabeth Donnan, *Documents Illustrative of the History of the Slave Trade to America* (1930–1933).

Ellsworth Faris, "The Mental Capacity of Savages," *American Journal of Sociology*, March, 1918, pp. 603–609.

Leo Frobenius, *The Origin of African Civilization* (1898).

Melville Herskovits, "The Negro in the New World," *American Anthropologist*, January–March, 1930, pp. 145–155.

Erich M. von Hornbostel, "African Negro Music," *Africa*, January, 1928, pp. 30–62.

Harry H. Johnston, *A History of the Colonization of Africa by Alien Races* (1913).

George P. Krapp, "The English of the Negro," *American Mercury*, June, 1924, pp. 190–195.

Bronislaw Malinowski, *Sex and Repression in Savage Society* (1927).

Peter Martyr's Decades (1511).

Newbell N. Puckett, *Folk Beliefs of the Southern Negro* (1926).

Friedrich Ratzel, *The History of Mankind*, Vol. II (1896–1898).

Corinne Sherman, "Racial Factors in Desertion," *The Family*, January, 1923, pp. 221–225.

Lindley Spring, *The Negro at Home* (1868).

Richard Thurnwald, "The Missionary's Concern in Sociology and Psychology," *Africa*, October, 1931, pp. 418–434.

Alfred M. Tozzer, *Social Origins and Social Continuities* (1925).

J. L. Wilson, *Southern Presbyterian Review*, March, 1848.

Clark Wissler, *Man and Culture* (1923).

CHAPTER VI

THE ORIGIN OF NEGRO SLAVERY

Slavery was not imported full grown into the American colonies. It evolved by gradual modifications in the law and custom of a type of servitude shared, at one period, by whites and Negroes alike. The English colonists who came to Virginia had no pattern of slavery to guide them in establishing this system which later proved to be so important to the material development of the country. As a matter of fact, the direction of growth ultimately taken by the colony, far from being planned, was apparently not even remotely suspected by those who came to America, or by those of the London Company who provided capital for the enterprise.

Virginia was an agricultural colony, but the first planters sent were gentleman adventurers, a few tradesmen and practically no one skilled in agriculture. England, coming late as a nation to the race for imperial expansion, and finding the field virtually preëmpted by Portugal and Spain, looked eagerly forward to finding lands no less rich in gold and spices than those already held by her two rivals. Overseas experience had been to this point very largely a matter of trading. Edgar T. Thompson calls attention to the fact that the first colonists settled on a marshy island on the north bank of the James river, a site most unsuitable for agriculture, but well adapted to trading.[1] Unlike the Mayflower party which came later, these first colonists did not bring wives. The early relations with the Indians were on the basis of trade, a fact which made them at first acceptable to the Indians.

When finally disillusioned in the quest for quick riches, and when successive decimations of their ranks from disease and starvation threatened the extinction of the party as well as the project, the adventurers appealed to the mother country for support. The manner in which support for the project was given by the mother country is curiously pertinent to the history of slavery. It was principally in the form of more labor and more funds, but these were in turn intricately involved with the accidental development

[1] "The Plantation," Ph.D. Thesis, University of Chicago, 1932.

of tobacco in the Virginia colony as a possible staple crop, and with social conditions in England.

So vital a rôle did tobacco assume in the colony that some historians have declared it is impossible to understand the colony, its social structure, its history, without taking tobacco into account. T. J. Wertenbaker says:

> It was this Indian plant so despised by many of the best and ablest men of the time, which determined the character of the life of the colony and shaped its destinies for two and a half centuries. Tobacco was the chief factor in bringing final and complete failure to the attempts to produce useful raw materials, it was largely instrumental in molding the social classes and the political structure of the colony, it was almost entirely responsible for the system of labor, it even exerted a powerful influence upon religion and morals. In a word, one can understand almost nothing of Virginia, its infancy, its development, its days of misfortune, its era of prosperity, its peculiar civilization, the nature of its relations to England, unless one knows the history of tobacco.[1]

In 1614, after two years of experimenting with the Indian weed which was then a weak, unpalatable product biting to the tongue, John Rolfe hit upon a product that was "strong and sweet and pleasant as any under the sun." Its success in England was immediate, and within a dozen years the exports mounted to a half million pounds. Furious and reckless development of the crop followed. It soon became the one hope of profit to the London Company, and all other measures were subordinated to its exploitation with both men and capital. This accidental discovery coincided with distressful social conditions in England, and provided for a next and vital step in the history of an institution.

The English system of apprenticeship, codified in the Statute of Artificers in 1562, was in one sense a System of Poor Relief. Patterned after the guilds, it bound the apprentice formally with a written indenture, fixing his term of indenture at seven years. It also restricted countrymen from entering most of the trades, reserving this for townsmen. Justices of the peace could, moreover, bind out any unemployed person under 21 as an apprentice to a trade or to husbandry. The arrangement was unequal since "the craftsman was taught a trade while the husbandman only worked for his master."[2] Later, by the Poor Law revision of 1601, children

---

[1] *The Planters of Colonial Virginia*, p. 23.
[2] Paul H. Douglas, *American Apprenticeship and Industrial Education*, p. 26.

of paupers, vagrants, and excessive children of large families were included under the power of the justice to bind out. Changes in English agriculture, with consequent displacement of large numbers of laborers, gave some point to this feature of the law. M. W. Jernegan notes that "a man worked forty weeks in 1600 for as much food as he received in 1500 for working ten weeks";[1] that the Poor Laws, while compelling each parish to support its poor and providing penalties for vagrancy, at the same time prevented desertion of the farms under the stress of helplessness. They prohibited anyone below the rank of yeoman from withdrawing from agricultural pursuits. Thus, as the sheep enclosures for example dispossessed thousands in the country, the development of the woolen industry dispossessed other thousands of their jobs in the towns.[2] Poverty and pauperism increased, burdening the parishes. Emigration was the most logical outlet, and the pattern of apprenticeship, particularly in its application to agricultural work, became the model for indenture.

In return for transportation the servant bound himself to work for a master for a specified number of years. The feature of transportation was not the only new one involved in the transition. Since apprentices were minors it became necessary to extend the age limits to include adults. In general, the exact number of years set under the apprenticeship laws became the practice for indenture. For nearly a century these indentured servants and redemptioners were brought to America and their services sold.

Philip A. Bruce, in his *Economic History of Virginia in the Seventeenth Century*, cites an instrument of indenture which suggests the rigid and almost feudalistic character of the arrangement:

> This indenture made the 6th day of June in the year of our Lord Christ 1659, witnesseth, that Bartholomew Clarke ye Son of John Clarke of the City of Canterbury, Sadler, of his own liking and with ye consent of Francis Plumer of ye City of Canterbury, Brewer, hath put himself apprentice unto Edward Rowzie of Virginia, planter, as an apprentice with him to dwell from ye day of the date above mentioned unto ye full term of four years from thence next ensuing fully to be complete and ended, all which said term the said Bartholomew Clarke well and faithfully the said Edward Rowzie as his master shall serve, his secrets keep, his commands most just and lawful he shall observe and fornication he shall not commit, not con-

---

[1] "A Forgotten Slavery of Colonial Days," *Harper's Magazine*, October, 1913, p. 746.

[2] Paul H. Douglas, *American Apprenticeship and Industrial Education*, p. 27.

tract matrimony with any woman during the said term, he shall not do hurt unto his master, nor consent to ye doing of any, but to his power shall hinder and prevent ye doing of any; at cards, dice, or any unlawful games he shall not play; he shall not waste the goods of his said master nor lend them to anybody without his master's consent, he shall not absent himself from his said master's service day or night, but as a true and faithful servant, shall demean himself, and the said Edward Rowzie in ye mystery, art and occupation of a planter which now . . . the best manner he can, the said Bartholomew shall teach or cause to be taught, and also during, said term shall find and allow his apprentice competent meat, drink, apparel, washing, lodging, with all other things fitting for his degree and in the end thereof, fifty acres of land to be laid out for him, and all other things which according to the custom of the country is or ought to be done.[1]

Once firmly established and essential, servitude took on even more rigid features. The right was eventually assumed by masters to assign their servant's contract without the servant's consent; time was added for misconduct, either actual or fraudulently charged; unexpired terms were sold; the right to corporal punishment was assumed; servants were rented and hired out by masters. In the end, as indentured servants began to be listed in the inventories of estates, in deeds and wills along with other property, their legal personality gradually approximated that of chattel. Some such servants brought by shipowners without indentures already made in England were, not infrequently, auctioned by the captain of the ship to the highest bidder. Abuses became so general that laws eventually were enacted by the Virginia and Maryland Assemblies in an attempt to curb the excesses. Maryland led in 1638 with these laws. Fifteen years later, this colony had to redefine the issue of the servant's age and length of service. Virginia took similar steps in 1643 and 1657.

As a necessary measure of control over these servants, and for the protection of the master, corporal punishment was legalized. Since the servants were without money to pay fines, and since length of servitude was fixed by law, something had to be done to protect the master in his rights. A law enacted in Virginia in 1662 provided "for the erecting of a whipping post in every county" and the General Assembly of the Colony in 1688 reassured the master of the right to whip the servant.[2] The severity of treatment of these

[1] Vol. II, p. 1.
[2] J. R. Davis, "Negro Servitude in the United States," *Journal of Negro History*, July, 1923, p. 270.

servants, ever increasing, created the serious problem of "runaways." Indeed, servants frequently ran away whether they had been abused or not. The legislative and customary measures designed to curb the practice of running off foreshadowed, and perhaps provided the actual model for, the later Fugitive Slave Acts and the Underground Railroad of the slavery régime. There were also foreshadowed in the expedients employed to control this servitude many features of the later slave codes. There were, for example, restrictions upon "unlawful assemblage," designed to prevent "plotting" and "insurrections." Not only was prolongation of servitude legalized as punishment for running away, but limits were established fixing the radius within which a servant might move around his master's home. In some states the limit was ten miles, in some only two miles. South Carolina permitted a fugitive servant, when caught, to be flogged by the constable in every town through which he passed in being returned to his master.[1]

All servants traveling were required to have a pass. There were advertisements for runaways in the newspapers. Provisions were made for the return of fugitives by one colony to another.[2] Even at the end of the period of servitude it was by no means certain that he would get his promised fifty acres of land. Indeed, little is known about the fate of this class after serving their time. James C. Ballagh states that the freedman formed a very strong type of peasant proprietor, and that he provided for the growth of a strong yeomanry,[3] but Douglas gives the opinion that, although the matter is shrouded in uncertainty, all evidence points to the opposite conclusion. "All that he received from his master when freed," says Douglas, "was some clothing, a few bushels of corn, a tool or two and sometimes a gun. It is evident that discrimination was made in the privilege of franchise between the recent freedman and the freeman, and that there existed a very definite suspicion of the ability of the freedman to exercise the suffrage judiciously." [4]

It was at the first turn of fortune for the colony, when labor was in high demand, that a Dutch frigate, manned chiefly by Englishmen, on its way to Bermuda touched at Jamestown around the latter

[1] Paul H. Douglas, *American Apprenticeship and Industrial Education*, p. 35.
[2] J. R. Davis, "Negro Servitude in the United States," *Journal of Negro History*, July, 1923, p. 274.
[3] *White Servitude in the Colony of Virginia*, p. 82.
[4] Paul H. Douglas, *American Apprenticeship and Industrial Education*, p. 38.

part of August, 1619, and disposed of the first twenty Negroes. The fact that the ship was a privateer, and had no rights of ownership over captives secured through piracy, would have determined the status of the Negroes even if there had been any design to sell them outright. For these captives were legally and theoretically under the protection of international law.[1] It is a matter of record that they were obtained by the settlers in Jamestown through exchange of public provisions, and that they were put to work on public lands to support the governor and other officers of the government.

The only question which seems to have occurred to the colonists concerned the right to the services of these Negroes, rather than the right to their persons.[2] They were accepted on the same conditions governing the white indentured servants brought from England. In all the records of the County Court of Virginia from 1632 to 1661 they were designated as "servants," "negro servants," or simply as "Negroes,"[3] although the term "slave" and its meaning were familiar to them.[4] The census of the colony made in 1624 and 1625 lists twenty-three persons of the African race, designating them merely as "servants."[5] Thomas Jefferson speculated that either the right to these first Negroes was common or they "lived on footing with the whites, who, as well as themselves, were under the absolute direction of the President."[6]

The most convincing evidence, however, of the status of Negroes during this period appears in certain court records of cases in which Negroes were litigants. One of these Negroes, Anthony Johnson, was probably a member of the first group of Negroes brought into the colony. There is evidence of his free status in the assignment to him in 1651, by the County Court of Northampton County in Virginia, of 250 acres of land in fee simple. The next year he petitioned the court and was granted an exemption from taxes for a

---

[1] James C. Ballagh, *A History of Slavery in Virginia*, p. 28.

[2] *Ibid.*

[3] John H. Russell, *The Free Negro in Virginia, 1619–1865*, p. 24.

[4] Indentured servants frequently referred to their lot as that of "slavery." There were, moreover, during this period acts referring to Indian slavery. "If the Indians shall bring in any children as gages of their good and quiet intentions to us . . . that we will not use them as slaves." H. W. Hening, *Statutes at Large, Being a Collection of All the Laws of Virginia, 1619–1792*, Vol. I, p. 296.

[5] John H. Russell, *The Free Negro in Virginia, 1619–1865*, p. 20, note 13.

[6] *Ibid.*, p. 24.

THE ORIGIN OF NEGRO SLAVERY 105

year because of loss of his property by fire. The following year he came to court again to answer the complaint of another Negro, John Casor, who accused Johnson of holding him in indenture "for seven years longer than he should or ought." [1]

In answer to this last complaint, Johnson contended that he had never seen any indenture papers of Casor's, and that he had the Negro for life. Casor still affirmed, with the aid of Captain Goldsmith, that when he came to Johnson he had the papers, and offered to produce witnesses who saw the paper signed by Mr. Sandys himself. In boldness, Casor threatened that if he were not freed he would take Johnson's cows in compensation for services rendered beyond his time. This was such a surprise that Johnson's wife, his son-in-law, and his own two sons, who were with him in court, urged him to give Casor his freedom. The old Negro, however, was wily, and although at first frightened, decided upon a course equally unexpected by the complainant. He entered suit against Robert Parker, a white man, and one of Casor's witnesses, charging that "hee detayneth one Jno Casor a negro the plaintiff's servt under pretense yt the sd Jno Casor is a freeman." [2] The Court, in a decision which marked a most significant step in the crystallization of slavery itself, rendered the following verdict:

> The Court . . . doe fynd that ye sd Mr. Robert Parker most unrightfully keepeth ye sd Negro John Casor from his rt Mayster Anthony Johnson . . . Be therefore ye Judgment of ye Court & ordered that ye sd John Casor negro shall forthwith return unto ye service of his sd Mayster Anthony Johnson and the sd Mr. Robert Parker make payment of all charges in the suite and execution.[3]

Thus was rendered, in strange and fateful irony, the first legal decision involving the right to the perpetual services of a Negro. The decision was obviously not made on racial grounds, as the chance position and relationship of the litigants in the suit well establishes.

Although servitude for life marked a step in the direction of slavery, it was not yet legal slavery. For many years, not only were Negro and white servants treated alike, but they associated freely with one another. White and Negro servants frequently ran away to-

---

[1] Edgar Tristram Thompson, "The Plantation," Ph.D. Thesis, University of Chicago, 1932, and John H. Russell, *The Free Negro in Virginia, 1619–1865*, p. 32.

[2] *Ibid.* p. 32.

[3] *Ibid.*, p. 33.

gether, intermarried, and were accused of plotting together against their masters. The stratification was one of class rather than race.[1] The colony was conscious of its mulattoes as early as 1638, and tried to do something about discouraging the matings responsible for this offspring. Several forces acting together eventually crystallized a next step in the transition from indenture to slavery.

One factor favorable to the continuance of Negroes in the status of servants was, no doubt, the headrights of fifty acres of land allowed planters for each servant introduced. There was no pattern for carrying over this privilege to cover a slave purchased outright. It is known that headrights were allowed on Negro servants.[2] The status of indenture for Negroes, having an element of profit, was not changed.

The extension, wherever possible, of the period of indenture of all servants, white, Negro, and Indian, was found to meet with less objection in the case of some than of others. The Indians represented hostile surroundings and evoked less sympathy; the Negroes were an alien people and were feared. This was evident in the practice of immediately separating them on arrival to prevent transmission of tribal traditions. The illiterate whites could not make their resentments felt effectively and they suffered accordingly. Other indentured whites were more often able to defend their rights.

While indenture for all three groups existed along with servitude for life, it could be noted that the incidence of life servitude tended to increase in the case of Negroes and Indians, and to decrease in the case of the whites. Moreover, punishments became more severe for Negroes and Indians than for whites, and tolerance of this further encouraged the practice. The Negroes were at a greater disadvantage than the whites in running away. Their color could always identify them.

The vicissitudes of tobacco, and notably the rapid exhaustion of the soil as a result of tobacco cultivation, brought on another situation. There could be relatively little stability in land-holdings where it was required that planters must constantly be on the move seeking new lands. Thompson suggests that the requirement of mobility in the labor force prevented serfdom, or attachment to the

---

[1] Philip A. Bruce, *Social Life in Virginia in the Seventeenth Century*, p. 53.

[2] "In 1651 there is specific record of headrights allowed on the importation of a Negro named Richard Johnson of Virginia." John H. Russell, *The Free Negro in Virginia, 1619–1865*, pp. 25, 26.

THE ORIGIN OF NEGRO SLAVERY

soil, and made imperative a status of "attachment to the person."[1] This encouraged planters to have the period of service extended, by whatever means available, to life.

Still another factor was that involving inheritance, and the status of children of indentured servants. In the contracts, as a rule, servants were forbidden to marry during the period of indenture. Marriage increased the burden of upkeep of the servant who had no other property or funds save those given by the master; it brought divided attention and obligation, and it introduced the problem of children, requiring further expense of upkeep and time from labor. Laws enacted by the Assembly, designed to cover this situation, in some instances extended the time of the mother, and there were planters who went so far as to permit extra-legal relations as a means of obtaining this legitimate extension of indenture.

This issue was accentuated in the case of Negroes because of the conspicuousness of the mulatto class. The colony officially regarded the unions with disfavor. It appears that the opposition to these relations was based as much upon the fact of religion as any other, since the relations were actually practiced, and it was the question of religion that still later became the test in determining who should and who should not be slaves. In 1630 the court ordered a man punished for "abusing himself to the dishonor of God and the shame of Christians by defiling his body by lying with a Negro,"[2] but this did not concern Negroes only. There were similar restrictions against Moors, Mohammedans, Turks, and Jews, representing difference in religion more consistently than difference in race and color.

The first bastardy laws, however, were designed as moral aids, to curb the impulses of both free and indentured women. Shrewdly, these laws protected the masters of servants more effectively than they protected the servants. They were, at base, laws against fornication, and provided that the woman, if free, be fined £15.0 or sold into service for five years; and if a servant, that she be given five additional years. A second law against fornication, in 1662, was aimed at relations between Englishmen and Negro women. It imposed the status of the mother on the child — i.e., servitude for life — and enacted a fine from the white offender just double that for other fornication.[3] By 1691 intermarriage of a free white with

---

[1] "The Plantation," Ph.D. Thesis, University of Chicago, 1932.
[2] James C. Ballagh, *A History of Slavery in Virginia*, p. 57.
[3] *Ibid.*, p. 57.

a Negro, mulatto, or Indian, bond or free, was punishable with perpetual banishment of the white, and the mulatto offspring, if any, was to be bound out for thirty years. However, the duty of carrying out the banishment was placed in the hands of the county justices without means of enforcing it, and in 1705 another law made the punishment more certain though less severe, and succeeded in checking intermarriage without seriously affecting miscegenation.

The doctrine of *partus sequitur ventrem*, enunciated in 1662, which provided that the child must follow its mother's status, became the next vital factor in the transition to slavery. Maryland followed Virginia the next year with similar legislation, Massachusetts in 1698, Connecticut and New Jersey in 1704, Pennsylvania and New York in 1706, South Carolina in 1712, Rhode Island in 1728, and North Carolina in 1741.[1]

The specific legislation which further contributed to the development of the institution of slavery was not followed up in Virginia and Maryland immediately, probably because of the depression in tobacco and the slackening in the demand for servants. But in the last quarter of the seventeenth century, when prosperity returned, the large planters, who alone were able to take advantage of this revival, based upon lowered cost of production rather than rise in price, turned frankly and flagrantly to direct purchase of Negroes from Africa. The Negroes were found more profitable than the white servants, and as their numbers mounted the whites were gradually eliminated from the plantations. They were pushed into the less productive areas or forced to migrate farther south and west.

The next important and final step occurred at the high point of prosperity in the colony. The justification of slavery, which was now getting fixed in custom, was a religious one. Christians might enslave the heathen as a means of "bringing them to a knowledge of Christ," but once a slave was brought to Christ there was the danger of losing him. The medieval theory of slavery which was developed in Europe under the influence of the Christian church was that slavery should be confined to the heathen, and that freedom should follow conversion. The first efforts to deal with this perplexing situation temporized desperately with the issue. The planters strongly opposed Christianization of Negroes because it meant loss of property. The Virginia Assembly in 1667 passed an act declaring

[1] James C. Ballagh, *A History of Slavery in Virginia*, p. 57.

that "Baptism doth not alter the condition of the person as to his bondage or freedom; in order that diverse masters freed from this doubt may more carefully endeavor the propagation of Christianity." This was followed by still another act three years later, which stretched the principle to make possible enslavement of those who had at any time been heathen. Maryland's law, which was passed the next year, was most specific, declaring that "the conversion of the Holy Sacrament of Baptism does not alter the status of slaves or their issue."

It was at this point that race, as such, was made to supplant religion as a test for slavery. In 1682, just sixty-three years after the coming of the Negroes to Virginia, the leaders in the colony found the solution consistent with the economic fortunes of the colony. A new law was then enacted which denied Christianity as a mode of gaining freedom to all Negroes, mulattoes, hostile Moors and Turks, and such Indians as were sold by other Indians as slaves; it repealed the Act of 1670 and made slaves of all such non-Christians thereafter coming into the colony, by land or sea, unconverted or converted, whether before or after captivity.

As a result very largely of social stratification in the colonies a planter caste had evolved, and the institution was complete. Tobacco, supported by Negro slavery, flourished until the American Revolution. By the end of the eighteenth century, following the final decline of tobacco as a major staple, and following the spirit engendered by the success of the Revolution, slavery lost much of its importance and slaves became an economic burden on the planters. Since the slavery evolved was essentially capitalistic, requiring a major investment in the legal ownership of labor itself, the system became wholly onerous when this labor, for any reason at all, became unproductive.[1] The importation of new slaves was stopped in 1776. The attention of planters and statesmen in states having large Negro slave populations was turned toward finding some means of ridding the states of their slave populations and the owners of their responsibility. While Thomas Jefferson was a member of the Virginia Assembly, he had proposed the utilization of vacant western lands for the increasing numbers of Negroes who were manumitted because of the expense of maintaining them. At the time of Jefferson's proposal the country was impoverished as a result of the

[1] Ulrich B. Phillips, "The Origin and Growth of the Southern Black Belts," *American Historical Review*, July, 1906, pp. 798-816.

Revolutionary War, and the proposal was tabled. The matter was seriously revived when several insurrections of Negroes were barely averted. These threatened slave uprisings prompted measures of restriction at the very time the slaves were least profitable. It is entirely probable that the system would have disintegrated from sheer inutility but for the sudden availability of another staple crop, through the invention of the cotton gin in 1793.

The invention of the cotton gin made possible the profitable cultivation of the short-staple variety of cotton which previously had required much labor in picking out the seeds by hand. Again, the confluence of favorable factors prepared the way for unprecedented extension and intensification of the system. The invention of the spinning jenny and the power loom, together with the establishment of the factory system in England, created a clamorous and insistent demand for cotton. Planters who once were anxious to rid themselves of the burden of their slaves suddenly discovered in them the possibility of a vast new wealth. Virginia tried to develop cotton in 1820, but the soil and climate were unfavorable. North and South Carolina swiftly came into the field, and new lands were rapidly opened to cultivation. Such cotton cultivation as there had been in the colonies had been limited to South Carolina and Georgia. These two states in 1791 raised about 2,000,000 pounds. By 1821 the area had included the South Atlantic States and the yield had jumped to 117,000,000 pounds. "Never in history, perhaps," says Frederick J. Turner, "was an economic factor more influential upon the life of a people. As the production of cotton increased, the price fell, and the Seaboard South, feeling the competition of the virgin soils of the southwest, saw in the protective tariff for the development of northern manufacturers the real source of her distress. The price of cotton was in these years a barometer of southern prosperity and of southern discontent." [1] Virginia, being unable to grow cotton, turned to supplying slaves for the more southerly states. South Carolina and Georgia in particular were finding the new turn of fortune profitable and were most sensitive to the privilege of retaining it undisturbed.

Abolitionist sentiment, just beginning to be felt, together with the developing sectionalism and political differences centering around economic issues, prompted impassioned rationalization of the system of slavery to insure its permanence. Said one writer in *DeBow's*

[1] "The South, 1820–1830," *American Historical Review*, April, 1906, p. 560.

Review, "This alliance between Negroes and cotton, we will venture to say, is now the strongest power in the world and the peace and welfare of Christendom absolutely depends upon the strength and security of it." The extensive area of the plantations, the impersonal relations, which, for the most part existed between master and plantation slave in the cotton belt, the heedless exploitation of the system for greater profit, the fear of insurrections, all combined to tighten the cords of slavery and to depersonalize it. The right to enslave was hotly defended by laymen and scholars as well as by the church. It was in this period of the supremacy of King Cotton that most of the literature appeared arguing the sub-humanity of Negroes and slavery as their natural state.

As the institution developed, the Black Codes were crystallized in both custom and law; there were enacted the Fugitive Slave Laws so clearly foreshadowed earlier in the efforts to protect the planters in the labor of indentured servants. Humane sentiments persisted but could scarcely keep pace with the material necessity for binding this productive chattel more and more closely to its station. In the end slavery became in theory not merely the lifetime status of Negroes in a special economy which demanded it, but a universal condition to which they were foredoomed from the beginning of time.

PROBLEMS FOR STUDY

1. Could American slavery have developed without a succession of staple crops?
2. Why did not the English settlers in Virginia, in the first years of their existence as a colony, import Africans to be used as slaves?
3. Why is so little known of the fate of white indentured servants after completing their terms of service?
4. Are there any close parallels between the development of slavery in North America and the development of the factory system?
5. Why was it necessary for the Virginia Assembly to declare that conversion did not alter the status of the slave?
6. How would serfdom rather than slavery have altered the direction of growth of the American colonists?
7. The status of the slave was mentioned in an early draft of the Declaration of Independence but omitted in the final draft. Why did the Fathers of the Republic deem this omission wise?

BIBLIOGRAPHY

James C. Ballagh, *A History of Slavery in Virginia* (1902).
James C. Ballagh, *White Servitude in the Colony of Virginia* (1895).
Philip A. Bruce, *Economic History of Virginia in the Seventeenth Century* (1895).
Philip A. Bruce, *Social Life in Virginia in the Seventeenth Century* (1927).
J. R. Davis, "Negro Servitude in the United States," *Journal of Negro History*, July, 1923, pp. 247–283.
Paul H. Douglas, *American Apprenticeship and Industrial Education* (1921).
H. W. Hening, *Statutes at Large, Being a Collection of All the Laws of Virginia, 1619–1792* (1809–1823).
Marcus W. Jernegan, "A Forgotten Slavery of Colonial Days," *Harper's Magazine*, October, 1913, pp. 745–751.
Ulrich B. Phillips, "The Origin and Growth of the Southern Black Belts," *American Historical Review*, July, 1906, pp. 798–816.
John H. Russell, *The Free Negro in Virginia, 1619–1865* (1913).
Edgar T. Thompson, "The Plantation," Ph.D. Thesis, University of Chicago, 1932.
Frederick J. Turner, "The South, 1820–1830," *American Historical Review*, April, 1906, pp. 559–573.
Thomas J. Wertenbaker, *The Planters of Colonial Virginia* (1922).

CHAPTER VII

RISE AND FALL OF SLAVERY IN THE NEW WORLD

At the close of the fifteenth century, Europe was drunk with the dream of fabulous wealth. The trade routes from India and the East were crowded with greedy adventurers, but the difficulties were great, and everyone longed for some shorter, less hazardous route by which this wealth might be brought to the courts of Europe. Among those who had such dreams, the most daring was Don Cristóbal Colón, better known as Christopher Columbus, who set sail in 1492, believing he could reach India by a westward water course. After sailing westward for ten weeks, his three little vessels came to anchor on Watling Island, which he named San Salvador, because of his deep gratitude for a safe journey. So kind were the natives that Columbus wrote to his patron sovereigns, Ferdinand and Isabella, that there "were no better people on the earth." After a brief stay on Watling Island, he sailed south and touched Long Island and Crooked Island, and after sixteen days he landed on the island of Cuba. He was so enamoured of the beauty of this island that he wrote a long letter, which he probably delivered in person to his sovereign, which describes what he found as follows:

> There is a river which discharges itself into the harbor which I have named Porto Santo, of sufficient depth to be navigable. I had the curiosity to sound it, and found it eight fathom; yet the water is so limpid, that I can easily discern the sand at the bottom. The banks of this river are embellished with lofty palm-trees, whose shades give a delicious freshness to the air; and the birds and the flowers are uncommon and beautiful. I was delighted with the scene, that I had almost come to the resolution of staying here the remainder of my days; for, believe me, Sir., these countries far surpass all the rest of the world in beauty and conveniency; and I have frequently observed to my people, that, with all my endeavors to convey to your majesty an adequate idea of the charming objects which continually present themselves to our view, the description will fall greatly short of the reality.[1]

The Indians on the island of Cuba told Columbus of the island of Bahio which lay to the east, on which they said he would find

[1] Thomas Coke, *A History of the West Indies*, Vol. I, pp. 78–79.

great riches. Columbus set sail in search of this land of gold, and landed on the island of Haiti, which the natives called Bahio (great country), on December 6. Columbus called this island Espanola, and the English later called it Hispaniola. One of Columbus's ships was grounded on December 24, and the native chief, or cacique, named Guacanagari, sent his canoes and swimmers out, rescuing all the crew and bringing the cargo ashore on Christmas Day. Out of the wreckage of the boat, Columbus built a fort. Then, leaving thirty-three (Coke says he left thirty-nine [1]) of his men under the leadership of his brother,[2] he sailed away to Spain to tell the world of his wonderful journey to the land of fabulous wealth. He did not know then — nor did he ever know — that he had not been on the mainland of India, which he had started out to seek. Instead he had opened up a new world of wealth and promise.

The inhabitants of the western portion of Haiti were Arawak Indians of whom Columbus wrote most enthusiastically: "The natives love their neighbors as themselves, their conversation is the sweetest imaginable; their faces always smiling; and so gentle and affectionate are they that I swear to your Highness there is not a better people in the world." [3] One of the earliest historians writes of these people as "hospitable, generous and unsuspicious. They engaged in no warfare, committed no depredations, and invaded no man's right." [4] Another historian says of them: "On the whole they were kind, polite, merciful. Their good qualities caused their ruin." [5]

The kindness of the natives was repaid by the Spaniards with cruelty, robbery, murder, and slavery. Some were put to work gathering cotton and tobacco, others were put to mining for gold. At first the Indians were not enslaved outright; but under the guise that they were being taught Christianity, each Spaniard had a number of Indians assigned to him and they were put at hard work. They were allowed to live in their own villages. But this did not produce wealth fast enough; so in 1506, pretending there was not enough time to teach them, and that going back to their

---

[1] Thomas Coke, *A History of the West Indies*, Vol. I, p. 109.
[2] *Ibid.*, Vol. I, p. 128.
[3] For fuller account see: Thomas Southey, *Chronological History of the West Indies*, Vol. I, p. 14 f.
[4] Thomas Coke, *A History of the West Indies*, Vol. I, p. 86.
[5] Jacques N. Léger, *Haiti, son histoire et ses détracteurs*, p. 21.

SLAVERY IN THE NEW WORLD 115

native huts at night undid most of the work of the day, on grant of Ferdinand, the Spaniards were assigned a certain number of natives each, who lived about them in actual slavery. "It was observed in behalf of religion, that so long as the natives were tolerated in their idolatrous superstitions they would never embrace the doctrines of Christianity; but that as this distribution of them would deprive them of an opportunity of worshipping idols, so it would place them more immediately under the care of their masters, who would be enabled to give them that necessary instruction which their case required. In behalf of policy it was urged, that while these Indians continued to live in hordes, agreeably to customs of their ancestors, they would be meditating revolts from their tributary state; and they would keep the Spaniards in perpetual alarm, and create an increasing expense to government to establish soldiers to prevent their insurrection and to protect the Spaniards and their Indian slaves." So severe were their tasks and so cruel was their treatment that twenty years of Spanish occupation sufficed to reduce the population from one million to a very few thousand in Haiti. The story of the stubborn resistance of Caonabo, and his beautiful Queen Anacaona, is one of the most thrilling accounts of early American history. "Five shiploads of the subjugated natives were sent to Seville to be sold as slaves, of which Queen Isabella, greatly to her credit, did not approve." [1] A little later two shiploads of natives were sent to Spain as slaves, and the Queen set them all free.

Not only were the Indians on the island of Haiti destroyed, but all the inhabitants on other islands of the West Indies group suffered a similar fate. The Indians were not robust physically, and they bitterly resented forced labor. They did not make good slaves — hence their rapid destruction. Seeing this, Las Casas, Bishop of Chiapa, went to Spain in 1517, and appeared before Charles V to plead the cause of this unfortunate people: "At my first arrival in Hispaniola, it contained a million inhabitants and now (twenty years later) there remains scarce the hundredth part of them." [2] It was therefore necessary to find some other labor supply, and Las Casas pleaded that Negroes whom he considered more robust should be secured to take the place of the poor Indians. "He proposed that the Spaniards might have Negroes, and that labourers with certain privileges might be sent them. Adrian, the

---

[1] Amos K. Fiske, *The West Indies*, p. 45.
[2] Quoted from: Anthony Benezet, *Some Historical Account of Guinea*, p. 43.

Cardinal of Toledo, approved of these expedients, and the officers of the India-house at Seville were applied to, to say how many Negroes would suffice for the four islands, Espanola, Cuba, San Juan, and Jamaica: they replied, 4000. The traffic in slaves was known to be a lucrative concern . . . and a Fleming who was major domo to the King, begged and obtained a licence to supply the islands: he sold it to some Genoese, for 25,000 ducats, for eight years. The King was not to grant any other licence. The Genoese afterwards sold it for a great deal more." [1]

The first Negro slaves had been introduced into the West Indies in 1502. Once started, almost every European nation entered the scramble for the wealth which might arise from the traffic. Carey estimated that a total of 2,130,000 slaves direct from Africa were introduced into the West Indies before the slave trade was finally abolished.

Thomas Southey tells us that, in making his second voyage to the West Indies, Columbus had on board his ships 1,500 men, twenty horses, and everything it was supposed the colony would want: ammunition, provisions, trinkets for barter, medicines, domestic animals, seeds, vine cuttings, and *sugar cane*.[2] Southey also quotes Martyr as saying of the sugar-cane growth, a year later: "Also the roots of the canes or reeds of the liquor whereof sugar is made, grow a cubit higher within the space of fifteen days, but the liquor is not yet hardened." [3]

There is however doubt whether cane was introduced by Columbus. Samuel Hazard thought sugar cane was introduced into the island of San Domingo in 1506, from the Canaries.[4] It was so thoroughly adapted to the climate and soil of the West Indies that it soon became the most important product of the islands. In the year 1506, wrote Southey, quoting Herrera as his authority, "Pedro de Atienca, Christoval de Tupia, and Francisco de Tupia erected a sugar mill, and pursued the making of sugar with great spirit. Their success induced others to follow their example." [5] R. Ligon in his *True and Exact History of the Island of the Barbadoes*, published shortly after he visited that island in 1647, states that "sugar has so much the start of all the rest of those that, were held as the staple

---

[1] Thomas Southey, *Chronological History of the West Indies*, Vol. I, p. 132.
[2] *Ibid.*, Vol. I, p. 24.   [3] *Ibid.*, Vol. I, p. 30.
[4] *Santo Domingo, Past and Present; with a Glance at Hayti*, p. 37.
[5] *Chronological History of the West Indies*, Vol. I, p. 104.

commodities of the Island and so much overtopped them, as they are the most part slighted and neglected." [1] He then proceeds to give a description of the method of raising sugar cane, and manufacturing sugar, which seemed to him to have progressed so far it "will admit of no greater or farther improvement." [2]

In order to give sufficient laborers for the new industry of the sugar-raising colonies, practically all the European nations redoubled their efforts in slave catching. The Dutch, who were among the earliest, first got their slaves from the Gold Coast, and a little later they wrested Angola from the hands of the Portuguese and used that as their base of supply. The Portuguese began their slave-catching career under Prince Henry the Navigator, whose captains, "Antam Gonçalvez and Nuno Tristas, in 1414 sailed down the African coast as far as Porto de Cavalleiro, and brought back the first captives." [3] Angola was for many years the seat of their operations, but for a short period after 1640, when Angola was controlled by the Dutch the Portuguese slaves were brought from Mozambique. The French and English first traded in the Senegal region, but later established factors on the Ivory Coast and as far down as the Congo section. Most of the crowned heads of Europe derived profit from the slave trade. Queen Elizabeth fitted out her personal ship for the trade, which by irony of fate was called the *Jesus*. Louis XIV held shares in the Royal Senegal Company. Reclus estimated that 413,000 slaves were imported into Cuba up to 1820, when legal importation was stopped and probably 500,000 more were smuggled in before slavery was abolished in 1887. H. C. Carey estimated the total imports to Jamaica at 750,000.[4] At the opening of the revolution in Haiti there were 500,000 slaves and 27,000 mulattoes mostly free.

From the very earliest days the English had fostered slavery in Barbados. In 1674 the number of slaves was perhaps 100,000,[5] and F. W. Pitman thinks the average yearly importation of slaves to Barbados was 3,000, so that 300,000 would probably not be an overestimate for the total number of slaves brought to this island alone.[6]

[1] *True and Exact History of the Island of the Barbadoes*, p. 86.
[2] *Ibid.*, p. 86.
[3] Joaquim P. Oliveira Martins, *The Golden Age of Prince Henry the Navigator*, p. 207.
[4] *The Slave Trade, Domestic and Foreign*, p. 12.
[5] Harry H. Johnston, *The Negro in the New World*, p. 212.
[6] *The Development of the British West Indies, 1700–1763*, p. 72.

With the single exception of Haiti, the slaves on none of the islands seemed to be able to perpetuate themselves. The figures for Jamaica are as follows: In 1702 there were 36,000 Negroes on the island. In 1775 there were 194,614, an increase of 158,614. But during that seventy-three years 497,736 Negroes had been imported, and only 137,114 has been exported to other islands or the states. It took therefore 360,000 imports to increase the population by 158,614. Of course a great number of the newly imported slaves died during the breaking-in season.[1]

The great amount of uncultivated land in the islands, together with the growing demand for sugar in Europe, kept the planters constantly clamoring for more slaves. As fast as a planter could buy new slaves, he opened up new land, on which he raised more sugar, on the profits of which he bought, or desired to buy, more slaves. It was a vicious cycle such as arose in the cotton belt of the southern states a century later. The planters bought from the English merchants on credit, and it was to the interest of the merchants to restrict slave importations so as to keep the price high. There was constant quarreling therefore between the merchants of the mother countries and the planters of the various islands. Since the slave supply could not keep up with the demand, overwork for the slaves was the inevitable tendency. Ill treatment was accentuated also by the fact of absentee landlordism. The horrible condition of the slaves in the English colonies was well brought out in the testimonies before a select committee of the House of Commons, which held its investigations in 1790. The abstract of this hearing published that year was republished in 1859 and used as a document by the abolitionists in the southern states. Long hours, scanty food, no Sabbath, severe punishments, inhumanity to women, were some of the terrible charges brought. The French *Code Noir* while more humane and liberal was far from ideal and it is to be doubted if the slaves under the French fared any better than under the English. The Spanish code, which granted certain privileges to the slaves, made their condition more tolerable and hence Spain held her slaves later than others. The Spanish codes of 1540 and 1641 gave to the slave the opportunity to buy his own freedom. The price set was $250, and in the case of an expectant mother $12 more would buy her unborn child. The Spanish code promulgated in 1789 carried provision for the religious instruction of slaves, it set a minimum for

---

[1] Henry C. Carey, *The Slave Trade, Domestic and Foreign,* p. 9.

food and clothing, it forbade certain work for women and children, it set aside the Sabbath as a day of rest, it set up a housing law whereby only two slaves could be lodged in one room, it encouraged matrimony among the slaves, it put a bar on severe punishment, and it made industrial training and care of slaves in old age obligatory upon all planters. Had all the colonies had so humane a code and lived up to it, there would have been more prosperity on the islands.

As a result of cruelty and their inherent desire for freedom, there was much dissatisfaction among the slaves. In Jamaica when the English took possession in 1650 many of the slaves fled to the mountains. Dwelling in the tops of these mountain fastnesses, they were first called Cimmerians or mountain dwellers, which was later shortened to Marons, and then became Maroons. From that time on there was constant warfare back and forth — much bloodshed, much destruction of property, and constant unrest.

The western portion of Hispaniola was ceded to France in 1697 and called St. Domingue, by which name it was known until after it became independent, when it took the name of Haiti. Here cruelty also reigned. According to Reclus: "Scarcely a single town in Haiti but recalls some siege, battle, or butchery. The very river marking the northern frontier is known by the name of Rivière du Massacre, in memory of a sanguinary conflict between the natives and the Spaniards." [1] Just as in Jamaica, so in this island the mountains became the asylum for fugitive slaves. As early as 1620 one thousand Negroes fled to these mountain fastnesses. Through the decades a Maroon colony was built up, which ultimately became so strong that it was recognized by the colonial government in 1784. Prior to this Morandal, a powerful leader of African origin, had led a dreadful revolt in 1758 which struck terror to the hearts of all the whites. In 1787 the English abolition society was organized, and in 1788 a similar society was organized in France with such prominent men as La Fayette and Mirabeau as most active members. The slaves on the island became again inflamed and the terrible revolution of 1791 took place. In 1801 Toussaint L'Ouverture, the Napoleon of the West Indies, led his people to a short-lived independence. Napoleon interfered, Toussaint was captured and exported, but the spirit of revolution lived on and Haiti was finally declared free in 1804. Most of the other islands ran a somewhat similar course.

Financially the West Indies can hardly be said to have yielded

[1] *The Earth and Its Inhabitants*, "North America," Vol. II, p. 410.

a satisfactory return. Tobacco, cotton, indigo, ginger, and sugar have always been the main crops, and most of these seemed to be best raised on large plantations. This was particularly true of sugar because it required a great deal of capital to provide the mill for grinding, and the apparatus for boiling and preparing the product. A small planter could not afford this large initial outlay, but must depend on his neighbor for such machinery; which dependence, owing to the shortness and emergency of the gathering season, was rather precarious. Bryan Edwards estimated that $150,000 was a minimum capital for running a sugar plantation. This demand for a large initial outlay resulted in an overwhelming amount of absenteeism. Most of the great estates were owned by the nobility and the rich in the mother countries, some of them, of course, being held by great companies. Investment in a plantation in the West Indies was to the mother countries what investment in mining prospects in the West has been to the wealthier and more settled populations of our eastern section of the United States during the last fifty years. A few men have made fabulous wealth out of their mining ventures, but most of those who have invested have never realized any profits and often they have lost their capital. However, the spirit of adventure is still strong in men, and on the basis of a chance men will continue to invest. So it was with the West Indian investors. They continued to buy land and slaves in the hope that some day they would "strike it rich." Most of them never did. It is due to this fact of absenteeism that so much of cruelty and hardship fell to the lot of the West Indian slave. The overseers, managers, and slave drivers were eager to make the best showing of profits and were not looking to a long-time policy of success.

Dr. Ulrich Phillips in his *American Negro Slavery* has given a full account of the poor returns of one of the great Jamaica plantations — Worthy Park.[1] The original outlay on this plantation was large, the loss of slaves heavy; the number who could not produce was high, bad crops had their effect, and the income did not average over a long period of years more than 4% on the investment. Because of unrest, poor management, a false economy, slavery in the West Indies really fell of its own weight. Thousands of slaves were transferred to the southern states, where some thought there were greater chances for success.

While the development of slavery in the West Indies was going

[1] P. 57 ff.

forward, the English, the French, and the Dutch were sending colonists to the continent of North America. Jamestown, as has been described earlier, was settled by men who wanted the freedom and power that goes with a landed proprietorship. Their great need was for laborers. Land was rich enough in the southern section of America to support workers and a gentleman class. Since there was so much free land, no freeman would hire himself to work on the land for another man, and the only means of securing large supplies of workers was by an indentured system or by slavery. The South being a section of warm climate and in the coastal plains and river bottoms marshy and unhealthful, those who could, preferred to have their work done for them. Furthermore, the crops raised in the southern states were just those which could best be handled by slaves. In Virginia and North Carolina the staple crop was tobacco, which involved a great deal of routine work, and hence was successfully worked with slave labor. Rice and indigo, the staple crops of South Carolina and the seaboard of Georgia, required marsh land, and since life in marsh lands was considered destructive of health, only Negroes, it was thought, could live in them. Sugar was the staple crop of Louisiana and lower Mississippi. It required very large investment of capital for machinery and hence could be profitably worked only on large plantations where there was great concentration of laborers. This again favored a slave régime. Lastly cotton, which was the great money crop of the interior, was a staple, which took the whole year to grow and harvest; hence it used the energies of a slave population continuously. Like tobacco, it ate up the fertility of the soil, thus demanding constant supplies of new land. The work of clearing this land, as well as the work of cultivating cotton, was distinctly routine; hence it offered an opportunity for the use of large groups of unskilled workers. If ever there was a land where every condition seemed most favorable for the development of a slave régime, the southern states seemed to be that land. From the earliest days the colonists had wanted servants, and we find the Puritans salving their consciences on the subject of slavery, just as did the Spanish, by seeking to convert the Indians to the Christian religion as a compensation for their loss of freedom. Thus, one Emanuel Downing wrote to his brother-in-law, John Winthrop, expressing hopes of a just war with the Narragansetts, first to stop their "worship of the Devil," and "2 lie, if upon a just warre the Lord should deliver them into our hands, we might easily have men, women and children enough to exchange for Moores (Negroes) which will be more gainful pillage for us than we conceive, for I do not see how we can thrive until we get into a stock of slaves sufficient to doe all our business, for our children's children, will hardly see this great continent filled with people, soe that our servants will still desire freedome to plant for themselves and not stay but for verie great wages." [1]

To supply this demand for workers almost every European nation had ships in the slave trade. The Assiento which the king of Spain had granted to a "Fleming," who sold it to some Genoese, was the royal permit to carry slaves to the West Indies. It was handed back and forth until it finally fell into the hands of the English through the Treaty of Utrecht. The Dutch landed their first group of Negroes at Jamestown in 1619; they were eagerly bought up by the planters, probably as indentured servants. In 1621 the first Dutch West Indies Company was formed, the policy of which was to furnish all Dutch colonies with all the slaves they could or would take. This company in the year of its organization was given a monopoly of trading privileges in the new Netherlands which is now New York. The purpose of the company was to develop the colony on the basis of forced or slave labor. They believed the colony would prosper if slaves were cheap and easy to secure. But because the colonists were more interested in trading with the Indians (which was the original idea leading to the opening of the colony) than they were in developing great plantations, the demand for slaves was nothing like as great as the company had hoped.

The English entered the West Africa slave trade in 1562, through John Hawkins, afterward knighted. Prior to this, "Elizabeth had lent her influence and assistance to a series of voyages to the African coast. Not only did she permit the use of four royal voyagers for the first expedition, but she spent five hundred pounds in provisioning them for the voyage. The value of these goods, sent to Africa, in these vessels, was five thousand pounds. According to the arrangement Queen Elizabeth received one third of the profits, which amounted to one thousand pounds." [2] In these voyages to Guinea the English trade had been for gold, elephants' teeth, and pepper. Trading in slaves had hardly occurred to these early adventurers.

[1] Quoted by Ulrich B. Phillips' *American Negro Slavery*, p. 101, from Massachusetts Historical Society Collections XXXVI, p. 65.

[2] *Journal of Negro History*, April, 1919, p. 138.

SLAVERY IN THE NEW WORLD   123

Nevertheless, as early as 1562, John Hawkins sailed for Sierra Leone with three vessels, and there captured three hundred Negroes whom he sold to the Spanish in Hispaniola. The success of this voyage was so great that in 1564 there was fitted out a second slave-raiding expedition, in which one of the Queen's ships, the *Jesus*, was employed. As before, Hawkins sold his slaves in the West Indies, this time with some difficulties, because the Spanish officials, who were forbidden to have any trade with foreigners, regarded the Englishmen as pirates.[1] On a third journey in 1567 Hawkins met with great disaster, losing all his ships save one, and barely escaping with his life. This practically put an end to English slave trading for a full century.[2]

W. O. Blake's *History of Slavery and the Slave Trade* says: "In 1790 the whole number of forts and factories established on the coast (West Africa) was about forty; fourteen belonged to the English, fifteen to the Dutch, three to the French, four to the Portuguese, and four to the Danes."[3] Blake further adds that the number of slaves carried away from Africa at this time must have amounted to at least 100,000 annually. He ventures a guess that 30,000,000 were exported from Africa in the entire history of the slave trade up to 1860. W. E. B. Du Bois thinks that in 1787 "the British were taking annually from Africa 38,000 slaves; the French 20,000; the Portuguese 10,000; the Dutch and Danes 6,000; a total of 74,000."[4]

At this time American ships were none the less industrious in importing slaves into America. From January 1, 1804, to December 31, 1807, there were 61 ships from Charleston engaged in the trade (carrying slaves to South Carolina, which was the only state with open port), 59 ships from Rhode Island, 4 from Baltimore, 1 from Boston, 2 from Norfolk, 1 from Connecticut, 1 from Sweden, 79 from Great Britain, and 3 from France, or a total of 211 ships. Among the consigners of these ships 13 were natives of Charleston, 88 natives of Rhode Island, 91 natives of Great Britain, 10 natives of France.[5] De Bow, giving these same facts quoted direct from the speech of Honorable Judge Smith, Senator from South Carolina, who had

[1] *Ibid.*, April, 1919, p. 139.
[2] Ulrich B. Phillips, *American Negro Slavery*, p. 34, citing: Gomer Williams, *History of the Liverpool Privateers with an Account of the Liverpool Slave Trade*.
[3] P. 108.
[4] *The Suppression of the African Slave Trade to the United States of America, 1638-1870*, p. 40.
[5] *Ibid.*, p. 90, citing: *Annals of Congress*, 16th Congress, 2nd Session, pp. 73-77.

procured his figures "from the hand of the collector" at Charleston, gives the names of all the 211 ships year by year, 1804, 1805, 1806, 1807, clearing from Charleston, and adds this caustic remark: "Note by the collector: It would appear from the foregoing, that of these importations of slaves into Charleston, there were imported by natives of countries and places now repudiating slavery, Foreigners 21,027, citizens of United States 14,605, by citizens of slave-holding states 3,443."[1] When one gathers the facts about the slave trade at this period it becomes very evident that the pot dare not call the kettle black. Almost every European nation had all the share it could have in the trade, and all sections of America were involved up to their full capacity to reap the rewards.

The slaves brought to America came almost exclusively from the west coast. The English brought captives from the Senegal and Gambia rivers, from the Gold Coast, slave coast, and even as far south as Angola. The Dutch had forts on the Gold Coast, and in 1640 captured the Portuguese forts at Angola, where they gathered many slaves. The French had Fort Louis at the mouth of the Senegal river, and other forts scattered down the west coast. Anthony Benezet, who made a careful study of the slave trade, said that slaves were regularly shipped from all points from the Senegal to Angola, a coast of nearly 4,000 miles.[2] The heart of the trade was the slave coast and the Gold Coast, and behind this a territory extending into the interior for 700 miles or more.[3] From this territory Senegalese Negroes, Mandingoes, Ibos, Efikes, Ibonis, Karamantis, Wydyas, Jolofs, Fulis, together with representatives of many of the interior Bantus were brought to America.

Slavery did not grow rapidly in America until 1700; a second great impetus was given to slavery in 1793, when the cotton gin was invented. In the earlier years there was much hesitancy lest the Negroes should become more numerous than the whites, and there was always some moral scruple about holding human beings in slavery. However, the slaves did multiply in this country as they did not in the West Indies. The gradual importations plus the natural increase therefore ultimately brought a large slave population. In 1714 there were 58,850 Negro slaves distributed through all the colonies.

[1] *The Industrial Resources, etc., of the Southern and Western States*, Vol. II, pp. 340–342.
[2] *Some Historical Account of Guinea*, p. 5 ff.
[3] *Ibid.*, pp. 18–19.

In 1750 there were 220,000 Negroes in America, and for each decade thereafter the figures were as follows:

1760	310,000	1820	1,771,656
1770	462,000	1830	2,328,642
1780	582,000	1840	2,873,648
1790	757,000	1850	3,638,808
1801	1,007,037	1860	4,441,830
1810	1,377,808		

Of the above numbers the great mass were slaves though there was a constantly increasing number of free Negroes.

As early as 1726, Virginia began protesting against the importation of so many slaves and to decrease the number imposed an import tax. This the Royal African Company got repealed. On July 12, 1736, William Byrd wrote to Lord Egmont:

> Your Lord's opinion concerning rum and Negroes is certainly very just, and your excluding both of them from your colony of Georgia will be very happy. I wish, my Lord, we could be blessed with the same prohibition. They import so many Negroes here that I fear this colony will sometime or other be confirmed by the name of New Guinea. I am sensible of many bad consequences of multiplying the Ethiopian among us. They blow up the pride and ruin the industry of the white people, who, seeing a class of poor creatures below them, detest work, for fear it should make them look like slaves. But these private mischiefs are nothing if compared to the public danger. It were, therefore, worth the consideration of the British Parliament, my Lord, to put an end to this unchristian traffic of merchandise of our Fellow Creatures. At least the further importation of them into our colony should be prohibited, lest they prove as troublesome and dangerous elsewhere as they have been lately in Jamaica.[1]

In 1712 Pennsylvania passed an act to prohibit slavery, but the act was annulled by the Crown. Massachusetts passed abolition measures in 1771 and in 1774, but both were disapproved by the colonial governors. The Virginia House of Burgesses in 1772 petitioned the king as follows:

> We implore your Majesty's paternal assistance in averting a calamity of a most alarming nature. The importation of slaves into the colonies from the coast of Africa hath long been considered as a trade of great unhumanity, and under its present encouragement we have too much reason to fear will endanger the very existence of your Majesty's American dominions. We are

---

[1] Beverly B. Munford, *Virginia's Attitude toward Slavery and Secession*, p. 17, citing unpublished Byrd manuscripts.

sensible that some of your Majesty's subjects may reap emoluments from this sort of traffic, but when we consider that it greatly retards the settlement of the colonies with more useful inhabitants and may in time have the most destructive influence, we presume to hope that the interests of a few will be disregarded when placed in competition with the security and happiness of such number of your Majesty's dutiful and loyal subjects. We, therefore, beseech your Majesty to remove all these restraints on your Majesty's Governor in this colony which inhibits their assenting to such laws as might check so pernisious a consequence.[1]

Right up to the hour of the American Revolution the English sovereigns and the influential leaders of England turned a deaf ear to all appeals for stopping the slave trade. Queen Anne, who held one quarter of the stock in the Royal African Company, charged that company to furnish full supplies of slaves to the colonies, and instructed the colonial governors to give all due encouragement to the business of the company. Other rulers followed her example, so rigidly that one writer declares: "British avarice planted slavery in America; British legislation sanctioned and maintained it; British statesmen sustained and guarded it." [2] And George Mason exclaimed in Congress: "This infernal traffic originated in the avarice of British merchants." [3]

In 1773 Patrick Henry wrote in a private letter the following indictment of slavery:

Every thinking honest man rejects it in speculation; but how few in practice, from conscientious motives! Believe me, I shall honor the Quakers for their noble efforts to abolish slavery; they are equally calculated to promote moral and political good. Would any one believe that I am master of slaves of my own purchase? I am drawn along by the general inconvenience of living without them. I will not, I cannot, justify it; however culpable my conduct, I will so far pay my devoir to virtue as to own the excellence and rectitude of her precepts, and to lament my want of conformity to them. I believe a time will come when an opportunity will be offered to abolish this lamentable evil; everything we can do is to improve it, if it happens in our day; if not, let us transmit to our descendants, together with our slaves, a pity for their unhappy lot and an abhorrence of slavery.[4]

[1] Beverly B. Munford, *Virginia's Attitude toward Slavery and Secession*, p. 18.
[2] Henry Wilson, *History of the Rise and Fall of the Slave Power in America*, Vol. I, p. 4.
[3] Beverly B. Munford, *Virginia's Attitude toward Slavery and Secession*, p. 30.
[4] George Bancroft, *History of the United States from the Discovery of the Continent to the Establishment of the Constitution in 1789*, Vol. III, p. 412.

The constant agitation of this matter on the part of the colonies finally irritated the statesmen of the mother country so much that it was suggested in Parliament that it might be a happy consummation to free the slaves and turn them into an armed force against the insubordinate colonists. Edmund Burke saw the utter foolishness of such a course and arraigned slavery and those who stood for its continuance in one of the most powerful speeches ever delivered in the House of Parliament:

With regard to the high aristocratic spirit of Virginia and the southern colonies it has been proposed, I know, to reduce it by declaring a general enfranchisement of their slaves. This project has had its advocates and panegyrists, yet I never could argue myself into any opinion of it. Slaves are often much attached to their master. A general wild offer of liberty would not always be accepted. History furnishes few instances of it. It is sometimes as hard to persuade slaves to be free as it is to compel freemen to be slaves; and in this auspicious scheme we should have both these pleasing tasks on our hands at once. But when we talk of enfranchisement, do we not perceive that the American master may enfranchise too, and arm servile hands in the defense of freedom? — a measure to which other people have had recourse more than once, and not without success, in a desperate situation of their affairs.

Slaves as these unfortunate black people are, and dull as all men are from slavery, must they not a little suspect the offer of freedom from that very nation, which has sold them to their present masters; from that nation, one of whose causes of quarrel with those masters is their refusal to deal any more in that inhuman traffic? An offer of freedom from England would come rather oddly, shipped to them in an African vessel, which is refused an entry into the ports of Virginia or Carolina, with a cargo of three hundred Angola Negroes. It would be curious to see the Guinea captain attempting at the same instant to publish his proclamation of liberty, and to advertise his sale of slaves.[1]

When Jefferson prepared the original draft of the Declaration of Independence he stressed the grievance of the colonies against George the Third, in his continual vetoes of laws suppressing the slave trade:

George the Third has waged cruel war against humanity itself, violating its most sacred rights of life and liberty, in the persons of a distant people who never offended him; captivating and carrying them into slavery in another hemisphere, or to incur a miserable death in their transportation thither. This piratical warfare, the opprobrium of infidel powers, is the warfare of the Christian King of Great Britain. Determined to keep open a market where

[1] *On Conciliation with the Colonies.*

men should be bought and sold, he has prostituted his negative for suppressing every legislative attempt to prohibit, or to restrain, this execrable commerce. And that this assemblage of horrors might want no fact of distinguished dye, he is now exciting these very people to rise in arms among us, and to purchase that liberty of which he has deprived them, by murdering the people on whom he obtruded them, thus paying off former crimes committed against the liberties of one people with crimes which he urges them to commit against the lives of another.[1]

The colonies were united to throw off the yoke of what seemed to them oppression and a form of slavery. They were therefore sensitive to the rights of their own slaves, since this was the basic principle of their own struggle. As a result most of the colonies took some legislative steps looking to freeing of the Negroes. Massachusetts passed a law in 1780 prohibiting slavery, and in 1788 passed another law prohibiting any of her citizens participating in the slave trade. Rhode Island, which had passed a law prohibiting slavery in 1774, passed one in 1787 forbidding all participation in the slave trade. New Hampshire prohibited slavery in 1792, Vermont in 1793; New York passed a law in 1799 providing for a gradual abolition of slavery. North Carolina in 1794 passed a law prohibiting the slave trade. Georgia, which had forbidden the entry of free Negroes in 1793, passed a most drastic law against all slave importations in 1798. South Carolina passed a five-year exclusion law in 1788, which law was reënacted in 1792 and continued in force until 1803. Maryland and Delaware both took action against the slave trade, with heavy penalties attached.

The spirit of freedom was evident in the Continental Congress in 1784. A committee consisting of Jefferson of Virginia, Chase of Maryland, and Howell of Rhode Island was appointed to draw up a plan of government for all territory ceded or to be ceded. In this report it was provided: "After the year of the Christian Era 1800 there shall be neither slavery nor involuntary servitude in any of these states, otherwise than in the punishment of crime, whereof the party shall have been duly convicted." [2] Unfortunately this measure failed to carry although it received a majority vote.[3] Had this meas-

[1] Beverly B. Munford, *Virginia's Attitude toward Slavery and Secession*, pp. 19–20, citing: George Bancroft, *History of the United States from the Discovery of the Continent to the Establishment of the Constitution in 1789.*

[2] Henry Wilson, *History of the Rise and Fall of the Slave Power in America*, Vol. I, p. 32.

[3] *Ibid.*, Vol. I, p. 32.

ure been adopted Kentucky, Tennessee, Alabama, and Mississippi, all of which were organized later, would have come into the union as free states. In 1785 a measure was introduced into Congress by Rufus King of Massachusetts calling for immediate prohibition of slavery, and in 1787 the famous ordinance prohibiting slavery in the territory northwest of Ohio was passed with the single dissenting vote of Yates of New York. It was evident that the struggle for political freedom of the colonies had had its influence on the whole question of holding human beings as slaves.

When the question of the importation of slaves came up in August of 1787, it was evident that another disposition prevailed. While South Carolina and Georgia voted to prohibit slavery in the Northwest Territory, they were not willing to forego what seemed to them their economic interest — namely, the importing of more slaves. The immediate debate arose over the question of whether the national government might levy a tax on all slaves imported. From this the debate moved on to the whole question as to the wisdom of prohibiting all imports. The discussion was long and bitter — with Baldwin of Georgia, the Pinckneys of South Carolina, and others declaring they would never consent to immediate prohibition, and Mason of Virginia, Martin of Maryland, and most of the New England representatives eager to see the trade abolished at once. Rutledge declared religion and humanity had nothing to do with the matter — it was distinctly a matter of interest. Ellsworth of Connecticut insisted that each state should be allowed to decide the matter of importation for itself, and Roger Sherman of Connecticut declared it would be better to let the southern states import slaves than to part company with those states. It soon became apparent that no unanimous decision could be reached; so a compromise was looked for. The East desired an export tax on the products of the slave, and a navigation act for the protection of the shipping business. To both of these measures the South was strongly opposed. The committee on details was composed of Rutledge, chairman, Randolph, Graham, Ellsworth, and Wilson. The committee brought in a report which provided (1) that no duty should be laid on exports, (2) that no navigation act should be passed without a two-thirds vote, (3) that importation of slaves should not be prohibited, and (4) that no tax should be imposed upon such imports. Debate continued, and finally the whole matter was recommitted to a committee composed of one representative for each state. This committee made a bargain which it reported back. The prohibition of export duties was retained, the slave trade was permitted until 1800, and the clause referring to the navigation act was left out. This report again raised a storm. Pinckney of South Carolina moved to extend the time for importations from 1800 to 1808, the restrictions on navigation laws were stricken out, and the enactment as it referred to slavery finally read:

ACT I, SEC. 9. The migration or importation of such persons as any of the states now existing shall think proper to admit, shall not be prohibited by the congress prior to the year one thousand eight hundred and eight, but a tax or duty may be imposed on such importation, not exceeding ten dollars for each person.[1]

Thus the North got a commercial right to lay a tax on shipping, which it considered to be to its economic interest, and the South got the right to import slaves for another twenty years if it so desired. The North again got the right to lay a tax on all such importations. It was a pure commercial bargain, each section sparring for the largest advantages to itself.

At the time the above ordinance was passed only three states — namely, South Carolina, North Carolina, and Georgia — permitted imports. North Carolina had a high import tax which was repealed in 1790. But a new motive was rapidly developing. The South always had a fear of insurrections, and the slaves of Haiti were just now in the midst of a bitter struggle for freedom, which was perceptibly affecting the thinking of the South. There was danger that slaves escaping from Haiti might come into the South and instigate revolution among the southern slaves. To prevent this South Carolina hurriedly passed a law in 1788 prohibiting importations for five years, which was renewed several times and did not expire until 1803. North Carolina in 1794 passed such a stringent law against importation that it made it embarrassing and difficult for a master to enter with his personal servants. Georgia alone enjoyed the notoriety of permitting imports, and in 1798 it passed a law forbidding importations under heavy penalties. Thus, from 1798 to 1803, there was not a state which permitted imports. All the border states strengthened their prohibiting laws, and the eastern states put very heavy penalties on any of their citizens who participated in the slave trade.

[1] For full discussion see: Henry Wilson, *History of the Rise and Fall of the Slave Power in America*, Vol. I, chap. 4.

It certainly looked as though slavery was tottering to its grave, and that of its own weight. In the North it had proved unprofitable; in the South it was feared because of the danger of insurrection; in the nation as a whole there was a growing moral sentiment against it. There were numerous petitions presented to Congress, both by abolitionists and by free Negroes praying for complete emancipation. Each petition was hotly debated. The North, with the exception of Rhode Island, was usually favorable to such petitions; the South, with the exception of Virginia, was usually opposed. In 1794 Congress passed a law against carrying slaves from the United States to any foreign port, and prohibiting a citizen of the United States from participation in the fitting out of slave ships. The law imposed a fine of $1,000 for each person engaged in the trade, and $200 for each slave carried. In 1803 this law was made much more stringent, calling for the forfeiture of the ship which brought any Negro or person of color into states which prohibited their importation. Thus all the states individually and the nation as a whole were solidly against the importation of slaves.

Just at this time South Carolina brought consternation to all by reopening its slave trade. The growing certainty that the United States would prohibit the slave traffic in 1808 as soon as the constitutional prohibition expired led South Carolina to take advantage of the few remaining years to replenish its stock of slaves for a greatly growing agriculture. Immediately a representative from Pennsylvania offered a resolution to tax imported slaves, but the bill presented was finally lost. Another event which brought consternation to those who hoped for the emancipation of slaves was the purchase of Louisiana in 1803. A long and bitter debate as to whether slave importation should be allowed in this territory followed. It was finally decided to allow an interstate trade with Louisiana, but only in slaves imported before 1798. That is, slaves could not be imported and bought in Charleston and immediately reshipped to Louisiana. It is quite apparent that the law was not well enforced, and many fresh slaves were evidently brought into New Orleans.

In spite of South Carolina's action the nation as a whole was bent on prohibition of importations. The abolition groups, seemingly defeated, again began marshaling their forces to prohibit the slave trade completely by national legislation. President Thomas Jefferson in 1806 sent a message to Congress urging immediate action, even though the law could not take effect until 1808. His message ran:

I congratulate you, fellow citizens, on the approach of the period at which you may interpose your authority constitutionally to withdraw the citizens of the United States from all participation in the violation of human rights which has been so long continued on the unoffending inhabitants of Africa, and which the morality, the reputation and the best interests of the country have long been eager to prescribe. Although no law you can pass can take prohibitive effect until the first day of the year 1808, yet the intervening period is not too long to prevent, by timely notice, expeditions which cannot be completely before that day.

A bill was finally passed in 1807 which prohibited the slave trade. There was practical unanimity both North and South in the desire to prohibit the trade, for the fear of insurrections due to the incoming of free Negroes from the West Indies, and also the fear that further importations would work havoc with the price of slaves, whipped into line all those who did not feel the pressure of moral and humanitarian arguments.

In spite of the fact that all sections were in favor of prohibiting further importations, there were three legislative difficulties which caused long and bitter debate. It was recognized that the law, to be effective, must carry penalties for violation. The first question involved was what to do with the slaves illegally imported; the second was what to do with those who did the importation; and the third was how to handle coastwise trade.

If imported slaves were confiscated by the government, what should be done with them? The South would not tolerate freeing raw savages and leaving them in its midst, nor did the North relish having them sent to its soil. But if the government must hold them in bondage or sell them, then the government would be embarking in the very business which it was seeking to destroy. It was a knotty question and the debate was long and bitter. Early of Georgia declared that if they were set free in the South not one of them would be alive at the end of a year. Barker of Massachusetts moved to amend by declaring that all imported slaves should be sent back to Africa, but the difficulties of reëstablishing them in their own land were so great that the amendment polled only nineteen votes. Quincy of Massachusetts declared that those imported into the South must become slaves, and those brought into the North must become vagabonds. Findley of Pennsylvania advocated the bonding out of all confiscated Negroes for a limited number of years — a suggestion which had much merit, but got little or no attention. Quincy then suggested that imported Negroes be confiscated, but the final disposition of them be left to the future.

Along with this discussion of what to do with the slaves ran the one of what punishment should be meted out to the slaver. All agreed he should be punished, but how severely was the question. Smilie of Pennsylvania, Ely of Massachusetts, and Talmadge of Connecticut strongly favored the death penalty. They were supported by others who considered slave importation as the acme of all crimes. Early of Georgia and other southern representatives declared the southern states would not execute the death sentence because they did not consider slavery a crime. He claimed slavery was an evil but not a crime. In the midst of the debate certain southern representatives called attention to the fact that most of the slave ships were from northern ports (mainly Rhode Island) and were captained by northern men. To this Mosely of Connecticut replied that he saw no reason why the southern representatives "should be so tender of these northern men." Stanton of Rhode Island stood with Early saying: "I cannot believe that a man ought to be hung for only stealing a Negro."

The third knotty question was what should be done with coastwise trade in slaves. It seemed likely that this would be prohibited altogether, but Randolph of Virginia declared, if it was so prohibited, "the southern people would set the law at defiance and he would set the example." The basis of such contention was the constitutional right of free use of property. A compromise was effected. The final disposition of the three questions was as follows:

As to the imported slaves the act said: "Neither the importer nor any person or persons claiming from or under him, shall hold any right or title whatsoever to any Negro, mulatto or person of color, nor to the service or labor thereof, who may be imported or brought within the United States, or territory thereof, in violation of this law, but the same shall remain subject to any regulations not contravening the provision of this act, which the legislatures of the several states or territories at any time hereafter make, for disposing of any such Negro, mulatto or person of color." [1]

For the men bringing in slaves the penalty was set as follows: "For equipping a slaver, a fine of $20,000. and forfeiture of the ship. For transporting and selling Negroes a fine of $1,000. to $10,000., imprisonment for 5 to 10 years, and forfeiture of the ship and Negroes.

[1] *Annals of Congress*, 9th Congress, 2nd Session, p. 1267.

For transporting Negroes, a fine of $5,000. and forfeiture of ship and Negroes. For knowingly buying illegally imported Negroes, a fine of $800. for each Negro and forfeiture." As to coastwise traffic it was decreed that "the transportation of slaves coastwise in vessels under forty tons with a view to sale" was illegal and would be punished accordingly.[1]

The burden of disposal of slaves was thus shifted to the shoulders of the various states, the penalty against the slave importer was decidedly softened, and coastwise trade was allowed in vessels of 40 tons or more. The compromises and indecisions remind one of the recent problems of prohibition of the sale of intoxicating liquor.

Congress thus finally prohibited the slave traffic, but the provisions for enforcing the law were quite inadequate. Just as the law for the prohibition of intoxicants has had inadequate provision for enforcement, with consequent laxness, indecision, and dallying, so the case stood with slavery. First the customs officials were made responsible for enforcement; then the navy was ordered to take the responsibility; but neither of these was effective, so the Department of State was charged with the responsibility; and finally it was shifted to the Department of the Interior. Just as New York and certain other wet states refused to support the national government on the prohibition of the sale of intoxicants, so the southern states were slow in passing laws for the disposal of imported slaves. The whole policy was so vacillating that importations went merrily on. Cargoes of slaves were landed in Florida and smuggled across the border into Georgia, or later they were landed at Galveston and brought thence into the states. Wilson states that an average of 15,000 slaves were annually landed in the states up to 1860,[2] and Du Bois estimates that 40,000 slaves were annually imported into North and South America from 1808 to 1820. By 1837, he claims, the volume had reached 200,000 annually, gradually declining thereafter up to the opening of the Civil War.[3]

Great Britain had in 1807 abolished all slave traffic within its empire and for more than fifty years she strove earnestly to suppress the whole illicit traffic. Again and again England attempted

[1] For full decision see: Henry Wilson, *History of the Rise and Fall of the Slave Power in America*, Vol. I, chap. 7, and *Annals of Congress*, 9th Congress, 2nd Session.

[2] *History of the Rise and Fall of the Slave Power in America*, Vol. I, p. 97.

[3] *The Suppression of the African Slave Trade to the United States of America, 1638-1870*, chaps. 8 and 9.

to get other nations to unite with her in this effort. The great obstacle was opposition to the right of search. England was really the mistress of the seas, and to give her the right of free search of all merchant ships was entirely too hazardous a business. The question was earnestly discussed at the Congress of Vienna in 1814, at the Treaty of Ghent in 1815, and at the Congress of Verona in 1822, always with sympathetic attitude by the contracting nations but with the same futile results.

As one reads the annals of slavery in America it seems evident that it was near to being abolished in 1780 and the years following, owing to the impulse of freedom inherent in the American Revolution. Again in 1800, when all the states had forbidden the importation of slaves, it looked as if it might come to an end. But an economic factor entered at this time which changed the whole complexion of the issue. Any social evil such as the present liquor power, and such as slavery was, when productive of financial profit will die a hard death. Slavery was not profitable in the North and had therefore gradually died a natural death from uselessness. But it was quite different in the South. Here millions of acres of fertile land waited the hand of labor to turn it into a great productive domain. The climate was congenial to the Negro, and the crops which grew best — namely, tobacco, rice, sugar, and cotton — required routine work best fitted to slaves. Cotton in particular was a crop which afforded work the year through and hence distributed the labor of the slave over the whole twelve months. There was little idle time; hence slavery could be made more or less profitable. The one thing which had stood in the way of cotton's becoming a great staple crop was the tedious method of seeding the lint. By the old hand process of seeding cotton with the fingers, the planter considered he had received a fair day's work if his slave removed the seed from six pounds of cotton lint. So severely did this limit the amount of cotton that could be produced that eight bags of cotton imported into England in 1784 were seized by the government on the ground that so much cotton could not be produced in America. Indeed, it is said John Teasdale of Charleston bought in 1785 the first bag of cotton ever sold in South Carolina.[1] The total American export to Europe in 1785 was only fourteen bags. But in 1793 Eli Whitney, a Yale graduate of 1792, who was then a guest of the widow of General Green on her plantation near Savan-

[1] Cf. J. D. B. De Bow, *The Industrial Resources, etc., of the Southern and Western States*, Vol. I, pp. 119–120.

nah, Georgia, produced a hand-propelled gin, which would seed fifty pounds of lint in a day. It was a very simple contrivance by which one cylinder with teeth a half-inch apart revolved against and in opposite direction to another cylinder in which the teeth were very closely set. The close-set teeth stopped the seed and the teeth on the other cylinder pulled the lint through, which was in turn cleaned off with a brush. The patent for this machine was granted March 14, 1794. In 1767 James Hargreaves in England had invented a spinning jenny, by which 120 threads at a time could be spun, instead of one as in the old hand process. Two years later Richard Arkwright had made noted improvements and soon Dr. Edmund Cartwright, a clergyman, had invented the power loom. Everything therefore was set for a greatly increased production of cotton. In 1793 only 500,000 pounds were exported to Europe, but the following year, when the new cotton gin was in operation, the export jumped to 1,667,000 pounds. The growth by five-year periods was as follows:[1]

1795	6,000,000 lb.	1825	176,000,000 lb.
1800	17,000,000 lb.	1830	298,000,000 lb.
1805	40,000,000 lb.	1835	389,000,000 lb.
1810	93,000,000 lb.	1840	740,000,000 lb.
1815	83,000,000 lb.	1845	873,000,000 lb.
1820	127,000,000 lb.	1850	1,026,000,000 lb.

The value of the crop in 1800 was twenty-four times the value of the crop in 1790. Eli Whitney's simple device changed a by-product of agriculture into the staple crop, raised at once the price of slaves, increased the size of plantations, and fastened firmly in the mind of planters the idea that slaves were not only profitable but necessary in the raising of cotton. Of this transformation Woodrow Wilson remarks:

> Before this tremendous development of cotton culture had taken place, slavery had hardly had more than habit and the perils of emancipation to support it in the South: southern life and industry had shaped themselves to it, and the slaves were too numerous and too ignorant to be safely set free. But when the cotton-gin supplied the means of indefinitely expanding the production of marketable cotton by the use of slave labor, another and even more powerful argument for its retention was furnished. After that slavery seemed nothing less than the indispensable economic instrument of southern society.[2]

---

[1] For full discussion of the cotton industry during this period see: J. D. B. De Bow, *Industrial Resources, etc., of the Southern and Western States*, Vol. I, pp. 114–242 *passim*.

[2] *Division and Reunion, 1829–1889*, p. 125.

The economic aspect of slavery concentrated great power in the hands of the planter class. It soon came to dominate political thinking. The phrase "Cotton is King," which came to its culmination in a ponderous volume of nine hundred pages written by a man in Cincinnati, was no idle boast. It meant that the slaves were more and more being concentrated into great aggregations by the great slave owners; it meant that these landed proprietors were more and more absorbing the power and influence in the South. It meant still more that these southern planters, backed as they were by the economic power of cotton, were more and more dominating the political thinking of the nation. The preliminary skirmishes of 1787 and of 1807 had tended to unify the planters in their defense of slavery, and cotton had now put into their hands the power to become a fighting force. "There was throughout southern society, something like a reproduction of that solidarity of feeling and of interest, which existed in the ancient classical republics, set above whose slaves, there was a proud but various democracy of citizenship and privilege." [1] "The ruling class in the South [was] small, compact and on the whole homogeneous; it was intelligent, alert and self conscious. . . . It had besides more political power, and clear notions of how it meant to use that power than any other class in the country." [2] The leisure which slavery allowed to a few had given opportunity to develop a statesman class represented by such names as Jefferson, Madison, Randolph, Calhoun, Jackson, and scores of others, who were unmatched in the rest of the country for bold and impetuous leadership. From 1807 on to the breaking out of the Civil War this group of leaders were able to hold the balance of power in Congress, even though they were fighting for a cause which must ultimately go against them. The great issue was whether the slave-owning states should continue to wield this power. The battle was fought out over the admission of Missouri, again over the admission of Texas, over the Kansas-Nebraska bill — each time with seeming victory for the slavery leaders. We must now briefly sketch these battles.

The first great struggle between the two sections came up over the formation of the territory of Arkansas and the admission of Missouri as a state. The North, led by John W. Taylor of New York, made an effort to forbid further importation of slaves into Arkansas and declare that all children born thereafter of slave parents

---

[1] Woodrow Wilson, *Division and Reunion, 1829–1889*, p. 107.
[2] *Ibid.*, p. 129.

within that territory should be free at twenty-five. Along with this came the request of Missouri for the privilege of calling a convention to draw a constitution looking to statehood. John W. Taylor of New York moved that slavery should be restricted in the new state if and when admitted. The debate was long and bitter. More than once disruption of the Union was hinted. Maine was at the same time applying for statehood, and should both states come in as free states the slave power would at once be outvoted. Hence the bitterness of the struggle. Finally the famous compromise which prohibited slavery in all territory ceded by France, under the name of Louisiana, lying north of 36° 30′, except in the case of Missouri, which was to be allowed to come in as slave if the inhabitants so desired, was hit upon. The feeling ran so high, and there seemed such imminent danger of a disruption of the Union, that many northern statesmen spoke earnestly for the bill. Kinsey of New Jersey, who strongly favored freedom and represented a free state, stated he could vote for the compromise lest "we break asunder on a dispute about division of territory." [1] Stephens of Connecticut declared he would vote for the compromise, for "a precipice lies before us at which perdition is inevitable." [2] Other speeches were of a similar import. Amidst such stirring appeals the vote was finally taken which resulted in 134 ayes and 42 noes. The equilibrium of the two forces of the country was thus held. According to Woodrow Wilson this opened the question of compromise, and gave the southern leaders to understand that "they had the sanction of the government to prosecute their efforts to extend their system and their political influence," [3] and Henry Wilson comments: "The victory of the slave power was now complete; slavery was fastened upon the territory of Arkansas and the new state of Missouri." [4]

The next great struggle arose over the Texas question. Texas and Coahuila had been united into a single state under Mexico in 1824, and provision had been made for the gradual abolition of slavery. But the state soon began filling up with settlers from Alabama, Georgia, North Carolina, Tennessee, and even Virginia, so that in

[1] Thomas H. Benton, *Historical and Legal Examination of That Part of the Decision of the Supreme Court of the United States in the Dred Scott Case Which Declares the Unconstitutionality of the Missouri Compromise Act, and the Self-Extension of the Constitution to Territories, Carrying Slavery along with It*, p. 94.
[2] *Ibid.*, p. 95.
[3] *Division and Reunion, 1829–1889*, pp. 131–132.
[4] *History of the Rise and Fall of the Slave Power in America*, Vol. I, p. 149.

the early thirties it was no longer a Spanish state but an American territory. Because of oppression by the Mexican government Texas seceded in 1836. After a sweeping victory over Santa Anna, the Texans, led by Sam Houston, a Tennesseean, declared their independence on San Jacinto day, April 21, 1836. In their new constitution slavery was recognized. The slave-owning states were therefore eager to recognize Texas as independent in the hope that this territory might be added to the Union and thus strengthen their position. The southern leaders were aided in their plans by the fact that both France and England were flirting with Texas, and fear lest one of these European nations might get possession of this broad sweep of territory led to hurried action with regard to annexation. The presidential election of 1844 was determined by the attitude of the candidate toward the annexation of Texas. Clay opposed it. James K. Polk, of Tennessee, favored it and was overwhelmingly elected. The election having settled the mind of the country, the retiring Congress passed a joint resolution of annexation which was signed by Tyler on his last day of office, March 3, 1845. This plunged the United States into war with Mexico over the boundary of Texas. In the Treaty of Guadalupe Hidalgo (1848) the United States agreed to pay Mexico fifteen million dollars for lands ceded, and the Rio Grande was made the southern boundary.

Florida was admitted to the Union March 3, 1845, of course as a slaveholding state. Iowa came in as a free-soil state December 28, 1846, and Wisconsin also as a free state May 29, 1848. Thus far there was parity between slave and free state additions.

The acquiring of Texas brought many disputes with Mexico. While the boundary question was being discussed and a bill appropriating two million dollars to facilitate its settlement was being considered, David Wilmot of Pennsylvania introduced an amendment (1846) which ultimately became famous as the "Wilmot Proviso." This provided that in any territory that might be acquired from Mexico neither slavery nor involuntary servitude should exist except for judicially determined crime. This caused heated discussion but was finally lost. Meanwhile the doctrine of "squatter sovereignty" was taking form. Leave the question to the settlers themselves. Just as the original states had the right to decide their own status with reference to slavery, without interference from the national government, so these new territories should have a similar right. But the men of the North answered by saying the status was not the same. The original states came in of their own right as members of the federation. These territories were carved out of lands which belonged to the Union, and hence the Union had a right to determine how they should be organized. It was this point of contention which gave meaning to every political move from 1846 up to the opening of the Civil War. In 1847, John C. Calhoun presented in the Senate a resolution which set forth clearly the slaveholders' view. It declared that, inasmuch as the territories were the property of all the states, Congress had no right whatever to exclude slaves from them, since this would be an abridgment of the rights of property operating against all persons who held slaves and who might want to move into those territories. If the sacred right of all property were granted, the contention seemed fair enough.

During Taylor's administration (1849 to July, 1850) the territories were confidentially urged to organize and express their preferences on the slavery question, and California, New Mexico, and Utah did so organize. The extremists of the North were urging disunion, and the extremists of the South were threatening withdrawal. At this juncture Henry Clay came forward with his famous compromise asking that Congress should admit California with its free constitution; should organize the rest of the Mexican cession without any provision concerning slavery, leaving that question to "squatter sovereignty"; should purchase from Texas certain portions of New Mexico which Texas claimed; should abolish slavery in the District of Columbia; and should enact a fugitive law. The bill was later broken up into three parts and each passed separately.

As early as 1793 Congress had passed a law facilitating the execution of a clause of the Constitution which provides that persons "held to service or labor in one state under the laws thereof, escaping to another" should be delivered up on the claim of the party to whom such services were due. The fugitive slave law was simply making that law explicit. It proved to be the most serious blunder of the famous compromise of 1850. Up to this time the return of fugitives from justice as well as fugitives from service had rested as a responsibility upon state governments. But there had been a growing laxness on the part of the officials of free states about returning fugitive slaves. Therefore, the compromise law of 1850 put the whole burden back on the central government. Warrants for arrest were to be issued by United States judges or commissioners; these warrants were to be executed by United States marshals; all citizens were commanded under heavy penalty to assist in the return of fugitives, and assistance of fugitive slaves was made an offense punishable by both fine and imprisonment. The affidavit of the master was made all that was necessary to demand a warrant for arrest of a slave. In the putting of this law into effect a great deal of bad blood was stirred up. Southern masters were disposed to push the law to the extreme, and Northern abolitionists were disposed to evade it wherever possible. Perhaps more than any other one item of the famous compromise, this law helped to hasten to its conclusion the tragedy of the country, bringing the settlement of the question to the arbitrament of war.

The beginning of the end came when, in 1854, Stephen A. Douglas with bold and impetuous leadership introduced into the Senate what became known as the Kansas-Nebraska bill. Kansas and Nebraska were a part of the Louisiana territory which had been set aside as "forever" free soil by the Missouri Compromise of 1820. But the addition of the Texas-Mexico territory in which "squatter sovereignty" had been set up threw the question open to debate as to why "squatter sovereignty" should not now be applied to the old Louisiana territory. No one, not even the southerners, had dreamed of so bold a stroke. But Douglas did. The passage of this bill really repealed the Missouri Compromise and opened the whole question of free or slave territories once again. Of this action Henry Wilson wrote:

> As both effect and cause it defies competition and almost comparison with any single measure of the long series of aggressions of the slave power.... No single act of the slave power ever spread greater consternation, produced more lasting results upon the popular mind, or did so much to arouse the North and to convince the people of its desperate character. Lulled by the siren song and drugged by the sorceries of compromise, they had learned to regard with equanimity and to acquiesce in the fixed facts of slavery as, exclusively and perpetually, a Southern system, confined within established limits, and kept back by impassable barriers. So long as it was only the slave that was crushed by its power, and the slaveholding States that were cursed by its presence, the North, sordid and safe, accepted its existence, and even welcomed its pecuniary and political aid, because it put money in its coffers and gave it votes, pleading ever the compact of the fathers as their confident reply to the simple claims, however urgent, of justice and humanity.[1]

The bold stroke of Douglas was followed in 1857 by a decision of the Supreme Court that a master might take his property in the form

[1] *History of the Rise and Fall of the Slave Power in America*, Vol. II, pp. 378–379.

of a slave into any free territory and still retain the right to that property. Thus the final breakdown of the old ordinance of 1787 relating to free territories was brought about and the final struggle was made inevitable.

Following these stirring events the various parties met to make their nominations. The northern Democrats nominated Douglas of Illinois; the Constitutional Union party, a group of conservatives, nominated John Bell of Tennessee; the radical southern group which withdrew from the Democratic party nominated John C. Breckinridge of Kentucky; and the Republicans nominated Abraham Lincoln of Illinois. It was of course a foregone conclusion that the Republicans would win, with the Democrats so thoroughly disorganized. The thorough disorganization of political life was indicated by the fact that the various Democratic groups polled 2,823,000 votes while the Republicans polled 1,866,000, but Lincoln carried the election on this minority vote. Woodrow Wilson has clearly interpreted the meaning of the election:

> The South had avowedly staked everything, even her allegiance to the Union, upon this election. The triumph of Mr. Lincoln was, in her eyes, nothing less than the establishment in power of a party bent upon the destruction of the southern system and the defeat of southern interests, even to the point of countenancing and assisting servile insurrection. In the metaphor of Senator Benjamin, the Republicans did not mean, indeed, to cut down the tree of slavery, but they meant to gird it about, and so cause it to die. It seemed evident to the southern men, too, that the North would not pause or hesitate because of constitutional guarantees. For twenty years northern States had been busy passing "personal liberty" laws, intended to bar the operation of the federal statutes concerning fugitive slaves, and to secure for all alleged fugitives legal privileges which the federal statutes withheld. More than a score of States had passed laws with this object, and such acts were as plainly attempts to nullify the constitutional action of Congress as if they had spoken the language of the South Carolina ordinance of 1832. Southern pride, too, was stung to the quick by the position in which the South found itself. The agitation against slavery had spoken in every quarter the harshest moral censures of slavery and the slaveholders. The whole course of the South had been described as one of systematic iniquity; southern society had been represented as built upon a wilful sin; the southern people had been held up to the world as those who deliberately despised the most righteous commands of religion. They knew that they did not deserve such reprobation. They knew that their lives were honorable, their relations with their slaves humane, their responsibility for the existence of slavery among them remote. National churches had already broken asunder because of this issue

of morals. The Baptist Church had split into a northern and a southern branch as long ago as 1845; and 1844 had seen the same line of separation run through the great Methodist body.

The Republican party was made up of a score of elements, and the vast majority of its adherents were almost as much repelled by the violent temper and disunionist sentiments of the Abolitionists as were the southern leaders themselves. The abolitionist movement had had an exceedingly powerful and steadily increasing influence in creating a strong feeling of antagonism towards slavery, but there was hardly more of an active abolitionist party in 1860 than there had been in 1840. The Republicans wished, and meant, to check the extension of slavery; but no one of influence in their counsels dreamed of interfering with its existence in the States. They explicitly acknowledged that its existence there was perfectly constitutional. But the South made no such distinctions. It knew only that the party which was hotly intolerant of the whole body of southern institutions and interests had triumphed in the elections and was about to take possession of the government, and that it was morally impossible to preserve the Union any longer. "If you who represent the stronger portion," Calhoun had said in 1850, in words which perfectly convey this feeling in their quiet cadences, "cannot agree to settle the great questions at issue on the broad principle of justice and duty, say so; and let the States we both represent agree to separate and depart in peace." [1]

South Carolina, Georgia, Florida, Alabama, Mississippi, and Louisiana immediately withdrew from the Union. They claimed they had a right to withdraw from a union they had freely entered, for mutual aid and protection, when the purposes for which they entered were no longer served by staying in it. Had not John Quincy Adams in 1842 read a petition from citizens of Massachusetts calling for dissolution of the Union? Had not the battle cry of 1843, "Annexation of Texas or disunion," been answered by Adams and other northern Whigs, by the statement that annexation would not only mean but justify a dissolution of the Union? Had not William Lloyd Garrison and his abolition society often and openly advocated dissolution of the Union as the only means of freeing themselves of the guilt of slavery? The threat of secession or dissolution had been so often made on both sides of the Mason and Dixon line that it seemed almost unreasonable to deny that any group of states had the right to such action. The contention seemed reasonable enough on the face of it, but it failed to take into account one significant fact: namely, that while each state entered the old confederation as a unit, independent

[1] *Division and Reunion, 1829–1889*, pp. 208–210.

in itself, it had not during the years remained independent. The states were no longer individual entities. The changing of boundaries, the purchase of new lands, the addition of new states, the acceptance into the Union of an independent republic — Texas — had all brought new responsibilities and new obligations. The obligations were not the obligation of any one state, but of all the states combined. The growth of the country had blended the states of the confederation into a unity from which no one could withdraw without great injury to all. Neither North nor South had fully realized this, but the South in particular did not see it. Its society was still more or less feudal. Its great estates were isolated and independent. Its sense of individual freedom was strong and its sense of social responsibility had not been fostered by the conditions of its social life. Therefore, it felt it was completely within its rights to withdraw. It was another case of lack of awareness of the tides of progress that surround society. The South therefore found itself fighting against the very spirit of the times. It went down in the bloody conflict which followed, and then began again to build a new civilization which was less individualistic.

PROBLEMS FOR STUDY

1. Would the large number of Negroes taken from Africa during the era of the slave trade help to explain the present backwardness of Africa?
2. What are the conditions most favorable to the development of slavery? Were they accentuated in the old South?
3. Why was slavery in the West Indies economically a failure?
4. Was slavery an economic failure in America? Would it have fallen of its own weight?
5. If slavery was an economic liability, why did the planters hold their slaves?
6. What were the effects of slavery on the economic development of the South?
7. Why were the slave states so powerful in the early history of America?
8. Slavery seemed doomed in 1780, 1808, 1820 to 1830, but at each period it revived. What were the causes leading toward its destruction, and what brought about the changed attitudes?
9. If the early colonies joined the Union of their own volition, why could they not withdraw when it seemed to their advantage to do so?

BIBLIOGRAPHY

Frederic Bancroft, *Slave-trading in the Old South* (1931).
William O. Blake, *The History of Slavery and the Slave Trade, Ancient and Modern* (1858).
Elizabeth Donnan, *Documents Illustrative of the History of the Slave Trade to America* (1930–1933).
George F. Dow, *Slave Ships and Slaving* (1927).
Jerome Dowd, *The Negro Races* (1907).
William E. B. Du Bois, *The Suppression of the African Slave-trade to the United States of America, 1638–1870* (1896).
Amos K. Fiske, *The West Indies* (1899).
Albert Bushnell Hart, *Slavery and Abolition 1831–1841* (1906).
Harry H. Johnston, *The Negro in the New World* (1910).
Beverly B. Munford, *Virginia's Attitude toward Slavery and Secession* (1909).
Ulrich B. Phillips, *American Negro Slavery* (1918).
Willis D. Weatherford, *The Negro from Africa to America* (1924).
Waldemar C. Westergaard, *The Danish West Indies under Company Rules* (1917).
George W. Williams, *History of the Negro Race in America, 1619–1880* (1885).
Henry Wilson, *History of the Rise and Fall of the Slave Power in America* (1875).
Woodrow Wilson, *Division and Reunion, 1829–1889* (1898).

CHAPTER VIII

ECONOMIC ASPECTS OF SLAVERY

The economic basis of slavery in its broadest aspects in America was cotton cultivation. Cotton was essentially a southern crop and Negro slaves the exclusive labor content of the institution. This alliance of cotton, Negroes, and the political power of the slaveholders, for more than seventy years, remained one of the strongest forces in American history.

It was, perhaps, the matter of climate and geography that first determined the sectional division of economic interests, permitting manufacturing industries to develop in one section and agriculture in another. That there existed from the beginning no purely moral scruples in any of the original states of the Union against slavery as a form of social accommodation is indicated in the fact of slavery, at some time, in all of them. But, just as slavery drove out indenture and free labor in Virginia, because in the cultivation of tobacco slave labor proved more satisfactory, indenture and free labor drove out slavery in Pennsylvania, because slave labor proved more costly in the competition.

The first general sectional division between industry and agriculture, however, helped to fix the logic of slavery as the "peculiar institution of the South," the defense of which became a part of the very social morality of the section. In this division the South received an enormous handicap, although this fact was not apparent at the beginning.

Agriculture depends upon soil and climate and yields different produce in different quantities according to the natural conditions imposed. Industries, and particularly manufacturing industries, have no such limitation. With the same skill and activity the product can be about the same anywhere.[1] Agriculture is a seasonal activity, while industry lends itself, more or less, to a regular distribution of the operation throughout the year. The division of labor in large-

[1] Edgar Tristram Thompson, "The Plantation," Ph.D. Thesis, University of Chicago, 1932.

scale manufacturing can be constant and standardized, while agriculture must readjust its processes with every stage of growth in the product. The goods of agriculture are perishable, both in the field and on the market. Industry can escape most of these inherently critical periods. In industry the defects of workmanship are immediately obvious, while in agriculture the results are deferred until the crop appears, thus lending themselves less easily to correction. To such disadvantages under normal conditions were added those inherent in slavery as an economic institution, and this double handicap has been ever apparent in the economic history of the South.

It was unfortunate, in the first place, that the economy adopted by the southern states fell outside the current of modern economic development. At the time of its beginning, the modern world was entering the age of industrialism, following the industrial revolution with its factories and cities. It was an age of economic nationalism rather than of sectionalism. It was an age of greater human freedom; the serfs had been freed in central Europe and this was followed by freedom of the blacks in the West Indies even before the institution of slavery had reached its nadir in America. Feudalism had been dead hundreds of years in Europe, but it found an opportunity to repeat itself in structure and in the psychology developed in America in the southern plantation.

Broadus Mitchell has drawn an arresting parallel between the economic structure of feudalism and that of the southern plantation. Both were based upon agriculture; in both systems there were decentralization, self-sufficiency, and a dominant class which constituted an aristocracy; in both there were an inevitable exploitation of labor, as such, and social stagnation. Indeed, many of the prime characteristics of feudalism were repeated, and much of its actual terminology was carried over to the plantation system, although removed in time by five hundred years.

The institution of slavery may, however, be studied independently, as one expression of our capitalistic culture. Slavery demanded that the capital be invested in slaves and land. The purchase of slaves, as Phillips points out, seriously drained off the earnings of the community which imported them.[1] Purchase was necessary if the labor was to be completely controlled, and the more the system grew, the higher the price of slaves mounted and the more speculative

---

[1] "The Origin and Growth of the Southern Black Belts," *American Historical Review*, July, 1906, p. 798.

the price of cotton became. Between 1810 and 1860, for example, the price of slaves increased from $900 to $1,800 at New Orleans, from $500 to $1,300 at Charleston, and from $600 to $1,800 in middle Georgia.[1] So bound up with cotton and prices were these slaves that the price of the slave, rather than the price of land, fluctuated with the demand for cotton. Moreover, in spite of the rise in price of slaves, cotton fell in price from 16 cents a pound in 1820 to 11 cents in 1860.[2]

The capital which normally might have gone into bank stocks or into commerce and trade went into slaves. The slave was a prospect as profit over and above the cost of his upkeep, and such profit was expected throughout the span of the working life of the slave. "The proclivity for buying slaves," says Phillips, "was the worst feature of the régime from an economic point of view, for it drained capital out of every developing district and froze the local assets into the one form of investment." Farmers in the North and West could hire labor to be paid from current expenses and invest their profits in further land improvements, railroads, factories, and banks, or accumulate some savings. Southern planters, under the eternal urge to secure more and more slaves, strained both cash and credit to buy slaves "whose life-time must be paid in advance."

There was a curious illusion which gave great satisfaction to southern planters when their per capita wealth was contrasted with that of the easterners. As Dodd observed, nearly one-half of the people of the cotton states were property.[3] The number of slaves was commonly taken as an index of wealth. It became evident to a few of the more discriminating speculators even before the end of the period of rapid expansion that there were economic limits to the size of the plantation. But worst of all, the system tended to operate in such a manner as to keep those large planters who had drawn to themselves a surplus of slaves scarcely more than custodians of the wealth created, while northern capitalists actually took off the major profits.[4]

The investment of capital in land was subordinated to investment in slaves. Land was plentiful and cheap. So long as wasted soil could be abandoned and new lands put into cultivation the system

---

[1] Ulrich B. Phillips, *American Negro Slavery*, pp. 370–371.

[2] William A. Yarbrough, *Economic Aspects of Slavery in Relation to Southern and Southwestern Migration*, p. 25.

[3] William E. Dodd, *The Cotton Kingdom*, p. 11.   [4] *Ibid.*, pp. 29–30.

tended away from giving increasing value to lands, and toward the tying up of capital in an uncertain and unfixed commodity. It became a vicious cycle of "cut down, wear out and walk off" which was condemned heartily enough but never seriously checked. As one writer of the period complained: "The Negro is the investment rather than the land. The value of the Negro is instantly affected by a change in the price of cotton, while the value of the land which grows the cotton is comparatively unaffected."[1] Far from being treated as a permanent investment, land came down to the category of current expenses. The dangers of this practice were reflected in an unstable population and working structure, and a system constantly on the move. "Mining the soil," Broadus Mitchell declares, "gave an unsatisfactory character to the economic life of the section. Nothing was rooted. Everybody was virtually poised for flight. This was the wrong keynote for any progressive society." To complicate the matter further, the enormous investment in slaves made any question of emancipation and freedom from the system and its economic consequences unthinkable. The very questionableness of the economic principles in operation prompted increasingly impassioned defense of the system.

Closely allied with the questions of capital and land are another group of problems inherent in the economics of slavery. A staple crop was imperative if the system was to endure and make profits; this crop had to lend itself to simple, routinized, year-round labor; there could be no scientific agriculture, no use of machinery, and no crop diversification; and as a requisite of profits, there had constantly to be opened up new lands to take the place of those worn out through the artless and unvaried cultivation of the staple. There was a limitation of habitat more drastic than that which conditioned industry. All soils were not conducive to the raising of the staple, and the use of slave labor depended to an important degree upon a public policy friendly to the system as a social institution. The extension of plantations was hedged about by the physical peculiarities of the country, as well as by the requisite internal balance of the plantation unit for highest administrative efficiency. Finally, slaves, however valuable, died, escaped, became old and useless, or were maimed, and thus could seriously affect, through any of these vicissitudes, the capital investment.

[1] William A. Yarbrough, *Economic Aspects of Slavery in Relation to Southern and Southwestern Migration*, p. 23.

There is evidence, from a period in the early history of the colonies, that through the lack of an adequate staple crop slavery was threatened with collapse from its own internal economic weakness. When tobacco, the first major staple, declined in importance, as a result of the inevitable soil wastage, overproduction, lowered prices, and the necessity for diversification of labor, slaves became a great burden. Slave prices were low, and their upkeep consumed as much as or more than could be earned through their labor. Individual manumissions reached such lengths as to embarrass the young republic with unwieldy and unwelcome numbers of free Negroes. Patrick Henry noted during this period that slaveholders were holding on to their slaves more from habit than any other motive, for they meant no profit.

At this critical period there developed, in a manner over which the South had little or no control, a fortuitous concourse of discoveries which elevated cotton to heights of dazzling promise as a new and profitable staple. These discoveries and inventions were the spinning jenny, Arkwright's water frame and throttle, Watt's steam engine, the fly shuttle, Crompton's water mule, the process of cylinder printing, calico printing, the power loom, Whitney's saw gin, the scrutching machine, the bleaching process, and, around 1840, the sewing machine. They combined an expanded demand with improved means of expanding the supply. The new staple had certain advantages within itself. It could, more successfully than other agricultural crops, engage labor throughout the year; it was not perishable when harvested; it could be routinized and it could be tended by simple labor.

The limitations upon this crop, however, were more serious than the advantages and were fatal over a long period. Routine was the key to effectiveness. The labor for these tasks was brought from Africa or, as was the case later, bred in Virginia and placed under the external coercion of the system. Compulsion took the place of yeomanly initiative. Essentially slave labor was an inert body, obviously without incentive, and with no more than a normal human love of drudgery. Since it was considered dangerous to educate the slaves, it was necessary to adjust the tasks to their unimproved and uninquiring minds. Such a limitation of tasks made necessary abandonment of all hope of scientific agriculture with this labor, and likewise the use of complicated machinery. The implements and methods thus remained as crude and as unimproved as the minds

ECONOMIC ASPECTS OF SLAVERY 151

of the slaves. Moreover, to permit free white labor to grow the cotton, assuming such labor to be superior, would have constituted promptly an argument against slavery.

Inherent in the nature of the system was the demand for rapid exploitation. On the question of soil exhaustion and wastage there is practically no disagreement among students of the system. Olmsted found the wasteful method of cultivation rationalized in the cotton states when at the height of their prosperity. The principal capital investment was in slaves. The method of cultivation encouraged waste. So long as land was reasonably plentiful and cheap, why should money be expended to restore the exhausted land when new land could be purchased for less than the cost of restoration? It cost twenty dollars an acre to manure, but new land could be bought, fenced and ready for the plough, for five dollars an acre.[1] Thomas Jefferson, in the latter days of his career, attributed his financial difficulties to a long succession of stunted tobacco crops. In South Carolina and Georgia, the first two important cotton states, a bare twenty-five years of exploitation brought serious results. Cotton production in the hill country, which, in 1821, amounted to half of the nation's output, fell off to such an extent that attention was forced to crop rotation. Hayne of South Carolina in 1832 referred in Congress to "mournful evidences of premature decay" in his state, and pointed with sadness to "fields abandoned, the hospitable manors of the fathers deserted; agriculture drooping, and slaves, like the masters, working harder and faring worse; the planter slaving with unavailing efforts to avert the ruin which is before him."

The only answer to this wastage was migration, ever westward to newer lands. The virgin lands of the lower South from 1800 onward drew off the population of the Atlantic slave states. In 1850, 34 per cent of the persons born in the seaboard slave states were living in other states and almost entirely in the states of the South and West.[2] The most casual examination of statistics of the period shows that the cotton industry declined in the older states in almost exact proportion to the expansion of the system in the direction of the Southwest. The new plantations with their imported slave populations drove out the white laborers and small farmers. They were in

---

[1] Frederick Law Olmsted, *A Journey in the Seaboard Slave States*, p. 272.

[2] William A. Yarbrough, *Economic Aspects of Slavery in Relation to Southern and Southwestern Migration*, p. 38.

a constant hegira before the advance of the great owners. The plantations were, indeed, most often assembled by buying up farms of independent small owners. The system was kept virile by the availability of new land. The exhaustion of free land meant its doom, and such exhaustion was bound to come.

The stupidity of the slaves has often been cited as responsible for the land waste. The masses of plantation slaves were, of course, ignorant, and it was considered wise to keep them so. However, it is perhaps more accurate to attribute this damage to slave culture. For after all, the slave labor was controlled labor, and foresight was the responsibility of the owners. Phillips insists that slave labor could have been used intelligently and constructively in agriculture, but the traditional methods of the plantation continued in the opposite direction.[1] Many factors abetted the practice. The value of overseers was measured by the amount of cotton they could raise and not by the amount of land preserved. As in the present issue of crop limitation to adjust cotton prices, no planter felt that he should be the one to make the sacrifice, or, indeed, to change his methods at all.

The complete concentration upon the staple not only caused neglect of other produce that had to be purchased from other sections, but ruled out stock raising, which would have aided in providing manure for fertilizer. The system militated against the use of improved methods of agriculture or the adoption of machinery on any important scale. There were few or no inventions in agriculture or otherwise. Inventiveness was killed by the reliance upon slave labor instead of machinery. The Patent Office records in 1840 show that the slave states received 76 patents while the free states received 564. It has been suggested that the mechanical aptness and inventiveness encouraged as a matter of course in the North played perhaps as decisive a part as any other factor in the military operations of the Civil War. Broadus Mitchell regards as a vital loss the failure of the slave states to devise some contrivance for putting back what was taken out of the soil. Beyond simple economics it was symptomatic to him of an avoidance of pressing social problems. Always the frontier stood as a safety valve.

The system tended to center control of wealth in the hands of a few. This might be considered especially disastrous in agriculture where yeomanry is still regarded as a symbol of national stability.

[1] *Life and Labor in the Old South*, p. 332.

ECONOMIC ASPECTS OF SLAVERY

Far from creating a self-sustaining class of sturdy farmers, the system virtually impoverished the majority of the white population of the South. Two-thirds of the white population had no connection with slavery and profited only slightly by its existence. A thousand families received $50,000,000 a year while 666,000 families received only about $60,000,000.[1] No economy, slave or otherwise, could be considered sound, in a democratic society, which kept the majority of its population in poverty. The economy of the plantation required no white people, except perhaps the proprietor, overseer, physician, and their families, and others were ruthlessly expelled.

George M. Weston speculated that if any state could be supposed to be made up of continuous plantations, the white race would not merely be starved out, but actually be squeezed out, and just so far as slavery falls short of effecting this result, it falls short of attaining its perfect development.[2] A free population is extrinsic to slavery.

The "Sand-hillers" of South Carolina, the "Crackers" of Georgia, were created by the system. These, of course, were the extremes of the class created by the pressure of the large plantations, but the actual numbers of non-slaveholders affected and kept poor was tremendous. For the system was inimical to the small planter. He could not compete with the large planter; his land, if fertile, was in demand as the plantations broadened, and he was either bought out or forced out. Benjamin Franklin anticipated this course of affairs in an essay on population written as early as 1751, when he pointed out that the Negroes brought into the English sugar islands greatly impoverished the whites there. "The poor," he said, "are by this means deprived of employment, while a few families acquire vast estates." In South Carolina in 1790 there were 107,094 slaves and 140,178 white persons; in 1850 there were 384,984 slaves and 274,563 white persons. Of the total white persons born in South Carolina only 58 per cent were living there in 1850.[3]

An effect even more profound was the restriction of another kind imposed by the system upon this element of the white population generally. Slave work was degrading and free white labor avoided it so far as possible. The avoidance was sentimental, but the result was economic. Again, the expulsion of the small farmer class and the poor whites carried with it a considerable hostility. There were

[1] William E. Dodd, *The Cotton Kingdom*, p. 24.
[2] *The Progress of Slavery in the United States*, p. 43.
[3] George M. Weston, *The Progress of Slavery in the United States*, p. 445.

exhibited toward them manifestations of behavior scarcely distinguishable from race prejudice, even though these poor whites were of the same basic stock as the more aristocratic planters. Olmsted, referring to the poor whites of North Carolina, said: "They are poor, having almost no property but their own bodies; and the use of these, that is, their labor, they are not accustomed to hire out statedly and regularly, so as to obtain capital by wages, but only occasionally by the day or job, when driven to it by necessity." [1]

Not only was there this blind and overwhelming competition of a system with an unorganized population of impoverished individuals, but in the direct work of the cities the leased slave labor kept down the number of white artisans. There are records of the bitter complaints and protests of this class against the custom of turning over the bulk of the important skilled work to Negro slaves. A petition, signed by about two hundred mechanics and laborers in Atlanta, Georgia, in 1858, read:

We, the undersigned, would respectfully represent to your honorable body that there exists in the city of Atlanta a number of men who, in the opinion of your memorialists are of no benefit to the city. We refer to negro mechanics whose masters reside in other places, and who pay nothing toward the support of the city government, and whose negro mechanics can afford to underbid the regular resident citizen mechanics of your city to their great injury, and without benefit to the city in any way. We most respectfully request your honorable body to take the matter in hand, and by your action in the premises afford such protection to the resident mechanics of your city as your honorable body may deem meet in the premises, and in duty bound your petitioners will ever pray.[2]

Economic restrictions were undoubtedly responsible for the general social condition of the non-slaveholding population of the South as compared with that of the North. The absence of schools, of literature, of science and art, has been conspicuous. In 1850 the white population of the 16 slave states was 6,222,418 and of the 18 free states 13,454,293. The *American Almanac* for 1858 states that the slave states had 15,000 schools and spent about $2,500,000 to support them, and that the free states had 87,000 public schools, and spent annually $16,545,288. Thus, with slightly more than twice the

[1] *A Journey in the Seaboard Slave States*, Vol. I, p. 388.
[2] Quoted from T. H. Martin's *Atlanta and Her Builders*, Vol. I, p. 139, in *Plantation and Frontier Documents: 1649–1863, Illustrative of Industrial History in the Colonial and Ante-Bellum South*, edited by Ulrich B. Phillips, p. 367.

population, the free states had over five and one half times as many schools, and spent nearly seven times as much to support them. Of illiterate native whites over 20 years of age there were 280,793 in the free states, and 552,605 in the slave states. One in every 10 free white persons over 20 years of age in the South was unable to read and write, as compared with one in 156 in the North.[1] One white person in 166 in Massachusetts could not read or write, and one in 17 in South Carolina; one white person in 568 in Connecticut was illiterate and one in 38 in Louisiana; one in 56 in New York, including foreigners and free Negroes, could not read and write, and one in 7 in North Carolina, excluding the Negroes. In the slave states there were 722 libraries, and in the free states 14,902.[2]

There has been attributed to the system the South's determined discouragement of foreign immigration, which has contributed energy, free man-power, and initiative to the building up of the industrial North. Alfred Holt Stone,[3] in an illuminating paper dealing with the economics of slavery, observes that the presence of the free Negro since 1865 deserves as much consideration, as a contributing cause of the course of immigration away from the South, as the presence of slavery before 1861. He attempts to draw a distinction between slave labor and Negro labor. The fact remains, however, that immigration avoided the South under slavery. Stone then questions how far the South really desired foreign immigration. The racial factor, he believes, during and after slavery has influenced southern opinion against complicating an existing racial difficulty through the addition of a foreign element to the population.

The existence of the system demanded solidarity of opinion and capacity for prompt adjustment to the various principles involved in the system. The condition of the non-slaveholding whites could not have been very inviting to free laborers from Europe who were escaping oppressive conditions in Europe. There is some suggestion of the force which contributed to the discouragement of immigrants to the South in the letter published in the Charleston (S. C.) *Mercury* for February 13, 1861, commenting upon the appearance of a number of European immigrants who had come to Charleston, following the withdrawal of several thousand slaves to the more productive

[1] Francis Newton Thorpe, *The Civil War: A Natural View*, p. 78.
[2] Census of 1850.
[3] "Some Problems of Southern Economic History," *American Historical Review*, July, 1908, pp. 779–797.

western lands. This writer saw great danger in the presence of the foreigners:

> When . . . more immigrant laborers shall come in greater numbers to the South, they will still more increase the tendency to exclusion; they will question the right of masters to employ their slaves in any works they may wish for; they will invoke the aid of legislation; they will use the elective franchise to that end; they may acquire the power to determine municipal elections; they will inexorably use it, and thus the town of Charleston, at the very heart of slavery, may become a fortress of democratic power against it. . . . It is probable that more abundant pauper labor may pour in, and it is to be feared that even in this state, the purest in its slave condition, democracy may gain a foothold, and that here also the contest for existence may be waged between them.[1]

During the year 1858 there came to New Orleans 13,913 Germans. Some 10,000 of these left within the year, going principally to St. Louis.[2] The secret of the dissatisfaction of the free white immigrant laborers who attempted to work in the South is suggested in the comment of a Welch miner to Olmsted. He reported the man as saying that "a man had to be too discreet here; if one happened to say anything that gave offense, they thought no more of drawing a pistol or knife upon him, than they would of kicking a dog that was in the way."[3] The incident was related to him of an English miner who had been placed at work with a gang of Negro slaves. Being unadjusted to the peculiar status of the Negroes, he talked freely with them. He was waited upon by a group of twenty or thirty armed white men and given fifteen minutes to leave the section forever.

The South, however, was not wholly without a foreign population. In 1860 the slave states had 9.0 per cent of the country's foreign immigrants. There has been an almost constant balance and adjustment between foreign-born and Negro labor both during and since slavery. In the slave states where Negro numbers declined, foreign immigration increased; where Negro numbers increased, the number of foreign-born declined or grew slowly. The difference, which has economic significance, between New England, for example, and the

---

[1] Extract from a letter of L. W. Spratt of Charleston, S. C., to John Perkins of Louisiana, from the Charleston *Mercury*, February 13, 1861, quoted in *Documentary History of American Industrial Society*, by Ulrich B. Phillips, p. 176.

[2] Ulrich B. Phillips, *Documentary History of American Industrial Society*, Vol. II, p. 184.

[3] Frederick L. Olmsted, *A Journey in the Seaboard Slave States*.

majority of the slave states on the matter of immigrant labor was that in the former section the proportions of persons in the most productive ages were higher and the proportions of dependents less. For the foreign-born came, as a rule, in the full vigor of manhood and could lend their energies and initiative to the building of the section, while the slave states had to support unproductive children, old persons, and a disproportionately large number of non-working women. In 1860 in the southern states 55.1 per cent of the white population was between the ages 15 to 69, while in New England 64.3 per cent fell within the productive period.[1]

The literature of the later period of slavery reveals how frequently it was pointed out, and particularly by the northern and European visitors, that free labor, in the long run, was superior to slave labor. The statistical comparisons were often so overwhelming as to be taken merely as hostile propaganda against the section's peculiar institution. Forced labor, at best, is grudging labor, which has to be kept at the point of profitable production by demoralizing exhibitions of physical violence or by elaborate systems of rewards. Slave labor, further, demanded a speculative capital outlay not involved in a system of free labor and wages. It was unfortunate that the labor precedent affected the psychology and habits of free white laborers to the point of making them exceedingly poor prospects for profitable production.

The difference in results is more clearly revealed in comparisons of the slave and free states. In agricultural products common to both sections, the free states greatly outstripped the slave states, even though the climate was more favorable to agriculture in the latter. In 1850 the hay crop alone of the free states exceeded by $3,533,275 the entire value of the six staples of the slave states, which included cotton, tobacco, rice, hay, hemp, and cane sugar.[2] The average value of land per acre in the South was $5.34; in the northwestern states $11.39; and in the northern states $28.07. One writer of the period noted that the land value on the free side of the Missouri and Ohio rivers was several times greater than on the slave side.[3]

[1] Alfred Holt Stone, "Some Problems of Southern Economic History," *American Historical Review*, July, 1908, p. 787.
[2] Hinton R. Helper, *The Impending Crisis of the South*, p. 53.
[3] Frederick Milnes Edge, *Slavery Doomed; or the Contest between Free and Slave Labour in the United States*, pp. 35–36.

Even in the South the comparisons were most often favorable to free labor. Phillips quotes Thomas Cooper of South Carolina as saying: "Nothing will justify slave labor in the point of economy but the nature of the soil and climate which incapacitate a white man from laboring in the summer time, as on the rich lands in Carolina and Georgia extending one hundred miles from the Seaboard." [1] The error of this belief, so commonly held, was not corrected by the fact easily observable, that the vast non-slaveholding population, numbering some 5,000,000, was then withstanding the climate and, as many of them as were permitted, were engaged in agricultural work. Alfred Holt Stone is insistent that there was nothing the Negro slaves did that free white workers could not and did not do. The difference was one purely of the limitation of the system, as the present engagement of these workers so completely proves. The soil and climate of the South have not changed, but attitudes toward work have undergone a significant revolution.

The economics of slavery involved another serious complex of handicaps in making it practically impossible to exploit other natural resources in the South than its agricultural products, and these in an unbalanced manner. The capital of the South inevitably became centered in the Black Belt cotton states. The system inevitably tended toward the concentration of the wealth of the section in a few hands, and it inevitably became tied up in slave property, to the extent of more than half the wealth of the South. Virtually no capital was available for developing mining, for which there was rich opportunity; or for developing manufacturing industries, which were essential; or for encouraging animal industry; or for utilizing its ever present water power and raw materials. Highways and railways could not be developed, and the section was forced to close itself generally to the unquestioned advantages of machinery. Even if there were capital available, the use of slave labor in mining on a large scale was considered impracticable, and free white labor was too often disdainful of such work. The system had produced lawyers, politicians, and theologians, but few scientists and practical engineers who could lead the way in exploitation of mineral resources. Railroad building was discouraged by the fact that, although plantations had to be near transportation, they could supply freight at only one season of the year, and this was not profitable.

A result of these limitations was an almost complete dependence

[1] *Life and Labor in the Old South*, p. 183.

ECONOMIC ASPECTS OF SLAVERY 159

upon the North and upon Europe for most of the necessities of life. From the North and West the section had to buy its cloth, shoes, hats, carriages, saddles, agricultural implements, and a considerable part of its food. The live stock, horses, cattle, and hogs had to be purchased from the West. De Bow's estimate of the value of the cotton crop in 1850 was $98,603,720. But the annual amount of merchandise sold to the South by the North alone amounted to $60,000,000.[1] This does not include the New England shipbuilding, so largely sustained by southern wants, nor does it include the goods purchased from Europe. No small part of the burden of these imports was upon that two-thirds of the whole population of the South who received none of the direct benefits of the institution of slavery.

This dependence of the slave states upon the North amounted to a secondary slavery for the southern slave masters themselves. "Dependence," says John G. Van Deusen, "was the one word which characterized the South during the entire ante-bellum period."[2] The neglect of banking and finance left this important field to the capitalists of the North. Only a small portion of the money from the export of cotton found its way into southern banks. It is estimated that less than a third of the returns on cotton shipped from New Orleans, one of the greatest of the southern exporting centers, came into the South's financial institutions.[3] New York and Philadelphia always had more money on deposit than the total value of the exports. In 1850 the total cotton, rice, and sugar sales amounted to $119,400,000 while the total bank deposits in the South were around $20,000,000. In 1860, when the value of crops reached $200,000,000, less than $30,000,000 was in southern banks.[4] For the ready capital for advances on cotton, or to sell bonds for the vital railways and such manufactories as the section tried to develop, the planters had to turn to Wall Street.[5] The exportations from Europe came through New York, and the northern broker took off his profit. New England manufactured the textiles; northern shipping lines carried the cotton away and brought supplies back. All the railroad iron and the machinery used in the cotton mills came

[1] George McHenry, *The Cotton Trade*, pp. 110–111.
[2] *Economic Bases of Disunion in South Carolina*, p. 328.
[3] William E. Dodd, *The Cotton Kingdom*, p. 28.
[4] *Ibid.*, p. 29.
[5] William A. Yarbrough, *Economic Aspects of Slavery in Relation to Southern and Southwestern Migration*, p. 328.

from the North, and after the stopping of the slave trade the cotton South had to depend upon Virginia and other border states to breed new slaves to keep the system going.

It was the contest of the two economic systems that led up to nullification in South Carolina, "the heart of the slave power," and eventually to the Civil War. Nullification was first aimed against the tariffs and did not immediately involve the issue of slavery, although it was the imperatives of the slave régime that forced the tariff issue. The industries and commerce of the free states flourished as the inevitable effects of slavery began to settle down upon these states. As a national measure tariff provisions were regarded as necessary, but in practice they protected the industries of the North more than the agriculture of the South. Almost as a whole, therefore, the South was opposed to all the important tariff measures.

The tariff of 1828 proved especially obnoxious to the South, and opposition to it was led by South Carolina. The contention was that it taxed the southern section disproportionately. It had few manufactories to protect, and it bought most of its goods outside the section. A tariff on the universally essential goods of the section decreased the purchasing power of its produce and, as Senator George McDuffie of South Carolina asserted with violence, shifted the tax to the producer. It was illegal to tax exports. Thus, the duties on a great portion of the goods imported by the South, for planters, slaves, and non-slaveholding whites, indirectly were paid by the cotton planter. For all goods needed had to be purchased either from abroad with these duties added, or from the North at increased prices.[1] It was estimated that the tax amounted to some 40 per cent of the value.

The European cotton market was vastly more important than the American, and exports had to continue if the cotton supplies were to be absorbed. The tax on imports from Great Britain, which restricted exchange of British manufactured goods for raw materials, prompted that country to investigate other sources of cheap supply, and this constituted a dire threat to the South's industry. In South Carolina, in particular, the effects of diminishing profits of cotton were being felt. Here was clear evidence that the economic life of the State was being choked by the cupidity of northern industrialists and capitalists. Many attempts at free trade were made without

---

[1] William A. Yarbrough, *Economic Aspects of Slavery in Relation to Southern and Southwestern Migration*, p. 328.

ECONOMIC ASPECTS OF SLAVERY

success. A compromise on the tariff of 1828 was of little effect. From 1832, when the state passed an ordinance nullifying the tariff and prohibiting enforcement, there was talk of disunion. Sectional feeling increased and took into its sweep the entire slavery issue. The inevitable crisis came, and it was more economic than moral at base.

It is in point to inquire how such a system, with all its manifest disabilities, could have been so long and so fervidly supported. Undoubtedly there were some advantages. It is likewise true that many of the inherent disadvantages were effectively concealed in the feverish expansion of the system, as it developed southward and westward. When Harrison A. Trexler made his study of slavery in Missouri, about twenty years ago, he tried to get from a number of former slaveholders an opinion about the economic value of slavery.[1] Four-fifths of them replied that slavery as an economic system was unprofitable.

It may be suggested that the system of forced labor, which had apparent merits at first, became an accepted social as well as economic institution in that section in which it could best thrive. Its rationalization as an economic value was not distinguished from its rationalization as a social value. Attacks upon slavery by the abolitionists came even while some of its economic aspects were beginning to be observable, but these attacks were made upon moral and humanitarian grounds, rather than upon economic grounds. The reaction of the section was a fierce and bitter defense of the whole institution, by many of the men who had been contributing, consciously and unconsciously, to its dissolution, and by many who were beginning to be aware of the economic evils involved. The voices of the anti-slavery advocates in the South fell silent under the sting of the abolitionists' charges of perverted humanity. The economic evils of the system were stubbornly and righteously defended along with the economic advantages.

There is another angle of explanation. Historically the South has been strongly represented in the political life of the nation. Eight of the first eleven presidents, and fourteen of the eighteen attorney-generals were southerners. They virtually controlled Congress during the first seventy-five years of its existence. A formidable strength was given to the system by the Constitution of the United States itself, which permitted slaveholders to count three-fifths of an enor-

[1] *Slavery in Missouri, 1804–1865*, Johns Hopkins University Studies in Historical and Political Sciences, 1914.

mous slave population as a free population in apportioning representation. Allowing one representative to every 70,680,[1] under the three-fifths apportionment after the census of 1840, gave the South 20 representatives on the basis of the slave population alone. For every 70,680 free men in the North required to elect a representative, 55,725 could elect one in the South. Virtually all the leaders of the South were of the slaveholding gentry. All the important judges and lawyers, the writers, the preachers and doctors and the press, were dependent upon the planters and reflected in turn their social and economic point of view. The fear of slave uprising, the uncomfortable prospect of millions of free Negroes to be incorporated into the body politic, the easy social habits fostered by the system, the strength of the ideal of an aristocratic ruling class, the toughness and persistence of social habits themselves, all contributed to a conservatism which forced the section out of step with the more progressive movements of the enlightened world, and prompted explanations of this relationship in terms of nature and the intention of Almighty Providence. To this end scholars lent their talents in proving, in scientific and Biblical language, that slavery was the natural condition of the inferior Negro and dominion the right and glory of those white men who owned them.

In order to survive, it was necessary not only that the institution should be defended, but that it should be aggressively active. Education was pro-slavery, religious doctrines were pro-slavery. Free speech was taboo; school textbooks carried the supporting point of view, and contrary opinions or facts were rigidly excluded. Publications advocating abolition of the system were kept from the mails, and individuals with independent views not consistent with the social philosophy necessary to the system were punished or expelled. The classics of world literature and science were admitted or rejected on the basis of this issue. Such standard college texts in moral philosophy as Wayland's *Moral Science* had to be reëdited and reinterpreted by southern instructors. There was a special *Sociology for the South*. The situation developed a unique philosophy of human relations, based upon subordination and domination. A result of it all was that the section not only sanctioned a caste system, but made it the unchangeable basis and mainstay of its economic life.

[1] Apportionment, after the Census of 1840.

PROBLEMS FOR STUDY

1. Many historians assert that slavery would have collapsed as an economic system without a civil war. What evidence is there to warrant this speculation?
2. How could slavery have been made profitable as an economic system?
3. It has been said that the Civil War was the result of the economic rivalry between the North and the South rather than the result of the moral issue of slavery. Could this economic question have been permanently settled without freeing the slaves?
4. What effect would the introduction and wider use of machinery have had upon slavery?
5. The plantation after slavery was modified to the tenant system. What difficulties of the plantation under slavery, if any, survive in this new arrangement?
6. Can a social system based upon class subordination exist independent of a corresponding economic structure?

BIBLIOGRAPHY

Census of 1840.
Census of 1850.
William E. Dodd, *The Cotton Kingdom* (1920).
Frederick M. Edge, *Slavery Doomed; or the Contest between Free and Slave Labour in the United States* (1860).
Hinton R. Helper, *The Impending Crisis of the South* (1860).
George McHenry, *The Cotton Trade* (1863).
Frederick L. Olmsted, *A Journey in the Seaboard Slave States* (1860).
Ulrich B. Phillips, *American Negro Slavery* (1918).
Ulrich B. Phillips, *Life and Labor in the Old South* (1929).
Ulrich B. Phillips, "The Origin and Growth of the Southern Black Belts," *American Historical Review*, July, 1906, pp. 798–816.
Ulrich B. Phillips, *Plantation and Frontier Documents, 1649–1863, Illustrative of Industrial History in the Colonial and Ante-bellum South* (1909).
Alfred H. Stone, "Some Problems of Southern Economic History," *American Historical Review*, July, 1908, pp. 779–797.
Edgar T. Thompson, "The Plantation." Ph.D. Thesis, University of Chicago, 1932.
Francis N. Thorpe, *The Civil War; A Natural View* (1906).
Harrison A. Trexler, *Slavery in Missouri, 1804–1865* (1914).
John G. Van Deusen, *Economic Bases of Disunion in South Carolina* (1928).
George M. Weston, *The Progress of Slavery in the United States* (1857).
William A. Yarbrough, *Economic Aspects of Slavery in Relation to Southern and Southwestern Migration* (1932).

CHAPTER IX

LIFE ON THE SOUTHERN PLANTATION

Alexis de Tocqueville, on visiting America, wrote about the section of America east of the Hudson (New England) and that section "Southwest of that river and in the direction of the Floridas," where, he says, some great English proprietors had settled, who had imported with them aristocratic principles and the English law of descent.[1] Not a few southerners believe that all the early settlers in Virginia were of aristocratic rank, and that all of them were landed proprietors. When James I in 1606 chartered the Virginia Company he had in mind the colonizing of America, by which means he would open up sources of trade for England. In the original company there were adventurers — those who were to subscribe funds for the adventure — and planters — who were to go as colonists. The planters were to receive free transportation to America, maintenance for a certain period while they were opening up the land, and then a certain portion of the land, which the advertisements for colonists said would in no case be less than five hundred acres for each colonist. The English people had always been a land-loving folk, and this offer appealed strongly to many young and adventurous natures. The first shipload which sailed for Virginia was composed of fifty who called themselves gentlemen,[2] and only eight who acknowledged themselves to be just common laborers, besides various skilled workers. This first group of men were evidently true to their title, for the colony came dangerously near starvation because so few were willing to work. Finally, in 1610, the whole colony was organized as a kind of labor battalion, and the severest penalties had to be fixed for all who would not work.

Land was granted in the earlier decades on the basis of headrights —

[1] *Democracy in America*, p. 29.
[2] John Fiske, *Old Virginia and Her Neighbors*, Vol. I, p. 96. Other records indicate that of 105 persons left at Jamestown when Captain Newport returned to England, 29 were gentlemen, 12 laborers, 6 carpenters, 1 mason, 2 bricklayers, 1 blacksmith, 1 sailor, 1 drummer, 1 tailor, 1 barber, and 6 councilmen. There were also the clergymen, the doctor, and 38 others not described.

LIFE ON THE SOUTHERN PLANTATION

that is, each head of a family got fifty acres for himself and an additional fifty acres for each member of his family, and a like amount for each indentured servant whom he brought out from old England, and who stayed a minimum of three years in the colony. This policy was pursued for two reasons. First, it limited the amount of land which any planter could claim; and second, it encouraged men to bring out more servants. Labor was the great need of the colony. The more enterprising men therefore strained all their resources to bring out as many indentured servants as possible in order that they might lay claim to lands lying on the river and in the most favorable localities. As years went by and more and more difficulties developed in the old country, large numbers of the younger sons of England's aristocracy came out to Virginia with an eager desire to establish estates in this new land. Thus there grew up a series of estates each more or less distant from all the others, and gradually growing in size and importance. In 1635 the average size of the land grants to these country gentlemen was 380 acres, but the size of these estates grew by added grants until in 1680 they averaged 600 acres. Of course there were some estates which ran into thousands of acres. John Fiske says that up to 1689 eighty-two grants of more than 5,000 acres had been made.[1] With the beginning of the reign of Charles II many famous English aristocrats moved to America, and we begin to find frequent reference to the names of Randolph, Pendleton, Madison, Mason, Monroe, Carey, Ludwell, Park, Robinson, Marshall, Washington, Lee, and others.[2]

The early settlers found the Indians cultivating tobacco, and it is said John Rolfe as early as 1612 began making experiments in tobacco culture. Columbus had recorded in his diary, in 1492, the finding of this strange weed, and Jean Nicot had introduced it into France as early as 1560 from Spain. Its use must have become popular in Europe, for Pope Urban VIII issued a bull against it early in the seventeenth century. There was ready sale for it all over Europe. It was therefore to the cultivation of tobacco that the early colonists turned their attention. In order to raise this product the very richest land was necessary, and also an ample supply of labor. The two went hand in hand in determining the social structure of old Virginia. As one planter after another pushed his way to the interior, land was cleared along the rivers, houses were built, and the early planta-

[1] *Old Virginia and Her Neighbors*, Vol. II, p. 24.
[2] *Ibid.*, Vol. II, p. 25.

tions began to take shape. In order to hold his land, which came to him by grant, the planter must build a house on it, must plant at least an acre of corn or tobacco, and must pay to the King a head rent of twelve pence for each fifty acres. The building of the house was no hardship, for most of the settlers desired to found homes, but the paying of tax was a bone of contention. As soon as a planter had cleared a tract of land and made his first tobacco crop, he was eager to bring over an additional laborer or laborers, in order that he might secure new grants of land to add to his plantation. This in turn would bring him increased quantities of tobacco, for which he got a good price, and immediately he converted all his spare cash into more indentured servants. In order to secure these indentured servants, Philip A. Bruce tells us, there were those in the seaport towns of England who made a livelihood of luring young people to their houses, cropping their hair, and then disposing of them to shipmasters who took them to the colonies.[1] When a planter had secured all the land he required, he must still continue to bring in more indentured servants, for there was a constant process of freeing those who had served their term of indenture, usually five to seven years. It would hardly be possible for one of these early planters to forego accepting additional land grants which his ever continuing succession of laborers entitled him to secure. Hence many plantations grew to enormous size.

It was no small relief to the planters when Negroes began to be delivered, first as indentured servants, but soon as slaves for life. It furnished one of the greatest necessities of tobacco raising: namely, an able-bodied and stable labor supply. Thus it came about that a Negro slave just from Africa sold for almost twice as much as an indentured white servant who would probably serve only five years.

The colonists shipped their tobacco direct to England and received in return manufactured goods, including clothing, furniture, tools, and all articles of comfort. The capital of the early planters was promptly absorbed in buying new laborers; hence there was no capital with which to start manufacturing plants of their own. Besides, the population lived in widely scattered plantations, which was not conducive to manufacturing processes. Thus early was the economic organization of the section determined, and in its wake followed the social life. While the smaller proprietors and laborers in general were always far in excess of the number of proprietors of landed estates,

[1] *The South in the Building of the Nation*, Vol. I, p. 54.

LIFE ON THE SOUTHERN PLANTATION 167

the latter gave the tone and color to early Virginia society. They became the vestrymen of the church — at first elected by the people, then elected by the vestry itself — and as such they were the virtual rulers of the parish.

The houses of the early settlers were crude indeed, built of logs felled in the forest, hewn square, and notched at each end so that they fitted close together. The cracks were "chinked" with small hewn-out boards and then daubed with clay, to keep the "weather" out. Many houses consisted of one large room only, but others had two large rooms with "lean-to's" and often with a loft — reached by a pole ladder — which was often used as sleeping quarters for the children of the family. The doors to these cabins were made usually of two wide boards hewn out of oak and strapped together at top and bottom with oak cleats, fastened on with oak pegs; the whole door was hung on a wooden swivel hinge. The chimneys were usually made of a pole boxing, daubed inside with clay and straw which baked hard. Hundreds of such chimneys can still be seen in the South in the mountain areas. The roof was made of clapboards about two feet long, and from six to twelve inches wide, hewn out from the oak trees. These were laid in tiers like shingles and often held down by long poles laid across each tier and tied down at the ends with hickory thongs. There were no nails, or at least very few, for all nails must be made by hand by the blacksmith. There are still some of these old cabins standing here and there in the remote sections of the South, and the workmanship, while crude, is remarkable. The furnishings in these earliest homes were simple indeed. The rough furniture was built out of native materials; pots and pans were imported from England; the fireplace with its hooks and cranes was the early stove; pewter plate and china were about the only items of luxury.

But of course the economic growth of the country soon brought enough wealth to begin to build more luxurious and more expensive houses. The first brick dwelling was built in Jamestown in 1639, and there still stand in old Jamestown a number of old houses which date back to very early days, two of which were planned by Sir Christopher Wren. These mansions were often placed on some prominent hillside or some neck of land that reached far out into the bend of a river, thus giving an ideal view in all directions. Often the house grew as the planter's family grew — addition after addition being made, until it covered a wide expanse of ground. About these buildings wide verandas gave ample space for life and leisure during the long, hot summers. The lawns were shaded by the primeval oaks and hickories, and the back yards always had both a vegetable garden and a flower garden. The gardens were usually the particular care of the mistress of the home. One who has visited one of these old flower gardens, with its honeysuckle hedge, its lilac bushes, its tangle of roses, its lilies, jonquils, and violets, can never forget it. They must have been a riot of beauty, filling the air with their sweet perfumes.

When slavery was at its height the slave quarters stretched away to the rear of the mansion, often in the form of a long street, with the overseer's house at the farthest end, and facing straight down the street; at other times they spread out in a great fan-shaped arrangement, all cabins facing into the center. The house servants lived nearest the "big house," and often the more favored of them, such as the "Mammy," a nurse, and the cook and butler had cabins within the yard proper of the big house.

Since people lived far apart and there were few means of communication, a visitor was quite welcome. Philip Fithian, a Princeton student who went to Nomini Hall, the home of Robert Carter in Virginia, as a tutor in 1773, found social life colorful and entrancing, and observed that the home was constantly thrown open to guests. Guests who were invited for meals came and made a day of it.[1] At these gay social parties men and women were well dressed, in the latest English fashion. In their camlet coats with sleeves that ended in lace ruffles, velvet breeches, shoes with brass or silver buckles, and powdered wigs, with snuff box and handkerchief in hand, the men must have been dashing beaux. Who would dare try to describe the beauty of the women's apparel, the broad hoop skirts, silks, laces, and brilliant scarfs and mantles of crimson? Thomas Nelson Page describes a social gathering of the times as follows:

> There were games and dances — country dances, the lancers and quadrilles. The top of the old piano was lifted up, and the infectious dancing tunes rolled out under the flying fingers. Haply there was some demur on the part of the elder ladies, who were not quite sure that it was right; but it was overruled by the gentlemen, and the master in his frock coat and high collar started the ball by catching the prettiest girl by the hand and leading her to the head of the room right under the noses of half a dozen bashful lovers, calling to them meantime to "get their sweethearts and come along." Round dancing was not yet introduced. It was regarded as an innovation, if nothing worse. It was held generally as highly improper, by some as "disgusting." As to the

---

[1] Philip V. Fithian, *Journal and Letters, 1767–1774,* passim.

LIFE ON THE SOUTHERN PLANTATION 169

german, why, had it been known, the very name would have been sufficient to damn it. Nothing foreign in that civilization! There was fun enough in the old-fashioned country dances, and the "Virginia reel" at the close. Whoever could not be satisfied with that was hard to please.[1]

Mrs. Susan Bradford Eppes, who grew up on a large slave plantation near Tallahassee, Florida, finds other reasons than that of isolation for the growth of hospitality in the South. She thinks the abundance of vegetation and fruits which the mild climate of the South provided made it possible to hold out a generous hand to all, while the culture of the landed class made them particularly desirous of social intercourse.

The tables of the wealthy citizens were loaded with a most varied abundance of food. The herds of cattle which ran almost wild supplied an inexhaustible quantity of milk, butter, cheese, veal and beef, while the hams were pronounced by travelers to be equal in flavor to those of Westphalia. Deer were shot in such numbers that the people were said to be tired of venison. On every plantation a flock of sheep nibbled the pastures; poultry abounded in every houseyard, partridges in the open fields, wild turkeys in the forests. Clouds of wild pigeons broke down the limbs of trees with their weight in the spring, and in autumn, countless duck and wild geese darkened the surface of the creeks, rivers and bays. Perch, bass, shad, pike and sheepshead were to be caught almost at the very door, while oysters and other shell fish could be raked up by the bushel from the bottom of the nearest inlet. Peaches, plums and apples were produced in every orchard, and figs and grapes in every garden. Sloes, scuppernongs and pawpaws were to be found along the banks of every shady stream. Wild strawberries were so plentiful that the domestic berry was neglected. Huge pumpkins and masses of peas sprang up in every cornfield between the stalks of maize. Potatoes, artichokes, onions, cymblins, watermelons — all were cultivated in profusion. Hickory and hazel nuts were to be picked up by the peck in the woods. Every table was supplied with homebrewed beer and cider. Perry was made from the juice of pears, punch from West Indian rum. The wines in domestic use were claret, Fayal, Madeira and Rhenish. It was a characteristic of the times that these fine wines could be bought in all the taverns. With such abundance prevailing, it was natural that the people should have been extraordinarily hospitable — a feeling further promoted by the secluded life of the plantation.[2]

Wealth to give leisure is evidently one condition of a highly developed social life, and this many of the planters had. The houses

---

[1] *Social Life in Old Virginia before the War*, pp. 98–99.
[2] Philip A. Bruce, in *The South in the Building of the Nation*, Vol. I, pp. 67–68.

were large and comfortable, and there were servants in plenty to take the load of entertaining off the shoulders of the mistress in the home. "So it came about that company came in crowds; they came mostly in carriages, they brought with them their maids and men, usually in a baggage wagon, along with all the necessary belongings of the visitors. Company in the mansion also meant company in the Quarter, and place and food to be provided for the horses as well. Often these visitors were relatives, sometimes dear friends, but occasionally they were barely acquaintances." [1]

Horsemanship was a mark of every southern gentleman, and women were scarcely less proficient. Equestrian parties were a regular diversion, and tournaments where the gallant young knights rode for the privilege of crowning their lady love were not an uncommon part of the social life of many communities. Horse racing was a favorite sport, and many a large plantation had its own race course. Near the city of Nashville there stands to this day the old barn and a part of the race course of one of these old plantations. The home of General Wade Hampton — Millworth — near Columbia, South Carolina, was built in 1818, and the race-horse barn with stalls for four horses is still standing; the race course was not far away. A Miss Kate Conyngham, who came from New England to Overton Lodge near Nashville in 1853 to be a governess in the home of Colonel Peyton, wrote that a Negro girl Eda was promptly assigned her as a maid in waiting, and a horse and saddle were put at her constant disposal. Not infrequently the governess and her charge — the fifteen-year-old daughter of Colonel Peyton — rode for two hours after breakfast before beginning the school routine of the day, while the late afternoon also found them in saddle again, for a scamper over the landscape.[2] No wonder the girls were almost as good riders as the men. Hunting was a great sport and took on a social aspect in the old South. Young women with their chaperons and escorts followed the baying of the hounds, and happy was the girl who could actually kill her own deer or be on hand when the hounds had overtaken Reynard. Young men were taught fencing, boxing, and marksmanship from early youth. Miss Conyngham tells of a young man of nineteen on a plantation near Natchez, Mississippi, who for her delight shot with a pistol three bumble-bees on the wing at six paces distance, and then, throwing in the air two quarter-dollar

[1] Susan B. Eppes, *Through Some Eventful Years*, p. 13.
[2] Joseph H. Ingraham, *The Sunny South; or, The Southerner at Home*, passim.

pieces, shot both of them with his pistol before either struck the ground.[1] When Andrew Jackson and Colonel Dickinson of Nashville went to the Kentucky line to fight their duel in which the latter was killed, Colonel Dickinson arrived at the appointed spot a day early, it is said, and regaled the curious crowd by throwing dimes into the air and shooting them with his pistol, never missing a shot.

Every plantation had three kinds of dogs: first, the tracking hounds, which were used to follow down the slaves who ran away to the swamp or woods; then the hounds trained to follow fox or deer; and lastly just the common hounds with which the "possum" and the "coon" were hunted. With these animals, with good horses, and with plenty of companionship many a moonlight night saw high revelry. One who looks into the social life of this period finds there were plenty of occasions for mingling of kindred spirits.

Life was strict and strait-laced in many ways. In the early days in Virginia, a man was fined twenty pounds of tobacco for taking a voyage on the Sabbath, except in going to church or in cases of extreme necessity. A man might not fire a gun on Sunday. Buying and selling futures — called "forestalling" — was strictly prohibited. Swearing was punished by fine of one shilling for each oath. The prices on all liquors were strictly set forth. Flirting was punishable by whipping in public. Women in particular lived much more circumscribed lives than do our modern girls. In most cases they were tutored in the home until fifteen and then sent to some famous "finishing" school where manners and music and a smattering of French made up a large part of the curriculum. Kate Conyngham described one of these plantation daughters as "a lovely girl, with beautiful hands, for she has never used them at harder work than tuning her harp, (and hardly at this, if she can trust her maid,) who rides like Di Vernon, is not afraid of a gun, nor, eke! a pistol, is inclined to be indolent, loves to write letters, to read the late poets, is in love with Byron, sings Jenny Lind's songs with great taste and sweetness, has taken her diploma at the Columbia Institute, or some other conservatory of hot-house plants, knows enough French to guess at it when she comes across it in an English book, and of Italian to pronounce the names of opera songs! She has ma's carriage at her command to go and come at her pleasure in the neighborhood, receives long forenoon visits from young gentlemen who come on horseback, flirts at evening promenades on the piazza with others, and is married at

[1] *Ibid.*, pp. 272–273.

sixteen without being courted!"[1] She was never left alone with her young man caller — it would not have "seemed proper." If the mother could not be present, a female slave sat at the parlor door. And yet social life revolved about her. She was gently bred, but knew little of the ways of the world. All her childhood she lived in the midst of social life and needed not to learn to be a lady. The old-fashioned southern girl did not "come out"; as Page remarked, she had never been "in."

Part and parcel of this plantation life, and so inextricably interwoven with it that these plantations without them would have been *Hamlet* with Hamlet left out, were the Negro slaves. In the whole South before the war, there were 2,300 plantations belonging to planters who owned one hundred slaves or more, and there were probably 100,000 planters who owned ten or more slaves. In Virginia there were 13,593 planters owning this number. The number of planters owning numerous slaves was small enough to give real distinction, and it was large enough to give these owners an overwhelming influence in the life of the South. On these plantations a close relationship existed between master and slave. Thomas Nelson Page, who was reared on a plantation of moderate size with a score or more of slaves, declares that while absenteeism in the case of some of the very large plantations, where hundreds of Negroes worked, may have led to abuses, "on most of the plantations the slaves and the masters were necessarily brought into fairly close contact, and the result of this contact was the relation of friendship which has been the wonder and the mystification of those who considered slavery as the sum of all villainies."[2] The loyalty of these slaves to their masters was beyond reproach. Reared side by side, sharing each other's joys and sorrows of childhood, often fed at the same table, hearing the same stories, visiting the same traps, riding the same horses, there was a mutual affection which even the Civil War could not destroy. The Negroes were "my servants" or "my people," and the masters were "my master," "my mistis," or "my white folks." The Negroes were proud of their "white people" and often boasted they were the best people in the world. In return the masters usually took a personal interest in their slaves, they were frequently united in marriage in the big house, they were tenderly cared for when sick, and when a trusted slave died, his funeral was conducted at the Mansion, and his

---

[1] Joseph H. Ingraham, *The Sunny South; or, The Southerner at Home*, p. 223.
[2] *The Negro: The Southerner's Problem*, p. 170.

humble shroud was followed to the grave by white and black alike. At Christmas and at "laying by of crops" all the Negroes had a wonderful time. No pains were spared to give them all the joy of which they were capable. There were usually gifts and small rewards for faithful service, a big dinner, dances, and a whole week of freedom from work. In July, when the last hoeing had been done and crops were laid by, there was always a celebration with a great hunt, a fishing party, or a barbecue. Mrs. Eppes describes an arrangement which her father had with two neighboring plantations, by which all the Negroes on the three came together annually for a great barbecue at "laying by time." This meant hundreds of Negroes, with of course loads of beef and potatoes and milk and bread.[1] It was a gala occasion, to which all the workers looked forward from the time Christmas festivities were over until the crops were "laid by."

Religion entered deeply into the life of white and black alike on the old plantation. The white planters of Virginia brought with them the rites of the established Church of England, which soon became the dominant social force in the colony. All free people of the parish were required by law to attend the Sabbath morning service, but this would have been unnecessary in most cases. The morning church service offered almost the only community meeting and every one eagerly went, to meet friends and exchange news, even if some of them were not attracted by the worship. Before and after the hour of service the men gathered outside the church door and exchanged ideas about the crops and about other problems of plantation management, and swapped yarns in neighborly fashion. Within, the women gathered in groups and discussed the latest gossip, along with questions of household management, the best remedies for children's diseases, and the latest recipes for favorite dishes. After the service, everybody invited everybody else home to dinner, those living farthest away usually being entertained by those living closer by. The remainder of the Sunday was spent in conversation and fellowship.

Place in every church was provided for the colored people. In most cases a gallery in the rear of the church took care of the house servants. A good illustration of this is the old stone church near Clemson, South Carolina, the ancestral home of John C. Calhoun. A stairway outside leads to the gallery in this old stone church which

[1] *Through Some Eventful Years*, p. 100.

was ample in proportion. In other churches the Negroes had a share of the main floor of the church. Such a situation as this is described by Miss Kate Conyngham of Overton Lodge near Nashville.

The second Sunday after I came here I was invited to attend service in the chapel with the family. Upon entering it, I found the body of the floor occupied by the black men and women of the plantation, seated in chairs with the utmost decency and quiet, and all neatly and cleanly attired. We took our seats in the gallery, while Isabel placed herself at the organ to play a voluntary. Until the old gentleman who officiated entered, I had time to look at the interior of this bijou of a church. On the right of the chancel was an exquisite group of statuary, executed in Italy expressly for this chapel by the colonel's order, at an expense of $800. It represented the Madonna and her child. On the opposite side was a table of the purest white marble, surmounted by a dove with its wings extended. It was a memento of the death of a little son of the colonel. There were no pews in the body of the church, only low chairs of oak, a chair to each worshiper, with an aisle between.

The service was very solemn; and my Puritanic objections to praying from a prayer-book, have been wholly removed by this day's experience. The singing was very remarkable. The African women all sing well, having naturally soft voices; with the organ, and full fifty fine voices swelling in harmony with it, the effect was very fine. "Is it possible," I asked myself, "that these are slaves? Is it possible that this rich voice which leads in such manly tones is their master's? Is it possible that the fair girl who unites, by an accompaniment upon the organ, her praise with theirs, is one of the 'haughty daughters of the South?'"[1]

This was the brighter side of the life on a slave plantation. Such a picture was true not of Virginia and North Carolina alone, for as these more wealthy planters moved westward in search of fresh and rich lands they carried with them their wealth, their manorial manners, their desire for luxury, and their pride of family. Scattered all over Kentucky, Tennessee, down through the lower South and even out into Texas, hundreds of these planters moved, carrying their culture with them. Some day a full story of these old plantations will be written, and when it is, it will be one of amazing luxury, of brilliant manners, of worthy achievement.

But this is only one side of the picture, albeit a most important one. The other side of the picture is not so pleasing, but it is none the less real. The sons of the landed proprietors of England were not the only ones who sought their fortune in the new country.

---

[1] Joseph H. Ingraham, *The Sunny South; or, The Southerner at Home*, pp. 67–68.

LIFE ON THE SOUTHERN PLANTATION

Hundreds of mechanics and day laborers who found life hard and almost hopeless looked with longing eyes across the sea to where an asylum for all who had not had a fair chance in life might offer conditions more nearly equal for all. Often these people were not able to pay their way overseas; so they sold their services for a certain length of time to the sea captains; and these captains, on landing in Virginia, sold this time to the planters on the basis of the highest bid. Abuses sometimes arose when unscrupulous planters tried to hold a man longer than his term of indenture. It therefore became necessary to protect these indentured persons by law. In 1660 a law was passed which required the planter buying such indentured service to have it legally recorded and the length of the indenture specified, so that the rights of the person so serving might be protected. Further protection of such persons was prescribed in that one could not be sent out penniless at the end of his service but must be paid stipulated amounts of clothing, food, and equipment for self-support. In this connection it is to be noted that many political criminals were sent over to the colonies, and it cannot be doubted that not a few malefactors came along. John Fiske thought that as many as 50,000 actual criminals may have been sent to America and the West Indies during the eighteenth century.[1] At least the numbers were large enough that Massachusetts in 1700 passed stringent laws, demanding every ship captain to furnish full lists of all passengers, together with a certificate of character for each person landed. This law was reënacted in 1722, and the fine for its violation was raised from £5 to £100, which is clear evidence that the law had been rather flagrantly violated. The facts seem to indicate that indentured white servants were made up of three classes: first, the honest, straightforward redemptioners, who came over to win for themselves a place in life, and who were perfectly worthy citizens; second, political criminals, who were progressive, even radical, eager for better political conditions and often men of real capacity; third, the criminal class which England desired to send away from her shores. This last group was probably much smaller than either of the other groups.

The first and second groups furnished many examples of thrift and leadership. Not a few of them became landed proprietors, and some of them were members of the House of Burgesses. Bruce tells us that the yeomanry of Virginia furnished 1,411 families owning one hundred acres or less at the beginning of the eighteenth century,

[1] *Old Virginia and Her Neighbors*, Vol. II, pp. 183-184.

and 2,693 families owning from one hundred to five hundred acres. At this same period there were 1,200 families owning estates in excess of five hundred acres. In other words, three out of every four landowners in Virginia at this time belonged to the yeomanry class.[1] It is possible that the land owned by these four thousand small proprietors may have equaled in acreage the amount owned by the twelve hundred gentry planters. But the total influence of this group was nothing like as great as that of the big planters. This latter group furnished most of the members of the House of Burgesses, they held the position of vestrymen in the church, and they provided the court officials; the ministers were almost exclusively sprung from this rank. The yeoman was independent, self-reliant, self-respecting, but he formed a distinct social class from the planter class. The third class in early Virginia society was the Negro slave. He was a distinct class from the beginning, having few civic and still fewer social privileges.

The social organization of Virginia undoubtedly had large influence on the whole South in these early years. The culture patterns which obtained there gradually diffused to the whole South, so that even down into Florida, Texas, and all the lower South and Southwest, a threefold social organization could be found. The most important social change in the lower South, perhaps, lay in the fact that the proportion of yeomen to landed proprietors was greater the farther west one went.

A picture of the yeoman in this southern country is given by Frederick Law Olmsted in his *A Journey in the Back Country*.[2] Riding on horseback from Texas to Virginia, spending the nights in the homes of the smaller planters who would receive him, stopping at roadside stores and conversing with all chance comers, he had a good chance of seeing life at first hand. He was probably biased somewhat by his opposition to slavery, but his detailed facts should speak for themselves. According to Olmsted, the average farm or plantation consisted of about six hundred acres, and the number of Negroes varied from ten to forty. Where the Negroes numbered less than twenty the planter himself frequently worked in the field and acted as his own overseer. When there were more than twenty Negroes, he did not work in the field, and often had a Negro driver and sometimes a white overseer. In Olmsted's opinion these small planters

---

[1] *Social Life in Virginia in the Seventeenth Century*, p. 99.
[2] Chap. 4.

had "more dignity of bearing and manner," "they give a stranger an impression of greater respectability than the middle class of farmers at the North"; they usually had "spent a short time at boarding schools, or institutions of a somewhat superior order, but their acquisition of knowledge subsequently to their school days . . . has been very small." They seemed to him to have "less active and inquiring minds" than northern farmers. The houses in which these small planters lived and the comforts of home seemed to him far below those of Northern farmers of one quarter of their wealth. The food consisted of "bacon, cornbread, and coffee," which "invariably appeared at every meal," but "at breakfast or supper a fried fowl, biscuit of wheat flour with butter were added." The "biscuits" were "invariably made heavy, doughy, and indigestible with shortening, and brought to the table in relays to be eaten as hot as possible with melting butter." "Molasses usually, honey frequently, and as a rare exception potatoes and green peas were added to the board." Olmsted did not find all the hospitality of which the South boasted. At many of the best plantations he could not get lodging, and at many of the smaller ones he paid for lodgings which were none too good. One cannot help suspecting that Olmsted was writing for propaganda purposes, and that hence his interpretations may have been much darker than the picture justified; but one cannot read the running diary which he kept without realizing that there was a shadow side to southern life. Slavery had undoubtedly prejudiced white people against manual toil, and on the smaller plantations where there was poorer organization, and where the Negroes took no pride in "the family," life must have often been at ragged ends. At least Olmsted often found homes where there were a dozen or more slaves, but where the commonest conveniences, cleanliness, privacy, and palatable food were almost wholly lacking. That the picture is not altogether false is amply proven by referring to other writers who would not thus be prejudiced. Thus De Bow, a South Carolinian by birth, a professor of economics at the University of Louisiana and an editor of high repute in New Orleans, wrote:

> If one unacquainted with the present condition of the southwest, were told that the cotton growing district alone had sold the crop for fifty millions of dollars per annum for the last twenty years, he would naturally conclude that this must be the richest community in the world. He might well imagine that the planters all dwell in palaces upon estates improved by every device of art, and that their most common utensils were made of the precious metals;

that canals, turnpikes, railways, and every other improvement designed either for use or for ornament, abounded in every part of the land; and that the want of money had never been felt or heard of in its limits. He would conclude that the most splendid edifices dedicated to the purposes of religion and learning were everywhere to be found, and that all the liberal arts had here found their reward and a home. But what would be his surprise when told, that so far from dwelling in palaces, many of these planters dwell in habitations of the most primitive construction, and these so inartfully built as to be incapable of protecting the inmates from the winds and rains of heaven; that instead of any artistical improvement, this rude dwelling was surrounded by cotton fields, or probably by fields exhausted, washed into gullies, and abandoned; that instead of canals, the navigable streams remain unimproved, to the great detriment of transportation; that the common roads of the country were scarcely passable; that the edifices erected for the accommodation of learning and religion were frequently built of logs, and covered with boards; and that the fine arts were but little encouraged or cared for.[1]

Mrs. Trollope, who visited this section in 1832, stopping at New Orleans, Natchez, Memphis, and other points, found it not at all luxurious. She declared she "would infinitely prefer sharing the apartment of a party of well conditioned pigs" to being confined in the cabin of a Mississippi river boat.[2] Mrs. Trollope found some "air of wealth and comfort" exhibited in New Orleans and its "immediate neighborhood," but up the Mississippi she saw "only two clusters of wooden houses, calling themselves towns" and so far as civilized habitation went she felt her party "might have thought" themselves "the first of the human race who had ever penetrated in this territory of bears and alligators." [3] The whole of life seemed to her crude and lacking in culture, so she flatly said: "I do not like their principles — I do not like their manners — I do not like their opinions." [4]

The towns and villages of the old South must have been rather desolate and almost pitiable. The larger towns like Mobile, Natchez, and others where the planter class went for recreation and amusement, may have had some air of brilliance and luxury, but most of these towns "were forlorn, poverty stricken collections of shops, groceries,

[1] *The Industrial Resources, etc., of the Southern and Western States.* Vol. II, p. 113.
[2] *Domestic Manners of the Americans*, Vol. I, p. 19.
[3] *Ibid.*, p. 27.
[4] *Ibid.*, Vol. II, p. 295.

and lawyers offices, mingled with unsightly and usually dilapidated dwelling houses."[1] Indeed, in the old plantation régime there was small place for the city. The planter was almost independent on his own estate, and should he desire to take some part in the life of the town he did so from his country seat. A good example of this is the case of Andrew Jackson, whose law office was located in his country mansion, The Hermitage, located twelve miles from Nashville, at which mansion his old law books and his great office chair are still exhibited.

The aristocratic organization of society was of course not so marked in the lower South and the Southwest as it was in Virginia. There was more of the rough and ready western or pioneer life, and many social distinctions were broken down, but the culture patterns of old Virginia still prevailed enough to make quite clear-cut classes. Miss Conyngham visited a large plantation near Natchez, Mississippi, in 1853, where she found a northern girl of "great mental accomplishments" acting as governess or teacher in the home. When the family were seated at the table Miss Conyngham did not find her old friend and acquaintance there — the meaning of which was that a teacher was considered to belong to a lower social class. On being shown to her friend's room she expressed her great grief at this social discrimination, to which her friend replied:

"It is not altogether disagreeable, as I do not wish to mingle in society where the ladies, however polite, would regard me as not their full equal; so I prefer dining in my room: though to tell you the truth, I am never invited at the dinner parties; nor when invitations are sent for the family am I included; and if I go, it is expected I shall keep an eye on my two sweet little pupils. Teaching here is by some families looked upon as beneath 'position,' as the phrase is. But I am content to endure all this neglect for the emoluments, which are seven hundred dollars per annum, which enable me to send four hundred dollars yearly to my mother, who has need of all the aid I can render her. . . . For these advantages I am content to hold an apparently inferior position."[2]

Because of this social discrimination most southern girls would not take places as governesses. They "would lose caste," which would be "an obstacle in the way of their marrying *en règle*."

The mechanics and laboring people in the South and Southwest

---

[1] Frederick L. Olmsted, *A Journey in the Back Country*, p. 159.
[2] Joseph H. Ingraham, *The Sunny South; or, The Southerner at Home*, p. 268.

formed a distinct class from the planters, while the business class held a position halfway between the two.

It was the plantation which dominated southern institutions and made the social organization so different from that of New England. The early settlers of the South were thoroughly English. They loved the land, and their desire for privacy and individuality led them to seek out spots where they could become lords of large estates. In old England it was the landed proprietor who controlled social and political life, and it was but natural that those who came from England bringing with them enough wealth to get a foothold on the land should be eager to perpetuate the old system. They therefore assumed the position of landed proprietors, which was the badge of a gentleman, and promptly put all others in a lower social class. When the slaves were first brought in, they were more nearly on a par with the indentured servants, but as slavery became more firmly established, and the indentured whites began to rise into positions of greater independence, the gulf between the two classes widened and there came to be a third distinct social class. The almost free land of Virginia and the advantage of raising tobacco on a large scale, together with the fact that slavery permitted the aggregating of large labor forces, fitted exactly into the culture traditions of the old country. What more natural thing than that this colony should develop a form of feudal institutions?

There were few people in the South during the seventeenth and eighteenth centuries who were not English, both in social ideals and by birth; so there was no tendency to break down the social pattern which had been set up.

No one who does not understand this background of the old South can understand the subsequent development of its institutions. The South was distinctly feudal up to the Civil War, and many marks of that old feudalism still survive.

While this system had many weaknesses, it also had elements of strength. It at least gave a small class the isolation and time for thought and meditation which are usually necessary to develop great men. Thomas Nelson Page, who was sprung from this line of plantation gentlemen, and who knew them as few men have known them since the Civil War, says there was about the master of the plantation "a contemplative expression due to much communing alone with weighty responsibilities resting upon him." "He reflected much. Out on the long verandas in the dusk of the summer nights, with his wide fields stretching away into the gloom, and the woods bounding the horizon, his thoughts dwelt upon serious things; he pondered causes and consequences; he resolved everything to prime principles." [1]

In spite of slavery and the elements of aristocracy in the social fabric, the southern planter was at heart a democrat. He was monarch of all he surveyed and expected every other man similarly situated to be the same. He had a self-confidence born of independence, and a tenacity of opinion which often took the form of dogmatic convictions. He wanted no man to tell him what he should do or think. He thought for himself and acted on his own convictions.

Nor did the situation fail to develop a sense of power and leadership. Lord of a great estate, with hundreds of persons living on it and dependent for sustenance on his good management, the very sense of responsibility made him a leader. Nor did he take that leadership lightly. No men were ever better sports or finer companions, but never were men more burdened with the weight of responsibility which was theirs. As the years passed and the richness of the land decreased, and as moral scruples arose over the question of slavery, which was the chief source of wealth, the planter became more and more serious, and his mind reached out to real statesmanship. It was out of such an environment that the Washingtons, Jeffersons, Madisons, Monroes, Lees, Marshalls, Jacksons, Georges, Calhouns, Claibornes, Hammonds, and scores of others sprang. Their names have made the pages of American history glorious, and their transmitted influence is still helping to mould the thinking of the world. From the prejudices and stubborn dogmatism of the old planter class the present South perhaps inherits some of its rigid conservatism, its dogmatic certainty in religion, and some of its attitude of class distinctions; but let us hope it has also inherited from this plantation régime some of its spirit of independence, some of its worthy convictions, and some of its vast ability for leadership. Of the influence of slavery on these men we must say a word later.

PROBLEMS FOR STUDY

1. Are large landed estates with their accompanying culture, wealth, etc., advantageous or disadvantageous in building a state?
2. The concentration of power in the hands of a few, before the Civil War, gave the South tremendous prestige in national politics. Was this good or bad? Why?

[1] *Social Life in Old Virginia before the War*, pp. 46–47.

3. Was the introduction of Negroes as laborers economically advantageous or disadvantageous to the colonies? Justify your answer.
4. Why was it impossible to develop manufacturing in the old South? Would it have been better for the South to have had factories?
5. Professor Josey, Lothrop Stoddard, and others claim that the Nordics must maintain leadership for the sake of the advancement of all. Was this principle applicable to the plantation system of the old South, and the class system that existed?
6. The southern girl of the plantation system has been held up as the ideal for womanhood. What social situation on the plantation made this type possible, and was it more admirable than present-day types?
7. What part did the independence and individualism of the plantation system play in developing theories of states' rights in politics and dogmatism in religious belief?
8. Were the personal contacts and responsibility of the old slave régime more likely to develop strong leadership than the present impersonal organization of business life?
9. The slave was sure of food and shelter and a certain type of protection; the present laborer is sure of none of the three. How would you characterize the hardships of both types?

BIBLIOGRAPHY

Philip A. Bruce, *Institutional History of Virginia in the Seventeenth Century* (1910).
Philip A. Bruce, *Social Life in Virginia in the Seventeenth Century* (1927).
James D. B. De Bow, *The Industrial Resources, etc., of the Southern and Western States* (1852–1853).
Susan B. Eppes, *The Negro of the Old South* (1925).
Susan B. Eppes, *Through Some Eventful Years* (1926).
John Fiske, *Old Virginia and Her Neighbors* (1897).
Daniel R. Hundley, *Social Relations in Our Southern States* (1860).
Frances A. Kemble, *Journal of a Residence on a Georgian Plantation in 1838–1839* (1863).
Howard W. Odum, *An American Epoch* (1930).
Frederick L. Olmsted, *The Cotton Kingdom* (1862).
Frederick L. Olmsted, *A Journey in the Back Country* (1860).
Frederick L. Olmsted, *A Journey in the Seaboard Slave States* (1860).
Thomas N. Page, *Social Life in Old Virginia before the War* (1897).
Ulrich B. Phillips, *Life and Labor in the Old South* (1929).
Ulrich B. Phillips, *Plantation and Frontier Documents, 1649–1863, Illustrative of Industrial History in the Colonial and Ante-bellum South* (1909).
Susan D. Smedes, *A Southern Planter* (1890).

CHAPTER X

THE ATTITUDE OF THE CHURCHES TOWARD THE NEGRO DURING SLAVERY

We have elsewhere noted that royal instruction was given the first settlers of Virginia that the "word and service of God" "should be preached, planted and used." They were specially commissioned "with unfailing kindness" "to draw them [the Indians] to the true service and knowledge of God." In 1609 the True and Sincere Declaration said the first object of the plantation was to preach and baptize into the Christian religion "those miserable souls" who were "wrapt unto death, in almost invincible ignorance." [1] In 1619, the year the first Negroes were landed, the authorities in each town and plantation were ordered to secure by peaceful means a certain number of Indian children, in order that they might be educated and brought up in the knowledge of the Christian religion. Many of the earliest wills among the colonists left bequests of money to be used for this specific purpose. As early as 1657 George Fox, the Quaker, had written "To Friends beyond sea, who have black and Indian slaves," urging them to give consideration to their slaves, since all nations were of one blood. When he visited Barbados in 1671, he was evidently under severe criticism; so he wrote a defense of the Quakers to "the Governor of Barbados, with his council and assembly," concerning the "scandalous lies and slanders" cast upon them as Quakers. One of these slanders he says was "that we teach the negroes to rebel, a thing we utterly abhor and detest in our hearts. . . . For that which we have spoken to them, is to exhort and admonish them to be sober, to fear God, to love their masters and mistresses, and to be faithful and diligent in their service and business." His *Journal* continues that slaves are a part of the family and every master is duty bound to "instruct and admonish those in and belonging to our families," and that an "account will be required" by

[1] Philip A. Bruce, *Institutional History of Virginia in the Seventeenth Century*, Vol. I, p. 4.

God for such care.[1] After leaving Barbados, Fox came to America, visiting Maryland, Virginia, North Carolina, and other sections and preaching to the Indians. He evidently labored also for the scattered slaves whom he found among his colonists,[2] for one of his convictions could hardly do otherwise.

In 1673 Richard Baxter published his *Christian Directory*, in which he has a chapter of "Directions to those Masters in Foreign Plantations who have Negroes and other slaves."[3] The first of these Directions reminded the masters that the Negroes had immortal souls "equally capable of salvation with themselves." The second reminded them they were trustees and guardians of these souls. The third charged the masters so to use their slaves as to prefer God's interest, and the slaves' everlasting happiness. The seventh and last Direction urged that they make it their first business to win their slaves to Christ.[4] In 1680, the Connecticut Assembly wrote the Lords of the Committee of Colonies that "great care is taken of the instruction of the people in the Christian religion by ministers . . . and also by masters of families instructing their children and servants."[5] In 1688 the yearly meeting of Pennsylvania and New Jersey had the matter of slavery brought before it by certain German Friends, but it was "adjudged not to be so proper for this meeting to give positive judgment in the case."[6] They were, however, not quite so careful when the matter came up again in 1696, for they gave the following advice to members: "Whereas several papers have been read relating to the keeping and bringing in of Negroes; which being duly considered, it is the advice of this meeting, that Friends be careful not to encourage the bringing in of any more Negroes; and that such that have Negroes, be careful of them, bring them to meetings, have meetings with them in their families, and restrain them from loose and lewd living so far as in them lies."[7] In 1699, when Nicholson was appointed governor of the Virginia colony, he was directed to see

[1] *A Journal or Historical Account of the Life, Travels, Sufferings, etc., of George Fox*, Vol. II, pp. 117–120.
[2] *Ibid.*, p. 121 ff.
[3] Charles C. Jones, *The Religious Instruction of the Negroes in the United States*, p. 6.
[4] *Ibid.*, pp. 6–7.
[5] *Ibid.*, p. 8.
[6] *A Brief Statement of the Rise and Progress of the Testimony of the Religious Society of Friends, Against Slavery and the Slave Trade*, p. 8.
[7] *Ibid.*, p. 8.

ATTITUDE OF THE CHURCHES

that proper laws were passed to insure the education of Indians and Negroes in the Christian faith. On presentation of this message, the House of Burgesses replied: "The Negroes born in this country are generally baptized and brought up in the Christian religion, but for Negroes imported hither, the gross bestiality and rudeness of their manners, the variety and strangeness of their languages, and the weakness and shallowness of their minds, renders it in a manner impossible to make any progress in their conversion." [1]

The Christians of the mother country were evidently not daunted by this message, for in 1701 the Society for the Propagation of the Gospel in Foreign Parts (S. P. G.) was organized with the patronage of William III, and the Bishop of Canterbury was made the first president. The purpose of this society was twofold: (1) to supply religious instruction to the colonists; (2) to preach the Gospel to Indians and Negroes. George Keith and John Talbot were sent out by this society as itinerant missionaries to spy out the land. They spent two years traveling and preaching from Carolina to New England, and like Caleb and Joshua, they brought back a good report of the land. The first regular missionary was Samuel Thomas, who went to South Carolina in 1702. His headquarters were at Goose Creek, where he preached to the Indians; he reported "that he had taken much pains also in instructing the Negroes, and learned twenty of them to read." [2] Dr. Le Jeau, who succeeded Thomas in 1706, "found parents and masters indued with much good will and a ready disposition to have their children and servants taught the Christian religion." [3] He reported that he baptized many Negro slaves. Le Jeau died in 1717 and was immediately succeeded by Mr. Ludlam, who probably found some opposition to his preaching to the Negroes, for he reported that all born in the country might be received into the church if the masters would heartily concur in the good work.[4] The opposition of masters to the preaching of the Gospel among their slaves grew out of two fears: first, that a slave would cease to be such when once he had been Christianized, which seems a tribute at least to their clear thinking; and second, that Negroes might become unruly or rebellious when once their minds had been opened to the larger conceptions of religion.

[1] Philip A. Bruce, *Institutional History of Virginia in the Seventeenth Century*, Vol. I, p. 9.
[2] Charles C. Jones, *The Religious Instruction of the Negroes in the United States*, p. 10. [3] *Ibid.*, p. 10. [4] *Ibid.*, p. 10.

The first church built in Charleston, South Carolina, was old St. Philip's, 1681, served first by Reverend Atkin Williamson, and later by Reverend Samuel Marshal. The work of the latter rector proved so satisfactory that the Assembly in 1698 appropriated to him and his successors one hundred and fifty pounds annually. The constitution of the colony drawn by John Locke in 1669, six years after the original charter by Charles II, had a provision for the established Church of England, though religious liberty was also granted. It was under this constitution that the Assembly acted in granting the annuity to the rector of St. Philip's. It is interesting as an indication of the attitude toward slavery that the Assembly also ordered that a Negro man and woman and four cows should be provided for the rector.[1] Twenty years later, when Alexander Garden became rector of this church (1719), he established a Negro school of seventy pupils, to which he gave constant time and attention.

In 1704 the S. P. G. established a catechizing school in New York City, of which Mr. Neau, a French Protestant, was appointed catechist. The school was practically destroyed by the Negro Plot of 1712, but later the work was revived, and Trinity Church, on the death of Mr. Neau (1722), requested another catechist, whom the S. P. G. appointed in the person of Reverend Colgan (1726), "who conducted the school with success and many Negroes were baptized." During all this period fear of insurrection was growing as the number of Negroes increased, and masters were sometimes indifferent, more often in open opposition to the preaching of Christianity to their slaves. The S. P. G., in lamenting the slow work of evangelizing the Negroes, complained: "But the greatest obstruction is the masters themselves do not consider the obligation which is upon them to have their slaves instructed." [2]

To meet this situation the bishops of the established church in England preached sermons and wrote letters of exhortation to the masters throughout the colonies. Dr. Fleetwood, Bishop of St. Asoph, preached a sermon in 1711 which was considered so valuable that the S. P. G. printed it and sent it in great numbers to all the plantations, including America and the West Indies. Dr. Gibson, Bishop of London, to whom the religious life of the plantations had been com-

---

[1] C. C. Tiffany, *A History of the Protestant Episcopal Church in the United States of America*, p. 225.

[2] Charles C. Jones, *The Religious Instruction of the Negroes in the United States*, p. 14.

mitted, wrote two letters of exhortation in 1727 — one to the masters and one to the missionaries, the former being printed in a lot of 10,000. These were sent out to all the British islands of the West Indies and to the American colonies. In the letter to masters the bishop deals with the difficulties of converting people reared in pagan rites, and the difficulty of language, since most of the Negroes as yet spoke little English. He then goes on to state that he cannot believe any Christian master would deny his slave the chance of salvation, or work him on the Sabbath, or refuse him time during the week for simple devotions. He also expresses surprise if any missionaries should not zealously embrace the chance to preach to the slaves, in cases where they are invited to do so by the masters. He deals fully with the thought that baptizing a slave sets him free. "To which," he says, "it may be very truely replied, that Christianity and the embracing of the Gospel does not make the least alteration in civil property, or in any of the duties which belong to civil relations." This he proves from Scriptural teachings. As to the fact that slaves become ungovernable when taught Christianity, he declares that Christianity has always made people more diligent and faithful for conscience' sake in whatever task they find themselves engaged. He closes with an appeal to masters to think of themselves as Christian masters who are under obligation to break the power of Satan and enlarge the kingdom of Christ.[1] The letter to the missionaries urges that time be given to this important part of their parishes, and that those who own slaves treat them in an exemplary manner, and fully instruct them in religion. He further urges that they enlist the services of schoolmasters in instructing the Negro youth in their leisure hours. Bishop Berkley was in Rhode Island from 1728 to 1730 and found a fear lest baptism interfere with the state of slavery. He procured from His Majesty's Attorney and Solicitor-General a signed statement that no such effects would follow, and in his report to the S. P. G. he expressed the hope that this statement would open the way for a more aggressive work.[2]

When John Wesley visited Georgia and the colonies in 1735, he found not a few Negroes interested in religion. He declared the best way to reach these Negroes was to travel from plantation to plan-

[1] For full text of these letters see: Charles C. Jones, *The Religious Instruction of the Negroes in the United States*, pp. 16-27.
[2] *Ibid.*, p. 28.

tation where the masters would permit, and preach to and catechize the slaves. He found numbers of planters who were desirous of such services.[1]

The first mission established exclusively for the Negroes, oddly enough, was planted in 1738 in Georgia, where slavery was at first prohibited. Count Zinzendorf, a Moravian, made a visit to London in 1737, and formed an acquaintance with General Oglethorpe, the founder of the colony of Georgia. Some of the trustees of the Georgia colony were also trustees of a fund left by a Dr. Bray to be used in establishing a mission to Negroes in South Carolina. They requested Count Zinzendorf to furnish them some missionaries to carry out this purpose. After settling the question that Moravians would be acceptable as representatives of the S. P. G., Zinzendorf appointed Peter Boehler and George Schulius, who set out in May, 1738, for Savannah, where they arrived in October. After many complications with Oglethorpe they finally established a mission at Purisburg, where there were only a few Negro children. Schulius died the following year, and Boehler abandoned the mission in 1740. So far as results went, the mission was a failure. The Moravians who had settled in Georgia moved to Philadelphia because they did not want to bear arms in Oglethorpe's army against the Spanish.

George Whitfield, the flaming evangelist, and one of the most popular preachers and orators the New World ever saw, came to Georgia in 1738 and worked faithfully with the colonists and Negroes alike. His habit was to meet all servants at seven in the evening and expound the catechism. Unlike Wesley, he believed slavery was both a blessing to the white man, because he needed laborers in so hot a climate, and a blessing to the Negro, because it gave him a chance to be Christianized. He was one of the most powerful advocates of opening the colony of Georgia to slavery.

Having thus taken a cursory view of the beginnings of interest in the religious instruction of slaves, let us now trace briefly the work of each of the denominations.

The Quakers were opposed to slavery from the time of George Fox's visit to Barbados in 1671. The Pennsylvania yearly meeting of 1691 discouraged the importation of slaves, and the yearly meeting of 1700 responded to Penn's appeal and appointed a special monthly meeting for Negroes; it also commanded the masters to give notice of the meeting regularly and to come with their slaves "as frequently

[1] Wesley's *Journal* (Everyman's Library), Vol. I, p. 48.

as may be."[1] The Chester quarterly meeting of 1711, which at that time included all societies as far south as Hopewell, Virginia, memorialized the yearly meeting to discourage further the bringing in of Negroes, which the yearly meeting did.[2] The yearly meeting of 1712 appealed to the London society, pleading that it correspond with all the plantations with a view to stopping the importation of more Negroes. This the London yearly meeting answered, and we find a note in the Pennsylvania yearly meeting minutes, 1714, acknowledging their advice and notifying the London meeting that no Friends in that colony were guilty of encouraging slave importations. The Chester quarterly meetings of 1715 and 1716 refer again to the subject, but seem not to have received much satisfaction. The yearly meeting "cautioned" Friends, without "censuring" any, against buying slaves.

The yearly meeting of Nantucket in New England ordered a compilation of important actions of the meetings of London, Pennsylvania, New Jersey, and New York in 1785, and in the record of this compilation we find a number of minutes on the question of slavery.[3] In 1727 it was voted: "It is the sense of this meeting that the importation of Negroes from their native country and relations is not a commendable or allowable practice, and that practice is censured by this meeting."[4] The matter of importation of slaves and buying and selling of slaves seems to have been up in every yearly meeting with a constant growing opposition to the practice. In 1743 the following query was adopted and directed to be regularly answered: "Do Friends observe the former advice of our yearly meeting not to encourage the importation of Negroes, nor to buy them after importation?"[5]

About this time John Woolman and Anthony Benezet, two Quakers, became deeply concerned about slavery. That the Quakers had not all heeded the injunction of the yearly meetings is brought out by Woolman's *Journal*. In 1742, when Woolman was twenty-two, his employer ordered him to write out a bill of sale for a Negro

[1] *A Brief Statement of the Rise and Progress of the Testimony of the Religious Society of Friends against Slavery and the Slave Trade*, p. 9.
[2] *Ibid.*, p. 10.
[3] *The Book of Discipline Agreed on by the Yearly Meeting of Friends for New England*.
[4] *Ibid.*, p. 101.
[5] *A Brief Statement of the Rise and Progress of the Testimony of the Religious Society of Friends, against Slavery and the Slave Trade*, p. 15.

woman. The purchaser was a member of the Society of Friends, and was waiting to take the slave away. Woolman wrote out the bill and said both to his master and to the purchaser that he "did not believe slave keeping to be a practice consistent with the Christian religion." [1] The *Journal* tells us that shortly after this a friend of Woolman asked him to prepare a bill of sale for a slave and he flatly refused to do it. In 1746 Woolman had become so deeply interested in the spreading of the Friends' message that his "mind was weaned of outward greatness," he turned down "several offers of business that appeared profitable," came to the conclusion "that a humble man, with the blessings of the Lord might live on a little," and gave himself to "the most steady attention to the voice of the true Shepherd." [2] He and Isaac Andrews set out on a journey through all the various meetings, visiting Pennsylvania, Maryland, Virginia, and North Carolina. Two things in the southern states impressed him: one was the vices that followed in the wake of slavery; the other was the fact that the entertainment which he received so freely was so often at the expense of the hard-worked slave that he could not rest easy. Slavery, for Woolman, cast a "dark gloominess" over the land, and he "frequently had conversations" with the masters concerning the evils of slavery.[3] This was but the beginning of long years of toil on behalf of the slaves, and equally on behalf of clearing the consciences of those Friends who still owned slaves.

In 1758 the Philadelphia yearly meeting appointed John Woolman, John Scarborough, John Sikes, and Daniel Stanton as an itinerant committee of four to visit all the quarterly meetings and urge that slaves be "set at liberty." [4] Up to this time the Quakers had concerned themselves about the importation of slaves, and the buying and selling of them. Here they come out clearly for the emancipation of all slaves, and they urge that quarterly and monthly meetings shall not permit slaveholders to "participate in the meetings for discipline, or be employed in the affairs of truth." [5] In 1760 certain of the yearly meetings followed the language of the London yearly meeting in warning all Friends against "reaping the unrighteous profits of that iniquitous practice of dealing in Negroes,"

---

[1] *The Journal of John Woolman*, p. 65.
[2] *Ibid.*, p. 68 *passim*.   [3] *Ibid.*, p. 74 *passim*.
[4] *A Brief Statement of the Rise and Progress of the Testimony of the Religious Society of Friends, against Slavery and the Slave Trade*, p. 22.
[5] *Ibid.*, p. 23.

alleging that it was unjust to the Negroes, made the owners haughty and tyrannical, and debased the morals of the children who observed it.¹ In 1774 the Philadelphia yearly meeting appointed a committee of thirty-four to study the whole question and report on ways and means of freeing the society of slaveholding. They brought in a report filled with considerateness, but clear in its conviction that all Friends should be brought to see that slaveholding was wrong. The procedure which had been followed from the beginning was to deal personally with each slaveholder and, in case he persisted, not to permit him to take part in the regular meetings. One cannot read the minutes of these meetings without being impressed with the calm persistence, the reasonable concern, and the Christian consideration displayed by those who were opposed to slaveholding. They were almost from the beginning vastly in the majority, and might have forcibly expelled from their midst all those who persisted in what to them seemed "an iniquitous practice." But they preferred to be patient and try by all reasonable means to bring their brethren to see the light. By 1782 it was possible to report that no member of the Philadelphia meeting held slaves.² In Virginia a similar course of persuasion was followed, but as late as 1787, it was still necessary for the yearly meeting "to bear testimony against these things."

As time went on the tone of action of the yearly meetings changed. Not only were slaves to be set free, but they were often to be indemnified for time spent as slaves after they were twenty-one years of age. An interesting account of one such transaction is that of T. W., whose father, W. W., ten years earlier (1768) had a slave named Cæsar. It seems Cæsar was thirty-one when freed, and T. W. felt an "uneasy conscience" because proper compensation had not been made. He mentioned his difficulty to his monthly meeting. A committee of five was appointed, which, after going into the case, awarded Cæsar five pounds per year for nine years, one year of the ten after he was twenty-one having been unprofitable because he had a severe spell of smallpox, through which his master nursed him. The award was entirely agreeable to Cæsar and to T. W.; so it was thus settled.³

¹ *The Book of Discipline Agreed on by the Yearly Meeting of Friends for New England*, p. 101.
² James Bowden, *The History of the Society of Friends in America*, Vol. II, p. 215.
³ *A Brief Statement of the Rise and Progress of the Testimony of the Religious Society of Friends, against Slavery and the Slave Trade*, pp. 35-36.

Instead of emphasizing primarily the freeing of slaves, more and more attention was devoted to caring for and teaching those who were set free. In the year 1779 the Chester quarterly meeting, the Concord quarterly meeting, the Burlington quarterly meeting, the Hoddanfield quarterly meeting, and the Salem monthly meeting all gave extended attention to meetings of worship for people of color and proper religious instructions of all colored people.[1] Following the Revolution, and as the Friends cleared their conscience of slaveholding in their own society, they gradually launched out in a campaign to stop the traffic in slaves all over the world. Anthony Benezet (1713–1784) was one of the great leaders in this work. He traveled extensively and wrote constantly on the subject. Some of his writings, which are still the best source material on the slave trade, are: *A Short Account of that Part of Africa, Inhabited by the Negroes*, Philadelphia, 1762; *Some Historical Account of Guinea: Inquiry into the Rise and Progress of Slavery*, Philadelphia, 1771; *Brief Considerations on Slavery, and the Expediency of Its Abolition*, Burlington, 1773; *Serious Considerations of Several Important Subjects, Observations on the Inslaving, Importing and Purchasing of Negroes*, Philadelphia, 1778; *A Caution to Great Britain and Her Colonies*, London, 1784; *Some Historical Account of Guinea* (another study), London, 1788.

The path of the Society of Friends in the South was beset with many pitfalls. As early as 1722 the yearly meeting of Virginia asked: "Are all Friends clear of being concerned in the importation of slaves, or purchasing them for sale?"[2] Almost every yearly meeting following that time discussed this subject. In 1790 an abolition society was formed in Virginia of which Robert Pleasants, a staunch Quaker, was president. Pleasants himself emancipated eight slaves, and worked for the establishment of schools for the instruction of "Blacks and people of Color."[3] It is interesting to note that as late as 1838 the Virginia yearly meeting warned Friends against the extremes of the abolitionists, although they, as members of the Society of Friends, had long since ceased to own slaves.[4] The laws against manumitting slaves in the southern states put the Quakers in a great dilemma. If they held their slaves, they violated their conscience and broke the law of the Society; if they freed them they violated the law of

---

[1] *A Brief Statement of the Rise and Progress of the Testimony of the Religious Society of Friends, against Slavery and the Slave Trade*, pp. 39–40 passim.

[2] Stephen B. Weeks, *Southern Quakers and Slavery*, p. 201.

[3] *Ibid.*, pp. 213–215 passim.   [4] *Ibid.*, p. 216.

ATTITUDE OF THE CHURCHES

the state. As early as 1796 the Friends of North Carolina protested against this state of affairs. In a petition to the Assembly they said:

For a legislative body of men, professing Christianity, to be so partial, as to refuse any particular people the enjoyment of their liberty, under the laws of the government wherein they live, even when the owners of such slaves are desirous from religious motives, that they might enjoy their personal freedom, as the natural right of all mankind, is so incompatible with the nature of a free republican Government, and repugnant to the spirit of the Christian religion, that the present case, perhaps, all circumstances considered, hath never been paralleled in Christendom. Therefore, we earnestly entreat and request that you may please to give your attention to this important and interesting subject, and pass an act whereby the free citizens of this state, who are conscientiously scrupulous of holding slaves, may legally emancipate them.[1]

The petition was not heeded; so the Society took other steps to relieve the conscience of its members. Beginning with 1808, the yearly meeting of North Carolina set up a system by which certain parties were permitted to hold the title to slaves whom the masters wished to free. The Society itself became slaveholder. By a law of 1796 any religious society or congregation might legally own slaves through its trustees, and the Quakers took advantage of this law. The legality of such action was tested by those who opposed manumission. In 1817 William Dickinson conveyed a slave to the Quaker society at Contentnea and the transfer was contested. It came to the Supreme Court in 1827 and Chief Justice Taylor declared that the practice of the Quakers was manumission in everything but name. He maintained that a religious society could hold slaves only for its own use. Justice Hall dissented from the decision, and nothing seems to have come of it, for the Society continued to accept slaves as a practical means of emancipation.[2] Friends coöperated with the Colonization Society; they attempted to help slaves to the free states by will of their masters; they organized manumission societies; they exhorted other churches to work for manumission; through Coffin and others they ordered the work of the Underground Railroad; and through Charles Osborne and Benjamin Lundy and Elihu Embree they published the first abolition papers: the *Philanthropist* of Mount Pleasant, Ohio (1817), the *Emancipator* of Jonesboro, Tennessee (1820), and later the *Emancipator* of Greeneville, Tennessee.

[1] Stephen B. Weeks, *Southern Quakers and Slavery*, p. 221.
[2] John S. Bassett, *Slavery in the State of North Carolina*, p. 32.

The Society was never large in numbers, but the steady conviction of its members, their "Christian prudence and forbearance," and their devotion to a great cause gave them an influence far out of proportion to their numbers. They were not only among the earliest advocates of the rights of the Negro; they were among the most consistent and faithful advocates of them.

The Episcopalians were not so fortunate in their constructive program as the Quakers. The church being larger, and having a particularly large following in the South, it would be natural that much internal dissension should be caused by slavery. However, the matter was handled, as we shall see, without a split in the church.

We have already seen that the established Church of England through the Society for the Propagation of the Gospel was active in evangelizing the Negro during early colonial days. After the Revolution the American church broke away from the mother church of England and organized the Protestant Episcopal church. The break was a trying experience, and the church was weak and struggling for several decades. So true was this that Bishop Wilberforce in his history of the church speaks of it as a period of depression, and Tiffany calls it the "Period of Suspended Animation and Feeble Growth."[1] However, by 1810 the Protestant Episcopal church in South Carolina could report 199 communicants in three churches; *viz.*, St. Philip's and St. Michael's, Charleston (120 and 73 respectively), and Prince George's, Winyaw (6). The other reports do not distinguish between white and colored communicants.[2] The report, for Charleston alone we presume, in 1818 was 289 communicants.[3] Bishop Dehan of South Carolina was active in preaching to the Negroes, and in 1823 he is reported as embracing every opportunity to converse with men of influence on this subject. Reverend Dr. Dalcho of the Episcopal church of Charleston in the same year (1823) issued a valuable pamphlet entitled: "Practical considerations founded on the scriptures Relative to the Slave Population of South Carolina."[4] He tells us that he had 316 Negro members, and 200 in the Sunday School.[5] In 1829, the Honorable Charles C. Pinckney, an Episcopalian, delivered an address before the Agricultural Society of South Carolina, in which he pleaded for the religious in-

---

[1] C. C. Tiffany, *A History of the Protestant Episcopal Church in the United States of America*, chap. 14.
[2] C. C. Jones, *The Religious Instruction of the Negroes in the United States*, p. 58.
[3] *Ibid.*, p. 62.   [4] *Ibid.*, p. 69.   [5] *Ibid.*, p. 69.

struction of Negroes.¹ Reverend Joseph Walker of Beaufort reported 57 Negro communicants in 1830, and Bishop Ives of North Carolina addressed the convention on providing the slaves with more adequate religious instruction.² Meanwhile Bishop Meade of Virginia was beginning his active work for the slaves. He published a letter (1834) to the ministers, members, and friends of the Protestant Episcopal church in the diocese of Virginia on the duty of affording religious instruction to those in bondage.³ The Episcopal Convention of 1838 passed strong resolutions calling on all slaveholders to support clerical missionaries and lay catechists for the religious instruction of all slaves.⁴ About this time a very trying experience came to the church. The General Theological Seminary was established by the whole church in 1836. In June, 1839, Alexander Crummell, a colored man, applied for admission and took up residence in the commons. Although there was no specific ruling which debarred him, when he consulted with the bishop he was advised to withdraw from the commons and simply attend classes as a visitor. This Crummell refused to do, on the ground of self-respect, and the matter finally came to the bishops, of whom all except Bishop Doane sustained the decision of the resident bishop.⁵ When Stephen Elliott was elected Bishop of Georgia in 1841, his "primary address" called attention to the importance of religious instruction of slaves.⁶ In the Ninth Annual Report of the Association for the Religious Instruction of the Negroes, Liberty County, Georgia, of which Reverend C. C. Jones was the missionary, we find encouraging word of the zeal of the Episcopal churches in the work. This report tells us that Bishop Jones, assistant to Bishop Meade of Virginia, "is very active in the work, and is of one spirit with Bishop Meade"; and it is remarked that "the uniting the whites and Negroes in one charge must be attended with happiest results." ⁷ This same account tells us that the Bishop of North Carolina was continuing his interest, that the Bishop of Georgia was most active, and that the "Episcopal church of South Carolina, taken as a whole, Bishop, Clergy and Laity, is more active and engaged than in any other

¹ Ibid., p. 70. ² Ibid., pp. 74–75.
³ W. P. Harrison, *The Gospel among the Slaves*, p. 80.
⁴ Ibid., p. 83.
⁵ Cf. Samuel Wilberforce, *History of the Protestant Episcopal Church in America*, p. 307.
⁶ C. C. Jones, *The Religious Instruction of the Negroes in the United States*, p. 93.
⁷ *Ninth Annual Report of the Association for the Religious Instruction of the Negroes*, p. 17.

state in the Southern Country." [1] The provisional Bishop of Florida, and Bishop Cobb of Alabama, and Bishop Otey of Tennessee are each referred to in 1845 as taking active interest in the slaves. It is clear that the whole church had become thoroughly aroused and interested in religious instruction for the Negroes, but there was a growing uneasiness between the wings of the church North and South.

When the South seceded, Bishop Meade of Virginia and Bishop Otey of Tennessee opposed the move, but joined with their states in loyal support, once the step had been taken. A call was sent out for a meeting of delegates from the Episcopal churches before the states of Virginia, Tennessee, North Carolina, and Arkansas had seceded. The representatives of South Carolina, Georgia, Florida, Mississippi, and Texas met at Montgomery (July 1861) and resolved "that an independent church was necessary." After drawing up a tentative constitution and canons, they adjourned to meet in October. Accordingly in October ten bishops convened at Columbia, South Carolina, and Bishop Meade of Virginia was made chairman. The constitution was adopted and submitted to the diocese. The church was to be called the Protestant Episcopal Church in the Confederate States. Under this rule R. H. Wilmer was elected Bishop of Alabama and consecrated by Bishop Meade of Virginia. This act declared to the world that they were an independent church. But the church in the North refused to concede that the church was divided. In the convention held in 1862 the names of the southern dioceses were called regularly, as if they were represented. They were considered as absent members. Bishop Hopkins of Vermont even claimed that the states had a right to secede if they felt it was to their best interest. His attitude perhaps helped to draw the southern wing back in 1865. Before the convention of 1865, Bishop Hopkins, who had then become the presiding bishop, sent out letters to all the southern bishops inviting them to the convention and assuring them of a warm welcome. The Bishop of North Carolina responded. When the convention opened, the secretary of the House of Deputies called the roll, the names of the southern dioceses being called just as in 1862. Tennessee, North Carolina, and Texas responded, so that the breach was already beginning to heal. All the southern dioceses returned to the united church and the Episcopal church of the Confederate States ceased to exist. We have thus seen that both the Quakers

[1] *Ninth Annual Report of the Association for the Religious Instruction of the Negroes*, p. 17.

ATTITUDE OF THE CHURCHES 197

and the Episcopal church really preserved their unity through the storm of those trying days of civil strife. We shall see how it fared with other churches.

The first presbytery ever held in America was in 1705 with six ministers and Francis Makemie as the moderator.[1] The first Presbyterian church in America was organized at Philadelphia in 1698. The first General Assembly did not meet until 1789. Shortly after this the Scotch-Irish migration set in and the Presbyterian church grew in numbers and influence. In 1717 the one presbytery of Philadelphia was divided into four, and these were united into a synod.[2] At the opening of the war for independence there were 17 presbyteries and 170 ministers. By 1837, the time when the great schism of a progressive versus a static theology split the church into the Old School and New School, it was the most influential religious body in the United States, Bacon says. At that time it had 135 presbyteries, 2,140 ministers, 220,557 communicants.[3]

The Presbyterians began work for the Negroes in Hanover, Virginia, in 1747. Reverend Samuel Davies organized so many congregations that he could not preach to them all; so in 1752 Reverend John Todd joined him in the work. It is evident from his letters that he took great interest in the "poor neglected Negroes . . . whom their masters generally neglect, [who] . . . sit adorned with so many black countenances, eagerly attentive to every word they hear."[4] Mr. Davies found the Negroes particularly apt in psalmody, for which he furnished books to those who could read, and he claimed that more than 1,000 attended his various places of preaching. Mr. Davies wrote to a friend that his greatest success was among the two extremes of society: namely, Gentlemen and Negroes. He evidently found difficulty even at this early time to attract the poor whites.[5] Other leaders evidently took great interest in the Negroes, Robert Henry of Cub Creek being notable among them. This man was a queer absent-minded rough and ready preacher. It is reported of him that after an ardent sermon he went to the place where he usually tied his horse, and mounted the horse of another man, without ever noting the difference. His crudeness and impetuous preaching appealed greatly to the Negroes.

[1] Leonard W. Bacon, *A History of American Christianity*, pp. 121–122.
[2] *Ibid.*, p. 136.   [3] *Ibid.*, p. 292.
[4] C. C. Jones, *The Religious Instruction of the Negroes in the United States*, pp. 35–36.   [5] *Ibid.*, pp. 37–38.

The first official action of the Presbyterian church seems to have been that of the synod of New York and Philadelphia, which was virtually the General Assembly of the church, the latter body not having been organized. At the meeting of this synod in 1787 it was "overtured that the synod of New York and Philadelphia recommend in the warmest terms to every member of their body, and to all the churches and families under their care, to do everything in their power, consistent with the rights of civil society, to promote the abolition of slavery, and the instruction of Negroes, whether bond or free."[1] The synod took action, urging that slaves be educated so that they might not be dangerous, if set free, that masters give their slaves a chance to win their freedom by industry, and that the goal of final abolition be set by all masters. The General Assembly was organized in 1789, and four years later it took official action (1793) by adopting the identical paper of the New York and Philadelphia synod.[2] The Assembly of 1795 reaffirmed the actions of 1787 and 1793, but took no further action. The matter came up again in 1815, and while the Assembly admitted that transfer of slaves might be necessary at times and in some places, nevertheless it affirmed that the "buying and selling of slaves by way of traffic was inconsistent with the spirit of the Gospel."[3] The matter was only indirectly up in 1816, but in 1818 it was more drastically treated. It was recommended to the Assembly that those who bought or sold slaves should be debarred from communion, but the committee to whom the matter was referred brought in a more moderate report, which recognized the difficulties of slave owners in the slave states, sympathized with them, asked them to deal wisely with the slaves, and closed by urging all to coöperate with the Colonization Society, recently organized. All masters were to instruct their slaves in religion; all church sessions were urged to see that all cruelty should cease, and that families of slaves should not be broken up.[4] In the Assembly of 1819, the Colonization Society was highly commended to the membership of the church; in 1824 the Assembly commended this society but refused to urge on the churches a collection for it; but in 1825 the General Assembly did recommend such a collection in all the churches; in 1835 the Assembly "resolved that this whole subject be indefinitely postponed."[5] Thus ended the

[1] John Robinson, *The Testimony and Practice of the Presbyterian Church in Reference to American Slavery*, p. 16.
[2] Ibid., p. 17.   [3] Ibid., p. 19.   [4] Ibid., pp. 23–28.   [5] Ibid., p. 32.

ATTITUDE OF THE CHURCHES

actions of the Assembly of the United Presbyterian churches, for, as we have noted before, the great schism of 1837 broke the church into two wings. The General Assembly of the Old School had this matter brought to its attention continuously up to the Civil War. In 1844 it tried to get rid of the subject by voting 115 to 70 to lay all memorials concerning it on the table, but it came back in 1845. At that session it was finally voted: (1) that slaveholding was not a bar to communion; (2) that slaveholding was not a matter of discipline. This did not satisfy the more radical element; so they brought resolutions back to the Assembly of 1846, but that body finally voted: "That no further action upon this subject is at present needed." [1] At the Assembly of 1847 the Reverend C. C. Jones of Georgia preached on the religious instruction of slaves and the board of missions of the church was directed to appoint a superintendent to coöperate in the work.[2] At the sessions of 1849 and 1850 it was further raised, but the Assembly reaffirmed its past action and declared nothing further need be done. This seems to be the last official action taken.

We turn back now to trace more fully the attitude of the Presbyterians in the South. In 1760 we find a Mr. Patillo in North Carolina laboring for the slaves. In 1792 Reverend David Rice in Kentucky published a pamphlet entitled "Slavery Inconsistent with Justice and Good Policy," and in 1794 the presbytery of that state resolved that "slaves should be taught to read the scriptures and prepare for freedom." [3]

During the great revival in Kentucky and Tennessee in 1799–1800 the Negroes were not neglected. Jones estimated that about 5,000 were taken into membership in the various denominations.[4] In 1807 we find the Presbytery of Hanover in Virginia exhorting the churches not to neglect their duty toward their servants.[5]

One of the most remarkable movements for the care of the slaves was an "Association for the Religious Instruction of the Negroes" organized in Liberty County, Georgia (1830). It was composed largely of planters who were solicitous for the religious well-being of their slaves. They employed as their missionary, or secretary, Reverend C. C. Jones, from whom we have quoted often in these pages. A yearly report was printed, and in 1842 Mr. Jones pub-

---

[1] John Robinson, *The Testimony and Practice of the Presbyterian Church in Reference to American Slavery*, p. 39.   [2] *Ibid.*, p. 40.   [3] *Ibid.*, p. 124.
[4] C. C. Jones, *The Religious Instruction of the Negroes in the United States*, pp. 55–56.   [5] *Ibid.*, p. 57.

lished, through Thomas Purse, Savannah, the little volume called *The Religious Instruction of the Negroes in the United States*, which is one of the fullest and most accurate statements extant of the attitude of the church toward slavery. Many similar associations in South Carolina and other sections were copied after this organization. Reverend Joseph Stiles of McIntosh County organized one of these. In 1834 the synods of North Carolina and Virginia met together and appointed a joint committee to work out a plan for the more thorough evangelization of the Negroes.[1] In the same year the synod of South Carolina and Georgia called upon all the presbyteries to include in their annual reports the increase in colored members, and voted "that this be a standing rule of the synod on the subject."[2] During this same year the synod of Mississippi and Alabama enjoined on all ministers their duty to preach to the slaves, and in Kentucky the various denominations united in a Kentucky union for the religious instruction of the Negroes.[3] In 1836 the synod of the Presbyterians of Kentucky appointed a committee which brought in a full and courageous report on "The Religious Instruction as Well as the Future Emancipation of the Slaves."[4] The plan was irenic, practical, courageous, and showed how deeply many southern Christians felt on the subject. In 1845 a very important meeting was held in Charleston, South Carolina, to lay plans for an advance in the religious instruction of the Negroes.[5] There were men in this assembly who bore the first names of the South; "men who have adorned the halls of our national legislature, the seats of literature, the pulpit and the bar." Daniel Huger, the successor of John C. Calhoun in the United States Senate, was the moderator of the assembly. Very aggressive measures were recommended to the churches. Various synods urged the local churches to give as much as half their ministers' time to work among the slaves. Reverend C. C. Jones prepared a special catechism for use among slaves (published in Charleston in 1834), and every possible incentive was set for an aggressive program of work.

Despite all this enthusiasm for evangelization there were many

[1] C. C. Jones, *The Religious Instruction of the Negroes in the United States*, p. 76.
[2] *Ibid.*, p. 77.   [3] *Ibid.*, pp. 77–78.
[4] Pamphlet entitled: "An Address to the Presbyterians of Kentucky — Proposing a Plan for the Instruction and Emancipation of the Slaves," published by Charles Whipple, Newburyport, 1836.
[5] *Princeton Review*, October, 1845, p. 590 ff.

Presbyterians who continued to hold slaves. The New School wing of the church had a strong contingent in the South. Unlike the Old School group, the New School assemblies were far from moderate. They constantly irritated their southern churches. The Harmony Presbytery in South Carolina, goaded by this attitude, finally passed a resolution which declared slavery was not opposed to the will of God, and the synod of Virginia declared the "General Assembly had no right to declare that relation sinful which Christ and His apostles teach to be consistent with the most unquestionable piety."[1] The New School body called upon all the churches in 1853 to report what they had done about slavery, and the presbytery of Lexington, Kentucky, replied "that its ministers and its members were slaveholders by choice and on principle."[2] This statement was condemned and six synods withdrew and organized the United Synod of the Presbyterian Churches. Perhaps no group of Christians worked harder or more intelligently to give their slaves every advantage of Christian instruction, and it seems a pity that the church should have been rent into warring factions over the issue. But great evils fortified by economic forces have a way of destroying harmony and breaking asunder the bonds of fellowship. One only need look about at present to see how economic advantage may color the attitude of groups of people.

The earliest impulse toward Methodism came from the visit of John Wesley. Wesley was strongly opposed to slavery and wrote in his journal on Wednesday, February 12, 1771, that he had read a book published by an honest Quaker, on that execrable sum of all villainies, commonly called the slave trade.[3] Whitfield, on the other hand, believed that the white man needed the Negro, and the enslaving of the Negro gave him a chance to be Christianized. The first organization of Methodism was a "class meeting" in 1766 in New York, under the leadership of Philip Embury. In 1768 a lot was purchased and a meeting house built on John Street. The first missionaries were commissioned in 1769 by John Wesley, and in 1771 Francis Asbury arrived in America. Asbury's work, Bacon thinks, was more fruitful than that of any other man in the history of the American church.[4] The first annual conference was held in

---

[1] Leonard W. Bacon, *A History of American Christianity*, p. 346.
[2] Charles L. Thompson, *The Story of the Churches*, p. 200.
[3] Wesley's *Journal* (Everyman's Library), Vol. III, p. 461.
[4] *A History of American Christianity*, p. 200.

Philadelphia in 1773, and ten preachers and 1,160 members were reported. The Methodists spread south very rapidly, and in 1776 in Virginia and North Carolina meetings were held where "hundreds of Negroes were among them [the worshipers] with tears streaming down their faces."[1] The annual conference held at Baltimore in 1780 asked if the assistant minister ought not to meet the colored people himself in order to give them instruction; a question which, of course, was answered in the affirmative.[2] As early as 1786 the Methodists reported 1,890 colored members, and by 1790 this number had reached 11,682;[3] in 1803 it had grown to 22,453.[4] The first African Methodist Episcopal church General Conference was held in 1816; at this meeting Richard Allen was elected bishop. Every General Conference reported increased membership. Bishop Capers prepared a short catechism, published in Charleston in 1832, for use among colored people. Another "Plain and Easy Catechism" with verses attached was compiled by Reverend Samuel J. Bryan, who labored on the Savannah river as a missionary of the Methodist church. This was published in Savannah in 1833.[5] The colored membership returned by the Methodists in 1820 was 40,588; in 1840 it was 94,532. This rapid progress was destined to be spoiled, however, by the growing controversy over slaves. As early as 1783 the General Conference warned local preachers about holding slaves, and intimated that the next conference would probably suspend any who were found neglecting this warning. In the year 1784 independent American Methodism was set up at the Baltimore Conference with Bishop Coke the first presiding bishop. This conference drew up a discipline which required all slaveholding members to set up plans for freeing all their slaves. Pastors were ordered to keep records of such transactions and see that every member lived up to the law. Following the conference Bishop Coke made an extended preaching tour through the South. In Virginia, while preaching in a barn, he attacked slavery as a system. Many were so infuriated that they withdrew and organized a mob, which planned to do him violence — one lady was so angry she offered £50 to anyone who would administer 100 lashes to the bishop. It was only the timely intervention of a military officer and others that saved the life of the bishop. Interesting enough is the remark of his biographer, Samuel Drew, that the magistrate of the community immediately freed fifteen slaves, and

[1] C. C. Jones, *The Religious Instruction of the Negroes in the United States*, p. 39.
[2] *Ibid.*, p. 39. [3] *Ibid.*, pp. 40–42. [4] *Ibid.*, p. 56. [5] *Ibid.*, p. 75.

others followed his example.¹ In North Carolina Coke did not speak against slavery because there was a law against emancipation. Drew says that Coke was received with "veneration" and "caresses" wherever he ignored the subject of slavery, but when this chord was touched "it instantly vibrated discord through the congregation, and applauses gave place to execration." ² Coke and Asbury ³ visited George Washington, dining with him at Mount Vernon, and laid before him their plan for emancipation. Washington signified his complete sympathy with their scheme, but refused to sign their petition. He did, however, promise that if the matter came to the Virginia Assembly he would write a letter favoring it.⁴ The next General Conference suspended the drastic rules about slavery. Coke's biography implies this was done with the sanction of both Bishop Coke and Bishop Asbury, on the ground that the government should act first, and not seem to be forced into such action by a religious body.⁵ Whether this was the real reason, there is some doubt. It is altogether likely that the rules of the church were too far in advance of the sentiment of the members, and hence had to be suspended.

The church for a period of years transferred its interest in the colored man from the field of emancipation to that of religious instruction. If it could not give him liberty it at least could give him religious instruction. Legislation in favor of emancipation flared up again in the General Conference of 1796, in which traveling preachers were forbidden to hold slaves, and slave sellers among the membership of the church must be expelled.⁶ But these regulations were never strictly enforced, and gradually there was a toning down of opposition to slavery. By 1808 every item that related to slaveholding among members had been eliminated from the discipline.⁷ This conference passed over the responsibility for dealing with slavery to the annual conferences. By 1824 the conference had so far changed front that it ordered all preachers to enforce prudently upon the members the teaching of the Bible to slaves; the colored preachers

---

¹ *The Life of the Rev. Thomas Coke*, p. 138 *passim*.   ² *Ibid.*, pp. 141-142.
³ Asbury had been ordained bishop by Coke at Baltimore in December, 1784. See Asbury's *Journal*, Vol. I, p. 486 ff.
⁴ Samuel Drew, *The Life of the Rev. Thomas Coke*, p. 143. See also Asbury's *Journal*, Vol. I, p. 496.
⁵ *Ibid.*, p. 144.
⁶ John N. Norwood, *The Schism in the Methodist Episcopal Church, 1844*, p. 16.
⁷ Lucius C. Matlack, *The History of American Slavery and Methodism, from 1780 to 1849*, p. 29.

and official members were to be given full privileges, and the annual conferences were urged to employ colored preachers to travel as missionaries among the slaves.[1] The anti-slavery spirit of the church seems to have spent itself before 1830, and from that time on for ten years there was little agitation in the General Conferences. One cause of this was the fact that the abolition societies were so violent during this period that others shrank from association with them. Also the colonization societies were flourishing, and many who opposed slavery spent their energy and found compensation for their feelings by taking part in these societies. During this time Orange Scott of Vermont became active and stirred up a great deal of opposition. William Lloyd Garrison began his *Liberator* in 1831. The American Anti-Slavery Society was organized in 1833. The social and political air was full of ferment. The New England churches issued an appeal to all Methodism in 1834, setting forth their reasons for abolition. This was answered by a counter-appeal. Seeing that the church was seething with strife, the bishops managed to keep discussion at a minimum in the General Conferences of 1832 and 1836. Two of the bishops had written letters to the New England conferences, pleading for peace lest the church be split asunder. The General Conference of 1836 refused to print the address of the fraternal delegate from New England because it dealt with slavery, and two preachers who spoke before anti-slavery societies in Cincinnati, where the conference met, were reprimanded. The conservatives were in the saddle and the radical abolitionists seemed on the retreat. In various annual conferences when anti-slavery resolutions and petitions were presented, certain bishops refused to refer them to committees, and refused to allow a debate upon them.[2] The Philadelphia annual conference refused to accept L. C. Matlack as a traveling minister in 1837, and again in 1838.[3] Orange Scott and Le Roy Sunderland were practically forced out of the church because of their radical abolition opinions. As an illustration of this tendency in the church the action of the Baltimore annual conference for 1836 might be given. It read as follows:

Whereas great excitement has pervaded this country, for some time past on the subject of abolition; and whereas such excitement is believed to be destructive of the best interests of the country and religion: therefore resolved

[1] L. C. Matlack, *The History of American Slavery and Methodism, from 1780 to 1849*, p. 32.   [2] Cf. *ibid.*, p. 166 ff. *passim*.   [3] *Ibid.*, p. 254 ff. *passim*.

ATTITUDE OF THE CHURCHES 205

1. That we are as much as ever convinced of the great evil of slavery.
2. That we are opposed in every part and particular to the proceedings of the abolitionists which look to the immediate, indiscriminate and general emancipation of slaves.
3. That we have no connection with any press by whomsoever conducted in the interest of the abolition cause.

The above resolutions were sent to all official Methodist papers with the signature of the members of the conference.[1] The New York conference the same year adopted a report prepared by Dr. Bangs and others, which declared: "It is the duty of the members of this conference, wholly to refrain from all abolition measures and movements"; the episcopal address to all the churches in this same year exhorted the churches "to abstain from all abolition movements and associations, and to refrain from patronizing any of these publications."[2] Joshua Soule and James O. Andrews were two of the bishops signing this letter.

When the General Conference of 1840 met there was a spirit of conservatism pervading the meeting. Certain bishops and presiding elders were arraigned for refusing to consider business of an anti-slavery nature which had been introduced into bodies over which they presided. The conference decided that these presiding officers had a right so to do. The conference also approved the minutes of the annual conferences of Georgia and South Carolina, in which were found resolutions declaring slavery was not a moral evil.[3] Silas Comfort, a presiding elder of the Missouri conference, was charged with maladministration because he allowed a Negro to testify against a white person in a church trial. He appealed to the General Conference. Mr. Comfort was exonerated, and immediately resolutions were introduced condemning the use of Negro witnesses against whites in church trials, but the vote was 69 to 69 and the presiding officer, Bishop Hedding, refused to cast a deciding vote.[4] But the most important single action of the conference came when a memorial from members of the Baltimore conference complained that the conference had refused to elect to ordination local preachers, on the single ground that they were slaveholders. A committee of nine, of which Henry B. Bascom (afterward bishop) was a member, brought in a report which was adopted, which declared: "The mere ownership of slave property, in states or territories where the laws

---

[1] *Ibid.*, p. 67.   [2] *Ibid.*, p. 43.   [3] *Ibid.*, pp. 81–82.   [4] *Ibid.*, p. 216.

do not admit of emancipation, and permit the liberated slave to enjoy freedom, constitutes no legal barrier to the election or ordination of ministers, to the various grades of office known in the ministry of the Methodist Episcopal church; and cannot therefore, be considered as operating any forfeiture of right in view of such elect and ordination." [1] This made it legal for any minister to hold slaves in the slave states and laid the foundation for the split of the church in 1844. Within a few weeks after the adjournment of the General Conference, Orange Scott called a Methodist anti-slavery convention to meet in New York. The call stated that the convention was to consider the disposition of money for missionary purposes, and "the formation of a General (Methodist) Anti-slavery Missionary Society, whose funds should be uncontaminated by the price of blood, as the contributions of slave-holders was significantly designated." [2]

In 1842 Orange Scott, despairing of the influence of the Methodist Episcopal church being cast against slavery, decided that he would withdraw and organize a new church, in which slaveholders could hold neither membership nor official position.[3] Accordingly the Wesleyan Methodist connection was formed in 1843, with an initial membership of 6,000 drawn from the mother church, which had grown to 14,100 by the meeting of the first General Conference.[4] The movement was a revolt not only against slavery, but against the dictatorial power of the General Conference, which in the 1840 meeting had declared that the presiding officers of quarterly and annual conferences had the right to decide what business might be brought before such a body.[5] This secession from the church immediately brought about a revival of anti-slavery feeling. Something must be done, it was thought, to stem the tide of disaffection. Conventions were called in Boston; Hallowell, Maine; New Market in New Hampshire, and other places. The church press, which had attempted to offer an open forum for discussion of both sides, immediately became belligerent on the side of abolition. Memorials to be presented to the General Conference which was to meet in New York in 1844 were broadly circulated and signed by great numbers. The first days of the conference were almost all taken up with the presentations of these resolutions. The fight was opened over the case of a Mr. Harding, a traveling preacher who had been sus-

---

[1] L. C. Matlack, *The History of American Slavery and Methodism, from 1780 to 1849*, pp. 221–222.
[2] Ibid., p. 224.   [3] Ibid., p. 237.   [4] Ibid., p. 349.   [5] Ibid., p. 237.

pended by his annual conference because he refused to free his slaves. He appealed to the General Conference and his trial focused attention upon the subject. But there was a far more difficult case to be handled.

Bishop Andrew held two slaves bequeathed to him by his first wife, and had recently married a second wife who owned slaves, which he had guaranteed to her by a deed of trust. He, of course, foresaw this would bring troubles in the conference. He earnestly desired to resign from the episcopacy to avoid the fight. The southern delegates, however, urged to the contrary. They claimed the General Conference of 1840 had specially legislated that the holding of slave property did not constitute a "legal barrier to the election or ordination of ministers to the various grades of office known in the ministry of the Methodist Episcopal church." The facts were clearly on the side of the southern delegates, but the spirit of the times had changed, and sentiment in the church was far different from what it had been four years earlier. The Wesleyan secession had thoroughly alarmed many northern preachers, and they believed that many more would leave the church if the conference temporized about slavery. The southern representatives recognized also that they were at the parting of the ways. To yield now was to throw over, once for all, the principle of slavery. In this situation there was nothing to do but part company. Accordingly a plan of separation was drawn up to be submitted to the annual conferences, and the General Conference adjourned.[1]

The southern delegates to the General Conference promptly called a meeting in Louisville, Kentucky, where the new church was organized, the name adopted, the discipline of the mother church accepted practically *in toto*, and plans made for the first General Conference, to be held in Petersburg, Virginia, in 1846. We are not here interested in following the further problems of the division of property and other constitutional questions involved in the relationships of the two churches. The one great fact that interests us is the way in which the separation liberated the southern church to carry forward an aggressive work of evangelization of the slaves. As long as there was so much division of opinion in the church, and so many were committed to abolition, the planters naturally looked askance at representatives of the church preaching to their slaves

[1] For full discussion of the division see: John N. Norwood, *The Schism in the Methodist Episcopal Church, 1844* (1923).

lest they stir up insurrection, but when once the southern church had withdrawn, this fear was removed, for "a man indorsed by the southern conference was considered by the owners of slaves as trustworthy, by virtue of that indorsement alone."[1] Quite likely the church found compensation for its feeling of defeat by a most aggressive work of evangelization. It may be also that some southerners desired to justify their stand in the conference of 1844 by a redoubled zeal on behalf of the slaves. Whatever the cause, a spirit of missions flared up in the church, and a zeal scarcely ever equaled showed itself in many of the outstanding members and preachers of this church. Some of the most prominent leaders of the church, such as Bishop Capers of South Carolina, Dr. Winans of Mississippi, and later Bishop Haygood of Georgia, became most ardent advocates of the cause. By 1849 fifteen annual conferences had established Negro missions, and there were 122 regularly appointed missionaries. This number constantly increased until 1861, when the Methodist Episcopal Church South had 327 full-time missionaries in this work; there were 329 independent missions, and there were 66,559 Negro members.[2] In addition there were scores of small missions attached to white churches, not included in this enumeration, and every white church had its gallery where the slaves received the Gospel along with the whites. Thus in 1846 the Kentucky conference reported only one colored mission, but had among its regular communicants 9,479 colored persons; and the Holston conference reported no colored missions, but had 4,133 colored members as communicants. The South Carolina Board of Missions declared: "As a general rule for our circuits and stations, we deem it best to include the colored people in the same pastoral charge with the whites and to preach to both classes in one congregation, as our practice has been. The Gospel is the same for all men, and to enjoy its privileges in common promotes good will."[3] Harrison shows that during the period from 1845 to 1860 this church expended $1,320,778 on these "plantation missions" as they were called, in addition to the large share which the Negroes had in all the regular white churches. Even

---

[1] W. P. Harrison, *The Gospel among the Slaves*, p. 297. This volume is one of the fullest statements of the work of the Methodist Episcopal Church South for the Negroes. Unfortunately, it is not carefully documented, but references which one can verify seem to be entirely reliable.

[2] *Ibid.*, chap. 15, *passim*.

[3] Holland N. McTyiere, *A History of Methodism*, p. 587.

ATTITUDE OF THE CHURCHES 209

in the year 1864, when the war had "bled the South white," the southern church contributed $158,421 toward this mission work among Negroes. All during the war period the white women of the South continued the work in the absence of most of the ministers and the other men of the region. If the southern church was mistaken in its judgment about the right of ministers and members to hold slaves, it certainly was not neglectful of its duty to do all in its power to ameliorate the conditions of slavery, and particularly to see that the entire Negro population had the Gospel preached to it. Speaking of the obligation of the church to carry forward this work, Charles Deems, editor of the *Annals of Southern Methodism*, in 1857 quoted from the report of E. W. Sehan, Missionary Secretary of the church, as follows:

The subject assumes an importance beyond the conception even of those more directly engaged in this great work, when it is remembered that these missions absolutely number more converts to Christianity, according to statistics given, than all the members of all other missionary societies combined. We have often adverted to the importance of this field of labor, and to the high estimate which should be placed on the faithful ministers of Christ who are laboring within its bounds.[1]

One cannot speak of all the outstanding leaders of the southern church in this work for the slaves. If one reads Deems' *Annals* of the annual conferences he will be surprised at the names of men who were the leaders of the church who at one time or another served as missionaries to the plantations. Such names as Kirkland, Capers, Wightman, Winans, Barbee, Andrew, and scores of others come immediately to the minds of those familiar with Methodist history. These were among the men who made the Methodist church. Bishop Capers was really the leader in this work. On his tomb at Columbia, South Carolina, there is written on the east front: "The Founder of Missions to the Slaves in South Carolina."[2] As early as the year 1829, Honorable Charles C. Pinckney, one of the largest planters in the state of South Carolina and a man of national political prominence, appealed to Dr. Capers to find a minister who could act both as overseer and preacher on his plantation. Capers said he could not find such a man, for the task of the overseer was not a very exalted one, and men who held such positions were not usually marked for their piety. He did, however, say he could send him a

[1] *Annals of Southern Methodism for 1857*, p. 134.
[2] William M. Wightman, *Life of William Capers*, p. 490.

missionary, which he ultimately did. Other planters, observing the good results, applied for similar services, and the colored mission was soon well under way. Capers, afterward elected bishop, never lost his profound interest in this work. When he died in 1855 "there were twenty-six (colored) missionary stations in South Carolina, on which were employed thirty-two preachers. The number of church members at that time was 11,546 (colored) in these mission stations."[1] The missionary revenue for that year was reported as $25,000 from South Carolina. With such leadership as this it is not surprising that the Methodist churches should have exerted great influence in converting the slaves, and in ameliorating to a considerable degree the rigors of a régime which at its best was fraught with much hardship.

The Baptists were early in the field. Beginning with Roger Williams in New England, they spread rapidly southward. Bacon says they were among the early dissenters from the established church in Virginia in the early years of the eighteenth century.[2] Since every church in the Baptist communion was free to determine its own policies, it would not seem that dissention should have arisen over slavery in the denomination. Members of this church, like those of others, early began to feel the importance of evangelizing the slaves. In 1773, Henry Sharpe of Burk County, Georgia, owned a slave named George Liehle. The last name came from his former master, on whose plantation in Virginia he had been born. George was converted in this year and joined the white Baptist church of his master. Mr. Sharpe gave his slave liberty to preach on the various plantations. In 1775 he was ordained and given freedom. About the same time David George and Jesse Peters, two Negroes, were preaching in South Carolina. The white planters encouraged their labors because of the good effect which Christianity had upon the slaves.[3] The Savannah colored Baptist church was organized about 1792.[4] Another famous slave preacher was Andrew Bryan, who was ordained at Augusta in 1788. He seems to have been a very powerful preacher, and one who was wholly committed to his work. Persecuted and abused, he declared he was willing to die for the cause. He was so genuine that he finally won the approval of the

---

[1] William M. Wightman, *Life of William Capers*, pp. 291, 292, 297, *passim*.
[2] *A History of American Christianity*, p. 53.
[3] Edgar G. Thomas, *The First African Baptist Church of North America*, *passim*.
[4] C. C. Jones, *The Religious Instruction of the Negroes in the United States*, p. 50.

ATTITUDE OF THE CHURCHES 211

white people.¹ The Baptists in America for the year 1793 were reported at 73,471, one-fourth of whom, it was estimated, were colored.² By 1806 there were 130 Baptist churches in South Carolina alone, with 100 ministers and 10,500 members, one-third of whom were Negroes.³ In 1822, Dr. Richard Furman, as president of the Baptist State Convention of South Carolina, addressed a letter to the governor of that state on behalf of the denomination, in which be declared the religious interest of the slaves made a serious claim on the masters, and the work of the masters was indispensable.⁴ In 1835 the Charleston Baptist Association addressed a memorial to the legislature, in which it stoutly maintained the right of slavery but insisted that Christian principles demanded that slaves be properly treated, and instructed in religion.⁵ That many of the leading Baptists owned slaves and thought it not incompatible with their religious profession can easily be proved. Furman himself left twenty-seven slaves to be disposed of along with two mules, one horse, and an old wagon.⁶ But the Baptists were no less zealous than other churches in preaching the Gospel to the slaves. They were even more liberal than most of the other denominations in permitting Negroes to have their own churches; hence they early got a great hold on the Negro people, which they have held up to the present hour.

The Baptist denomination tried hard to steer clear of the slavery question. When the American Baptist Home Mission Society was organized in 1832, its constitution was silent on the question of slavery, and in practice it elected slaveholding officers, accepted funds from slaveholders, and sent out slaveholding missionaries.⁷ The triennial convention held in Boston admitted slaveholders and non-slaveholders on equal footing according to its constitution. The first president was Richard Furman of South Carolina, a slaveholder. He was succeeded in 1820 by Robert Semple of Virginia, another slaveholder. The third president (1832–1841) was Spencer Cone of New York, not a slaveholder, whose successor was William B. Johnson of South Carolina (1841–1844), a slaveholder, and he was succeeded by Francis Wayland, an anti-slavery man, who held office until the division of the church. Thus three out of five presi-

---

¹ *Ibid.*, p. 52. ² *Ibid.*, p. 53. ³ *Ibid.*, p. 57. ⁴ *Ibid.*, p. 69.
⁵ William Goodell, *Slavery and Anti-Slavery; a History of the Great Struggle in Both Hemispheres; with a View of the Slavery Question in the United States*, p. 184.
⁶ *Ibid.*, p. 186.
⁷ A. T. Foss and E. Mathews, *Facts for Baptist Churches*, p. 63.

dents were slaveholders.¹ It was the problem of slaveholding missionaries which ultimately split the church, just as the problem of a slaveholding bishop split the Methodist church. Spencer Cone tried in 1841 to prevent the split by a compromise which declared that no new tests should be set up for membership save those specifically set forth in the Bible.² This resolution did not quiet the agitation, for a Mr. Fuller of South Carolina carried through the Philadelphia meeting of the society in 1844 a resolution declaring that the business of the society was to expend the funds placed in its hands, and "did not imply any sympathy with slavery or anti-slavery." ³ The triennial convention of 1844 held in Philadelphia took practically the same position.⁴ A long and heated argument between Wayland and Fuller followed. The whole church became sensitive and nervous.

The Alabama State Convention, meeting at Marion, November 25, 1844, drew up resolutions which demanded a final statement from the Baptist General Convention as to whether slaveholders "had all the privileges of non-slaveholders and especially to receive any agency, mission or other appointment" which the church or its societies might make.⁵ The Board of the Triennial Convention answered that slaveholders did have all the immunities of membership, but they would not appoint a slaveholder as a missionary.⁶ So the argument was really ended. The Executive Committee of the Georgia Baptist Convention and the Board of the Alabama Baptist Convention immediately passed resolutions looking to separation. The Board of the Tennessee Foreign Missionary Society declared the Board of the Triennial Convention had gone beyond its authority and its action would not be sustained by the convention itself. There was an implication that Tennessee Baptists would withdraw if the ruling was sustained by the convention.⁷ On May 8, 1845, delegates from Maryland, Virginia, North and South Carolina, Georgia, Alabama, Louisiana, Kentucky, and the District of Columbia met in Augusta, Georgia, and on May 10 a constitution of the Southern Baptist Convention was presented and adopted. Thus slavery had become the rock on which another great denomination had split asunder.⁸

¹ A. T. Foss and E. Mathews, *Facts for Baptist Churches*, p. 15.
² *Ibid.*, pp. 75–76.   ³ *Ibid.*, pp. 89 and 93.   ⁴ *Ibid.*, p. 94.
⁵ *Ibid.*, p. 104.   ⁶ *Ibid.*, p. 106.   ⁷ *Ibid.*, pp. 112–113.
⁸ For full description of this meeting see *Niles' Weekly Register*, Vol. 68, pp. 187–188.

ATTITUDE OF THE CHURCHES 213

The Baptist denomination was from the beginning very active in the evangelization of slaves. The earliest records in Rippon's *Annual Register* report members of the churches in Rhode Island as interested in the salvation of Negroes.[1] This same record gives a full account of the Baptist church in Savannah under the leadership of George Liehle and Andrew Bryan and others.[2] Reports from Virginia, Kentucky, and other states indicate a deep interest in the welfare of slaves. By 1800 the Negro church at Savannah had become so large that Andrew Bryan thought it should be divided.[3] In some of the early churches slave members were even given a vote, but by 1802 this practice was falling into disuse, as the slave members were not considered capable of making decisions on policy.[4] A Baptist missionary to the Negroes of New Orleans was appointed in 1818, and work for the Negroes was begun in earnest.[5] Similar work was beginning all over the South. The minutes of the conventions and annual meetings are filled with references both to domestic missions for Negroes and to the African mission started by Lott Carey. The mission to Haiti was organized in 1835.[6] Many Baptist associations did as the one at Charleston did in 1835; namely, called upon all churches and members to accept "responsibility in regard to the religious instruction of this class of people."[7] The Welch Neck Baptist Association circularized the churches in 1841 on the subject: "How can we best promote the religious instruction of our black population?"[8] The question was based on three considerations: (1) that the black people belonged to the family of the masters; (2) that they were in deep need; (3) that the means were at hand to meet this need. The family altar, pastoral visitation, and public worship were among the means urged. One of the very first actions taken by the Southern Baptist Convention was: "Resolved, that the Board of Domestic Missions be instructed to take all prudent measures, for the religious instruction of our colored population."[9] The records of many other associations bear testimony to the fact the Baptists

---

[1] John Rippon, *The Baptist Annual Register for 1790*, p. 88.
[2] *Ibid.*, pp. 339–343.
[3] *Ibid.*, 1798–1801, p. 366.
[4] R. B. Semple, *History of the Rise and Progress of the Baptists in Virginia*, p. 130.
[5] John T. Christian, *A History of the Baptists*, p. 204.
[6] *Proceedings of Baptist General Convention in Richmond* (1835), p. 24.
[7] *Minutes of Charleston Baptist Association* (1835), pp. 6–7.
[8] *Minutes of Welch Neck* (S. C.) *Baptist Association*, (1841), pp. 15–22.
[9] *Minutes of Southern Baptist Convention* (1845), p. 15.

were not lacking in zeal for the Negroes' religious life. The split in the church made no change in either section of the church as to this zeal for evangelization. Jones, in his report to the Liberty County Association for the Religious Instruction of the Negroes, for 1848, said that Alabama was the leading state in the country in its interest in the religious life of the Negro, and he intimated that the Baptists were the leaders of the work in that state.[1] This same report says there were 10,716 Negro Baptists in Georgia in 1847. There were 130,000 Negro Baptists in 1849,[2] and the report of the Board on Domestic Missions at the Southern Baptist Convention held in Richmond, Virginia, 1859, estimated that the number of colored members was 150,000.[3]

We have seen in this study two tendencies which seemed at war with each other. First, there was a constant tendency to invoke the Bible as a defense for slavery. So blind does man seem, when his economic welfare is affected, that we do not doubt these Christians were honest and sincere. But the fact that they were attacked, and that to yield meant the loss of property, drove them to use religion as their defense. The literal interpretation of the Bible so common in that day was a tower of strength in their arguments. It is just possible that the desire for defense may have driven the church deeper and deeper into this literal interpretation. Certain it is that the dogmatic attitude assumed at that time has lived to plague the southern churches ever since. The overemphasis on creed and dogma, and on correctness of belief, which played so large a part in defending slavery, has not been completely shaken off by our southern churches even to this good day.

The other influence at work among the southern Christians was a genuine desire to see their slaves enter into the fullest blessing of Christian experience. While this statement may seem to contradict the last one made, it is certainly true. Human nature is often better than its theories. The interpretations of the churches justified slavery, but the Christian spirit of the church members was eager and alive to human need and suffering. This was so true that southern states became the greatest mission field ever known to the church. One is amazed that the churches could not see the in-

---

[1] *Thirteenth Annual Report of the Association for the Religious Instruction of the Negroes* (1848), p. 24.
[2] *Proceedings of the Southern Baptist Convention* (1849), p. 64.
[3] *Ibid.* (1859), pp. 60–61.

justice of slavery, but one cannot help but rejoice in the high and heroic endeavor which made a whole race Christian.

PROBLEMS FOR STUDY

1. What was the earliest objection to evangelizing the Negroes?
2. Was religion compromised when its advocates asserted that they did not teach the slaves to desire freedom?
3. When the churches divided over the question of slavery, the southern or pro-slavery wings became very active in preaching the Gospel to the slaves. Can you explain this?
4. Why was there greater liberty granted the slaves in religious worship than in any other kind of assemblage?
5. How do you account for the fact that some of the denominations which were bitterly opposed to slavery in the eighteenth century toned down their opposition during the first three decades of the nineteenth century?
6. Judging from the present Negro church, how effective was the religious work of the early white churches with and for the Negro?

BIBLIOGRAPHY

Leonard W. Bacon, *A History of American Christianity* (1901).
A. T. Foss and E. Mathews, *Facts for Baptist Churches* (1850).
W. P. Harrison, *The Gospel among the Slaves* (1893).
Charles C. Jones, *The Religious Instruction of the Negroes in the United States* (1842).
Lucius C. Matlack, *The History of American Slavery and Methodism, from 1780 to 1849* (1849).
John N. Norwood, *The Schism in the Methodist Episcopal Church, 1844* (1923).
John Rippon, *The Baptist Annual Register.*
John Robinson, *The Testimony and Practice of the Presbyterian Church in Reference to American Slavery* (1852).
Edgar G. Thomas, *The First African Baptist Church of North America* (1925).
Charles L. Thompson, *The Story of the Churches* (1903).
Willis D. Weatherford, "The Attitude of the Churches toward the Negro during Slavery" (Manuscript).
Stephen B. Weeks, *Southern Quakers and Slavery* (1896).

CHAPTER XI

SOCIAL DOGMAS IN RACE RELATIONS

To the social psychologist it makes little difference whether or not a group has actual reality as it is pictured; the social behavior based upon the concept of this group tends to be the same. Walter Lippmann provided an apt phrase to describe our stereotyped way of thinking when he referred to the "picture within our heads." This is but little different from Wilhelm Wundt's "apperceptive masses," or Vilfredo Pareto's "residue," or Émile Durkheim's "collective representations." These stereotypes help to define situations, to make easier the classification of individuals as well as groups, and to provide a framework and continuity for the kind of social relations deemed desirable.

Stereotypes, as well as the images around which they are formed, are crystallizations of attitudes, and these attitudes are in turn the result of social and cultural conditioning. They are usually acquired in early childhood as a part of the informal education process: through suggestion, inference, observation of the behavior of others, and the manifold implications of these institutions which make up so large a part of the cultural environment. Not only are the stereotypes a means of defining situations, but they have an additional function of social control. It is natural, where groups conspicuously contrasted in physical features are in association, and where there is special advantage, economic or otherwise, in defining relations in terms of superior and inferior character, that the resulting behavior patterns should be rigid, and take on the character and sanctity of a creed. So long as codes of conduct are generally understood there is little danger of conflict. They become an established "etiquette" which it is unnecessary to articulate, except in the forms of behavior themselves. But these codes may not be completely understood by everybody. Moreover, they may frequently be understood but not accepted. It then becomes necessary to define them, and the less defensible the definition, as a rule, the more exacting the dogma of definition. Thus it happens that much of the dogma of race relations offers little explanation, is highly toned emotionally, and utilizes those images of the group which are most likely to maintain a fixed social distance.

Dr. Thomas Pearce Bailey, formerly Dean of the Department of Education and Professor of Psychology of the University of Mississippi, was one of the first serious students of the South to articulate, in the spirit of scientific study, the orthodoxy of the South with reference to the Negro. This orthodoxy, or race attitude, he noted, was "not so much a code of cases as a creed of a people, a part of their morality and of their religion." This creed was summarized as follows: "Blood will tell. The white race must dominate. The Teutonic peoples stand for race purity. The negro is inferior and will remain so. This is a white man's country. No social equality. No political equality. In matters of civil rights and legal adjustments give white man, as opposed to the colored man, the benefit of the doubt, and under no circumstances interfere with the prestige of the white race. Let there be such industrial education of the negro as will best fit him to serve the white man. Only southerners understand the negro question. Let the South settle the negro question. The status of peasantry is all the negro may hope for, if the races are to live together in peace. Let the lowest white man count for more than the highest negro. The foregoing statements indicate the leadings of Providence." [1]

In any study of the influence of racial dogma upon race relations we are dealing with three important elements: the facts upon which this dogma rests, the theories about these facts, the actions based upon the theories. There are, again, generalizations and theories built upon these assumed and actual facts that do change as society develops and as false statements are refuted and new facts come to light. It is on these theories that the layman is most frequently confounded. Yet upon these as a basis he is most constantly acting. These dogmas are founded in the historical relations of whites and Negroes in America and given both permanence and continuity by what Dr. Robert E. Park so aptly calls the "high visibility of the Negro." Associated with them are numerous taboos, from shaking hands and eating together to intermarriage. That these taboos are more concerned with status than contact is suggested in the acceptability of contact with favorite servants when the relationship is mutually understood, and in the long tolerance of race crossing with-

[1] *Race Orthodoxy in the South*, p. 93.

out benefit of clergy. With respect to these dogmas there is a disposition to assume that the theories about the facts are as unchanging as the facts themselves; a disposition to deny the fact when it contradicts the theory, and to see facts when they do not exist because the theory demands them.

The growth of feeling in the United States on the question of the Negro is a natural process. The greatest difficulty in objectively analyzing these beliefs lies in the fact that we quite generally and naturally regard our views and beliefs, whatever they are, as founded on eternal and unchanging principles. It is not often that we care to question the origin of our most firmly rooted convictions. As James Harvey Robinson points out, "we like to continue to believe what we have been accustomed to accept as true, and the resentment aroused when doubt is cast upon any of our assumptions, leads us to seek every manner of excuse for clinging to them. The result is that most of our so-called reasoning consists in finding arguments for going on believing as we already do."

Only within recent years have we begun to study our own thinking processes, and the conditions and tendencies of our social life; and only recently have we ceased to bow down with unquestioning acquiescence to the locally familiar as the universal intention of nature and the ordinance of God. John Stuart Mill, in his attack upon the particular justifications, theories, explanations, and philosophies which, wholly without substantial reason, held women in subjection, made an observation which applies today, with scarcely a single modification, to the question of the Negro:

> When there is feeling mixed with an opinion, it tends to gain rather than lose by having a preponderant weight of argument against it. If accepted as the result of argument, the refutation of the argument might shake the foundation; but when it rests on feeling, the worse it fares in argumentative contact, the more persuaded its adherents are that their feeling must have some deeper ground which arguments do not reach, and while the feeling remains, it is always throwing up new entrenchments to repair the old.

The analogy between the struggle of women for status and that of the Negro population is interestingly close. Anatomically, mentally, and by an alleged special act of God, both have been arranged in the scheme of creation a little lower than supreme man of the particular race making the comparison. Less than seventy-five years ago women were held unfitted for college education. Governor Winthrop of Massachusetts thought such training would certainly induce insanity. A few scientists are still saying, but with a perceptibly weakened sense of conviction, that women measure five ounces less brain matter than men and lack reasoning capacity. It is more than a historical accident that Negro suffrage and woman suffrage were proposed and fought for at the same time. The facts about woman — as, for example, that she is different from man — had not changed in 1920 when universal suffrage was granted. The theories about the facts, however, had undergone an almost complete revolution.

There are three cardinal beliefs at the basis of practically all of our racial dogmas, and these serve to control, in one form or another, most of the thinking about Negroes: first, that they are mentally inferior; second, that they are immoral; and third, that they are criminal. About the question of the Negro's mental disabilities there is and has been for many generations the greatest cocksureness, and this is not unnatural. Most races, when in a position of physical dominance, feel a similar superiority to all other races, and entertain a derogatory opinion about subject races. They believe, not merely in their own superiority, but in the absolute and unchangeable character of this superiority. The French feudal lords felt it toward their vassals; the Russians toward the Jews, who in turn, once regarded themselves as the chosen of the Lord. As George Elliot Howard observes, the Magyars of Hungary felt their absolute and eternal superiority over the Croatians, Slovacks, and Roumanians, although Kossuth was a Slovack and the Roumanians in large part derived from the old Roman masters of the world.[1]

Attitudes at the core of racial dogma frequently vary widely within the same area. It is not clear how these variations occur among individuals exposed to what is apparently the same environment. Sometimes members of the same family vary widely in their attitudes on race. The differences may involve temperament and other intimate personality traits, in combination with the cultural and physical environment. There are extremes in these attitudes, but commonly there appears a heavy deposit of racial sentiment, as reflected in the racial dogma, notably in the South, where there has been historically this long association with Negroes and with slavery.

It would be useless to attempt to illustrate all types and degrees

[1] "The Social Cost of Southern Race Prejudice," *American Journal of Sociology*, March, 1917, p. 581.

of expression of these attitudes as reflected in the dogma. A few examples may be cited, briefly, from current sources. A man moderately prosperous, born and reared in Georgia and at present the southern correspondent for two metropolitan newspapers, gives this personal reaction to Negroes, which embodies many of the familiar aspects of the dogma:

Fundamentally and originally all Negroes are similar. However, to understand them properly they should be divided into two classes, the urban and the suburban Negroes — the city and the country types. Elementally they are identical. The suburban or country Negro is a pure type of secondary animal. He has but two ambitions or desires — to eat as much as he can get at any and all times, and to sleep when not eating. His instincts are those of a monkey or a dog, to seize an object or thing that to him seems desirable, but like the dog he can be trained, not to recognize property rights of others from a standpoint of moral obligation, but from fear of punishment. He will work, not because he wishes or is willing to, but because his elementary instincts have taught him that if he does not work and has no opportunity to steal he cannot eat. He is but one short step in advance of his original status of raw barbarity.

The city Negro presents a little different object. Constant association with white people, a crude knowledge of simple things absorbed from whites and pounded into him by persistent repetition, some little elementary education in schools and colleges, and the example of white people have given the urban Negro a little surface finish that qualifies him for a grade of effort and production of which the country relative has no idea or appreciation and could not equal.

But it is a painful fact that the urban Negro is so totally ignorant of all skilled knowledge in what, in the North, East and West, is called "skilled labor," that he is actually but a short step in advance of his suburban relative.

Truly, the Negro at his best is a real, lamentable "white man's burden." You cannot make a silk purse out of a sow's ear, because it is a sow's ear and nothing else.

I am convinced that the African Negro race, as in this country, is but a step in the evolution from the Eastern plains, and that a very slow and painful process of education covering many years of effort is the only practical plan that can raise the Negro as a mass and a class to the higher, not only intellectual plane, but to a better material plane.

The American Negro as a race is not immoral, but unmoral. They have little or no sense of moral obligation or responsibility. They are animals whose spiritual sense is almost entirely dormant, if not entirely missing.

In bringing the African Negro to this country the barbarous, primitive methods and ways of life and existence of thousands of years ago have been transplanted into the garden of the highest civilization that the earth has known. To expect this civilization of the present to accept this ancient barbarianism, except as a convenience and a possible useful detail of material and daily life, is a dream that is not even a possibly true one, and which can only be dreamed of in the regions of the dream world and that can have no possible grounding outside of ignorance of real conditions and intangibilities.[1]

It is apparent that while most of the dogma is present it is expressed in the facile manner of a semi-serious magazine article. It actually disguises, however, a serious conviction. This is, perhaps, an extreme statement, but it is not infrequently encountered whether it leads to extremes in actual social behavior or not.

Within the same city, another man, born and reared in the state, moderately prosperous and manager of an automobile assembling plant employing some 500 men, reveals both a very different attitude and different stresses in the racial dogma. There is evidence that difference in the fundamental conviction regarding mentality or educability supports broader social tolerance. There is obviously less emotional reaction, and some evidence of reflection in the rational conflict between the dominant social dogma and the foundation of American principles of government. There is less crass certitude on ethnology, but the attempt to reconcile opinion with observation is a curious and recognized factual contradiction at the basis of his new opinion.

I believe the Negro should be educated to take a place of leadership and see no reason why he should not. I admire the Negro who tries to hold himself up, educate himself, and make something out of himself. It is the low class of Negro who doesn't try to make anything out of himself that I have no patience with. I think he should take his place in educational circles when so educated. I would not like to have one as instructor in a school I had anything to do with, but probably the reason for that is public opinion.

The Negro has no place in the political world in the South today, but the time is coming when he will have such a place, and when his name will be on the tickets to be voted for or against. I think, however, that day is a long time off, although there is nothing except race prejudice which prevents it. While I would not vote for a Negro for Mayor, if a Negro is capable and will do the right thing I don't see why he shouldn't become a political leader.

I am entirely against the social side of the Negro question, and think that the two races, especially in the South, should be kept entirely apart socially.

[1] Unpublished document from a Study of Racial Attitudes being made by Charles S. Johnson, Fisk University.

There should be coöperation between the races, but not social equality. I do think, however, that the Constitution of the United States gives the Negro equal rights with the white man, and that that part of it should be enforced, and that the Negro should have an equal opportunity to develop himself along with the white man. If he prepares himself he should have equal opportunity. The trouble now is that they never have had the opportunity. Generally speaking I think the capacity of the black man for work is inferior to the white man's, but I would say this is because they are not so far removed from savagery as we are. I believe the black man's brains, if properly developed, would be as good as anyone's. The Negro is more interested in things that are happening and is quicker to catch on than the average white person, and I believe this is due to the fact that the Negro knows now that he must watch things in order to learn, and that he is on the alert to pick up all he can this way.

I think a better understanding would help in the proper approach to a solution of the race problem. The main problem is the extreme prejudice against the black man, particularly in certain sections of the country. This prejudice leads all the way back to slavery. Of course, in slavery times in the South the Negro had no chance whatever. I think the Negro is just about as desirable as the Italians or Poles.

I have worked some Negroes, and have also observed them as servants in the home, but have had personal contact with very few highly educated Negroes.

It isn't the educated Negro that's giving us trouble. It's the uneducated.[1]

The peculiar racial dogma in American race relations appears to have some foundation in purely local situations. It is by no means certain that patterns formed in one section will carry over to another section intact; or that either dogma or behavior will be the same when detached from local traditions. The editor of a South Carolina paper, born and reared on a Black Belt plantation, and a person of considerable intelligence along with his thorough incorporation in the mores of his locality, makes this thoughtful confession of feeling:

It is hard to define my feeling of race difference. If I were in a restaurant in New York I would resent having to sit next to a Negro, though perhaps not bitterly, and I am as broad minded as anyone on the earth. Once I went into a restaurant and a Negro came in and I heard him talking French perfectly. That was a different cast of countenance, as he was from a French colony. I felt he was from a different world. The English haven't a much different attitude toward the East Indian from my attitude toward the Negro,

[1] Unpublished document from a Study of Racial Attitudes being made by Charles S. Johnson, Fisk University.

and yet I have no feeling toward the Oriental. I have had them here in —— and taken them to my club. Prejudice seems to arise from the nature of the association. California has little prejudice toward the Negro because he is not a factor in their lives.[1]

Nevertheless, for many individuals in the setting, the traditional heritage has a powerful appeal and, from the strength of the emotional factors surrounding the physical fact, can create in intelligent men a tremendous conflict between reason and emotion. The provincial rarely challenges tradition; more commonly, in cases of such conflict, he rationalizes the situation. A judge and lawyer in South Carolina gives frank articulation to the confused sentiments beneath certain of the racial dogmas in his own racial attitude as follows:

> A nigger is a nigger no matter how high he rises. I would find it difficult to treat him with the same courtesy. I'm not great enough; it would be embarrassing to me. I would help an old Negro woman cross the street, but I would cut off my hand before I'd offer that courtesy to a younger one. In the court room I have called them 'Mr.', but only because I expected them to be regular witnesses. It would hurt me in the estimation of people if I tipped my hat to a colored woman, and my own feeling would be that it was indescribably unpleasant. That's imbued in me by tradition. It must be racial. Certain animals have certain dislikes, and so have people. There was intermixture, of course, but the old southerners who did it felt the racial difference. The relation was essentially bestial and there was little or no tenderness involved. It is not as degrading for a white man to have relations with a colored person as for a white woman. Men are less affected by such experiences than women. They get fewer consequences; there isn't the same lowering of standards. The male is the master and his standards dominate. As for respect for womanhood; respect is not what you *should* feel but what you *do* feel, and the white man simply doesn't respect the colored woman.[2]

The alleged innate mental inferiority of the Negro was once held to be due to a difference in species, later to the more recent emergence of this race from primitive life, and to backwardness in ascending the scale of civilization. A natural deduction follows: the mind of the Negro cannot be improved beyond a given level; so, in any effort to adapt American education to his capacities, he ought to be taught mainly to use his hands. It is not uncommon, however, to hear it advanced, as an argument against the entrance of Negro workmen to skilled trades, that they are not capable of performing tasks which require either dexterity or sustained mental activity.

[1] *Ibid.* [2] *Ibid.*

On the theory of uneducability a school principal in one large northern city, who imagined that she had discovered that "colored children are restive and incapable of abstract thought and must be continually fed with novel interests and given things to do with their hands," altered her curriculum to teach them handicraft instead of arithmetic, and singing instead of grammar.

The dogma of mental inequality provided at one time one of the strongest objections to expenditures for Negro education in states where there are separate schools for Negroes. That the dogma persists in the present dual system of education is suggested in the results of a study by Dr. Dennis Hargrove Cooke, of the George Peabody College for Teachers, of the white superintendent in relation to Negro schools in North Carolina. Among other things, he found that the typical superintendent does not believe the white and Negro pupil should be given the same type of education; nor does he believe that the Negro should be given as much education as the white; furthermore, he believes that the average Negro pupil does not have as much capacity to learn as the average white pupil.[1]

How these attitudes were first developed would make, in itself, an interesting study. The holding of slaves by a Christian nation demanded some kind of justification. If it were ethically wrong for one human being to enslave another, conscience would best be satisfied by providing that these slaves were either outcasts or less than human. Accordingly, Biblical arguments founded on Noah and the ark and his three sons, one of whom was cursed, conveniently supplied support for the unscientific. Charles Carroll, as late as 1900, rationalizing these sentiments, wrote a book to establish from Biblical texts the fact that man was created in the image of God; and since God, "as everybody knows," is not a Negro, it follows that the Negro is not a man. John C. Calhoun, the statesman, at the time when Negroes were everywhere by intention deprived of the elements of education, ventured the assertion that if he could find a Negro capable of giving the syntax of a Greek verb, he would be disposed to call him human. Thomas Jefferson observed that a Negro could scarcely be found who was capable of tracing and comprehending the investigations of Euclid. It was probably true that there were not many Negro scholars in evidence when these observations were made.

Science helped to bolster up both the theories and the dogma. In

[1] *The White Superintendent and the Negro Schools in North Carolina*, pp. 128–130.

1870 Dr. Jeffries Wyman of Harvard discovered that the Negro afforded the point "where man and brute most nearly approached each other." A. H. Keane, author of an anthropology still used in our libraries, found that the black and white human types had no sanguinary affiliation, and that the black was inferior because he registered a lower cranial capacity. Dr. Karl Vogt, an eminent German scientist, deduced the inferiority of the Negro race from the examination of the skull of one Hottentot woman. In 1906, Dr. Robert B. Bean, who is quoted in most discussions on the intelligence of Negroes, seized upon a theory advanced by Spitzka, that brain weights determined genius, and applied it to 150 white and 150 Negro brains. He announced that he had found constant and important variations according to race.[1] Under remarkable circumstances, the accuracy of his findings was tested by Dr. Franklin P. Mall, an associate, who used the same brains and more precise instruments, and took the precaution of concealing the racial labels until the measurements were made. Dr. Mall announced that almost invariably the Negro brains had been underweighed by Dr. Bean, and the white brains overweighed.[2] His final result showed no such differences as Dr. Bean reported.

Sir Francis Galton, scientist and the father of eugenics, based a rather remarkable conclusion concerning the mentality of Negroes upon accounts he had read and heard of the stupidity of Negro servants in America. Such an unscientific basis would have been rejected for any of his other conclusions. E. B. Tylor, author of another textbook on anthropology, assumed from the accounts of European teachers of children of backward races that after the age of 12 the mentality of colored children is arrested; G. Stanley Hall fixed 14 as the age at which Negro mental growth comes to a partial standstill. There is an interesting assumption which connects the "arrested mentality" of Negroes with sexual overdevelopment, thus combining two popularly accepted racial traits.

The delusion of the scientists on this question can be traced back as far as 1856, when, in a discussion in a meeting of the Anthropological Society of Paris, Louis Pierre Gratiolet asserted that "the cranium

---

[1] "Some Racial Peculiarities of the Negro Brain," *American Journal of Anatomy*, September, 1906, pp. 353-389.

[2] "On Several Anatomical Characters of the Human Brain, Said to Vary according to Race and Sex, with Especial Reference to the Weight of the Frontal Lobe," *American Journal of Anatomy*, February, 1909, pp. 1-32.

[of the Negro] closes itself upon the brain like a prison." This was the famous theory of the closing of the frontal sutures, and it was explained technically that it was characteristic of the Negro to have the coronal suture close before the lambdoid. It is this union between the forehead and top of the brain case that was then thought to be the seat of intelligence. Dr. T. Wingate Todd of Western Reserve University, in referring to the persistence of this conviction, says: "Today we are quite uncertain about the brain functions which cluster under the coronal suture, but we do know that the power of learning by experience occupies that part of the brain under the lambdoid. If the facts indeed were as Gratiolet stated, our present knowledge would merely assure us of preëminence of the Negro in ability to store up and, later, utilize his experiences, surely a most valuable asset today. Secondly, were the facts as Gratiolet stated, the situation would look very black for the white man." [1] But this, we know, despite the persistence of the uncritical dogma, is not what is intended by referring to the evidence on the closing of the brain case.

A few years ago, before a meeting of the Eugenics Education Society in England, Dr. A. F. Tredgold, M. D. F. R. S., in an address on the inheritance of mental qualities, cited as his evidence of the racial difference in potentiality for development along educational lines a comparative racial study made by Dr. M. J. Mayo [2] in the public schools of New York City. This study was taken as a fair test because the black and white races in the New York schools were being educated side by side. This study has also been quoted in most discussions of Negro intelligence. Whatever the facts are, Dr. Mayo's study could not possibly have discovered them. In the first place, his study was made from records which had to be classified according to race by the memory of the teachers extending back as much as four years. The gradings by which they were measured were largely subjective with the teachers, and admitted by the investigator himself to be unscientific. Many of the Negro children were from migrant families, and the southern schools from which they had come were inferior and backward institutions, which fact might reasonably be offered as an explanation of their retardation.

[1] "An Anthropologist's Study of Negro Life," *Journal of Negro History*, January, 1931, p. 36.
[2] *The Mental Capacity of the American Negro*, New York, Science Press, 1913. Also in *Archives of Psychology*, No. 28, 1913.

And finally, as evidence of the subjective character of the gradings, the Negro children made their lowest scores in English and their highest in mathematics, where subjective grades are less possible. In spite of all this the difference between Negro and white children finally amounted to about 4 per cent.

Then came the Army intelligence tests, which, it was at first insisted, are a measure of innate intelligence. Again the Negroes were consigned to their familiar station. The Army tests were an expedient of the World War, and the tests were devised as a means of rapid selection of men. The Negroes were needed in largest numbers as laborers and fewest in the higher branches of the service; and by admitted design the lowest classes of Negroes were accepted unless totally unfit, while these classes among whites were freely eliminated. The Surgeon General's instructions to the Psychology Division explicitly state that "in the examination of Negro recruits camp procedure should be determined by the practical needs of the army, and the collection of scientific data always incidental to this main purpose."

The Negroes in most camps, accordingly, were marched in a body to the Beta tests designed principally for the non-English-speaking recruits; this was done in spite of the objection in practically all the camps that these tests unnaturally limited Negroes. (Specifically 65.6 per cent of the Negroes as compared with 24.7 per cent of the whites were given the Beta tests.) Discrimination was further shown when it came to reëxamination; only 20 per cent of the Negro failures were reëxamined, in spite of the fact that 86.9 per cent of these improved their score anywhere from 3 per cent to 30 per cent. Yet the results have been used and in some quarters continue to be used as though they were the results of scientific measurement under properly controlled conditions.

Quite apart from the question of a controlled experiment, there are other seldom mentioned facts about what was actually found but not made explicit. The intelligence gap between southern Negroes with practically no schools and Negroes living in the North with better educational facilities was eight points greater than the difference between native whites and Negroes. When the native white populations of northern and southern states, presumably of the same stock, are compared a similar difference is found; for instance, Connecticut with only a 35 per cent native white population registered 30 points higher for white recruits than North Carolina with a 99 per cent native-born white population. This is a difference greater by 50 per cent than that shown between the native whites and Negroes. When the factors of bad schools, mass handling, and, to a large extent, examiners with a bias concerning Negro mentality were eliminated, as in the case of Camp Lewis in a northwestern section, Negroes registered a median score superior to the white recruits in Camp Gordon in the South. The Negro recruits from Ohio registered a score higher than the white recruits from every state in the South except Florida. And finally, the Negroes recruited from New Mexico registered a score equivalent to the highest rank of whites — the officers.

The support lent by science to this dogma simply shows that scientists are only human, and many of them choose the easy path to acceptance and popularity. Says Professor Wilson D. Wallis, "We go through life lopsidedly maintaining one thesis and moved from it, if at all, only to some other extreme. . . . We confuse 'facts' with theories, inference with observation, postulate with induction, and relative values with absolute ones. . . . An Aristotle may be able occasionally to regard himself searchingly and dispassionately — but certainly not the ordinary man. Here we come back to the inferiority complex. The truth seeker forgets it, and so comes to grief. He forgets that the ordinary man, at bottom, is always afraid of himself, as of some horrible monster. He refuses to sanction the lie whereby the ordinary man maintains his self respect." [1]

During slavery, when it was against public policy to educate Negroes, and for a period after emancipation, when over 90 per cent of the Negro population were illiterate, it could easily be believed that their illiteracy was a mark of their incapacity, inescapable and eternal. But now educability has been demonstrated; illiteracy has been reduced to 18 per cent; thousands have graduated from standard universities; and thousands have entered the professions. In spite of such facts as these, and in spite of the questionable support of the dogma, belief in the innate mental inferiority of the Negro persists. It tends to crush the Negro's hope of improvement through education; it insists by implication that Negro education is useless; it has for many years tended to distort desire for education into a desire to avoid hard work; and to make of efforts at independent thinking a brand of impertinence and radicalism.

[1] "Some Phases of the Psychology of Prejudice," *Journal of Abnormal and Social Psychology*, January, 1930, p. 418.

The second cardinal belief which constitutes an important element of the dogma concerns the constitutional immorality of Negroes. They are sometimes in charity called unmoral. Dr. Frederick L. Hoffman, after assembling an array of figures on the question, concluded that "all facts prove that education, philanthropy, and religion have failed to develop [among the Negroes] higher appreciation of the stern and uncompromising virtues of the Aryan race."[1] Not long ago, a professor in an eastern college made the statement that less than 2 per cent of the Negro women are virtuous. It got credence in spite of the fact that it is as impossible of proof as a similar statement about any other race. The statistical evidence of immorality consists largely of figures on illegitimacy. Records here are meager, and where found tend to shield those with greater means of secrecy and knowledge of birth control. It is an undoubted fact that the lack of a stable family under the institution of slavery, and the different moral values imposed by the imperatives of the slave market, account for a larger amount of recorded illegitimacy among certain classes of Negroes than among whites. The fact, however, that these differences appear strikingly between classes of the Negro population, and that these rates decline with increased education and developed culture, points to the temporary and circumstantial character of these records rather than to any inherent and unchangeable weakness. However, the number of illegitimate mulattoes and even the prevalence of venereal disease may be said to point at least to a mutual lack of restraint. It is accepted as a fact that in most of the unions of whites and Negroes the Negroes, as a matter of course and for a period as a matter of property, were not the aggressive parties. Records of sales and inspections of Negroes brought to this country as slaves carry no mention of venereal infection. Indeed, it is given as an explanation of the seriousness of its ravages among Negroes that it was a disease new to them, against which they had not developed adequate immunity. There is, however, a theory to explain the mulatto population in what is called the "biological urge" of females of inferior races to mate with males of the superior race. This for many years absolved the dominant group from moral responsibility but did not diminish the immorality. Fortunately the practice is becoming considerably less common.

There are, of course, immoral Negroes; in fact, many such. The

[1] *Race Traits and Tendencies of the American Negro*, p. 329.

assumption in the dogma, however, that this immorality is the result of a constitutional laxity which is peculiar to Negroes as a race, has no certain foundation, and is extremely ungracious; it implies that there is no hope for moral improvement. Another aspect of this dogma is revealed in the well-intentioned act of certain judges in trying cases involving the immorality of Negroes among themselves. They are less severe than the situation would warrant on the belief that the offense is less.

The third cardinal belief noted is closely allied with the second: that Negroes are criminal by nature; that an alleged peculiar emotional instability predisposes them to crimes of violence, particularly sex crimes, and a constitutional character weakness addicts them to petty thefts. In practically every city with a large Negro population their crime rate exceeds their proportion in the population. There are Negro criminals, as no one denies, but the dogma of the criminal nature of Negroes seems unnecessarily severe. It must be urged that a constitutional criminal nature would most certainly have shown itself during the Civil War when the protective hand of the slave master was withdrawn from his family, and the Negro slave stood guard. Figures on Negro crime rarely escape factors completely vitiating for comparative purposes. Thus, judges, prosecuting attorneys, and jury foremen testified before the Chicago Commission on Race Relations that in Chicago, a northern city, there was an unvarying tendency to arrest and convict Negroes more readily than whites, and on less evidence, and to give them longer sentences. The police officers, jurors, and court officials are members of the public and hold the common beliefs about Negro traits. The Negroes, further, have less money to fight their cases, to escape detection, to pay fines, or even, so far as some records go, to bribe officials.

The question of rape is regarded as the most serious of Negro crimes, and it usually gets most serious punishment if it is a case involving a Negro man and a white woman. A predilection for sex crimes is attributed by the dogma to the criminal nature of Negroes. Comparison of statistics on rape, however, does not show as many crimes of this type among Negroes as among certain non-Negro groups. In one part of New York City, to take one example, there were in one year more white persons *indicted* for rape in the first degree than there were Negroes even *accused* of the crime throughout the United States over a period of four years; and more evidence is required by a New York jury than by a hostile mob bent upon lynching. A predilection for sex crimes could scarcely be assigned to a race, with an average population of eight million over a period of thirty years, of which number 675 were charged with the crime. Yet this belief, deepened by its association with the most elemental of human passions, prompts constant and innumerable perversions and extremes of conduct. This sex motif is still an excuse for lynching in the South, and it ran, with more or less prominence, through each of the race riots which occurred in the North around the period of the Negro migration.

It will be found that certain elements of the dogma are being modified among more advanced individuals. Instead of assuming that Negroes are immoral or criminal by nature, they assume that Negroes are immoral or criminal as a result of their inescapable cultural heritage from Africa; that while the condition is not eternal it is one that will require many decades to alter.

Although the three cardinal beliefs listed are among the most dangerous, there are others, less important, perhaps, but worth questioning. (1) The Negro race is believed to be physically repulsive — one encyclopedia, in describing the Negro in 1880, stated that Negroes "emit an odor similar to that of a goat." This dogma is entertained less by those whose children were reared by Negro "mammies" than by those who read about Negroes or are expecting this peculiarity. (2) They are believed to be constitutionally incapable of resisting the ravages of the white man's diseases. Such dogma, until very recently, discouraged programs of health improvement among Negroes as hopeless, although by a little effort their mortality has been reduced 21 per cent in eleven years. (3) They are described as "happy-go-lucky" and "thriftless," although they own farm lands valued at more than two and one-half billion dollars; nearly two million are insured in one large insurance company alone, and one of every four families owns its home.

Some of the familiar and perhaps less serious stereotypes of the Negro will be quickly recognized. For example, that they are boisterous, over-assertive, lacking in civic consciousness; that they usually carry razors, play with dice habitually, are inordinately fond of red and of watermelon, are afraid of ghosts and graveyards. Mr. H. L. Mencken [1] in *The American Credo* has caught up other points: "A Negro's vote may always be readily bought for a dollar." "Every colored cook has a lover who never works and she feeds him

[1] Pp. 111–191 *passim*.

by stealing the best part of every dish she cooks." "Every Negro who went to France with the army has a liaison with a white woman and won't look at a nigger wench any more." "All male Negroes can sing." "If one hits a Negro on the head with a cobblestone, the cobblestone will break." "All Negroes born south of the Potomac can play the banjo and are excellent dancers." "Whenever a Negro is educated, he refuses to work and becomes a criminal." "Every Negro servant girl spends at least half of her wages on preparations for taking the kink out of her hair." "All Negro prize fighters marry white women and they afterward beat them." "All Negroes who show any intelligence are actually two-thirds white and the sons of United States Senators." "The minute a Negro gets eight dollars he goes to a dentist and has one of his front teeth filled with gold." "A Negro ball always ends up with a grand free-for-all fight in which several Negroes are mortally slashed with razors."

Jokes about Negroes, news stories, anecdotes, gossip, the stage, the motion picture, the Octavus Roy Cohen, Hugh Wiley, and Irvin S. Cobb type of humorous fiction, repeated with unvarying outline, have helped to build up and crystallize a fictitious being unlike any Negro. Usually one of two things happens when a Negro fails to reflect the type: either he is considered an exception, or he is "out of his place." The sources of information covering this group that might be useful in dispelling many of these notions are most inadequate. Few white people read Negro periodicals or books; they come in contact with only a few Negroes, usually their servants, whom they erroneously regard as being able to articulate the aims and ideals of all Negroes, and to appraise accurately the significance of racial incidents and personalities.

It is this mass of ideas about the Negro, accumulated through experience, passed on through tradition, embedded in the mores and absorbed even without conscious attention, which is the present concern of students. These are the background of recognition, of classification, and of behavior itself. Compounded of time-saving generalizations, stereotypes, myths, conventions, they determine the attitudes which control racial dogma. They determine the ways of interpreting facts, and even the way of seeing facts. To quote Walter Lippmann again, "Except where we deliberately keep prejudice in suspense, we do not study a man and judge him to be bad . . . we see a bad man." [1]

[1] *Public Opinion*, p. 119.

False notions, if believed, and false preconceptions may control conduct as effectively as true ones. The moral eruptions observed in the reckless unrestraint of the mob mind are, from one point of view, merely an acute phase of the same opinion held by those who condone even while not actually participating in the unpleasant work of the mobs. The "hoodlums," those members of the public least able to sublimate their impulses or restrain their resentments, however acquired, are, in a sense, merely the executioners for prevailing sentiment. The judgment is passed by the community. The riots that have taken place in Washington, Atlanta, Chicago, East St. Louis, and Omaha are striking examples of the accumulated resentments, unchallenged mutual beliefs, of the one race about the other.

It would be interesting to inquire into the effects of this dogma upon the Negroes themselves. It is evident that so long as they are exposed to the dogma they are constantly receiving intimations, both subtle and direct, of their own inferiority. There are many of them who are either insensitive to these implications, or are convinced of their inferior rôle and regard the question as a purely academic one. This is in part an effect of the tradition itself of which they are a part. From the beginning, all Negroes born in the setting characterized by this dogma are "saturated in a tradition of their own incompetence." This is a poison, as one writer puts it, "at the very centers of growth." They grow up in the system inferior not only to other races, but to their own potential selves. They are in the midst of an advanced social system of definite cultural influences, but denied full participation, and they are never permitted to escape the insistent implications of their status and race. Attention and interest are centered upon themselves. They gradually become race conscious. Opinions and feelings on general questions must always be filtered through this narrow screen that separates them from their neighbors. Their opinions are therefore largely a negative product — either disparagement of difficulties or protest.

This enforced self-consciousness has developed strange distortions of conduct: it has increased sensitiveness of many Negroes to slights, and prompted the fabrication of compensations for their inferior station. Natural impulses and desires are balked. Their conduct becomes unintelligible. The processes of thought by which opinions are reached and translated into action are, as a result of their isolation, concealed from outsiders. It has been observed, for example, that the "old-time darky" is passing. This is probably but another way of putting the very real fact that rapidly developing industrialism, increased literacy, mobility, and means of communication, and the irresistible trend of present-day forces, which are upsetting the old order and creating new desires generally, have affected the Negro as they have all others. One student of world race problems observed realistically that the "peaceful co-existence of ruler and ruled is possible only where relations between classes remain static for long periods of time." Such a condition is favorable to the growth of traditions, to the love of common things, and the manifestations of kindliness and loyalty. Those who picture the Negro of four or five decades ago forget that he is being swept along by the same tide that wrecked the institution of slavery and increased the tempo of our whole national life. He is indeed not the same, and it is probably unreasonable to expect him to be.

The World War and the new economic release expressed in migration brought about another shock to traditions, and simultaneously a different outlook on life for Negroes. Over a million and a quarter moved North within the period of fifteen years. The motives have been both economic and sentimental. Both desires are evidences of dissatisfaction and unrest, and these dissatisfactions are in large part the result of changing standards among the Negroes.

The "back to Africa" movement among Negroes was a dramatic demonstration of their attitude toward their status. This rather absurd dream, to which more than a million Negroes, at one time, were contributing their small funds, was more than a gesture to escape America. It was a movement of the class lowest down to fabricate a background and a racial self-respect, to compensate for the prestige and power they have habitually lacked. The extravagant titles of the movement, like those of the Ku Klux Klan, helped to clothe little men with the importance and prestige they otherwise would not enjoy. The movement was significant further, not because of any possibilities of realization, but because it demonstrated the psychology of escape.

Still another expression of the restlessness has been registered in escape of quite a different sort. It is that of leaving the Negro race entirely — "crossing over" it is called. When a person of partial Negro descent, who is to all appearances indistinguishable as a Negro, elects to class himself as a Negro, he voluntarily assumes all of the limitations placed upon that group. But he is an equal of the white man and eligible to all the privileges of his citizenship so long as he forgets the black twig on his family tree. The subject from its very nature does not lend itself readily to statistical treatment, but it is a fact that as the ring around the Negroes grows tighter, it is squeezing out many who can easily escape, and is thus carrying on a process which the most zealous supporters of the American race dogma have declared could never occur, and which they are most anxious to prevent.

It is important to recognize that the most serious clashes of interest come in that vague and intangible world of feeling where reason ceases to function. Attitudes and opinions have been set and ground into tradition. Demand for reasons is absurd and infuriating, because they are perhaps the least important and least convincing factors in a confirmed attitude. Where there is general agreement on the premise they are unnecessary, but where, as in the case of a less prejudiced person, the premise is questioned and it is necessary to support one's attitude, there is a temptation, rarely avoided, to compensate for deficiency in fact by embellishing it to fit the feeling. A Negro becomes a "burly Negro." Objection to the presence of Negroes in a public meeting is based on smell. Instead of smiling, Negroes "grin" or "expose a gleaming row of ivory from ear to ear." The French Military Mission stationed with the American Expeditionary Army circulated (but later withdrew) at the request of Americans and under protest of the French government a clear-cut example of this disposition. It read in part:

> American opinion is unanimous on this [The Negro Question] and permits no discussion of the matter. The kindly spirit which exists in France for the Negro profoundly wounds Americans who consider it an infringement of their national dogmas. . . . We should not sit at the table with them and should avoid shaking hands with them . . . the merits of Negro soldiers should not be too warmly praised, especially in the presence of Americans. . . . The vices of the Negro are a constant menace to the American who has to repress them sternly. The black American troops in France have by themselves given rise to as many complaints for attempted rape as all the rest of the Army. The black is constantly being censored for his lack of intelligence and discretion, his lack of civic and professional conscience. . . .

On the basis of the prevailing dogma, race discriminations are faultlessly logical. When the practices vary it is because the fundamental beliefs vary. The questions raised in this chapter are based largely upon the theories about existing fact which, questionable in themselves, have blinded the eyes of observers to factual contradictions, and prompted hallucinations of fact to support the theory. This body of beliefs expressed in the dogma, compounded of a mixture of truth and fiction, self-interest and passion, forms the structure of public opinion on the question of the Negro. These beliefs, unchallenged, not only magnify themselves and breed others, but react upon the Negro group, distorting its conduct. This distortion tends to provide in turn a sterner pronouncement of these dogmas, and so on indefinitely, and with every step the isolation increases, each group building up its own myths and stiffening its own group morale. If the element of error in the stereotypes can be dissolved; if, indeed, they can even be honestly questioned, many of the inhibitions to normal, rational, and ethical conduct could be removed. As Artemus Ward, famed for his homely wit, once remarked, "It's not ignorance that hurts, but knowing so much that ain't so."

PROBLEMS FOR STUDY

1. The stereotype of the Chinese is a laundryman; the stereotype of an Irishman a pugnacious "Paddy" with long upper lip and pipe; the stereotype of an American Indian is a redskin in war paint with tomahawk, etc. Do these stereotypes facilitate in any way essential understanding of these peoples?
2. List the parallels in the arguments by which women and Negroes were declared inferior.
3. How do children acquire race prejudice?
4. The Army intelligence tests show southern whites inferior in "intelligence" to northern whites. Is this a matter of nature or nurture?
5. The racial dogma insists upon "keeping the Negro in his place." What is meant by the Negroes' place?
6. Does racial dogma change in a progressive society?
7. Racial dogma holds
    a. That a mixture of the races results in a mongrel inferior to both parent stock, and
    b. That mulattoes are superior to unmixed Negroes because of their white blood.

    Does this contradiction reveal any characteristic of dogma generally?

BIBLIOGRAPHY

Thomas P. Bailey, *Race Orthodoxy in the South* (1914).
Robert B. Bean, "Some Racial Peculiarities of the Negro Brain," *American Journal of Anatomy*, September, 1906, pp. 353–389.

Dennis H. Cooke, *The White Superintendent and the Negro Schools in North Carolina* (1930).
Frederick L. Hoffman, *Race Traits and Tendencies of the American Negro* (1896).
George E. Howard, "The Social Cast of Southern Race Prejudice," *American Journal of Sociology*, March, 1917, pp. 577–593.
Charles S. Johnson, Unpublished Documents from a Study of Racial Attitudes being made by Charles S. Johnson, Fisk University.
Walter Lippmann, *Public Opinion* (1927).
Franklin P. Mall, "On Several Anatomical Characters of the Human Brain, Said to Vary according to Race and Sex with Especial Reference to the Weight of the Frontal Lobe," *American Journal of Anatomy*, February, 1909, pp. 1–32.
Marion J. Mayo, *The Mental Capacity of the American Negro* (1913).
Henry L. Mencken and George J. Nathan, *The American Credo* (1920).
T. Wingate Todd, "An Anthropologist's Study of Negro Life," *Journal of Negro History*, January, 1931, pp. 36–42.
Wilson D. Wallis, "Some Phases of the Psychology of Prejudice," *Journal of Abnormal and Social Psychology*, January, 1930, pp. 418–429.

CHAPTER XII

THE FREE NEGRO

The institution of slavery was guided in its growth very largely by economic considerations. So long as personal relations could be maintained between master and slave in the small household it was impossible to escape in individual cases the normal development of sentiments of attachment. Living and working together tended inevitably to humanize these relations. But a master, while feeling attached to his own Negro servant or slave, whom he considered a part of his household, was not always constrained to extend these sentiments to other Negroes whom he did not know. They were aliens, and part of the abstract conception of the Negro, which was feared. Similar distinctions between the personally known Negro and the abstract conception appear even today in many southern communities. White men known to be hostile to the abstract Negro, to his presumed character and aspirations, may go to extreme lengths to protect and help individual Negroes of their acquaintance whom they detach completely in their thinking from all other Negroes.

Under slavery the necessity for Negroes was bound up with the necessity for labor and, in large measure, alien labor. To give stability and security to this economic system the rights of owners had to be protected and the labor made sufficiently mobile to meet the exigencies of production. Thus, the general tendency to conceive this labor supply in the abstract went along with the individual tendency to humanize the relations. This, no doubt, accounts for the extraordinary paradox of increased legislative restrictions upon the slave at the same time that slaves were being manumitted, frequently by the very masters who in their official rôles were responsible for the restrictions. Masters could be certain that they would deal kindly with the slaves attached to their own families but not so certain that other masters would feel the same sentiments. Rather than sell their slaves, therefore, many were disposed to liberate them unless, of course, some strong financial circumstance forced other measures. When it is considered how much of the wealth of the slave owner was represented by the slave himself, it is surprising how many manumissions did occur by will or deed or direct certificate of freedom. This same conflict between economics and sentiment was, without question, responsible for the fact that the legislation of control was almost always more severe in its terminology than in its actual application, and that manumissions continued despite the most drastic prohibitions against this practice.

Slave trading, which became an increasingly important part of the system of slavery in its new economic stress, tended to introduce impersonal relations, breaking the primary bonds between master and slave, and contributing to that ruthlessness by which the institution latterly became known. The development of large plantations and of large labor gangs made impossible the kind of personal relations between master and slave which would support these humanizing sentiments.

It can be noted that in the upper slave states like Virginia and Maryland, where plantations were few and relations close, the number of free Negroes was large, while in such lower plantation states as Mississippi and Alabama free Negroes were extremely few.

There had always been free Negroes in the American colonies. Beginning with the free and indentured Negro servants in the early seventeenth century, this original free status was not affected even

GROWTH OF THE SLAVE AND FREE NEGRO POPULATION IN THE UNITED STATES, 1790–1860 [1]

Census Year	Total Negro Population	Free Negroes		Slaves	Decennial Increase			
					Number		Per Cent	
		Number	Per Cent	Number	Free	Slave	Free	Slave
1860	4,441,830	488,070	11.0	3,953,760	53,575	749,447	12.3	23.4
1850	3,638,808	434,495	11.9	3,204,313	48,202	716,958	12.5	28.8
1840	2,873,648	386,293	13.4	2,487,355	66,604	478,312	20.9	23.8
1830	2,328,642	319,599	13.7	2,009,043	85,965	471,021	36.8	30.6
1820	1,771,656	233,634	13.2	1,538,022	47,188	346,660	25.3	29.1
1810	1,377,808	186,446	13.5	1,191,362	78,011	297,760	71.9	33.3
1800	1,002,037	108,435	10.8	898,602	48,908	195,921	82.2	28.1
1790	757,181	59,557	7.9	697,624				

[1] From E. Franklin Frazier, *The Free Negro Family*, p. 5.

after slavery had become crystallized as an institution. The first census in 1790 showed 59,557 free persons of color in a total Negro population of 757,181; in 1860, the end of the institution, there were 488,070 in a total Negro population of 4,441,830. The largest proportion of free Negroes in the total population was noted in 1830, just before slavery reached its apogee as an economic institution.

John H. Russell lists five sources of increase for the free Negro population: (1) children born of free colored persons; (2) mulatto children born of free colored mothers; (3) mulatto children born of white servants or free women; (4) children of free Negro and Indian parentage; and (5) manumitted slaves.[1]

The extent of increase in the free Negro population due to children born of free colored persons is difficult to ascertain. The fluctuations of public sentiment on the question of manumission introduced qualifying elements which prevented statistical separation of natural and artificial increase. The pressure of life for the Negroes who had been freed would be expected to militate against rapid natural increases. Moreover, the unbalance in the sexes, with a considerably larger number of females than males, and the usually advanced age at manumission of a large proportion of these persons would be expected to affect the number of children born. Frazier notes that of 32 family groups in Richmond County, Georgia, with an average of 5.3 persons to each family, a woman was the head in twenty cases.[2] There is reason to believe that natural increase was slow in this group.

Increase through mulattoes born of free Negro women has some significant documentation in the legislation largely designed to check such increases. Some of the earliest laws of the colonies of Virginia and Maryland were directed against this "abominable mixture, and the spurious issue, which may hereafter increase in this His Majesty's colony and dominion, as well by English and other white men and women intermarrying with them, as by their unlawful coition with them." The stress of the first laws was against intermarriage, and while this practice was checked by the penalty of imprisonment and forfeiture of money for the parties engaged and the officiating minister, it promptly raised the question of illegitimate offspring from the same types of unions unsanctioned. There were so many illegitimate children who were becoming public charges that it was necessary to legalize the binding out of such issue after the manner of

---

[1] *The Free Negro in Virginia, 1619–1865*, pp. 40–41.
[2] *The Free Negro Family*, p. 24.

the indentured servants, and to provide the penalty of a public whipping for the white man involved. Virginia, in 1630, punished soundly a white man, Hugh Davis, by whipping before an assembly of Negroes, for "abusing himself to the dishonor of God and shame of a Christian by defiling his body in lying with a Negro." In 1662 double fines were imposed for fornication with a Negro.

The influence of these laws extended to such northern colonies as Pennsylvania, Massachusetts, and Rhode Island. In 1780, in Chester County, Pennsylvania, mulattoes were one-fifth of the Negro population, and by 1860 they were one-third of the Negro population of Pennsylvania.[1] A further circumstance pointing to increase from this source is in the actual numbers of mulattoes within the free population. In 1850 about 37 per cent of the free Negroes were mulattoes as compared with one-twelfth of the slave population. It is by no means certain, however, to what extent this free mulatto increase was due to issue through white men and free Negro women and to what extent through the manumission of the offspring of slave women and white masters. The laws directed against the unions of white men and free Negro women eventually became so drastic as to keep such issue low.

It seems likely that increase through mulatto children of white servants or free white women, though it did occur, was small. In the early stages of the colony this was fairly frequent, and as in the opposite type of union provoked laws to curb the practice. Benjamin Banneker, the Negro astronomer and mathematician who lived in Maryland (1731–1804), was the mulatto child of a white mother. Cases arising in law and involving this type of admixture and free increase were not wholly uncommon. In 1826, in the case of the *State of South Carolina vs. Mary Hayes*, the defendant, a mulatto, was indicted for keeping a disorderly house. When she was brought up for sentence the judge refused to pass sentence because, although she was an obvious mulatto, which made her a Negro and subject to trial by a court of magistrates and freeholders, it was brought out that she was the daughter of a white woman and thus, logically, subject to trial by a court of General Sessions. The court finally decided that "it was not sufficient that she derived her ancestry from a white mother. The African father reduced her to the same degraded state as if she were a free Negro."

[1] Carter G. Woodson, *Free Negro Heads of Families in the United States in 1830.* p. 12.

In a like case (*State of South Carolina vs. Richard Scott*) the court had to determine whether, under the constitution of the state, the son of a white woman by a Negro father could be allowed to vote or take seat as a legislator. It was decided that "when the words 'Negro, mulatto,' etc. are used in the act (of 1740, Section 1) for the purpose of designating a *class*, they are to be interpreted by their common acceptation ('offspring of a black and white') and not by the rule of *partus sequitur ventrem*, which was only intended to operate on the question of slavery or freedom." [1] Thus, the interpretations of the laws tended to give equal status (or lack of it) to mulatto offspring, whether of Negro or white mothers, despite the principle just enunciated, that the child should follow the status of the mother. Such a practice would naturally tend to obscure the number of cases of the latter type. For practical purposes it is difficult to see how it could have been otherwise if the class distinctions were to be held as rigid as the social arrangement made it necessary to hold them.

The offspring of free Negro and Indian parentage has significant reflection in the present extent of Negro and Indian admixtures in the population which go back to an early period. Herskovits estimates the present extent at about 30 per cent. Conditions of life, slave and free, says one writer on the subject,[2] often led to the union of the Indian and the Negro, and the final extinction of Indian slavery was in part due to the absorbing of the Indians by the more numerous Negroes. There is evidence of the feeling of unity between Indians and Negroes in the fact that in certain of the massacres the Indians murdered every white man and spared the Negroes. There was frequently concerted action in time of insurrection. The Seminoles freely mixed with Negroes. Many Negro slaves escaped to this tribe and were given refuge by them. The Seminole Wars have been described as "not so much Indian wars as Negro wars." Osceola, one of the greatest and fiercest of the Indian leaders, was of mixed Negro and Indian blood, and his own wife had been captured by slave catchers. In the discussion of the Seminole Wars of 1836–1837, in Congress, they were defended on the ground that the Indian fathers of Negro-Indian children were fighting to defend their children

---

[1] Helen T. Catterall (Ed.), *Judicial Cases concerning American Slavery and the Negro*, Vol. II, p. 339.

[2] J. Hugo Johnston, "Documentary Evidence of the Relations of Negroes and Indians," *Journal of Negro History*, January, 1929, p. 26.

from slave takers. When force was used by masters to capture the children of these intermarriages the Seminoles decided upon a course of extermination of the whites.

In Virginia the relations of Negroes with the Indians resulted in the most extraordinary confusion of family lines. Although the original effect was largely that of free increase through the escape of Negro slaves and their intermarriage with Indians, the state is experiencing at present considerable embarrassment in defining racial status where Indian heritages have persisted. The Pamunkys, who are reputed to be the only surviving Indian group in Virginia, are so mixed with Negroes as to make any valid racial distinction impossible. Of the Mattopomys, Thomas Jefferson, in 1800, said, "There remain three or four men only, and they have more Negro than Indian blood in them."[1] The same situation is found in many other Indian tribes remaining in the states of the South and the North as well.

The increase in the free Negro population through manumission was extensive, though subject to fluctuations of public sentiment on the issue of slavery itself. There were sectional differences in this attitude between the North and the South, due largely to the difference in the practicability and usefulness of slavery in the two sections. The climate and work of the North were less hospitable to the institution than in the South, and since it was less profitable in the North there were more frequent occasions for granting slaves their liberty and placing them on their own resources. This section abolished slavery en masse for this reason long before the rise of organized abolition sentiment.

The spirit of freedom and independence which found expression in the Revolutionary War stimulated the manumission of many slaves as an extension of the logic of this movement. Economic conditions were favorable to manumission, since there were no important staple crops which demanded slave labor or made slave property valuable. Between 1790 and 1800 the free Negro population increased 82.2 per cent and continued this rate of increase until the discovery of the cotton gin changed fundamentally the economics of the South and multiplied the value of Negroes as slaves. Between 1810 and 1820 the rate of increase dropped to 25.3 per cent. As the new system developed under the domination of cotton, public sentiment against manumission increased and got further reinforcement in stringent legislation. The increase in the free Negro population

[1] *Ibid.*, p. 33.

dropped still further. In 1860 the increase was only 12.3 per cent. At no period, however, was it completely checked.

To understand that interesting process by which manumissions occurred in spite of opposing laws it is useful to inquire into the motives behind certain types of the manumissions. States were by no means uniform in their legislative regulations, and in practically all of the states the legal efforts to curb the practice reflected local circumstances. They were inspired in varying degrees by economic considerations, or fear of insurrections, or fear of free Negroes becoming public charges, or fear of demoralization of the slave population by the presence of free Negroes, or fear of creating a large free Negro population which could not be incorporated into the body politic. In states like Virginia, Maryland, and Tennessee the curb upon manumission was never extremely severe. It was estimated by the census directors of 1860 that about 20,000 manumissions had occurred between 1850 and 1860. The number is considerable in view of the stringency of laws against manumission and the apparent economic arguments at this period in favor of slavery. Indeed, the figures bear eloquent testimony to the increased humanization of sentiments on the matter among slave owners at the very moment of greatest activity to preserve the institution.

The distribution of the free Negro population by states in 1860 shows striking differences with respect to the policy of the states toward manumission. In such states as South Carolina and Mississippi the laws were more severe. In practically all of the states of the lower South the laws increased in severity up to 1860, and at the most stringent stage there was included, in the rare manumissions sanctioned, the provision that all such manumitted persons must leave the state within a brief stated period or be returned to slavery. But manumissions continued.

Some of the motives behind the liberating of individual slaves were as follows: (*a*) distinguished or meritorious service performed by a slave to the State (in some states this constituted the only grounds on which a slave could be liberated without the consent of his owner, but practically none were ever so freed); (*b*) meritorious or distinguished service to the master of the slave; (*c*) personal interest in the welfare of the slave; (*d*) protest against the evils of the system; (*e*) affectional ties developed between a master or mistress and a slave, and fear that the slave might fall into the hands of unkind masters; (*f*) affectional ties between a master and his mulatto

THE FREE NEGRO

DISTRIBUTION OF THE FREE NEGRO POPULATION ACCORDING TO STATES IN 1860 [1]

State	Population	State	Population
Maine	1,327	Georgia	3,500
New Hampshire	494	Alabama	2,690
Massachusetts	9,602	Mississippi	773
Rhode Island	3,952	Louisiana	18,647
Connecticut	8,627	Tennessee	7,300
Vermont	709	Kentucky	10,684
New York	49,005	Ohio	36,673
New Jersey	25,318	Indiana	11,428
Pennsylvania	56,949	Illinois	7,628
Delaware	19,829	Missouri	3,572
Maryland	83,942	Michigan	6,799
Virginia	58,042	Arkansas	144
North Carolina	30,463	Florida	932
South Carolina	9,914	District of Columbia	11,131
Minnesota	259	Oregon	128
Iowa	1,069	California	4,086
Kansas	189	Texas	355

[1] Adapted from Table II, *The Free Negro Family*, by E. Franklin Frazier, p. 8.

children by slave mothers; and (g) manumission by purchase and self-purchase. Many other motives prompted acts of manumission, but a great proportion of the cases could be grouped under the general classifications listed.

Instances of manumission for meritorious service to the state are by no means unusual, but these nearly always had the consent of the owners, and not infrequently came at the instance of these owners. Cæsar, a South Carolina slave, was liberated for his service to medicine, in compounding a cure for snake bite which was a mixture of hoarhound, lye, and some other ingredients. The legislature freed him and made public the formula. Another Negro slave in South Carolina rendered to Governor Rutledge such important service in the Revolutionary War that a special act of the legislature in 1783 freed him, his wife, and his children.[1]

More numerous were the manumissions for distinguished service to the master. One of the most interesting of these appears in the records of Mississippi, where manumissions for any purpose were rare, because each manumission required a special act of legislation

[1] Carter G. Woodson, *The Negro in Our History*, p. 128.

on the petition of the owner and other white citizens of the community. The case, as cited by Charles S. Sydnor from the records of the Laws of the State of Mississippi, is explained in the act of legislation itself.

An Act, to emancipate Bill, a person of color.

WHEREAS, William Smith, of the county of Hancock, was in his early childhood, by the dispensation of Heaven, deprived of his parents and thrown on the cold charities of the world, with no other patrimony than the negro slave hereinafter mentioned, who by unwearied industry and fidelity, sustained his young master through this helpless season of life, and enabled him to acquire an education adequate to discharge the various duties of a free citizen, and in addition hath accumulated for his master property sufficient to enable him to obtain an easy competency: Therefore, on the petition of the said Smith,

SEC. I. Be it enacted by the Senate and House of Representatives of the State of Mississippi, in General Assembly convened, that William Smith, of the county of Hancock, be, and he is hereby authorized to emancipate from the bonds of slavery, his negro man named Bill, saving the rights of creditors, and provided that the said Smith shall give bond to the State of Mississippi, with good and sufficient surety, to be approved by the county court of said county, and recorded by the clerk thereof, in the penal sum of one thousand dollars conditioned for the good behavior of the Said Bill, and that he shall not become a public charge.[1]

Reflections of personal interest in the welfare of slaves are fairly common in the wills of owners who attempted during their lifetime to maintain humane relations, and who wished their slaves, after the death of the master, to escape the bonds of slavery entirely. This generosity was not confined to wills, but often was extended to large groups of personal slaves to enable them to go to some free state or to Liberia and establish themselves as free citizens. Captain Izard Bacon of Virginia around 1800 liberated and led his 53 slaves to Pennsylvania, where he hoped to find means of transporting them somewhere overseas; and another Virginian, James Smith, trudged to Ohio with his slaves, seeking vainly to colonize them in free territory. John Randolph of Virginia liberated his 385 slaves by will and had them migrate to Ohio, where land was to be purchased to enable them to settle in a colony. The will of Mrs. Hannah H. Coalter of Virginia, probated in 1857, is typical of the sentiment described, and disposed of her 93 slaves in the following manner:

[1] *Laws of the State of Mississippi, 1827*, pp. 56–67.

Fourth. I hereby manumit my faithful servant Charles, and direct my executors to provide him with a fund sufficient to take him to such state or country as he may elect to live in, and pay to him an annuity of one hundred dollars during his life. Fifth. I direct in regard to the balance of my negroes, that they shall be manumitted on the last day of January 1858. And I Authorize and request my said executors to ascertain what fund will be sufficient to provide the usual outfit, and to remove, said negroes to Liberia. And I hereby direct my executors to raise said fund, or such an amount as in their judgment may be sufficient for that purpose from my said estate, and to use the said fund in removing and settling my said servants in Liberia, or any other free state or country in which they may elect to live, the adults selecting for themselves, and the parents for the infant children; and I further direct that if any of my said servants shall prefer to remain in Virginia, instead of accepting the foregoing provisions, it is my desire that they shall be permitted by my executors to select among my relations their respective owners; said election to be made by the adults and parents as aforesaid.[1]

Personal protests of members of a slaveholding society against the general evils of the system could be expressed either by declining to own slaves or by freeing those inherited or otherwise in their possession. The Quakers as a sect were opposed to slavery and for the most part refused to own slaves. Consistent with their conviction, though frequently against community sentiment, they purchased slaves for the sole purpose of liberating them. Such opposition, however, was not confined to Quakers, as numerous court cases explicitly testify. In the case of *Jones vs. Bennet* in which the freedom of certain Negroes was contested in Kentucky (May 1840), the testimony cites:

> Early in the year 1830, John Bennet, who though once an owner of slaves, seems to have been in principle opposed to slavery, liberated a female slave, then the mother of four children, and the wife of a colored man named Levi Jones, once also a slave, and who was emancipated by his master, William Chenault, on the 31st day of May, 1830, in the county of Madison in this state, where both Bennet and Chenault then resided . . .[2]

Such opposition may be attributed as the motivation to the act of Thomas Jefferson in sending his slaves to Ohio, and in a milder degree to George Washington, who expressed himself late in life as being deterred from ridding himself of his slaves only by certain financial considerations which would prove embarrassing.

The affectional ties developing between master and slave, as men-

---

[1] Helen T. Catterall (Ed.), *Judicial Cases concerning American Slavery and the Negro*, Vol. I, p. 246.   [2] *Ibid.*, p. 349.

tioned before, constantly confounded the system, and created a conflict of principles in men who were both officials of the state and owners of slaves to whom they were personally attached. In North Carolina a case was brought by several free persons of color who had been slaves of Major Absolom Tatom, who, though a member of the General Assembly that had been responsible for stringent restrictions on manumissions and on free Negroes, had nevertheless made secret provisions in his will for their emancipation at his death. His will read, in part:

> I give . . . to my friends . . . my negroes George, Cate, Sally and her child with their future increase, young George, and Jack . . . in trust . . . that they will use their best endeavors to procure them to be emancipated . . . for meritorious services rendered me.[1]

The circumstance of his position appears to have been such as to require that the emancipation be effected indirectly. The executors, true to their trust, united in an application to the county court to emancipate them. The court quietly ordered them emancipated, but the clerk for some reason failed to enter the record. The slaves believed themselves free and for fifty years had acted and been accepted as free persons. Then it was discovered that there was no record, and they were confronted with the sudden prospect of loss of freedom. The judgment of the court carried this striking statement:

> An aged man without . . . any descendant . . . is about to descend to the grave. Between him and his slaves exists a tie . . . unknown to the master and the hireling. . . . He does what he can to confer upon them the boon that they hold most dear! Half a century passes away; . . . it is discovered that the records are silent . . . immediately the birds of prey are upon the wing. . . . It would indeed be a reproach to the law, if there were no way in which it could correct the evil, growing, in a measure, out of its negligence.[2]

They were allowed to retain their freedom.

The evidence is abundant that the free Negro population increased through efforts of white slave owners to liberate their children by slave mothers. Wilberforce University in Ohio was originally established as a place for the education of such children of the white planters who were accustomed to visit the summer resort at Tawawa

---

[1] Helen T. Catterall (Ed.), *Judicial Cases concerning American Slavery and the Negro*, Vol. II, p. 189, footnote.   [2] *Ibid.*, p. 189.

Springs.[1] Charles S. Sydnor, in commenting upon the free Negro population of Mississippi,[2] observes that the free Negro increase in the State was at the same time "a monument to the best and worst traits in human society." The "sordid side of the story" was, in Mr. Sydnor's opinion, "that many instances can be given in which the slave owner emancipated a mulatto slave and in the deed or will of manumission acknowledged his own blood relationship to the slave." Of the 773 free persons of color in 1860 in Mississippi, 601 were of mixed blood and only 172 were black.

A case coming into the courts of South Carolina in 1839 for settlement contains enough of the circumstances involved in this type of free Negro increase to be illuminating. An attempt was being made to prove that undue influence had been used by a Negro woman in the making of a will by her former master. Farr, the former master, was unmarried and lived with his mulatto slave woman, Fan, the child of a half-brother of the testator of the will, as his wife. She not only assumed the position of a wife, but controlled all of the domestic arrangements of the family. The issue was a boy, named Henry, who was acknowledged by the testator as his son. It appears that Farr was extravagantly henpecked in this relationship. Fan forced him, out of jealousy, to sell all his other female slaves, threatened on one occasion "to knock his teeth down his throat," and on another to "beat the skin off his back" with a whip. Nevertheless Farr was fond of both the mother and their son. He tried to send the boy to the local white schools, and when refused, sent him away to school. Long before his death he had petitioned the legislature to emancipate the boy. Unsuccessful, he sent the boy away finally to Indiana and provided him with considerable sums of money. His will in part read as follows:

> I want Fan and Henry to be free, I want Fan to have one-half of my estate, and Henry the other half. When Fan Dies I want Henry to have half of Fan's half, and you [Judge J. B. O'Neall] the other half, for your care . . . and should Henry die, leaving no wife or child, I want you to have the whole. I want you to give Henry a good education, and do the best you can with him, and deal out his share. . . . As you think he will improve it. . . .[3]

[1] "Concerning the Origin of Wilberforce," *Journal of Negro History*, July, 1923, p. 336.

[2] "The Free Negro in Mississippi before the Civil War," *American Historical Review*, July, 1927, p. 787.

[3] Helen T. Catterall (Ed.), *Judicial Cases concerning American Slavery and the Negro*, Vol. II, p. 375.

Many of the issue of such unions passed over into the white population. Aside from illustrating one important channel of increase of the free Negro population this type of case also helps to explain the social and economic advantage frequently held by mulattoes and free Negroes, generally, over unmixed Negroes, when the Emancipation Proclamation was issued and for many years afterward.

Manumission by purchase or self-purchase might be a matter, on the one hand, of financial profit to the owner, or, on the other, an act of humanity in which the financial consideration was incidental. An owner indifferent to community sentiment on the principle of slavery might, without financial loss, allow a slave to purchase his freedom, or sell to a free Negro his slave wife or child, instead of selling them to another slave owner. And this happened often. Some skilled Negro slaves bought their freedom with money earned through overtime work. This was true in the case of Lott Carey, the Negro who later became an important figure in the founding of Liberia. The largest number of slaves owned by Negroes belongs in this category.

The condition of free Negroes during the period of slavery was always an anomalous one. A few of them followed the prevailing pattern and held slaves themselves. In 1830, the year for which fullest figures are available, there were 3,805 Negro owners of 12,905 slaves. In a large majority of these cases only one slave was owned. The evidence seems to indicate that the Negro purchases of slaves were primarily acts of philanthropy rather than of profit-making. Their slaves became, most of them, members of the family group and frequently were natural members. Free husbands purchased slave wives or children, and free wives purchased slave husbands. In some cases it was found that formal manumission entailed more difficulty than simple purchase; in others it appears that both husbands and wives used the power of resale as an instrument of family control.

Virginia had the largest number of Negro owners of slaves. There were in this state 983 such owners of 2,236 slaves. In the upper South slavery was not so completely divorced from the pattern of indenture as in the lower South, and Negroes had always been free and privileged to hold Negro servants. Next in numbers of Negro slave owners was the state of Louisiana, where conditions were favorable to this practice in the existence of a mulatto caste, with special privileges and relationships to the white population, strongly French and Spanish in composition. In this state were 956 Negro owners of

4,277 slaves. Certain individuals owned as many as seventy-five slaves. Maryland, a border state, ranked next, with 655 owners of 1,575 slaves, and South Carolina, where another mulatto caste existed, had 467 owners of 2,788 slaves.

TABLE SHOWING NEGRO OWNERS OF SLAVES AND NUMBER OF SLAVES OWNED[1]

State	Number of Negro Slaveholders	Number of Slaves
Alabama	48	197
Arkansas	1	3
Connecticut	1	1
Delaware	9	21
District of Columbia	133	242
Florida	15	92
Georgia	61	205
Illinois	7	11
Kentucky	120	265
Louisiana	956	4,277
Maryland	655	1,575
Mississippi	17	74
Missouri	4	6
New Hampshire	3	3
New Jersey	16	32
New York	21	41
North Carolina	192	624
Ohio	1	6
Pennsylvania	23	50
Rhode Island	3	3
South Carolina	467	2,788
Tennessee	69	153
Virginia	983	2,236
	3,805	12,905

Compiled from Census records of free Negro owners of slaves in the United States, republished in the *Journal of Negro History*, January, 1924, p. 41.

The great majority of the free Negroes, however, found conditions of life inhospitable to their status. There were differences between North and South, and their status was adversely affected by successive codes during the later period of slavery. In the North, despite a theoretical freedom from codes, economic competition was severe, and jobs for them were scarce. Actually there were fewer opportunities for skilled work in the North than in certain of the southern cities. Race prejudice in the North took the place of restrictive codes. There were frequent race riots between the Negroes and the Irish immigrants that were largely economic at base. In 1834 one of the most serious of these riots occurred in Philadelphia, followed by another in 1838, and still another in 1843. There were serious race riots in Cincinnati in 1827, 1836, and 1841. New York, Pittsburgh, and Portsmouth, Ohio, were scenes of other serious outbursts against the free Negro residents.[1]

Although nominally free, in the North they were not allowed suffrage, and were excused from the militia and excluded from the jury. They were taxed as citizens but given few of the privileges of citizenship. The free schools were closed to them, and such separate schools as were available were poorly equipped. The professions and trades were closed to them, since they were not used as apprentices or admitted to the professional or theological schools. Such persistent individuals as James McCune Smith, the physician, who could not enter the American medical schools, went to Scotland for an education. In travel by stage they rode with the baggage or out with the driver. In travel by railway they rode in the smoker. Hotels would not accommodate them, and places of amusement barred them or shut them off in the gallery. Most of the churches confined them to "Negro pews" or to the organ loft. They held jobs on the whole that were menial, or they engaged in domestic service as waiters, coachmen, grooms, barbers.[2] The ministry offered opportunity to some because it required no professional preparation.

In the South the tradition of "Negro jobs" protected both slave and free Negroes in the performance of many skilled occupations. As pointed out, many of the free Negroes had been able to purchase their freedom through their skill, which enabled them to accumulate sufficient for that purpose in overtime work.

In Charleston, South Carolina, in 1850, the slaves were listed as performing 46 different occupations and the free Negroes 50.[3] The latter number did not, however, represent merely an extension of the slave occupations, for while the free Negroes could be tavern and hotel keepers, milliners, storekeepers, the slaves could not; the slaves, on the other hand, were sailors and boatmen, while no free Negroes were so listed.

Frequently, in work, free Negroes were classed with slaves, especially if this was skilled work. The records of southern states show

---

[1] Carter G. Woodson, *Free Negro Heads of Families in the United States in 1830*, p. xl.
[2] George W. Williams, *History of the Negro Race in America, 1619–1880*, pp. 131–132.   [3] Charles H. Wesley, *Negro Labor in the United States* p. 36.

petitions from white workers to the legislatures to pass laws restricting or removing the free Negroes. In Georgia, an act was passed on December 27, 1845, in response to these petitions, and resulted in the severe handicapping of the free Negro labor. It was called: *An Act to prohibit colored mechanics and masons, being slaves, or free persons of color, being mechanics or masons, from making contracts.*[1] The official register of Richmond County, Georgia, in 1819, showed 194 free persons of color, most of these in family groups. Among the 136 adult occupations listed, there were 9 house servants, 30 laundresses, 32 sewers and weavers, 36 skilled workers representing such trades as steamboat pilot, carpenters, saddlers, rafters, and barkers.[2]

The restrictions upon free Negroes in the South were largely of a social nature. The assumption prevailed, supported by the opinion of the courts, that all persons of color were slaves unless they could prove the contrary. Every free Negro was required to give proof of his freedom. His only protection was a certificate with full description, supported by the testimony of white persons. These certificates had to be renewed at stated periods. If his certificate of freedom was not available, he was subject to imprisonment and, after a lapse of time, to sale at public auction. It was illegal for a free Negro to sell goods in other than narrowly prescribed places. He could not sell spirituous liquors or maintain houses of entertainment. Typesetting was barred, and death was the penalty for free Negro or mulatto who printed or circulated literature which could be regarded as inciting unrest among the slaves. He could not vote, serve on a jury, or be a witness in a case in which a white man was a party.

The first achievement of free status had its natural difficulties, and the increasingly repressive legislation brought others. Not all of the free Negroes had trades, and not all of those with trades could practice them. Altogether they constituted a most unfortunate and uncomfortable group. Their associations, especially in the South, were chiefly with slaves. They were hounded out of southern states and mobbed in the North. The state of Louisiana finally enacted an ordinance banishing them sixty days after manumission. South Carolina forced them, poor as they were, to put up bond of $500 or be resold into slavery. After the Missouri Compromise the welcome

[1] *Acts of the State of Georgia* (1845).
[2] Ulrich B. Phillips, *Documentary History of American Industrial Society*, Vol. II, p. 143.

to fugitives and free persons alike chilled into intolerance in the new states. Joel Chandler Harris' classic picture of Free Joe describes the lot of most of them in the South. They were exiles from their own people, without status with the whites, secretly envied and openly despised by the slaves, eternally suspected and hounded by their quondam masters.

The fear of these free blacks, together with the normal difficulty of survival, created a most unfortunate picture in the minds of their contemporaries: their condition was pointed to as proof of the inability of Negroes to support themselves. A contemporary issue of the *Christian Spectator* presents a poignant picture of this class:

> Who are the free people of color in the United States? In what circumstances does philanthropy find them? There are indeed individuals and families who are sober, industrious, pious. But what are the remainder, the mass? Everyone knows that their condition is deep and wretched degradation; but, only a few have ever formed any accurate conception of the reality. The fact is, that as a class they are branded. They have no home, no country, no such personal interest in the welfare of the community, as gives a certain degree of manliness to almost every white man. . . . Three hundred thousand freemen in this country, are freemen only in name, forming only a little else than a mass of pauperism and crime. . . . Here the black man is paralyzed and crushed by the constant sense of inferiority. He has no effectual incentives to manly enterprise. He stands in a degraded class of society; and out of that class he never dreams of rising.[1]

The masses of free Negroes were accused by virtually all communities of being indolent and thievish. The extent to which this was true cannot be determined from simple records of crimes, since, as frequently happens today, the class suspicions often made unwarranted charges. On the other hand, poverty and the difficulty of getting regular employment as free labor in a slave environment could indeed offer strong temptations to theft as the alternative to starvation. There were, in the midst of the general charges against them, some responsible voices raised in defense of their character. Governor William B. Giles of Virginia, in 1829, in a letter to General Lafayette on the question of slavery had this to say about the free Negroes in Virginia:

[1] Quoted in: William Lloyd Garrison, *Thoughts on African Colonization, or an Impartial Exhibition of the Doctrines, Principles and Purposes of the American Colonization Society, together with the Resolutions, Addresses and Remonstrances of the Free People of Color*, p. 128.

In relation to the free people of color, I am far from yielding to the opinion expressed by the intelligent Committee of the House of Delegates of Virginia, and the enthusiastic memorialists of Powhatan, respecting the degraded and demoralized condition of this *caste;* — at least in degree and extent. It will be admitted that this *caste* of colored population attract but little of the public sympathy and commiseration, — in fact, that the public feeling and sentiment are opposed to it. It is also admitted, that the penal laws against it have been marked with peculiar severity; so much so, as to form a characteristic exception to our whole penal code. When I first came into the office of Governor, such was the severity of the penal laws against that *caste*, that for all capital offences short of the punishment of death, and for many offenses not capital, *slavery, sale and transportation,* formed the *wretched doom* denounced by the laws against this unfavored despised *caste* of colored people. About two years since this extreme severity of punishment was commuted into the milder one of confinement and labor for stated periods in the penitentiary. I have also reason to fear, that under the influence of general prejudices, the laws, in some instances, have been administered against them more in rigor than justice. Yet, notwithstanding all these deprecated circumstances, the proportion of convicts to the whole population has been small. During the existence of those extreme punishments, up to the present period, the whole population of this description of people may be considered, at the beginning, to be about 35,000, now increased to about 40,000 in despite of all the efforts of the Colonization Society, and notwithstanding the operation of the laws in favor of emigration, and against immigration. During the existence of these extreme punishments, the annual convictions for offences did not exceed eleven, (11) upon an increasing population of 35,000. Since the commutation of the punishment, the annual average of convicts upon the increased population of 40,000 is reduced to eight, (8) as will be seen by an official report of the Superintendent of the Penitentiary, forwarded herewith. The proportion, therefore, of the annual convictions, to the whole population is as 1 to 5,000. These facts would serve to prove, almost to a demonstration; 1st, That this class of population is by no means so vicious, degraded and demoralized, as represented by their prejudiced friends (friends!) and voluntary benefactors. And 2d, That the evils attributed to this *caste* are vastly magnified and exaggerated.[1]

Despite the general condition affecting this class there did emerge a number of outstanding individuals. In New Orleans property owned in 1860 by free Negroes amounted to $15,000,000.[2] A report of the National Convention of Colored Americans in Philadelphia in 1856 estimated the property and business valuation of free Negroes

[1] Cited in *The Anti-Slavery Record*, August, 1836, p. 8.
[2] Charles H. Wesley, *Negro Labor in the United States, 1850–1925*, p. 50.

in New England at $2,000,000; in Ohio, Illinois, and Michigan at $1,500,000; in New York and Pennsylvania at $3,000,000. James Forten, a Philadelphia Negro sailmaker, was rated at $100,000. When Negroes were barred from the local public schools in New Bedford, Massachusetts, Paul Cuffe (1759–1817), a Negro ship owner, navigator, and trader, built a finer one from his own resources and gave it to the town for all children.

In the uncomfortable situation of the majority of free Negroes there were three courses of action possible which promised some measure of relief: (*a*) return to slavery; (*b*) work toward total abolition of slavery; (*c*) colonization. In certain of the states of the lower South some slaves actually refused freedom in the face of a more miserable existence in nominal free status. Some others voluntarily returned themselves to slavery. In the laws of Mississippi, 1859–1860, is this document of defeat and disillusion:

An Act for the relief of James Wall, a free man of color.

SECTION 1. Be it enacted by the Legislature of the State of Mississippi, that Jim Wall, a free man of color, of the county of Wilkinson, be, and he is hereby authorized, to become the slave for life of Daniel Williams of said county, and for that purpose may appear before the police court of said county, by petition or otherwise, setting forth his desire to become such slave.

SECTION 2. Be it further enacted, That should the said Daniel Williams appear in said police court, at the time of said application by the said Jim Wall, or at any time thereafter, and signify his assent to become the master of the said Jim Wall, it shall be the duty of said police court to order and decree the said Jim Wall to be the slave for life of the said Daniel Williams, as fully to all intents and purposes as other slaves are held in fee simple, giving to the said Daniel Williams as full, and complete and absolute ownership of the said Jim Wall as if the said Jim Wall had been born the slave of the said Daniel Williams, subject to all the laws of descent and distribution in this State.

SECTION 3. Be it further enacted, that this act take effect and be in force from and after its passage.[1]

Approved, February 11, 1860

Virtually all free Negroes in the North were abolitionists at heart although there existed in instances a marked social distance between

---

[1] Charles S. Sydnor, "The Free Negro in Mississippi before the Civil War," *American Historical Review*, July, 1927, p. 781.

them and fugitives and more recently manumitted slaves. The phenomenon is paralleled in more recent times in the attitude of northern Negroes toward more recent migrants to the North. From the free Negro group, however, there came some of the foremost abolitionists. Frederick Douglass of Maryland, James McCune Smith of New York, Lunsford Lane of North Carolina, and a long, distinguished list, were among the most effective figures of their day in advancing the cause of abolition. Free Negroes in the South were restrained by the threat of death from abolitionist activities. However, it was a free Negro, Denmark Vesey, who planned the slave insurrection in Charleston, South Carolina, in 1822, which almost succeeded. The reaction was an immediate blanket of terror over the whole South and more drastic restrictions on both the slave and the free Negro population.

Colonization seemed the one clear way out. It was proposed, at first on purely humanitarian grounds and later as a political measure, to rid the country of an embarrassing population of free Negroes, to send the free Negroes to western states in America, to Haiti or San Domingo, to South America, to Madagascar, and finally to Liberia, on the west coast of Africa. This last proposal, the only one actually put into action, was to be a return to the motherland for the Negroes, and a relief of America from the anomaly of their presence.

The free Negroes were divided on the issue of colonization. Some refused to be banished to a country about which they actually knew no more than the whites, and preferred to continue the struggle for their own rights as free men and for the total abolition of slavery. Others considered that any fate would be better than their present anomalous and hopeless position in America as free Negroes. The largest numbers transported to Liberia during the first important years of the Colonization Society were those who had been freed by masters on condition that they migrate.

It is of sociological importance that the free Negro population, by their longer apprenticeship in freedom, their peculiar relationship to situations and individuals of this earlier society, and their advantage of many years in the acquirement of some property and education, became one of the most valuable forces in the process of Negro family organization following their general emancipation. As a class they correspond to the *Mayflower* party as symbols of stability and mature respectability. They reflect in the larger background and its significance that prestige which revered traditions alone can confer.

When emancipation came there were a half-million free Negroes in America. This about equaled the number of white holders of Negro slaves. The process of individual manumission, by which so large a group had been technically released from the institution, was one of the most interesting in American history. It revealed in its spread and variety and intensity much of the nature of human nature itself. It reflected the long contest between material advantage, by which survival was possible, and those intimate and humane sentiments by which survival is made worth while. It foreshadowed the troublesome problems to be faced in our democracy by the presence of a free population of Negroes now numbering twelve million, for whom neither extinction, nor fixed and universal subordination, nor colonization is a solution.

PROBLEMS FOR STUDY

1. Is there any evidence that total emancipation of Negro slaves would have been accomplished through individual manumissions?
2. Why were there more free Negroes in Virginia and Louisiana than in Mississippi and Alabama?
3. Manumissions increased at a rapid rate immediately after the War of Independence. What factors were chiefly responsible for this increase?
4. Was there a cultural anomaly in the fact of Negro owners of slaves?
5. Why does free Negro ancestry give status to Negro families?
6. Why could not free Negroes before the Civil War establish relationships similar to those established between former slaves and masters after the Civil War?
7. Compare the free Negro in the North before the Civil War with the Negro in the South today.

BIBLIOGRAPHY

The Anti-Slavery Record, August, 1836.
Helen T. Catterall (Ed.), *Judicial Cases concerning American Slavery and the Negro* (1926).
E. Franklin Frazier, *The Free Negro Family* (1932).
William Lloyd Garrison, *Thoughts on African Colonization*, etc. (1832).
Acts of the State of Georgia (1845).
J. Hugo Johnston, "Documentary Evidences of the Relations of Negroes and Indians," *Journal of Negro History*, January, 1929, pp. 21–43.
Laws of the State of Mississippi (1859–1860).

Ulrich B. Phillips, *Documentary History of American Industrial Society*, (1909).
John H. Russell, *The Free Negro in Virginia, 1619–1865* (1913).
Charles S. Sydnor, "The Free Negro in Mississippi before the Civil War," *American Historical Review*, July, 1927, pp. 769–788.
Charles H. Wesley, *Negro Labor in the United States, 1850–1925* (1927).
"Concerning the Origin of Wilberforce," *Journal of Negro History*, July, 1923, pp. 335–337.
George W. Williams, *History of the Negro Race in America, 1619–1880* (1885).
Carter G. Woodson, *Free Negro Heads of Families in the United States in 1830* (1925).
Carter G. Woodson, *The Negro in Our History* (1928).

CHAPTER XIII

SLAVE LAWS AND INSURRECTION AMONG THE SLAVES

The laws for the control of slaves were detailed and minute. Besides those which controlled free persons, and applied also to slaves, there were numerous laws in every slaveholding state which applied to slaves alone. Some of these laws were designed to protect the slave against cruel treatment and guarantee to him a certain modicum of health and happiness. The laws of Georgia as enacted 1833 say:

> Any owner or employer of a slave or slaves, who shall cruelly treat a slave or slaves, by unnecessary or excessive whipping, by withholding proper food or sustenance, by requiring greater labor of such slave or slaves than he or she or they are able to perform, or by not affording proper clothing, whereby the health of such slave or slaves may be injured or impaired, or cause or permit the same to be done, every such owner or employer shall be guilty of a misdemeanor, and on conviction shall be punished by fine or imprisonment in the common jail of the county, or both, at the discretion of the court.[1]

Georgia also had a law against working slaves on Sunday which read as follows:

> If any person shall on the Lords day, commonly called Sunday, employ any slave on any work or labor, (works of absolute necessity and the necessary occasions of the family only excepted) every person so offending shall forfeit and pay the sum of ten shillings for every slave he, she, or they shall so cause to work or labor. (Act of May, 1770)[2]

Other states had similar laws. South Carolina fixed the fine for working a slave on Sunday as £5 current money (act of 1740) and by the same act fixed the maximum hours of labor from March 25 to September 25 at fifteen hours, and from September 25 to March 25 at

---

[1] George M. Stroud, *A Sketch of the Laws Relating to Slavery in the Several States of the United States of America*, p. 13.

[2] *Ibid.*, p. 13.

fourteen hours. Judge J. B. O'Neall of South Carolina, commenting on this law in an elaborate article in *The Industrial Resources of the Southern and Western States*, said: "The time limited and allowed for labor in this section is too much. Few masters now demand more than twelve hours from 1st of March to 1st of October and ten hours from the 1st of October to 1st of March." [1] Louisiana in 1806 passed a law governing hours of work and meals for slaves which read as follows:

As for the hours of work and rest which are to be assigned to the slaves in summer and winter, the old usages of the territory shall be adhered to, to wit: The slaves shall be allowed a half hour for breakfast during the whole year; from the first day of May to the first day of November they shall be allowed two hours for dinner; and from the first day of November to the first day of May, one hour and a half for dinner: Provided however, that the owners who will themselves take the trouble of causing to be prepared the meals of their slaves, be and they are hereby authorized to abridge by half an hour per day the time fixed for their rest.[2]

Cruelty to slaves was a finable offense. The South Carolina law of 1740 said:

If any person shall wilfully cut out the tongue, put out the eye, castrate, or cruelly scald, burn, or deprive any slave of any limb or member, or shall inflict any other cruel punishment, other than by whipping, or beating with a horsewhip, cowskin, switch, or small stick, or by putting irons on or confining or imprisoning such slave, every such person shall, for every such offense, forfeit the sum of £100 current money.[3]

The writer of the article just quoted comments that the punishment is too light for such scandalous offenses.

Most of the states had specific laws protecting the slave in sickness and old age: "For the master is bound by the most solemn obligation to protect his slave from suffering, he is bound by the same obligation to defray the expenses in services of another to preserve the life of his slave or to relieve the slave of pain and danger." [4] In

---

[1] J. D. B. De Bow, *The Industrial Resources of the Southern and Western States*, Vol. II, p. 278. See this article for full discussion of South Carolina's laws.

[2] G. M. Stroud, *A Sketch of the Laws Relating to Slavery in the Several States of the United States of America*, p. 15.

[3] J. D. B. De Bow, *The Industrial Resources of the Southern and Western States*, Vol. II, p. 277.

[4] Judge Wild's decision, quoted by De Bow in *The Industrial Resources of the Southern and Western States*, Vol. II, p. 278.

1669 Virginia law declared: "If any slave resists his master and by the extremity of coercion should chance to die, that his death should not be accounted felony but the master be acquitted from molestation since it cannot be presumed that prepensed malice should induce any man to destroy his own estate."[1] This presumption was evidently not warranted by practice; so all the states passed laws later which defined the conditions under which the death of a slave from punishment was considered a crime by the master. The earlier of these laws punished such offenses by fine, but by 1821 all the states included imprisonment in the punishment. The law of Tennessee in 1799 declared: "If any person shall wilfully or maliciously kill any negro or mulatto slave, on due and legal conviction thereof, etc., shall be deemed guilty of murder, as if such person so killed had been a freeman, and shall suffer death without benefit of clergy.... Provided, this act shall not be extended to any person killing any slave in the act of resistance to his lawful owner or master, or any slave dying under moderate correction."[2] Stroud comments that the fact that correction which causes death can be called moderate is a "solecism too monstrous for sober legislation." Slaves and even free colored people were specifically forbidden to strike or in any way resist a white person under most severe penalties. The Louisiana law read: "Free people of color ought never to insult or strike white people, nor presume to conceive themselves equal to the whites; but on the contrary they ought to yield to them on every occasion, and never speak or answer them but with respect, under the penalty of imprisonment according to the nature of the offense."[3] The Virginia law of 1680 declared that if any slave "shall presume to lift up his hand in opposition against a Christian" he shall be punished with thirty lashes.[4] The South Carolina statute of 1740 provided that "a free Negro, mulatto or mestizo cannot lawfully strike any white person, even if he be first striken ..." and "such slave on conviction shall suffer death."[5] The slave therefore was robbed of all legal self-protection. Furthermore, the slave could not testify against a white person, and hence had no recourse through the courts. Even when

---

[1] John C. Hurd, *The Law of Freedom and Bondage in the United States*, p. 232.

[2] G. M. Stroud, *A Sketch of the Laws Relating to Slavery in the Several States of the United States of America*, p. 23.

[3] *Ibid.*, p. 69.

[4] J. C. Hurd, *The Law of Freedom and Bondage in the United States*, p. 234.

[5] J. D. B. De Bow, *The Industrial Resources of the Southern and Western States*, Vol. II, p. 281.

testifying against another slave, free Negro, mulatto or mestizo, he did so without oath in South Carolina.[1] If, therefore, no other white man was present when a master abused his slave, there was no evidence for convicting such a master.

Another serious problem which affected the protection of the slave lay in the fact that any agent, deputy, or overseer had the same power conferred on him by law as was inherent in the legal rights of the master. The Louisiana law read: "The condition of a slave being merely a passive one, his subordination to his master, and to all who represent him, is not susceptible of any modification or restriction." [2] Most of the abuses of the system arose out of this provision, for the overseer had no such interest in the slave as had the master, and furthermore he usually belonged to a very low and inferior type.

The Supreme Court of North Carolina in 1829 rendered a decision in the case of *State vs. Man* in which it said: "The end [of slavery] is the profit of the master, his security and the public's safety. The subject is one doomed in his own person and his posterity to live without knowledge and without the capacity to make anything his own; who surrenders his will in implicit obedience to that of another." [3] In a North Carolina case (1830) in which a mother was on trial for the murder of her child Judge Ruffin refused to convict the woman of murder because in so doing he would rob the master of his property.[4] The South Carolina law declared: "Slaves shall be deemed sold, taken, reputed and adjudged in law to be chattels personal";[5] except that slaves were exempt from levy for debts until all other property of the debtor had been levied upon.[6] In earlier times, while all slaves were held as chattels, it seems likely that conversion to Christianity changed their status to legal persons held for life.[7] But in later years this provision passed out of sight. If a slave was injured by a third party, the third party was liable to

[1] *Ibid.*, p. 279.

[2] G. M. Stroud, *A Sketch of the Laws Relating to Slavery in the Several States of the United States of America*, p. 28. [3] *Ibid.*, p. 10.

[4] William Goodell, *The American Slave Code in Theory and Practice*, pp. 317–318.

[5] G. M. Stroud, *A Sketch of the Laws Relating to Slavery in the Several States of the United States of America*, p. 11.

[6] J. D. B. De Bow, *The Industrial Resources of the Southern and Western States*, Vol. II, p. 276.

[7] J. C. Hurd, *The Law of Freedom and Bondage in the United States*, p. 210.

the master of the slave, for his hire during his disability, or for his price if permanently disabled. In the latter case the disabled slave was turned over to the one who had paid for his disability.[1] Goodell, writing in 1853, declared: "Slaves are better protected as property, than they are as sentient beings." [2]

In most of the slaveholding states Negroes were forbidden to assemble without having white people present. The South Carolina law forbade as many as seven male slaves traveling on the public road together, unless accompanied by some white person.[3] This of course was a precaution against plots for insurrection. Slaves were not permitted to possess, carry, or make use of firearms or other weapons unless accompanied by a white person, or unless they had a written permit from the master or overseer, or could prove they were employed on their master's estate as a hunter or as a destroyer of mischievous birds or beasts.[4] By the South Carolina law of 1740 slaves were prohibited from blowing horns, beating drums, or in any other way making loud noises, the master being finable for each such offense of his slave.[5] Slaves were not permitted to leave the plantation on which they lived without a written permission from their master or his representative, and any slaves violating this law were subject to punishment by any white person who might choose to question them.[6] Neither could a slave go into the plantation of another without a written permit from his master sending him on business.[7] For loosing a canoe or boat, for its lending, he might be beaten with thirty lashes, and for the second offense have an ear cut off.[8] There were laws against his riding horseback without written permission, against his killing deer, against his having a dog, and against innumerable other petty offenses.[9]

Of course the slave was subject to the laws against major crimes: theft, arson, murder, rape, concubinage, incendiarism, counterfeiting, etc. In all such crimes the punishment for slaves was extremely heavy — usually death. According to Stroud there were sixty-eight offenses in Virginia law in the case of which the punishment for slaves was death.[10] In major crimes trial by jury was common, but

[1] Cf. William Goodell, *The American Slave Code in Theory and Practice*, pp. 205–206.   [2] *Ibid.*, p. 201.
[3] J. D. B. De Bow, *The Industrial Resources of the Southern and Western States*, Vol. II, p. 280.   [4] *Ibid.*   [5] *Ibid.*
[6] G. M. Stroud, *A Sketch of the Laws Relating to Slavery in the Several States of the United States of America*, p. 69.   [7] *Ibid.*, p. 71.
[8] *Ibid.*, p. 71.   [9] *Ibid.*, pp. 72–75 *passim*.   [10] *Ibid.*, pp. 77–80.

in minor crimes trial by justices, or justices and freeholders, was the practice. In Virginia slaves were tried for all save capital offenses by five justices, a unanimous decision being necessary for conviction. In Georgia three justices conducted the trial; in Louisiana one justice and three freeholders; in South Carolina one justice and two freeholders; in Mississippi one justice and two slaveholders. In South Carolina a majority only of the court was necessary for conviction, and in Louisiana half of the court. In Kentucky one justice of the peace could try and condemn a slave. Whipping was the most ordinary punishment, and this was often applied by masters without recourse to courts, and the patrolmen — the "patter-rollers" as the Negroes called them — were licensed to whip Negroes whom they caught away from home without permits. As a result of this loose procedure the overwhelming mass of punishment of slaves never found a place in the criminality records.

Many people have had an idea that there was little or no crime by Negroes during the slave régime. This impression will be quickly dispelled if one consults the elaborate studies contained in *Judicial Cases concerning American Slavery and the Negro*. Here the Carnegie Foundation has compiled many hundreds of decisions in the courts of Virginia, West Virginia, Kentucky, North Carolina, South Carolina, and Tennessee. In these lists can be found cases of murder, rape, attempted rape, arson, theft, burglary, and practically every conceivable crime.

The Virginia file of crime for 1780 to 1864 included 90 slaves convicted for arson, of whom 29 were women; 257 for burglary; 15 for highway robbery; 20 for stealing horses; 24 for other types of stealing; 346 for murder (including murder of masters 56, mistresses 11, overseers 11, free Negroes 7, slaves 85, children 12, and others); 56 for poisoning; 111 for assault; 73 for rape; 32 for attempted rape. We shall discuss later in this chapter the cases of insurrection.[1] Such a catalogue of crimes forever lays to rest the boast that there were no criminal slaves, and that the régime worked with such harmony and good will that there was little friction between whites and blacks. One must not forget also that most of the minor offenses, and often the major offenses of one slave against another slave, never got to the courts at all. They were settled by the master, with the whip or by confinement, and occasionally by selling the offending slave farther South.

[1] Cf. pp. 267–273.

The number of Negro prisoners in state prisons and penitentiaries in the slave states in 1850 was, according to W. O. Blake, 323, as against 988 native whites; in the northern or non-slaveholding states the corresponding figures were 565 and 2,271.[1] Louisiana and Virginia kept more careful records than other states, and their criminal reports show great variety in crime. In Louisiana in 1860 there were 96 slave prisoners and 236 white prisoners; 11 free colored prisoners and 83 of the slaves were serving life terms. Classed by crime, 12 of them had been sentenced for arson, 3 for burglary or housebreaking, 28 for murder, 4 for manslaughter, 4 for poisoning, 5 for attempts to poison, 7 for assault with intent to kill, 2 for stabbing, 3 for shooting, 20 for striking or wounding a white person, 1 for wounding a child, 4 for attempts to rape, and 3 for insurrection. This catalogue is notable for its omissions as well as for its content. While there were four white inmates of the prison who stood convicted of attempted rape, there were no Negroes who had accomplished that crime. Likewise as compared with 52 whites and 4 free Negroes serving terms for larceny, there were no slave prisoners in that category. Doubtless on the one hand the Negro rapists had been promptly put to death, and the slaves committing mere theft had been let off with whippings. Furthermore there were no slaves committed for counterfeiting or forgery, horse stealing, slave stealing or aiding slaves to escape.

It would go without saying that punishment of crime would be harshly administered in a primitive society such as that represented in the early colonies. Henry S. Cooley, in his study of slavery in New Jersey, quotes an old authority on the punishment of a Negro convicted of murder as follows: "Thy hand shall be cut off and burned before thine eyes. Then thou shalt be hanged up by the neck until thou art dead, dead, dead; then thy body shall be cut down and burned to ashes in a fire, and so the Lord have mercy on thy soul, Cæsar." [2] It is to be hoped the Lord did have mercy, for the judge had none. Many cases of burning at the stake are on record in the old colony of New Jersey. The crimes for which this severe punishment was meted out varied from burning of barns to murder and rape. The southern slave states were no whit behind New Jersey in their cruelty of punishment. In North Carolina, if a slave was found to have testified falsely, he should have one ear

[1] *The History of Slavery and the Slave Trade, Ancient and Modern*, pp. 818–819.
[2] *A Study of Slavery in New Jersey*, p. 39.

nailed to a pillory, where he must stand for an hour, and then this ear was cut off, and then the other ear was nailed to the pillory and at the end of a second hour the second ear was cut off. The slave was then whipped with thirty-nine lashes.[1] In case a slave in North Carolina was caught stealing hogs, cattle, or horses, his ears were cut off and he was whipped according to the statutes of 1741.

In case a slave lost his life during punishment the master was reimbursed by a poll tax levied on all slaves of the county. In 1758 this law was so amended that instead of execution for certain crimes, the slave was to be castrated, and for a second offense might be put to death. The law was so revolting that it was not long enforced. In 1729 Maryland passed a law which recited that former punishments had not been sufficient to deter crime and that Negroes in the future convicted of petit treason, murder, burning of dwelling houses, etc., should be condemned "to have the right hand cut off, to be hanged in the usual manner, the head severed from the body, the body divided into four quarters, and the head and quarters set up in the most public places of the county where such act was committed."[2] It is unnecessary to cite further instances of cruelty in punishment, since those who are interested in further detail may read them *ad nauseam* in Stroud's *A Sketch of the Laws Relating to Slavery in the Several States of the United States of America*, Goodell's *The American Slave Code in Theory and Practice*, or Hurd's *The Law of Freedom and Bondage in the United States*. These works were published in 1856, 1853, and 1858, respectively, and are replete with all the horrible details which could be gathered together to turn the public against a system in which such evils could exist.

The basis of much of the severity of punishment was undoubtedly an ever present fear of insurrection. Goodell quotes Wheeler's *Law of Slavery* as saying: "It must be remembered that the primary object of the enactment of penal laws is the protection and security of those who made them. . . . And the severity of those rules will always bear a relation to that danger, real or ideal of the other class."[3] The laws against assemblage of slaves, the laws against education of slaves, the laws against Negroes having firearms, the laws against

---

[1] Cf. John S. Bassett, *Slavery and Servitude in the Colony of North Carolina*, p. 30 f.

[2] G. M. Stroud, *A Sketch of the Laws Relating to Slavery in the Several States of the United States of America*, p. 185.

[3] *The American Slave Code in Theory and Practice*, p. 310.

runaway slaves, and scores of others were undoubtedly partly due to the fear of insurrection. It was fear of insurrection also which tightened the laws against the liberties of free Negroes, for the South constantly feared that this class would stir up strife and incite insurrection. Joshua Coffin says that no free Negroes were leaders of slave insurrections, with the exception of Denmark Vesey, who led an uprising in Charleston in 1822;[1] but this seems not to have had much weight in southern opinion. H. M. Henry calls attention to the fact that South Carolina in 1690 provided the death penalty for an attempt to instigate an uprising, which could mean nothing else than that such uprisings were feared. The first of the great insurrections occurred in New York in 1712. As narrated by Coffin it took place as follows: "The Negroes sat fire to a house in York City, and Sunday night in April about the going down of the moon. The fire alarmed the town who from all parts ran to it; the conspirators planted themselves in several streets and lanes leading to the fire and shot or stabbed the people as they were running to it."[2] The conspirators were soon overpowered; eighteen were put to death and many killed themselves. Mr. Neau, who ran a school for colored children, was charged with being responsible for the uprising, but it was proved that his school had nothing to do with it. "However, a great jealousy was now raised and the common cry very loud against instructing the Negroes."[3] In 1720 there was a small uprising in South Carolina. In 1722 a group of Negroes on the Rappahannock river in Virginia gathered for killing the people at church, but were dispersed without bloodshed. So great were the fears of insurrection in Boston in 1723 that two Negroes were not permitted to idle together, and "in addition to the common watch a military force was not only kept up, but at the breaking out of every fire a part of the militia were ordered out under arms to keep the slaves in order."[4] A law was also passed that on the breaking out of a fire no Negro, Indian, or mulatto should leave his master's house during the continuance of such fire. In 1728 there was an insurrection of slaves in Savannah, Georgia; in 1730 such an insurrection occurred in Williamsburg, Virginia, and another in South Carolina.

---

[1] *An Account of Some of the Principal Slave Insurrections, and Others, Which Have Occurred, or Been Attempted, in the United States and Elsewhere, during the Last Two Centuries*, p. 7.   [2] *Ibid.*, p. 10.
[3] *Ibid.*, p. 10.
[4] *Ibid.*, p. 12.

SLAVE LAWS AND INSURRECTION 269

There were also other uprisings. Thus, there was an insurrection at Portsmouth, New Hampshire, in 1732 and at Burlington, Pennsylvania, in 1734; there were three in South Carolina in 1739, and one in New York in 1741; in 1755 there was an uprising of house slaves in Cambridge, Massachusetts; there was an insurrection in Boston in 1768; and one in Virginia in 1775. Many of these were frustrated before any damage was done.[1]

One of the first uprisings in the South was that at East Jersey, near Somerville, in 1734, which was put down with severity. One Negro was hanged, others had their ears cut off, many were whipped.[2] Another uprising was that at Stono, South Carolina, in 1739. This insurrection was incited by the Spanish in Florida — twenty-one white people were murdered, and forty-four Negroes were executed.[3] Another formidable uprising was the insurrection in New York in 1841, after which thirteen Negroes were burned alive, eighteen were hanged, and eight transported.[4] Still more formidable was the Gabriel plot in Richmond, Virginia, in 1800. It was reported afterward in the papers that two Frenchmen and certain other profligate and abandoned whites were conniving with the Negroes. Gabriel, known as General Gabriel, who was the slave of a Mr. Prosser, was to lead the Negroes. "The conspirators were to have seized the magazine, the treasury, the mills and the bridges across the James River. They were to have entered the city of Richmond in three places with fire and sword, to commence an indiscriminate slaughter — the French only excepted. . . . The city of Richmond and the circumjacent country are in arms and have been so for ten or twelve days past. The patrollers are doubled through the state and the Governor impressed with the magnitude of the danger has appointed for himself three Aides-de-camp."[5] So runs the account given in a letter from a resident of Richmond at the time. Thirty-six or more Negroes were executed immediately. Gabriel was captured on board a boat at Norfolk and was executed. The legislature met in secret session and resolved; "That the Governor [Monroe] be requested to correspond with the President [John Adams] on the subject of purchasing

---

[1] *Ibid., passim.*
[2] Henry S. Cooley, *A Study of Slavery in New Jersey*, p. 43.
[3] Cf. Howell M. Henry, *The Police Control of the Slave in South Carolina*, pp. 149–150.
[4] Joshua Coffin, *An Account of Some of the Principal Slave Insurrections*, etc., p. 15.   [5] *Ibid.*, p. 25.

land without the limits of this state, whither persons obnoxious to the laws, or dangerous to the peace of society may be removed." Not being successful in this attempt, the legislature in 1805 passed the following resolution:

> Resolved that the Senators of this state in the congress of the United States, be instructed, and the representatives be requested to exert their best efforts for the obtaining from the General Government a competent portion of territory in the country of Louisiana, to be appropriated to the residence of such people of Color as have been or shall be emancipated, or may hereafter, become dangerous to the public safety.[1]

In Coffin's opinion, it was this insurrection which was directly responsible for the formation of the Colonization Society in 1817.

Still another major plot was the plan of the slaves in Camden, South Carolina, to fire the powder magazine on July 4, 1816, and then collect in another section of the town, falling upon the whites unawares. The plot was revealed by a loyal slave; seventeen were arrested, and five were executed.

In 1822, Denmark Vesey, a free Negro of Charleston, South Carolina, in company with slaves — notably, Gullah Jack, Monday Gill, and Peter Payas — planned to rise suddenly, burn the town, murder the inhabitants, and sail for the West Indies. Again a loyal slave betrayed the plot. One hundred and thirty-one were arrested, thirty-five were executed, and thirty-two were deported.[2] There had been a little African church in Charleston led by one Morris Brown, a Negro (he later moved to Philadelphia and was elected Bishop of the African Methodist Episcopal church in 1828), and suspicion was at once fastened on that church, but Brown and his members seemed to be innocent. Denmark Vesey was a native-born African who in 1800 had drawn a prize of $1500 from the East Bay St. Lottery in Charleston. With this money he bought his freedom. At his home there had gathered from time to time the Negroes who made up the conspirators. John B. Adger, who afterward (1847) established a Presbyterian church for Negroes in Charleston, found great opposition to his scheme, because of the 1822 uprising and because some people still felt the little African church was connected with it. He says of the plot: "A very profound impression was made by these occurrences upon both the white and black population of the City."

[1] Joshua Coffin, *An Account of Some of the Principal Slave Insurrections*, etc., p. 29.
[2] Cf. H. M. Henry, *The Police Control of the Slave in South Carolina*, p. 152.

After twenty-five years he found "public sentiment" very "sensitive" in the "good old city."[1]

Perhaps the most serious uprising, and certainly the one that created the most profound impression on the white people of the South, was that which occurred in Southampton County, Virginia, in 1831, and which because of its leader was commonly called Nat Turner's Rebellion. Nat Turner was born October 2, 1800, as the slave of Mr. Benjamin Turner. He was later purchased by Mr. Thomas Moore and belonged to Mrs. Joseph Travis at the time of the rebellion. Mrs. Travis was the widow of Thomas Moore. The chief henchmen of Nat were Henry Edwards and Hark Travis. Nat Turner was an extraordinarily bright child, and was given instruction by his owners in reading and writing. He later accumulated considerable knowledge. In his confessions after his arrest he stated that he had received certain revelations in his childhood which convinced him he was to play some kind of remarkable rôle in life. As he grew up he became fanatically religious and frequently heard voices and saw visions. He became a person for whom the slaves had the greatest reverence, and since he was a preacher he had full access to all the slaves. He was shrewd enough to remain in seclusion enough to keep up the hoax of his being a special or inspired personage. From all sources it seems clear that his mistress was most lenient and excessively kind. On the evening when the uprising was to start (Sunday, August 21, 1831) Nat feigned sickness, for he feared that if he went to supper and saw all the old surroundings his heart would soften and he could not carry out his threat. Mrs. Travis, his mistress, is said to have prepared him a special supper and taken it to him herself. Late that night, after all the white people were asleep, Nat and six other conspirators went to the home of Joseph Travis, where they were joined by Austin, another slave. Here Will, Hark, and Henry brutally murdered Travis and his wife and three children, Nat Turner saying he could not kill his own master and mistress. From there they proceeded to one house after another until fifty-five white persons had been murdered. By this time a band of sixty Negroes, mounted and armed, were moving on their terrible march of destruction. As the massacre went forward many faithful slaves who had become aware of the danger hid their masters and mistresses and thus saved them from massacre. The insurgents, who could not withstand the temptation of the wine cellars of these

[1] *My Life and Times, 1810–1899*, pp. 50–55 and 164–165 *passim*.

prosperous Virginia farmers, soon became intoxicated and unmanageable. Because of this fact they were easily dispersed on the afternoon of August 22 by a small band of white men who had come together for the protection of their homes. Many Negroes were shot on sight. Many others were given trials and executed. It is estimated that at least one hundred Negroes lost their lives. But Nat Turner was still at large. Hiding in a cave which he had dug not far from the scenes of the terrible massacre, he was not captured until October 30. The trials of the conspirators seem to have been conducted in an orderly fashion — at least as orderly as could be possible under such great provocation. Turner's trial began on Saturday, November 5, and on the following Friday he was hanged. Officially the terrible orgy was over.[1] But its effect was far-reaching. Many false alarms followed one after another. A general hysteria was spread throughout the whole of Virginia and North and South Carolina. Indeed the whole South shuddered to think what might happen in any community. Almost every slaveholding state passed much more stringent laws for the control of the slaves, and a fear and hatred of the free Negroes began to grow. Many people felt that free Negroes must be sent out of the South. Indeed, many of the states passed drastic laws forbidding the freeing of slaves save for very meritorious conduct. The insurrection also gave a text for the abolitionist which was hard to answer. If slaves who were greatly in the minority were willing to risk life and all for freedom, then freedom must be a dear hope for them. Drewry says it was the forerunner of the great slavery debates and was indirectly responsible for bringing about abolition.[2] This is perhaps too strong a statement, but it undoubtedly was a very telling blow at the slavery system.

One wonders as he reads history, not why insurrections occurred, but why they did not occur more often. Of course, the slaves must have known they had little chance of success. Nevertheless, humanity has the spirit of freedom planted deep within it, and will risk all in the barest hope of gaining it. Furthermore, the ruthless murders in the various uprisings, together with the other crimes committed

[1] The account here given was taken from a pamphlet printed within a month after the events and called "An Authentic and Impartial narrative of the Tragic Scenes which were witnessed in Southampton County"; also from the very excellent volume by W. S. Drewry, *Slave Insurrections in Virginia (1830–1865)* — a doctor's dissertation at Johns Hopkins University, 1900. The facts here are carefully gathered, but one would be forced to dissent from the conclusions.

[2] William S. Drewry, *Slave Insurrections in Virginia (1830–1865)*, p. 181.

every year by slaves, prove they were not altogether craven and cowardly. There must have been some bonds of friendship between slave and master which eased the burden of slaves and prevented more uprisings. The Negro slaves were human. They could and did commit heinous crimes, they could and did revolt against injustice, but also they could be, and were, as faithful a group of people as the world ever saw. That there was as little crime as there was, and that there were as few revolts as there were, must always be the marvel of those of us who look back upon this civilization.

PROBLEMS FOR STUDY

1. Why was the killing of a slave in punishment not usually considered murder?
2. What crimes would be most likely to be committed by slaves?
3. Were there motives which led the planters not to report slave crimes to the officers of the law?
4. What influence did the uprisings in the West Indies have on the slave owners in America?
5. How much influence did fear of insurrections have on the making of stringent laws for the control of slaves?
6. Were free Negroes responsible for slave insurrections or not?
7. Were insurrections due primarily to cruel treatment or to man's desire to be free?
8. What influence, if any, has the fear of insurrection left in the psychological reactions of the white South?

BIBLIOGRAPHY

Helen T. Catterall (Ed.), *Judicial Cases concerning American Slavery and the Negro* (1926).

Joshua Coffin, *An Account of Some of the Principal Slave Insurrections, and Others, Which Have Occurred, or Been Attempted, in the United States and Elsewhere, during the Last Two Centuries* (1860).

William S. Drewry, *Slave Insurrections in Virginia (1830–1865)* (1900).

William Goodell, *The American Slave Code in Theory and Practice* (1853).

Howell M. Henry, *The Police Control of the Slave in South Carolina* (1914).

John C. Hurd, *The Law of Freedom and Bondage in the United States* (1858–1862).

George M. Stroud, *A Sketch of the Laws Relating to Slavery in the Several States of the United States of America* (1856).

CHAPTER XIV

THE EFFECT OF SLAVERY ON THE NEGRO

Slavery is frequently referred to as the school through which the Negro race passed in its progress from a primitive state to civilization. It was, indeed, the means of introduction of African natives to the American culture. The effects of this racial experience have been more or less manifest in the life of this group since its sudden emancipation. These effects may be classified for convenience of treatment as physical, social and economic, and psychological.

The physical effects of slavery are often overlooked or understressed because, in certain significant respects, they are more closely related to the commercial than to the social aspects of the slavery system. Nevertheless, if there is any value in physical selection and survival, there is perhaps no more sensitive example of this in history than the cold and almost organic selection for which the slave trade was responsible. For every slave introduced into the routine of the American slave system, from two to five died or were killed on the way. Thomas F. Buxton estimates that for every slave landed safely on a plantation five were lost,[1] and he is supported in this estimate by Norman Leys.[2]

The African slave trade was aided by the intertribal warfare which kept numerous slaves in the possession of tribes. As the trade became widespread and highly profitable, there were deliberate slave raids which entailed great loss of life. The march to the coast, hunger, the harsh measures of the slave drivers, the exposure to contagion in the close quarters of the slave barracoons, and the horrors of the notorious middle passage, the long ocean voyage on which the victims were packed close in the foul and unsanitary holds of the slave ships, resulted in an excessively high toll. It has been estimated that the mortality on the journey from the interior to the coast amounted to five-twelfths of the entire number cap-

---

[1] *The African Slave Trade and Its Remedy*, pp. 66–67.
[2] Cf. Louis Le Fevre, *Liberty and Restraint*, p. 101.
[3] *Ibid.*, p. 103.

tured.³ Since no careful records were kept, this may be an extreme figure, but it is known that this mortality was extremely high.

There are better estimates for the mortality of the middle passage. A journey required about fifty days. Slaves were cheap in Africa but high in America, and this fact encouraged overcrowding. The records of the English African Company, for the period 1680 to 1688, show 60,783 Negro slaves shipped, of which number 14,387 were lost in the middle passage. This is 23.7 per cent of the number. Altogether, this was an experience calculated to eliminate weaklings. Says Le Fevre: "From the standpoint of the American slaves, the most significant aspect of the slave-trade was its frightful efficiency in weeding out feeble bodies and easily depressed minds. Every Negro who survived proved by the mere fact of being alive, his physical and mental capacity for endurance." [1]

There is some reason for attributing to this drastic selection the fact that under the average conditions of slave life in the United States this slave population increased at a rapid rate and reached an almost unprecedented rate of fecundity. Dr. Louis Dublin asserts that the birth rate among the American slaves approached the limit of reproductive capacity.[2] It was, no doubt, this physical stamina which made survival possible. To this fact might be added the reasonable speculation that the matings for the purpose of breeding came as close to the physical ideal of the eugenists as is possible in human society. It is not likely that a slave owner, with responsibility for the unproductive years of life of children, and of weaklings, would be less careful about the breeding of his slaves, when this could be controlled, than about the breeding of his cattle. Nor would he, if reasonably careful, permit obviously inferior physical strains to be propagated.

A first important effect of slavery, thus, was upon the physique of the Negro, and to his physical stamina may be, indeed, attributed the special capacity for work usually regarded as racial. This stamina seems to be qualified by the high mortality of Negroes during the first years of freedom. However, as noted elsewhere in this volume, the mortality of slaves from tuberculosis, the chief scourge, was less than that of the white population generally, during slavery. The fecundity has remained high, and the balance of births over deaths, even at the point of greatest disparity in these rates, was never so fatal to the Negro as to the Indian.

[1] Cf. Louis Le Fevre, *Liberty and Restraint*, p. 108.
[2] *Health and Wealth*, p. 257.

The social effects of slavery have been of such a pronounced character as to make of the Negro population an extraordinarily valuable laboratory case for the study of social organization. In one sense normal social life with them began with their emancipation. They entered this new free status so recently that it is possible to trace the stages of social organization almost within the span of one long life. This is notably true of the Negro family.

Under slavery it was neither possible to continue the family pattern of Africa nor to build up a family structure on the pattern of the American culture. There could be quasi-unions but none binding within themselves. There could be no effective internal discipline, nor family tradition through which stability is assured, nor control over the children, nor inheritance of property by which the material structure of the family is given reinforcement. The structure lacked, essentially, the moral codes which are expected to operate in normal American family life. A natural result was that the emancipated slave entered upon his freedom with a looseness and insecurity in his family life and a vagueness about the moral codes which should support it.

E. Franklin Frazier's studies of the Negro family reveal this process of organization after slavery. He points out that with the acquirement of property, education, and a measure of economic security, stability has increased. Except in the more isolated culture pockets, inaccessible to contact with the dominant culture patterns, there are few areas in which pronounced development in this respect has not been shown. There is, however, no escaping either the fact or the cause of the first condition.

Involved in the question of the family are certain other social problems, not the least important of which is that of illegitimacy, because of the relationship of this problem to social and moral codes. The illegitimacy rates have been excessively high among Negroes since slavery, and it is evident that the tendencies have been merely extensions of habits and values instilled during slavery. What was natural and non-moral mating or breeding of slaves during slavery took on the name and stigma of illegitimacy in the changed political status of the Negro. There has probably never been the amount of uncontrolled relations suspected, and in the comparisons of rates of illegitimacy usually made with the white population the figures are influenced by the fact that more Negro cases find their way into the records, and more suspected cases involving Negroes are classified as illegitimate. Nevertheless the rate has been excessively high. Du Bois estimated the rate at 25 per cent in 1908.[1] Frazier, in a comprehensive survey of studies of illegitimacy and of recent figures, estimates that illegitimate births constitute about 15 per cent of total Negro births at present.[2]

The low economic status of Negroes at the time of their emancipation was a natural result of slavery. Slaves did not own property; they were property. The transition in status likewise demanded those accompanying traits of thrift, providence, the sense of money values and the whole complex of vested interests, which the institution had no obligation to pass on to the slave. Except among the free Negro class, there was little ownership of property. But the slaves did acquire skill and habits of routine labor which served many of them well in their freedom.

The higher valuation placed upon skilled slave artisans in the slave market, and the increased interest on the investment for their masters through the leasing or hiring of the skilled slaves, early encouraged schooling in the crafts. For thirty years after slavery their skill and the position which it gave to them in the industrial life of the South were sustained by Negro artisans against the serious competition of the free white laboring class. Much of the economic self-sufficiency attained by Negroes after slavery may be attributed to this advantage. It was, undoubtedly, one of the most important heritages of the institution.

With respect to the economic factor, a distinction should be made among Negroes themselves. For the institution neither served all Negroes alike nor drew from them the same type of response. Not all Negroes were good slaves any more than all slave masters were cruel, or kind, as one tradition or the other would have it. The most common habit which the system would be likely to inculcate was that of dependence. The slave had no need to think of providing his food or clothing, or of taking care of himself in his useless days. Such providence would not only have been needless, but most certainly would have been interpreted as a discourtesy to the master, or supererogation. All that was expected of slaves was labor and loyalty and enough animal intelligence for labor without too much waste. It would be expected that generations of such dependence would have some effect on the habits of life of many Negroes after slavery, and it

[1] W. E. B. Du Bois (Ed.), *The Negro American Family*, p. 152.
[2] E. Franklin Frazier, "An Analysis of Statistics on Negro Illegitimacy in the United States," *Social Forces*, December, 1932, p. 257.

did. There are today distinct survivals of these habits of dependence, stronger perhaps among the older generation of Negroes than among younger Negroes. This appears in the practice, once very common, of electing some friendly white family to serve as guardian angel in the matter of support; and of relying rather benignly upon their "white folks" for intimate advice as well as ultimate relief from distress. Sometimes the relationship was based upon affectional ties established during slavery and sustained afterward. In perhaps too many cases the Negroes, out of their long habit of dependence, were avoiding the serious responsibility of self-support. Booker T. Washington, in a memorial address for Samuel C. Armstrong, founder of Hampton Institute, declared that the greatest injury that slavery had done Negroes was that of depriving them of a "sense of self-dependence, habit of economy, and executive power." [1]

The economic and social system in which Negroes were set after slavery had something to do with this dependence; perhaps reinforced it. For these conditions were only slightly altered from the original situation under slavery. More especially was this true in the matter of personal safety and security. The protection of some responsible white person was often needed against other white persons, or against the too drastic operation of the social system. Accordingly, it has been, and is still, regarded as a wise measure to have some white person upon whom to depend in an emergency. The attendant flattery and the sense of personal power and benevolence which this confers upon the white person so selected help to sustain this type of relationship. It frequently happens, also, that the favors cover a wide range and that the Negro most apt in flattery, whatever his other qualifications, is the one most readily favored. For a number of years, for example, appointments of Negro school teachers were made very largely on this basis, with no little damage to Negro education.

Just as slavery enabled certain Negroes to develop skill, it instilled in others slovenly habits of work which have not yet been entirely overcome. The unintelligent performance of routine tasks under the prodding of a master or overseer could accomplish habituation to routine, but such labor could scarcely be depended upon, unstimulated or unguided, to perform new tasks. It was thus most fortunate for Negroes emerging from the institution that they were, in so large a degree, cast upon their own resources to reëducate themselves

[1] E. Davidson Washington, *Selected Speeches of Booker T. Washington*, p. 27.

under the cold and stern selection of free and bitter economic competition. Too much tutelage would have been unsalutary. There was an immediate reflection of this economic selection in the rocketing of death rates, and especially the infant mortality rates, and the collapse of the weaker ones from the fresh ravages of tuberculosis.

No less damaging than these unfortunate habits of work was the artificial division of labor under slavery, especially in the case of those Negro slaves who were parts of large households. This artificial division merely gave them something to do, rather than set them to the intelligent accomplishment of a round of tasks, which would have proved a more useful education. Miss Sara Haardt, in an amused and amusing discussion of the etiquette of slavery, comments upon such highly specialized and often useless exclusive assignments as fanning flies away from "ole Mistiss," or the dry rubbing of a mahogany floor to the point of inutility. "This was ruinous business," she said, "this waste of labor, or rather this triumph of labor, and in the end, even without the war, it would probably have bankrupted the South." [1] It was bad not only for the South, but for the habits of the Negroes trained under it. Dr. Du Bois (in an Atlanta University monograph on the morals and manners of the Negro, in 1914) had to say of the slavery environment: "Slavery fosters certain virtues like humility and obedience, but these flourish at the terrible cost of lack of self-respect, shiftlessness, tale bearing, theft, slovenliness and sexual looseness." [2]

With respect to education, slavery may be said to have stimulated various reactions, not all of them, however, of equal value. It placed the traditional stamp of approval, through censure and praise, upon the sufficiency of mother wit as a substitute for education. Older Negroes, who managed to get along although illiterate, felt the adequacy of their good sense, and especially their sensitiveness to the expectations of their station, in the struggle for existence. From the security of enough to eat, they could and did ridicule effectively the first clumsy efforts of other Negroes to educate themselves.

Still another reaction to education among the slaves which continued after slavery was the profound curiosity over and fascination of the mystery of "pen and pencil." "It can tell you everything you want to know." The methods devised by certain slaves to

---

[1] "The Etiquette of Slavery," *American Mercury*, May, 1929, p. 39.
[2] W. E. B. Du Bois and A. G. Dill (Eds.), *Morals and Manners among Negro Americans*, p. 16.

steal the elements of education provide some of the most interesting examples of inventiveness among slaves. They subtly coaxed the meaning of words from unsuspecting white children; they eavesdropped and pieced together the fragments of overheard instruction; they patiently fumbled through the Bible to get the shape of letters; they met clandestinely with other slaves who had mastered the elements. There was a tremendous lure in this locked-up magic. The first impulse of many of those who had been deprived of education under slavery was to see that their children got it under freedom. This zeal has been marked in the educational efforts of Negroes since slavery.

The first attempts of the Negroes to educate themselves reveal a further influence of the institution. The exposure of the slaves to the formal process of education and its end-result of educated persons was, in the nature of things, casual and incomplete. What was impressive to the slave in the magic of education was not an appreciation of the profound implications of knowledge, but of the more easily recognizable surface accompaniments of this condition. "Educated" people did not perform manual labor; they spoke in polysyllables, wore collars, quoted Greek and French, and spent their time communing with other educated people, or with books. The ridicule of the first experiments of Negroes in education both by white observers and other Negroes had a real basis. To escape drudgery and the complete status associated with slavery was naturally a first objective. Where there had been no education, a little education gave a feeling of great superiority. But this "superiority," awkwardly accompanied by the mannerisms of scholarship, became merely grotesque imitation. The most serious and sustained effect of this first interpretation of education may be noted in the long and bitter objection of the first educated Negroes to industrial education. There was insistence upon classical education, as if to have "higher education" would in itself suddenly reverse the social order. As education becomes more generally widespread, and less novel, these first false glamours disappear and its deeper values take their place. This attitude toward work and toward education may not be regarded as peculiar to the Negro. It was likewise true of many whites, and for much of this, slavery was likewise responsible.

The psychological effects of slavery have been pervasive and will, perhaps, continue longest. The infrequency of actual slave uprisings points to a mental adjustment of the slaves to their position of subordination. Human beings can become adjusted to almost any condition of life. From the vantage point of the experience of freedom, it is difficult to understand how any people, unless they are innately adjusted to slavery, can live in it without protest. But even free men who for one reason or the other lose their freedom, as in confinement to prison, if this confinement is sustained, become adjusted to the loss of freedom. The serfs under feudalism were adjusted to their station for hundreds of years. Women were, until recently, adjusted to a subject rôle. There were no widespread uprisings of the Helots of Sparta, or of the Phrygians, Cretans, Corsicans, Dalmatians, Britons, Syrians, Ionians, Alexandrians, who were used as slaves under the Romans.

The intellectuals and humanitarians are more concerned about the exploited cotton mill operatives in the South, and the slum dwellers in the North, than are these less fortunate ones about redeeming themselves from a status of perpetual or perennial insecurity. The Russian revolution was not the result of a wholesale uprising of the Russian peasants themselves, but of the activities of a relatively few intellectual strategists.

It is characteristic of such a subordination or subjection that the first control is by force; inevitably, and before many years, habituation to the status takes the place of a direct show of force. These habits persist, and have persisted long after slavery, in the psychology of Negroes. It is the "marginal" man, the individual who gets partially out of this zone of habituation and partially into another, who is restless, discontented, and dangerous to the fixed order of things. It is persons of this type that are most sensitive to insults, because such individuals resent the implications of a lowly place in society by foreordination. They are the ones who, when balked, develop psychoses of oppression and become the radicals who are either suppressed by force or expelled by it.

What is frequently overlooked is that American society is not a fixed society, and that movement and growth are communicated. The processes of education, migration, and communication inevitably break up old relations. It is well to point out here what seems to be a difference in the character of "marginality." The older generation of Negroes are frequently recognized as more agreeable types than the younger generation, and they occasion less concern for established social relations. This is to be expected from the nature of their mental habituation to their rôle. Their children have not entirely the same social background; they are less isolated from other experiences of Negroes; they read, travel, and are generally in communication with a wider public. The new life of this generation brings its own impact to destroy the old cultural patterns under which their parents lived. It creates less respect for authority, and more insistent challenges of the order of relations. The "bad nigger" is, from one point of view, merely an ignorant "marginal man." The old cultural and social controls are weakened without the resourcefulness of a substantial new culture. This is probably what is meant by the observation that the education of Negroes tends to diminish crime as well as other forms of social disorganization.

The mental adjustment to slavery has been responsible for other manifestations in the later behavior of Negroes. It has in many cases instilled a belief in their own actual inferiority, which extends beyond themselves to the conviction of the inferiority of all Negroes. Without raising the point of racial equality or inequality, it is rather generally acknowledged that for the most wholesome social growth of any group there should be respect for qualities of accomplishment in character, culture, and education without the hopeless implication of limitations fixed by racial lines. Such fundamental self-depreciation not only prevents the development of racial self-respect but creates actual distrust of Negro leadership of any sort. For many years Negro doctors had difficulty in persuading Negro patients to use their services, and the distrust continues to a marked extent.

Another expression of the sense of inadequacy may be noted in the attempt to compensate for it in devious ways. One such compensation is through the acceptance of the limited racial field, and constricting the horizon of accomplishment to yield superiority merely over other Negroes. This is implicit in the boastful description of persons as being the "best Negro doctor in town," and in the proud reference to a "Black Billy Sunday." Another expression is in the behavior which stresses the external aspect of culture without the substance; or which, on the other hand, resignedly attributes personal deficiency to race, where lack of industry is more responsible for failure. Still another expression is the scornful hopelessness about improvement. With this attitude, not infrequently, goes ridicule of the professional skill and competence of Negroes.

The more recent training of Negroes in medicine, perhaps, accounts in part for the distrust of them by many Negroes; but there is evidence of uncritical preference for white doctors when there is the option of an established Negro physician and a white hospital interne. Recently in a clinic in a rural county in the South, in which hundreds of Negroes were being given inoculations, a white and a Negro physician were stationed on opposite sides of the room. It was the first time a Negro physician had been used in any work connected with a public clinic. When the subjects lined up for the inoculations, all of them, except a handful of adventurous and sacrificially polite ones, went to the white physician. So matter-of-fact and usual was the choice that no one gave it special notice until, in the serious effort to distribute the burden of work, the white physician told them that the Negro physician could inoculate them as competently as he. The scepticism persisted in the frightened aspect of those who, in responding to the accustomed authority, extended nervous arms to the Negro physician.

It is not a myth that many Negroes object to other Negroes in positions of authority over them, or that they prefer to be directed by a white person. This is an extension of basic convictions instilled during slavery, which continue in many relations at present. The admission that a Negro may be as capable as a white man is an admission of a double personal inferiority. The preference of Negroes for white authority carries an element of flattery, and cannot be regarded as evidence of the incapacity of Negroes to direct Negroes. The extent to which it is not evidence of such incapacity may be said to be a measure of the psychological influence of slavery.

A subtle effect both of slavery and of the culture that it represented is the persistent evidence of acceptance by Negroes of standards of beauty and physical appearance which are not wholly adjustable to themselves. It is recognized that this is an inevitable part of the adoption of a new culture, since æsthetic codes and judgments of value are as definite elements as moral or material standards. A part of the Brobdingnagian scorn of blackness familiar in some intra-racial appraisals reflects this, as does the valuation on mulattoes and other approximations to whiteness and straight hair. Along with the difference, Negroes absorbed under slavery a contempt for blackness. The implications are everywhere: "Black is evil." It has been and still is associated with witchcraft, devils, sin, bad luck, and "all the other distressing and horrible aspects of human experience."

The core of this psychological problem, and resentment of it, get expression in the following remarks by Dr. C. V. Roman, a Negro physician of some distinction:

Slavery taught the Negro to accept without question the white man's opinion on every subject. This he does yet to the injury of both races. When a white man believes the white people are the best looking people in the world, he is wise and in harmony with nature. When a Negro believes that, he is a fool and out of harmony with nature. Because that belief will make the white man proud of himself and his race, while that same belief will make of the Negro a creature that neither God nor man has yet found any use for, namely, a man ashamed of his race. This by-product of the slave system has confused ethnic values and hindered social progress. It is an insidious poison that has perverted the reason of many men, so that they have not only forgotten justice but are blind to their own interest. The white man is right when he insists that the Negro cannot be a white man, but wrong when he insists all men are white. The Negro who does not accept the first proposition is a fool; but the one who does accept the second is a fool with an adjective in front of it.[1]

So long as scorn of blackness is in the tradition, it will be "evil" for Negroes until they can succeed in emancipating themselves from its implications.

The humor of the Negro has been regarded as one of his native characteristics. It is, indeed, one of the useful contributions of the race to the grim struggle of America for progress and wealth. This humor has enlivened the public and private stage, the joke columns of the press, and countless after-dinner speeches. It has made entertainment without end for the smoking cars of the railroad trains. Since the native African is not a very humorous person, it seems most likely that this quality of humor was developed in slavery, and there is just as good reason for regarding it as a survival trait. No master could be thoroughly comfortable around a sullen slave; and, conversely, a master, unless he was utterly humorless, could not overwork or brutally treat a jolly fellow, one who could make him laugh. The famous black-face minstrels by white performers get their suggestion from the plantation entertainers. The most important use of humor to the Negro, however, was in his personal relations with his white master. The master says to a young slave, "You scoundrel, you ate my turkey," and the slave replies, "Yes, suh, Massa, you got less turkey but you sho' got more nigger." The slave lives to eat another turkey and the master has another entertaining story. The trait continues as a survival measure, and it will, no doubt, prove a great loss when the full grimness of the American culture is captured by American Negroes.

[1] An Address to the National Medical Association in 1914.

THE EFFECT OF SLAVERY ON THE NEGRO

Allied with the early utilitarian value of humor is a less naïve counterpart, similarly a survival trait acquired in slavery. It is the protective coating of humor, with an obsequiousness which shields beneath it a more sober philosophy and criticism of life. Lunsford Lane, a slave in North Carolina who managed to steal an education, buy his freedom, and move away, could write about this trait fairly objectively. Speaking of the period during which he was saving money, he said:

> Two things I kept constantly in mind. First, to make no display of the little property or money I possessed; but in every way I wore, as much as possible, the aspect of poverty. Secondly, I never appeared to know half so much as I really did. On no occasion did I intrude my intelligence in my conversation with white people. The latter rule the people of my race in the South, both free and slave, find it peculiarly necessary, for their own comfort and safety to observe.[1]

Sixty years later, L. M. Hussey, a Philadelphia white man, who had been sent out to interview leading Negroes on the value to their race of various charitable and social institutions, made a discovery which is not wholly without basis. He got the answers for which he was looking, but he was troubled by "a subtle something, a vocal color, an insinuation of the gesturing hand," that somehow bade him pause. When he had encountered enough of it, he concluded that:

> These posturings of the mime in every tinted gentleman of my acquaintance, from the elegant pastor of the First (African) M. E. Church to the corner bootblack, were all mere manifestations of a simple defense mechanism. . . . In sheer self-protection he has made of himself a slick, slippery, deceptive fellow. On the one hand the object of half-affectionate derision, the butt of the immemorial watermelon and pork-chop jokes, the eternal clown, and on the other hand, in darker representations, the ceaseless, potential menace to every one-hundred-proof virgin south of Mason and Dixon's line, he is no more what he appears to be to the naïve Caucasian eye than the girl three rows back in the chorus, exhibiting herself under half an inch of cinnabar, antimony and talc.[2]

Slavery introduced the Negro to Christianity. This was, no doubt, a much more complicated cultural process than is normally supposed. Whether there is predicated an African cultural base or no certain

---

[1] William G. Hawkins, *Lunsford Lane, Another Helper from North Carolina*, p. 99.
[2] L. M. Hussey, "Homo Africanus," *American Mercury*, January, 1925, p. 85.

cultural base at all, the process of taking on the dominant religion of the western culture was a momentous one. In the first place, Christianity presupposed an intelligence and habits of thought developed in the western culture; it was an abstract religion, and the philosophic foundation of its doctrines was in great measure removed from the elements actually dominant during the early struggling period of the American colonies. This was an acquisitive and imperialistic age, and not one calculated to put too seriously into practice the chief tenets of the religion of Christianity. Humility and brotherhood, and commonalty of worldly goods, could serve as important and necessary counter forces to the spirit of the age, modifying and softening them, but they were not, it would appear, the popular religion of practice.

The exposure of Negroes to Christianity was an uneven one. There was, at first, some reluctance about converting them. The strength of religious doctrines, however, made planters uncomfortable about their own souls until slaves had been admitted to some type of religious instruction. When they discovered that Christianization made better slaves, the practice was encouraged. Again, not all slaves had the same access to competent religious instruction. There has arisen out of differences between domestic and plantation slaves a distinction which regards somewhat disdainfully the "corn field religion" of the plantation.

The doctrines of the Anglican Church, which was the denomination first in favor with the slaveholders, were too highly formalized and abstruse for the untutored and simple slave minds. When the Baptists and Methodists came along with their more simple and literal rendering of the Scriptures; their doctrines of man's sinfulness, and his need of redemption; their vivid picturing of the rewards of the good life called Christian, and their even more vivid pictures of the punishment of the sinful; their camp meetings and protracted meetings; and, most important of all, their deliberate efforts to proselyte the slaves, they brought something that the slaves could understand.

The slaves took over what they could understand of the Christian religion, and reinterpreted it to meet their own needs. Thus their religion stressed otherworldliness, which offered an escape from the discomforts of their present life. It may be presumed that the constant inhibitions necessary in some phases of their life could get approved vent in the emotional expression of religion for which the hysteria of the camp meetings provided a pattern. A relationship was established between religion and social life, through the sociability almost exclusively possible in religious worship.

It seems never to have been clear to the slaves generally that Christianity and morals or ethics were, or should be, reinforcing currents of the same stream of culture. In this failure they are perhaps not wholly to blame. Even if they had understood this relationship, it would not have been possible for them to insist upon the principle of morality, as understood in free society, over against the necessities of their status as slaves. Many of these patterns set in slavery survived in the religious life of the freedman.

So far as Christian virtues are concerned, the situation of Negro slaves gave them a certain practical advantage over their masters. Religion has been and remains for them a large part of their lives. For many years after slavery it was the major social as well as spiritual outlet for them. Their naïve and kindly interpretation of the Scriptures has helped to re-create the positive virtues of a Christian life. For it appears that the otherworldly element of the Christian religion selected by the Negroes was the more pleasant one. They stressed going to heaven in contrast to the emphasis of the white Methodists and Baptists on the avoidance of hell fire and damnation. Associated with this religious life of the slave is the creation of the Negro spirituals, which have been recognized as a distinct and distinctive contribution to the art of America, and music of deep emotional appeal.

An effect of Christianity upon the slaves, both during and after slavery, was to constitute the Negro church as their most important social institution; to give, for more than fifty years, an unchallenged position of influence to the Negro preachers, most of whom were at first of a low level of education; and to provide an emotional outlet for worldly discomfort, which became an important survival trait. The church was the first social organization brought to completion, unaided, by Negroes. The greatest single unit of Negro wealth is "frozen" in church edifices. While failing in this respect to follow the dominant American pattern of investing capital productively, Negroes have provided for themselves through this means a most important instrument of social control, and at least some simple, understandable codes of living.

Any attempt to appraise the social effects of any institution upon individuals or groups necessarily involves a great deal of speculation. In the case of the American Negroes it is impossible to determine which traits are directly and exclusively traceable to slavery, and which are inherent in their status as a minority group. Since, however, slavery is responsible both for their presence here and for their minority status, it may take the major responsibility. Where pronounced personality types and situation patterns are observed in the Negro group, differing both from the African and the American patterns of culture, it seems not unreasonable to attribute them to the long dominating influence of slavery.

PROBLEMS FOR STUDY

1. One student of the Negro has observed that the Negroes nearest to slavery believed that they were completely inferior to all white persons and acted as if they were; the next generation acted as if they were but did not believe it; and the next generation of Negroes neither believed that they were nor acted as if they believed it. How closely does this analysis correspond with your observation or with the impressions you have derived from literature on this subject?
2. Is there any difference in manner and bearing between a Negro who has experienced slavery and a native African who has been a person of status in his own culture?
3. To what extent should Negroes rely upon white leadership for their racial guidance?
4. As successive generations of Negroes are removed from the influence of slavery, are not more occasions made for racial friction?
5. What habits socially valuable to good citizenship did slavery instill in the Negro?
6. What habits that should not be encouraged in a free society did slavery develop in the Negro?

BIBLIOGRAPHY

Thomas F. Buxton, *The African Slave Trade and Its Remedy* (1840).
Louis I. Dublin, *Health and Wealth* (1928).
W. E. B. Du Bois and A. G. Dill (Eds.), *Morals and Manners among Negro Americans* (1914).
W. E. B. Du Bois (Ed.), *The Negro American Family* (1908).
E. Franklin Frazier, "An Analysis of Statistics on Negro Illegitimacy in the United States," *Social Forces*, December, 1932, pp. 249–257.
Sara Haardt, "The Etiquette of Slavery," *American Mercury*, May, 1929, pp. 34–42.
William G. Hawkins, *Lunsford Lane, Another Helper from North Carolina* (1863).

L. M. Hussey, "Homo Africanus," *American Mercury*, January, 1925, pp. 83–89.
Louis Le Fevre, *Liberty and Restraint* (1931).
C. V. Roman, An Address to the National Medical Association in 1914.
E. Davidson Washington, *Selected Speeches of Booker T. Washington* (1932).

CHAPTER XV

THE EFFECT OF SLAVERY ON THE WHITE PEOPLE

When de Tocqueville visited America in the early part of the nineteenth century, he was eager to discover what effect democracy had had upon American institutions and American people. Oddly enough, the impression made upon him was that "equality of conditions" was "the fundamental fact" from which all influences flowed. He felt that "the gradual and progressive development of social equality is [was] the past and future of their history." [1] This was a general observation made on the country as a whole. But when he floated down the Ohio river, with the fertile fields of Ohio (a free state) on one side and the less prosperous plantations of Kentucky (a slave state) on the other, he made the observation, that slavery "affects the character of the master, and imparts a peculiar tendency to his ideas and tastes. Slavery not only prevents the whites from becoming opulent, but even from desiring to become so." [2] While we would not agree with de Tocqueville's last conclusion, we must agree with him in his earlier one, that slavery had a marked effect on the master class. Indeed it had a profound effect, not only upon the masters and the non-slaveholding whites of the South, but also upon the whites of the whole country. For it must never be forgotten that even the sturdy Puritans could drive a good slave bargain; it is recorded in early New England history that one Emanuel Downing, brother-in-law to John Winthrop, "was in hopes of a war with the Narragansett's for two reasons, first to stop their worship of the devil, 2 lie, if upon a just warre the Lord should deliver them into our hands, we might easily have men, women and children enough to exchange for Moores [Negroes]." [3]

The first influence exerted on the white man by slavery came

[1] *Democracy in America*, Introduction, *passim*.
[2] *Ibid.*, p. 344.
[3] Quoted by Ulrich B. Phillips, *American Negro Slavery*, p. 101, from Massachusetts Historical Records, Collections XXXVI, p. 65.

THE EFFECT OF SLAVERY ON THE WHITE PEOPLE 291

through the economic system which resulted from the slave régime. Slavery tended to separate the leaders of the people on to large plantations, and hence set up a form of individualism which has been strangely characteristic of the South, up to the present hour. Every planter became the mayor of his own small village. He must run his own store, grind his own corn, gin his own cotton, mend his own tools in his own blacksmith shop, make his own syrup, and cobble his own shoes; not infrequently he had his own tailor shop, and the millinery and dressmaking room of every big plantation house was a busy place. It thus happened that life on the individual plantation became self-contained, independent, individualistic. The distance from the big house to the next nearest neighbor was often miles, so that the planter could not rely on collective action. There were few towns, and these were comparatively uninfluential. They did not have in them the leadership which they had in other parts of America. Even the leading lights of the law, the ministry, and medicine usually were rural dwellers. In the early days of the South even the colleges were not established in the town, but in isolated places. The whole trend of southern life was toward isolation, independence, hence individualism. Furthermore, the slave system tended toward sectional independence and isolation. Slavery effectually cut off all migration of labor from the North, and to this day a very small proportion of the immigrants from Europe have come to settle in the South. Since northern and European peoples shunned the South, capital from these same places tended to stay at home; so the South attracted few outside investors seeking favorable places to use their money. There was therefore no outside money for manufacturing, and the slave régime absorbed all local money as the planter continued to expand his acres and increase his slave holdings. The widely scattered population gave no stimulus to the processes of manufacturing. Commenting on this situation in 1849, Charles T. James, a cotton manufacturer of Providence, Rhode Island, wrote a monograph for a Mr. Hamilton Smith of Louisville, Kentucky, in which he proved, to his own satisfaction at least, that there was much more profit to be made out of turning cotton into cloth than there was to be made from turning the results of land and labor into cotton itself. According to Mr. James' figures based on the cotton returns of 1847, the southern states furnished four-fifths (or 480 million pounds) of all the cotton to the British manufacturer, for which the South received $30,000,000. For turning this raw cotton into cloth the manufacturer in England got $118,000,000. Mr. James, therefore, argued that if the South would build cotton factories to use its own raw product most of this $118,000,000 could be retained in this country. He claimed, furthermore, that the outlay for machinery to do this work would be no greater than the outlay for land and slaves to raise the cotton. Hence, it seemed to him the South was following the less lucrative end of the business.[1] De Bow's *Industrial Resources* placed the comparative profit of raising the cotton to that of manufacturing it at $11\frac{1}{2}$ per cent to 24 per cent on the capital invested.[2] Whether or not Mr. James was entirely right in his contention, it must be said that others had similar opinions. De Bow estimated that in 1849 there were 606,772 bales of cotton manufactured in the United States, or some 300,000,000 pounds. Of this only 75,000 bales were consumed in the South itself, and De Bow believed that the proportion should be much larger.[3] A Mr. Huntington writing in 1848, in the January issue of *De Bow's Review*, declared that, owing to the fact that Great Britain is so far removed from the place of growth of the raw cotton, "it is impossible that they can ever again compete with us in this branch of industry."[4] He further insisted that the seat of American cotton manufacture must be transferred from New England to the South, just as it had been transferred from Old England to New England. But of course he overlooked many important factors in the problem. One was that the "Surplus Capital" of which he spoke glibly was entirely lacking in the South. It was easy enough to make an argument like that on paper and no one could pick a flaw in it, but the trouble was that it did not work out in practice.

Not only was free capital wanting, but trained labor was also completely absent. The slaves on the whole were not adequately trained for manufacturing processes. It is true that certain experiments were tried, in which slave labor tended the machines in cotton factories,[5] such as that conducted at Saluda, South Carolina, but either because the labor was so inefficient or because there was fear of

[1] Charles T. James, *Practical Hints on the Comparative Cost and Productiveness of the Culture of Cotton, and the Cost and Productiveness of Its Manufacture*, pp. 25–26.
[2] *The Industrial Resources of the Southern and Western States*, Vol. II, p. 126.
[3] *Ibid.*, Vol. I, p. 217 ff.
[4] P. 13.
[5] J. D. B. De Bow, *The Industrial Resources of the Southern and Western States*, Vol. II, p. 127.

THE EFFECT OF SLAVERY ON THE WHITE PEOPLE 293

what might happen if slaves were congregated and trained, the practice never became general. It is altogether likely that fear of congregating Negro labor was a great deterrent, for when the Honorable Abbott Lawrence of Boston visited Richmond, Virginia, in 1837, and brought with him ample backing from eleven other wealthy New Englanders, to establish cotton mills run by water power of the James river, he met with "abuse and insult" from the Richmond *Enquirer*, because he was "interfering with the beloved institutions of the South."[1] Both Helper, who was a North Carolinian, and James, who was a New Englander, made a plea for manufacturing because it would give employment to the poor white people of the South, who James claimed would apply in greater numbers than could be used. This New England advocate became almost an evangelist in his plea that cotton manufacturing would afford opportunity to educate the poor whites thus brought together in villages, and besides it would give the wealthy planters a chance to aid this unfortunate class, which James was magnanimous enough not to charge up to the slave system.[2] Even De Bow believed this would be one way of relieving the terrible condition of the poor southern whites.[3] But all the arguments availed little, for the amount of manufacturing carried on in the South was so small that Henry A. Wise could say to a Virginia audience, "You have no commerce, no mining, no manufactures,"[4] and Mason of the same state could say, "Slavery discourages arts and manufactures."[5] The matter was so obvious that an orator in the Southern Commercial Convention meeting in New Orleans, in 1855, exclaimed: "It is time that we should look about us, and see in what relation we stand to the North. From the rattle with which the nurse tickles the ear of the child born in the South, to the shroud that covers the cold form of the dead, everything comes to us from the North. We rise from between sheets made in Northern looms, and pillows of Northern feathers, to wash in basins made in the North, dry our beards on Northern towels, and dress ourselves in garments woven on North-

---

[1] Hinton R. Helper, *The Impending Crisis of the South*, pp. 106–108 *passim*.

[2] Charles T. James, *Practical Hints on the Comparative Cost and Productiveness of the Culture of Cotton, and the Cost and Productiveness of Its Manufacture*, pp. 41–43, *passim*.

[3] *The Industrial Resources of the Southern and Western States*, Vol. II, p. 124, ff., *passim*.

[4] Hinton R. Helper, *The Impending Crisis of the South*, p. 90.

[5] *Ibid.*, p. 209.

ern looms; we eat from Northern plates and dishes; our rooms are swept with Northern brooms, our gardens dug with Northern spades, and our bread kneaded in trays or dishes of Northern wood, or tin; and the very wood which feeds our fires is cut with Northern axes, helved with hickory brought from Connecticut and New York." [1]

Another economic influence of slavery was found in the tendency of wealth to be concentrated in the hands of a few. Cotton, tobacco, and rice could be more economically grown on large plantations, and sugar could hardly be profitably grown at all save on a large scale. The cutting and grinding season was short, and the necessity of getting the work accomplished before frost bit the stalks made it almost imperative that every planter have his own sugar mill. This was very expensive; hence sugar tended to be raised on larger and larger plantations. Besides, the prestige of a planter was measured by the extent of his acres and the number of his slaves, so that every planter constantly stretched his resources to buy more land and more slaves. Francis P. Blair in 1856 declared before the Republican Convention of Maryland that the continuance of slavery had "resulted in the monopoly of the soil to a great extent in the hands of slaveholders." [2] Also the big planter often did not want the little individual farmer at his side. Olmsted said that every inquiry he made of large planters about their small farm neighbors elicited habitual irritation.[3] They feared the bad effect of poor white farmers working as freemen alongside the slaves. It was calculated to make the slaves dissatisfied and prone to run away; "hence the desire of every planter to get possession of the land of any poor — non-slaveholding neighbor." William Chambers of Edinburgh, having made a journey through America, quoted approvingly from *De Bow's Review* of December, 1855, as follows: "Of the $20,000,000. annually realized from the sales of the cotton crop of Alabama, nearly all not expended in supporting the producers, is reinvested in land and Negroes. . . . One will discover numerous farm houses, once the abode of industrious and intelligent freemen, now occupied by slaves, or tenantless, deserted and dilapidated." [4] Professor J. E. Cairnes of Queens College, Scotland, writing during

[1] Quoted from Frederick L. Olmsted, *A Journey in the Seaboard Slave States*, p. 544.
[2] Quoted from Hinton R. Helper, *The Impending Crisis of the South*, p. 213.
[3] *The Cotton Kingdom*, Vol. II, p. 355 ff.
[4] *American Slavery and Colour*, pp. 9–10.

THE EFFECT OF SLAVERY ON THE WHITE PEOPLE 295

the early days of the Civil War, pointed out exactly the same tendency of the big plantations to become bigger and the little farmers to be crowded out.[1] The tendency was so obvious that no economist writing at the time could overlook its effects, and this carried with it the other tendency of wearing out the land.

The single crop system was foisted on the South largely because the slaves were ignorant and were kept so; hence it was difficult to teach them new processes. When once they had been taught to raise tobacco or cotton it was thought more profitable to keep them at the same routine task. Hence the land was mined instead of being cultivated. C. C. Clay, Jr., of Alabama, speaking before the Chunnenugie Horticultural Society of Alabama in 1855, said: "I can show you, with sorrow, in the older portions of Alabama and in my native county of Madison, the sad memories of the artless and exhausting culture of cotton. Our small planters often taking the cream off their lands, unable to restore them by rest, manures, or otherwise; are going further West and South in search of other virgin lands, which they may and will despoil and impoverish in like manner. . . . If the planters of Alabama would prevent the shameful decadence of agriculture so palpable in Virginia and the Carolinas, they must banish the wild illusion, which holds them spellbound to the changeless, artless, exhausting culture of the cotton plant. They must abandon a system which is at war with nature and condemned by experience. . . . They must learn the physical fact that all nature loves a change, and diversify their field labor by the introduction of other plants."[2] While the soil of the South is on the whole light, one may claim that it was quite fertile. It needed careful treatment to be sure, which was just what slave labor could not give it. The planting of one crop year after year wore it out rapidly. Hence new lands must be constantly introduced and old lands often left to wash away. Olmsted, who journeyed through the whole South and was himself an expert agriculturist, called the land "generally rich" — "as rich as possible" and similar phrases are used throughout his book — but he found it badly worn by routine crops, "the hillsides gullied like icebergs, . . . its productiveness rapidly decreasing" and the soil "washing into adjoining swamps."[3] Fannie Kemble, who lived a short time on the Georgia plantation of her husband, a Mr. Butler,

---

[1] *The Slave Power*, chap. 2, *passim*.
[2] *De Bow's Review*, December, 1855, p. 727.
[3] *A Journey in the Back Country*, chap. 1, *passim*.

wrote: "The land is being exhausted by the careless and wasteful nature of agriculture itself, [and] suggests a pretty serious prospect of declining prosperity; and indeed unless these Georgia cotton planters can command more land or lay abundant capital upon that which has already spent its virgin vigor, it is a very obvious thing that they must all very soon be eaten up by their own property." [1]

It was just this constant supply of new lands that made the continuance of the slave system possible. The planters of the upper and middle South gradually moved down to the lower South in search of these richer lands, and finally pushed on west into Texas, where land was still abundant. This process is clearly revealed in a letter from Lamar to Howell Cobb of Georgia, whose plantation he managed:

> Lord, Lord, Howell, you and I have been too used to poor land to know what crops people are making in the rich lands of the new counties. I am just getting my eyes open to the golden view. On those good lands, when cotton is down to such a price as would starve us out, they can make money. I have moved one-third of my force to Sumpter. I shall move another one-third this fall or winter, leaving the remaining one-third to cultivate the best lands on my Bibb place. This year I shall do better than I ever have done, and next I shall do better than I ever expected to do. This year I shall cultivate very little poor land and next year I shall not waste labour on a foot of unprofitable soil. All will be of the 1st quality. When I work through I will try and help you onward to the promised land. But for 2 years after the present one I shall be up to my chin in responsibility. I hate responsibility, but I have figured it out, that unless I take some as other prudent folks do, I shall be like John Grier of Chack farm cultivating poor land all my life, which I am resolved not to do.[2]

But of course this process of cultivation ultimately spelled economic ruin for the South and bankruptcy for many of the big planters. Helper of North Carolina burned this truth into the minds of the southern people with the red-hot iron of his statistics, and made the whole South writhe under his withering sarcasm.[3]

The political effects of slavery were no less marked than the economic. We have noted earlier that the system put large wealth into the hands of a few, and hence produced a leisure class which was able to give itself to statesmanship. Washington, Jefferson,

---

[1] *Journal of a Residence on a Georgian Plantation in 1838–1839*, p. 164.

[2] Ulrich B. Phillips, *Plantation and Frontier Documents, 1649–1863*, Vol. I, pp. 177–178.

[3] *The Impending Crisis of the South*, chap. 1.

THE EFFECT OF SLAVERY ON THE WHITE PEOPLE

Madison, Monroe, Randolph, Calhoun, and a host of other names flash before the mind as one thinks of the brilliant galaxy of leaders who were sprung from the system. A tradition of political leadership grew up in the old South which fired the imagination of every boy. The gentleman of the old South was proud, dignified, eloquent. His tongue and his pen alike held caustic power. As the manager of a great plantation where hundreds of souls were under his care and subject to his will, he acquired an ability to govern which impressed men from the North as a spirit of domineering — almost tyranny. He knew large responsibilities and shrank not from assuming his full share. He read widely, often traveled to Europe, and frequently had read law as a young man, so that the whole trend of his life was toward political leadership. But slavery gave the tone and color to all this leadership. In the earlier colonial days the planters had tried hard to rid themselves of slavery, but the mother countries had forcibly interfered. Later, when cotton and tobacco and sugar were in demand all over the world, and slaves seemed necessary to raise these commodities, there gradually grew up a tolerance for slavery and then a spirit of defense. The political leaders were driven into a fighting unit, to sustain their economic privileges. This gave a fire and an imperiousness to the southern leaders which marked them as impetuous orators, dogged debaters, and men who knew all the tactics of political warfare. In 1850 only one man in five owned slaves; but according to the Constitution, every five slaves counted as three citizens in giving representation in Congress; hence this minority of slave owners, backed by the political power conferred by their very slave ownership, became a small oligarchy. They were alert, intelligent, homogeneous, and united. They knew what they wanted and were determined to have it. The constant attacks upon the slave system drove them into complete agreement on almost every minor issue. Just as the presence of the Negro has tended to keep the South a solid political unit, so slavery broke down every petty barrier and welded the old South into a fighting unit.

This sectional solidarity inevitably cut the South off from the rest of the nation, and made it more self-conscious, more individualistic, and hence less progressive. While the other sections of the Union were becoming nationalized and internationalized the South remained apart. It did not change because its institution of slavery admitted of no change — as an agricultural section it had stood against all high tariffs. The great need of the old South was a completely free interchange of commodities with the Old World. It needed to send its cotton, tobacco, and sugar there (products in which it had no competition) and receive manufactured goods in return, without the penalty which a high tariff surely attached to the exchange. This was not in accord with the needs of the North; hence an economic conflict arose which must be fought out in the political arena. Furthermore, since the South believed its economic welfare depended upon slavery, and much more the prestige of its great landed proprietors, it was the business of its statesmen to protect it against attacks of criticism from without. This could only be done by keeping a balance of power between the sections, and that meant continual expansion of slave territory. Since internal improvements and high tariffs out of which to pay for them went hand in hand, the old South stood firmly against appropriating national government money for that purpose. Besides, there were no great cities in the South where concentrated wealth demanded great harbors and rapid transportation. To be sure the South was feverish about transportation between the West and the South, and *De Bow's Review* and similar magazines exploited the idea again and again; but the conservative spirit of the southern statesmen did not permit much progress. Again, in relation to finance the South was more individualistic. The planters' crops moved at one time of the year, and at that time they needed much capital. Hence they wanted banks near at hand which could be easily reached and could lend them on all forms of security. A national bank could not do this so well as state banks; hence the South supported "Old Andy" in his bitter fight against the Second United States Bank. Thus the political as well as the economic interests of the South clearly conflicted with those interests of the North. The North was in favor of strong centralized government, and the South, with its strong individualism, was in favor of power distributed to the several states. The whole trend of slavery was away from putting too much power into the hands of the national government. In short, the presence of slavery committed the South to a patriarchal form of life which affected both its economic and political culture patterns.

Who among us has not seen how the presence of the Negro has moulded our political history since emancipation? We have been slow to pass laws for compulsory school attendance lest we tie ourselves to the task of classical education of the Negro. We were slow enough about extending the suffrage, lest the colored man should become too influential. No major political issue has faced the South, in the last hundred years, that has not been decided largely in the light of the presence of the Negro. As is always the case when economic advantages inhere in any system, there grew up a small class of unscrupulous persons who profited by the injustices and cruelties which were inherent in slavery. These slave breeders and slave dealers were scorned by every true gentleman; yet they were a necessary part of the system. When any gentleman died his estate must be settled, and the slave dealer often had to be called in. So the landed proprietors were of necessity put in communication with, and sometimes greatly influenced by, this vulgar group. As Lincoln once wrote: "The slave-breeders and the slave-dealers are a small odious and detested class among you; and yet in politics they dictate the course of all of you, and are as completely your masters as you are the masters of your Negroes."

The original settlers in Virginia were deeply religious, or at least firmly committed to the support of the established church. From the very beginning there was a passionate devotion to the work of converting the Indians to Christianity. The original adventurers were commanded by royal decree to see that the "word and service of God were preached, planted and used" among the Indians, as well as among themselves. It is reported that Sir Thomas Dale arrived at Jamestown in May, 1611, as the governor of the colony, and his first act was to go to the church and listen to a sermon by the rector. His later correspondence shows that he thought of himself and his work as much in the light of a missionary of religion as of a political administrator. In the early wills, money or property was often left for the rearing of Indian children, in order that they might be converted to Christianity, and religious books were among the most precious possessions conveyed by many wills. Indeed the whole social organization was more religious than it was political.

From the beginning the church vestry was a most influential body. It was composed on the whole of men of the best intelligence, and the largest influence, as well as the largest financial resources. Bruce tells us that most vestrymen were able to read and write, which in that time was considered an accomplishment,[1] and later they were

---

[1] For a full discussion of the early religious life and church organization in Virginia see Philip A. Bruce, *Institutional History of Virginia in the Seventeenth Century*, Vol. I, Part I.

all required to be freeholders. The vestry was usually elected every third year at a meeting of all parishioners. Their duties were threefold: (1) to appoint the clergyman to serve the parish; (2) to act as a kind of grand jury to ferret out all immorality or lax practices among the people and bring them to the attention of the court; (3) to levy the tax for the support of the parish church and clergyman. In the carrying out of these duties there were usually two or more church wardens who acted for the vestry. It will readily be seen there was no such clear-cut distinction between the church and the state as we now suppose is necessary for the well-being of society. Church attendance was required of all citizens, and dissenters were often fined for staying away from the regular service. Toward the middle of the seventeenth century the Quakers arose in Virginia, and the records are full of petty persecutions of them. The Puritans who began to trickle into the colony from about 1650 on were soon branded as dissenters also. This was in keeping with the spirit of the mother country which passed the Act of Conformity in 1662. It was not until the eighteenth century that the Presbyterians, the Methodists, and the Baptists began to have any considerable influence. During all these early decades a doubter, one who denied the authority of the Bible or questioned the existence of the Trinity, not only was at fault morally but became a criminal. This situation held in the mother country and also in the New England colonies.

But the other colonies gradually underwent a change in the direction of liberalizing religious thinking. The South stood still in its religious interpretations. This was in part due to the nature of society, largely controlled by a landed proprietor class which feared all change. Those who have large wealth secured to them under the laws of any régime are usually loath to change lest there be less security for their wealth under any new régime. But the fact of slavery itself tended to keep the southern people conservative. At first there was some fear lest the conversion of slaves to Christianity alter their status as slaves. But in 1667 the House of Burgesses passed a law that ". . . baptisme doth not alter the condition of the person as to his bondage or ffreedome; that divers masters, ffreed from this doubt, may more carefully, endeavor the propagation of Christianity."[1] This question once settled, the Bible and religion seemed

[1] Joseph B. Earnest, *The Religious Development of the Negro in Virginia*, p. 22. (Quoting H. W. Hening, *Statutes at Large, Being a Collection of All the Laws of Virginia, 1619–1792*, Vol. II, p. 260.)

THE EFFECT OF SLAVERY ON THE WHITE PEOPLE 301

to become the allies of slavery. Did not the Bible give numerous examples of patriarchs owning slaves? And even the New Testament had the example of Paul exhorting Onesimus to return to Philemon his master. As late as 1893, thirty years after emancipation, one doughty defender of the faith wrote: "It is impossible to read the Bible with attention without perceiving that the inherent sinfulness of human slavery is not taught in the word of God." [1] In the famous volume, *Cotton Is King*, edited by E. N. Elliott, president of Planters College, Port Gibson, Mississippi, with contributions from Governor Hammond of South Carolina, Bledsoe, and other eminent southerners in 1860, there is one chapter given up to "Arguments from the Scriptures" in favor of slavery. The argument was reduced by the abolitionists to a syllogism which ran: "Whatever God sanctioned among the Hebrews he sanctions for all men and at all times. God sanctioned slavery among the Hebrews; therefore, God sanctions slavery for all men and for all times." [2] Of course the southern ministers denied so bold a statement, but their belief in a literal interpretation supported them in their defense of slavery, and their defense of slavery tied them hard and fast to a literal interpretation of the Scripture. Supporting this view may be mentioned such volumes as *The Bible Defense of Slavery, Slavery Not Sinful, A Scriptural Examination of the Institution of Slavery, The Christian Doctrine of Slavery, Slavery Ordained of God, Slavery Sanctioned by the Bible, Proof of Slavery from the First Chapter of Genesis as Founded in Organic Law, Emancipation Inconsistent with Teachings and Doctrine of the Bible.* The list could be indefinitely extended. So true was this that James G. Birney wrote a book called *American Churches the Bulwark of American Slavery*. While the South was using the Bible to prove that slaveholding was right, the North was quoting Scripture to prove it wrong. The difference lay in the fact that the southern view drove its defenders into a more and more literal interpretation of Scripture, and the northern view drove its defenders to a more and more liberal interpretation. How much influence this difference has had on present religious interpretations it would be difficult to tell, but certain it is that the defense of slavery tended constantly to make southern churches conservative and individualistic.

There was a romance about the old South which has often and well been told, albeit the picture has often been one-sided. But no

[1] W. P. Harrison, *The Gospel among the Slaves*, p. 27.
[2] E. N. Elliott, *Cotton Is King*, p. 337.

one can appreciate the influence of slavery who does not see the romance as well as the sordidness which the system produced. On a thousand southern hills, and hidden away in a thousand groves, still stand the old mansions, many of them now fallen into decay, where the glory and the culture of an age flourished. If one wants to know of the setting of this colonial life he would do well to read *Homes and Gardens in Old Virginia*,[1] which will make the beauty and romance of that early day live again. The libraries in these old colonial homes were not large, but the volumes were well selected. In the early days they were mostly in Latin and Greek, and evidently could be read by those who owned them. Most of them treated of government and religion, but there was a sprinkling of the great classics, such as the works of Ovid, the *Æneid*, and others. One daring dweller on the James river prepared translations of some of these. On the other hand, how much of stupefaction to real intelligence may have been produced by slavery it would be hard to tell. The presence of an ignorant class undoubtedly hampered liberty of speech and freedom of the press. Mr. C. K. Marshall of Vicksburg, Mississippi, head of the committee on home education appointed by the Southern Commercial Congress, wrote a lengthy article for *De Bow's Review* (December, 1856) in which he pleaded that the South should produce its own textbooks and its own literature, to be sure that no word crept in to destroy the belief in its system of slavery. The men in the large homes were dignified almost to austerity, but they had about them an atmosphere of good comradeship which came to the surface in the social gatherings or in the fox hunt. They could easily be distinguished by their walk, by the carriages in which they rode, by the manner of their dress. The women were no less distinctive. Someone has said they were the "Magnolia grandiflora of a race of Cavaliers." They possessed a charm, a poise, a grace of manner, which has been excelled nowhere else in the world. If their education in the schools was rather superficial, they at least had an education in the home which was unsurpassed. They were far from being the wallflowers that some have painted them. The responsibility of a big household sobered them, and if it did not break them it gave them the rich natures which come only from great responsibility and great love.

The romance and beauty must never be forgotten, but if slavery gave a chance for leisure and the cultivation of statesmanship, it

[1] Edited by Susanne W. Massie and Frances A. Christian.

THE EFFECT OF SLAVERY ON THE WHITE PEOPLE 303

also gave a chance for harshness and tyranny. It was a southerner who wrote: "They used their power cruelly at home, for contact with slaves bred contempt for the weak, and unscrupulously at Washington, aiming always to protect themselves in their peculiar rights of property."[1] No people have had a more severe test of character than those among whom human beings have been held as slaves. It is not to be wondered that many southern people fell before so terrible a temptation. Imperialism was of the very air the child of the manor breathed. Not infrequently, when the child was born, he was laid in the arms of a young slave, and the slave was charged to serve him well for life. As the boy grew he had complete command of his body servant. His every wish was law. Often his parents rejoiced in his imperious manner. They felt sure it destined him to great leadership. What wonder that he grew up to be proud, overbearing, not infrequently irascible, and even at times cruel. Jefferson summarized the matter thus: "The parent storms, the child looks on, catches the lineaments of wrath, puts on the same airs in the circle of smaller slaves, gives a loose rein to the worst of possessions, and thus nursed, educated and daily exercised in tyranny cannot but be stamped by it with arduous peculiarities."[2] Colonel Mason of Virginia said before the Constitutional Convention, in speaking against slave importation: "Every master of slaves is born a petty tyrant. They [slaves] produce the most pernicious effect on manners."[3] This very pride and imperiousness served to cut the landed proprietor off from all normal contacts with the mass of men which would have tended to correct his faults. As in the case of the very wealthy of our day, there were few people who could or would hold up to them their weaknesses. Being shut off from such normal contacts, the planter class tended to become conservative and develop a characteristic narrowness of view. If wealth gave a man an opportunity to be independent, it also gave him a chance to be seclusive, and seclusiveness has never been known as a great antidote for weakness. Perhaps he was driven into a deeper seclusion because he was sensitive to criticism and the system to which he was pledged was one which brought against him an ever greater storm of protest. Hence there was naturally

---

[1] William G. Brown, *The Lower South in American History*, p. 30.
[2] *Notes on the State of Virginia with an Appendix Relative to the Murder of Logan's Family*, p. 221.
[3] Hinton R. Helper, *The Impending Crisis of the South*, p. 209.

a heightening pride and a constantly growing stubbornness of mind.

But imperiousness and intolerance were not the worst effects of the system on the ruling class of the South. Jefferson said, "The whole commerce between master and slave is a perpetual exercise of the most boisterous passions." [1] A Mr. Moore, speaking in the legislature of Virginia in 1832, said that slavery carried an "irresistible tendency which it has to destroy everything like virtue and morality in the community." [2] That the presence of a slave class of women, who were completely at the disposal of hot-blooded youth, was a continual menace to high morality is not to be wondered at. The real wonder is that such a large proportion of southern white men, reared under these conditions, retained their purity of life and developed a type of chivalry which was as a pure white lily springing out of a miasmic swamp.

Perhaps the most serious effect of slavery was that which it had upon the poor whites. It has been stated before that not more than one man out of five owned slaves. The mountains of the Carolinas, Virginia, Kentucky, and Tennessee were inhabited by white people who owned no slaves and did not want them. The sandhills of Georgia and Alabama, and the pine barrens of these and other states were populated sparsely by an indigent type of whites who had been crowded out of the richer valleys. Probably one-fourth of the white people of the South fell into the class of the poor whites. They furnished the overseers of the big plantations, and a rather crude and sorry lot they were. They did not hire out on the farms, since manual labor was supposed to be the lot of slaves alone. Charles Yancey of Buckingham County, Virginia, wrote in 1847: "As to agricultural labor we have none. Our poor are poor because they will not work, therefore are seldom employed." [3] De Tocqueville in his comparison of Ohio and Kentucky noted that in Kentucky labor was confounded with slavery and that "no white laborers can be found, for they would be afraid of assimilating themselves to the Negroes." [4] Thomas Jefferson noted also that slavery destroyed the industry of the people. Olmsted found the poor whites in very

---

[1] *Notes on the State of Virginia with an Appendix Relative to the Murder of Logan's Family*, p. 221.
[2] Hinton R. Helper, *The Impending Crisis of the South*, p. 101.
[3] Quoted from Frederick L. Olmsted, *The Cotton Kingdom*, Vol. I, p. 115.
[4] *Democracy in America*, p. 343.

THE EFFECT OF SLAVERY ON THE WHITE PEOPLE 305

desperate condition. "They would not hire out by the month"; "never would work steadily at any employment"; "their wages were from fifty cents to a dollar" per day; they were "worse off in almost all respects than the slaves." He found "badly educated American women who choose to die as seamstresses, rather than live as cooks or chamber maids, because they are taught that the position of a servant or of those who sell their labor or skill by measure of time and not by measure of amount, is worse than that of a slave." He found that even the work of the craftsman was in competition with slave labor and that therefore it was "less honorable than that of the tradesman, the clerk or the professional man."[1] Not only was the work of the skilled craftsman degraded by the fact that it became a part of slave labor, but opportunity to pursue a skilled craft was almost denied the whites, because so many masters took their most capable slaves and trained them as skilled laborers. Every big plantation had its blacksmith, its carpenter, its shoemaker, its cooper. The whole time of these skilled workers was not needed on the plantation; so these workers were hired out by the month and sometimes by the year for good wages. This effectually limited the opportunity for the white skilled worker. At the opening of the Civil War almost all the skilled trades were in the hands of slaves. With every avenue for labor closed to the poor white, subsistence was of the barest and most meager sort.

The influence of that period still lives in the South. Every job where a skilled worker is required about one's home finds that skilled worker bringing a Negro day laborer along to do the rough work. Through all the decades since slavery was abolished white people have had a dislike for certain types of labor. A white girl will hardly work as a cook for ten dollars per week and room and board, but she will work in a department store for eight dollars per week without room and board. How much of this is a hangover from the social patterns of slave days one cannot say, but one fears we are still dominated by the slave pattern.

All those effects on the white people were seen by the best type of southern men. Washington, Jefferson, Lee, Mason, and scores of others recognized that slavery degraded both the black and the white, and that no permanent and enduring civilization could be built upon a system which had such evil effects upon both.

---

[1] *A Journey in the Seaboard Slave States*, pp. 83, 202, 210, 266, 712, *passim*.

PROBLEMS FOR STUDY

1. Is slave labor ever as efficient as free labor?
2. What influence did slavery have on the attitude of white people toward labor?
3. Would slavery tend to heighten or to decrease the master's respect for persons?
4. Did the slave system feed a despotic attitude among whites as some think?
5. Was slavery the basis of aristocratic attitudes?
6. Did the defense of slavery have anything to do with religious dogmatism in the South?
7. Does the presence of light-colored Negroes indicate lax moral relation with slave women on the part of the master class?
8. What relation did slavery have to the reputed spirit of hospitality in the old South?

BIBLIOGRAPHY

William G. Brown, *The Lower South in American History* (1930).
Philip A. Bruce, *Institutional History of Virginia in the Seventeenth Century* (1910).
Philip A. Bruce, *Social Life in Virginia in the Seventeenth Century* (1927).
Hinton R. Helper, *The Impending Crisis of the South* (1860).
Daniel R. Hundley, *Social Relations in Our Southern States* (1860).
Thomas Jefferson, *Notes on the State of Virginia with an Appendix Relative to the Murder of Logan's Family* (1803).
Frederick L. Olmsted, *A Journey in the Seaboard Slave States* (1860).
Ulrich B. Phillips, *American Negro Slavery* (1918).
Willis D. Weatherford, *The Negro from Africa to America* (1924).
Charles K. Whipple, "The Family Relation, as Affected by Slavery" (1858).

PART III

THE PRESENT STATUS OF THE NEGRO AND
RACE RELATIONS

CHAPTER XVI

PRESENT ECONOMIC RELATIONS

The contribution of Negroes to the development of the New World has been only partially recognized, because it has lacked glamour and dramatic incisiveness. This contribution, however, constitutes an element of some importance in the rapid rise of American civilization. The Greeks had a name for such a contribution because it symbolized the embodiment of an idea which, in its growth and cycles of growth, marked both the surface and the depths of a profound social philosophy. They called it *ponos*, and meant by it "work," although the word has the same root as the Latin *poena*, which means "sorrow." To the Greeks "work" carried the meaning of a heavy burdensome task — drudgery; and it applied to all forms of physical work. This was the major contribution of Negroes to the New World, and it has not infrequently carried for them this serious double meaning. The pertinence of this reference to the Greeks and their attitude toward work lies in the extraordinary change which has been experienced in the American philosophy about work. Not only has there been a change in the philosophy, but there have been profound changes in the manner of living which involves this concept. From the shadow of the Greek ideal of the aristocratic scorn of labor we have moved through rapid stages of industrial expansion to the philosophy of work for its own sake and a dignification of labor.

Actually no group in America reflects so completely the whole course of our industrialization and its growing pains as do the Negro workers. They are the oldest surviving labor group; they are linked historically with the founding and the successive stages of development of the New World. It was upon their early labors that tobacco, rice, indigo, sugar, and cotton, each in its turn, gave to the New World a means of prosperous survival. The essence of the early agricultural economy demanded their presence and got them in irretrievable numbers. They were in large part the foundation of our present machine culture and actually performed most of the early industrial tasks. Their labor, in so far as it has contributed to the present industrial age, has finally created a situation which renders them virtually non-essential and unnecessary. There are no more frontiers to conquer; the machine has taken the ascendancy over the crude artifact of the institution of slavery; there is no longer a contemptuous scorn of work, but a righteous and insistent demand for it. Most important, however, there has been conferred upon this race, since its transplantation from Africa to America, a new social status, with theoretical rights to equal citizenship which were utterly unanticipated in the beginning.

The Negroes are not the only unnecessary laborers in the new industrial period. But, regarded as *Negro labor*, they are unnecessary in the same sense that *slave labor* is unnecessary in this age. Their chief heritage of status from the past is that undifferentiated one of mass labor for certain tasks. And in this status, valuable as it once was, they can neither be completely absorbed nor completely expelled.

In the South until the Civil War they were the blind content of an institution which held a vast white working population relentlessly to the ground. This period witnessed the beginning of a bitter enmity, economic at base, but racially focused, which survives today in practically every detail of race relations in the South. For the institution of slavery required no white workers, and they were simply eliminated from the picture and very largely by their own blood kin of another class. These whites were driven off to the barren hills, forced into a degrading poverty at times beneath even the Negroes, reasoned out of the right to work as the Negroes were reasoned out of the right to enjoy the fruits of their own labor. It was this period that found Negro workers both capable of and acceptable for all grades of work, from the rough labor of the plantations to the skilled work of the towns. They did most of it, in the South at least, and, so long as their services were profitable to the owner and could be leased, like one of our present-day business machines, they were bluntly defended in their monopoly.

The use of Negroes as artisans came about, incidentally, in a quite natural manner. It was during the early period of the dominion of tobacco, with its reckless venturing of all available hands and fortunes in this crop, that the field was left open for the training of Negro artisans. The mother country, England, not yet convinced of the independent spirit of the colonies, needed and demanded raw materials for fabrication which, in turn, could be sold back into the colonies. She needed spars, beams, and like naval stores. In the midst of the development of a profitable staple there was demand for diversification. Moreover, too much concentration of attention on the staple tended to overproduction. Even the making of barrels and staves for the shipping of the tobacco called for specialists. A rise in standards of living called for better houses, landings, warehouses. Finally, the shortage of manufactured goods from England and extravagantly high prices, due to poor transportation facilities as a result of wars and other causes, forced the colonies to do manufacturing of their own. Taxes on imports, together with England's restrictive commercial and trade policy, made impracticable the shipping of much of their raw material.

These factors would have brought diversification even if there had not been the factor of soil exhaustion. As a pure matter of profit, therefore, the settlers trained their Negro servants and slaves for the skilled work. Since both the white planters and indentured servants wanted to be farmers this move encountered no difficulty. Virginia took the lead in training Negro slaves as artisans, and was followed in time by practically all of the other colonies. In the files of the *South Carolina Gazette*, M. W. Jernegan found, from 1732 to 1776, references to Negroes in 28 different trades; among these were sawyers, squarers, coopers, house carpenters, ship carpenters, cabinetmakers, curriers, tanners, shoemakers, wheelwrights, bricklayers, silversmiths.[1] From training Negroes for these positions on the plantation the practice extended to that of leasing their skill for profits. Eventually the practice encompassed most of the skilled work of the South, squeezing the white workers out, and creating deep antagonisms. This bitterness, which was engendered during the last period of slavery, gathered itself into gall during the period of reconstruction when the poor whites first began to emerge from beneath the grinding weight of the institution.

Between 1880 and 1907 every southern state enacted laws intended to separate the races and limit the privilege of franchise. In effect, this legislation, backed by a solid sentiment, threw up an economic breastwork of protection for white workers against the free competition of the blacks who had the advantage of actual possession of the trades as a heritage of three hundred years of slavery. In 1880 the census showed an absolute decline in the number of Negroes in skilled

---

[1] "Slavery and the Beginnings of Industrialism in the American Colonies," *American Historical Review*, January, 1920, pp. 220–240.

trades; there was intense economic conflict, employing fiery racial arguments. By 1900 these jobs had not only been successfully challenged by white labor, but the racial arguments had advanced to the point of denying the capacity of Negroes for skilled work.

Another force, however, must be taken into account in order to understand the changed character of Negro labor. The wasteful methods of crop cultivation had exhausted the soil in those rich delta stretches to which the Negroes had been moved by the exigencies of cotton. The search for new land, shared by both white and Negro agricultural workers, has been evident since the Civil War. This restlessness has been unmistakable and is reflected in various social reactions. The center of the Negro population moved southward and westward uninterruptedly for 130 years. The Negroes were being crowded off the land, and under the rigid conditions of their life their death rate reached such enormous proportions around 1890 that Dr. Frederick Hoffman [1] predicted the race question would soon solve itself by the extinction of the Negro. Each year the descendants of non-slaveholding classes were emerging and contesting and winning many of the old strongholds of Negro labor.

It is well to point out another situation of importance in Negro status generally. For many decades the Negro remained not only in the South but in the rural areas of the South. There has been a rapid rate of urbanization among the general population, but the Negro element of the population, until recently, has been slowest of all in deserting the rural areas. As the general rate of urbanization declines, however, the Negro rate becomes more rapid. Since 1900 about 2,225,000 Negroes have left the farms and small villages of the South. And during the decade 1920–1930 alone nearly 1,225,000 southern Negroes deserted the farm. In 1910 the total population was 45.8 per cent urban; in 1920 it was 51.4 per cent urban. The concentration of the foreign-born white stock in cities gives a certain distortion to the normal urban trends. Present trends imply that the native whites of native parentage and Negroes will both pass the mid-mark in urbanization about 1935. Despite the fact that there has always been a much lower proportion of urbanization among Negroes than among whites of native parentage, the recent rapid urbanization of Negroes indicates that they will have passed native whites of native parentage in degree of urbanization by 1940.

In the North the inconsiderable numbers of Negroes, until recently,

[1] *Race Traits and Tendencies of the American Negro*, p. 329.

have made them a negligible factor in mass. Even free Negro labor before the Civil War had limited opportunity. For the past forty years, immigrants from South Europe have been the grist of the expanding mills. And although there survive memories of clashes with the Irish in the middle eighties, over the rough work of the cities, and still later with the Italians in the vast railway extension projects, the essentialness of Negroes to the North began virtually with the hectic, artificial acceleration of the World War emergency. Negro workers were employed first in the Connecticut tobacco fields to take the place of the Slavic workers who had been attracted to the better-paying war industries. Later the use of Negroes was extended to other states. One northern railroad brought up thousands from the South for the essential road work, and all but a few of these went into the surrounding mills of Pennsylvania. The stockyards in Chicago and the mills of the adjacent industrial towns drew Negroes from the lower Mississippi Valley. In the fourteen-year period 1916–1930 over 1,200,000 Negroes moved from South to North. Not all remained, but a vast deposit was left. They entered iron and steel mills, stockyards, railroad maintenance and repair work, light manufacturing, the textile industry, and construction, and scattered themselves in smaller numbers over a large range of work.

Now that the northern expansion is checked and a residue of at least a million and a quarter of this restless army of black workers remains in the North, a serious question arises concerning their future. For it is clear that their future is bound up with American industry and business generally, and with the very structure of American life.

It is entertaining at times to indulge in the reflection that the temperament of the Negro is the one mass quality in America which is resisting the corruptive influence of mechanization; that he has his own racial rhythm; that in a folk sense he creates so many new and quaint variations of any given pattern as to render him helpless in the midst of those higher, unvaried rhythms of mass production. This would be a solution if it were possible for Negroes to make use of some unique racial temperament in commanding a sufficiency of material goods for existence in a highly competitive society. But this does not appear to be the case. The romantic view of the Negro and of Negro labor is of very little value in a situation of a competitive struggle with workers who have adjusted themselves to the exacting tempo of the machine.

Cheap Negro labor is more and more being supplanted by machinery or cheaper Mexican labor, and the traditional "Negro jobs" are disappearing. Cotton culture is passing out of the hands of Negroes; cotton fabrication has never included them, and apparently has no intention of doing so. Menial public service jobs such as street-cleaning and garbage collection, to which "no self-respecting white man" would stoop a decade or so ago, are rapidly becoming exclusively white men's jobs, under the more euphonious label of "white wings" and "sanitary squads." Personal service positions—those of hotel waiters, bellmen and porters, barbers, caterers, and bootblacks — are comfortably distributing themselves among the French, Italians, Germans, and Greeks.

The changing character of industry itself has resulted in erratic employment fluctuations in all classes of labor. An effect not to be ignored here is the excess of workers created who are not too proud to compete in the lower ranges of labor. The rapid introduction of machinery into industry has brought vast displacements in mining, road building, brick making, tobacco handling and rehandling, and farming, and threatens among other fields cotton picking, from which hundreds of thousands of Negroes at present get a living. The entrance of women into industry since the war provides an even cheaper labor source for light manufacturing than Negro labor and excludes, in large part, Negro women, except in laundries and certain tobacco industries, where adequate machinery has not yet been devised to do the work which they are doing.

The increased urbanization of rural workers following the decline of agriculture in sections and, in turn, following the use of labor-saving machinery on the farm, and the disappearance of free land, are crowding the cities with cheap and eager labor. The reduction of man power generally in factories, following technological improvements and efficient economies in the handling and routing of materials, until quite recently hailed as a triumph of the skill of the industrial engineer, is now unmistakably felt as inevitable displacement for the eternal marginal men in industry. The heartlessness of the process is evident in such an instance as this: when the army of unemployed in the depression which began in 1930 reached disturbing proportions, many workers, without prospects of other jobs, found that they could eke out an existence of a sort by selling apples. Then some inventive genius placed on the market an automatic apple-vending machine which, with ironic thoroughness, crashed this last defense against the bread line.

From a somewhat exaggerated position of importance as labor the vast bulk of Negroes find themselves in a somewhat insecure position. They have been carried through the conditioning of the cotton era, and are just emerging from it with mentality and musculature adjusted to its simple and almost elementary routine. Like the rest of America they have passed from an agricultural to an industrial economy, but with two significant differences: (1) the struggle for economic security, which is characteristically one of class, is complicated for them by the added factor of race and color with its highly charged emotional complexes; (2) the shift from agriculture to industry which has left them very largely without traditional skills has made necessary the acquirement of new skills without the aid of apprenticeship, or special training, or the effective protection of labor organization.

Unskilled labor has been most seriously affected by machinery and by the industrial changes, and the largest proportions of Negro workers (75 per cent or more) are unskilled. In the building trades the structure of buildings is changing from lumber to steel. There have been many Negro carpenters but few structural steel workers and few chances for apprenticeship in this new field. The number of carpenters per thousand of the population has, thus, actually declined since 1910. The painters, glaziers, and varnishers have suffered a similar decline since 1910, because much of their work is now done in factories. Brick and stone masons and plasterers have declined more than 50 per cent since 1890, because of the shifted emphasis in trade. Wheelwrights and coopers are gone, probably forever. This work is done in factories by machinery. Moreover, steel drums, pails, sacks, and other containers have replaced the wooden barrel. Machinists have increased sevenfold, but the machinists' unions bar Negroes. Trucks are replacing drays and also competing with railway transportation; and trucking, increasingly, is becoming a chain proposition instead of an individual venturing.

Dr. Julius Klein, while in the Department of Commerce, pointed out with respect to power that there has been a world-wide shift from coal to oil and hydro-electric power. The coal industry reflects this shift in its decline, and in the consequent disintegration of the industry in Kentucky and West Virginia. The particular figures for Illinois mines give a picture which well characterizes the situation. Between 1918 and 1928 there were fewer mines operated, fewer men employed, and fewer days of employment for miners; less coal was produced, but there was an increase in average tons per man per day. Negro workers have formed 7.3 per cent of the workers in the coal industry but a negligible percentage of the oil industry. There are fewer factory workers generally than there were in 1920, but increasingly more goods are being produced. Hand laundering is giving place to machinery requiring skill and permitting the entrance of white women workers, and one of the most recent and powerfully effective laundry advertisements suggests that housewives should "avoid contagion in shanty washed clothes." In the name of hygiene, a blow is struck at the Negro washerwoman who has been the backbone of stability for the Negro laborer's family. Moreover, washing machines in the homes are doing their bit in further reducing the necessity for Negro washerwomen. Oil-burning furnaces with thermostat control strike at the Negro janitor, as do manless elevators. Ditch-digging machinery has quietly eliminated thousands of Negro road workers as the new hoisting machinery is eliminating the well-known Negro job of hod-carrying.

Stuart Chase traces the process of the new industry as follows: first the specialization and the machinery which merely gives more power to the skilled worker; then the subdivision of the manufacturing process, which makes use of many unskilled workers on dull routine; finally the elimination of the unskilled workers (the robots) by more complicated machinery, calling back the skilled worker.[1] The Negro workers do not seriously profit by the first and third, but share to some extent the second stage with new women workers. The vital fact is that the most important fields of Negro work have been affected by both the temporary and permanent depressions. The changes have placed white and Negro workers more acutely in competition for the same jobs, since race is here given greater value than class, with the result that white workers are most frequently given preference by employers.

The field of skilled work, which absorbs, at least temporarily, a portion of the excess workers, is coming increasingly under the control of labor organizations which either restrict or do not encourage Negro memberships. The new industries which are expanding — the radio industry, airplane transportation, automobile service, the manufacture of complicated labor-saving machinery, trucking — restrict Negro employment to certain grades of work, and are making apprenticeship for the new trades extremely difficult. The pressure

[1] *Men and Machines*, pp. 171-175.

for the few new jobs has, in known instances, stimulated efforts of anxious protective organizations to urge employment of white workers before placing Negroes. These have not excluded women's clubs and Junior Leagues, but have found most notorious expression in the Ku Klux Klan and the Black Shirts.

Since 1910 more than 500,000 Mexicans have entered the country, unrestricted by the quotas applied to Europeans and others. They are finding the lowest American wage and living scale for fruit and cotton picking in Texas and California superior to their agricultural wages at home. From the Southwest they have moved into Illinois, Michigan, and Pennsylvania, invading the tentative borders of the very recent Negro migrants. The truth is that they are no more incapable of skill than the Negroes, granted a long enough exposure to that range of work. It is inevitable that the cycle will include the semi-skilled and skilled ranges of work as it has moved geographically from Texas and California to Illinois and Pennsylvania.

The situation of labor unions in normal times takes this general pattern: the availability of Negro workers, at times at a lower cost, constitutes a menace to organized labor, which would, it seems, ignore the group unless under pressure to do otherwise. This ever present menace has tended to soften the first hostility to inclusion, and in lines in which Negroes have been freely employed in the past the unions have extended membership. The less skilled lines have had the largest numbers of Negro members. These were the longshoremen and the hod-carriers. However, the carpenters' union, which before the period of general depression of 1930 set in had 340,000 members, had less than 600 Negro members, and the painters' union with 120,000 members had less than 300 Negroes, although there were 34,000 known Negro carpenters and more than 10,000 Negro painters. Eleven internationals exclude Negroes by constitution or ritual. These eleven had in 1928 a total membership of 436,000 workers and controlled a field in which 43,000 Negroes were employed. Where the unions are freely open the Negroes have entered with the general movement of workers. Most frequently, however, it appears that with the continued disposition to disproportionate assignments of work among white and Negro union members, advantage for Negro workers lies outside present forms of organization.

What happens to the Negro worker in periods of acute economic stress is indicated in the unemployment records since 1929. The first workers to be affected are the unskilled and the casuals, the newest comers are the first goers, and this can be viewed as a simple matter of priority; jobs easy to learn are easy to dispense with. The few unemployment studies made where there is an important body of Negro labor reflect the weight of these factors. In Baltimore, for example, the Bureau of Labor statistics showed that the Negroes were 32.6 per cent of the unemployed although only 14.7 per cent of the population. The New York State Department of Labor at the end of 1930 found the Negroes ranking below the native white and foreign-born in amount of full-time employment. Of native white men, 64.2 per cent were employed full time; of foreign-born, 53.8 per cent; and of Negroes 42.5 per cent, while only 31.9 per cent of the Negro women as compared with 74.7 per cent of the native white and 63.4 per cent of the foreign-born were employed full time. For both sexes, just about twice as many Negroes as native-born whites were totally unemployed.

Dr. Earle Eubank of the University of Cincinnati early in 1933 directed a study of unemployment among white and Negro families in Cincinnati. His results indicate the disproportionate pressure of prolonged unemployment upon these two groups of workers: "Among the white workmen whose former weekly average wage was $35.62, the income dropped to an average of $7.61, an average reduction of $28.01, or 78 per cent. Among the Negro workmen, the average weekly income dropped from $26.47 to $4.32, a reduction of $22.15, or 83 per cent." [1]

Dr. Joseph H. Willits, of the University of Pennsylvania, conducted in Philadelphia one of the most careful studies of unemployment according to race. With his assistants he studied this factor among several groups for the four-year period 1929–1933, thus tracing the impact of unemployment over successive years. In 1929, when 9.0 per cent of all white employables were unemployed, 15.7 per cent of the Negroes were unemployed. In 1930 it was 13.8 per cent for whites and 19.4 per cent for Negroes; in 1931 it was 24.1 per cent for whites and 35.0 per cent for Negroes; and in 1932 it was 39.7 per cent for whites and 56.0 per cent for Negroes.[2]

From the beginning of the unemployment period, the Negroes have shown a larger percentage of unemployment than the whites, but as the depression continued, the percentage by which the Negro

[1] "The Consequences of Unemployment in Cincinnati."

[2] An address before the Conference on the Economic Status of the Negro, sponsored by the Julius Rosenwald Fund, Washington, 1933.

ratio exceeded that of the white tended to narrow slightly. Nevertheless in 1930 the percentage of Negroes still unemployed was half as high again as the percentage of whites. If to these proportions the 20 per cent doing part-time work had been added, the unemployment rates would have been tragic as well as startling.

In the matter of made work in the city, which offered another unemployment index, actually more Negroes were counted among the applicants than there were Negroes in the city's gainfully employed occupations. The question of willingness or inability to work did not enter and has never been raised. For 90 per cent of the unemployment among Negroes was due to the fact that they had been "laid off" or that the firms that had formerly employed them had become bankrupt, merged with others, or moved away.

The marginality of these workers is further reflected in the industrial histories of the unemployed secured by the Industrial Research Bureau. The average length of the longest job of Negroes was 3.8 years as compared with 6 years for whites. Earnings of whites were from $5 to $10 more weekly in the same general labor classification; the median savings, before losing their jobs, were $86 for Negroes and $204 for whites. Nearly twice as many Negroes as whites were in arrears on their rents; a third more of the whites could get loans and just twice as much in amount. Finally, as the climax of this impact in appeals for public relief, in 1931-32, while Negroes formed 20 per cent of the city's unemployed, 27 per cent of the children under relief care were Negroes.[1]

In 1933, the Julius Rosenwald Fund held in Washington a conference on the economic status of the Negro, and made possible an appraisal of studies in special lines by authoritative students of this question. Many of the analyses were based upon the 1930 census figures on occupations, but most of them were supplemented by additional special studies. From these reports, it appears that over the past forty years there has been an increase of Negroes in industry, larger in manufacturing and mechanical industries than in trade and transportation; that the occupational status of women has not changed materially over the past twenty years, while in the South there has been a pronounced shift from agriculture to domestic service. In mining and in steel the proportion of Negroes has declined but not excessively when total decline is considered. The largest

[1] *Report on the Economic Status of the Negro*, published by the Julius Rosenwald Fund, pp. 19-20.

numbers of Negro industrial workers, however, have gone into the building and construction industries, which have been affected most seriously of all by business depressions. In the food industries the numbers have been insignificant and remain so, except in the meat-slaughtering plants. In skilled lines the number of Negroes has been declining in both the South and North, and their present proportions are higher in those trades that are waning in importance than in the new industrial skills. Negro women form 9.7 per cent of the female population 10 years of age and over, but are 17.1 per cent of the working women.

It is, in a sense, very largely a matter of attitudes which constitutes for these workers a problem different from that of other working groups in America. Dr. Herman Feldman of Dartmouth in treating racial factors in industry reduced the problem wholly to the sphere of racial attitudes. He pointed out that:

> In the South there is a greater fixity of habits, mores, traditions, and prejudices. The problem there is to secure a loosening and relaxation, while in the North there is often merely an unawareness of the extent of racial discriminations and an uncertainty which presents the opportunity for considering the question anew. Also, the North shows less rigidity because the community sentiment is less unanimous, permitting a clash of opinion on the ethical and social questions of race relations.[1]

The interplay and uncertainty of these factors are well illustrated in one of the marginal areas in which Negroes are in competition with several types of workers. A study made recently of 456 industrial plants and 23 labor unions in Los Angeles, California, reveals the various configurations of policy possible, all of which are imagined to be founded upon the same racial instincts.[2]

The most frequently encountered policy was one based upon the belief that "Negro and white workers will not 'mix.'" Investigation showed that they did mix, however, in over fifty of the plants studied. In certain plants where Mexicans were regarded as white, Negroes were not allowed to mix with them; where Mexicans were classed as colored, Negroes not only worked with them but were given positions over them. In certain plants Mexicans and whites worked together; in some others white workers accepted Negroes and objected to Mexicans; in still others white workers accepted Mexicans

[1] *Racial Factors in American Industry*, p. 13.
[2] Charles S. Johnson, "The Negro in Los Angeles Industries." Unpublished study, National Urban League, 1926.

and objected to Japanese. White women worked with Mexican and Italian women, but refused to work with Negroes. Mexicans and Negroes worked under a white foreman; Italians and Mexicans worked under a Negro foreman; Mexicans were in some places refused entirely because of plant policies against mixing. In a hospital Negro nurses attended white patients, but were segregated from white nurses; in a manufacturing plant white workers refused to work with Negroes, but worked under a Negro foreman. Brick manufacturing was declared by some employers to be too hot and dusty for Negroes; yet the Negroes were said by others to be the best brick workers, and were given a better scale of wages than Mexicans. Peoples from southern climates were regarded as better adapted to work in the presence of heat; but the Consolidated Ice Companies found the Mexicans best fitted to handling and storing ice. Because white elevator men and attendants in a department store disturbed the morale of the organization by constant chatting and flirtations with the salesgirls, Negro men were brought in to take their places and the morale was restored, in spite of the fears of other employers that the two races could not work side by side in these positions.

Labor union practice in this situation followed the same uncertain pattern of plant practice. Negroes were admitted freely to unions when they were regarded as a menace to white workers, or when it was conceded that they held distinctly favorable positions with employers. The bricklayers were indifferent to Negro membership and refused to mix with them until they discovered that Negro bricklayers were "working independently for whatever wages they could get." The asbestos workers barred Negroes, Mexicans, and Italians. The three reasons given were: "Negroes cannot stand the heat of the work"; "there are no Negroes in the trade"; and "if we begin mixing the races they will get all of the good jobs." The iron workers are certain that their work is "too dangerous for Negroes"; besides, the work pays well. While Negro musicians were in public favor and frequently given preference over white musicians, there was a drive to preserve working standards for all musicians, and they were freely taken into the unions, without regard to the question of racial difference and the impossibility of mixing. The white painters could not have Negroes or Mexicans in their locals, but they frequently worked for Negro contractors when they could improve their jobs by doing so.

The fluctuations of racial feeling according to circumstance can be reduced to these generalizations. Racial feeling increased when, in instances of the unions' assignment of work, white workers were given preference and Negroes complained. It increased as white workers were exclusively favored by employers in work once shared by Negroes. It decreased when the question of job assignment was not present and the membership of Negroes was considered essential to the success of the white members. It appeared on first contact where Negroes were taken into a trade, and disappeared as members became accustomed to Negro members. It increased in unions of trades in which Negroes were given about the same chance for work as whites on some notion of their special fitness or on grounds of "fairness." It increased to the point that Negroes were sometimes given more than their numerical proportion of offices in locals of trades in which Negro workers were given actual preference over white workers by employers.

The objections to Negro labor in industry which constitute their major problem may be summarized as follows:

1. Traditional policy of the plant not to employ Negroes.
2. Fear of racial difficulties if whites and Negroes are introduced into the same plant.
3. Fear of the objection of white workers and resultant labor difficulties.
4. Traditional beliefs about Negroes which concern their mentality and character, and general inability to perform the work required.
5. Fear of bringing Negroes into contact with white women workers.
6. Lack of training of Negroes for certain jobs.
7. Unsatisfactory experience with Negro workers in the past.
8. Advocacy of certain jobs as belonging exclusively to the white race.
9. Expense that would be involved in making alterations in the building to accommodate white and Negro workers separately.
10. Objections of labor unions.[1]

The response of Negro workers to the special limitations is manifest in the various means by which they acquire new occupations:

1. Personal interest of an employer in an individual Negro.
2. Superior efficiency.
3. Labor shortage.
4. Elimination of prejudice among employers and employees.
5. The practice of "passing" for white.
6. Political influence.

[1] Charles S. Johnson, *The Negro in American Civilization*, p. 13.

7. Gradual introduction of Negro workers by beginning with persons of fair complexion and adding successively darker ones.
8. Accepting segregated facilities.
9. Accepting lower wages.
10. Strike-breaking.
11. Training and apprenticeship.[1]

The problem of training of these workers centers largely upon the vocational schools which have been thought to be inadequately equipped to prepare Negroes for modern industry. However, these schools insist that their graduates are in demand, and that when they leave school they receive higher wages and are better fitted for promotion to advanced positions than other workers. A vital criticism of present educational methods and policy condemns the disposition of Negro teachers and leaders to ignore vocational training as lacking in dignity and social position, thus increasing the waste of the process. Of 3,000 Negro high-school graduates in North Carolina schools who were asked to name the careers for which they were preparing themselves, 41 were planning to enter agriculture although 75 per cent of the Negroes of the state derived their living from agriculture; 207, or about 6 per cent, were planning to enter trades, and 2,062, or 68 per cent, were dreaming of professions.

Now that vocational training in high schools has been proved a wise social expedient for white students and the cost considerable, there is a new and suspicious willingness on the part of school boards to give Negroes the inexpensive classical training which some of their leaders clamored for several years ago as a requisite of status and culture.

Agriculture has always been an important occupation for Negroes. Although there has been a decrease in the number of farm operators, both white and Negro, for the country as a whole during the period 1920–1930, agriculture is still the occupation engaging the largest number of Negroes. About one-third of all Negro workers are farmers. In 1900, the percentage engaged in farming was 53.7; in 1920 and 1930 this occupation still maintained first place, although the percentage had decreased to 44.4 in 1920 and to 36.1 in 1930. The trend is toward an increase of Negro managers (40.5 per cent), a decrease in the number of Negro owners (13.1 per cent), and a slight decrease in Negro tenants (1.6 per cent). The trends for Negroes and whites are not similar for the period except in the case of white owners,

[1] *Ibid.*, p. 11.

which shows a corresponding decrease of 9.1 per cent; while white tenants increased (12.3 per cent), and white managers decreased (20.3 per cent).

Some of the decrease, particularly for the period preceding 1920, was due to the migration to northern states, and this is notably true of owners. Later, at the beginning of the decade, a great part was undoubtedly due to the development of industries in the South and the consequent movements of both white and Negro populations to the cities. But the provocation to migration is more important. Agricultural production, despite this depletion, has been greater during the past decade than ever before, because of the fact that a decreasing proportion of the population engaged in full-time farming is able now to produce plenty for everyone in the nation to eat. As a consequence, there has been an inescapable forcing out of farm people to the cities. Farm areas have contracted or shifted, the value of farm lands has suffered heavily, and there is a persistent surplus of farm products carrying prices so low that an adequate living is difficult for even the best of farmers. One unmistakable observation, whatever the approach, is that agriculture, one of the most essential fields of labor, is not now very profitable.

The farmer was experiencing a depression long before the effects of the 1930 depression became widespread. When the collapse in prices came the farms were seriously overwhelmed. In this situation of agriculture generally, it is not difficult to understand the plight of the Negro farmers. The bulk of these, who are tenants, are part of a system the features of which admit of considerable exploitation, both deliberate and undeliberate.

In the plantation credit system, seizure of saleable produce for a tenant's debts is not uncommon, but there is less of it when prices are low than when prices are high. The large plantations utilize the most productive lands, and the masses of agricultural workers in these areas are very dependent and as a rule poor. It has been found that accumulations are very slow. According to the study made in 1927 by the North Carolina State Tax Commission, the average annual cash income of white farmers is $556, while the incomes of Negro farmers are still lower; in Dr. Arthur Raper's study of Greene and Macon counties, Georgia, the average total income for Negroes was $399 in Greene County and $448 in Macon County.[1]

[1] An unpublished study by Dr. Arthur Raper, under the Commission on Interracial Coöperation, Atlanta, Georgia.

Lack of sufficient equipment was one of the penalties for failure to accumulate, but it also limited income and made chances of accumulation less.

Credit plays a vital part in agriculture; it is necessary for the conduct of farming enterprise. Federal mortgage agencies occasionally make loans to Negro farmers, but Federal Land Banks limit loans to members of loan associations. Negro farm owners, excluded from membership and having none among themselves, are without these credits. Merchants are almost the only credit agency which will grant loans for the whole of the crop season and covering all the needs of the farmers. Among Negro farmers one-third of the owners and two-thirds of the tenants received credits from time merchants at an average interest of 25 per cent.

There is a vicious circle, with poor farming methods, lack of knowledge and education, concentration of production on cost crops, and methods of living being partially responsible for the dependence upon the high cost of merchant credit, while, on the other hand, the low income and high cost of credit are partly responsible for continuing these conditions.

Improving the Negroes' use of credit seems to involve not only a change in the habit on the part of the farmer himself, but also an accompanying change in their whole economic situation. It is doubtful, indeed, if much will be accomplished by merely raising the Negro farmer to the level of the white farmer, for the prospects under the present system seem no brighter for one than for the other.

The easiest way to dismiss the troublesome economic future of the Negro is to put the responsibility for change hopefully upon Providence or some sudden social enlightenment. If dominant industry and labor which aspires to dominance would only forget color, the lot of the Negro worker would be easier. This seldom happens by and of itself. But it can be and is often disregarded when it is profitable to do so. So long, however, as color carries the connotation of inefficiency and unnecessity to employers, and of an unwarranted and menacing usurpation of jobs to labor, it will ever be the badge of the marginal worker. And such a worker need never hope for full participation in the dominant American economy. With the disposition of labor organizations to oppose sharing the available work on grounds of race, these black workers are on the mercies of employers. Except where some favorable personal factor enters, or wages are to be reduced, or there is a strike or a sudden emergency, their chances for employment are uneven. It seems an unsound principle, to say the least, for Negro workers to have to pin their security in work upon the misfortune of their fellow-workers.

It should be evident, however, despite the fact that there is no single source of responsibility for their drastic exclusion from some industries and the limitation of the opportunity to work in others, that the community must pay for the policy which it countenances. It usually pays indirectly in the magnified costs of relief and of protection against crime, in the support of offenders against the law, in illness and the loss of earning as well as spending power. For whether wise or not this group most nearly approaches the antidote to depressions in keeping most of its earnings in circulation. Most significantly, however, though less impressively, the community pays in what the system of exclusion and humiliation does to the sense of fair play itself. The blanket policies against special jobs or special ranges of skill mean a loss of efficient man power to the extent at least of that proportion of the Negro working population that earlier showed an exceptional capacity for skilled performance.

At any step forward an interesting paradox interposes: the acquirement of status and security by Negro workers is the only means by which they can develop their moral powers and full value as citizens; but this very development frequently renders more acute the conflict of racial policies and relations. It has been pointed out that Negro labor in its old concept is not essential to present industry; that this labor has, nevertheless, along with all America, been carried on the wave of general advance; and that in its present status it cannot be expelled, and is yet not desired for incorporation. This is merely a reflection of that curious paradox of present American life which makes it impossible for Negroes either to develop their own culture or to share fully the dominant one. In this relationship they are unique. The American Indians, who until recently were wards of the government, kept their cultural autonomy but became economically dependent; the Orientals, as soon as they had reached a point of acute competition, were expelled; the Jews, who represent a minority group in America, have both the cohesive influence of a religion and an economy which sustains itself through a special financial skill. The South Europeans, once a minority, are affected adversely by economic factors, but may lose themselves in the second generation. The Negroes remain a recognizable bloc, ever wearing the visible livery of their station.

In the mood of the present implications of the Negro's place in industry, it would be entirely logical to look forward to the complete separation of industries according to race. It is perfectly clear that this would be as economically unsound as it would be socially absurd. There survives out of the most recent changes in industry a tendency to employ Negroes in iron and steel, on "heat" jobs; and in longshoring, which demands a combination of strength and agility. The first of these is based upon a favorable myth, which is as groundless as that larger group of myths by which Negroes are excluded from other lines; and longshoring, perversely enough, is being affected by declining river transportation and the introduction of loading machinery. It might be possible to found, upon preference for them in certain limited fields, a cult of competence which would automatically eliminate competition, but this in a sense would be as unfair as the practices against which protests are now made. Again, it might be rationally urged that Negroes should receive a prorated share of unskilled, skilled, and even professional positions according to their population proportion. But there is no dictator to enforce such specious even-handedness. The closest approach to such an opportunity has been the authority of the National Recovery Act inaugurated under President Roosevelt in 1933. Almost revolutionizing in its approach to industrial problems, it has favored workers by offering them a first opportunity for class recognition and bargaining power. The first tendency observed in the operation of the various industrial codes has been to sharpen the issue of competition along racial lines, except where this has been expressly warned against. The recombination of tasks to meet the requirement regarding minimum hours and wages without increasing the burden of labor costs has pushed many Negroes out of positions. It is possible that, for the security of the structure itself, the wisdom of guarding labor against itself may be seen, and the Negroes more equably introduced into the country's major industries.

The situation, it would seem, demands deliberate education and strategy to overcome the emotional opposition to the full inclusion of Negro workers in the pattern of American industrial life. What appeals to good-will and the generosity of their hard-pressed and scarcely sympathetic white fellow-workers cannot accomplish may thus be accomplished with the aid of economic laws. To enjoy anything approaching an independent status the Negro workers must achieve it by some effort of their own. This, then, is their new economic frontier. The task ahead is the creative one of making Negro labor to fit the exigencies of the new age, if they are to survive in it.

It is scarcely worth while to dwell upon the present character of Negro labor. It is by no means an abused mass of undifferentiated competence. The extent to which only moderately competent and even incompetent Negroes have been able to exist at all is one of the best auguries for this labor under a new discipline which makes superior competence in all ranges of skill the price they must pay now for being Negroes. The fundamental lack, strange to say, has not been skill, but a developed sense of those more generalized patterns of precision and craftsmanship. The ease with which the Japanese could shift from an age-old eastern culture to that of the west is due not so much to the precision of imitation as to a well-developed technique for manipulation which could be transferred to any given set of problems. Such is the value of a college for providing a student with a technique which, though not related to any given occupation, may be transferred to any field. Such is the value and should be the insistence of all the elementary schools where Negro youth are in attendance, and such is the special task of the Negro technical schools, which, one fears, are less concerned with the development of these mental and physical habit sets than with caps and gowns.

Although it has scarcely been recognized, the new age of machinery has rendered archaic and ruinous the dual and mutually exclusive chambers of white and black labor; only the shell of the social customs remains. Black labor as a group asset is linked with the institution of slavery which created it. The institution of slavery did not completely expire with the Civil War. It owes as much of its death as has been accomplished quite recently to the relentless course of a more efficient, even if less idyllic, system. It probably would have expired without a civil war. The logic of this new economy permits no specific sphere for black labor of all grades and degrees of competency, without an enormous waste both to industry and to national life. The present transgression of the boundaries of those spheres by white workers, in their acceptance of "black jobs," even to the point of passing ordinances to insure street cleaners' jobs and shooting Negro railroad firemen, is only an admission of the cold color blindness of this process.

The Negro workers face today one of the most intense periods of their history, and in the struggle for survival they have the weight of many factors against them. But it is becoming increasingly clear that, at bottom, the contest is not as much between white and black labor as it is between the imperatives of our new economic system and the surviving social orthodoxies of the old.

PROBLEMS FOR STUDY

1. What result may we expect as machinery increasingly invades the field of unskilled labor? Will this mean greater and constant Negro unemployment, or will Negroes be forced back to competition with white labor in semi-skilled and skilled lines?
2. Is it conceivable that economic lines can be drawn on a racial basis without danger to the security of labor or our present economic structure?
3. Will increased Negro efficiency increase the intensity of racial competition?
4. In the drawing up of the industrial codes for the southern industries under the National Recovery Act, it was urged that a differential wage scale should be inserted for Negroes since these industries were accustomed to paying Negroes a smaller rate of pay. Would not the smaller rate of pay for Negroes permit greater profits for industries and in turn encourage employers to use Negroes in preference to white workers, thus creating further racial strife?
5. Negro workers are prevented from joining unions either by the policy of direct exclusion or discriminatory treatment in work assignments after joining, and they are condemned for breaking strikes. What policy should they follow in securing a foothold in industry?
6. Fifty years ago it required about half of the working population to supply the food of the nation. About half of this number today can produce more than enough. Should the excess Negro working population in cities be induced to return to the farm?
7. A Mississippi county in an unemployment emergency voted to give the Negro unemployed a small measure of relief and white unemployed the "made work" for which some funds were available. Did this act indicate greater sentimental concern for the Negro unemployed? Was this a fair division of unemployment relief?

BIBLIOGRAPHY

Stuart Chase, *Men and Machines* (1929).
Earle E. Eubank, "The Consequences of Unemployment in Cincinnati" (unpublished study).
Herman Feldman, *Racial Factors in American Industry* (1931).
Frederick L. Hoffman, *Race Traits and Tendencies of the American Negro* (1896).

Marcus W. Jernegan, "Slavery and the Beginnings of Industrialism in the American Colonies," *American Historical Review*, January, 1920, pp. 220–240.

Charles S. Johnson, *The Negro in American Civilization* (1930).

Charles S. Johnson, "The Negro in Los Angeles Industry." Unpublished study, National Urban League (1926).

Report on the Economic Status of the Negro, published by the Julius Rosenwald Fund (1934).

Arthur Raper, An unpublished study under the Commission on Interracial Coöperation, Atlanta, Georgia.

Joseph H. Willits, An Address before the Conference on the Economic Status of the Negro, Sponsored by the Julius Rosenwald Fund, Washington, 1933.

CHAPTER XVII

NEGRO MIGRATIONS

One characteristic of the status of peasantry is attachment to the soil. It is quite possible that the factor of mobility, inherent in the agricultural situation of the Negroes in the South, prevented the crystallization of a definite and widespread Negro peasant class. Indeed, mobility has been an essential characteristic of Negro labor. It was first brought from Africa. It was constantly moved from one area to another as new plantations were developed. Without this ease of mobility there could have been little profit in cotton cultivation. As a consequence, first, of the exigencies of cotton cultivation under slavery, and later, of the continued search for new lands, the center of the Negro population moved southward and westward without a break for 130 years. Actually, it did not turn northward until the period of the World War. With the theoretical freedom permitted in emancipation, it might seem strange that the great mass of movement was farther and farther southward. There were hundreds who strayed into northern fields seeking work, but these numbers remained small, and for good reasons. The celebrated Negro, Frederick Douglass, could observe blandly of these ineffectual flurries of escape: "The dust will fly, but the earth remains."

There has always been this restlessness and migration of both whites and Negroes in the South. The Negro movement has been immeasurably complicated, however, by acute social and economic conflicts and problems, within and between the two racial groups. The two movements have not always been regarded as the same basic economic phenomenon. But it now appears that this Negro movement was a part of the whole southward and westward movement; and that as free lands became increasingly scarce, competition increased; and that as this competition became increasingly severe upon the Negroes they sought means of escaping the situation entirely. Thus, the opening of the West marked the first notable attempt of Negroes to escape the cotton belt. The numbers going into Kansas and Indiana in 1879 were sufficiently large to earn for the movement the term "Negro Exodus."

The background of the first movement should be briefly sketched. Political freedom was perhaps the one definite and immediate boon of the general emancipation of the slaves, and this was qualified. When reconstruction was firmly accomplished, the Negro freedman, in many instances, worked for his former master with little more return from his labors than before the war. The mores of the South regarding his social and political participation changed slowly, as would naturally be expected. However, it was clear that the only sound economic course for them to pursue was to remain in the South. General Clinton B. Fisk, head of the Freedmen's Bureau in the states of Kentucky and Tennessee, was realistic when he advised the freedmen to remain in their homes, and to make contracts with their former masters; but if their owners would not make good contracts with them, giving them good wages or an equitable share of the crop, they would have "a perfect right" to go where they could improve their condition.[1] There was no market for their labor elsewhere and they were needed in the rehabilitation of the South. The new relationship with their former masters, themselves impoverished by the war, could not yield large returns, however good the intention. In the majority of the southern states the actual money paid to the freed Negro in 1867 was less than that paid to the hired slave in 1860.[2] But not all intentions were good. Promises of wages were made, but instances in which these promises were not kept mounted at times to disconcerting proportions. Moreover, the South, far from conceding this dependence on black labor in its new and unprecedented aspect, was studying the possibilities of a new and, perhaps, cheaper labor supply. Its bids for white immigrant labor were not wholly successful against the more attractive call of the West. The Mississippi Immigration Company, capitalized at $1,000,000, inaugurated a movement to import Chinese coolies, but was unable to carry it through. In the end the Negro remained an important element in the labor supply of this section.

Complicating the readjustment of relations between master and former slave, there were to be reckoned with the new energy and opportunity of the non-slaveholding whites, the emerging white

---

[1] Charles H. Wesley, *A History of Negro Labor in the United States, 1850–1923*, p. 127.

[2] *Ibid.*, p. 132.

labor group. The conflict was both political and economic, and the economic pressure upon these Negroes, colored by the emotions engendered by reconstruction, became exceedingly uncomfortable. The election years 1868 and 1876 were marked by numerous instances of violence, aimed largely at consolidating the program of white Democracy. As early as 1869 there were advocates of emigration voicing the disappointment of Negroes, and urging migration as the only remedy for the ills they were experiencing. These leaders declared that the promised "forty acres and a mule" had not materialized; that the Negroes labored with little pay, and often with no pay at all. But, since there was no market outside the South for Negro labor, the restlessness continued, without drawing off any important numbers of the Negro population. "In 1869 Negroes were reported leaving Virginia in large numbers for the cotton plantations of Georgia, Alabama, and Mississippi because better wages were being paid there than in the tobacco area."[1] In 1871 the National Immigration Bureau was organized in New York. Laborers were needed in Arkansas and Kansas and these states were willing to accept Negro workers. In 1872 Jefferson Long, a Georgia Negro, attempted to organize a State Immigration society "to encourage migration to the fertile lands in the West." About 35,000 Negroes migrated to the Southwest between 1875 and 1878.[2]

The "exodus" to Kansas and Indiana in 1879, however, marked the peak of the migration into the West. Prominently featured as its leader was Benjamin "Pop" Singleton. He had induced a few Negroes to go from Tennessee to Kansas in 1869, and each year thereafter more came through his efforts. Accounts of freedom and plenty came back from emigrants. Handbills were circulated, agents moved actively among the people. In the spring of 1879 Nashville steamship lines exported his Tennessee and Kentucky delegations at a cost of $10 for each person. As the movement gathered momentum, excitement increased. In Louisiana, Henry Adams, another Negro, announced that he had 98,000 ready to move, and he actually led a large number of these to Kansas. North Carolina and Texas delegations joined the trek. Kansas became disturbed over these hordes pouring in, and made efforts to dissuade others from coming. Agents were sent south to discourage them

[1] Charles H. Wesley, *A History of Negro Labor in the United States, 1850–1923*, p. 211.
[2] *Ibid.*, p. 213.

gently, by explaining what every immigrant would need in order to get properly settled in the state. Frederick Douglass raised his voice against the mass movement, but the Negroes continued to move to Kansas. Many of them were indigent, and a Freedmen's Relief Association was formed there in April, 1879. The superintendent, in a report before the association in February, 1880, said 60,000 Negroes had come into Kansas; that 5,000 had gone to other states. Thirty thousand of these migrants settled on farms and 25,000 remained in the towns and cities.[1] Five or six important colonies were established, the most important of which were Baxter Springs, Nicodemus, Monton City, and Singleton.[2]

There was considerable concern in many quarters over this unexpected mass movement. Democratic politicians in the Senate made an investigation and, in their report, attempted to prove that it was a Republican conspiracy to get more votes.[3] However, the Mississippi Valley Labor Convention meeting at Vicksburg, Mississippi, May 6, 1879, with General N. R. Miles as president, gave the causes of the emigration: (a) the low price of cotton, (b) the system of credit, (c) the partial failure of the crop, (d) the system of plantings, (e) the fear of Negroes that their civil rights would be removed, and (f) opportunities of plenty in Kansas as reported to the Negroes.[4] They recommended, as a means of encouraging Negroes to remain in the South, that the disabilities on Negro laborers by the whites should be removed. After the peak of this movement, interstate migration continued, but without reaching the volume of a mass movement.

In 1888–89 there was a movement of about 35,000 Negroes to Arkansas, but the decennial increases were beginning to be felt in several of the western states. Between 1900 and 1910 Arkansas gained 105,516 Negroes, Oklahoma 85,062, and Texas 19,821; while all the eastern, southern, and central states suffered corresponding losses in the Negro population. In 1910, 52.3 per cent of the migration from southern states was to the area west of the Mississippi.

Negro migrations attracted comparatively little attention until

[1] George W. Williams, *History of the Negro Race in America, 1619–1880*, p. 537.

[2] Carter G. Woodson, *A Century of Negro Migration*, p. 142.

[3] *Congressional Record* — Senate, 46th Congress, Vol. 10, part 5, Washington, D. C. 1880, p. 4141.

[4] Charles H. Wesley, *A History of Negro Labor in the United States, 1850–1923*, p. 216.

the direction changed northward. The conquest of the frontier and the end of free land had marked the beginning of migration of the white population to cities. The Negroes followed shortly afterward, and, although at first much slower in their movement cityward, momentum increased until the rate, during the last decade, 1920–1930, about equaled that of the whites. Since 1900 the urban Negro population has increased almost three and one-fifth millions, of which number less than a million is attributable to excess of births over deaths in these cities and towns. Approximately two and one-quarter millions, or about one-fifth of the present Negro population, have left the farms and villages of the South. This, according to Frank A. Ross' estimate, was distributed by decades as follows: one-third of a million between 1900 and 1910, three-fourths of a million between 1910 and 1920, and one and one-fourth millions between 1920 and 1930.[1]

Urbanization in the South has gone along with northward migration. It has not been as conspicuous because it has been more widely distributed.[2] Of the 78 cities in 1930 with more than 10,000 Negroes, in a total population of not less than 25,000, only one (Los Angeles) is in the West; 25 are in the North, and 52 in the South.[3]

Ross cites five distinct types of Negro population origin: (1) widespread drawings to many of the larger and more northerly of the northern cities as exemplified by Chicago; (2) accretion to certain northern Atlantic coast cities, almost exclusively from southern states on the Atlantic seaboard, as in Baltimore; (3) strictly local increase in most of the cities of the deep South, as demonstrated by Atlanta; (4) acquisition from the Mississippi basin by cities of the middle western border and lower tier of states, as in the case of St. Louis; (5) increment to far western cities from east south-central and more west south-central states, as in Los Angeles.

Up to the period of the World War the labor supply for the unskilled processes of industry had come from Europe, and during the later years from the countries of South Europe. Northern industries, ever growing, had been able during the decade preceding the war to absorb as many as ten million of these foreign workers. The sudden stopping of immigration occasioned by the war, and along with this the call of the mother countries for their nationals abroad, created a critical demand for a new labor supply.

The most obvious source of labor for this emergency was the

[1] *Urbanization and the Negro*, p. 118.   [2] *Ibid.*, p. 121.   [3] *Ibid.*, p. 122.

surplus Negro labor of the South. The demand corresponded with a combination of extraordinarily depressive circumstances in the South: the boll weevil had destroyed millions of acres of cotton in the Southwest for successive years, and had spread its blight eastward into the heart of the Black Belt; there had been a serious drought, bringing further ruin to crops; the flocking to the cities from the farms had created a surplus of labor. Wages, usually lower than in the North, were further depressed, and with the still lower rate of pay current for Negroes, the amount which a Negro laborer could earn was extremely small. R. H. Leavell of Mississippi, who made a study of this migration while it was in progress, reported that in spite of the need of labor in such states as Mississippi, few appeared to be getting really more than 75 cents a day, although a range of from 40 and 50 cents up to $1.00 was reported to him.[1] The wages of laborers in twenty-one Black Belt counties in Alabama averaged 50 and 60 cents a day.[2] Alabama industries paid Negroes from 50 cents to $2.00 a day.[3] In Georgia in 1916, when farm hands were getting 50 and 75 cents a day, the oil mills and fertilizer works paid 80 cents, $1.00, and $1.25 a day.

At this same time the northern industrial centers were offering from $3.50 a day upward. Abraham Epstein [4] in Pittsburgh in 1917 compared the wages being received by Negroes in the Pittsburgh industries with their former wages in the South, and found that whereas 56 per cent of them received less than two dollars a day in the South, only 5 per cent received such a wage in Pittsburgh. The average wage for thirty-six industrial concerns in Chicago in 1917 was 48.7 cents an hour. Common laborers received from 50 cents to $1.00 an hour, and women in industrial establishments from $9 to $35 a week.[5]

With such inducements in the North a stream of labor turned in that direction. The stream became a torrent as the movement reached mass proportions, and exhibited all the hysteria of a mass movement. Labor agents, the Negro press, letters from the first

[1] "The Negro Migration from Mississippi," in *Negro Migration in 1916–1917*, United States Department of Labor, p. 117.

[2] Tipton R. Snavely, "The Exodus of Negroes from the Southern States," in *Negro Migration in 1916–1917*, United States Department of Labor, p. 66.

[3] *Ibid.*

[4] *The Negro Migrant in Pittsburgh*, p. 23.

[5] *The Negro in Chicago* (Report of the Chicago Commission on Race Relations 1922), pp. 366–372.

adventurers to the North verifying the reports of high wages and different mores, churned enthusiasm to the point of heedless emotional precipitation. The Negroes, under this new stimulation, moved and gave their reasons for it afterward. Some of the migrants had felt social grievances deeply; others had been adjusted to their positions and were moved only by the prospect of bettering their economic lot.

The towns were the first to feel the effect. There, the "pass rider" — that is, the labor agent — could move about more freely. People in the towns lived in closer contact, and news circulated more rapidly. The newspapers came in regularly, and the Negroes themselves could observe large numbers of migrants as they left. On Saturday, the market day, when the country folk came to town they could not escape this excitement, and soon began to share it. Not only the adventurous youth suddenly quitted the quiet isolation of the farm, but sturdy, dependable farmers, whose whole lives had been spent on the farm, could not resist the temptation. They returned to the country saying: "They are leaving town by the thousands," and, "Man, colored folks are leaving in droves for the North." [1]

The state of mind of communities under the influence of the first effects of the "fever" is illustrated in authenticated accounts of persons who witnessed the exodus from different cities. Said one of these:

> The most interesting thing is how these people left. They were selling out everything they had or in a manner giving it away; selling their homes, mules, horses, cows, and everything about them but their trunks. All around in the country, people who were so old they could not very well get about were leaving. Some left with six to eight very small children to feed and babies half clothed, no shoes on their feet, hungry, not anything to eat and not even a cent over their train fare. Some would go to the station and wait there three or four days for an agent who was carrying them on passes. Others of this city would go in clubs of fifty and a hundred at a time in order to get reduced rates. They usually left on Wednesday and Saturday nights. One Wednesday night I went to the station to see a friend of mine who was leaving. I could not get in the station, there were so many people turning like bees in a hive. Officers would go up and down the tracks trying to keep the people back. One old lady and man had gotten on the train. They were patting their feet and singing and a man standing nearby asked, "Uncle, where are you going?" The old man replied, "Well, son, I'm gwine to the promised land." [2]

[1] Emmett J. Scott, *Negro Migration during the War*, p. 41.   [2] *Ibid.*, p. 41.

The devout and religious attributed the movement to some Divine plan. Proof of this inspiration was to be found in the very numbers of Negroes, all obsessed at once with the same impulse. There were rumors that a calamity was about to befall the Southland. "In Georgia and Alabama," says one investigator of the period, "hundreds believed that God had cursed the land when he sent droughts and floods and destructive pests to visit them." The number of Negroes needed in the North was counted in millions; the wages offered were fabulous, and the letters that came from the vanguard painted pictures of a land of plenty.

From some communities, says another report, a small group would leave, promising to inform those behind of the actual state of affairs. For a week or more there would follow a tense period of "watchful waiting" and never ending anxiety, when finally there would arrive a card bearing the terse report "Everything pritty," or "Home ain't nothing like this." On this assurance, a reckless disposition of household effects would follow.[1]

The white labor agent was an important first means of acquainting Negroes with the superior wages of the North, and with the greater degree of equality of treatment in the courts, in the schools, in the cars, at the polls, and elsewhere.[2] In Alabama these agents found it advantageous to employ Negro sub-agents to work for them among the Negroes. Discussion played its part, but the Negro press, notably the *Chicago Defender* and *New York Age*, were of great influence. The very fact that Negroes were leaving in large numbers was a disturbing factor. It was the custom to review in discussion all of the instances of mistreatment and injustice which fell the lot of the Negro in the South.[3]

The southern white press, while opposing the movement, contributed unwittingly to the hysteria with each notation of unwise numbers and each bit of counsel against going. The letters from the emigrés to their friends and relations at home, as a rule, had wide circulation. They carried alluring pictures of the North against which most counter propaganda was unavailing. When a migrant

[1] Monroe Work and Charles Johnson, "Report on the Migration during the World War," in Emmett J. Scott, *Negro Migration during the War*, p. 40.

[2] R. H. Leavell, "The Negro Migration from Mississippi," in *Negro Migration in 1916-1917*, p. 27.

[3] Charles Johnson, "Report on the Migration from Mississippi," in Emmett J. Scott, *Negro Migration during the War*, p. 36.

wrote home, "I gits as much by the day as I got by the week at home and don't have to humble to nobody," he touched a long hidden spring of hope.

The movement carried away all types of Negroes, from the vagrants and "ne'er-do-wells," hanging out at the barber shops and pool rooms, to steady professionals following their clientele. Because of its mixed character it has not been possible to confirm either of the opposing rationalizations: that it carried off the floaters and surplus labor, and that it carried off the more alert and pioneering individuals.

The means employed to check the movement were at first neither wisely chosen nor wisely executed. Rather, they served to intensify the desire to leave, and to provide further reasons for going. In one city five young men reading poetry on a migration theme were charged with inciting to riot, and two of them were sent to prison for thirty days. Everything from persuasion to actual force was employed by authorities to prevent Negroes from boarding trains.

The strongest measures, it appears, were directed against the labor agents. In Alabama, licenses were issued only at prohibitive costs. In Birmingham and Bessemer the license cost was $1,250 and $1,050, respectively. In Jacksonville, Florida, emigration agents were required to pay $1,000 for a license. The Macon, Georgia, city council raised the license fee from a nominal sum to $25,000, and required that each agent be recommended by ten local ministers, ten manufacturers, and twenty-five business men.[1] A next and sounder step was that of raising wages for Negroes in the South to reduce the competition, and stimulating new public efforts to provide better schools for Negro children. This period marked also the beginning of organization of interracial committees.

One writer has referred to the "push" and the "pull" of the migration. Extremely unfavorable conditions in the South constituted the "push"; the expansion of northern industries and the cessation of immigration constituted the "pull." The actual annual rate of absorption was 1,200,000 new workers each year. The checking of these numbers by the exigencies of war was followed shortly by immigration restriction when the war ended. Roughly, where we might have had about nine and one-half million potential workers between 1914 and 1922, we had actually only about three million, or about one-third. The 3 per cent quota law contemplated the

[1] Monroe Work and Charles Johnson, "Report on the Migration during the World War," in Emmett J. Scott, *Negro Migration during the War*, p. 73.

entrance of about 360,000 persons annually, or 45 per cent of the usual influx. When emigration was deducted and actual man-power considered, the percentage was reduced to about 11. A revision of the Immigration Act further reduced the quota to 2 per cent of the total immigrants in the country. The increase of prejudice against South Europeans, who were the rough manual laborers, tightened the bars even more against the traditional northern competitors of Negroes, giving preference to North Europeans, who did not so readily turn to rough manual occupations. Ordinary losses by death, retirement, and advancement require annually about 214,000 laborers. The population increases by about 1,400,000 annually, or about 14 per 1,000. To keep pace with the growth there were needed about 368,000 new laborers annually, not possible through immigration.

In the migration of 1916–1918 there was a net increase of 340,260 in the northern Negro population. The newcomers crowded into cities. Their wages were from 100 to 250 per cent higher than in the South, and although living costs in many instances were correspondingly high, there was in the thrill of earning and spending, in increased standards, greater mobility, freedom, and excitement, the emotional satisfaction required by most people.

The causes of the migration of 1916–1918 were similar to those of the movement of 1879. From the factors surrounding this phenomenon, and from the migrants themselves, these causes may be grouped as follows:

1. Better wages
2. Better social treatment
3. Better cultural advantages; schools, stimulating contacts, wholesome diversion, etc.
4. Mass psychology, and the hysteria of a mass movement
5. Desire to travel
6. Direct importation to the North through labor agents for individual concerns

All of these, more or less, had some influence on each of the migrants, and in but few instances was there one cause acting alone. Most commonly, one motive was dominant, with one or more of the others added to give complete stimulus to action. In 1918 a study was made of some 4,000 letters written by Negroes from all parts of the South to northern persons and agencies, expressing a desire to move. Of these, 71 per cent gave as their dominant motive economic improvement. This was described as meaning more wages, more regular wages, shorter hours, opportunity for advancement, more agreeable work.

The question of better treatment had many interesting angles. So long as people know nothing better than the conditions to which they are accustomed, they can adjust themselves to them, but discontent comes by comparison. Travel and reading afford such comparison, and the initial movement of Negroes, probably for economic motives, carried them to their first contacts with other modes of living. Natural but obscure forces had also been at work breaking down the isolation of farm-reared Negroes. The coming of good roads, cheap automobiles, telephones, undoubtedly had great effect in making for discontent and a desire for wider experiences.

The end of the war, which brought a slump in business activity, was no doubt largely responsible for the changed attitude toward immigrant laborers, which quickly resulted in the Immigration Acts restricting their numbers. It also checked the migration of Negroes from the South. The return of prosperity around 1923 was followed by a second migration of southern Negroes. This movement lacked the hysteria of the first and seems to have been chiefly characterized by the reuniting of families. The first movement carried an excess of men without their families. In the second, it is noted that women and children constituted large proportions.

The difference in character of these two migrations may be observed in a study of the table on page 342. While these figures are given by decades, they reflect what happened at the peak of the movement within each decade. The Negro population increased 6.5 per cent between 1910 and 1920. While in the northern states the increase ranged from 251 per cent in Michigan, in which the Negro population had been small, to 19.5 in Massachusetts, it showed decreases in the east south-central states ranging from 0.8 in Alabama to 9.8 per cent in Kentucky. None of the southern states, with the exception of West Virginia and the District of Columbia, showed significant increases above that of the general population increase. In many of the southern states showing an increase, the increase was less than 6.5 per cent. Indeed, the general flux of this period and the separation of families may explain the abnormally small rate of increase between 1910 and 1920, which returned to its normal rate the following decade.

Niles Carpenter [1] observes that in the normal migration from rural

---

[1] *The Sociology of City Life*, p. 171.

CHARACTER OF THE MIGRATIONS OF 1916–17 AND 1923 AS INDICATED IN THE CENSUS REPORTS OF 1920 AND 1930

States	Negro Population Increase Per Cent		Males to 100 Females			Increase in Number of Children between Ages 5–20 Per Cent	
	1910–20	1920–30	1910	1920	1930	1910–20	1920–30
UNITED STATES							
Whole Population	14.9	16.1	106.0	104.0	102.5	11.6	15.4
Negro Population	6.5	13.6	98.9	99.2	97.0	3.2	8.7
NEW ENGLAND							
Massachusetts	19.5	15.2	97.1	101.6	99.3	14.4	37.3
Connecticut	38.7	39.5	91.0	105.0	98.6	37.1	48.4
MIDDLE ATLANTIC							
New York	47.9	108.0	91.3	92.6	93.5	42.3	122.3
New Jersey	30.5	78.3	94.5	96.2	97.2	33.8	82.6
Pennsylvania	46.7	51.5	97.7	108.8	102.6	43.6	61.5
EAST NORTH-CENTRAL							
Ohio	67.1	66.1	108.5	116.4	106.0	62.0	190.9
Indiana	34.0	38.6	106.0	107.2	103.9	26.8	39.3
Illinois	67.1	80.5	109.1	106.1	99.9	56.8	85.3
Michigan	251.0	182.0	111.1	132.6	110.5	195.5	218.1
Wisconsin	79.3	106.5	103.7	132.6	117.9	83.2	114.3
WEST NORTH-CENTRAL							
Missouri	13.2	25.6	104.6	104.3	100.0	1.7	25.7
Kansas	7.2	14.5	107.3	105.5	105.0	− 1.8	12.1
SOUTH ATLANTIC							
Delaware	− 2.7	7.5	105.5	106.6	108.7	− 12.2	− 4.5
Maryland	5.3	13.0	97.7	102.0	103.4	*	8.8
District of Columbia	16.4	20.1	82.2	86.0	89.1	14.5	17.1
Virginia	2.8	− 5.8	97.1	98.6	97.8	− 0.9	− 2.8
West Virginia	34.6	33.1	132.8	120.2	112.7	33.2	26.0
North Carolina	9.4	20.3	94.8	96.0	94.6	10.4	22.5
South Carolina	3.5	− 8.2	95.4	95.4	91.5	3.7	− 4.5
Georgia	2.5	− 11.2	97.2	95.9	92.1	2.7	− 11.9
Florida	6.7	31.1	109.5	103.0	99.3	5.8	21.8
EAST SOUTH-CENTRAL							
Kentucky	− 9.8	− 4.2	101.0	101.0	100.9	− 17.7	− 6.4
Tennessee	− 4.5	5.7	97.6	97.2	94.9	− 7.9	0.4
Alabama	− 0.8	4.9	97.2	95.4	93.7	0.7	0.4
Mississippi	− 7.4	8.0	99.2	98.0	97.4	− 6.9	2.2
WEST SOUTH-CENTRAL							
Arkansas	6.6	1.3	101.7	100.7	98.1	4.3	4.1
Louisiana	− 1.9	10.9	98.3	97.0	95.5	− 3.9	4.7
Oklahoma	8.6	15.3	109.5	104.3	101.7	8.5	6.7
Texas	7.5	15.3	100.0	100.3	97.7	2.8	7.0
PACIFIC: California	79.1	109.1	109.3	104.8	97.7	70.9	110.9

* Less than one-tenth of one per cent.

to urban areas women are in excess of men. The Negro population of New England and the Middle Atlantic states in 1910 showed the number of males per 100 females to be less than their proportion in the whole population. In the North Central states, probably because of the nature of the industries there, the proportion of men to women was much in excess of the proportion for the whole population. In the South, generally, except in the cases of those states showing marked population increase, the proportion of men was lower than for the total population. The sex ratio in 1920 showed an increase of less than 1, while states to which the population was moving, excepting Illinois and West Virginia, with large mining populations, showed increases of from 1 to 28 in the ratio of men to women. The migrations tended to even the ratio. The rate of increase in children between the ages of 5 and 20 above the rate of Negro population increase suggests the extent to which families migrated during the second period.

Migration itself may have been marked by a high emotionalism, little discretion, and disregard of practical considerations, but settling in the North, despite first enthusiasms, was a serious problem. Establishment in urban industrial centers required a vast reorganization of the Negro's social life. Transformation of rural agricultural workers into urban dwellers and industrial workers was not a simple process. The initial problem facing new arrivals was housing. In virtually all the northern cities Negroes lived in more or less contiguous neighborhoods. The migrants were housed in the older parts of the city, where buildings were old, and they were held there, both by economic and racial considerations. These areas could not expand rapidly enough to keep pace with the sudden population growth. A result was overcrowding, high rents, accentuation of physical problems of sanitation, and the social problems growing out of close contact with all types of characters. Miss Louise V. Kennedy notes that the migrations tended to increase residential separation of the two races "both by enlarging the Negro group within the colored districts and, at the same time, by intensifying the opposition of white people whenever the Negroes attempted to enter new neighborhoods." [1] Objection to Negro "invasions" reached the point of violence in several cities. Even violence, however, proved an ineffective check to territorial expansion when the pressure at the source of population increase was at its height.

[1] *The Negro Peasant Turns Cityward*, p. 46.

The migrants were charged from 10 to 100 per cent higher rentals than other groups. In New York City between 1919 and 1927 the Negro rentals in one area studied increased nearly 100 per cent (from $21.66 to $41.77), while average rentals increased during the same period only 10 per cent.[1] In one of the old areas of Chicago where Negroes had been living for many years and few improvements had been made, the rents doubled between 1911 and 1931; and in some instances they reached the astonishing extent of a 250 per cent increase.[2] But these increased rentals did not insure better care of the property on the part of owners and agents.

The condition of housing in the North for these migrants undoubtedly registered more acutely with the social workers than with many of the Negro migrants themselves. These migrants, and especially the rural ones, had lived in dwellings even worse in the South. There were not in these southern rural homes, however, the congestion, the exposure to disease and to severe weather, and the other hazards associated with northern urban life.

A certain amount of social maladjustment of Negroes in the cities was to be expected, and there were striking reflections of this maladjustment in the amount of crime, juvenile delinquency, dependency, and family disorganization. The prophecy that "migration would result in a tremendous increase in the problems of crime and vice in northern cities" was justified, for practically every important center to which migrants flocked witnessed an increase in the number of Negroes brought before the police court.[3]

However, it was also observed that comparisons of criminal tendencies inherent in Negroes and whites are usually made on the basis of the number of arrests and convictions, which does not furnish an adequate measure of the amount of actual crime. When the number of arrests and convictions is used, the criminal proclivities of Negroes are likely to be exaggerated because Negroes are handicapped by the tendency of authorities to arrest them more freely than whites, to book them on more serious charges, to convict them more readily, and to give them longer sentences.[4] Wherever figures that measure the amount of actual crime have been obtained

---

[1] *Negro Housing.* Report of the Committee on Negro Housing of the President's Conference on Home Building and Home Ownership, p. 14.

[2] *Ibid.*, p. 16.

[3] Louise V. Kennedy, *The Negro Peasant Turns Cityward*, p. 182.

[4] *Ibid.*, p. 186.

in northern cities, however, Negroes have contributed a proportion of delinquents larger than their proportion in the total population.

Conditions in the public schools were aggravated by the problem of retardation of the southern children. This retardation produced restlessness, a sense of defeat and rebellion in these backward children who had been handicapped by less efficient schools in the South and home habits. It also raised the question of separating classes on the basis of the rate of progress of children, which would have resulted practically in racial segregation. Over several years of exposure to these schools the southern children, on the whole, overcame their handicap and became adjusted to more normal rates of educational achievement.

Many of the children of migrants thrown without guidance into the strange environment of the city found it difficult to make the complicated adjustment to city life, and ended in the juvenile courts. The importance of surroundings in the problem of delinquency among Negro children in northern cities [1] is revealed in a study recently made by Clifford Shaw. He points out that the increase in delinquency follows the same fundamental processes, whatever the race of the newcomer, introduced to the deteriorated areas of residence. He says:

In such cases [referring to population influx into Chicago] the process has been the same. The most recent immigrants enter and secure a footing by invading the areas of lowest rank in the deteriorated areas adjacent to the Loop and the large industrial centers. In time another group enters and displaces the population ahead of it and pushes it out into what may be called areas of second settlement.[2]

The highest rates of juvenile delinquency have invariably been in those areas of the Negro community which are characterized by deterioration and social disorganization. As the process of urbanization goes on, delinquency tends to decrease. The disorganized immigrants, from whatever source, begin life in the city in the blighted areas, and as their economic level is raised and there is increasing stability they move into better residential sections, making way for newer waves of immigrants, who in turn follow the same pattern. Frazier [3] has given an illuminating analysis of the Negro family in

[1] *Ibid.*, pp. 189, 190.
[2] *Negro Housing.* Report of the Committee on Negro Housing of the President's Conference on Home Building and Home Ownership, p. 145.
[3] *The Negro Family in Chicago*, p. 211.

Chicago — most of them migrant families — dividing the city Black Belt into seven zones. Each zone, in a series from the oldest to the newest areas, shows less disorganization than the one preceding. The percentages of marriages and home ownership increase, while overcrowding, crime, and delinquency decrease. According to Frazier's study, delinquency decreased from 42.8 per cent in the disorganized zone of first residence to 1.4 per cent in the seventh zone. The period of social disorganization of these migrants varies in intensity according to their intelligence and their ability to make the readjustment. The greater the number involved, the more noticeable the process becomes.

One general result of the northward Negro migration has been to disturb the heavy concentration of Negroes in the Black Belt section of the South. However, the special direction and inspiration of the northward movement tended to create new centers of concentration in a few northern cities. Nine metropolitan regions contain 55.5 per cent of all Negroes in metropolitan areas. These nine regions, as defined broadly by the census monograph on Metropolitan Districts, Population and Area, are as follows:

District	Negro Population
Boston, Massachusetts	33,820
Columbus, Ohio	35,033
Indianapolis, Indiana	44,598
Kansas City, Missouri	60,763
Cincinnati, Ohio	60,917
Pittsburgh, Pennsylvania	108,897
St. Louis, Missouri	125,269
Great Lakes region [1]	578,450
Middle Atlantic seaboard region [2]	985,456
	2,033,203

Monroe N. Work of Tuskegee further notes that there has been a decrease in the South and an increase in the North and West in the number of counties in which there are no Negroes. He suggests that, as a result of the new and more serious depression which set in around 1929, the Negroes are tending to move from the rural and small town districts of the North and West into the more populous centers.

[1] Metropolitan districts from Buffalo to Milwaukee; also the Akron, Canton, and Youngstown metropolitan districts in Ohio, the Flint district in Michigan, and the Fort Wayne and South Bend districts in Indiana.

[2] Metropolitan districts from New York City to Baltimore, by way of Philadelphia.

Always there has followed mass migrations a return of some of those who found life too strenuous or too strange in the new environment. Thousands of Negroes returned to the South; but, as the census returns and practically all the special studies made of the migrants in the North show, the vast majority have remained in the North. Exposure to industries, to the more highly developed even if more exacting measures of hygiene, and to the superior schools have resulted, on the whole, in a lifting of their general level of well-being. Their numbers, however, have served to transfer to the North some of the racial problems more commonly associated with the southern states. The severity of the most recent economic depression has taken a serious toll among these newcomers to northern industry, creating among them a larger amount of unemployment than either the native white or foreign-born experience. Northern cities, after attempting without marked success to assist these migrants in returning to their homes in the South, have accepted the relief load as a part of their normal burden.

The movement to the North is perhaps a much deeper symptom of the declining importance of agriculture than of disagreeable social relations. One indication of this is the consistent trend to the cities, South and North, and another the continued residence of these Negroes in the South for fifty years, until economic opportunities developed elsewhere. Despite the volume of these migrations, almost four-fifths of the Negroes remain in the South.

PROBLEMS FOR STUDY

1. Booker T. Washington once observed that the Negro could earn a dollar in the South but could not spend it, and that he could spend a dollar in the North but could not earn it. To what extent does this hold today in the broad sense of his observation?
2. Explain the Negroes' mobility in the light of their being bound to certain staple crops and not to the soil.
3. How may the negligible change in the status of the Negro following the Civil War be explained by tenacity of the mores?
4. While the North offered freer participation in the social life, why did Negroes continue to move south and westward until the World War?
5. In the trend toward urbanization why do not Atlanta and Chicago draw from the same radius?
6. The migration of Negroes suffering from economic reverses may easily be explained on an economic basis; what factors entered into the movement of comfortably situated Negroes?

7. How does the impact of the urban environment produce disorganization in rural migrants?
8. What possible complication of the South's race problem may arise if any situation should result in a return to the South of a majority of the migrants to the North?

BIBLIOGRAPHY

Niles Carpenter, *The Sociology of City Life* (1931).
Congressional Record, Senate 46th Congress, Vol. 10, Part 5, p. 4141 (1880).
Abraham Epstein, *The Negro Migrant in Pittsburgh* (1918).
E. Franklin Frazier, *The Negro Family in Chicago* (1932).
Charles S. Johnson, "Report on the Migration from Mississippi," in Emmett J. Scott, *Negro Migration during the War* (1920).
Louise V. Kennedy, *The Negro Peasant Turns Cityward* (1930).
R. H. Leavell, "The Negro Migration from Mississippi," in *Negro Migration in 1916–1917*, United States Department of Labor (1919).
Negro Housing. Report of the Committee on Negro Housing of the President's Conference on Home Building and Home Ownership (1931).
The Negro in Chicago. Report of the Chicago Commission on Race Relations (1922).
Frank A. Ross, *Urbanization and the Negro*. Publication of American Sociology Society. Vol. 26, No. 3, August, 1932, pp. 115–128.
Emmett J. Scott, *Negro Migration during the War* (1920).
Tipton R. Snavely, "The Exodus of Negroes from Southern States," in *Negro Migration in 1916–1917*, United States Department of Labor (1919).
Charles H. Wesley, *A History of Negro Labor in the United States, 1850–1923* (1925).
George W. Williams, *History of the Negro Race in America, 1619–1880* (1885).
Carter G. Woodson, *A Century of Negro Migration* (1918).
Monroe N. Work and Charles N. Johnson, "Report on the Migration during the World War," in Emmett J. Scott, *Negro Migration during the War* (1920).

CHAPTER XVIII

PROBLEMS OF EDUCATION

When the first Negroes were introduced into America they were raw and ignorant folk from the bush of central Africa. The first Negroes taken to the West Indies were taken by way of Portugal, where they could be baptized and given the first elementary instruction in Christianity. But no such condition held for the Negroes introduced into the American colonies. Hence, these first servants were without any training whatever. Two motives, however, induced the early colonists to give their slaves some training. In the first place, these early American settlers were deeply religious, and hence they desired their slaves to be instructed in the meaning of Christianity. This of course called for teaching them to read the Bible, and was the earliest educational motive on behalf of colored people. There were some qualms about holding as slaves Negroes who had been converted to Christianity, but this question was soon put at rest, and the work of instructing the slaves went forward.

The second motive for teaching slaves was that it would make certain of them more efficient. Those slaves who were kept about the house as cooks and nurses, and also as skilled workers, needed to be able to read instructions. It was clear that a Negro carpenter who could not use figures or read simple instructions was greatly handicapped. As a matter of economic advantage, therefore, the early slaves were taught.

These two motives worked side by side in the early years and there seems to have been little or no opposition to such instruction. But when the Negroes began to be more numerous, and particularly when a few of them became restless and desirous of freedom, there gradually grew up opposition to the training of Negroes either slave or free.

So far as we know, the first formal education of Negroes in America was undertaken by the Society for the Propagation of the Gospel in Foreign Parts, at Goose Creek, South Carolina. Reverend Samuel Thomas, the first missionary sent to the Negroes, in 1702, worked here four years, and in his first report claimed "he had taken much pains in instructing the Negroes, and had learned twenty of them to read."¹ In his report of 1705 he wrote: "I have here presumed to give an account of one thousand slaves so far as they know of it and are desirous of Christian knowledge and seem willing to prepare themselves for it, in learning to read, for which they redeem the time from their labor. Many of them can read the Bible distinctly and great numbers of them were learning when I left the province."²

Through the influence of the Society for the Propagation of the Gospel in Foreign Parts a second school was opened, in New York City in 1704, under the direction of Elias Neau. This man went from house to house and succeeded in getting a few masters to send their slaves to him for instruction. When the Negro riot of 1712 broke out in New York, it came near to wrecking this school, but it was finally proved that the leaders of the riot had never received instruction in the school. The governor again gave it his protection and recommended that masters have their slaves instructed. Neau taught until his death in 1722, but there were some masters who continued to fear that training "would be a means to make the slave more cunning and apter to wickedness." One of Neau's successors, Mr. Auckmutty, who served in the school from 1747 to 1764, wrote that not one single Black admitted by him to the Holy Communion had "turned out bad, or been in any scrape or disgrace to our Holy Profession." ³

In 1741 Bishop Secker brought forward the suggestion that the society should train some Negroes to carry forward this work among their own people. Accordingly two slaves, Harry and Andrew, were purchased and qualified for the work, and in 1744 they started their first school in Charleston, South Carolina, in a building which is said to have cost £380. Sixty students were enrolled the first year, but it is not likely that any of these were slaves, for South Carolina had in 1740 passed a law which read: "Whereas those having slaves taught to write or suffering them to be employed in writing, may be attended with great inconvenience, any person who shall teach any slave to write, or employ any slave as a scribe in any writing shall

---

[1] Cf. Charles C. Jones, *The Religious Instruction of the Negroes in the United States*, p. 10.

[2] *Journal of Negro History*, 1916, p. 350.

[3] C. F. Pascoe (Ed.), *Classified Digest of the Records of the Society for the Propagation of the Gospel in Foreign Parts*, pp. 59–66.

forfeit one hundred pounds."[1] Georgia in 1770 passed laws which were almost identical with those of South Carolina,[2] these two states being the only ones which prohibited the instruction of slaves during the eighteenth century. Because of the growing fear of insurrection, practically all the states passed such laws during the period from 1800 to 1860.

In spite of handicaps the double motive of religious duty and efficiency of slaves led many slave owners both North and South to continue to give instruction to their slaves. Not even the fear of insurrection could deter many southern owners from teaching their slaves to read the Bible.[3] The Quakers were among the most ardent advocates of the instruction of Negroes, working in North Carolina and on up to Philadelphia. Three early advocates of education for the Negro were Anthony Benezet, Robert Pleasants, and Kosciuszko, the Polish general. The first two were Quakers and left sums to establish schools for Negroes; the latter put into the hands of Thomas Jefferson a fund with which to buy the freedom of slaves and give them an education. Jefferson seems not to have done anything with this fund, for in 1835 the heirs of Kosciuszko were suing to recover it.[4]

A continual and growing interest in the education of the Negro was manifest up to the more serious Negro insurrections: that of Gabriel in 1800, that of Vesey in Charleston in 1822, and that of Nat Turner in 1832. North Carolina and Delaware passed restrictive laws in 1831. Florida and Alabama followed in 1832, Missouri in 1847. Tennessee and Kentucky, interestingly enough, did not pass such laws. In 1833 Prudence Crandall, a Quaker woman who was conducting a school for girls at Canterbury, Connecticut, admitted a Negro girl. The white parents immediately objected, but the Quaker woman stood firm. Thereupon the white girls withdrew, and the school was threatened with violence. The legislature passed a law forbidding anyone to teach colored children who were not inhabitants of the state, and then only when written permission was granted by the authorities in the township where the school was conducted. Under this law Miss Crandall was arrested, and she finally abandoned the school. Such stormy scenes were the constant

---

[1] John C. Hurd, *The Law of Freedom and Bondage in United States*, p. 307.
[2] *Ibid.*, p. 311.
[3] Cf. Chapter X.
[4] *African Repository*, Vol. XI, pp. 294–295.

concomitant of Negro education before the Civil War. However, it was still possible for a Negro to learn to read and write: "The education of colored people as a public effort," says Woodson, "had been prohibited South of the border states [and he might have said in almost all the states], but there was still some chance for Negroes of that section to acquire knowledge. Furthermore, the liberal white people of that section considered these enactments, as we have stated above, not applicable to southerners interested in the improvement of their slaves, but to mischievous abolitionists. The truth is that thereafter, some citizens disregarded the laws of their states, and taught worthy slaves whom they desired to reward, or use in business requiring an elementary education. As these prohibitions in slave states were not equally stringent, white and colored teachers of free blacks were not always disturbed. In fact, just before the middle of the nineteenth century, there was so much winking at the violation of the reactionary laws that it looked as if some southern states might recede from their radical position and let Negroes be educated as they had been in the eighteenth century." [1]

The second period of Negro education opens with the Civil War. No sooner had the northern armies come into the South than slaves began to flock to the camps. These gave no little trouble to the army, and in many cases they were not permitted to stay. General Halleck issued an order that no slaves should be permitted within the lines of the army. But other generals found the slaves useful in manual labor; hence they were more lenient. Some of the generals, because they had abolitionist ideas, or because they thought the receiving of the slaves would weaken the South, received those arriving at their camps. This necessitated keeping them occupied; so, as a means of self-protection, schools were started. At Port Royal, South Carolina, large numbers of fugitive slaves had entered the union camps, and E. E. Pierce, agent of the United States government for contrabands at that point, urged that something be done. Accordingly, at the Young Men's Christian Union on Friday, February 7, 1862, an Educational Commission for Freedmen was organized and aid of the government was solicited. The first official report of this commission, printed in May, 1863, indicates that eighteen thousand Negro men, women, and children came under

---

[1] *The Education of the Negro prior to 1861*, p. 205. This is the fullest account of this period of education; though at times it appears to be trying to make a case derogatory to the South, it carries much valuable data.

the charge of the teachers at this place alone during the first year of activities.¹ Plantations were taken over, crops were cultivated, discipline was established, and the colored people were instructed. This work was taken over by General Rufus Saxon and became quite efficient.² Soon work was established at Fortress Monroe in Norfolk, Virginia; Beaufort, South Carolina; New Orleans, Louisiana; Vicksburg and Corinth, Mississippi; Columbus, Kentucky; Cairo, Illinois; Newbern, North Carolina, and other places. General Banks in Louisiana seems to have organized the refugees into schools and had nearly fourteen thousand in attendance.³ By Act of Congress, March 3, 1865, the Freedmen's Bureau was set up with General O. O. Howard as commissioner and J. W. Alvord as inspector of schools. Abandoned lands were seized, crops planted, taxes assessed on all the populations, and plans made to push the establishment of the freed slaves economically and educationally. This work was so well done that Alvord reported to the War Department on January 1, 1866, that there were enrolled 90,589 students, with 1,314 teachers in 740 schools.⁴ These schools were supported, he says, first by contributions from various benevolent societies, second by tax commissions, and in Louisiana by a military tax. The government furnished transportation for teachers, gave furniture, and provided the use of buildings.⁵ The buildings were mostly churches or school buildings which belonged to the white people of the South. That there had been some effective educational work going on in the South before the Civil War is proved by Alvord's statement that out of seventy-six teachers employed in South Carolina, twenty-four were colored.⁶ The report also tells us that a number of southern white teachers had been employed,⁷ and of their unselfishness and courage the inspector speaks in highest terms. But of course many were very sceptical. The report tells us of one legislator in Louisiana who, on passing one of these schools during recess, inquired of Inspector Alvord if this was a school. On being assured it was he raised both hands and exclaimed: "Well, well, I have seen many an absurdity in my lifetime, but this is the climax of absurdities."⁸ Reports detail the growth of educational work. By Act of Congress it was

¹ *First Annual Report of the Educational Commission for Freedmen*, p. 8.
² *Ibid.*, pp. 8–9.
³ John W. Alvord, *Report on Schools and Finances of Freedmen*, January, 1866, p. 8. ⁴ *Ibid.*, p. 3. ⁵ *Ibid.*, p. 3. ⁶ *Ibid.*, p. 5. ⁷ *Ibid.*, p. 9.
⁸ *Ibid.*, p. 10.

provided that "the secretary of war may direct such issues of provisions, clothing and fuel as he may deem needful for the immediate and temporary shelter and supply of destitute and suffering refugees and freedmen, and their wives and children." Under this provision considerable aid was given to the schools but no funds were provided for paying teachers. The act, however, was amended in 1866 and much larger educational powers were conferred by it. Half a million dollars per year for 1866 and 1867 was voted specifically for educational purposes. In 1870 General Howard reported that 4,239 schools had been established, 247,333 pupils had been instructed, 9,307 teachers had been employed.[1] The total amount expended from 1865 to 1872 was probably nearly sixty million dollars.

But the resources which the government could provide were not sufficient; hence we find voluntary organizations springing into existence to meet the urgent need. General Howard in his circular dated May 19, 1865, made it clear that the government did not mean to take over the educational work of the independent associations; rather, he declared, it would coöperate with them in every way possible.[2]

"At Nashville, a square of land has been purchased by northern associations for sixteen thousand dollars, on which a high school building has been erected for teaching the children of freedmen in all the higher branches. It is expected that this institution will equal in its advantages the best schools of the same class in New England. The building was dedicated on the 9th of January last and has now 1,100 pupils."[3] This was the beginning of Fisk University. This sprang up under the influence of the American Freedmen's Association, of which there were a number of principal branches. This organization started a magazine called *The American Freedman* in April, 1866. The second issue of this magazine, in May, 1866, reported a total of 613 schools under the direction of these independent societies. These schools were located as follows: 41 in the District of Columbia, 61 in Maryland, 104 in Virginia, 80 in North Carolina, 129 in South Carolina, 31 in Georgia, 29 in Florida, 28 in Alabama, 20 in Mississippi, 6 in Louisiana, 65 in Tennessee, 5 in Kentucky, 8 in Missouri, 10 in Arkansas, 4 in Kansas,

---

[1] Cf. George W. Williams, *History of the Negro Race in America, 1619–1880*, Vol. II, pp. 380, 385.
[2] Cf. *Protestant Episcopal Freedmen's Commission — Occasional Papers*, January, 1866, p. 22.   [3] *Ibid.*, p. 12.

PROBLEMS OF EDUCATION 355

3 in Illinois, and 1 in Ohio. The report indicates that during the year ending January 1, 1866, these independent societies had spent more than $700,000.[1]

In addition to these independent associations the leading churches North and South promptly organized to help in the education of the Negro. On October 5, 1865, the Protestant Episcopal Board of Missions meeting in Philadelphia appointed a committee of seven, of which the Bishop of North Carolina was chairman, which on October 13 recommended the organization of the Protestant Episcopal Freedmen's Association. The recommendation was adopted, and the association went into operation.[2] The American Baptist Home Missionary Society; the American Missionary Association; the Board of Missions and the Woman's Home Missionary Society of the Methodist Episcopal Church; the Board of Freedmen's Missions of the United Presbyterian Church; the Board of Home Missions of the Reformed Church in the United States; the Five Years Meeting of the Friends in America; the Board of Missions for Freedmen of the Presbyterian Church in the United States of America; and numerous other church societies began active work at once following the freeing of the slaves. All of the southern churches had been active long before the Civil War, and continued their activities in some degree following the war.[3]

It was during this period that the southern states established their public free school systems. Mississippi, Arkansas, Louisiana, South Carolina, and Georgia all provided for such systems in 1868, Florida and North Carolina followed in 1869, Virginia in 1870, and Tennessee in 1873. The struggle to maintain these schools was long and discouraging. The war had reduced the South to dire poverty. The valuation of two billions of agricultural wealth at the beginning of the war was reduced to not more than half a billion at the close of the war. It was not until 1900 that the farm valuation in the South amounted to two billions again. In other words, it took the South forty years to win back the financial status which it had in 1860. Under such conditions one would expect that the school system would be starved and inefficient. Indeed, many people expected the South to set aside the schools for Negroes as soon as the military

---

[1] Cf. *The American Freedman*, May, 1866, pp. 21, 25.

[2] Cf. *Protestant Episcopal Freedmen's Commission — Occasional Papers*, January, 1866, pp. 1–2.

[3] Cf. Willis D. Weatherford, *Interracial Coöperation*.

pressure was removed. But those who held such fears did not know the spirit of the old South. Having once set their faces toward a fair chance for the Negro child, they never turned back. It was a long time before this Negro child could find a real chance, but the hope of such a chance was never abandoned. A double school system was a heavy load on a poverty-stricken section, and education in the South is still handicapped by this double load, but the South has struggled long and hard to remedy defects. It is common knowledge that the Negro child did not have as much spent on him as did the white child — and for this we know there was no adequate excuse — but the South did what most parents under similar circumstances would do: if there was insufficiency for their own children and others, they would almost surely favor their own. Such was the action of the white South.

If the Freedmen's schools marked a second stage in Negro education, the third stage would be an emphasis on agricultural and mechanical arts. General Howard in 1865 had said, "Education must of course extend rather to the practical arts than to theoretical knowledge." [1] He well knew that the destiny of the Negro people was wrapped up in their ability to make a living. Among the subcommissioners of the Freedmen's Bureau under General Howard was a young man named Samuel C. Armstrong. He was a graduate of Williams College, had served in the Union army in charge of colored troops, and was mustered out of the army in November, 1863, as Brevet-Brigadier General. He was appointed by General Howard in 1866 to supervise the Bureau's work in nine counties of Eastern Virginia. Armstrong had earlier determined he would establish a school for these people.[2] In 1868 General Armstrong established Hampton Institute with the aid of the Freedmen's Bureau, the American Missionary Association, the Peabody Fund, and the Land Scrip Fund.[3] Booker T. Washington went to Hampton as a student, and was sent by General Armstrong in 1881 to Alabama to found Tuskegee, which was to be wholly a product of the Negro's ability in education. These two schools, which are still among the most powerful influences in Negro life in the South, dominated the ideas of Negro education for the remainder of the nineteenth century.

[1] *Protestant Episcopal Freedmen's Commission — Occasional Papers*, January, 1866, p. 24.

[2] Franklin Carter, *General Armstrong's Life and Work*, pp. 8–9.

[3] *Journal of Negro History*, April, 1925, p. 146.

They put emphasis on skill in doing daily tasks, and were dedicated to fitting Negro students to live in the environment in which they found themselves. The philosophy of this education was well set forth by Washington in his speech before the Atlanta Cotton States and International Exposition in 1895. Speaking to his own people in the audience he said: "Cast down your bucket where you are. Cast it down in making friends in every manly way of the people of all races by whom you are surrounded. Cast it down in agriculture, mechanics, in commerce, in domestic service, and in the professions. . . . We shall prosper in proportion as we learn to dignify and glorify common labor and put brains and skill into the common occupations of life." [1] This philosophy found a ready response on the part of the southern white man and laid the foundation for a much friendlier attitude toward the training of the Negro. It must be said it did not find such a favorable response from the Negroes. To many of them it seemed to be an acquiescence in the old policy of forcing the Negro to live in the field of manual labor alone. It meant to them deliberate abandonment of the idea that Negroes could attain intellectual leadership. Not all of that idea has yet disappeared. But in spite of this opposition, schools of the industrial type sprang up all over the South, and found support of both white and colored people. Hampton and Tuskegee have had a large influence in moulding white schools to a more practical application of knowledge and have become world-wide influences in this field of education. As one visits these schools he is struck with the sanity and constructiveness of their work. The work of the rural industrial supervisor of Negro schools under the Anna T. Jeanes Fund is but a broader application of their theory of education.

The fourth period of Negro education — or what might be called modern trends in Negro education — began about 1900. In that year the history-making conference at Capon Springs, Virginia, was held, and white men, North and South, dedicated themselves to a fair opportunity for the Negro. It was in 1901 that the Southern Education Board was organized, and in 1900 to 1902 that Governor Acock of North Carolina gave such large impetus to general education. The moving spirit of this Southern Education Board was Robert Curtis Ogden, member of the firm of John Wanamaker, President of the Board of Trustees of Hampton Institute, President of the Board of Trustees of Union Theological Seminary, elected

[1] Booker T. Washington, *Up from Slavery*, pp. 219–220.

President of the Conference for Education in the South, 1900, and elected President of the Southern Education Board in 1901, both of which offices he held until his death in August, 1913. These boards held annual meetings in the South which aroused interest in education and became, as it were, the source of a renaissance of southern education. They were not in any special sense interested in Negro education, but the general impulse given to education made a large contribution to the improvement of the Negro. The report of the Seventeenth Conference for Education in the South, issued shortly after Mr. Ogden's death, states that while the percentage of illiteracy had dropped from 9.5 to 4.0 between 1900 and 1914, "the figures for the reduction of illiteracy among the colored children would be still more astounding." [1]

Clearly this period marks the beginning of a new era in Negro education in the South. At the beginning of this period only 31.3 per cent of the Negro children between 5 and 20 years of age were enrolled in school; by 1910 the figure had been raised to 45.4, by 1920 it stood at 54 and in 1930 it was 60.[2] While this latter figure is very low it shows tremendous progress over 1900. Illiteracy among Negroes 10 years of age and over in 1900 was 44.5 per cent, in 1910 it was 30.4, and by 1920 it had been reduced to 22.9;[3] in 1930 this figure stood at 16.3.[4] At the beginning of this period there were glaring weaknesses in the public school system for Negroes.

The first great weakness lay not simply in inadequate funds, since all schools, white and colored, suffered from this weakness; but among the colored it was still further aggravated by the fact that the Negroes got on the average perhaps less than one-fourth their per capita share of the small funds available. Thus in South Carolina in 1909, although there were more colored children than white, the colored received $308,153.16 and the whites $1,590,732.51 — or less than one to five. In Alabama the corresponding figures were $287,045.43 and $2,143,662.15 — or less than one to seven. In North Carolina the corresponding figures were: for colored, $366,734.28; for whites, $1,851,367.57 — or one to five.[5] The other southern

[1] *Proceedings of the Seventeenth Conference for Education in the South, and Twenty-fifth Annual Meeting of the Southern Education Association*, p. 4.
[2] Cf. Census of 1930. Population. Vol. III, p. 17.
[3] Cf. Census of 1920, Vol. II.
[4] Cf. Census of 1930. Population. Vol. III, p. 18.
[5] Cf. William E. B. Du Bois and A. G. Dill (Eds.), *The Common School and the Negro American*, p. 29.

PROBLEMS OF EDUCATION

states showed similar figures. The figures summarized for eleven southern states by McCuistion for 1930 are as follows:

> ... approximately 75 per cent of the total enrollment was white, and 25 per cent Negro.
> Of the $240,180,140 expended for current operation, $23,461,919 was spent for colored schools. Current expenditures per pupil enrolled in white schools averaged $44.31, while the average per pupil enrolled in colored schools was $12.57, with an average for both white and colored of $35.42. The average for the United States for the same year was $87.22, or two and one-half times the amount of the average for the South and seven times the amount spent for Negroes.[1]

Another weakness of the schools for Negroes lay in the fact that the school term was so short that children forgot most of what they learned in one term before they were given further instruction. According to Bulletin 90 of the United States Bureau of Education, the average length of term in schools for colored children in 1918 was 111 days, whereas in schools for white children it was 148 days. "In the elementary schools of six southern states the average term provided for colored children is 106 days, while the corresponding term for white children is 145 days."[2] Much progress has been made in this regard in the last few years. In 1930 the average length of term for all Negro children in fourteen southern states was 134 days.[3] Still another weakness at this earlier period was the poor school equipment. As late as 1920 the State Superintendent of North Carolina reported 126 Negro districts without any schoolhouse, and 1,020 Negro schools without modern desks.[4] In 1921 the State Educational Commission of Kentucky claimed that nine out of ten of all rural school buildings were one room "box-like structures" and "almost all bad." These buildings were unpainted, "the roofs leak," and the buildings were in general bad repair. "These neglected school houses," the report continued, "teach eloquently the doctrine of shiftlessness, disorder and indifference. Their silent lessons will undoubtedly be reproduced in the home, on the farm, in the fac-

---

[1] Fred McCuistion, *Financing Schools in the South, 1930*, p. 18.

[2] U. S. Bureau of Education, *Biennial Survey of Education in the United States, 1916–1918*, p. 126.

[3] Fred McCuistion, *Financing Schools in the South, 1930*, p. 25.

[4] *Biennial Report of the Superintendent of Public Instruction of North Carolina for the Scholastic Years 1918–1919 and 1919–1920*, p. 230.

tory and the store."[1] The other southern states could show no better conditions on the whole. Salaries of teachers were still another weakness. In 1919 the average annual salary for white rural teachers was $298.80; the salary for colored was $157.15. In Alabama the corresponding figures were: for white male teachers, $408; for colored male teachers, $186; for white female teachers, $391; for Negro female teachers, $157. In 1927–28 the annual salary to Negro teachers varied from $268 in Georgia to $990 in Maryland.[2] This disparity in salary shows up in the amount of training teachers are able to secure and the length of experience they acquire.

The Negro schools of this earlier period were almost without supervision. County superintendents rarely visited these schools, and young Negro girls as teachers, without encouragement of a supervisor, must have done a miserable job of teaching. Most of these weaknesses have been largely eliminated or are in process of elimination at the present time. But there is one weakness in the Negro school which does not seem to be in a fair way of solution. Perhaps the weakest point in the Negro school is its maladjusted course of study. Most of the Negro children are located in the rural districts. These children, like the white rural children, are being taught from books made almost entirely by city teachers and adapted to city children. They talk about problems and situations arising in urban communities. The city is glorified and the country neglected. This has a tendency to make the rural child dissatisfied with the rural surrounding, and desirous of getting away to the city. I remember once going into a rural Negro school in Virginia and finding a third reader group spelling out the words of some court scene enacted in England. I would not have rural children, either white or colored, shut off from any of the culture of the world, but if nine-tenths of the material in their readers and histories relates to things that do not concern their daily life, how can we expect their school work to give them any appreciation of their surroundings? We must remember that if the rural curriculum is unadapted to rural children, it is not the fault of rural teachers, either white or colored, for the course of study is outlined and the texts are written almost entirely by those who have long been removed from the rural environment.

[1] *Public Education in Kentucky.* A Report of the Kentucky Educational Commission published by General Educational Board, 1921, pp. 72–73.

[2] U. S. Bureau of Education, *Biennial Survey of Education in the United States, 1928–1930,* p. 46.

We cannot blame the Negro teacher, therefore, if the school tends to urbanize the mind of the Negro child.

There is great need that we have two sets of textbooks, one for rural children and one for urban children. Into the book of the urban child will go something of the best of rural life, and into the text of the rural child will go something of the best of city culture. But the body of the text for the rural child will deal with the materials at hand. It will teach him the beauty of nature, and it will help him observe the birds and bees, the flowers and plants and trees; it will help him see new beauty in the growing crops and the fallow fields. Who would dare say there was not as much real culture in studying the life about him as in studying the life offered by the city zoo? I am not sure that a country boy who knows all about a cow but has never seen a lion is not fully as cultured as a city boy who has seen numerous lions and knows about their native home but knows nothing about a cow and could not get a drop of milk from her even if he were starving. Culture and outlook on life are not determined by the kind of facts we have, half so much as by the interpretation we give to the facts we have. We may see the whole of life in a "flower in a crannied wall," or we may treat it as a noxious weed. What the rural child needs — and especially is this true of the Negro child — is a new ability to interpret the life that surrounds him. At Tuskegee the boys and girls are brought close to nature. In their arithmetic they learn how to measure, not bushels, but bushels of corn or potatoes. They study chemistry, not in the abstract, but the chemistry of making soap or preparing specific foods. And that is what every child needs — adaptation to his daily need.[1]

In the educational renaissance of the South the great education boards have played a large part. First of all the Anna T. Jeanes Fund has helped to give impetus to the small county school. This fund was established by a Quaker lady of Philadelphia who in 1908 decided that the small schools were the most needy and should be helped most. It was quite a problem to find out how they could be helped. But Mr. Jackson Davis, county superintendent of Henrico County in Virginia, and Miss Virginia Randolph, a remarkable Negro teacher in that county, worked out a plan which was adopted. This plan calls for a rural industrial supervisor who goes from school to school in a county and helps the teachers in the small schools to

[1] Cf. Willis D. Weatherford, *The Negro from Africa to America*, pp. 376–378.

organize their domestic science, their gardening, and their simple carpentry work. The idea is to put the children more in touch with the immediate needs of their homes and give them a sense of pride in doing the home work well. Miss Randolph was the first worker of this kind, her salary being paid by the Jeanes Fund. So successful was she that the idea spread rapidly, the Jeanes Fund paying the salary to start with, but decreasing its appropriation year by year until the work was taken over entirely by the county school board. Almost every county in the South which has any considerable Negro population now has a county supervisor.

I have visited numbers of schools where these rural supervising teachers have been at work and I have seen the marked results of their work. One school I visited in Henrico County is more or less typical of the results being achieved all over the South. We arrived at the school building — located eleven miles from the city — at about eleven thirty in the morning. The first thing we noticed was that the yard had been fenced, and we afterward learned that the teacher and children had raised the money to do this. We noticed the grounds were very clean, no paper and no trash to be seen. We went to the well and found the dirt drawn up to the curb so that the water which might be spilled would run away instead of seeping back into the well to contaminate the supply. We examined the outhouses and found them whitewashed, screened, clean and sanitary. As we entered the schoolroom our eyes were at once attracted to a row of nails driven into the wall, on each of which hung a tin cup, and above each of which was pasted the name of a pupil. "Individual drinking cups in a rural Negro school!" Somebody seemed to know about the danger of spreading disease through a common drinking cup. Some of us remember the time in our small town schools when even the white boys did not have a cup, but all drank out of the bucket at the well, allowing any water spilled to run back into it. Two girls in this schoolroom were preparing a dinner. They were twelve and thirteen years old. A little screen around the table, stove, and cupboard made the kitchen in the corner private and kept activities there from disturbing the other children. The teacher asked us if we would not sample the cooking of these two girls. Fried chicken, sweet potatoes, hot chocolate, and hot rolls with butter, all prepared by these two girls, were served us. It was a delicious meal and proved to us at least that the school training of these two girls was really effective. One of the weakest points in the rural Negro home is the food. Every girl who gets the kind of training these girls were getting will help to remedy this condition.[1]

The next step in supervision was supplied by the General Education Board, under the wise direction of Dr. Wallace Buttrick. This board recognized that state supervision was absolutely necessary if schools were to be kept up to standard. It further recognized that the state superintendent could not give the time necessary to direct the Negro schools. The Board therefore decided to provide funds for the employment of a state supervisor of Negro schools in each state, who would be directly related to and under the direction of the state superintendent. It was fitting that Mr. Jackson Davis should be the first such worker (1910), serving in the Department of Education in Virginia. Agents are now maintained in all the southern states, and a finer group of men could not be found in educational work. Both Mr. Davis of Virginia and Mr. Favrot of Louisiana have been promoted to be general supervisors for the General Education Board; Mr. S. L. Smith, who was the first supervisor for Tennessee, has become the agent of the Rosenwald Fund for the South; Mr. Sibley, who served first in Alabama, went to Africa to establish educational work and there gave his life for the cause. Mr. N. C. Newbold, who was the first supervisor in North Carolina, is still at that task and has become one of the real educational statesmen of the South. Perhaps no one thing that has been done for the Negro schools of the South has been more statesmanlike than this.

In 1914 Mr. Julius Rosenwald furnished a small fund to Dr. Booker T. Washington to aid in building a few model school buildings in Macon County, Alabama. The experiment worked so well, and the enthusiasm of the Negroes was so great, that Mr. Rosenwald decided to extend the work to the state of Alabama, agreeing to give one-third of the funds required for the erection of a rural school building, provided the school authorities with the aid of white friends and the Negro people themselves would furnish the other two-thirds. Sixty-nine such buildings, costing seventy thousand dollars, were erected the first year. Other states then applied for aid, and a broad program of Negro school building was begun. Mr. S. L. Smith, the director of this work, furnishes the following figures as of July 1, 1932. Up to this date 5,357 schoolhouses had been completed in fifteen states, at a cost of $28,408,520. Of this amount

[1] Cf. Willis D. Weatherford, *The Negro from Africa to America*, pp. 381–382.

the Rosenwald Fund contributed $4,364,869; the Negroes $4,725,871; white friends $1,211,975; and the public school funds $18,105,805. Mr. Rosenwald had thus supplied buildings with a pupil capacity of 663,615, or two-fifths of all the Negro children enrolled in the fifteen states. He had contributed 15 per cent of the cost and stimulated the South to supply the 85 per cent. These Rosenwald schools have set the pattern for all rural schools, white and colored. White men were not willing to see their own children taught in buildings which were inferior to those in which the Negro children of the community were taught. Hence, during the nearly twenty years covering the growth of these Negro school buildings, perhaps two or three times as much has been spent in similar buildings for white children. The Rosenwald Fund has also encouraged libraries in rural schools. A total of $146,936 has been spent in establishing 1,189 rural school libraries. The fund has furnished buses for 159 schools at a cost during the last three years of $440,000, of which amount the local committees paid about two-thirds. The fund has thus put at the disposal of 40 per cent of the Negro children of the South school facilities which are entirely adequate for the purpose.

Another important element in this progress of Negro schools has been the better training of teachers. The John F. Slater Board, under the leadership of Dr. James H. Dillard, undertook to improve this situation by establishing county training schools, in connection with the best public school in a county. By paying the salary of a well-prepared teacher of pedagogy, the Board made it possible to equip many of the best high school students to teach in elementary schools. The Slater Fund also furnished special teachers to a number of the denominational schools for the same purpose of training teachers. From 1882 to 1931, this fund expended $3,690,714 on Negro education, all but a few hundred dollars of which was spent in the South.[1]

The development of higher education for Negroes has been under way ever since the Civil War. A number of the northern churches undertook to establish colleges during the first years of reconstruction. Thus Shaw University, Fisk University, and the theological school which was the forerunner of Virginia Union were all established in 1860. Rust College and Roger Williams were established in 1866. Morehouse College, Biddle (now John C. Smith), Atlanta University, and St. Augustine were established in 1867; Hampton,

[1] *Report of John F. Slater Fund, 1931*, p. 9.

not then a college, was established in 1868, Claflin and Straight in 1869, and Benedict in 1870. None of these were really colleges, for the reason that there were no students qualified to enter college classes. But the determination to make them colleges was there, and the beginning of a system of higher education was in evidence. The actual working out of this system was slow and tedious. When Dr. Thomas Jesse Jones made his exhaustive study of Negro colleges in 1917 he found a respectable number of college students enrolled in these colleges, and the Bureau of Education in its study of 1928 found 15,930 collegiate students enrolled in Negro colleges.[1] This same survey found there were 3,500 Negro doctors, or one for every 3,343 Negroes, while the white people have one doctor for every 553. Of course many Negroes go to white physicians. In 1928 there was one Negro dentist for every 10,540 Negroes. There were 19,600 Negro preachers but only a very small percentage were college trained. Ignorance in a Negro preacher may be even more disastrous than ignorance in a white preacher. The Negro, who is by training highly emotional, needs some wholesome preaching if his religion is to bear fruit in moral living. This kind of preaching cannot be done by men who are ignorant and unlettered. Out of the 1,046 teachers in colleges, in 1928, only 412 held graduate or professional degrees. These facts are sufficient to show the desperate need for college training of Negroes. By no possible line of sound reasoning can one arrive at the conclusion that we do not need greatly to augment the college education of the Negro people.

Progress during the last two decades has been great. In 1916, when Dr. Jones was working on his report, there were 31 Negro institutions offering college work; in 1926 there were 77, while the increase in enrollment was 550 per cent. The annual income of the 79 colleges studied was $2,283,000 in 1916, and it had increased to $8,560,000 in 1926. The total capital invested had increased in the same ten years from $15,720,000 to $38,680,000. Endowments had mounted during these ten years from $7,000,000 to $20,000,000.[2]

The collegiate institutions of the Negro youth are listed by the Bureau of Education studies under four heads: (1) institutions governed by independent boards of trustees; (2) publicly supported and controlled institutions; (3) colleges controlled and administered by

[1] United States Bureau of Education, *Survey of the Negro Colleges and Universities of the South*, p. 33.
[2] *Ibid.*, p. 32.

state Negro church organizations or conferences; (4) colleges under control of white church boards. Of these groups the first have by far the largest incomes; they have on the whole the best equipment and the largest teaching staffs. The missionary colleges, under group 4, have the poorest incomes and the smallest average teaching staffs. Some of these have gone out of existence during the hard years of 1929 to 1932. Others will undoubtedly have to disband. The state schools are destined to make rapid progress in the near future. With the tax funds behind them, with a more sympathetic attitude on the part of southern politicians, and with the demand for a more intelligent citizenship there can be no doubt that these institutions will get more and more funds to do their work. This is as it should be. The state is in the business of education to make an intelligent citizenship. The Negro people of the South make up more than 30 per cent of the population. Unless they are given intelligent training they will be a drag on the progress and constructive life of the section. As a matter of self-protection the southern white man would need to be interested in the education of Negro youth. But increasingly the best element of the South is rising above bare self-interest and is willing to coöperate in giving the Negro boy and girl every advantage which the white boy and girl wants and needs.

PROBLEMS FOR STUDY

1. Do you think the planters were right in supposing that Negroes who learned to read and write thereby became dissatisfied and ready for insurrection?
2. Does education at the present time unfit Negroes for life, since many of them must make their living at manual toil?
3. Does education make all workers, including Negroes, better citizens, or does it make them restless, or do both results follow an education?
4. If the state is educating people for citizenship in a democracy, should it spend more money on those who have had considerable advantages or on those who have had little? How would this affect the division of public school money between white and colored children?
5. Professor Coon of North Carolina claimed that Negroes paid more taxes than they received back in schools and other public benefits. Could you verify this?
6. Is industrial training more important for Negro boys than it is for the mass of white boys in the United States?

7. Since a dual system of education is very expensive, have you any suggestions as to how the problem of education for two races can better be organized?
8. Should there be separate textbooks for Negro children and white children, for city children and rural children?
9. Would it be wise or possible to include poetry and prose by Negroes in textbooks used by white children?
10. Do you think the various educational boards have helped or hindered Negro education?
11. Why do you suppose there has been so much opposition to higher education of Negroes?

BIBLIOGRAPHY

Dennis H. Cooke, *The White Superintendent and the Negro Schools in North Carolina* (1930).
William E. B. Du Bois and A. G. Dill (Eds.), *The College-bred Negro American* (1910).
Leo M. Favrot, *A Study of County Training Schools for Negroes in the South* (1923).
Oscar F. Galloway, *Higher Education for Negroes in Kentucky* (1932).
Atticus G. Haygood, *Pleas for Progress* (1889).
Nolen M. Irby, *A Program for the Equalization of Educational Opportunities in the State of Arkansas* (1930).
Lance G. E. Jones, *The Negro Schools in the Southern States* (1928).
Ullin W. Leavell, *Philanthropy in Negro Education* (1930).
Hollis M. Long, *Public Secondary Education for Negroes in North Carolina* (1932).
United States Bureau of Education, *Negro Education: A Study of the Private and High Schools for Colored People in the United States* (Bulletin No. 39, 1916).
United States Bureau of Education, *Survey of the Negro Colleges and Universities of the South* (1928).
Carter G. Woodson, *The Education of the Negro prior to 1861* (1919).

CHAPTER XIX

HEALTH OF THE NEGRO

The excessive mortality of Negroes in America has been so persistent as to prompt the belief that they are constitutionally defective and incapable, to the same degree as white persons, of physical survival. This, indeed, is strongly implied in the consistently high Negro mortality from respiratory diseases. In 1929, the last year for which it is possible to get figures from the registration area of the United States, the general Negro mortality was 16.9 per thousand as compared with 11.4 for the white. This is a crude death rate for Negroes which is 47 per cent greater than the rate for whites. The urban rate for Negroes for this same year was 20.6 as compared with 12.4 for the whites, and the Negro rural rates 14.9 as compared with 10.4 for whites.

The racial disparity is not only greater in the city than in the country but it is greater in the North than in the South. For eleven northern states the death rate averaged 19.0 per cent for Negroes and 11.5 per cent for whites; thus the rate for Negroes was 65 per cent higher than the rate for whites. For eleven southern states it averaged 15.9 for Negroes and 10.0 for whites; in other words the rate for Negroes was 59 per cent higher than the rate for whites. The rates for whites and Negroes are generally lower in the South than in the North, a fact which may be due either to inadequate registration in the South, or to larger urban concentration and accompanying stress of life in the northern states. The Negro rate is greater for the southern cities than for the northern cities, and the rural Negro death rate is greater in the North than in the South.

Despite the present disparity in white and Negro rates, however, it has been considerably greater in the past.

CRUDE DEATH RATE OF WHITES AND NEGROES IN THE REGISTRATION AREA OF THE UNITED STATES, FOR SELECTED YEARS

Year	White	Negro
1929	11.4	16.9
1926	11.6	18.8
1910	14.6	25.7
1900	17.1	29.4

HEALTH OF THE NEGRO 369

There is a slightly greater rate of decline since 1900 in the Negro rates, and it will be noted that the Negro rate for 1929 is less than the white rate in 1900. This is, in a sense, the measure of a lag which is, obviously, more social than physiological, for a race cannot change its fundamental constitution in thirty years. As early as 1910, Bulletin 112 of the Census Mortality Statistics series pointed out that the differences in the death rates of the native white and Negro populations should not be interpreted as essential racial differences, but rather as due to economic and other social causes. For, although the Negro rates were consistently higher than native white rates, they were also consistently lower than white rates in the great majority of European countries.

The difference between Negro urban and rural rates is actually more than twice as great as the difference between white urban and rural rates. Urban rates tend to decline for both whites and Negroes the further north the area, while just the opposite is true in the case of rural rates. Mary Gover and Edgar Sydenstricker,[1] in calculating the mean age at death of all persons for the three decades preceding 1920, for white males found these mean ages to be 48, 50, and 54 years, respectively, and for white females 51, 54, and 56 years. For Negro males it was 33, 34, and 41 years, and for Negro females 35, 38, and 42 years. The lag noted in the reduction of Negro mortality rates is again strikingly evidenced in death for Negroes about 15 years earlier than for whites.[2]

The chief causes of Negro deaths have been, in order of importance, tuberculosis of the respiratory system, organic diseases of the heart, pneumonia, external causes (excluding suicide and homicide), congenital malformations and diseases of early infancy, cerebral hemorrhage and softening, and cancer. In 1925 for the first time organic diseases of the heart took first place over tuberculosis. In 1929 Negro deaths from organic diseases of the heart stood 27 per cent higher than deaths from tuberculosis of the respiratory system; pneumonia remained third, nephritis fourth, cerebral hemorrhage and softening fifth, congenital malformation sixth, and cancer seventh. For the whites heart diseases lead, followed in turn by cancer, ne-

---

[1] *Mortality among Negroes in the United States*, Public Health Bulletin 174 (1928).

[2] These calculations were based upon the original registration area, and since only about 4 per cent of the Negro population lives in these states the Negro life expectancy is understated.

phritis, pneumonia, cerebral hemorrhage, congenital malformations, and tuberculosis. The significant difference is in the relative positions of cancer and tuberculosis. Cancer is second in importance among white deaths and seventh among Negro deaths, while tuberculosis is second in importance among Negro deaths.

The greatest disparity between Negro and white death rates has been in the rates for tuberculosis of the respiratory system. Some of this difference may be due to the fact of unequal importance of this disease as a cause of death. It was, nevertheless, responsible for 76,624 total deaths in 1929, of which 20,000 were Negro deaths. On the basis of relative population proportions this is two and one-half times as many Negro as white deaths.

The highest rates for Negro tuberculosis deaths are in cities, and these fluctuated widely, from 50 per 100,000 in Syracuse, New York,

WHITE AND NEGRO DEATHS PER 100,000 FROM TUBERCULOSIS FOR TWENTY SELECTED CITIES IN 1931 [1]

City	White Tuberculosis Death Rate per 100,000	Negro Tuberculosis Death Rate per 100,000	Both
New York City	58	286	69
Chicago	49	283	66
Philadelphia	61	247	83
Detroit	56	307	76
Baltimore	74	313	117
Milwaukee	67	528	73
Buffalo	68	491	79
Washington, D. C.	66	262	120
Cincinnati	68	468	112
Indianapolis	61	277	87
Houston	65	137	81
Columbus	73	244	92
Atlanta	39	198	92
Dallas	53	234	80
Birmingham	41	233	114
Memphis	77	303	164
Akron	31	145	36
San Antonio	166	147	165
Syracuse	50	51	50
Kansas City, Kan.	61	195	83

[1] Taken from figures compiled by Godias J. Drolet, New York Tuberculosis and Health Association, 1932.

to 528 per 100,000 in Milwaukee in 1931. In the same year white rates varied from 31 per 100,000 in Akron, Ohio, to 166 per 100,000 in San Antonio, Texas. The table on page 370 gives these rates for twenty northern and southern cities.

Tuberculosis is a disease which has its greatest incidence among the lower economic groups. Its seriousness is closely related to social and economic factors, and its prevention has become as much a sociological as a medical problem. Poverty, poor food, bad housing, overcrowding, overwork, and worry diminish resistance. Improvement in economic well-being usually carries with it improvement in resistance to its fatal ravages. Dr. Louis I. Dublin, of the Metropolitan Life Insurance Company, one of the foremost authorities on this question, has pointed out that tuberculosis is not uniformly distributed in the population as a cause of sickness and death; that it is a workingman's disease.[1] In the experience of the company, which insures millions, the death rate among industrial policyholders in the lowest income group from all forms of tuberculous diseases in 1930 was 81.3 per 100,000. Among the "ordinary" risks, which include persons holding policies of more than $1,000, it was 48.7 per 100,000. For the group carrying $5,000 or more there was a mortality rate of only 17 per 100,000. Within this industrial classification tuberculosis is found concentrated primarily among males and among colored persons. A glance at the occupational figures for Negroes in cities in which these rates are highest will show that over 75 per cent of the Negro workers are engaged in unskilled lines of work, and that 54 per cent of the women are workers. The table on page 372, adapted from the Metropolitan figures, shows these rates for whites and Negroes, male and female, over a period of years.

Tuberculosis mortality among Negroes has its heaviest incidence at younger age periods than for whites. It greatly exceeds white rates between the ages of 20 and 45, and reaches the highest point of disparity around the age of 25. In 1930 it was seven times as great for Negro boys (159.8) 10 to 20 years of age as for white boys (21.1), and six times as great for Negro girls (245.6) as for white girls (41.8). Control of tuberculosis alone, it is estimated, would increase the Negro life span by five years. The facts that between 50 and 90 per cent of the population are infected when they reach adulthood; that the disease is now declared not in itself hereditary; and that its

[1] "Tuberculosis among Industrial Workers," *American Journal of Public Health*, March, 1932, pp. 281–291.

DEATH RATES PER 100,000 FROM TUBERCULOSIS — ALL FORMS — 1911 TO 1930

Year	Male		Female	
	White	Negro	White	Negro
1930	68.0	223.8	57.1	213.0
1929	73.1	226.4	63.0	220.1
1927	77.9	227.6	70.9	228.4
1925	84.3	224.9	76.7	228.0
1923	97.9	242.9	88.2	245.7
1921	99.5	249.1	95.2	285.8
1919	145.2	319.7	125.2	328.9
1917	194.3	414.9	135.0	371.7
1915	201.1	432.8	141.5	394.2
1913	218.2	428.6	147.7	363.1
1911	230.8	422.2	105.4	415.1

incidence is heaviest among the poorer classes, raise the question whether the lack of resistance among Negroes is not more economic than biological.

Considering this phase of the problem as a whole, 67 per cent of all Negro workers are confined to two of the poorest paid occupations, agriculture and domestic service. Just 100 per cent more Negroes than whites are so placed economically. Taking the rural group, which, by the way, constitutes about 43 per cent of all Negro workers, 56 per cent are laborers and 32 per cent tenants. The 33 per cent of Negro workers not farmers and domestics are for the most part in industry. About 75 per cent of these receive the wages of unskilled laborers. In skilled work Dr. Raymond Pinchbeck's study of the Negro artisans and tradesmen in Virginia indicates that they receive wages from 20 to 50 per cent less than those of white workers.[1] The study of Negro families in Richmond, Virginia, in 1929, made by the Council of Social Agencies, shows that the total weekly income of Negro families from all sources was less than $25 in over 80 per cent of the Negro families, and under $15 weekly in over 40 per cent of the families. This is, assuming unemployment, less than $750 annually.[2] The United States Department of Labor

[1] Raymond Pinchbeck, *The Virginia Negro Artisan and Tradesman.*

[2] *The Negro in Richmond, Virginia.* Report of the Welfare Survey Committee, Richmond Council of Social Agencies (1930).

study of living costs and incomes in Richmond, Virginia, for the year 1924 finds that only 2 per cent of the white families from an average population studied, earned under $900.[1]

The mortality of Negroes from tuberculosis, if the premise of social responsibility holds, gets very direct reflection in the Richmond, Virginia, situation, for in 1927 the Negro mortality was 147, and that of the whites 49.2. In this connection it might be noted that the provisions from public funds for the care of Negro and white cases after tuberculosis has been developed show a similar disproportion. While the Negro rate is three times the white rate, there are 6.8 white and 1.4 Negro cases under supervision per death. During the year there were 90 beds for whites and 67 deaths, while for Negroes there were 30 beds and 82 deaths. In Nashville, in 1929, of 500 Negro families included in a study by the Department of Social Science at Fisk University, 325 heads of families, or 64 per cent, earned less than $20 per week.[2]

Occasionally it is possible to get comparisons of the tuberculosis death rate by race and economic class. In Cincinnati, Ohio, Dr. Floyd P. Allen compared these rates for two census tracts of Cincinnati. In tract 36 the Negro population was of low economic status, and in a population of 4,131 there was a tuberculosis mortality of 290 per 100,000. In tract 37, adjoining but with a Negro population of 1,763, for the most part representing a higher range of occupations and incomes, there were no deaths from tuberculosis. Again, in tract 5, with a very poor white laboring population, the tuberculosis death rate was 673 per 100,000. The general mortality rate was two and one-half times higher for the white population in tract 5 than for the Negro population in tract 37.[3]

The Negro tuberculosis mortality rate has not always been so much greater than the white, if we are to take the earlier figures and findings seriously. The physicians of Louisiana, assembled in convention several years before the Civil War, appointed Dr. Samuel A. Cartwright of New Orleans to prepare for them a report on the diseases and physical characteristics of the Negro race. Thirty years

---

[1] United States Bureau of Labor Statistics, *Cost of Living in the United States* (Bulletin No. 357), p. 98.

[2] Charles S. Johnson, "One Thousand Negro Families in Nashville (Tennessee)." Unpublished study made by Department of Social Science, Fisk University.

[3] "Physical Impairment among One Thousand Negro Workers," *American Journal of Public Health*, June, 1932, p. 579.

of practice in the South and a reputation for scholarship warranted this assignment and gave confidence later in the acceptance of his findings. This is, in part, what he found:

To the question, "Is not Phthisis very common among the slaves of the slave states and unknown among the native Africans at home?" I reply in the negative, that Phthisis, so far from being common among the slaves of the slave states, is very seldom met with. As to the native Africans at home, little or nothing is known of their diseases. They have no science or literature among them, and never had. The word Consumption is applied to two very different diseases among negroes. The Cachexia Africana, Dirt-eating of the English, and Mal d'Estomac of the French, commonly called Negro Consumption, is a very different malady from Phthisis Pulmonalis, properly so called. The Cachexia Africana, like other spanoemic states of the system, may run into Phthisis, or become complicated with it. . . . Phthisis is *par excellence* a disease of the sanguineous temperament, fair complexion, red or flaxen hair, blue eyes, large blood vessels, and a bony encasement too small to admit the full and free expansion of the lungs, enlarged by the superabundant blood, which is determined by those organs during that first half-score of years immediately succeeding puberty. Well-formed chests offer no impediment to its inroads, if the volume of blood be out of proportion to the expansibility and capacity of the pulmonary organs. Hence it is most apt to occur precisely at, and immediately following, that period of life known as matureness, when the sanguineous system becomes fully developed and gains the mastery, so to speak, over the lymphatic and nervous systems. With negroes, the sanguineous never gains the mastery over the lymphatic and nervous systems. . . .

Phthisis is a disease of the master race, and not of the slave race — that it is the bane of that master race of men, known by an active haematosis; by the brain receiving a larger quantity of aerated blood than it is entitled to; by the strong development of the circulating system; by the energy of intellect; by the strength and activity of the muscular system; the vivid imagination; the irritable, mobile, ardent and inflammatory temperament, and the indomitable will and love of freedom. Whereas the negro constitution, being the opposite of all this, is not subject to Phthisis, although it partakes of what is called the scrofulous diathesis.[1]

This same conviction had the support of no less important a person than Thomas Jefferson.

During slavery, when it was economically profitable to preserve the years of service and strength of the chattel property, and under

[1] *Cotton Is King and Pro-Slavery Arguments* comprising the writings of Hammond, Harper, Christy, Stringfellow, Hodge, Bledsoe, and Cartwright (Slavery in the Light of Ethnology), pp. 691-706.

HEALTH OF THE NEGRO

the rigid dietary discipline of the institution, the Negro death rate, from such records as we have, was no more than, and in many cases less than, the white. Dr. Frederick L. Hoffman, in the first extensive research into Negro mortality trends, states that "the opinion of southern physicians who practised among Negroes before the Civil War was almost unanimous that consumption was less frequent among the colored population than among the white."[1] Mortality records extend backward to an early period in Charleston, South Carolina; Mobile, Alabama; Savannah, Georgia; and New Orleans, Louisiana. In Charleston the death rate for whites and Negroes for consumption between 1822 and 1848 was as follows:

Period	White	Negro
1822–1830	437	447
1831–1840	231	320
1841–1848	368	266
1822–1848	347	342

Dr. Hoffman calculated general mortality rates from records in three other southern cities which extended back as far as 1843.

City	Period	White	Negro
Mobile, Alabama	1843–46	45.83	23.10
	1847–50	42.53	31.19
	1852–55	54.39	34.70
Savannah, Georgia	1856–60	37.19	34.07
New Orleans, Louisiana	1849–60	59.6	52.1

Additional evidence of the history of tuberculosis appears in the number of rejected recruits per 1,000 examined for the Civil War.[2] For white recruits generally it was 264.1, and for colored recruits 120.2. For consumption, the number of rejections of white recruits was 11.4 and of Negro recruits 4.2. The curious consistency of the figures in different cities may in some degree balance their defectiveness otherwise. When the slaves were emancipated they were thrown suddenly upon their own economic resources. They were ignorant and propertyless for the most part, and their mortality, if we are to follow the figures, took an abrupt upward trend. In Charleston, South Carolina, where the white rate for consumption had been 268 and the Negro rate 266 in the period 1841–1848, they

---

[1] *Race Traits and Tendencies of the American Negro*, p. 69.
[2] *Medical Statistics of the Provost Marshal General's Bureau*, Vol. II, p. 431.

shifted to 198 for whites and 411 for Negroes in the year just following the Civil War. In 1890, the most recent year for which the figures were available for Dr. Hoffman, the white tuberculosis rate was 355.4 per 100,000 and the Negro rate 686.3. Said he: "In the plain language of the facts brought together the colored race is shown to be on the downward grade, tending toward a condition in which matters will be worse than they are now, when diseases will be more destructive, vital resistance still lower, when the number of births will fall below the deaths, and gradual extinction of the race take place." [1]

During the long period of acceptance of the high Negro tuberculosis rate as a fundamental and inescapable mark of inferior physique and racial lack of resistance, little was done to reduce the startling decimation in this race from the disease. General public health programs, which began to be effective about twenty-five years ago, reached this group tardily. In the white race, tuberculosis, which once led as cause of death, has been reduced to a minor rank, and among Negroes, where they have been exposed to preventive measures, control, and hospitalization, there have been corresponding improvements. Where no important measures of control have been taken the rates have remained high.

The importance of heart disease among Negroes has only recently been recognized, and even yet it is not given the place of importance it deserves above tuberculosis in actual seriousness. The present Negro rate is about twice that of the whites, and the rates for both Negroes and whites have been mounting over the past thirty years. This is, to some extent, to be expected, statistically, with the decline in the rates of certain other diseases, since the heaviest incidence of diseases of the heart is in the later age periods.

The Negro infant mortality rate continues to be extremely high. It was 102.2 in 1929 as compared with 63.2 for whites, and the Negro rate for stillbirths was nearly three times that of the whites. Infant mortality is greater in the cities than in the country, and the racial disparity is likewise greater in the cities. The Negro rates were in 1917 higher in northern than in southern states, but the decline has been more rapid in the North. Amanda L. Stoughton, acting Assistant Surgeon, and Mary Gover, Associate Statistician of the United States Public Health Service, have pointed out that whites and Negroes have shown corresponding trends in both North and South,

---

[1] *Race Traits and Tendencies of the American Negro*, p. 312.

but that in the matter of rate of decline, infant mortality appears to be more closely associated with geographic locality than with racial difference. They add that it is to be assumed that sanitation and infant welfare measures, which were initiated earlier and have been more actively carried out in the North, have been the chief factors in the decline of the rates of both races.[1] The infant mortality rate for whites has been reduced from 82.1 in 1920 to 60.2 in 1930, while that for Negroes has been reduced from 135.6 to 95.1 in the same period.

It has been pointed that some of this excess may be due to faulty birth registration, especially in the southern states where the largest numbers of Negroes live. Nevertheless, the rates are extremely high. Premature birth is the most frequent cause of death for both white and Negro infants; the second cause is respiratory diseases for Negroes and gastro-intestinal diseases for whites.

A question demanding serious attention, in connection with the high mortality from organic diseases of the heart, the infant and maternal mortality, and other notable end results is that of venereal diseases. The most recent and complete figures on the prevalence of gonorrhoea and syphilis in the United States are those obtained by the United States Public Health Service. These were published in 1930. These surveys of persons under treatment in a population of 24,498,000 in various localities show a rate per thousand of 7.46 for both sexes. Separately they are 10.0 for males and 4.86 for females. These, of course, represent only cases under treatment and thus are minimal rates.[2] The prevalence of venereal diseases among Negroes has been the subject of much speculation, sound and unsound. It has, as a rule, been readily assumed to be high and related to an undisciplined moral nature, as well as to ignorance of principles of hygiene. The estimates have ranged from 3.0 to 75 per cent of the population, but few of these estimates have been based upon sources which could be regarded as representative of the Negro population. The most common source of figures has been free clinics; figures from this source have been overweighted by the fact that the Negroes, being poorer, could less often secure the services of a private physician, especially for such costly treatment as venereal

[1] *A Study of Negro Infant Mortality.* United States Public Health Reports, Vol. 44, No. 45, Nov. 1929.

[2] Lida J. Uselton, *Prevalence of Venereal Disease in the United States*, United States Public Health Service, Venereal Disease Information, December 20, 1930.

diseases involve. Conservative estimates more recently have placed incidence of general diseases among Negroes as about two and a half times their incidence among whites.

An experiment in 1930 by the Julius Rosenwald Fund, in the mass control of syphilis, provided what is perhaps the most thorough survey available anywhere of the prevalence of syphilis, hereditary and acquired, over large areas in selected groups of the Negro population. Six counties in the South were intimately studied, and Wassermann blood tests made of families representing from 20 to 40 per cent of the entire Negro population of these counties. A total of 33,234 examinations were made, of which number 6,800 or 20.5 per cent were positive. The percentages of positive Wassermann reactions varied from 8.9 in Albemarle County in Virginia to 39.8 in Macon County, Alabama. In explanation of these striking differences it was pointed out, suggestively, by Dr. Taliaferro Clark of the United States Public Health Service, who prepared the report for the Rosenwald Fund, that in Macon County the extremely low levels of literacy and of economic, social, and cultural status were initially responsible for the high rates, and that to this situation was added the fact that less than 3 per cent of those who gave positive reactions had ever had any treatment at all. In the two lowest counties, Albemarle (8.9)[1] and Pitt, North Carolina (12.5),[2] he said, the social and economic status of the Negro population was found to be on a higher educational, social, and economic level. These figures may not be taken as representative of either urban or northern Negro groups. Examinations in two Negro educational institutions drawing students from a wide range of families throughout the states of Alabama and Texas showed 7.0 and 8.0 per cent, respectively, hereditary and acquired. No study of similar thoroughness has yet been made of the white population.

The extent of physical impairment among Negroes, and particularly among Negro workers, has only been surmised from occasional examinations by industrial concerns. It is, however, a question of serious importance to this population group. In Cincinnati in 1930, one thousand Negro factory workers were examined by the local Public Health Federation and Anti-Tuberculosis League, in coöperation with the Heart Council Life Conservation Program. Their findings for the thousand workers were as follows:

---

[1] *The Control of Syphilis in Southern Rural Areas*, pp. 21–22.
[2] *Ibid.*, pp. 13–14.

Physical Findings [1]

	Number Involved
Weight — 10 pounds or more over weight	358
10 pounds or more under weight	275
Vision — 20/30 or more in one or both eyes	508
Dental defects	787
Defective hearing	107
Enlarged thyroid	39
Significant cardio-vascular lesion	556
Valvular lesions	125
Cardiac enlargement	249
Myocardial insufficiency	68
Hyper tension	249
Hypo tension	119
Arteriosclerosis (Markey)	11
Pulmonary defects............(findings incomplete)	82
Hernia	147
Hemorrhoids	147
Dermatoses	212
Flat feet	816
Traumatic defections	22
Albuminuria	170
Glucosuria	4
Wassermann positive	300*

* Estimated on basis of 85 positives out of 362 Wassermanns obtained.

A group of white workers which, unfortunately for an exact comparison, included many office workers, showed 33.5 per cent defects, with significant circulatory defects as compared with 55.6 per cent for the Negroes.

The voluminous report embodying the findings of the study of the costs of medical care made under the direction of I. S. Falk, C. R. Rorem, and M. D. Ring, while recognizing the question of Negro health as having special features and stresses, does not, however, include specific studies either of the prevalence of sickness or of medical costs among them. For the white population the investigators found (as evidenced in a study of 9,000 families) a morbidity experience of 844.5 illnesses of all types and durations per 1,000 persons in the course of a year. Of the Negro families they had only this to say: "Although it cannot be expressed quantita-

[1] Floyd P. Allen,"Physical Impairment among One Thousand Negro Workers," *American Journal of Public Health*, June, 1932.

tively, it can be said that the need for medical care is in general greater among Negroes than among white persons." The rate per 1,000 for hospital cases was 60.1 for the white families studied in 130 communities.

The *Journal of the American Medical Association* lists 6,807 hospitals of all sorts in the United States with 853,318 beds and an average of 671,830 patients daily. This is one bed for each 139 of the population. The number of known Negro hospitals in 1926 was 210, of which only 7 were approved, and these had 6,780 beds. This was one bed for each 1,941 Negroes. In the northern cities it is possible for them to get admitted to wards of public hospitals; in the South, while certain limited provisions are made in special wards of public hospitals in the large cities, it is a fact which has often been given dramatic and fatal acuteness, that the great majority of hospitals, public and private, will not admit Negro patients under any circumstances.

Negro health is not simply a question of medicine, or of hospitals, or of doctors. It is bound up securely with the elusive factors of cultural status, economic levels, and the progress of medical science itself. The present problem of Negro mortality cannot be adequately understood out of relation to these questions. It is not enough to know that the Negro mortality is higher than for any other people in the population. What is important is the reason why it is higher. Strangely enough the sociologist, the economist, the psychologist, have a rôle in this unraveling that is quite as vital as the rôle of the physician and the public health officer. There is a significant correspondence between the amount of Negro illiteracy, low economic status, and high mortality. Folk cures, superstitions, various incantations, throw up a formidable barrier to proper treatment of sickness.

For many years, and even to a certain extent today, the belief in a different racial physiological pattern has retarded efforts at improvement of Negro health. Quite apart from the external restrictions with respect to admission to hospitals and full participation in various public health programs, there are throttling economic handicaps which have a direct influence upon the disease and death rates. The diseases which, authorities agree, are due to insanitary conditions and to low economic status show the greatest disparity between whites and Negroes.

Dr. Dublin points out that, during the war in Europe, when economic reverses came, the tuberculosis death rate in Germany increased from 157 in 1913 to 287 in 1917, and in Warsaw from 306 in 1913 to 840 in 1917. After 1920 the Warsaw rates declined to 338 again. Miss Grace Abbott, of the United States Children's Bureau, in commenting upon the excess mortality of Negroes and of Negro infant mortality, reached the conclusion that it was largely a reflection of low economic status. Robert Morse Woodbury found infant mortality rates varying directly with the father's earnings, and that for infants over one month of age the death rate was lowest for the highest income group.[1] The only available study of white and Negro families of the same low economic class — those earning less than $50 per year — made in Baltimore, shows the Negro and white mortality approximately the same.

The United States Women's Bureau studies show, for the occupations covered, that in Georgia 89 per cent of the Negro women receive less than $10 weekly as compared with 21 per cent of the white workers, and the white workers are underpaid. That is, four times as many Negro as white women workers receive less than $10 weekly. Thirty-five per cent of the Negro and 10 per cent of the white women received less than $5 a week. In Tennessee 28 per cent of the Negro women and 12 per cent of the white women received less than $5 a week; 85 per cent of the Negro and 41 per cent of the white women received less than $10 weekly.

It is necessary to view this factor as a community rather than a personal one before it is fully convincing. Eventually the community pays for Negro illness. It pays, not alone through taxes for public health and relief programs, but for the support of prisons and police. It pays in philanthropy and the personal aid doled out to the individual Negro dependents whom many of the white families of the South find it difficult to escape. The community further pays in the loss of both a producer and a consumer in the shortened span of a Negro's life. For at the present mortality rate they are cut off before the community can fully compensate itself for the expense of rearing them to the age of self-support. Dublin and Whitney have calculated that a loss of one year of life is equivalent to a money loss of $100 in national wealth, and that every tuberculosis death subtracts an average of 2.5 years from the life span of each individual, meaning a loss per person of $250. But for each death there are six to eight persons constantly ill from the disease. Here again is a burden in impaired income which the community sustains.

[1] *Infant Mortality and Its Causes*, p. 48.

The placing of major emphasis upon the improvement of economic well-being is not intended to minimize the value of other measures in overcoming Negro disabilities. One of the most acute problems is that of illiteracy and ignorance. The distinction is made because in matters of health there are so many ignorant literates. Schools exist already but these have their own problems of insufficiency and inadequacy. Public health is beginning to approach future problems in health and industrial efficiency by early examination and, to some extent, correction of defects. The prevailing ignorance about disease, and the seriousness of disease and the early signs of illness, and ignorance about the manner of promoting health, still constitute a handicap to health programs.

The health programs of late have increasingly been bearing in upon the Negro population; their illiteracy has been reduced to less than 18 per cent; the migration of over a million from the South to the North has exposed them to better wages and certain measures of improved sanitation; and along with these factors has gone a consistent improvement in health. Between 1911 and 1927, although this covered the period of the northern Negro migration, with its new climatic as well as industrial stresses, the mortality rates (in the experience of the Metropolitan Life Insurance Company) declined from 17.5 to 14.0. This was a drop of more than 20 per cent. Within the same period of time there was an actual increase of five years in the Negro life span. The Negro rates today are where the white rates were about 25 years ago; and where conditions are at all favorable similar results are registered in life conservation.

PROBLEMS FOR STUDY

1. Can the high rate of Negro mortality from tuberculosis be dissociated from low income, bad housing, and poor sanitation?
2. Is it more plausible that the decline in Negro tuberculosis mortality is due to improved income rather than to change in physiological constitution?
3. What is the scientific explanation of the higher mortality of an immigrant group than that of the residents?
4. A Negro family of six living in a two-room house on an income of $20 a week contracts tuberculosis. What are the chances of their receiving proper care?
5. How does the lack of regard for Negroes in health programs make for lag in health?

6. What explains the lower relative mortality of Negroes from cancer and diabetes?
7. The inadequacy of hospitalization for Negroes even in emergency cases is responsible for a portion of the higher Negro mortality. Since Negroes who are most in need of these services are least able to support hospitals, should not the state assist them to the extent that it assists the white population?
8. Can any sound medical ethics refuse emergency treatment of Negroes in a white hospital when no other hospital is available?

BIBLIOGRAPHY

Floyd P. Allen, "Physical Impairment among One Thousand Negro Workers," *American Journal of Public Health*, June, 1932, pp. 579–586.

Taliaferro Clark, *The Control of Syphilis in Southern Rural Areas* (United States Public Health Service, published by Julius Rosenwald Fund, 1930).

Louis I. Dublin, "Tuberculosis among Industrial Workers," *American Journal of Public Health*, March, 1932, pp. 281–291.

Isidore S. Falk, C. Rufus Rorem, and Martha D. Ring, *Costs of Medical Care* (1933).

Herman Feldman, *Racial Factors in American Industry* (1931).

Mary Gover and Edgar Sydenstricker, *Mortality among Negroes in the United States* (Public Health Bulletin 174, 1928).

E. N. Elliott, *Cotton Is King and Pro-Slavery Arguments* (1860).

Charles S. Johnson, "One Thousand Negro Families in Nashville, (Tennessee)." Unpublished Study by the Department of Social Science, Fisk University.

Medical Statistics of the Provost Marshal General's Bureau, Vol. II.

Raymond Pinchbeck, *The Virginia Negro Artisan and Tradesman* (1926).

The Negro in Richmond, Virginia. Report of the Welfare Survey Committee, Richmond Council of Social Agencies, 1930.

Amanda L. Stoughton and Mary Gover, *A Study of Negro Infant Mortality* (Public Health Reports, Vol. 44, Part 2, November 8, 1929).

United States Bureau of Labor Statistics, *Cost of Living in the United States*. Bulletin No. 357 (1924).

Lida J. Uselton, *Prevalence of Venereal Disease in the United States* (United States Public Health Service, Venereal Disease Information, December 20, 1930).

Robert M. Woodbury, *Infant Mortality and Its Causes* (1926).

CHAPTER XX

HOME LIFE OF THE NEGRO

Every city with any Negro population at all has its "Negro quarter." With such regularity does it appear in the structure of the city, and so unvarying is its general aspect, it may be taken as one of the distinctive features of the American city. These Negro residence areas tend to follow a pattern in location: they are, in the older town especially, somewhere near the center of town; the buildings have an old and deteriorated aspect; they are set close together and commonly in proximity to such business structures as warehouses, garages, and automobile repair shops, junk shops, secondhand furniture stores, fish markets, and pawnshops. Old clothes dangling from store fronts clutter and flutter; unkempt merchandise from vegetables to hardware juts out on the sidewalk; and a lazy litter fills the unswept city streets. Within this rather dismal area move Negroes of every description: bustling housewives goodnaturedly bent on shopping, and visiting from the street; hardhanded workingmen leaving or going home, grimy and perspiring in overalls; loungers, dragging their bored bodies from one empty crate to another; hard-eyed dark women shuffling along in cotton aprons and carpet slippers; and children, unkempt but city wise, darting about and shrieking petulantly.

There is a grimy gloom about the picture as a whole — the unpainted and sagging houses with their dark interiors, and the narrow alleys leading back from the street. The area has a tangy swarthiness, like the color of its inhabitants, and a first inescapable impression is this association. It is difficult to visualize Negroes living away from it. But it must be tolerated, unbeautiful as it is, because it serves the essential function of concentrating this disrepair, this shuffling indifference to freshness and to beauty, this squabble and noise, within a zone. The Negroes seem to be satisfied where they are; they have built their churches there; and all their public service places, barber shops, restaurants, pool rooms, theaters, and other assembling places are there. It can be shut off and left to its own devices as the city grows in its own way. It need not be disturbed unless some of its residents break their bounds and cross the law, or otherwise too seriously disturb the peace. When such crime is committed, officers are expected to "scour the Black Belt" in search of the culprits, and this they can well do through a special technique which these Negroes have learned to respect.

A curious visitor may be carried through to see how the Negroes live; a kindly white family may enter in search of an old servant of the family; insurance and rental agents, and collectors of payments for furniture, musical instruments, and clothing, bought on installment, affect an easy familiar air. A trolley car may pass through the business street. The sight becomes familiar with a faintly unpleasant association to be tolerated.

One does not have to search far for the hub of this world: Beale Street in Memphis; Cedar Street in Nashville; Auburn Avenue in Atlanta; Rampart Street in New Orleans; Milan and Prairie Streets in Houston; Druid Hill Avenue in Baltimore; Central Avenue in Los Angeles; South Street in Philadelphia; State Street in Chicago; and Lenox Avenue in New York. On and abutting these are the dwelling places of the race. A most natural assumption is that the life which goes on behind these fuliginous walls is just what gets reflection on the street, or in the records of the domestic relations and juvenile courts, or in the humorous or exaggerated accounts of brawls that appear in the press, or in the gossip of housewives about their tribulations with Negro servants.

There are three factors of importance to any social appraisal of the homes in which Negroes live and the life that goes on within them. The first of these is the natural factors which aid in the making of Negro areas and their almost unfailing location near the center of the city. The second is the fact that these recognized Negro residence areas characterize only one part and phase of Negro housing and home life. The third is the fact that the physical character of the dwelling is never an adequate index to Negro home life.

In the normal process of growth the city expands radially from the center, or business district, to the exclusive suburban residential areas about the rim. These characteristic zones have been very well described by Burgess.[1]

Just beyond the business zone is almost always an area in transition from residence to business. Here the first residents once lived.

[1] Robert E. Park, Ernest W. Burgess, and Robert McKenzie, *The City*, p. 50.

Although these earliest occupants have been long gone, and the character of the residence area has faded, the buildings remain to be rented cheaply by successively lower income groups, until the land can be profitably sold as business sites. The Negroes, constituting so largely this lowest income group, are drawn into it.

A great measure of the initial unsightliness of the area is due to the advanced age and natural deterioration of the structures. The Negro residents, largely renters, come in last; and even if they were zealously and universally devoted to the physical improvement of things, they could have but little effect upon them. Most often, however, they drift along with the tide of decay. They share with the landlords and municipal authorities the temptation to negligence and hopelessness. If one should try to overcome it by purchasing his home and beautifying it, the weight and reputation of the area would be sufficient to keep down the value, whatever the investment. There is little encouragement to buy. The city authorities might be induced to clean the streets and collect the garbage and keep up the street lighting; but practically in no cities have Negroes sufficient political power to command these improvements. If they move out of their area there is, at least at first, opposition to the invasion of "white" areas. If they move to the outskirts of the city, they must be able to persuade the city to extend lights, streets, and sewerage, and in this they practically never succeed. In the end not many of them ever protest the surroundings, although some of them eventually move away.

There is scarcely ever a single Negro residence area in a city; there are commonly one large area and several smaller ones in different parts of the city. These differ in character and aspect, as a rule. It is difficult at first to identify some of these as Negro residence areas unless Negroes are observed in the neighborhood or about these homes. It is not always possible to determine the race of the occupant of a Negro home that gets completely detached from these areas through accident, or a fortunate purchase of long standing, or through withstanding the initial hostility against moving into a white neighborhood. They are thus not normally counted as Negro homes, because they do not reflect the type.

In the smaller zones away from the central one, more of the dwellings are owned and consequently better kept. But it is rarely possible to keep an area secure against the natural agencies of disintegration. The Negro areas are rarely the choice sites of a city, and if one is a relatively new site, the proof of its lesser desirability is the fact that Negroes live in it. They are usually the areas next in order of abandonment as the white residents move farther out. Cheap rental houses are established, municipal neglect increases, the low incomes of the newer Negro population accretions prevent improvements, the property valuations begin to decline, and the cycle completes itself. It is this process that accounts largely for the mixed character of Negro neighborhoods, the ceaseless milling and moving about, the general atmosphere of decrepitude which obscures many individual values, and the frequent discrepancy between the aspect of the dwelling and the home life of the occupants.

The home life of these Negroes is so extremely varied that it is never safe to attempt generalization about it. Practically all treatments of it disclose the fault of understatement or overstatement, or arrive at a type which reveals little of the intimate routine of life. It is the purpose of this chapter to present certain phases of the home life of Negroes out of intimate, objective studies of it. Because of the wide variations in pattern, the immediate problem is that of the quantitative importance of the types. Since physical housing does not in itself give a useful correlation with home life, occupational classes will have to be used. Even in this division there are extraordinary and unique factors which qualify this division, in such circumstances as the abnormal occupational restriction upon Negroes, and the difference in social significance within the Negro group of familiar occupational designations. A messenger, for example, ranks low in the general scale of occupations, but a Negro messenger is, not infrequently, in a specialized position, which includes a variety of tasks from bookkeeping or clerking to ushering in visitors and depositing the money of the firm. A Negro janitor may, in some special cases, be doing the work of a building superintendent. If he were called a building superintendent, however, or received a building superintendent's pay, it would no longer be a Negro job. Similarly, "porter" has usually a lowly meaning. But the Negro Pullman porter is a distinctive character, fairly well educated, and in some instances far above the general average of the population in education. Almost invariably he represents a level of home life above the average. Thus, the name of the occupation does not always convey the social character of the occupation.

The actual range of Negro occupations is wider than supposed. Although the bulk of the working population falls within the classification of unskilled workers, there are some Negroes in all but four of the 534 occupations listed by the census. As a reference structure for understanding the further discussion of types of Negro home life, it might be indicated that this vast unskilled group includes tenants on farms, domestics, industrial workers in coal, iron, steel, and meat packing; porters, janitors, and messengers, laborers in construction and public service, and some others. There is a semi-skilled group of no less than 200,000, which includes helpers in industry, chauffeurs, and minor factory operatives. A third general group is skilled and includes such artisans as carpenters, bricklayers, machinists, tailors, shoemakers, and electricians. In addition to these there is a so-called Negro middle class, numbering about 370,-000, and among these are merchants, technicians, managers and officials, and some 120,000 professional and semi-professional workers. There is a range within specific occupations. For example, the businesses may be small restaurants doing a gross business of $1,500 a year, or they may be insurance companies handling millions annually. These individuals in the different classes of work represent, in part, family groups, since it is most often the head of the family and the adult males only who are listed in connection with the occupation.

Obviously it is not possible to picture the home life of Negro families in any brief summary or in selected sketches. All that can be accomplished is to indicate through a few selected fragments some of the intimate concerns of selected types of families as they are revealed in the experiences of members of these families. An immediate difficulty arises in the selection of these types, and in the selection of phases of life which are most illuminating. Home life is a subtle blend of affectional ties and sentiments, personality, inter-relations, and adjustments within given physical surroundings. Every family has its codes, its traditions, weak or strong, its own reaction to its environment. These do not lend themselves readily to generalization. The types selected include a laborer's family, a domestic worker's family with a slight conflict situation, a small-town Negro family of stable character and strong family ties, a business man, and a physician. They are neither the worst types nor the exceptional ones with respect to income and family traditions.

The J——s live deep and securely in the Negro quarter of a southern city. Theirs is a four-room dwelling, set close against its neighboring building, unpainted and growing brown with age and the weather.

The entrance room is a sleeping room, and the bed, high with a collection of mattresses, and covered with a quilt of varicolored squares, is the center of attention. There is no rug; the curtains are starched lace in which the patterns have been raggedly distended. A dresser is covered with old and dusty photographs, the colored faces cut from advertisements, a comb and brush, and a collection of plain and decorated bottles. There is a trunk, covered with a cloth and used as a seat. Across the window is a new settee, and in another corner an upright piano with several rolls of music on top of it. On the walls are crayon enlargements of relatives, posturing rigidly and uncomfortably in high collars, and surrounded by heavy gold-painted frames. Before the fireplace is an easel holding another portrait, presumably of the favorite among the relatives carried away by death or migration. The other rooms are more utilitarian and less decorative. They are used by the children for sleeping and playing. About the rooms are scattered homemade toys, clothing, and the more useful remains of worn furniture.

The husband is a day laborer and the wife works occasionally as a domestic. The ages of the children are fourteen, twelve, ten, and three. The fourteen-year-old girl, when not in school, works in a poultry yard. Frequently, however, when neighbors cannot care for the baby while the mother is working, the daughter stays at home. The father is a hard-working man, unemotionally wedded to the routine of day labor, who earns a small pay but wisely lets his wife budget it. They are proud of the fact that the children are in school. Even when the husband is out of work, they manage on the wife's earnings in service. "We get along," she says, "and I don't bootleg either. I always have something to eat; can't always get meat, but there's butter, bread, milk, coffee, potatoes, and the children don't have to stay out of school to work."

Two of the rooms are used for sleeping, but during the winter all the family sleep in one room to save coal. The husband and wife have separate furniture accounts; the husband makes the payments on the piano and settee and the wife is buying the chairs. "I have a furniture bill," she said, "but my furniture man is just a good man. I haven't paid anything in three months." They are trying to buy the house, and pay $19.75 a month including interest. The wife likes to talk about the kind of house they want to make of it. The husband is content to let her plan and fuss and dream. "I want steam heat and everything," she says. She also wants a modern bathroom with toilet inside and a bathtub. There is an outhouse in the back yard, but they do not like going out there when it is cold or wet. The mother thinks what her children need most is a place to play. There is a back yard, but it is low and damp. The requirement of their work keeps the family in broken contact except on Sundays. The father is out early; the mother, when working, does not eat at home; the children cook for themselves a great part of the time.

The wife says they always had a little money until they started buying the house, but they never have any now. "Lord, I believe somebody put bad luck on me. I can't keep a nickel. If I get it there's always somebody here to take it." They once had nine head of hogs in the country where her mother lives, but had to sell them to pay the wife's hospital bill. The family does not put in winter coal. They can always get it when they need it, and the children can get wood and kindling from the dump and railroad which are nearby. The mother is emphatic in saying that they never ask help from anyone, and never expect to. In speaking of her neighbors she said, "I have neighbors and enemies as the saying goes. I have pretty fair neighbors. I don't bother them. I did have one that sort of meddled once, but I called her and told her that I take and take and then you got to whup me. She didn't give me no more trouble."

The wife is cheerful and sees nothing to worry about. She is just as happy, she says, with one penny as she would be with lots of money, for something always happens just when they think they cannot make ends meet. For instance, at Christmas time, the family had no money — "not even enough to buy nuts for Christmas" — but her mother and friends happened to have some and gave them cake, a hen, nuts, and fruits, and they had a big time. They have enough plans for the future to keep them in good spirits.

The K——s represent a type of family in which the children have varied and sometimes conflicting interests. The father is dead, the mother and two older sisters run the household. Two sisters are hotel maids, a brother is a porter, and another sister works in a cafeteria. The mother has about a fourth-grade education; the eldest daughter finished grammar school; the second one went to seventh grade; the third daughter and the only son, who is 25 years old, went as far as the fifth grade. One of the girls finished high school and it is she who comments about their family life:

My father died about three months after my baby brother was born. That is why we have so much trouble with him, he didn't have a father to tell him nothing. Mother tried the best she could but you know a woman just can't raise a boy without a husband. We get very disgusted with my brother and want to put him out of the house but mother won't hear to it. He is her baby and I guess he is spoiled. He works and dresses himself but he don't give us one penny to help run the house. He has got some habits we can't stand but we have to put up with him. My sister and me run the house. She is here with three children. Her husband deserted her. We won't let mamma work 'cause she is too feeble. It takes so much to live and just us two women working we have it pretty hard. If we had a father bringing in about twenty-five dollars a week it would be fine. Some of my friends say, "Girl, I would rather teach than do just ordinary work like you do now," but I ain't ashamed of what I've done with no more opportunity than I have had. I went to normal school about one year and I had to stop. My aunt died who supported me. Then there was no money to continue on. I would like to have finished. Since I began working every year I say I'm going to go back but it looks like it gets so unconvenient for me to get off to go that I just never have gone back. Then there ain't no money to spend for that. Rent to pay, food to buy, insurances to keep up, clothing, etc. I just don't make enough to go to school. I appreciate what learning I have got. I look at all these girls around here where I live who have not had as much as I have and I see how they act and carry on and I just thank the Lord I got what I did. Living where we do I meet up with every kind of thing. I have experienced life so much. The reason I'm single now is because I don't mingle with the class around me and the class that I am thrown with. I wouldn't marry any of these men I have ever met. Wish I could find a man like I would like to have. Course I don't expect any doctor or any professional man to want me but I would like an honest hard-working man who would take care of me. I had rather take care of myself than to take care of two and then the possibility of children. My brother has a lot of men hanging around the house all the time but I don't associate with his company. Course we don't allow them to drink and carry on their bad habits here but they come here full of liquor. Mamma won't let us put them out. She says so many boys my brother's age would not stay at home; so she just lets him do as he likes. He lived a great part of his life up at —— Street and that part of the street is worse than this end. Well, when we lived up there he got to running around with those folks up in that section and mamma just could not keep him in school; he stopped in the fifth grade.

Of course, I could be worse off. I don't have to take the lowest kind of job that folks take who don't have no education at all. I make salads. I learned how to do all those things in high school. I make delicious mayonnaise. If I could have gone on in school I would have specialized in domestic science.

I don't belong to anything except the church, —— Christian Church. I had to get out of all my clubs because of my work.

The R——s are an excellent example of the small-town self-respecting Negro family of moderate means. They may safely be regarded as typical of a large and growing class of Negroes in town and city who are integrated in their society, but whose more intimate life is, as a rule, little known about and less understood. Because of the usefulness of the document in reflecting a variety of aspects of family life, it is given at some length:

My father is a small merchant in a small town, but he has built up a reputation for shrewd buying and carefully paying his debts. The importance of this reputation to the family has been observed by all eight of us children and it has thus not been necessary to indulge in repeated lectures on thrift. There was not always large margin of money above our family needs, but there was always plenty of food; the children were kept neat and clean and in school, and by careful planning the things we wanted were eventually made possible. However much in need, or however close our financial margin, mother could keep up family morale by her even optimism and her domestic resourcefulness.

To us, our family has always been an interesting one; to a great many others, perhaps, a clannish one. Because our parents had certain ideals for us and certain ideas about other families, we learned early to live a great deal to ourselves. The first I remember was filial respect and devotion which developed through our observation of harmony between the parents and a devotion to the children. At twenty-four I cannot remember an acrimonious disagreement between my mother and my father. There have been times when they have had different opinions, when one was not most pleased with the actions of the other, but I do not recall ever seeing my mother angry with my father, and I have never heard them argue.

Both being strong personalities, there must have been disagreements, but these were between themselves; the children should not and did not sense them. Each parent religiously taught us that we must show utmost attentiveness to the other. We had to run out to meet Papa, to swing on to his arms, to get him a comfortable chair, to see if he wanted the paper before we read the funnies, to consider his responsibilities before our childish whims. Likewise, our father drilled into us the same sort of attentiveness to our mother. "Tip lightly so you won't disturb your mother"; "Bring mother some candy"; "Lighten the work for your mother"; etc.

With parents who could agree, there was not much legitimate excuse for the children to quarrel. When we went to them with our arguments they reminded us that they managed to live without quarreling and this was evident. So after filial devotion, there was developed a strong tie among the children. My father told how he had always wanted to be in position to look out for his sisters and brothers and hoped we would always do the same. "Look out for one another" was the advice on their lips. Not only were we to consider one another but we were to develop pleasure in one another's company. I can hear my mother saying how that in the last analysis your own family would always be your solace, comfort, and protection, so one should learn early to enjoy being with one's own family. So we read together, we got our lessons around the dining-room table together, we went out, at least, in pairs. Even now, though grown, when we are all at home in the summer, we stay together perhaps much too closely — our own card games, picnics, parlor entertainments. But we were taught that it made a person common to be seen too much. And somehow we contented ourselves with not a great deal of movies, rides, and visiting.

My parents believed thoroughly in education and in well-rounded development. They supervised our study, and counted times while we practiced our scales and arpeggios. They gave parties for us and planned the entertainment, had swings built for us and our friends, bought games that we would enjoy, carried us to the most important of the town's "concerts." Usually, too, they kept the guest artist in our home so that we might be inspired and learn to be at home with people "who stood for something."

There were several ceremonies observed in my family. Every morning before breakfast the daily Bible verse had to be read, and every Sunday at dinner each member had to repeat a not too much repeated Bible verse. If a verse had been said too often, the person saying it had to get up from the table and learn a new one, or we all had to sit and listen while Mamma read a chapter or more from the Bible. Always on Sunday, we had to go to Sunday School, and not singly, although going all together might make us late. My father, as Chairman of the Trustee Board of the church, usually took up collection on Sunday — in the days when one eloquently told the congregation of the need for funds. As children we all profoundly admired him as he played this rôle. Likewise, my mother, as President of the principal woman's club, always introduced the guest artists at school concerts. We all sat together and nudged one another as we felt she grandly played her part.

In the eyes of our small-town people my oldest brother and sister were fairly good musicians, and no program was complete until H—— had played some favorite "variations" or he and D—— had played a duet. And whenever we went to a musical recital we came back believing that one day our parents would be proud of similar artists in our own family.

Methods of discipline in our family were more or less orthodox. It is true, however, that my mother did not like to administer corporal punishment, not so much because she had no faith in its results as in her wish that her children might be "reasoned with." She had always hoped that she might discipline her children by appeals to pride, and self-respect. But when she sometimes found this ineffective, she would report to Papa, who hated to whip as much as she did. I have always believed that our other relatives believed that we were not whipped enough, although we did get a judicious share.

Our parents' status in the community, however, was an effective means of control over our behavior. When other children planned certain outings, Sunday afternoon "get-togethers," it was simply understood that the R—— children would not be present, unless every participant was well known and his character well known to the family. My father, as business manager of his lodge, might rent the hall for a public dance even to some of our own family friends, but his daughters could not dance at the hall. At home they might dance as long as they wished. The principal of the school found this a useful example for some of the less careful families. He would say he never saw us out late unaccompanied, that our parents were wise, that we would make "pure men and women." And so we believed that as R—— children there were certain things that we simply could not do. We believed that ours would be the greater, fuller lives in the future. Our friends might have new party dresses, more clothes, more spending change, but we knew that our parents had another sort of a goal for us; that we all had to go to college. We knew that those who outdressed us would probably not be able to go. Somehow we believed that we were financially able to have more, but that it was not wise or expedient at the time to spend too freely.

Our family was large, but with thrifty parents we usually got what we needed and there was always room for visitors and relatives. So much company did we have that we called our home "Wayside Inn." My father's relatives always felt more at home with him, so it was not unusual for us to have three or four, sometimes five, relatives visiting us. There were times when as many as sixteen of us sat down to the table together and always there managed to be plenty to go around.

Another type of family life is that of the successful business man, who is able to provide a level of comfort somewhat above the average. While representing a higher standard than the usual Negro working family it is not an extreme example of the class which he represents.

The present head of the B—— family is a business man. He traces his ancestry for three generations on his father's side and two generations on his mother's side. As long as he can remember, there has been a consciousness in his family, especially on his father's side, that they should own their property. Mr. B—— boasts of owning land unmortgaged, much of which was handed down. The urge to own and accumulate property conflicted with his aspirations for advanced education in his youth. His own education thus stopped at the ninth grade. His wife, however, completed normal school, and had planned to teach if she did not marry. They have four children, one daughter and three sons. The girl was given a musical education, one boy is studying business at New York University, and another is at Hampton. The father believes in "both practical and higher education." The third son is still in high school. They have been living in their present home fifteen years. It was built by a Negro contractor and designed to meet the family needs and interests. It has, for example, a music room for the daughter, an enclosed conservatory for flowers, to which the wife is devoted, a combination office and study for the father, and a game room for the boys. In the set-up of the home the only break in consistency with the prevailing styles in furnishings is the addition of Chinese rugs and several pieces of teakwood which they have purchased.

The contact of the family with the community is largely through the father. The wife and children are restricted in their social contacts to a small group of families of business and professional men. They are seldom on the street; their social affairs are held in the home, except on the rare occasion of a formal social function, which requires a public auditorium. When this occurs, the entire auditorium is leased and only their friends are admitted. For other recreation, living as they do in the South, they visit friends living in the North. This is not difficult since they own a good car. The annual visit is a ritual with the family. The boys are being trained into the business, and the daughter has recently married one of the young officials of her father's company.

One other example is being given because, in addition to the factor of intimate home life and its discipline and codes, there is revealed an exposed racial facet. Dr. —— is a professional man in a southern city. His income is not exceptional; neither is his status very different from that of the normal successful Negro doctor. The struggle against the environment to maintain respectability, and to bring up children free from the corrupting influences, demands a rigid discipline and the creation of an artificial world. This gets interesting reflection in the story of a daughter in this family.

My father had been at college perhaps a year when my mother came. He was regarded as a handsome man and my mother also was beautiful. They fell in love and married two days after my father's graduation from medical school. They went first to Mississippi to live and spent about a year, but the curiosity of the whites became intolerable to the extent that mother insisted that they return to ——. Two months later I was born. My father was terribly disappointed in my sex, but mother believed me the most precious little mortal in the world. But I almost escaped staying here — when I was about an hour old the nurse laid me on a table and in some way or other I fell off.

For more than a year I was the darling of the family. My grandparents, with whom my mother and father lived, fairly worshipped me and I knew it. But the paradise couldn't last always — a little brother had to come. At first my position was not severely challenged — so all was well. Eventually it was, for he became a very sickly baby and of course every one's time and attention was given to him. It was "the baby this" and "the baby that."

All the people who had previously played with me and brought me pretty toys now gave things to the "poor little baby." It was terrible that I should be so neglected, I thought. I guess grown ups don't realize how easily little children can be hurt, and how easily their whole disposition can be changed by jealousy and unintentional neglect. There was one person, however, who always found time to bathe and dress me prettily, and to tell me that I was the loveliest child in the world — that was my grandmother. That's one reason, I think, that I believed that she was my mother for such a long while instead of my own mother.

I became terribly jealous of my little brother. When no one was looking I would pinch or bite him. Once I tried to hit him with a stick. Everybody then began telling me how mean I was and punishing me for the crying spells I'd have — blaming it on temper. My grandmother and grandfather knew, however, that I wasn't really a cruel, mean child; they realized that attention was what I wanted — and they gave it to me.

Eventually I learned to love my invalid baby brother intensely and joined the others in making him happy. When I began music lessons I'd teach him everything I'd learned. When I entered kindergarten I insisted that he be allowed to go also. He was soon put out though for fights he'd have with the children; he was nervous and irritable. When we started to public school I spent more time looking after him than studying. I fought the boys who bothered him, I was impertinent to teachers who scolded him. My tempestuous babyhood had done good as well as bad things to my disposition. I was independent to a superlative degree, I demanded attention, I allowed nothing to interfere with my desires. My brother was sweet natured and a bit submissive but he *would* start fights — fights I'd have to finish. I had, I fear, a most condescending attitude toward children of lowly birth. This attitude toward common people I attribute to two sources — first my grandfather's utter contempt for them, and second, the fact that they treated me with such contempt — calling me "half-white," "fay," and the like. I guess I showed my contempt too, and consequently we were constantly at war.

I never thought about color whatsoever in regard to race until I was about eight years old. I thought that some people were just brown, some tan, some white. My grandmother was brown, my mother was tan, and I was cream colored; they had black hair and mine was yellow. There occurred an incident one day that changed my whole attitude toward people. I remember it most distinctly. My mother had me in town with her; we were standing in front of a large department store. A white woman and her son were standing there also — he must have been ten or eleven years old. Evidently he hadn't seen us when he first walked up, for suddenly he turned to stare at me. He then picked up one of my curls and exclaimed: "Mother! this nigger has hair like mine!"

My mother flew into a rage, slapped the boy's hand, and to the astonishment of the white woman who was trying to say that the boy meant no harm she said coldly:

"It's as gross an insult to have your son lay his hands on my little daughter as it would be for my son to touch yours" — then took me by the hand and walked away, leaving the crowd gaping with astonishment. I shall never forget that day — nor my mother's words. From then on I have shunned even the most impersonal contact with white men. That was the birth of my race consciousness. Most of the time I forget I'm a Negro, but some remark or stare always brings me back with almost a shock to the reality that I am one of those discriminated against.

I entered high school with a most absurd determination to finish with a minimum amount of study. I did but two things: read and get "crushes" on pictures of good-looking brown-skinned men. I've always had a mania for brown-skinned men.

I had greater access to books than to moving pictures and actually enjoyed reading far more. I fairly devoured them — both the good and the bad ones. I'd read a magazine from cover to cover; many novels I've read through twice. I was particularly fond of Sax Rohmer's *Fu Manchu* stories — I craved the mystical and weird. My imagination became so vivid and my mind so full of the gruesomeness of his stories that I became afraid to go from room to room at night for fear some unseen hand would reach to choke me. That whole period of my life was one of romantic craving. The contact that I was denied with people my age was substituted by constant day dreams. I wished bitterly that I didn't have to be "high-brow" to the extent that I couldn't have fun like other children I knew. But I didn't in the least blame my mother for the way she was rearing me. I believed that she was under the impression that she was doing the correct thing, so I wouldn't for the world rebel and hurt her. I did have many an opportunity to deceive her and have my own way, but I never did — that is only once.

She never permitted any contact with boys, and above all things forbade note writing — pointing out numerous wrecked homes on account of some foolish letter, or cases of blackmail that I knew of. Once a boy I rather liked wrote me a note which I answered. She found the answer and casually mentioned the fact. That was enough for me. I was afraid that she had lost confidence in me and that I had done irreparable damage to her heart. I worried for weeks over the thing.

When I was about a junior in high school I lost all interest in boys, and by the time I was a senior I was so thoroughly disgusted with them that I resolved never to marry and to perhaps enter a nunnery. I got so I didn't believe in God or anything. Nothing had happened to disillusion me in any way — life was just so stagnant. Nothing ever happened to relieve the monotony of my drab existence. I wished repeatedly that I had been a boy so I could run away to Algeria or Singapore — some notorious place. I decided to "run away" to college instead and complete my education, then perhaps be a physician or something that would enable me to mix with people. I was bored stiff with the "family background" prerequisites that my family so insisted upon. I couldn't attend parties because "there was no telling who wouldn't be there," I couldn't visit a girl unless mother knew her mother. I wanted so to be democratic, but just couldn't. Deep down in me I was as conventional as my family — and am to an extent yet. But they did make me rather tired sometimes by being "so careful."

I had thought myself fairly wise before entering college — and I was wise enough to keep my mouth shut and conceal some of my ignorance. But the moment of my arrival drove home the utter naïveté of myself to me and to everyone else. I wore curls, low-heeled shoes, little make-up, had never had a 'feller,' and had been to but two dances before in my life. I was by no means shy or bashful — I was as sophisticated as a twelve-year old. Innocence was written all over me.

I remember how shocked I was upon going to the bathroom my first morning at college and seeing a nude woman. It was the first time in my life that I had ever seen anyone but little babies without clothes on.

The multiplication of examples of home life would perhaps not illuminate the subject more, and indeed presents a certain dilemma: examples which are too individualistic are not typical, and, in such a large proportion of the examples, the home life follows so closely the general American pattern for the social group represented by the Negroes that description is gratuitous. There will be found, of course, minor variations which are perhaps more characteristic of Negro families than white families. In the matter of physical setting, there are frequently adaptations of furniture to meet the fixed limits of dwelling and income; a motley array of second-hand furniture, or inexpensive installment house furniture; an emphasis upon color and decoration, and musical instruments; an accumulation of belongings to the point of overcrowding, rather than a bare and colorless interior.

In general, the Negroes who represent a higher economic level purchase their goods at the local shops. Not infrequently one encounters an excellence of taste in selection and arrangement, and a regard for cleanliness to match it. In the northern cities, especially, it would be difficult for them to do other than follow the common pattern in equipment. Many homes show a carefulness of planning and a taste and expense in decoration which simply obscure them among the good homes of a city. It is usually a surprise to white visitors to this type of Negro homes to find them fitting the pattern consistently. There are, too, the "show places," for the designing of which decorators have been responsible; and likewise the households in which various motifs, French, Italian, Spanish, modernistic, early American, have been carefully worked out over years of leisurely selection by the owners themselves.

In the matter of family habits there is a like tendency to conformity to the local pattern. The Negro family disorganization gets its reflection in divorce, desertion, delinquency, loss of control over children. Such disorganization, however, although perhaps greater among Negroes in proportion, is after all but a small measure of the whole life, which is in greatest measure normal.

This does not mean that the families which escape the courts or separation are homes without conflict. The cultural conflicts within these families frequently become most intense and far-reaching in their social consequences. There are differences among the children in response to their environment; there are difficulties based upon color; the changes brought about by education introduce problems and sometimes lead to breaks; migration brings about such changes and, as in the case of European immigrants, helps to break parents' control over their children. One of the unique problems in the Negro home, and one of the inescapable ones, is the color problem. It is not merely the question of frequent differences in shades of children in the family to which the outside world gives difference in valuation in one direction or the other, but the question of educating the children to live in a race-conscious world.

These questions, naturally enough, are never real to any but the Negro families, and thus can be dismissed as the vain pretentiousness of a negligible few of the Negroes. In the training of children, nevertheless, there are questions for which Negro parents seem to have no adequate answers. When Negro children ask why they cannot go where other children go; why they must go to a poorer school; why white children may call them names and not be punished; why the mother regards it as a serious life and death issue if the father proposes to defend the child against whites; why there are adequate areas of play space in parks with attractive equipment for white children which colored children are not expected to use; why nothing can be said or done if one of them is slapped by a white person — there are really no satisfactory answers. Should children be taught that their color does not make them less as human beings than other children? If so, how can parents make them feel proud of their heritage? Are they to be taught that their color does not diminish their worth, other things being equal? This is not realistic, and the child soon discovers it. There is no answer, and when there is no answer all sorts of expedients must be employed to conceal the unpleasant truth.

The easiest adjustment is to avoid discussion altogether and let the environment do the conditioning. This is what most often happens. The children grow up "knowing their place." And while it may be avoided in conversation, and the children taught that, like the mystery of life, this is one of the subjects not to be asked about, there is no escaping entirely a measure of concern about it. On such grounds they may urge getting more education, but just as often they realize that getting more education may mean more sensitiveness and more trouble. On such grounds also they permit the children to leave home early to seek their careers where they can grow up under a minimum of racial restriction. Some parents teach their children to defend themselves and count upon taking the social consequences. Others attempt the feat of protecting them against all contact, hoping thereby to protect them against all race consciousness. The greatest aid in this situation is in the fact that, living wholly within the Negro quarter, with all types of Negroes, keeps them out of touch most of the time with all types of whites. Thus, another cord of sentimental self-interest binds them to the Negro quarter.

Adjustment to the race factor becomes an important feature of the Negro home in other and broader respects. The limitation of wholesome recreation tends to emphasize the home as a social center.

The usual Negro restaurants in most cities, it will be noted, have as patrons workingmen without homes, floaters and strangers without connections in the town for the most part. The institution of "dining out" is not established among careful families — it is a reflection on the home to eat in a restaurant; it simply is not done. The absence of suitable restaurants and the unavailability of hotels for Negroes in turn encourage families to extend their hospitality to strangers of similar station. This broadens the range of personal contact with other Negroes, and contributes to sociability within a congenial group.

So skillfully are these adjustments worked out between Negro homes in the South, connected by this thread of common social necessity, that it is possible for a Negro to pass through the South without coming into direct contact at any point with the characteristic racial orthodoxies and institutions of the section. They may escape the "Jim Crow" car and the separate railway station waiting room by riding in their own automobiles. If the trip is a long one they may route themselves through the homes of friends in different cities. They escape the restaurants by going to these homes which are expecting to extend this courtesy even though they might be strangers. Negro residents of southern cities refrain frequently from entering the general theaters through the alley entrance, or from attending the poorly kept Negro theaters, with their gross burlesque performances and inferior or uninteresting selections of motion pictures, by developing social clubs within their homes. The number of such clubs is large and varied, but they offer an important substitute for the public accommodations which are not possible. All these devices reinforce the importance of the home of this group, and at the same time contribute to a distortion of the popular view of Negroes.

The Negro population cannot be represented adequately either by its broken homes or by its normal ones. There are many of both types and innumerable varieties of integration and disintegration. The disintegrated homes, sooner or later, become a matter of public record. But the more normal ones, obscure in a vast social distance, run one of the greatest risks to their normality from the reputation of the first.

PROBLEMS FOR STUDY

1. What are the characteristics of the zone of first residence in a city that make it the home of newer immigrants and lower income groups?
2. How may the position of the Negro in the succession to these areas of first residence account for the impression one gets of Negro areas?
3. What factors prevent physical improvement in the conditions of Negro residence areas?
4. What are the possible effects upon Negro children from the injustices of the racial situation and the powerless position of their parents?
5. How do cultural advancement and educational training make for isolation of the Negro upper class family?
6. What differences are there in the social pattern of the Negro family from that of whites, due to their respective positions in the community?
7. Is it possible for a person who has not been admitted intimately to the home life of a Negro family to make a safe judgment of its character from external evidences?

CHAPTER XXI

CIVIC AND POLITICAL STATUS OF THE NEGRO

When the first Negroes were brought to Virginia there was no such prejudice against them as afterward developed. They were probably bought as indentured servants just as white people from England were so bought.[1] Not infrequently white indentured women became mothers of children by Negro men, and the general status of the Negro was simply that of a hired servant. Prior to 1723, there was no limitation against free Negroes voting in Virginia. "All freemen and servants having served their time were permitted to take part in elections" provided they would "fairly give their votes by subscription and not in a tumultuous way."[2] But in 1723 stringent laws were passed, by which the free Negro was denied the right to testify in court except in cases where Negroes only were concerned, the right to serve as a juror or a judge, and the right of suffrage. He could not bear arms or hold office.

In Maryland the constitution of 1776 expressly gave the right of suffrage to all freemen of age and owning a certain amount of property. In 1783 certain limitations were placed on this right, but it was not until 1810 that the right of suffrage was restricted to whites alone. In 1807 heavy restrictions were put on the movements of free Negroes. Free Negroes or mulattoes were forbidden to enter the state as residents. Those coming in as servants of non-residents could stay only two weeks, on penalty of a ten-dollar fine for each week thereafter. In case they could not pay the fine they could be sold by the sheriff for a term sufficient to pay the fine and costs.[3] The journals of the legislature of Maryland are full of petitions for redress from the border counties, against the entry of so many free Negroes from Virginia. In cases where such Negroes were very skilled and proved an asset to the community, we find petitions that they be allowed to remain in the county. After Nat Turner's

[1] Cf. John H. Russell, *The Free Negro in Virginia, 1619–1865*, p. 24.
[2] *Ibid.*, p. 118.
[3] Jeffrey R. Brackett, *The Negro in Maryland*, p. 176.

rebellion in 1831, there was still greater fear of the free Negro class; hence much more drastic laws were passed forbidding their entry into Maryland. Negroes going out of the state of Maryland were declared non-residents and not permitted to return. There was a series of more and more drastic laws of similar nature passed in Maryland right up to the time of the Civil War.

In North Carolina during early colonial times the rights of the Negro were broader than they were in later times. "They had most of the rights and duties of the poor white man; they fought in the revolutionary armies, mustered in the militia, voted in the elections, and had the liberty to go where they chose." [1] Troubles with the Negroes in the West Indies soon made the white people of the South wary about having free Negroes who were free to move about and perhaps plot insurrection. In 1787 restrictions began to be put on the free Negroes in North Carolina. They could not entertain slaves in their houses, and they could not marry a slave. After 1795 free Negroes could not come into the state without giving bond of £200 for good behavior, they could not be aboard a ship at night or on Sundays, and they might not sell or peddle goods without a license from the county court.[2] This last item of the law was doubtless to prevent petty stealing of cotton, tobacco, or other products, and vending them to petty buyers.

In South Carolina there seems to have been no specific law giving the right to vote to free Negroes, although the law of 1704 providing a property qualification for voting made no reference to race, and hence might be supposed to legalize the vote of the free Negro.[3] This presumption is strengthened by the law of 1716, which restricted voting to "every white man, and no other, professing the Christian religion, being of age and having certain property." [4] As early as 1735 all manumitted slaves were ordered to leave the state. The law of 1740, the substance of which remained in effect up to the Civil War, permitted free Negroes to testify in cases against other Negroes only; set up special courts of three justices and three slave owners to try Negroes; forbade the carrying of firearms by Negroes; made stringent rules against harboring Negro runaways; refused to Negroes the right to keep inns or sell liquor; and forbade

---

[1] John S. Bassett, *Slavery in the State of North Carolina*, p. 34.
[2] Cf. *Ibid.*, p. 34 ff.
[3] John C. Hurd, *The Law of Freedom and Bondage in the United States*, p. 298.
[4] *Ibid.*, p. 301.

the ownership or use of horns by Negroes. Along with these rules it set up certain regulations for the protection of Negroes. The laws of Georgia were almost a verbatim copy of those of South Carolina.

The northern states were almost equally drastic in dealing with free Negroes. The first constitution of Indiana (1816) did not debar free Negroes from voting, but in the following year a law was passed which read: "No Negro, Mulatto, or Indian shall be a witness except in pleas of the state against Negroes, Mulattoes or Indians, or in civil cases where Negroes, Mulattoes or Indians alone shall be parties."[1] In 1831 this state demanded bond of free Negroes coming into the state. In 1851 laws were passed forbidding Negroes to serve in the militia, placing heavy fines on white persons employing Negroes coming into the state, and specifically denying the franchise to Negroes and mulattoes.[2] Illinois limited the franchise to whites in 1818, and imposed numerous limitations on the free movements of Negroes. To prevent runaway slaves settling within its borders, who might become a charge on the state, Ohio early passed laws which required all Negroes to show a certificate of freedom, and making it a serious offense for white people to employ Negroes without such certificate.[3]

It will thus be seen that even free Negroes were gradually deprived of most of the advantages of freedom before the Civil War, because the planters lived in constant fear that free Negroes would become centers of infection for insurrection. The vote was taken from them, freedom of movement was limited, they were not permitted to testify against white people, they could not carry firearms, they could not buy or sell except under certain restrictions, they were not permitted to assemble freely, and in some states they could not preach the Gospel save in the presence of at least one white man. They could not be taught to read and write, and in many northern states the chance to make a living was practically denied.[4]

The free Negro could own property, could transmit it by will, could sue and be sued, and had, therefore, certain economic rights. But the slave had not even these rights. He was a chattel pure and simple. Laws drawn for the protection of slaves were primarily

---

[1] George W. Williams, *History of the Negro Race in America, 1619–1880*, Vol. II, p. 121.   [2] *Ibid.*, pp. 121–122.   [3] *Ibid.*, p. 111 ff.
[4] Cf. William Goodell, *The American Slave Code in Theory and Practice*, p. 355 ff.

meant to protect property and not to safeguard persons. Thus the law of South Carolina (1740) read:

> If any Negro or other slave who shall be employed in the lawful business of his master, owner, overseer, etc., shall be beaten, etc., by any person or persons, not having sufficient cause or authority for so doing, and shall be maimed, or disabled, by such beating from performing his or her work, such person or persons, so offending, shall forfeit and pay to the owner or owners of such slaves, the sum of fifteen shillings current money, per diem, for every day of his lost time and also the charge of the cure of such slave.[1]

According to the laws of Louisiana, when a slave was so injured

> If the slave be forever rendered unable to work, the offender shall be compelled to pay the value of such slave, according to the appraisement made by two free holders, appointed by each of the parties; and the slave thus disabled shall forever be maintained at the expense of the person who shall have thus disabled him, which person shall be compelled to maintain and feed him, agreeably to the duties of master and slaves, as ordered by this act.[2]

The point of view of the law in all the states was that of protection of property. Not a shred of protection of the slave against suffering is contained in any of these laws. Indeed one could hardly imagine a more cruel fate than that which bound an injured slave over to be fed and maintained by the one who willfully and cruelly injured and incapacitated him. "The end of slavery," said Judge Ruffin, "is the profit of the master. The slave is doomed to toil that others may reap the fruits."[3] The slave was without economic rights. He could not own property, he could not buy and sell, he could not bequeath anything. Anything he might possess was held by the sheer good will of his master. The code of Louisiana said:

> All that a slave possesses belongs to his master, he possesses nothing of his own except his peculium, that is to say the sum of money or movable estate, which his master chooses he should possess.[4] ... One general principle prevails in all the states, and in the British, Spanish and Portuguese West Indies, and that is, that a slave cannot make a contract, not even a contract of matrimony.[5]

Not only did the master have complete power over the slave, but his representative or overseer had similar rights. Masters were

---

[1] William Goodell, *The American Slave Code in Theory and Practice*, p. 202.
[2] *Ibid.*, p. 203.   [3] *Ibid.*, p. 79.   [4] *Ibid.*, p. 90.
[5] *Ibid.*, p. 93, quoted from Wheeler's *Law of Slavery*, p. 190.

forced by law to provide certain food and clothing and to treat slaves humanely, but such laws were difficult to enforce. Since the slave could not testify against a white man, there was usually no witness in case of the violation of these laws. It was a capital offense in most states for a slave to strike a white person, even in self-defense. The killing of a slave was usually punishable by fine. In other words, it was not usually considered murder, and Goodell claims there are no cases on record where white men were convicted of the murder of slaves.[1]

When such absolute power could be delegated to persons of low standards of morals such as the overseers usually were, it robbed the slave not only of all legal protection but of all moral protection. Stroud, in commenting on this situation, declares: "All the power of the master over the slave, may be exercised, not by himself only in person, but by anyone whom he may depute as his agent." [2] He gives as evidence in proof of this statement a case in which May sued Brown and Boisseau for breaking into his Negro quarters and beating his Negroes, but Brown claimed to have a written permit to visit these quarters and chastise any of his slaves who might be found acting improperly.[3] But a special mandate did not seem to be necessary; the fact that a person was set over slaves seemed enough to enable him to act completely in the capacity of the owner.[4]

Most slave offenses of minor character were never carried to court, but were settled by the owner. Whipping and sometimes more cruel treatment were usually the punishment. Occasionally an unruly Negro was sold "south." In case of crimes involving life or limb, the slave of North Carolina was tried before a jury. After 1816, slaves charged with murder were tried in the Superior Court, and the slave might, on the advice of his master, ask for change of venue. In case of charge for conspiracy the slave was to be tried by a special commission.[5] In 1823 the Supreme Court of North Carolina declared that the killing of a slave might be tried as murder at common law. Justice Hall dissented from this decision on the

[1] Cf. William Goodell, *The American Slave Code in Theory and Practice*, chap. 14.

[2] George M. Stroud, *A Sketch of the Laws Relating to Slavery in the Several States of the United States of America*, p. 71.

[3] *Ibid.*, p. 72.

[4] John S. Bassett, *Slavery in the State of North Carolina*, p. 12.

[5] *Ibid.*, p. 12.

basis that it was a civil and not a criminal offense to destroy property.[1] In 1834 the North Carolina Supreme Court, in the case of *State vs. Will*, ruled that a slave when barbarously attacked by his master had a right of self-defense.[2] In most of the states, if a slave was convicted of crime and sentenced to be put to death, the public was required to pay the master a fair price for his slave. South Carolina in 1758 hit upon an expedient to obviate this expense. The Assembly decreed that from the first offense the slave, if a male, should not be executed but should be castrated, the sheriff being allowed a fixed sum for the operation and an additional sum for the curing of the same. If the slave died the master was to be compensated, the price being fixed in advance. This law soon became a dead letter, perhaps because the sensibilities of South Carolina revolted against a procedure so lacking in all moral decency.[3] Most drastic punishment was meted out to any slave testifying falsely against another slave or a free Negro.[4] Virginia permitted officers of the law to kill, without any guilt, slaves which were runaway or who resisted arrest.[5] The law of 1748 forbade the whipping of a white servant naked — which by implication meant that Negro servants might be so whipped.[6] It set forth that any Negro lifting his hand against a white person should be whipped with thirty lashes. It forbade the assembling of slaves, and made it an offense to be away from the plantation without written leave.

It will thus be seen that slaves had no political rights and not many civic rights. They could not sell or hold property, they could not assemble freely, they could not travel without specific permit, they could not testify except against their own kind — and they usually resisted ill treatment at the peril of their lives.

At the close of the Civil War a new situation arose. There were then four classes of society in the South. First, there were the planters, an aristocratic class who up to this time had dominated the social, civic, and political life of the section. Most of these were owners of considerable numbers of slaves, and the most influential were plantation owners. A few were men of intellectual

[1] John S. Bassett, *Slavery in the State of North Carolina*, p. 21.

[2] *Ibid.*, p. 25.

[3] John S. Bassett, *Slavery and Servitude in the Colony of North Carolina*, p. 31.

[4] *Ibid.*, p. 30.

[5] J. C. Hurd, *The Law of Freedom and Bondage in the United States*, p. 236.

[6] *Ibid.*, p. 243.

and professional leadership who by sheer force of character and ability made a place for themselves in the midst of this aristocratic society. This landed group at the close of the war were completely bankrupt. Their slaves were freed; they could not hire laborers; the tools with which to farm the land had rotted in the fields during the war; there were no work animals, for these had been taken away to the war; there was no capital and no means of getting any. Many of the plantation houses had been burned and the land was almost worthless. It was a sad and discouraging world that this group faced.

The second class was the poor whites. The war had not borne so heavily on them for the simple reason that they had little or nothing to lose. Most of them owned little land, they had no property, and slaves were a handicap to them because all the skilled labor was in the hands of slaves. The poor whites hated the slaves because their own degraded status was fixed by the presence of slaves. They were all too eager to use this new situation to achieve their own freedom. They were eager to see that the slave lost his monopoly of skilled labor, and of course they had no desire to see the Negro acquire political power.

The third class was the free Negro. He had always had limited civic rights, but just prior to the war had lost most political rights because of the fear that he would stir up insurrection. The war opened the way for him to enter into political power as the leader of the newly emancipated slaves.

Lastly, there were the slaves just set free and now known as freedmen. Most of them were ignorant. They had on the whole only two types of training — that of agriculture and that of the mechanical training which was useful about the plantation. There were among them skilled wheelwrights, good carpenters, good blacksmiths, good machinists. But these men had had little or no training in managing business affairs. Great masses of the unskilled laborers were unwilling to stay on the plantations, and they could not do anything in the towns. Hence they became wandering, homeless men, without responsibility and without restraint.

There was a fifth class, perhaps, made up of some well-bred men who had not been sympathetic with secession, and did not join in after the states seceded. Many like Lee were opposed to secession but believed firmly in the sovereign right of states; hence they joined the Confederacy as soon as it was clear that the Union would use force to keep the states in the Union. But there were others who did not share that view and held out permanently. To a few high-minded people of this class there were added others who, in the hope of preferment by the Union or for other selfish reasons, stayed out of the Confederacy. Many of these last were eager to become leaders of the freed slaves. They became known as Scalawags. To them was added a group of men who swarmed in from the North to grab the political offices and to fatten on the spoils of the Union régime. These were called Carpetbaggers, because they were so impecunious as to be able to carry all their worldly possessions in a carpetbag. Many of them were sent down to become agents of the Freedmen's Bureau. They had large powers, they controlled relief funds, and many of them used these for their own selfish aggrandizement. Human nature being what it is, one would expect a certain percentage of such persons to prove recreant to their trust. These agents in many cases stirred up the freedmen and fostered in them false hopes. General Grant reported to the President:

> The belief widely spread among the freedmen of the southern states that the lands of the former owners will, at least in part, be divided among them, has come from the agents of the bureau. This belief is seriously interfering with the willingness of the freedmen to make contracts for the coming year . . . The effect of the belief in the division of lands is idleness, and accumulation in camps, towns and cities.[1]

With the group of poor whites unsympathetic to the freedmen, with the landowners proud and somewhat aloof, and with some of the Bureau agents the Scalawags and Carpetbaggers eager to use the Negroes for their own selfish purposes, it is no wonder that a period known as "reconstruction" should be attended with all the horrors of an uncontrolled mob.

In the midst of such conditions the southern states set about reorganizing their governments. On May 29, 1865, President Johnson issued a proclamation to North Carolina, that had been worked out and approved by Lincoln before his untimely death, which looked to the restoration of civil government in that state. Proclamations to other states followed promptly, that to Georgia being issued June 17, and the one to Alabama June 21. In all these proclamations it was assumed that the seceding states were to be taken

---

[1] Hilary A. Herbert, *Why the Solid South?* pp. 17–18.

back into the Union as soon as they had laid down arms and rescinded their acts of secession. This view was repeatedly expressed in Congress by northern representatives.[1] Indeed, Abraham Lincoln had specifically stated this would be the case. In Lincoln's last message to Congress, December 5, 1864, he said: "They [the seceded states] can at any moment have peace simply by laying down their arms and submitting to the National Authority under the Constitutions." Lincoln's plan for restoring these states to the Union never contemplated anything but that they should reorganize their governments on the basis of loyalty to the Union. He never had the remotest idea of dictating the basis of suffrage. Before his death he had written to Governor Hahn: "Now you are about to have a convention which, among other things will probably define the elective franchise, *I barely suggest,* for your *private consideration,* whether some of the colored people may not be let in, for instance the very intelligent and especially those who have fought gallantly in our ranks. But this is only a suggestion, not to the public, but to you alone."[2] Andrew Johnson, adopting Lincoln's policy *in toto,* wrote to Governor Sharkey of Mississippi: "If you could extend the elective franchise to all persons of color who can read the constitution of the United States in english and write their names, and all persons of color who own real estate valued at not less than two hundred and fifty dollars, and pay taxes thereon, you would completely disarm the adversary, and set an example that other states will follow."[3] Lincoln had already fought out with Congress in 1864 the question whether the President or Congress had the right to restore the southern states, and had apparently won recognition for his contention that the President had such power. Had he lived, Presidential reconstruction would probably have been carried through. But Johnson, although in agreement with Lincoln's policy and thoroughly loyal to it, had not the influence with Congress to see it through.

With the assumption that Lincoln's policy would be sustained the southern states met, reorganized their governments, rescinded the secession ordinances, abolished slavery, ratified the Thirteenth Amendment, and under considerable pressure repudiated the bond

[1] Cf. Henry Wilson, *The History of the Rise and Fall of the Slave Power in America,* Vol. III, chap. 43.
[2] Hilary A. Herbert, *Why the Solid South?* p. 7.
[3] *Ibid.,* p. 7.

indebtedness accumulated during the process of the war. This last step brought financial ruin to many widows and old people who had invested their all in the success of the Confederate cause. The suffrage was confined to the white people just as it was so confined at the time in Ohio, Michigan, Pennsylvania, Kansas, Connecticut, and numerous other northern states. There were many men in these constitutional conventions that favored a limited suffrage for Negroes on some such basis as Mr. Lincoln had suggested, but the time was hardly ripe for such a step.

Everything seemed set for a peaceful return of the states to the Union until Thaddeus Stevens on December 14, 1865, declared: "According to my judgement they ought never to be recognized as capable of acting in the Union or of being counted as valid states until the constitution shall have been so amended as to make it what its makers intended, and so to secure perpetual ascendency to the party of the Union."[1] Stevens was bent on enfranchising the Negro and disfranchising the whites of the South. In order to allow time for the northern states to come to his opinion, a commission of fifteen was appointed to study the situation in the South and determine whether the people were loyal to the Union. Although both Lee and Grant testified that the people on the whole were loyal, certain of the Carpetbaggers and some of the Freedmen's Bureau agents testified to the contrary, and the commission decided to take their testimony rather than that of Lee and Grant and others of their type. Mr. Davis, representative of Maryland, in submitting a bill for the reinstatement of the seceded states (March, 1864), declared that the majority of the people not only were now but always had been in sympathy with the Union.[2] In furtherance of the view of Thaddeus Stevens, and others whose hatred and rancor had grown with the months, the southern states had made one fatal blunder — they had passed the "Black Laws."

As we have remarked before, and as General Grant testified, the unrest in the South due to idle and wandering Negroes was a sore trial. Laborers could not be secured to till the soil. The presence of large numbers of ignorant and unemployed Negroes, and the fact that many of these owned firearms, were a cause for

[1] Hilary A. Herbert, *Why the Solid South?* p. 13.
[2] Henry Wilson, *History of the Rise and Fall of the Slave Power in America*, Vol. III, p. 522.

great concern. The presence of Carpetbaggers and Scalawags, who were false guides of the ignorant, made the southern leaders very fearful of what the immediate future might hold. What they did can easily be understood, but it can just as easily be seen that they greatly harmed their own cause, and completely tied the hands of the President. The Black Laws put Thaddeus Stevens and his followers in complete control. No greater calamity could have befallen every class than this. It swept the northern man into a bitter persecution of the South; it united the southern whites in a stubborn opposition and created in their minds a bitter feeling toward the blacks; and it put into the minds of the ignorant freedmen false hopes which they were not then capable of realizing. Just as the war itself might have been averted had it not been for hotheads both North and South, so "reconstruction" might have been averted had it not been for stubborn prejudice on both sides. The North felt the South was virtually trying to enslave the Negro again, and the South felt the North was trying to put an ignorant class in charge of them as masters.

The Black Laws in most of the southern states treated as vagrants all persons who could not show a legitimate occupation. They were to be arrested on a warrant from any justice of peace. If the person arraigned could not show that he was employed, and if he could not put up bond as surety for his good behavior, he could be sent to prison or to the workhouse. In binding out apprentices, the former masters were given the first opportunity to bid for the services of Negro boys and girls. The law declared that apprenticed youths must be well treated and must be given a certain amount of schooling; and should the master fail in these respects, the court could take the ward away and give him to another. But in case the master performed faithfully his part of the contract and the apprentice ran away before finishing his apprenticeship, damages could be recovered, and the court had the right to decide how much the apprentice should pay. The master holding an apprentice had the power of parents over such person. Laws fixed the hours of labor and guarded against impudence on the part of the laborers. Negroes could sell farm products only under specific conditions and with written permit. In some states a Negro could not hold certain types of real estate, he could not engage in certain types of business, he could not assemble with other Negroes with complete freedom, he could not testify against a white man, he could not sit on juries, and he could not vote or hold office.[1] It is entirely beside the case to say that laws similar in intent were in the statutes of most of the northern states. These states were not in question, and they had no class just emerged from slavery. The laws passed by southern states may have been provoked by the conditions prevailing, but they in turn provoked a bitter attack in return. As a result Congress on March 2, 1867, passed the Reconstruction Act, which put the whole South under military law again, and which laid the ground for such bitter antagonism between whites and blacks in the South.

As soon as Congress had acted, the provisional state governments were automatically disbanded, and under military control new conventions were called. In these, Negroes, both free and freedmen, were given full voice. In Virginia 90,000 Negroes voted for representatives in the convention and twenty-five Negroes were elected as members.[2] In North Carolina 93,006 Negro votes out of a total of 125,967 were cast for the reconstruction convention. There were twelve Carpetbaggers and nineteen Negroes in the first legislature which met.[3] In South Carolina the convention consisted of forty-eight white men and seventy-six Negroes.[4] In Georgia 95,973 out of 192,235 votes were cast by Negroes, and thirty-three out of one hundred sixty-six delegates to the convention were Negroes. In the first legislature of the state, twenty-eight Negroes sat as legislators.[5] In the Alabama convention there were eighteen Negroes.[6] In Mississippi the first election under congressional reconstruction placed five Negroes in the Senate and thirty in the House.[7] The policy of Congress worked out to make the voting South as black as possible, and to exclude the leading whites as far as possible from the vote. The Fourteenth Amendment, adopted in 1868, excluded all white leaders of the Confederacy from the exercise of the franchise. The

---

[1] Cf. James B. Browning, "The North Carolina Black Code," *Journal of Negro History*, October, 1930, pp. 461–473; Hilary A. Herbert, *Why the Solid South? passim;* Henry Wilson, *History of the Rise and Fall of the Slave Power in America*, Vol. III, chap. 43; Paul Lewinson, *Race, Class and Party, passim; The South in the Building of the Nation*, Vols. I and II; William A. Dunning, *Reconstruction, Political and Economic, 1865–1877.*

[2] *The South in the Building of the Nation*, Vol. I, p. 131.

[3] *Ibid.*, pp. 502–504.   [4] *Ibid.*, Vol. II, p. 98.

[5] *Ibid.*, Vol. II, pp. 223–224.   [6] *Ibid.*, Vol. II, p. 302.

[7] *Ibid.*, Vol. II, p. 436. For detailed statistics see *Negro Year Book, 1925–1926*, p. 236 ff.

Fifteenth Amendment, adopted in 1870, was a still further attempt to force the South to permit the Negro to rule. These early conventions, composed so largely of ignorant and untried men, made assemblies which were pitiable in their unfitness.[1] The constitutions drawn by these conventions were adopted under great protest.[2] The new officials elected were mostly northern whites. Thus, of the states restored to statehood in 1868, ten of the fourteen United States senators, twenty of the thirty-five representatives, and four of the seven governors,[3] were Carpetbaggers. The petty offices were filled by Negroes and Scalawags. The enforcement act of May, 1870, laid heavy penalties on any who interfered with the right to vote as secured by the Fifteenth Amendment adopted in 1870.

But as Ray Stannard Baker wrote forty years later, "Mankind is reconstructed not by proclamations or legislation or military occupation, but by time, growth, education, religion, thought."[4] Most of the power of thinking after the war was still in possession of white men, and they resolved to get back their political power. The abuses and extravagances which followed the reconstruction organization have been so often told that they need only mention here to bring to mind the conditions against which the South reacted. The most outstanding abuse was the piling up of heavy bonded debts. "A very conservative figure in 1872 put the increase of indebtedness of the eleven states since their reconstruction, at \$131,717,777.81."[5] Much of this went into railroads which were never completed, much of the remainder went into exorbitant salaries for Carpetbag officers. The result was a revolt on the part of the white leaders, the wresting of the ballot from the Negroes, by a series of grandfather clauses which enabled anyone who was a voter in 1860 still to vote, and enabled anyone to vote who was a descendant of those who were then voters, or who were descendants of those who fought in the Revolution. The purpose of all these laws was to give the vote to the white people regardless of educational or property qualification, while general barriers were raised against others who could not read and interpret the constitution, etc. Thus most of the Negroes were excluded from the right to vote. The process

---

[1] William A. Dunning, *Reconstruction, Political and Economic, 1865–1877*, p. 112.   [2] *Ibid.*, pp. 117–118.   [3] *Ibid.*, p. 120.

[4] *Following the Color Line*, p. 235.

[5] William A. Dunning, *Reconstruction, Political and Economic, 1865–1877*, p. 208.

of exclusion stretched over a period of twenty years — indeed was not really completed until the beginning of the present century.

In all this turmoil, the poor whites stood usually against the Negro and also against the white planter class. Slavery had shut the poor whites out from opportunities of occupation and had robbed them of all political power. The slaves held the skilled positions, and the planters held all political power. Hence the war had as truly given freedom to the poor whites as it had to the Negro slaves. These people were therefore determined to come into their own as soon as possible. Their hatred of the slaves was only inflamed by the bitter conditions of the reconstruction period. These were the people who flocked to the Ku Klux Klan and who went to the polls with shotguns to intimidate Negroes who might want to vote.

In the first stages of the disfranchisement of the Negro, the aristocrats came back into power, but the poor whites hated the aristocrats only a little less violently than they hated the slaves, and aristocratic rule in the South was doomed. This condition partly explains the rise to power of men like Ben Tillman, Cole Blease, Vardaman of Mississippi, and Huey Long of Louisiana. They are the outcroppings of a widespread upheaval among the common people. The South has not yet seen the end of the influence of reconstruction. The whole movement has been one of blind democracy hitting out against any thing or any class that stands in its way. It was as inevitable as are the incoming tides. The old aristocracy of the South was doomed from the beginning. It had many wonderful qualities, and the beauty of its social graces kept it in power much longer than one would have expected; but, like the Russian revolution, reconstruction in the South with its later rise of the masses was a terrible rebuke to all special privilege.

Before the Civil War the South was "solid" because the economic interest of the South seemed to dictate that the planter class should act as a unit. Twenty-three hundred planters, owning an average of more than one hundred slaves each, made a compact, intelligent, and determined group which could completely dominate southern politics. After the war and during reconstruction the South was almost solid, because the common white men were united against the disfranchised aristocrats and the newly enfranchised Negroes. Since 1900 the South has continued solid because Vardaman, Tillman, Hoke Smith, and others of their class have continually declared that all white men must stand together or be dominated by the Negro. Some of these men have believed this; others have used this fear of Negro domination as a horse to ride into office. When the grandfather clauses were being passed men were told that the elimination of the Negro from politics would free the white South to discuss issues, and to divide when needed on matters of policy. It has not proven so. The Negro still dominates the South. Indeed one could hardly find an issue of any import, which has come before the white South for decision during the last hundred years, that has not been decided largely in the light of the Negroes' presence. Our social customs, our educational systems, our political life, even our religion, have been deeply colored by the presence of the Negro. Much of the energy of the South has been expended over this problem. The white man has been constantly concerned about maintaining his supremacy; the colored man has been trying constantly to come into his own. It is in the light of this fact that the present political situation takes on large social significance.

That the Negro does not at present have equal civic rights with the white man, no one who has his eyes open can fail to see. If he goes to school he must in many cases sit in a poorer building than that provided for the white child. He is taught by a more illiterate girl, who is paid a much smaller monthly wage, and often for fewer months, than is the teacher of white persons. If he rides on a train he must pay the same fare as a white person, but sit in a small cramped Jim Crow car with all classes mixed together indiscriminately, often with only one toilet for both men and women; the car itself is usually an old wooden one, long since out of use for white people. If he is called into court he has much less chance for real justice than has the white man. If he has a white man friend and his offense is not too serious he usually gets far less punishment than justice demands. The white man says, "That's my nigger and I'll be responsible." So he is released. If he has no white sponsor he usually gets more punishment than justice demands. His sentence is usually more severe, his chances of a fair trial are much smaller, than in the case of the white man. If he makes a business deal his smaller economic resources force him to pay larger prices, carry higher rates of interest, and often get inferior goods.[1] At every turn he is handicapped. Many Negroes claim this is so because the Negro has no power to protect himself through the ballot. Indeed, Dr. Du

[1] Cf. Willis D. Weatherford, *The Negro from Africa to America*, chap. 13.

Bois charges almost every evil of the Negro to his disfranchisement,[1] and almost every forward step is attributed to the fact that he is having an increasing chance to express himself at the polls. The fullest study of this subject is that of Lewinson.[2] He lists three influences which are making for a larger enfranchisement of the Negro: first, favorable white sentiment; second, skilled Negro leadership; third, a growth in economic and cultural status on the part of the Negro.[3] There can be no doubt that all three of these factors are working. Sentiment in the South has become much more liberal in the last twenty years. In particular the college trained youths of the South are open-minded and tolerant. The student Young Men's and Young Women's Christian Associations have led the way. They have invited colored students, men and women, to their conferences and hence have come to know them personally. Knowing them personally, they are eager to see that they have full chance of self-expression. The progress of the Negro educationally and culturally, and also his great advances in economic independence, have been powerful factors in giving him a right to vote.

But these factors have not made it possible for all Negroes to vote freely and without intimidation. The Republican party, which has held almost the solid vote of the Negro since emancipation, has of late come almost to repudiate him, because as long as the Negro voted solid for Republicanism there was no chance to win any considerable number of southern white votes. If the Negro stands as a solid unit, it is fairly certain that the southern whites will stand as a unit. Hence, a "lily white" movement has sprung up in the Republican party. Following up this move of the Republicans Mr. Hoover in 1928 made an appeal for the reorganization of the party program in the South, which the press assumed to mean that Negro political bosses in that section were to be pitched out. Commenting on this the Baltimore *Evening Sun* said: "He [Mr. Hoover] is aware that, while millions of southerners represented by Bishop Cannon could vote for him . . . without losing caste, they cannot without losing caste put themselves under the leadership of such Negro politicians as etc., etc. Therefore, when he flung the Negro out, the President evidently did take a long step toward

---

[1] Cf. Charles S. Johnson, *The Negro in American Civilization*, chap. 29.
[2] *Race, Class and Party*.
[3] *Ibid.*, p. 103.

assuring the permanency of the Republican South. It is rough on the Negroes but it is first-rate politics." [1]

The attitude of indifference of the Republican party to the Negro who had solidly supported it in the South called forth a protest following the Kansas City Convention, in which the Negro Republicans declared they desired to work for full enfranchisement of the American Negro, they wished to find their exact standing in the Republican party, and they desired to bring to the light of publicity the acts of those Negroes who vote against race interest and yet desire to get the emoluments of any race advancement.[2] If the "lily white" movement of the Republican party splits the Negro vote in the South, it may ultimately bring about a larger amount of freedom in voting on the part of the southern white man. As long as the Negro votes solidly the Republican ticket, it is not likely that the white vote will be greatly divided in national issues.

But there is also opposition to the Negro having any voice in the Democratic party. The white primary, which excludes in most cases the Negro, settles the election in the South. To get the Democratic nomination in most states means to get the election. If the Negro has no voice in the primary, his vote counts for nothing in the election. Because Negroes protested this procedure, Texas passed a white primary law in 1923, which was tested by Dr. A. L. Nixon (colored) of El Paso. The case came to the Supreme Court of the United States, and Justice Holmes handed down a decision which was unanimous, March, 1927, declaring that the Texas law barring Negroes voting in the primary was unconstitutional. The fruits of this victory have, however, been since set aside by a political dodge of allowing the executive committee of the party to decide who might be members of the party. In some places in Texas the Negro is now admitted to the Democratic primary,[3] but this depends entirely on the attitude of the local committee. In certain other southern states the primaries are being opened to Negroes.[4] In the border states like Tennessee, Kentucky, West Virginia, and even Arkansas, the Negro has less trouble in registering his vote than in many of the states of the lower South. In cities like Memphis, Tennessee, with a 42 per cent Negro population, and Nashville, with a 35 per cent Negro population, the Negro vote is something really to be reckoned with. More than once in the last ten years the Negro vote

[1] *Negro Year Book, 1931–1932*, p. 94. [2] *Ibid.*, p. 85.
[3] *Ibid.*, p. 102. [4] *Ibid.*, pp. 103–104.

in Nashville has been the deciding factor in the election. Certain Negro papers claim that Negroes will vote Democratic when the Democratic primaries are opened to all alike. Whether this would be so or not, there seems no fairness in charging the Negro with voting solidly against the southern whites, and then blocking his way to vote with the majority of southern white voters.

But there are other obstacles besides the primaries in the way of the Negro casting his ballot. The procedure of registration is peculiarly difficult for the great mass of Negroes. In the first place a Negro must pay his poll tax long months in advance, and he must keep his receipt and show it to the registrar on registration day. This is often overlooked by ignorant Negroes as, of course, it is by many whites. But often white men may register without being challenged to show their poll tax receipt. Not infrequently the registrars have dummy receipts made out in advance which they can furnish to the improvident white man. The Negro can make no such dodge. Filling out the blank for registration often gives technical basis for the name being thrown out. The registrar in some states has a right to examine the applicant on his ability to interpret the constitution. The registrar alone is the judge of whether the explanation is adequate. Lewinson reports one colored school official in New Orleans as saying: "Had I been requesting registration to practice law, the examination could have been but little harder."[1] In many cases Negroes applying for registration are browbeaten and embarrassed, so much so that many of them will not face the ordeal. Still other Negroes are prevented from registering and voting because they feel it will hurt their standing with the white people of the community. In some small communities the white people will tell you frankly they don't want "Negroes who are mixed up in politics." Whenever the "red necks" or "poor whites" or members of that class are in control the Negro has little chance for a vote, even if the law does guarantee such right. This situation cannot be changed by law; it must be changed by an educational process.

Perhaps the Negro can help in this if he will come to view community issues from the standpoint of a good citizen and not from the standpoint of a good party member.

The problem that at once faces the Negro in his effort to exercise his franchise is political leadership. There are not many educated Negro men with a capacity for leadership who care to enter politics.

[1] *Race, Class and Party*, p. 117.

It immediately makes them a target for severe criticism and robs them of any fair chance to become economically efficient or successful. There is bitter prejudice on the part of many white communities against any Negro who enters politics. Part of this is a hangover from reconstruction days when Carpetbaggers, Scalawags, and Negroes ruled the South. The politically-minded Negro is still classed with the Scalawags.

So long as the Negro does not have full power of suffrage he is helpless to protect himself against the discriminations which arise. Might is not right, but it often helps to bring rights. If the Negro has no vote for municipal officers, he has no way of seeing that men are elected who will be just in their treatment of the Negro. He can do nothing about the unpaved streets, the lack of sewerage, and the lack of street lighting in the Negro section. There can be no doubt that the voter has power to influence public administration of justice, provided there are sufficient numbers and there is intelligent leadership. Far too long we have looked to the good will of the white man to protect the Negro in his rights. Let us hope that the spirit of *noblesse oblige* will never die out of the heart of our best white people in their dealings with the Negro people, but we must not count on that to give full justice. The Negro must become a man in his own right in taking his own responsibilities and carrying his privileges.

But it is not the Negro alone who suffers from lack of political justice. The whole South and the white man suffer also. Much of the corruption in southern politics is directly traceable to the treatment of the Negro. Dishonest officials play fast and loose with the Negro vote. If it is to their advantage they register the Negro; if not, he cannot pass the registration list. Here is a constant temptation to corruption. It was said in the nineties that buying the Negro vote was a source of corruption; hence that vote must be eliminated in order to purge politics in the South of dishonesty. One wonders whether the constant unfairness to Negroes may not produce equally bad effects on the character of the southern whites. Not only the white man, but the whole southern community, suffers from this unfair treatment of the Negro. As long as the South is forced to vote "solid" — as long as southerners feel they must think alike and stand together to prevent so-called "Negro domination" — no statesman-like policies can be initiated. Free discussion of public policies, and free action on the basis of conviction, are the only hope of progress. But the South has no freedom. We are slaves to a caste system. For two hundred years the Negro has sat in the shadows of every civic and political assemblage. He has dominated the thinking and action of every section of our land. We dare not think independently, because in so doing we would have division, and that would mean Negro domination. One can hardly conceive a more abject slavery than this — slavery to our ever present fear. The hope of the South politically, economically, socially, and, one would almost say, religiously, is that we shall throw off this fear. Let us set up high standards of civic and political participation. Let us make them high enough and rigid enough to eliminate all the unfit — white and black. Then let us administer these tests with rigid justice to white and black alike. There are more than two white persons to every Negro in the South. If we eliminate those who by ignorance, shiftlessness, and crime are unfit, it would hardly be conceivable that the Negro would anywhere dominate. Such a procedure would open the way for a progressive South; it would stimulate once more civic and political leadership among the whites, and it would set an incentive for educational and property progress before the Negro people of the South. Some such step would seem necessary if the South is once more to take a place of leadership in the affairs of the nation.

PROBLEMS FOR STUDY

1. If the southern states disfranchised free Negroes and slaves because they feared restlessness or insurrection, why did most of the northern states discriminate against and disfranchise free Negroes, and refuse them the privilege of testimony against whites?
2. If the slave laws were drawn primarily with a view to protecting property, can we find a parallel in factory laws which primarily protect profits and not persons?
3. On what basis during reconstruction did the common people (poor whites) fear that the slaves would follow the leadership of the master class rather than make common cause with the poor whites?
4. If Lincoln had lived and the seceding states had been restored by him, rather than reconstructed according to Thaddeus Stevens' plan, what would have been the effect on the relation of the white and colored people?
5. In the presence of an idle class of freedmen, what measures could have been taken in the South which would have been more constructive than the Black Laws?

6. In the state of Mississippi, where there are as many Negroes as whites, and where there are many delta counties with the overwhelming majority black and ignorant, what is the practical way of handling the franchise?
7. Is there any parallel between the rise of the Soviet leaders of Russia, and the rise of the poor white leaders during reconstruction?
8. Will the "lily white" policy of the Republicans during recent years play into the hands of the Democrats, or will it probably divide the South, thus strengthening Republicanism?
9. In what ways can the grip of the "Solid South" be broken, and a national rather than a sectional spirit be developed?
10. Is it to the advantage both of the South and of the nation that the South cease to be "solid"?

BIBLIOGRAPHY

William G. Brown, *The Lower South in American History* (1930).
Jerome Dowd, *The Negro in American Life* (1926).
William A. Dunning, *Essays on the Civil War and Reconstruction and Related Topics* (1904).
William A. Dunning, *Reconstruction, Political and Economic, 1865–1877* (1907).
Walter L. Fleming, *Documentary History of Reconstruction, Political, Military, Social, Religious, Educational, and Industrial, 1865 to the Present Time* (1906–1907).
William Goodell, *The American Slave Code in Theory and Practice* (1853).
Archibald H. Grimke, "Why Disfranchisement Is Bad," *Atlantic Monthly*, July, 1904, pp. 72–81.
Hilary A. Herbert, *Why the Solid South?* (1890).
Charles S. Johnson, *The Negro in American Civilization* (1930).
Paul Lewinson, *Race, Class and Party* (1932).
Negro Year Book, 1925–1926, 1931–1932.
William F. Nowlin, *The Negro in American National Politics since 1868* (1931).
The South in the Building of the Nation, Vol. I (1903).
Gilbert T. Stephenson, *Race Distinctions in American Law* (1910).
Woodrow Wilson, *Division and Reunion, 1829–1889* (1898).

CHAPTER XXII

NEGRO CRIME AND THE TREATMENT OF CRIMINALS

A great deal of discussion has been carried on around the question of the comparative criminal record of white and colored people in America. Some have maintained that the Negro is much more criminal than the white man, others have felt it is simply the economic and social situation in which the Negro lives that makes the difference in his criminal record. The latter point to the record of the Negro during slavery, maintaining that few Negroes were criminals during that period. While the facts are not widely known there was, on the contrary, considerable criminality among slaves. The records do not show nearly all the crimes of the period, for all minor and many major offenses were dealt with by the master and never came to the attention of the courts. The laws of South Carolina expressly permitted a slave master to punish his slaves by "whipping or beating with a horsewhip, cowskin, switch or small stick, or by putting irons on, or confining or imprisoning." [1] The law of Louisiana said: "The slave is entirely subject to the will of his master, who may correct and chastise him, though not with unusual rigor, nor so as to maim or mutilate him, or to expose him to the danger of the loss of life, or so to cause his death." [2] In the case of *Slave vs. Man* in the courts of North Carolina (1829) the defendant had hired one Lydia for a year. During the term the defendant undertook to punish Lydia for some minor offense, and she ran away. Being ordered to stop, she refused, and was shot and wounded. The owner of the slave brought suit, and in the final decision Judge Ruffin said:

The power of the master (in this case the employer became the master) must be absolute to render the submission of the slave perfect. I must freely confess my sense of hardness of the proposition. I feel it as deeply as any man can. And as a principle of moral right every person in his

[1] William Goodell, *The American Slave Code in Theory and Practice*, p. 160.
[2] *Ibid.*, p. 161.

retirement must repudiate it. But in the actual condition of things it must be so. There is no remedy. This discipline belongs to the state of slavery. They cannot be disunited, without abrogating at once the rights of the master, and absolving the slave from his subjection. It constitutes the curse of slavery to both the bond and the free portions of our population. But it is inherent in the relation of master and slave.[1]

These three illustrations are samples of the working of slave law. The master was free to go to any length in punishing a slave, so long as he did not permanently injure him, and even that prohibition seems to have been abrogated in the North Carolina court in order to preserve discipline among slaves. Under such conditions most masters never took the trouble to bring their slaves to court, which was both bothersome and expensive. They summarily dispensed "justice" as it seemed wise and expedient. Hence we are justified in assuming that a small proportion of slaves committing crime got into the criminal records. But if one supposes that there were no criminal procedures against slaves, one will have a rude awakening when he studies the facts. The South Carolina law of 1690, which with slight modification held down to the time of the Civil War, provided that any justice of the peace hearing of a crime by a Negro should forthwith dispatch his constable to arrest such Negro; the justice must also summon another justice and at least three freeholders, and a trial must be held in three days. There was no appeal from the decision of this court. Under this law, the record indicates, there were many executions of Negroes, sometimes with scant justice.[2] Louisiana kept careful records of its criminal court procedures, and these reports show that crime among slaves was not infrequent. In 1860 there were 96 slave prisoners in the state prison, 83 of whom were serving life sentences. "4 of these slaves were convicted for attempt at rape, and 3 for insurrection."[3] In Virginia all slaves convicted and thus taken out of active labor were to be paid for by the public; hence careful records or vouchers were kept. "The gross number of convictions" from 1780 to 1864 "was 1418, all but 91 of which were males. . . . For rape there were 73 convictions and for attempt at rape 32."[4] It is thus quite clear that practically

---

[1] William Goodell, *The American Slave Code in Theory and Practice*, pp. 172–173.

[2] Howell M. Henry, *The Police Control of the Slave in South Carolina*, chap. 6.

[3] Ulrich B. Phillips, *American Negro Slavery*, pp. 456–457.

[4] *Ibid.*, pp. 457–458.

every type of crime is recorded against slaves. Even the crime of rape was not unknown. Referring to this crime in Louisiana, J. E. Cutler says: "The record stands, three slaves and one free Negro legally executed for rape and two slaves legally executed for attempted rape. There are some instances reported of summary punishment, not death, being administered to Negroes for inducing white girls to run away with them, or for living with white women."[1] Whatever we shall find as to the state of present Negro crime, it appears, therefore, that slavery did not prevent the commitment of crime in the days prior to the Civil War.

When one turns to the present situation the criminal record of the Negro, at least on the face of it, seems quite discouraging. Many writers, including some of the best representatives of the Negroes themselves, such as Washington, Du Bois, and Work, recognize this fact, and the actual figures all appear to be against the Negro. The special government report on Negro population from 1790 to 1915 gives the Negro criminality for 1910 as 21.9 per cent of the total criminality for the country, while they constituted only 10.7 per cent of the total population. Fifty-six per cent of those committed for grave homicide, 49 per cent of those committed for lesser homicide, and 41.1 per cent of those committed for assault were Negroes.[2] Thus Monroe N. Work puts the record: "The Bureau of Census reports on crime show that the per cent commitments by race was in 1910 white 77.1; Negro 21.1; others and unknown races 0.7. In 1923, the per cent of commitments by race was white 74.6; Negro 23.2; others and unknown races 2.0. The per cent commitments by race in 1926 was white 75.6; Negro 21.4, others and unknown races 3.0."[3] The Negro represented less than 10 per cent of the population. Careful studies of comparative crime of whites and Negroes in North Carolina indicate that, according to the census of 1920, the Negroes constituted 28 per cent of the population of the state, and yet they furnished approximately 44 per cent of the indictments for crime. For each 1,000 white population there were 4.65 indictments, while for each 1,000 Negroes there were 8.71 indictments. The Negroes furnished just about one-third of the indictments for violation of prohibition laws, practically half for

[1] *Lynch Law*, p. 126.

[2] United States Bureau of the Census, *Negro Population in the United States, 1790–1915*, p. 438.

[3] *Negro Year Book, 1931–1932*, p. 279.

gambling, nearly two-thirds for murder, and more than half for carrying concealed weapons and for assault.[1] In Richmond, Virginia, in 1929, the Negroes constituted 28.7 per cent of the population, but the number of arrests were as follows:

	White	Colored
Males	10,162	8,607
Females	918	1,824
	11,080	10,431

Of the 2,360 adults before the court of domestic relations in Richmond in 1927, 1,108 were Negroes. The numbers of juvenile probationers at the end of 1927 in Richmond were:

	White	Colored
Males	134	85
Females	40	37
	174	122

In the detention home there were 146 more Negro children listed than white.[2] In the city of Nashville, Tennessee, with approximately one-third of the population colored, the numbers of juvenile delinquents for white and colored from November 1, 1929, to November 15, 1930, were:[3]

	White	Colored
Males	278	189
Females	73	68
	351	257

Contrary to public opinion, the Negro rate for the crime of rape is not nearly so high as the rate for either native whites or foreign-born. Thus the figures for 1926 are: Negro, 2.6 per cent of commitments; native whites, 4.0; Indian, 9.4; foreign-born whites, 5.5. Even if all Negroes lynched that year should be charged with rape the percentage committed for the crime would be decidedly below that for the native whites.[4] The figures for 1904 are thoroughly in keeping with these proportions.[5]

[1] Francis S. Wilder, "Crime in the Superior Courts of North Carolina," *Social Forces*, March, 1927, pp. 423–427.

[2] *The Negro in Richmond, Virginia*, p. 97.

[3] Francis H. Hiller, *The Treatment of Juvenile Offenders in Nashville, Tennessee*, p. 14.

[4] *Negro Year Book, 1931–1932*, p. 284.

[5] *Annals of the American Academy of Political and Social Science*, September, 1913, p. 76.

The figures do not always show a larger proportion of Negro criminals than whites. Records of the county jails of Georgia for 1927, 1928, and 1929 showed respectively 25,056, 24,893, and 27,276 Negro prisoners, while the numbers for the white prisoners were 20,157, 20,110, and 23,040. The Negro and white populations in Georgia are almost equal. "In 1921, 66 per cent of the jail population" of Georgia "was made up of Negroes and 33.9 per cent of whites. In 1929 the proportion of Negroes had fallen to 54.2 per cent and that of the whites had increased to 45.8 per cent."[1] Similar changes in proportion seem to have taken place in other southern states during the same period. On the whole, however, it seems to remain true that the number of annual commitments and the annual jail population show disproportionate numbers of Negroes. The question which must at once be asked is whether these facts indicate a more criminal tendency on the part of blacks or whether they indicate differences in social treatment which might account for the disparity.

First of all let us look at the juvenile delinquency situation. We have full studies of at least two southern cities. The report on Nashville says:

The Negro boy in Nashville, as a delinquent, has been studied, but not apart from other delinquents, by the National Probation Association and by the Department of Sociology of Vanderbilt University.

This is a report on a survey to secure data as to the amount, nature, and treatment of cases of juvenile delinquency among Negro boys in Nashville. The data were secured directly from the records of the Humane Commission and the secretary to the judge of the Juvenile Court. Frequent reference was made to the report of the National Probation Association on the Treatment of Juvenile Offenders in Nashville, Tennessee.

The Negro boy in Nashville has been treated in such a manner as not to minimize his delinquency but to aggravate it. The most serious defects of the Juvenile Court which affect the Negro boy are: The lack of sufficiently well trained probation officers; the failure to coördinate the operation of the probation department with the work of the judge; the complete absence of any effective organization for the direction of probation work; inadequate or, in most of the cases, non-existent social investigation; failure to consider the needs of the boy, resulting in too frequent commitment to institutions; failure to use the existing social agencies in treatment of the boy and his family; the detention of these boys in the city and county jails until called for by the juvenile court officer; the detention of boys in the Colored De-

[1] *Negro Year Book, 1931–1932*, p. 285.

tention Home for long periods of time; the lack of physical and mental examination; and the lack of an adequate system of records, both of social information relative to each child brought before the court, as well as of all proceedings and decisions of the court.[1]

The Richmond survey, commenting on the larger crime record for the Negroes than for the whites, calls attention to a score of conditions which may affect the proportion:

If parental control is a valuable factor in the training of children, does the absence of many Negro mothers from home during the day explain Negro juvenile delinquency in part? If Boy Scouts and Girl Scouts establish good habits and high ideals for white children, are Negroes handicapped by their almost total absence in Richmond? If community centers upbuild white citizenship, what serves that purpose among the Negro population of the city? If summer camps are good for white boys and girls why not for Negroes? If gymnasiums and a modern Y.M.C.A. program for white men and boys are necessary agencies in Richmond, do the Negroes suffer by their absence? If the Federation of Mothers' Clubs and Parent-Teacher Association justifies itself as a white member of the Community Fund, why not a similar Negro organization? If poverty and poor homes relate themselves to the misconduct of whites, as every study ever made seems to indicate, how do Negroes escape the depressing and demoralizing effects of their low economic status? If feeblemindedness plays a part in crime, who can doubt that feebleminded Negroes, for whom no local training and very little institutional care is provided, are at an enormous disadvantage in making adjustments in the complex city life of Richmond? If defective and diseased bodies sometimes explain abnormal human behavior, why not accept that explanation for Negroes who suffer the same physical diseases and weaknesses as other men but in larger numbers in Richmond? If education tends to protect and stabilize a white man, why should it be expected that the ignorant Negro will be able to save himself from temptation? If special classes for subnormal children and the case work of visiting teachers are of value in adjusting Richmond's white school children to life, why assume that Richmond's Negro children will make the grade unassisted?[2]

In the Nashville study of the Negro boy the peak of arrests seemed to be at the ages of fourteen and fifteen, just as the Negro boy was getting away from the influence of the home, and there was no place for play or recreation.[3] Of 679 Negro boys in junior and

[1] Willis D. Weatherford (Ed.), *A Survey of the Negro Boy in Nashville, Tennessee*, p. 70.

[2] *The Negro in Richmond, Virginia*, pp. 98–99.

[3] Willis D. Weatherford (Ed.), *A Survey of the Negro Boy in Nashville, Tennessee*, p. 73.

senior high schools in Nashville in 1932, 61 or 9 per cent had been before the juvenile court. In the cases of 330 of these high school boys there was some disruption of the family, either by the mother or the father being away from home for work at night, or by the permanent separation of the parents. In 264 cases there was permanent separation of the fathers and mothers either by death, divorce, or desertion.[1]

The economic condition of the Negro would also account for much juvenile crime, as well as a great deal of adult crime. In the case of Nashville, of 359 boys arrested during 1930, 158 cases involved larceny in some form. There can be no doubt that the economic helplessness of the Negro adult exposes him to arrest and conviction when a white man with more resources would never be arrested. Negroes are frequently decoyed into crap shooting, or other petty crimes, by officers who get a fee for all arrests made. This would rarely ever happen with white men. Also Negroes are not infrequently arrested simply because they apparently have no work to do, and are classed as vagrants. Also it happens often that a crime committed by a white person is laid at the door of a Negro who is not able to defend himself. His status makes him an easy mark for such injustice. The legislature of Mississippi in 1930 voted a $500 bonus to a Negro who had thus been imprisoned for five years, though innocent.[2]

The fact that a Negro may be "framed" or that he may not get a fair trial undoubtedly tends to make all Negroes think of those arrested as martyrs rather than as criminals. This would gradually break down one of the most powerful deterrents of crime: namely, the loss of status among those who are of the same class as the possible criminal. Closely akin to this is the fact that the Negro has no voice in making the law in the South, and only small voice in administering it. He is in some places a policeman, and sometimes a juror, but he is never the judge, and not often does he have a real voice. If our colleges have found it necessary to give students a share in self-government, not only to develop character but to improve discipline, it would seem high time that the Negro was given a larger voice in the making of his own laws and in administering them.

It is altogether likely that the disparity of percentages for white

[1] Willis D. Weatherford (Ed.), *A Survey of the Negro Boy in Nashville, Tennessee*, p. 78.

[2] For other cases see *Negro Year Book, 1931–1932*, p. 289 ff.

and colored commitments may be affected materially by the fact that in the South the white man often escapes punishment. "It must be poor consolation to the foreign born, the Indian, the Negro, and the ignorant generally, to learn that the law has punished only the guilty of their class or race, and to see that the guilty of the class, fortunate by reason of wealth, learning or color, are not so punished for like crime."[1] But Judge Thomas recognizes that this condition does prevail in southern courts. Anna J. Thompson, in an article on Negro crime in Philadelphia, expresses the opinion that Negroes in that city are more apt to get the full penalty of the law than are white men.[2] Judge William H. Samford of Montgomery, Alabama, maintains that in counties where Negroes are greatly in the majority, the white man gets much less than due punishment, and the Negro usually gets fair justice; but in counties where the population is almost entirely white the white man gets fair justice and the Negro gets almost no chance for justice.[3] This is an opinion based on long observation and not on statistical facts. The Chicago Commission on Race Relations found that the number of arrests was no accurate record of criminality, because there were often wholesale arrests in the attempt to locate one criminal. Much less care to avoid arresting innocent persons was taken in the case of Negroes than in the case of whites, "since police officers share in the general public opinion that Negroes are more criminal than whites," and "there is little risk of trouble in arresting Negroes."[4]

If one bases his judgment of criminality on the comparative prison population, there is an obvious unfairness to the Negro, because the penalties given him are generally recognized to be much more severe than those given whites. Thus, for a crime for which a white man would be given a prison sentence of one to five years, the Negro is apt to get a sentence of from five to ten years. Many writers on Negro crime have not recognized this fact. Thus, C. H. McCord, writing in 1914 on the American Negro dependent, defective, and delinquent, uses again and again gross figures of prison population. But he gives the comparative sentences for white and colored for each class of crime, and these figures show that the average sentence

---

[1] Judge William H. Thomas in *The Call of the New South*, p. 207.

[2] *Opportunity*, August, 1926, p. 251.

[3] *Annals of the American Academy of Political and Social Science*, September, 1913, p. 76.

[4] *The Negro in Chicago*, p. 345.

for a Negro is one-third longer than that for a white man committing the same crime.¹ It is perfectly obvious that in the long run one Negro sentenced for two years will add as much to the total prison population as two white men sentenced one year each for the same crime as that for which the Negro was sentenced. Not only are Negroes sentenced for longer terms than white men for the same degree of crime, but the Negro rarely gets the benefit of pardons or paroles. Speaking of indeterminate sentence and parole in the southern states, McCord says: "So far as I have been able to learn, these provisions have not been applied to any great extent among Negro offenders." Governor Bickett, addressing the students of Hampton Institute in 1921, declared he had discovered in the North Carolina prisons many Negroes "literally buried alive," forgotten even by their own families, and never thought of by society. He found one man who had been committed when he was eleven years old and was still in prison after twenty years.³ In the light of these facts it is perfectly clear that gross figures for criminal population fail to represent the actual status of criminality of the Negro. But even if arrests were equally justified, trials equally fair, sentences completely equalized, and pardons and paroles equally distributed between white and colored — which of course is a big if — still the number of convictions and the proportion of prison population would not be a fair measure of the Negro's criminal propensities.

One could easily give statistics which would show that the vast proportion of white criminals come from the ignorant, the poor, the disadvantaged. The conditions under which many of these live tend to drive them into crime. If this be true for the submerged white man it must be doubly true of the Negro. He is in the lowest-paid class of American workers. He is the last hired and the first fired. He has a higher rate of illiteracy in the South than has the white man. He lives, on the whole, in the slum of the city. If the figures for the whole country are being considered, we must remember that practically all the Negroes of the North live in the city, and the criminal statistics for cities are far higher than for rural districts. In short, there are no statistics of Negro criminality as compared with white which represent the actual criminal attitude

[1] *The American Negro as a Dependent, Defective and Delinquent*, Part II, chaps. 1, 5 p. 188 ff., and p. 289.
[2] *Ibid.*, p. 287.
[3] *Southern Workman*, June, 1921, p. 250.

of the Negro. While the figures which we have, and which have some value, do show the Negro in a bad light, we should be careful not to base too rigid a conclusion on any facts so far recorded.

It is not possible to treat the subject of the care of criminals in this chapter. That it is bad now and has been bad for many years is evident to one who studies the facts. George W. Cable, more than forty years ago, protested against the treatment of the Negro criminal in the South.[1] John L. Spivak in 1932 wrote a terrible story of the "Georgia Nigger" which he claims is typical of much of the treatment of the criminal Negro all over the South.[2] Data for the treatment of juvenile delinquents can be found in the surveys of the Negro boy in Nashville, Tennessee, and of the Negro in Richmond, Virginia, to which we referred earlier in this chapter.

Let us turn our attention to a phase of Negro crime and punishment which perhaps is the basis of more race hatred than any other. It makes the white man hate the Negro because of the supposed heinousness of the crime, and also because it degrades the Negro to the status of the beast; it makes the Negro hate the white man because of the rash injustice of it, because it so often punishes the wrong person, and because it robs the Negro people of any sense of security or protection. Lynching is a crime practiced almost exclusively in America, and practiced much more extensively in the South than in the North, and practiced against Negroes four times as frequently as against whites, or nearly forty times as frequently in proportion to population.

From 1889 to 1929 — a period of forty years — there were 3,703 persons lynched in the United States, of whom 787 or 21.3 per cent were whites. The number of whites lynched has been gradually declining. During the first decade of this forty-year period the percentage of whites to all persons lynched was 32.2; during the second decade 11.4 per cent were whites; during the third decade the percentage was 8.9. The figures for the last decade have grown somewhat, to 10.3.[3]

The justification for lynching has usually been the heinousness of attack on white women. But when one looks into the record he finds that only a small proportion of the persons lynched were men

---

[1] *The Silent South.*
[2] *Georgia Nigger.*
[3] *Lynchings and What They Mean*, p. 10. The *Negro Year Book, 1931–1932*, p. 294, gives the number lynched for these years as 3,714.

charged with this specific crime. The *Negro Year Book, 1931–1932* classifies all lynching for the years 1889 to 1929 as follows: homicide 1,399, felonious assault 214, rape 622, attempted rape 247, robbery and theft 267, insult to white people 66, all other causes 897. It will thus be seen that those charged with rape and attempted rape form only 23 per cent of the total number lynched.[1] It should be remembered that in many of these cases the charge was not only not proved but not even investigated. The simple report of the guilt of the victim was all the evidence given or desired. Some years ago in the city of Nashville a lynching was narrowly escaped because a business girl claimed she was raped by a Negro student. It later developed that she had had criminal relations with her sweetheart, and was trying to cover up the fact. Had the Negro been lynched the facts would never have come to light. Anyone who studies the record with an unbiased mind must come to the conclusion that a considerable percentage of the lynchings for rape are completely without evidence of guilt. In not a few cases where lynchings have been prevented, and the criminal charged with rape has been legally tried, the court has found him not guilty. Had the lynching occurred, no further investigation would have been made. It is usually to the advantage of a mob to make the accusation rape, because it immediately quiets further investigation. The Southern Commission on Lynching after exhaustive case studies of many lynchings came to substantially the conclusions stated here.[2] The Commission found among the accusations classed under "all other causes" the following: "Inciting race troubles, bringing suit against white men, frightening school children, operating house of ill fame, from which white girls were taken, trying to act like a white man, refusing to pay note, seeking employment in a restaurant, forcing white boy to commit crime, expressing sympathy with murder of white men, participating in fight between white and Negro . . . stealing hogs . . . boasting remarks," and many other petty misdemeanors.[3] The evidence is clear that many lynchings are a pure matter of vengeance, with no serious crime committed to incite such a terrible revenge. This should not be taken as treating lightly any such heinous crime as rape. Even Dr. Du Bois, after making allowance for all the false charges, admits: "There still remains enough well authenticated

---

[1] *Negro Year Book, 1931–1932*, p. 294.
[2] Cf. its report, *Lynchings and What They Mean*, p. 19.
[3] *Ibid.*, p. 19.

cases of brutal assault to make every Negro bow his head in shame. Negroes must recognize their responsibility for their own worst classes, and never let resentment against slander allow them even to seem to palliate an awful deed." [1]

Lynching has been resorted to in primitive communities of America because there has not been adequate legal protection for the citizens, or at least because it has been thought that there has not been adequate protection. In similar manner lynchings have been justified on the basis of the slow action of courts and the frequent failure of justice, and on the assumption that such terrible punishment will deter further crime and hence protect citizens against criminals. In the case of rape it is frequently urged that court procedure submits the woman to humiliation in a trial, and lynching obviates that. Of course this is a mere subterfuge. The trial might be held behind closed doors, or the woman's deposition might be taken. Furthermore, nothing could expose a woman to more vile and odious conversation than a lynching. The white women of the South have gone on record against this false basis for lynching. The Alabama women declare: "We protest against the claim that lynching is necessary for the protection of white womanhood"; in Georgia they say: "We find in our hearts no extenuation for crime, be it violation of womanhood, mob violence, or the illegal taking of human life"; the Kentucky women say: "We hold that no circumstances can justify the disregard for civil law and human rights involved in lynching"; the Mississippi women say: "As Southern women we hold that no circumstances can ever justify mob action"; those of North Carolina say: "We resent the assertion that criminality can be controlled by lawless outbreaks, and woman's honor protected by savage acts of revenge"; and the women of South Carolina declare: "There is no greater fallacy, than that which holds up the shield of womanhood in defense of the crime of lynching." [2] Certainly so far as the best womanhood of the South is concerned there can be no justification of lynching in order to protect womanhood.

Lynching does not deter crime, but rather tends to become epidemic. Kelly Miller long ago pointed out the fact that the criminal element of the Negroes who are already hardened may be made all the more

[1] *Some Notes on Negro Crime, Particularly in Georgia*, p. 56.

[2] The declarations are those of state gatherings of women under the auspices of the Commission on Interracial Coöperation. Quoted in *Negro Year Book*, *1931–1932*, pp. 297–298.

callous by the crimes committed against the race.[1] Lynchings seem to go in waves, and tend to recur in the same or neighboring localities. Thus in Shelby County, Tennessee, three Negroes were lynched in 1892, another Negro was lynched in the same county in 1893, and in 1894 six more were lynched. In Lauderdale County, Tennessee, where there had never been a lynching before, so far as I can ascertain, there occurred a lynching in Ripley in 1898. In 1900 there were four more lynchings, in 1903 one, and in 1904 one. The first record we have of lynching in Obion County, Tennessee, is that of 1900, when a Negro was lynched in Tiptonville; another Negro was lynched in the same town in 1901, another in the same county in 1907, three more in the same town and county in 1908, and two more in the same town and county in 1910. The first lynching in Dyer County, Tennessee, of which we have record took place in 1901, when one Negro was lynched; another lynching occurred in the same county in 1902; and there was a lynching in each of the years 1913, 1916, and 1917 in this same county. In Lamar County, Texas, the first recorded lynching was in 1892, when four were killed. True to form, lynchings recurred again in the county in 1893, in 1895, in 1897, and in 1901. These lynchings for the five specified years all occurred in the one town of Paris, showing still more conclusively the epidemic character of the disease. Grimes County, Texas, had lynchings in 1890, in 1892, and in 1893, in 1914 and 1917. Many other illustrations could be given. Anyone who will take the records of lynchings for the last thirty years will see for himself just how epidemic it is. Of course, no one would maintain that isolated lynchings do not occur.

To the charge that the courts are slow and uncertain the obvious reply is that no court has ever been known to free a Negro when the proof was clear that he had violated a white woman. Such a thing is almost unthinkable. It just would not happen. The lack of genuineness of such a charge is proven by the frequent attempts to take a prisoner out of the court and lynch him, and it has happened that a Negro who had been tried and condemned to summary death has been taken by the mob — purely that they might wreak vengeance upon his person.[2] The mob mind is hysterical, dogmatic, and brutal. It asserts beyond peradventure of doubt the proof of guilt when often no proof is at hand. It is dogmatic about the proper

[1] *Race Adjustment*, p. 69.
[2] *Lynchings and What They Mean*, p. 40.

person having been caught and lynched when often no one knows whether it is true or not. It assumes that the court will not act, when everyone in his right mind knows the court will if the charges are proved.

The courts have not dealt adequately with those who perpetrated lynching. In many cases nothing is done at all. In others where indictments are brought they finally are dismissed because no one will testify against other white men. Even good white citizens will not break the white bond of unity in cases like these. In fifteen cases of lynching in the South in 1930, the coroner returned a verdict that the parties came to their death "at the hands of parties unknown."[1] Of forty-nine persons indicted for lynchings in 1930 all but four were acquitted, two of those convicted being given light sentences and only two being given life sentences.[2] Some reasons for this laxness in the execution of justice were given by the Southern Commission on Lynching. They included divided responsibility between grand juries, trial juries, and judges, indifference on the part of officers, and fear of white people that any lack of white unity would result in further outrages by the Negro.[3] Thus again the South is tried by the presence of the Negro.

The terrible effect on the South cannot be exaggerated. That the Negro is made sullen and bitter cannot possibly be doubted. I have had good Negroes tell me that their people were being drawn into more crime because of this brutal practice. It certainly brutalizes the youth of both races. I have talked with scores of high-school students, and not infrequently have found boys who take the practice for granted as the only means by which a more advanced race can deal with a crude and uncultured race. It certainly writes all Negroes down, in the minds of such youths, as scarcely above the beast. It vulgarizes and brutalizes the atmosphere of life. When women will go to a lynching and take their children in arms, when they will incite men to the crime, when a whole community sees such cruelty — when these things can happen the whole morale of the inhabitants is lowered.

Yet again lynching defeats its own avowed purpose. It is said that lynchings must be had to deter crime. But we have shown that lynching increases crime. Again, it is said that lynching inspires respect for the law — but it does the opposite. At all times lynchings have broken down and destroyed the power of law. In the 1830's a

[1] *Ibid.*, p. 49. [2] *Ibid.*, p. 49. [3] *Ibid.*, p. 51.

series of mob actions disturbed the whole country. At that time Abraham Lincoln said of this phenomenon:

> Accounts of outrages committed by mobs form the every-day news of the times. They have pervaded the country from New England to Louisiana; they are neither peculiar to the eternal snows of the former nor the burning suns of the latter; they are not the creature of climate, neither are they confined to the slaveholding or the non-slaveholding States. Alike they spring up among the pleasure-hunting masters of Southern slaves, and the order-loving citizens of the land of steady habits. Whatever then their cause may be, it is common to the whole country.
>
> It would be tedious as well as useless to recount the horrors of all of them. Those happening in the State of Mississippi and at St. Louis are perhaps the most dangerous in example and revolting to humanity. In the Mississippi case they first commenced by hanging the regular gamblers — a set of men certainly not following for a livelihood a very useful or very honest occupation, but one which, so far from being forbidden by the laws, was actually licensed by an act of the legislature passed but a single year before. Next, negroes suspected of conspiring to raise an insurrection were caught up and hanged in all parts of the State; then, white men supposed to be leagued with the Negroes; and finally, strangers from neighboring States, going thither on business, were in many instances subjected to the same fate. Thus went on this process of hanging, from gamblers to Negroes, from Negroes to white citizens, and from these to strangers, till dead men were literally dangling from the boughs of trees by every roadside, and in numbers almost sufficient to rival the native Spanish moss of the country as a drapery of the forest.
>
> Turn then to that horror-striking scene at St. Louis. A single victim only was sacrificed there. This story is very short and is perhaps the most highly tragic of anything of its length that has ever been witnessed in real life. A mulatto man by the name of McIntosh was seized in the street, dragged to the suburbs of the city, chained to a tree, and actually burned to death; and all within a single hour from the time he had been a freeman attending to his own business and at peace with the world.
>
> Such are the effects of mob law, and such are the scenes becoming more and more frequent in this land so lately famed for love of law and order, and the stories of which have even now grown too familiar to attract any thing more than an idle remark.[1]

A cartoon recently appeared in one of our southern papers in which a Negro hung from one limb of a tree and "The Law" hung from another. The law had as surely been lynched as had the Negro. Notwithstanding all these facts about lynching there are not a few

[1] James E. Cutler, *Lynch Law*, pp. 111–112.

white people who still defend it. A most highly educated acquaintance of mine has recently done so, and only a few years ago a man who held a Ph.D. degree wrote a book which was a sorry defense of the practice.¹

Much concerted action has been had in the South during the last twenty years to stop this practice, and it is undoubtedly having marked effect. The Georgia Interracial Commission drew up some years ago a program which they felt would help to put a stop to it:

1. In order to secure convictions more frequently it is suggested that the Attorney General and Chief Justice of Georgia be given power to shift judges and solicitors for these special cases. This provision is in effective operation in several states, notably Alabama.

2. In order that more lynchings may be prevented it is suggested that a state police force, similar to the Texas rangers, be added. This force would be very valuable in coping with any other cases where the criminals operate in several counties, such as cases of automobile theft and liquor running. Such a force is very effective in Tennessee, Pennsylvania and Alabama.

3. An immediate measure suggested is one which was originally asked for by Governor Northern in 1892, Governor Atkinson in 1896, and Governor Dorcey in 1919, and hinted for by Governors Hoke Smith, Candler and Slaton. This measure would provide for the removal of a sheriff who is proven derelict in his duty. South Carolina, Kentucky, and Florida have given the governor power to remove the sheriff. In Alabama the matter is still further from politics by providing that the sheriff be tried before the Supreme Court.

4. More vigorous local action in the counties is also suggested. Sheriffs and solicitors should be more strongly backed up. The action of the citizens of Athens and Clarke County in this respect was especially praised and recommended to other counties. In this place eight hundred citizens signed up to help the sheriff protect a prisoner if he thought it necessary. Because this was generally known, no mob formed. ²

In 1917 a group met at Blue Ridge, North Carolina, and for two days discussed causes and remedies. They printed a report which went to all sheriffs in the South.³ The National Association for the Advancement of Colored People issued a monograph in 1919 in which were gathered careful data for use in this attempt to eradicate lynching.⁴ And recently a study has been made by a

¹ Winfield H. Collins, *The Truth about Lynching and the Negro in the South.*
² Willis D. Weatherford, *The Negro from Africa to America*, pp. 363–364.
³ Willis D. Weatherford (Ed.), *Lawlessness or Civilization — Which?*
⁴ *Thirty Years of Lynching in the United States, 1889–1918.*

very representative commission appointed and financed by the Commission on Interracial Coöperation.[1] All this indicates that the people of the South are aware of the destructive influence of this immoral practice, and they are determined to cast it out — root and branch.

The South can be at peace, prosperous, and progressive when all its citizens have equal and rigid justice; until that time the Negro will dominate our every thought and action.

PROBLEMS FOR STUDY

1. Were conditions on the plantation as conducive to crime as conditions in the modern city?
2. Have you any explanation of the fact that the criminal record in a highly civilized community is often higher than that of a less advanced society?
3. If crime is more frequent among the poor and uneducated, is crime a matter of low social and economic status?
4. What environmental conditions in the life of the Negro are most conducive to crime?
5. If the Negro has no voice in making or executing the laws, what effect is that likely to have on his criminality?
6. Why do Negroes, on the average, receive heavier sentences for the same crime than do white people?
7. Is there ever any possible excuse for lynching?
8. Does disregard for law in one area tend to destroy respect for law in all areas? What bearing would this have on lynching and disregard for prohibition laws?

BIBLIOGRAPHY

Helen T. Catterall (Ed.), *Judicial Cases concerning American Slavery and the Negro* (1927).

James E. Cutler, *Lynch Law* (1905).

William E. B. Du Bois, *Some Notes on Negro Crime, Particularly in Georgia* (1904).

Howell M. Henry, *The Police Control of the Slave in South Carolina* (1914).

Francis H. Hiller, *The Treatment of Juvenile Offenders in Nashville, Tennessee* (1930).

Lynchings and What They Mean. Report of the Commission on Interracial Coöperation (1931).

Negro Year Book, 1931–1932.

[1] *Lynchings and What They Mean.*

The Negro in Chicago. Report of the Chicago Commission on Race Relations (1922).

The Negro in Richmond, Virginia. Report of the Richmond Council of Social Agencies (1930).

Arthur Raper, *The Tragedy of Lynching* (1933).

John L. Spivak, *Georgia Nigger* (1932).

Gilbert T. Stephenson, *Race Distinctions in American Law* (1910).

Thirty Years of Lynching in the United States, 1889–1918. Monograph issued by the National Association for the Advancement of Colored People (1919).

Willis D. Weatherford, *Lawlessness or Civilization — Which?* (pamphlet, 1917).

Willis D. Weatherford (Ed.), *A Survey of the Negro Boy in Nashville, Tennessee* (1932).

CHAPTER XXIII

THE CULTURAL DEVELOPMENT OF THE NEGRO

When we speak of the cultural development of the Negro it must be made clear in what sense the term "culture" is used. It is, of course, familiar in the literature of inspiration, of education, and of manners and etiquette. In recent years, however, the concept of culture, once almost exclusively employed by the ethnologists, has been taken over and incorporated into the language of the whole social science group. By the term is now rather generally meant "the complex whole, which includes material goods, knowledge, beliefs, art, morals, law, custom, and any other capabilities and habits acquired by man as a member of society." Culture in this sense is almost synonymous with civilization, and the more highly developed the civilization, the more confounding the number and variety of culture traits, which are the material and non-material units of culture.

It seems desirable to cast this discussion in the second and broader meaning of culture. There are several reasons for doing this: the Negroes in America, by implication at least, are symbols of a culture widely different from that of the Euro-American culture in which they now live. This is implicit in the references to the success, or failure, or ineptness of the Negro in taking on the white man's civilization. When this is applied to the American Negroes it is clearly meant that they represent a basically different culture. On the other hand, there is some basis for the view that the Negro has been stripped of the greater part of his original culture heritage, as a result of his American life. Thus, any appraisal of his development must be made against the background of the civilization to which he has been exposed. No discriminating treatment of the Negro in America could fail to take into account the wide cultural differences existing contemporaneously in America; nor could it fail to recognize the equally wide cultural differences among Negroes themselves.

A derivation of the concept of culture is the culture-pattern. It helps to explain how there can be, within any given culture, many patterns, or traits and complexes in combination, which are adaptations to peculiar situations. "America," says Robert Bowden, "cannot be appraised in the light of a single culture pattern . . . we have to deal with all grades of life, from the frontier to the metropolis." [1] The culture of the western world has the American culture as one important variety. But within the American culture there are numerous patterns. There is, for example, a significant difference between an American agricultural and an urban culture. But more than this, there are obvious differences in the quality of the same types of culture. William F. Ogburn's references to greater or less technology, and to the utility of culture forms,[2] carry the suggestion of differences in efficiency in the same type of culture. It should not be necessary to postulate the notion of *planes* of culture to express these differences in quality, or to indicate the measure of integration of an individual or group with a given culture pattern. This is just what one finds in the broad picture of American civilization. The pattern of American cities is essentially the same, but no one denies the wide cultural differences between them. Similarly, there are cultural differences between groups within a given area. A notable example of this is the slaveholding and non-slaveholding white populations of the South under slavery. Both represented the same basic European cultural background, and both lived in the same agricultural area. The Scotch-Irish of Pennsylvania and the Scotch-Irish of the highlands of Tennessee and North Carolina, within the same general cultural background, reveal this difference in quality. Whether the difference is described as cultural lag, or inefficiency, or cultural isolation, it is clear that these groups, representing the same stock and background, lived on different planes of the culture.

The differences between these two groups may be attributed to a number of factors: to social isolation, as a result of geographical isolation or of class division on economic lines within the same area; to lack of acquaintance with the accumulated social heritage through formal education; or to weakness in what Professor Ogburn describes as the "adaptive culture." In our present society there are these different planes of life, shared interchangeably by entire groups within the larger pattern, which differ significantly among themselves in their use of common culture tools. The situation is frequently obscured by the fact of a constant movement from one plane to the other, thus reflecting to a certain extent one of the character-

[1] *In Defense of Tomorrow*, p. 7.   [2] *Social Change*, p. 154.

istics of our democratic society. This general principle is important to an understanding of the cultural development of the Negro.

Perhaps no other group in America represents so wide a range of planes of culture as does the American Negro. There are fairly well integrated groups and individuals, on practically every level of the American culture, from the isolated relics of the plantation system in the back country of the South, to the sophisticated æsthetes of the metropolitan centers. It is not possible to speak of any of the backward groups in our American society as being wholly without a culture; and in so far as the Negroes do not seem to manifest traces of the African quite so much as they do traces of early American culture, any study of this cultural development becomes a study of the extent to which the social and cultural isolation of the group is being broken down. The measure of this development thus is the measure of their increased knowledge of the objective world, of their social participation, and of their adjustment to the most important elements of growth in the American civilization.

This notion of the changes in cultural planes can be given pertinent illustration in the observation made by Dr. Robert E. Park regarding changes in race relations. At one time race relations could be represented by a horizontal line, with all white folk above and all the Negro folk below the line. At present these relations are assuming new forms, and, as he says, changing in character and meaning. "With the development of industrial and professional classes within the Negro race, the distinction between the races tends to assume the form of a vertical line. On one side of this line the Negro is represented in most of the occupational and professional classes; on the other side of the line the white man is similarly represented." [1] The situation was this:

All White
—————
All Colored

It is now this:

White	*Colored*
Professional occupation	Professional occupation
Business occupation	Business occupation
Labor	Labor

The result has been development, in every occupational class, of professional and industrial bi-racial organizations. These bi-racial

---

[1] "The Bases of Race Prejudice," *Annals of the American Academy of Political and Social Science*, November, 1928, pp. 11–20.

organizations preserve race distinctions, but change their content. The distances which separate the races are maintained, but the attitudes involved are different. The races no longer look up and down, they look across. An explanation of this change in relations is suggested in the fact that during slavery and for several years after its abolition all Negroes virtually belonged to the same cultural plane. With the development of elements of the Negro population, as a result of education, migration, broadened contacts, and reading, there naturally followed this division in cultural efficiency and achievement.

The thesis of this chapter is: that American Negroes vary in their cultural development according to the extent of their social and cultural isolation, and according to the character of the culture patterns to which they are or have been exposed; that the variation is as great among these Negro groups, living contemporaneously under different environments, as any of the variations that have existed within the Negro group as a whole at different periods of its history; that different planes of culture may be found among different Negro groups within the same community; and that the extent of the movement from one plane to the next provides a measure of the cultural development of this group.

It will be useful, in explanation of this thesis, to describe several Negro groups which are representative of these different cultural planes, and to select various groups from the same general area. Fortunately, there is at hand a study of a plantation community in Macon County, Alabama, which provides an intimate view of the life of several Negro groups representing varying degrees of social and cultural isolation.[1] These Negroes are for the most part tenant farmers who were living upon the plantations of the area during slavery, or who are direct descendants of Negroes who were. There has been little mobility; the traditions of the plantation survive, only slightly modified by the accident of the formal abolition of slavery. The customs, attitudes, and general mode of life are intimately related to this early pattern. There are few schools, low literacy, and an economic position which holds the group profitlessly but continuously to the earth. They reflect in this cultural lag the persistence of virtually all the material traits of the culture in which the plantation existed under slavery, and virtually all the customs and attitudes of the slaves reared under this régime. Patterns of family life, relations between the sexes, religion, and play

[1] Cf. Charles S. Johnson, *Shadow of the Plantation.*

life are based upon this earlier culture situation. There has been developed in this situation an interesting organization of life in the course of the adjustment to the social and physical fact of slavery.

The position of women in the organization of the life of this group may be taken as one example of several relationships. Under slavery, the position of the Negro woman was always a strategic one. Children belonged more to the mother than to the father; as a matter of fact the father was often purely accidental. There could be no formal marriage. The mother "belonged" to the master rather than to the husband, and, as a result, the Negro man had little family control. The Negro woman always had greater advantage in dealing with the white master than the man, who would more readily be punished for insolence. In cotton cultivation the labor of the woman for most of the year is almost as valuable as that of the man.

The result of this strategic position of Negro women has been manifold in such social survivals as the present communities represent. There is a notable dominance of women in the families, and a marked economic, as well as sexual, independence of the women. Those most completely adjusted to this pattern of life may select the fathers of their children, and marry them before children are born, or afterward, or not at all, as suits the exigencies of the situation. The question of morals does not seem to be seriously involved. The unions which are not given legal sanction are, on the whole, as stable as those with legal sanction. The children belong to the mother. If she is living with her parents and unmarried, they belong to her parents. These groups, in their degree of isolation, are in a sense in cultural pockets; they are better integrated, certainly, than families of the same low level of education and lack of urban experience, under the first shock of city life. It is when new cultural standards are introduced that there is consciousness of shame about children born out of wedlock, or about forming a more efficient economic family unit involving a different male, without the legal procedure of divorce. One mother who was not married and whose daughter, also a mother, was not married remarked: "I ain't want no husband myself, and I don't care if Alder [the daughter] marries or no. Alder's father asked me to marry him, but I tole him I don' want no husband." She was not an irresponsible person; indeed, she was one of the hardest-working and most dependable women in the community. Self-reliant and capable, she wanted children but did not need a husband. Under the situation, when new standards appear, both Alder and her child become illegitimate and develop a disabling sense of guilt. For the dominant culture has different codes of conduct. A point to be noted is that such a mode of life is not African any more than it is Russian; nor is it necessarily disorganized.

The rural public schools in this area are introducing gradually knowledge of the outside world and the standards of the dominant culture, through the textbooks, through the teachers from the outside, and through the ability of the children to read about what is going on, and pass it on to their parents.

In this community are certain other Negro families which appear to respond to standards and social codes from the outside. As a consequence this group reflects a different pattern of sentiments, and a quite different organization of life. Although living in the community and in daily contact with others, the members of these families take but small part in the intimate phases of community life. Numbers of them are farm owners; they send their children to school; their homes, mostly small, are owned and stand out from the others in rigid contrast. These homes have paint on them instead of whitewash; there are flowers around the house instead of the bare beaten earth; there are window panes instead of the crude wooden shutters.

When the families of this second type are more closely observed even wider and more significant differences appear. The M—— family can be taken as fairly typical of the group. The father and mother are both in their fifties; there are three children, aged 27, 25, and 17 years. The father is not a farmer, and thus escapes some of the dominant imperatives of the tradition. He is a machinist and works in a railroad shop in a city about a hundred miles away. His two sons, however, are farmers, and of a different quality from their neighbors. The father comes home every two months for a week-end. All the children have been sent away to normal school, and are back at home, one teaching, the other two farming. Family association is with a small number of other persons in the community of similar situation and habits and standards. There are courtship codes; illegitimacy would be a shock and disgrace. There is indeed a problem of suitable mates in the locality for the girl of the family in question. They go to church, and occasionally to social affairs in the large nearby city. They own a small automobile and a piano, and subscribe to a city daily and a Negro weekly newspaper. The home is equipped in simple conventional southern small-town style;

in the living room are a duofold, table, straight chairs, a bookcase with about 200 volumes, and a victrola. It is an unpretentious but comfortable home.

Still another Negro community in the same county is an even more highly selected one in which there is a large and important but all-Negro educational institution. Teachers, officials, professional men, and their families constitute a close society, on a distinctly different plane from both of the other types described. All are of advanced education, experienced in travel, easy in manner, intimately acquainted with the changing traditions of the Negro and the social heritage of Americans, through an equivalent formal education. They know good music, and some of them can create it; they appreciate art, and reflect in their home setting what æsthetes refer to as "taste." Within this group are physicians of exceptional skill, a scientist, a scholar, and an educator of international reputation. It was of this group that Will Rogers, the humorist, said, they spoke English so correctly he could not understand them.

All three types are Negroes living in the same area. It is the same local culture, but manifestly different levels of it are exemplified. These distinct planes of cultural development represent both the fact of the extraordinary variety of cultural development among Negroes and a method by which this cultural development of the Negro group in America may be measured.

Another set of examples descriptive of these different planes may be drawn from the Negro population of a southern city. There is evidence of varying degrees of social distance between groups in this urban community, based on isolation, education, and like factors. There is also consciousness and recognition of this distance, as evidenced in the references of Negroes on one plane, in a mood of class-conscious humility, to "the upper classes," or sarcastically to "the high muck-a-mucks," or scornfully to "the educated niggers"; and, on the other hand, in the reference of Negroes on this plane benevolently to "the masses of our people" and "the underprivileged group," or in good-natured, somewhat condescending sympathy, to "poor Sam," or "Aunt Hagar's children."

This cultural distance, as well as the cultural mobility, is evident in the statement of a Negro minister of the city who had in his congregation individuals representing several different groups.

There's a war between the educated and uneducated people in our race. The educated ones need something to keep them from getting swell headed

They are just critics, and they don't do any church work at all. There's a great partition between them. Some preachers see an educated person in his audience and he'll just preach to him and talk all over the heads of his congregation, but I don't do that. I preach their style about a fourth of the way, just to let them know that I have some sense, and then the rest of the sermon I preach for the common people. You know the common people have to have something to appeal to their emotions and I give it to them.

To one distinct plane, undoubtedly, belongs a group of 100 Negro families in this city whose living costs were studied.[1] They were unskilled workers for the most part. Few were illiterate, but the average years of schooling for the men was six and a half years, and for the women slightly more. The income ranged between $400 and $600 annually. About 35 per cent had, by long saving, bought small homes. About 90 per cent of them "belonged to church," Baptist and Methodist principally. They were poor but neither disorganized nor vicious, and appeals to charity were a last resort. Their recreations were simple, and centered about home or church. They took pride in staying out of trouble. Some of the children were progressing normally in school; others had stopped school out of a simple feeling of the needlessness of much education. As the mother in one of these families said:

There's nothing that a colored man can be improved in here. Nothing for him to do except what he is doing. They're educating themselves and nothing for them to do. They may just land out there in the fertilizer works and stay. I sent my daughter to school, but she didn't like teaching or clerking, so there was nothing for her to do but get married.

A third of these families had telephones, a few had bought small second-hand automobiles, and an eighth of the families had radios. There were about 3.5 books per family, and about half of the families read newspapers and magazines. They were honest, self-respecting, and hard-working folk. They had grossly inadequate material goods, but they were not impoverished. Their home life was fairly stable, and by careful living they got along.

Another type can be represented by the family of B——s. The husband is a dentist, who received his medical degree after marrying; the wife is a high-school graduate. There are three children. Fragments from the life history of the mother in this family reflect, even

[1] Julia M. Johnson, "The Standard of Living of 100 Negro Families of Nashville," M.A. thesis in sociology, Fisk University, 1933.

better than description, intimate aspects of this family life, its interests, associations, desires and satisfactions, and something of its standards of value.

I married when I was twenty years old. Neither of us wanted a wedding so we married secretly. My husband finished medical school in 1926 and college in 1920. He served one year during the war in camp. . . .

I lived in good environment. Most of the children that I played with have grown up and done something. There is ——. She finished college and married, and —— she married and finished college this year and graduated with highest honors. Then there is Dr. —— and Dr. ——, they were all good friends; we all played together and everyone of them is doing well.

I was single almost two years after I finished high school. I took music and stenographic work for a while. After I found out that the teacher didn't give certificates in stenographic work I quit. My uncle tried to get me to go to college. I was very much interested in college but just didn't go. I really wanted to complete that course in stenography because that's what I really wanted to do. I like stenography even now. I had other ambitions too — I wanted to teach school and I wanted to take nurse training. I would have gone to a nurse's training school when my husband studied dentistry, but my husband wouldn't allow it — you know how men are; he didn't want me in school with him. If I had it all to do over again I would finish college. I don't feel that I have missed anything, however. I'm pleased with myself. If I had to make a change — in case I should lose my husband, I would go to college. My children came very early, and I'm happy with them. My husband is successful and I haven't needed college.

My high school education has allowed me to be thrown in contact with people, and to be well benefitted by the class of people I've been thrown with. You have to have a little learning to get along and you have to have a little education to move around in certain classes. Of course my husband's friends and my friends all run in the same circle. I haven't missed anything by not having a degree. They say professional men's wives should have certain contacts, but I haven't missed a thing. I get to go all I want. One of my neighbors dropped a hint one day to somebody else and they told me. She said all professional men should marry wives with degrees. Of course my husband got his degree after we married. It's all in knowing how to stay in your place, that's all. I don't think she should have said that. All she does is wash and iron for a living. I don't think a degree would make me get along better with my husband. You need to know how to treat people. I never throw my head up in the air.

I haven't taken an interest in clubs, social life and things like that. When you accept courtesies you have to return them. And I don't have the time and don't have the place to entertain. I don't like display and popularity. I just treat everybody alike. Of course I don't associate with everybody but I'm nice to everybody. Because my husband has a fine office and a car, nobody's going to say I'm "uppish."

I'm looking forward to give my children everything though. I want to equip them for life. I want them to go all the way through — as far as the average student can go. The two boys are 7 and 8 years old and are in the 3rd grade. I sent them to kindergarten before they went to public school. The girl is 6 years old. I sent her to school at five but they wouldn't take her. One of the boys wants to be a physician and the other a dentist. The girl wants to be a music teacher. I carry my children to school and bring them back every day.

There are no children in the neighborhood for them to play with except two or three. Most of them are too old or else they are babies. There are some down the street but I don't allow them to associate with them.

It is difficult to escape the feeling of an intense striving in this family, in an effort to reach and realize the security of a more advanced cultural position. Nevertheless, it represents a distinctly different picture from the first group, and from still another type which will be described.

The N——s are both descendants of free Negroes, and have distinguished parents. Both received college education at least fifty years ago. In their home, behind deep curtains, are furnishings rich in quality and character and family association. Beside the gold and silver plate presented to the parents of the wife on their fiftieth wedding anniversary are the gold and silver plate presented to this couple on their own fiftieth wedding anniversary. The husband, an attorney and business man now in advanced years, is the unmistakable gentleman, with a courtliness and grace of manner which seems instinctive. The wife, who was reared to womanhood by an English governess, has a poise and charm which is more English than American. They have lived for periods in national diplomatic circles, and had two presidents as friends. In their ancestry are individuals who were important figures in the stirring days preceding the emancipation of Negroes. The surge of life around them has never disturbed this deep-seated calm and culture. They have not withdrawn from this life but have mingled freely with it. There is neither apology nor self-consciousness when they say, "we Negroes," although there is a certain grotesqueness in the swift association of pictures of some race-mates a few blocks away, who, honest and hardworking, have rationalized the pattern of their lives in these sentiments: "I ain't doing no thinking bout the future. I don't know how long I'm gonna be here. I'm just working and trying to make an honest living while I'm here because we plan today and God come and displan tomorrow. I just want to live while I'm here."

The fact that these three urban types belong to the same race and general culture clearly does not mean that they share the same plane of this culture. The types are not selected to represent, by any means, equal numerical distribution; they merely represent variety. But this variety also reveals the range of culture possible, and suggests the progressive nature of this development.

A person who lives within a given cultural situation is not commonly conscious of its elements. Such a person is described as naïve. The Negro spirituals are in this sense naïve creations. They happen, however, to have a tremendous and universal emotional appeal. There is a difference between the naïve Negroes who contribute to the creation of a spiritual, and such Negro poets as James Weldon Johnson, Langston Hughes, and Sterling Brown, who can objectively recognize the artistic value of these materials and give them conscious treatment, distilling new beauty and charm from their rich and varied motifs. All are Negroes, but the cultural distance within the race is sufficiently great to permit those from one plane of this culture to objectify situations on a different plane. Between these two extremes are many others. Not the least interesting of these are the individuals who are made self-conscious by any reference to slave songs, despite their beauty, and who refuse to sing them or to have anything to do with them.

There is, as has been indicated, mobility from one group to the next. Lines are not fixed, and in this respect the democratic tradition of the American civilization gets expression. There is no better example of this than is revealed in the experience of a family in the first tenant group described. The mother and father were illiterate, and bound by the firmest elements of the plantation tradition. Two of the sons, by their own efforts, left the community, found their way to a school, and later passed through several educational institutions. One of them became the president of a Negro college in another state. His parents and all but one other of the five children remained in the old community, and did not change. They have little in common; their modes of life are as far apart as two cultures. They speak to one another from different worlds. It is a separation almost as complete as the removal of the race from Africa.

The range of these planes of culture is given poignancy in the experience of a well-known Negro writer and scholar. Dr. W. E. B.

THE CULTURAL DEVELOPMENT OF THE NEGRO 453

Du Bois may be described as a sensitive and cultured Negro. He was born in Massachusetts and received his education at Fisk University, Harvard, and Heidelberg. One of his first positions after graduating from Fisk University was teaching in a rural Negro school in Tennessee. Reared outside this pattern he could see the life in its sharpest angles:

> At first I used to be a little alarmed at the approach of bed time in the one lone bed room, but embarrassment was very deftly avoided. . . . Across the road, where Fat Reuben lived, they all went out doors while the teacher retired, because they did not boast the luxury of a kitchen. . . .
>
> Tildy's mother was incorrigibly untidy, Reuben's larder was limited seriously, and herds of untamed insects wandered over the Eddingses' beds. . . . For two summers I lived in this little world. . . . Hither my world wended its crooked way on Sunday to meet other worlds, and gossip, and wonder, and make weekly sacrifice with frenzied priest at the altar of the "old time religion."

And then this comment which is a significant document on the two worlds in which they lived but not entirely apart:

> I have called my tiny community a world, and so its isolation made it, and yet there was among us but a half awakened common consciousness, sprung from common joy and grief, at burial, birth or wedding; from a common hardship to poverty, poor land and low wages; and above all, the sight of the Veil that hung between us and opportunity. All this caused us to think some thoughts together; but these, when ripe for spirit, were spoken in various languages.[1]

The intra-racial cultural differences and the changing cultural status of Negro groups create interesting and new racial situations. Misunderstandings and, frequently, conflicts arise out of the failure on the part of the white community, consciously or unconsciously, to recognize these essential cultural differences. The stereotype "Negro" is one which, in the nature of stereotypes, is of long standing. It is usually this stereotype, with all the implications of the character imputed, which obscures all other lines of character or culture. It is undoubtedly true that the stereotype was evolved from the most numerous group. If conditions were static, the picture which was compounded out of fact and impression would not be quite so harmful. But conditions have never existed exactly according to the stereotype, and there has been rapid movement away from it over the past fifty years.

[1] W. E. B. Du Bois, *Souls of Black Folk*, p. 67.

Another of the vital aspects of these cultural differences lies in the fact of this constant movement from one plane to the next. Being Negroes, in the American culture, there is not the same opportunity for those who have advanced their culture to escape the others of their race, even if they desired to do so. A result is that, although there are these differences, there is and probably will continue an intimacy and inter-group sympathy. The Polish aristocracy is closer to other European aristocracies than to the Polish peasantry of its own country. In the case of the Negroes, the superior minds developed do not move off entirely into an exclusive world of advanced cultures, across the line of race, but are turned back, as teachers, ministers, and professionals, to the least advanced levels, where they may accelerate the cultural development of the mass. The majority of the college graduates return South, and chiefly to teach. One reason why this happens, of course, is that all of the colleges in which they may teach, with few notable exceptions, are in the South. Once returned, however, they have the opportunity to contribute vital leavening for the whole of the group.

This cultural development yields itself to a certain amount of quantitative consideration. The means of measurement are, of course, not entirely satisfactory, because there are so many imponderable factors to be taken into account. However, there are some objective indices. Educational development can serve as one of these. When Negroes were emancipated in 1863, between 8 and 15 per cent of them could read and write. This percentage included the literates among a fairly large group of free Negroes. In 1930 the position had been almost completely reversed. Less than 18 per cent were unable to read and write. In 1870 there were, under the Freedmen's Bureau, which was largely responsible for making provisions for Negro education, 3,300 schools with 149,581 pupils. In 1930 in eighteen southern states there were in the public elementary schools 2,133,353 Negro students, in the high schools 106,275, and in the colleges approximately 25,000. In 1911 there were 5,000 Negro graduates of colleges and nine doctors of philosophy; in 1933, the number of these graduates had mounted to 16,000 and the doctorates in philosophy to ninety. There were 400 more graduates in the year 1932 alone than there were total graduates for the whole period from 1820 to 1890. There are 89 Negroes listed in *Who's Who in America*, four in *Who's Who in American Medicine*, and five in *American Men of Science*. Up to 1930 the national scholarship fraternity, *Phi Beta Kappa*, had elected 116 Negroes to membership.

The "middle class" is expanding. A recent census release shows 25,701 retail stores operated by Negroes in the United States, with total annual net retail sales of over $100,000,000. The professional classes have shown a most significant increase. Since 1890 the number of Negroes in the professional classes has increased from 32,879 to 137,263, or 417.4 per cent. This number includes 3,805 physicians and 56,829 teachers, 430 artists and art teachers, 210 librarians, and 425 authors and editors.

It should be remembered, of course, that the census figures are subject to two important qualifications: the listing under the name of the occupations does not indicate quality; on the other hand, the persistent restrictions upon occupations for Negroes tend to depress the numbers in these occupations to an undetermined extent.

Social well-being may be used as a further objective index to cultural development. As a test of the ability to survive under the new condition of freedom, it might be pointed out that the mortality of Negroes has declined about 30 per cent since 1910, and their span of life increased by seven years. The crime rate has shown a decline. The *Negro Year Book*[1] estimates that the number of Negro families owning their homes increased from 12,000 in 1860 to 750,000 in 1930. Reading has increased enormously with literacy. The American Library Association has noted the greatly expanded book circulation among Negroes.

During the past fifteen years there has been such a pronounced increase in creative literary expression as to be characterized as a "Negro Renaissance." There have been notable advances in music, both in the Negro idiom and in classical fields, climaxed by an award to Clarence Cameron White of the Bishpan medal for the composition of an opera, and the appearance of two Negro artists in 1933 in metropolitan opera. For several years the artistic abilities of Roland Hayes and Paul Robeson have received international recognition. The record need not be expanded into further detail to illustrate the range of this development. As late as twenty-five years ago, the appearance of a Negro in any of these fields was regarded as a phenomenon, and he was detached and treated as a special example, unrelated to the general capacity of the race for

[1] *The Negro Year Book, 1931–1932*, p. 118.

such cultural development. The fact that this no longer happens is in itself an indication of development.

The question not infrequently arises as to how these cultural differences develop, and what factors are responsible for change. At least four sources of the current cultural differences may be noted: (*a*) free Negro origin, (*b*) racial intermixture, involving race crossing, (*c*) migration, and (*d*) education.

The free Negro families had an advantage of a number of years in adjusting themselves to the American culture. Historically they were concentrated in the towns and cities. Many of them had some skill. Community acceptance of the free status during slavery would be expected, especially in the South, to give them a superior status over the more recently emancipated Negroes. They tended to form a class-conscious group, with some traditions and with a developed group and family pride.

The families of mixed racial origin had similarly a position of advantage in point of history. They also tended historically to be concentrated in the towns, and, since much of their early employment was domestic, they were in closest and most sustained exposure to the most advanced members of the white population. Codes and standards implicit in the culture of the white group could thus more readily be absorbed. They sought for their children the same education provided for the white children. There were, too, many who were related by blood to these families, and took a pride in their heritage similar to that of the full white issue of their fathers. It is a familiar fact that for many years mulattoes were favored in the matter of occupations. Their marginal position made them more restless under restrictions which were the common experience of Negroes. They have often been most bitter in their racial attitudes. Many of the early Negro leaders were of such mixed origin; and for many years the cultural advance of this group over unmixed Negroes was explained as a result of their "white" blood. This explanation is not so often heard in recent years since the emergence of the unmixed Negroes, largely of the plantation type, and their rapid cultural development.

The last two factors of migration and education have been chiefly responsible for the emergence of the Negroes from that vast group indiscriminatingly classified as "the masses." The movement away from the farms, between sections and to cities, which began promptly after Negro emancipation, has gradually extended the cultural horizon of all Negroes. It has brought a greater knowledge and sophistication, and exposure to those standards implicit in the complexity of city life: schools, hygiene, newspapers, and the myriad tools by which one gains control over the forces of his civilization.

The northward migration with all its shock and initial disorganization has, on the whole, tended to advance the general culture of the group. It is frequently overlooked that disorganization in family life or disorganization expressed in crime is the inevitable accompaniment of the complexity of an advanced culture. In any complex civilization the two elements of balance and imbalance are found together. The test of a "civilized" or "cultured" person is the ability to reorganize his personality upon a new basis of greater control. Negro migrants from the South to the North have to a considerable degree achieved this balance.

Finally, the factor of education has proved, perhaps, most important of all aids to this cultural development. The access to schools from kindergartens to universities has been a positive influence in the transmission of the best in the American and European cultures. Education has diffused knowledge and skills, and opened channels, through literacy, to contact with the best that has been thought and done in the world. In early American society and in many other cultures, the function of passing on the heritage has been very largely the responsibility of the family. Such a method inevitably made for a more rigid channeling of classes and cultures as well. Increasingly the schools are taking over this function from the family. Dr. Harold Rugg has well pointed out that the home, although ideally selected for this task of education and of passing on the social heritage, "is rapidly disintegrating under the impact of the increasing tempo and restless variety of urban life." [1]

Whether the family is or is not failing in this function, it is a fact that education itself, through formal and informal channels, is for most individuals in our society now the dominant agency for transmitting the social and cultural heritage. Increasing control and development in this respect offer both the explanation and further prospect of the Negroes' cultural development.

PROBLEMS FOR STUDY

1. What distinctions can be made between the notion of culture planes suggested in this chapter and that of economic classes?

[1] *Culture and Education in America*, p. 292.

2. How do the *nouveaux riches* reveal the difference in culture planes when the accident of an advanced economic status admits them to a culturally advanced group?
3. Students wishing to study the purer forms of the English ballad go to the mountains of Tennessee. How does this illustrate cultural lag?
4. How does the theory of open classes in democracy make for a multiplication of social planes?
5. How do trade-unions and interracial student organizations illustrate Park's notion of the new vertical relation between races?
6. Where the white community knows only its Negro servants and bases its judgment of the Negro group upon their qualities and characteristics, can the most wholesome community race relations exist?
7. How do crime and family disorganization reflect a phase of cultural development?
8. Race friction frequently arises when types of Negroes from one cultural plane respond negatively to the etiquette of race relations founded upon master and slave relations. To reduce this friction, should there be withdrawal and isolation of these disharmonious types? Should the Negroes in this case adjust themselves to the old etiquette, or should the white persons adjust themselves to the new cultural plane of these Negroes?

BIBLIOGRAPHY

Robert D. Bowden, *In Defense of Tomorrow* (1931).
William E. B. Du Bois, *The Souls of Black Folk* (1903).
Charles S. Johnson, *Shadow of the Plantation* (1934).
Julia M. Johnson, "The Standard of Living of 100 Negro Families of Nashville" (M.A. thesis in sociology, Fisk University, 1933).
William F. Ogburn, *Social Change* (1922).
Robert E. Park, "The Bases of Race Prejudice," *Annals of the American Academy of Political and Social Science*, November, 1928, pp. 11–20.

CHAPTER XXIV

NEGRO LITERATURE

If one is to understand the contribution of the American Negro to literature he must look far back to its source material, in the jungles of Africa where the favorite occupation around the camp fire or on the moonlight night is to tell stories, which are the never ending delight of the primitive inhabitants. Professor Edward B. Reuter and others claim that African culture patterns can hardly be found in America, but one cannot read the folk stories of the ante-bellum Negro and the folk stories of the west coast of Africa without being convinced that much of the old folk lore did find its way across the Atlantic. Professor Newbell N. Puckett has carefully traced certain words which are common in the South to their African origin,[1] even though the wide scattering of fellow tribesmen in slavery meant that native languages must be almost completely abandoned. Such words as *hoodoo, goober, Gullah, buchra,* and even *oona* of St. Helena Island, meaning *you,* are in fairly common usage in the South. But while the language of the slaves was of necessity dropped, the ideas expressed by those languages were far more persistent. If one takes groups of African folk tales, such as those given by Robert H. Nassau,[2] John H. Weeks,[3] Richard F. Burton,[4] or numerous other writers, and compares them with Negro folk tales of the old South, one will be immediately convinced of the striking similarity. Similarity does not necessarily indicate common origin, but when one traces down a number of these folk stories he can find no other source save Africa. Gerber[5] has thus traced many of the stories of Uncle Remus. "One thing is certain," says Joel Chandler Harris, in the introduction to the 1916 edition of his *Uncle Remus,* "the animal stories told by the Negroes in our southern states and in Brazil, were brought by them from Africa." A. O. Stafford in a little volume of animal stories says: "It is now admitted that the great number of quaintest animal stories once so frequently told

---

[1] *Folk Beliefs of the Southern Negro,* 1926.   [2] *Fetichism in West Africa.*
[3] *Congo Life and Jungle Stories.*   [4] *Wit and Wisdom from West Africa.*
[5] "Uncle Remus Traced to the Old World," *Journal of American Folk-Lore,* October-November, 1893.

among the slave population of our southern states in their odd dialect were brought to America by their ancestors from the shores of Africa."[1] In like manner Natalie Curtis Burlin, after careful study of the Negro spirituals, came to the conclusion: "That Negro folk song is indeed an offshoot from an African root, nobody who has heard Africans sing or ever beat the drum, can deny."[2] James W. Johnson, in his *Book of American Negro Spirituals*, calls attention to the fact that Africa has a culture rich in music, art, and folk lore. He further refers to the fact that the Negro slaves thus brought with them a native endowment and that "the Spirituals possess the fundamental characteristics of African music."[3] One who would trace the rich color of Negro literature to its origin must thus familiarize himself with the rich heritage of the Negro found in Africa.

One of the most striking examples of a folk tale from Africa appearing in America almost word for word is that of the tar-baby. In Joel Chandler Harris' story, it is Brer Fox who sets a tar-baby to catch Brer Rabbit, and of course the rabbit, incensed because the tar-baby will not speak to him, slaps her jaw and his front foot sticks. He slaps the other jaw with his other front foot and it sticks. Then he kicks and butts her, and his hind feet and head stick. The African parent of this story is given by Weeks in his *Congo Life and Jungle Stories*.[4] Here the Gazelle is the one who sets the Nkondi, a wooden fetish, to catch the Leopard which had been stealing maize from the Gazelle's field.

That night as the Leopard left the maize field the Nkondi said: "Oh, you are the thief, are you?"

"If you talk like that," growled the Leopard, "I will hit you."

"Hit me," said the Nkondi. The Leopard hit him, and his paw stuck to the image.

"Let go," cried the Leopard, "or I will hit you with my other hand."

"Hit me," repeated the Nkondi. The Leopard hit him with the other hand and that stuck also to the image.

"Let go," angrily cried the Leopard, "or I will kick and bite you." Which he at once did as the Nkondi would not let him go, and his feet and mouth stuck to the image; then both the Leopard and the Nkondi fell to the ground together.

By and by, the Gazelle arrived and when he saw the Leopard sticking to the Nkondi he said: "Oh, you are the thief!"; and having punished him, he cut some leaves and made a charm to set the Leopard free.

[1] *Animal Fables from the Dark Continent*, p. 3.
[2] *Negro Folk-Songs*, Book II, p. 4.   [3] P. 19.   [4] Pp. 389–390.

There are two striking variations in these stories. First the Nkondi, possessing a spirit, had power to hold the Leopard; but in America, where the belief in spirits was somewhat weakened, a little tar is smeared on to compensate and hold the rabbit. The second is the method of releasing the one caught. In the Nkondi story the spirit had to be appeased; so the Gazelle cut leaves and made a charm, presumably of some more powerful spirit. In the American version the Fox catches Brer Rabbit by the hind legs, jerks him loose, and flings him into the brier patch. There may be some symbolism in the brier patch as a kind of substitute for the charm which freed the Leopard.[1] It is most interesting to note that the favorite animal in Africa is the gazelle, a perfectly harmless and helpless animal. He always wins by guile and shrewdness. In America the rabbit, another harmless animal, takes his place in the folk stories. This is true to the life of the Negro. He is not usually a fighter, but wins by shrewdness and politeness. The slaves turned many a hard corner because they knew that a "soft answer turneth away wrath."

These folk stories were the first form of literary expression which the American Negro had. They were told by parents to their children, they were related around the camp fire on hunts, and as Harris stages them, they were told to the children of the "big house." They carried in them a real philosophy of life, with many a moral lesson, though they were not always discriminating as to the moral issues involved. Along with these stories were proverbs and bits of wisdom which passed from mouth to mouth and formed a rough and ready practical philosophy. On the question of the slaves' industry, they had such pithy sayings as these: "Nigger dot gets hurt wukkin oughter show de skyars"; "Rails split fo breakfus'll season de dinner"; "Looks won't do ter split rails wid"; "Hits a mighty deaf nigger dat don't hear de dinner-ho'n."

On the weaknesses of the slave they had such sayings as these: "You kin hide de fier, but w'at you gwine do wid de smoke"; "Licker talks mighty loud w'en it git loose from de jug"; "Ef you wanter see yo' own sins, clean up a new groun'." And as a kind of philosophy of consolation in the midst of hardship they used to say: "Troubles is seasonin', simmons ain's good twel dey'er fros' bit"; or "Watch out w'en you'er gittin all you want, fattenin' hogs ain't in luck."[2]

[1] Joel C. Harris, *Uncle Remus, His Songs and His Sayings*, Stories II and IV.
[2] *Ibid.*, pp. 173–177.

Folk stories and folk sayings were thus the beginnings of self-expression on the part of the slaves. As such, they merit the attention of all serious students of Negro literature.

Early in the life of the slaves there arose those consolation songs which we call the spirituals. The Negro brought with him from Africa a remarkable sense of rhythm. Those who are in position to know claim that African music has little or no melody, but is beyond compare in its rhythm — while the Africans do sing, they express this rhythm more often in the drum beat. For some unexplained reason the American Negro slave did not bring his tom-tom with him; that is, he did not make or use such an instrument much in America. But he did not leave his sense of rhythm behind. No sooner had he learned a little of English and a little of Bible lore than he began to pour out his sorrows in a rhythmical form which soon grew into the most wonderful music America has produced. These spirituals are a combination of music, religion, and suffering, and they arose out of the life of the people. They were not composed by any one author, but were the spontaneous creation of groups, under the stress of religious emotion and with a background of hardship and suffering. Some have tried to take from the Negro the credit for producing such music. They have claimed that these songs were adaptations of the folk music of Europe, but it would be hard to show that slaves on southern plantations had enough contact with European life to make such a theory plausible. Others have claimed that this music was absorbed from the religious music of the planters themselves. If so they improved on that music so much and changed it so completely that it became a new creation.[1] To those who know the Negro and have come to know and love his music, such criticisms seem nothing more than the biased opinions of prejudiced minds. The critics cannot see how an ignorant slave could produce such music. Indeed, as James Weldon Johnson has so well said:

> There is a wide, wide wonder in it all
> That from degraded rest and servile toil,
> The fiery spirit of the seer should call
> These simple children of the sun and soil.[2]

---

[1] For answer to these critics see: Henry E. Krehbiel, *Afro-American Folksongs;* James W. Johnson, *The Book of American Negro Spirituals;* Natalie C. Burlin, *Negro Folk-Songs.*

[2] From his poem, "O Black and Unknown Bards."

But the facts are that they did produce it, and in so doing they have given to the world the finest piece of artistic creation which America has so far had to offer.

The conditions of the old South were conducive to such a production. The plantations were scattered, there was leisure even in the midst of hardships, there was suffering, and religion was a regnant force. The slaves were ignorant; few could read or write. They must find some means of expression; hence, the folk tale and the folk song became their one way of release. Nowhere else in America save in the South were the conditions such as to give rise to this rich expression. This music not only arose out of the social situation of the South; it helped to mould that situation to its own rich but sad melody. "Whom the gods will destroy they first make mad." Thus in the old South the folk stories and the folk songs threw such a halo of glory around the old plantation that many were blinded to the sterner aspects of plantation life. The story of the influence of these literary expressions on the life of the white planters is yet to be written, but when it is written it will be both a wonderful and a tragic chapter.

The Negro songs boxed the compass of human feeling. Dr. Work of Fisk University used to say they were all religious, and in the sense that they grew out of experience, and religion is as broad as experience, that is true. But surely they are not all couched in religious terminology. They had dignity, they had power, because they were the expressions of the deepest emotions of life. The words were often absurdly simple and when sung now tend to provoke laughter, but they were never meant for humor, and to those who enter into the feeling of them, to hear people laugh when they are sung carries something of sacrilege with it.

During the Civil War Thomas Wentworth Higginson and others gathered some of these simple slave songs and published them.[1] Soon after the war Fisk University, then only a struggling elementary school, saw the great possibilities in these songs. George L. White in 1871 gathered a group of Fisk students and started on the road to sing these songs. At first they met an unsympathetic world, when the newspapers called them a Negro Minstrel, but White gave them the name of Jubilee Singers, and as such they sang their way into the hearts of two continents. I have before me as I write a copy of the first edition of these "Jubilee Songs," as they were then

[1] Cf. *Atlantic Monthly*, June, 1867.

called, published in 1872. The critic who wrote the preface, not quite so sure of their value as are we, says: "It is certain that the critic stands completely disarmed in their presence. He must not only recognize their immense power over audiences which include many people of the highest culture, but, if he is not thoroughly incased in prejudice, he must yield a tribute of admiration on his own part, and acknowledge that these songs touch a cord which the most consummate art fails to reach." [1] He goes on to say that the songs were all the more moving when people remembered that the singers were but recently slaves, but he adds that "the power is chiefly in the songs themselves." After hearing these singers in Henry Ward Beecher's church in Brooklyn, Dr. Cuyler, then one of New York's most famous divines, wrote: "The weird melodies of these emancipated slaves touched the fount of tears, and gray haired men wept like little children." [2] From that day to this these spirituals have had a powerful moulding influence on the life and institutions of the Negro. The white artists of the present day, as well as the great Negro composers like Robert N. Dett, Henry T. Burleigh, and Rosamond Johnson, are using the rich material in these songs to color our present American music. Who will say how much we owe to the musical creation of these simple slaves?

The earliest form of written literature produced by the Negro was that of a slave narrative. Briton Hammond, a Massachusetts slave, set forth in 1760 "A Narrative of the Uncommon Suffering and Surprising Deliverance of Briton Hammond, a Negro Man." He seems to have set a precedent, for from that time on it was the fashion for a runaway slave to publish the "Narrative" of his life and sufferings. I have before me more than a hundred such narratives, including some most famous ones. "A Narrative of the Lord's Wonderful Dealings With J. Marant, A Black" was published in 1785. Othello, a Negro, published "An Essay on Slavery" in 1788. In 1789 Gustavas Vassa, a Negro born in Africa but captured and enslaved at the age of eleven, wrote the story of his life, which is full of adventure. The story of Paul Cuffe, a freeman and owner of his own ship, appeared in 1811. David Walker's famous "Appeal" against slavery appeared in Baltimore in 1829. Frederick Douglass began lecturing against slavery in 1841 while he was yet a slave, and soon after (1845) the "Narrative of the Life of Frederick Douglass"

---

[1] "Jubilee Songs," published by Biglow and Main, 1872.
[2] Quoted from the press notices of "Jubilee Songs" (1872).

appeared and continued to be revised and reprinted right up through the period of the Civil War. The most important of all these narratives is Booker T. Washington's *Up from Slavery*, published originally in the *Outlook* in 1900. It has been translated into many languages and is one of the most widely read books of this century.

Many of these narratives were probably written *in toto* by others, and some were taken down from the dictation of the slave himself. One such famous narrative was written by none other than John Greenleaf Whittier. This was first printed in the *Anti-slavery Examiner* of New York. In the preface to the article Whittier writes a scathing account of slavery and attaches a series of runaway slave advertisements gleaned from southern papers to prove his contention. The advertisements bear the dates 1836 and 1837. Thus this issue of the *Examiner*, which bears no date, must have been published in the latter part of 1837 or early in 1838. This narrative aroused a great deal of criticism in the South, some of the southern critics claiming that Whittier made it out of whole cloth. I believe Whittier was never quite able to substantiate all the facts set forth therein.

Another narrative which holds deep interest, because of its connection with Harriet Beecher Stowe, is that of Henry Bibb. This little volume of 204 pages has an introduction by Lucius C. Matlack in which he says he prepared the manuscript as to "orthography and punctuation, merely" and that the whole narrative was the work of Bibb. In his narrative, Bibb claims that he was born in Shelby County, Kentucky, in 1815, and that he was "brought up or flogged up" in Shelby, Henry, Oldham, and Trimble Counties. He asserts that he was the son of James Bibb, of one of the old planter families, and that his mother was a mulatto descended from her master's family. Then follow harrowing tales of suffering and escape. The significance of this narrative is that it fell into the hands of Mrs. Stowe and is said to have furnished not a little of the background material for *Uncle Tom's Cabin*. Another slave who influenced Mrs. Stowe was Josiah Henson, to the second edition of whose narrative, published in 1858, she wrote an introduction. This slave claimed to have been born in Charles County, Maryland, in 1789, his mother and father being slaves on neighboring plantations. His story opens with a harrowing account of the whipping of his father because he had defended Henson's mother against the attack of a licentious overseer. The story is written in clear and lucid English — indeed too clear to be the complete product of an unlettered slave. Henson made a trip to England and was introduced to the Archbishop of Canterbury. The Archbishop, impressed with his information and good conversation, inquired at what university he had graduated. "At the university of adversity," he replied. He then told his distinguished host he had never been to school and had never read the Bible in his youth. He continues that the Archbishop was astonished at the eloquence of his language, which he claims he learned from hearing good speakers.[1] The explanation does not seem very satisfactory, and the narrative must have been written or revised by another. Be that as it may, the first edition of this narrative fell into the hands of Mrs. Stowe and along with that of Henry Bibb had much to do with moulding her ideas of slave conditions.

The influence of these slave narratives was far-reaching. They had about them a directness and an emotional appeal which went straight to the heart of those who were opposed to slavery. Experience is always interesting, and if the element of tragedy or suffering is central in the experience it has a mighty and moving power. As literature the narratives are on the whole very poor reading, but as a social influence helping to destroy slavery they were among the most powerful of all the anti-slavery documents.

It is interesting to note that in the same year in which Briton Hammond wrote his "Narrative" (1760), another Negro, named Jupiter Hammon, published a poem called "An Evening Thought: Salvation by Christ with Penitential Cries." The subtitle goes on to say that the author was the slave of Mr. Lloyd of Queen's Village, on Long Island. This poem consisting of eighty-eight lines was composed of stanzas of four lines each — the alternate lines rhyming.

> Dear Jesus, unto thee we cry,
> Give us the preparation;
> Turn not away thy tender eye;
> We seek thy true salvation.

The Lloyds were evidently very lenient with their slave, for in 1787 he wrote an address to the Negroes in the state of New York, in which he admonishes them to honesty, faithfulness, and obedience. He declares it is good to be free, but because his lot has been cast with very kind masters he does not desire freedom. Hammon also wrote a "Poem for Children," "A Dialog Entitled the Kind Master and the Dutiful Servant," and "An Address to Miss Phillis Wheatley,

---

[1] Josiah Henson, *Truth Is Stranger than Fiction*, pp. 196–198.

Ethiopian Poetess." His poetry has significance not because of its intrinsic worth — though as religious poetry of the eighteenth century it was not wholly bad — but because he was the first slave in America to attempt poetry. He antedated Phillis Wheatley's first poem by eleven years, and hence is the first in a growing line of Negro poets.[1]

The first American Negro poet to attract national attention was Phillis Wheatley. John Wheatley in his introduction to her poems, published in 1772, says that she was brought to America in 1761 at an age between five and eight. Later her biographer, who was a relative of Mrs. Wheatley, says she was about seven years old. In sixteen months she learned at home (taught by Mrs. Wheatley's daughter) the English language, and also "learned something of latin."[2] The preface to the 1802 edition says that these poems were written in her leisure moments and for her own amusement, and were never intended for publication. In 1770 she published a poem on the "Death of the Rev. George Whitefield" which made her name known in two continents, and laid the foundation for the hearty welcome that she received in England, which she visited in search of health in 1773. There she was the guest of Lady Huntingdon, and was given every attention. It was in 1770 that she joined the old South Meeting House, and her biographer assumes that she wrote at that time the poem "On Being Brought from Africa to America," which runs:[3]

> 'Twas mercy brought me from my pagan land
> Taught my benighted soul to understand,
> That there's a God, that there's a Saviour, too;
> Once I redemption neither sought nor knew
> Some view our sable race with scornful eye,
> "Their color is a diabolic dye."
> Remember Christians, Negroes, black as Cain,
> May be refined and join the angelic train.

An "Ode to George Washington" published in 1775 brought forth a courteous letter from the General, in which he declared the "style

---

[1] For a fuller statement concerning Jupiter Hammon see: Oscar Wegelin, *Jupiter Hammon, American Negro Poet*. This gives five facsimiles and a good brief biography.

[2] Cf. Advertisement to 1802 edition of Poems, printed by Thomas and Thomas, Walpole, New Hampshire.

[3] Cf. *Memoir and Poems of Phillis Wheatley, A Native African and a Slave, also Poems by a Slave*, 3rd ed. (1838), p. 16.

and manner exhibit a striking proof of your [Phillis'] poetical talents," [1] and it was this poem which afterward led to her presentation in person to General Washington.

Phillis Wheatley's life from the time of her purchase by Mr. Wheatley in 1761 to the death of this kind master in 1778 was one of peculiar good fortune. She had comfort, care, love, and every attention. After the death of her benefactor and the upheaval of the Revolution, she was thrown on her own resources, and finally married John Peters (April, 1778). Peters was a ne'er-do-well and provided poorly for her. She bore to him three children, the last of whom, along with herself, died in utter wretchedness in 1784.

The poems of Phillis Wheatley were mostly written on occasions of the death of friends, the visit of persons of distinction, and on some special occasion which touched her imagination. They are almost all deeply religious and are written in a stilted English which is much influenced by Pope. As poetry they can hardly be said to have permanent significance, save for the conditions out of which they arose, and the very singular fact that they were penned by one who had been a slave. As such they do have significance, and perhaps they show some genius as Washington thought they did.

The next Negro poet of any importance was George Moses Horton, born in North Carolina in 1797. He seems not to have been very valuable as a farm worker; so he drifted away to the University of North Carolina in 1830. He attended camp meetings often, and absorbed the atmosphere and language of Bible, sermon, and song, all of which are evident in his writings. In 1829 he published at Raleigh his first poems, *The Hope of Liberty*. With the sale of these poems Horton hoped to purchase his freedom, but the venture was a failure and Horton remained a slave until emancipation.[2] A second edition of this volume was published in Philadelphia in 1837,[3] and in 1838 the poems were published in conjunction with poems of Phillis Wheatley. *The Poetical Works of George M. Horton* appeared in 1845; and a volume called *Naked Genius* was published in Raleigh in 1865. The first poem printed in the 1838 edition was "Praise of Creation," which runs:

---

[1] *Memoir and Poems of Phillis Wheatley, a Native African and a Slave, also Poems by a Slave*, 3rd ed. (1838), p. 37.

[2] Cf. *Memoir and Poems of Phillis Wheatley, a Native African and a Slave, also Poems by a Slave* (3rd ed., 1838), p. 120.

[3] *Ibid.*, p. 123.

> Creation fires my tongue!
> Nature thy anthems raise;
> And spread the Universal song
> Of thy creator's praise!

The fourth poem in this series is "On Liberty and Slavery."

> Alas! and am I born for this,
> To wear this slavish chain?
> Deprived of all created bliss,
> Through hardship, toil and pain!

Another poem, entitled "The Slaves Complaint," begins:

> Am I sadly cast aside
> On misfortune's rugged tide?
> Will the world my pains deride
>   Forever?

He wrote poems on "Spring," "Summer," "Winter," "The Evening and Morning," and numerous other subjects.

On February 27, 1843, some contributor who signs himself "G" wrote from Chapel Hill, North Carolina, to the editor of the *Southern Literary Messenger:* "A volume of manuscript Poems was lately placed in my hands by their author, George Horton, a Negro boy, belonging to a respectable farmer residing a few miles from Chapel Hill." He sent two poems and said if they met with favor he would send others. One of these poems was an "Ode to Liberty":

> O! Liberty, thou dove of peace,
> We must aspire to thee,
> Whose wing thy pris'ners must release,
> And fan Columbia free.

The poem is sixteen lines in length and is one of the best penned by Horton.[1]

For years Horton lived at the University of North Carolina, his chief patron being Dr. Caldwell, president of the university. During those years he is said to have hired his time from his master at fifty cents per day. He did menial service about the campus and wrote poems on the side. Many of these poems were written for a price — some young university student wanting to impress his fair lady with his own poetic genius. It was probably some such occasion as this that called forth the second poem published in the *Southern Literary Messenger* referred to above:

[1] Cf. *Southern Literary Messenger*, April, 1843, p. 237.

LINE TO MY ——

I would be thine when morning breaks
On my enraptured view;
When every star her tow'r forsakes,
And every tuneful bird awakes,
And bids the night adieu.

* * *

Let me be thine, altho.' I take
My exit from this world;
And when the heavens with thunder shake,
And all the wheels of time shall break,
With globes to nothing hurl'd,
   I would be thine.

Here again one cannot claim that the poetry is either good or permanent, but the conditions under which it was produced give it a place in early American verse.[1]

Ellen Watkins Harper, born in 1825, and James Madison Bell, born in 1826, are two minor poets, better known for their anti-slavery lecturing. Bell was a voluminous writer and speaker. Most of his poems are recitative verse on slave subjects such as "The Dawn of Freedom," "Emancipation," "Lincoln," etc. Ellen Watkins, who later married Fenton Harper, was also an anti-slavery lecturer, an active worker in the Underground Railroad, and a voluminous writer. Her first volume of poems appeared in 1854. One of the best known of her poems is "The Slave Mother":

Heard you that shriek? It rose
So wildly on the air,
It seemed as if a burden'd heart
Was breaking in despair.

* * *

She is a mother, pale with fear,
Her boy clings to her side,
And in her kirtle vainly tries
His trembling form to hide.

* * *

They tear him from her circling arms,
Her last and fond embrace.
On! never more may her sad eyes
Gaze on his mournful face.

---

[1] For fuller study of Horton see: Stephen B. Weeks "George Moses Horton: Slave Poet," *Southern Workman*, October, 1914, pp. 571–577.

No marvel, then, these bitter shrieks
Disturb the listening air:
She is a mother, and her heart
Is breaking in despair.

In Alberry A. Whitman, a Kentucky slave, we have something more of poetic genius and certainly more of skill in writing. His two most important poems were "Not a Man and Yet a Man" and "The Rape of Florida," published in 1877 and 1884, respectively. The volume published in 1877 contains more than two hundred pages and in spots is lighted with the fire of real poetry, as is also the lengthy poem on Florida. Here race consciousness is distinctly uppermost and the militant attitude finds strong expression.

However, it is not until we reach Paul Laurence Dunbar that we find real poetic genius in the Negro. Dunbar was born in Dayton, Ohio, in 1872, of ex-slave parentage. His father escaped from Kentucky during slavery and went to Canada; his mother was only seventeen years old when the Emancipation Proclamation was published. This she told me herself in her home in Dayton. Dunbar attended the public schools in Dayton, where he won a reputation as editor of a school paper and as a good student in literature. Being poor he had to work as an elevator boy, but he continued his literary interest. His first volume, *Oak and Ivy*, was published in 1892, and a second one, *Majors and Minors*, in 1896. William Dean Howells reviewed this second volume, which immediately brought Dunbar into prominence. Within a year *Lyrics of Lowly Life* with an introduction by William Dean Howells gave Dunbar a national reputation. In this introduction Howells said frankly he did not value Dunbar's work because he was born of slave parents or because he was poor, but because it was real creative art. "What struck me in reading Mr. Dunbar's poetry was what had already struck his friends in Ohio and Indiana, in Kentucky and Illinois. They had felt as I feel, that however gifted his race had proven itself in music, in oratory, in several of the other arts, here was the first instance of an American Negro who had evinced innate distinction in literature. . . . So far as I could remember, Paul Dunbar was the only man of pure African blood and of American civilization to feel the Negro life æsthetically and express it lyrically." [1]

This sober judgment of the critic agrees most thoroughly with what we have found. While the writers of narratives had value

---

[1] Cf. *The Complete Poems of Paul Laurence Dunbar*, pp. vii–viii.

as products of slavery and as a voice which helped to break the shackles of the slave, and while Wheatley and Horton showed power, they were not, and cannot be made to appear to be, writers of great literature. The honor of being the first American Negro to produce genuine poetry must, it seems to me, rest with Dunbar. He had literary insight such as none of his predecessors possessed. He had a sincerity which meets one in every line of his poetry. He had humor which is distinctly marked in his dialect poems. He had a sympathy which none had equaled. Most of all, Dunbar wrote of his people without bitterness or malice. I remarked this to his mother when I visited the old home in Dayton and wondered that she, an ex-slave, should have given such a legacy of good will to the boy. She denied that she had done so, but he got it somewhere, and one is inclined to think it must have come out of his home environment. He knew the life of the old South and yet he had never had any real contact with it. Here again he must have been greatly indebted to his mother.

Some of Dunbar's best and most finished poems are not dialect. "Ere Sleep Comes Down to Soothe the Weary Eyes" has a clear poetic insight and imagination which makes it one of the best pieces of American verse written by white or black. His "Ode to Ethiopia" and "Slow through the Dark" express his passion for his race in dignity and beauty. There is a strength in these poems which marks them as the work of a master. Perhaps the dialect poems of Dunbar were the ones which first arrested attention; they are probably the best known of his poems, particularly among white people. "When De Co'n Pone's Hot" has a musical lilt and a whimsicalness that immediately catch the ear and heart of the reader. "Little Brown Baby" and "When Malindy Sings" have a hominess and a human sympathy which go straight to the heart. Some think this last the very best of Dunbar's dialect poems. His insight into the old South is beautifully shown by such poems as "The Deserted Plantation" and "Christmas on the Plantation." The depth of feeling of the man can be seen in such a poem as "Sympathy":

> I know what the caged bird feels, alas!
> When the Sun is bright on the upland slopes;
> When the wind stirs soft through the springing grass,
> And the river flows like a stream of glass;
> When the first bird sings, and the first bud opes,
> And the faint perfume from its chalice steals —
> I know what the caged bird feels!

While his dialect poems established Dunbar's reputation, and started a school of dialect writers, he was nevertheless dissatisfied with them. He felt dialect to be a temporary form which must ultimately pass. Pass it probably will, but in power of portrayal of a past age it will probably never be surpassed by any other literary form. The social significance of Dunbar's achievement is tremendous. It brought white people to realize that the pure Negro could do first-class work, and by the same sign it inspired the Negro to a new confidence in himself. Perhaps these two aspects of Dunbar's work are more important than the work itself.

In a single chapter one can do no more than mention a number of colored people who have written verse. George Marion McClelland of Tennessee in 1895 published a *Book of Poems and Short Stories*, which are thoroughly worthy of mention. Daniel Webster Davis of North Carolina published *Idle Moments* and *Weh Down Souf and Other Poems*, the latter appearing in 1898. Charles R. Dinkins published *Lyrics of Love* in 1904, in which "We Are Black but We Are Men" is perhaps the most striking poem. Thomas Fortune of Florida, Maud Allen of Alabama, Clara Thompson of Ohio, Joseph Cotter, Sr., of Kentucky, James David Carrothers of Michigan, Joseph Cotter, Jr., of Kentucky, and numerous others have furnished verse for most of the anthologies.[1]

In recent years a number of Negro writers of real power have come to the front. Johnson and Cullen in their anthologies have given full space to most of these. We can here only take note of a few of them. Among women writers perhaps Jessie Fauset and Georgia Douglas Johnson are the most outstanding. The work of Jessie Fauset will be touched upon later, in our discussion of novelists, but she has produced some real verse. Her poem "Oriflamme" shows genuine power. It is a picture of Sojourner Truth, the great emancipation worker.

> I think I see her sitting bowed and black,
> Stricken and seared with slavery, mortal scars,
> Reft of her children, lonely, anguished, yet
> Still looking at the stars.

---

[1] Aside from the regular anthologies of American poetry, there have been four good anthologies of Negro verse: James W. Johnson's *The Book of American Negro Poetry* (1922), Robert T. Kerlin's *Negro Poets and Their Poems* (1923), Newman I. White and Walter C. Jackson's *An Anthology of Verse by American Negroes* (1924), and Countee Cullen's *Caroling Dusk* (1927).

> Symbolic mother, we thy myriad sons,
> Pounding our stubborn hearts on Freedom's bars,
> Clutching our birthright, fight with faces set,
> Still visioning the stars!

There is a note of disillusionment in her poems although she says "she finds life perpetually enchanting."

> I that had found the way so smooth
> With gilly-flowers that beck and nod,
> Now find that same road wild and steep
> With need for compass and for rod.
> And yet with feet that bleed, I pant
> On blindly, — stumbling back to God!

The most lyric voice of the Negro is probably Mrs. Georgia Douglas Johnson. Born in Atlanta, educated at Atlanta University, later moving to Washington where she was married, she has the passion of the poet in her. She has published three volumes, *The Heart of a Woman, Bronze,* and *An Autumn Love Cycle.* Her life has not been a hard one, but has evidently been full of lonely hours. The death of her husband in 1922 created a void in her life, though she has two sons. The bands that restrain a woman are clearly seen in all her poetry — as perhaps the "irony of her situation" as a woman of color comes out constantly. Her mood is that of a quest not always fulfilled.

> The phantom happiness I sought
> O'er every crag and moor;
> I paused at every postern gate,
> And knocked at every door;
>
> In vain I searched the land and sea,
> E'en to the inmost core,
> The curtains of eternal night
> Descend — my search is o'er.[1]

In the introduction to *The Heart of a Woman* Braithwaite says that "sadness echoes its tender and appealing sigh in these songs and lyrics," but since "sadness is a kind of felicity with woman . . . Mrs. Johnson creates just that reality of woman's heart and experience with astonishing raptures."

---

[1] Quoted from *The Heart of a Woman*, p. 11.

> The heart of a woman goes forth with the dawn,
> As a lone bird, soft winging so restlessly on,
> Afar o'er life's turrets and vales does it roam
> In the wake of those echoes the heart calls home.
>
> The heart of a woman falls back with the night,
> And enters some alien cage in its plight,
> And tries to forget it has dreamed of the stars
> While it breaks, breaks, breaks on the sheltering bars.

Perhaps the most lyric of all the poems she has so far published is one entitled "Joy."

> There's a soft rosy glow on the whole world today,
> There's a freshness and fragrance that trembles in May,
> There's a lilt in the music that vibrates and thrills
> From the uttermost glades to the tops of the hills.
>
> Oh! I am so happy, my heart is so light,
> The shades and the shadows have vanished from sight,
> This wild pulsing gladness throbs like a sweet pain.
> O soul of me, drink, ere night falleth again!

Nothing which I have read in American verse surpasses this for sheer beauty of expression. Here then is an influence in Negro life which must ultimately tell. A life filled with poetic passion, along with a deep longing which finds itself hemmed in by racial bars, which cannot be broken. It is the power that is moulding the future of the Negro people.

Cullen, Hughes, Braithwaite, James Weldon Johnson, and Claude McKay, among the more recent Negro poets, have done brilliant writing. Cullen, a man of scholarly instincts, graduate of New York University and Harvard, "arrantly opposed to any form of enforced racial segregation," [1] "a rank conservative" as to poetic form, a protester in thought, has appeared in each of the anthologies of magazine verse since 1923. His attitude toward some white people may be summed up in four lines, "For a Lady I Know":

> She even thinks that up in heaven
> Her class lies late and snores,
> While poor black cherubs rise at seven
> To do celestial chores.

[1] *Caroling Dusk*, p. 180.

His rebellion against racial handicaps may be summed in the closing lines of "Yet Do I Marvel":

> Yet do I marvel at this curious thing:
> To make a poet black, and bid him sing![1]

Cullen is still a young man, born in 1903, and we may look for poems of real power from his pen, which will undoubtedly be filled with a social passion for his race.

William Stanley Braithwaite (born in 1878), on the other hand, seems not at all conscious of race. He is a critic who has read all poets alike without reference to race. His anthologies, beginning in 1906, have appeared annually since 1913 up to the present time. If the growing size of these anthologies is any indication, he and others have done much to stimulate the spirit of poetry in America during the last twenty years. Detached as Braithwaite is from racial problems, he has had less of tragedy in his life and more of calm. His poems are marked by a delicacy and charm which make of them lyrics of rare beauty. One can illustrate his mood by quoting his little poem, "Sic Vita":

> Heart free, hand free,
> Blue above, brown under,
> All the world to me
> Is a place of wonder.
> Sun shine, moon shine,
> Stars, and winds a-blowing,
> All into this heart of mine
> Flowing, flowing, flowing!
>
> Mind free, step free,
> Days to follow after,
> Joys of life sold to me
> For the price of laughter.
> Girl's love, Man's love,
> Love of work and duty,
> Just a will of God's to prove
> Beauty, beauty, beauty.[2]

Langston Hughes (born in 1902) is another one of the younger Negro poets who write of race. He has lived a most colorful life, which is reflected in his poems. He has issued two volumes of poems, *The Weary Blues* and *Fine Clothes to the Jew*. His style is independ-

---

[1] Quoted from *Caroling Dusk*.   [2] *House of Falling Leaves*.

ent and original, and follows the rhythm of the "blues" about which he writes. Much of his poetry deals with the more sordid strata of life, but at times he lifts into higher levels. The note of his racial attitude is struck by the "Proem" to *The Weary Blues*.

> I am a Negro:
> Black as the night is black.
> Black like the depths of Africa.
>
> I've been a slave:
> Caesar told me to keep his door-step clean.
> I brushed the boots of Washington.
>
> I've been a worker:
> Under my hand the pyramids arose.
> I made mortar for the Woolworth building.
>
> I've been a singer:
> All the way from Africa to Georgia,
> I carried my sorrow songs.
> I made ragtime.
>
> I've been a victim:
> The Belgians cut off my hands in the Congo.
> They lynch me now in Texas.
>
> I am a Negro:
> Black as the night is black.
> Black like the depths of my Africa.[1]

Another poet who cannot escape the facts of race is Claude McKay. Born in Jamaica, he wrote his volume of poems about the scenes of his own land — *Songs of Jamaica*. Coming to the United States as a student, he worked awhile at Tuskegee and then at Kansas State University. His first volume published in the United States was *Harlem Shadows*, a series of powerful, passionate, sarcastic poems, portraying the wrongs of his people in this country. He voiced the bitter hurt and disappointment of the Negro soldier returned from France. He saw the injustice of our whole American attitude and gave it powerful voice. Speaking of this land he says:

> Altho she feeds me bread of bitterness,
> And sinks into my throat her tiger's tooth,
> Stealing my breath of life, I will confess
> I love this cultured hell that tests my youth![2]

[1] P. 19.   [2] Quoted from "America" in *Harlem Shadows*, p. 6.

In the same mood he writes of New York:

> My being would be a skeleton, a shell,
> If this dark Passion that fills my every mood,
> And makes my heaven in the white world's hell,
> Did not forever feed me vital blood.[1]

But the terrible passion and hatred of the man came out in "The Lynching" and "If We Must Die." Here all the injustices to his race are put into words of fire. Nothing ever said about the suffering of a race has been more withering. The first of these poems closes:

> The ghastly body swaying in the sun
> The women thronged to look, but never a one
> Showed sorrow in her eyes of steely blue;
> And little lads, lynchers that were to be,
> Danced round the dreadful thing in fiendish glee.[2]

Perhaps the most influential single voice among the Negro poets is James Weldon Johnson — not because he has more power than McKay, or because he had more poetic insight than Cullen, but because his sympathies and understanding are broader than theirs. He has caught as few have the wonder of the early members of his race. His introductions to the first and second *Book of American Negro Spirituals* are poems written in prose. His tribute to the makers of these spirituals in "O Black and Unknown Bards" is the finest word that has yet been said about these songs. In his "God's Trombones" he has caught the essential poetry of the Negro preachers' sermons, and has helped to immortalize that worthy group. His plea to the South for larger vision and a new spirit could not but find response in every noble heart:

O SOUTHLAND!

> O Southland, fair Southland!
> Then why do you still cling
> To an idle age and a musty page,
> To a dead and useless thing?
>
> Tis spring time! Tis work time!
> The world is young again!
> And God's above, and God is love,
> And men are only men.[3]

---

[1] Quoted from "America" in *Harlem Shadows*, p. 23.
[2] *Ibid.*, p. 51.
[3] Quoted from *Fifty Years and Other Poems*, pp. 8–9.

His deep sympathy for his own race is set forth in "Brothers":

> See! there he stands; not brave, but with an air
> Of sullen stupor. Mark him well! Is he
> Not more like brute than man? . . .
>
> How came this beast in human shape and form? . . .
>
> I am
> No more than human dregs; degenerate;
> The monstrous offspring of the monster, — sin;
> I am — just what I am. . . . The race that fed
> Your wives and nursed your babes would do the same
> Today, but I —
>
> What did he mean by those last muttered words,
> "Brothers in spirit, brothers in deed are we"? [1]

Poetry is a powerful medium for passion, and when it speaks the sorrow of a race it will be heard. America will do well to heed the voice of its Negroes, which swells in the rising tide of their poetry.

Among the writers of slave narratives which had a large influence on the abolition of slavery, William Wells Brown was one of the most powerful. His narrative was first published in 1847, and the introduction to the second edition, published in 1848, says that the three thousand copies of the first edition were sold in six months. The narrative is no more remarkable than many others, although written in clear English. But it takes on larger significance when one knows that Brown became the first historian of his race; he was its first novelist, and while not a poet, he did collect and edit a book of songs for anti-slavery meetings. In the original edition of this *Anti-slavery Harp* I find one headed "Jefferson's Daughter," to which there is appended a note: "It is asserted on the authority of an American newspaper, that the daughter of Thomas Jefferson, late president of the United States, was sold at New Orleans for $1,000." The first verse of this hymn ran as follows:

> Can the blood that, at Lexington, poured o'er the plain,
> When the sons warred with tyrants their rights to uphold,
> Can the tide of Niagara wipe out the stain?
> No! Jefferson's child has been bartered for gold! [2]

In 1849 Brown went to Europe to lecture on slavery, and in 1852 he published a volume, *Places I Have Seen and Peoples I Have Met*,

[1] *Ibid.*, pp. 14–17.   [2] P. 23.

which had a wide sale due to the excitement over slavery in England. In 1855 he published a book in America called *Sketches of Places and People Abroad*. These books are dreary enough reading, but they helped to establish the reputation of this man who was up to 1854 legally a slave.

In 1853 Brown published a novel called *Clotelle*[1] or *The President's Daughter*, a narrative of slave life in the United States. The scene is laid at Richmond; the time is the opening of the nineteenth century; Currer, the mother, and Clotelle and Althesa, the daughters, are the chief characters. They are all slaves of a rich Virginian, whose death causes them to be sold, and we follow the daughter first to Natchez, then to New Orleans. The sordidness of the slave market, the slave drivers, the tracking of slaves with bloodhounds, and other features of slave trading are all portrayed in harrowing detail. Like most of the Negro novels which have followed it, *Clotelle* is weak in plot, and the characters are poorly developed. But as the first attempt of the American Negro to write a novel it is not without merit.

Brown tried his hand at writing a play in *Escape*, and later turned historian, in *The Black Man, His Antecedents, His Genius and His Achievements*, a volume of 310 pages, copyrighted in 1863, which soon ran through four editions and was exceedingly popular. It contains a brief memoir of the author, then a discussion of the capacity of the Negro and his relation to ancient civilization, and then biographical sketches of fifty-seven Negroes, including among others Nat Turner and Denmark Vesey, who led two famous slave uprisings. The general discussion of the place of the Negro in civilization was much enlarged upon by Brown in his volume *The Rising Son*, a book of 555 pages, copyrighted in 1873.

Shortly after the Civil War (1867) Brown wrote *The Negro in the Rebellion*, which attempts to set forth the capacities of the Negro as a soldier. These three volumes made Brown the best historian of the Negro which that race had up to that time produced.

Perhaps the nearest approach to literary merit in Brown's writings is *My Southern Home*, a series of twenty-nine sketches of life in the old South. It sets forth the tragedy as well as the joyous side of the slave civilization. All of these books were widely read and had a large influence in moulding public opinion in the North during these days of bitterness and misunderstanding.

[1] It is usually spelled *Clotel*, but this spelling is taken from Brown's *The Rising Son*, published in 1876.

Another Negro who wrote about colored people as soldiers was William C. Nell. In 1851 he published a pamphlet called "Services of Colored Americans in the Wars of 1776 and 1812." Nell calls attention to work done on this subject by John Greenleaf Whittier, a Quaker, from which work he acknowledges he got his inspiration. This simple pamphlet was later (1855) enlarged into a full volume which added to the general emancipation literature which was flooding the country.

Jaret Smith wrote public letters to Reverend James Smylie in Mississippi in 1837, and to Henry Clay in 1839, which were the first printed utterances of one destined to play a considerable part in the abolition movement. From that time on to the Civil War, he had frequent articles in the press, and produced books, the most influential of which was probably *Autographs for Freedom* (1854). Martin Delany was another writer of this same period, who published in 1852 a volume called *The Condition, Elevation, Emigration and Destiny of the Colored People of the United States, Politically Considered*. He later published parts of a novel called *Blake* or *Huts of America* which was much in the style of *Uncle Tom's Cabin*. Brown[1] tells us Delany first came into prominence through his newspaper, the *Mystery*, which he published in Pittsburgh, of which no copies are preserved. At about this same period William Cato and William Douglas wrote histories of the African Presbyterian and Episcopal churches of Philadelphia. Brown[2] says that Douglas was a man of finished education well "versed in Latin, Greek and Hebrew." These church histories called attention to the religious progress of the Negro, and helped establish a faith and confidence in his ability; hence they added to the abolition idea.

Henry Hyland Garnett was a prominent New York preacher and an abolition orator, a kind of firebrand, but withal a man of power.[3] W. C. Pennington, a Presbyterian preacher, born a slave, was given the doctor of divinity degree of Heidelberg University, and during the last ten years of the slave régime was a prominent antislavery orator.[4] Perhaps the leader of all the preachers, orators, and writers of this period was Alexander Crummell, a man of

---

[1] *The Black Man, His Antecedents, His Genius, and His Achievements*, p. 174.
[2] *Ibid.*, p. 271.
[3] *Ibid.*, p. 149 ff.
[4] *Ibid.*, p. 276 ff.

"unadulterated blood," as Brown calls him, a graduate of Cambridge University, a clergyman of the Episcopal church. His oration on Clarkson (1846) and his oration on "The Duty of the Rising Christian State to Contribute to the World's Well-being and Civilization" (1855) make him out a man of power, a man sane in his ideas, passionately devoted to his people, and one who was destined during the whole last half of the century to influence the social thinking of the Negro people.

The era of the modern Negro novel was ushered in by Paul Laurence Dunbar, in his *Uncalled*, the *Love of Landry*, the *Fanatics*, and the *Sport of the Gods*. These novels are not up to the standard of Dunbar's poetry. They are written in clear English but have no particular social significance. In Charles W. Chestnut we find a novelist of great ability. He was distinctly race-conscious; all his stories and novels center around the relation between the races. His most powerful novel, *The House behind the Cedars*, is the story of a brother and sister, children of a slave mother and planter father, who attempt to pass. The frustration of their plan brings tragedy to them and to the white people connected with them. Chestnut handles his material in such manner as to make one sympathize with the mulatto girl. The plot of the story is good, and the action is swift and direct. In this regard it is superior to most of the modern Negro novels. There is nothing of the sordid in Chestnut's novels and stories, and one wishes he could say as much of more recent Negro novels. Among the modern novelists there seems to be a "preference for sordid unpleasant or forbidden themes."[1] Most of these stories center around Harlem's life, which, as Professor Brawley remarks, must of necessity restrict and throttle freedom of literary production on the part of the Negro.

Jessie R. Fauset's *Plum Bun, Chinaberry Tree*, and *There Is Confusion*, and Nella Larsen's *Quicksand* and *Passing*, are all concerned with the problem of the mixture of races. The plots in all of them are poor and the material is more or less commonplace. Claude McKay's *Home to Harlem* and *Banjo* are running stories of the roving Negro and deal with the crudest type of life. When one reads stories like these and *Ginger Town* by this gifted Negro writer, one feels either that the author has mistaken the purpose of literature or that he has become so realistic as to lose his sense of values. It is

[1] Benjamin Brawley, *The Negro in Literature and Art in the United States*, p. 117.

this kind of writing which brings out the protest of Professor Brawley in the *Southern Workman* for December, 1932: "If we read of one coarse and ignorant Negro, then of another, and another and another, it is by a very simple induction that we conclude that all Negroes are coarse and ignorant." It is not enough that we should answer that this is simply realistic presentation of types and is not meant as characterization. Whatever we may say about it, literature is characterization, and if it is not it is not real literature.

Rudolph Fisher's *Walls of Jericho*, while dealing with the swearing, swaggering, laboring type of Negro, has something more of the genuine in it, and shows Shine at least as a real man. His *Conjure Man Dies* is more a detective story than it is a novel, and deals with the rougher element of Harlem.

Countee Cullen's *One Way to Heaven* tries to make heroic the professional religionist, but even his final deception for the sake of his wife hardly rises into the realm of the heroic.

Langston Hughes' *Not Without Laughter* strikes a finer note, and is a better portrayal of character, than most of the modern novels.

Walter F. White's *The Fire in the Flint* and *Flight*, while purely racial, have more of plot and real power. They show the difficulty of the educated Negro living in the South and trying to walk the narrow path of service to his own people without offense to the whites.

William E. B. Du Bois' *Dark Princess*, dealing with the embarrassment of a Negro student who finds himself balked in his education because he is black, is a story with satire and deep passion. The plot is poor and the action hardly well motivated. His earlier novel, *The Quest of the Silver Fleece*, concerned more with the economic problems of the Negro, is truly more successful as a novel.

All these novels of the Negro writers are intensely propagandist, they are often bitter, frequently sarcastic, they are lacking in power of sustained plot, and often become a series of episodes strung on a rather precarious thread of story. The Negro does not seem at his best in his effort at novel-writing.

One cannot do justice in a brief record to the Negro drama. Negro life is colorful and picturesque. It is full of both comedy and tragedy. Because the Negro has been a member of a submerged group and because he has come out of much tribulation he offers to the dramatist much rich material. It is not strange, therefore, that Eugene O'Neill and Paul Green, leaders of the new drama among white people, should turn to the Negro for subjects. Nor is it strange that the most powerful play on the New York stage during the last ten years — Marcus C. Connelly's *Green Pastures* — should have a Negro theme. Alain Locke and Montgomery Gregory have compiled twenty such plays,[1] about half of which are written by Negroes, and half written by white people using Negro themes. These plays are rich in dramatic color and have within them powerful passions which make them vital. The Negro not only lives in the midst of dramatic settings but he has great power as a dramatist. His ability to see the other man's point of view, and sympathize with it, will carry him far in this field of endeavor. The plays of Negro life presented to enthusiastic audiences throughout America have gone far and will go further in breaking down racial prejudice.

It remains only to say a word about the Negro press. As early as 1827 Samuel E. Cornish and John Russwurm published the first number of *Freedom's Journal*. Another paper, called the *Colored American*, appeared ten years later, edited in turn by Cornish, Phillip A. Bell, and James McCune Smith. Ten years later (1847) Frederick Douglass established his famous paper, the *North Star*, for the founding of which funds had been subscribed in England. Frederick G. Detweiler tells us that twenty-four Negro periodicals appeared before the Civil War.[2] Douglass tells us he established his paper, the *North Star*, to demonstrate that Negroes had ability, and doubtless others were established with similar intent, though the ultimate aim of all these papers was winning freedom for the Negro slave.

After the Civil War weekly papers began to arise, the *Washington Bee* and the *Indianapolis World* being among the first. It was not until the first and second decades of the present century that successful dailies could be established. The *Baltimore Daily Herald* seems to have been one of these. Ten years ago Detweiler listed eighty-three religious papers, forty-five organs of fraternal orders, eighty college publications, thirty-one trade journals, and two hundred fifty-three periodicals and newspapers.[3] This is a very formidable list when one remembers that at least one of these, the *Chicago Defender*, claims 150,000 circulation. Detweiler thinks the combined circulation of all these papers is over a million.[4] Almost every important city in America has one or more such Negro publications. Philadelphia has fifteen, Baltimore has seven, Chicago has fifteen, and New York has seventeen; many of the southern cities have two

[1] *Plays of Negro Life.* [2] *The Negro Press in the United States*, p. 39.
[3] *Ibid.*, p. 4. [4] *Ibid.*, p. 7.

or more, besides having large lists of subscribers for some of the prominent northern publications. Magazines of the type of the *Crisis*, established in 1910, have had a large influence.

These papers are widely and eagerly read and are doubtless having a large influence in moulding public opinion among Negroes. They have large significance in building morale among colored people, through giving them a sense of independence and self-respect. They are therefore a large social force. It is important to know what they represent. A careful clipping of forty representative papers for a year brought the following convictions. Negro papers are first of all race papers. They are first and foremost interested in the advancement of the race. A large percentage of the editorials are concerned with justice to the race, with equal privileges, with facts of race progress, or with complaint against conditions as they are. Of course there occur from time to time well written editorials on topics of general interest, such as world peace, better political adjustment, or the progress of civilization; but it still remains true that most of the editorials are distinctly racial. The articles in these papers are usually propaganda — that is, they follow the line of the editorials. A great many are genuinely inflammatory. Robert T. Kerlin quotes scores of such articles.[1] From the standpoint of world news it can hardly be said that many of these publications are real newspapers, although there are an Associated Negro Press and a National Negro Press Association. The purpose of both these bodies is to pool the interest of all the papers and provide common news for all. But as in the case of many white papers, the funds of many papers are too limited to permit them to avail themselves of the full services of these general agencies. The majority of the Negro papers are therefore purely local, just as are hundreds of papers edited by whites.

That these papers are having a large influence in unifying the Negro people, and that they are building up a sense of the difficulties which the Negro faces, cannot be doubted. It will be well for the whole of America to become aware of this very potent force. We believe its influence is for good; we believe it is on the side of progress; but we are aware that it may become a powerful influence for dissatisfaction unless there is a larger interest in human justice on the part of the whole American people.

The literary expression of the Negro is certainly here to stay. It is voluminous, it is often very well done, it is undoubtedly powerful.

[1] *The Voice of the Negro.*

If properly encouraged it can and will make a real contribution to the whole of American civilization. It should not remain neglected and unnoticed by the white people, for no one can understand the social processes of Negro life without knowing Negro literature.

PROBLEMS FOR STUDY

1. Would it be derogatory to the American Negro if we should find that he brought certain culture traits with him from Africa? Of what significance would it be?
2. Can we be sure that certain culture traits found both in America and in Africa have an African origin, rather than an origin in some other part of the world?
3. What elements in southern life were most conducive to producing a folk music? Why did not the Negro in other sections of America produce such music?
4. Have the folk stories of the American Negro either moral or social significance?
5. How do you account for the fact that a race completely untrained in music has given to America its most distinctive musical creations?
6. How much influence did the early slave "Narratives" and Harriet Beecher Stowe's *Uncle Tom's Cabin* have on the social thinking of ante-bellum times?
7. Can the Negro hope to produce a race literature? Would he be wise to do so if he could?
8. What qualities of Negro character lend themselves most readily to the creation of drama?
9. Can you account for the Negroes' somewhat modest success in producing novels?
10. What influence does the Negro press have in moulding social opinion among Negroes?

BIBLIOGRAPHY

Benjamin G. Brawley, *The Negro in Literature and Art in the United States* (1930).
Natalie C. Burlin, *Negro Folk-Songs* (1918).
Countee Cullen, *Caroling Dusk* (1927).
Frederick G. Detweiler, *The Negro Press in the United States* (1922).
Joel C. Harris, *Uncle Remus, His Songs and His Sayings* (1931).
James W. Johnson, *The Book of American Negro Poetry* (1922).
James W. Johnson, *The Book of American Negro Spirituals* (1925).
James W. Johnson, *The Second Book of Negro Spirituals* (1926).
Robert T. Kerlin, *The Voice of the Negro* (1920).

Henry E. Krehbiel, *Afro-American Folk-songs* (1914).
Alain Locke and Montgomery Gregory, *Plays of Negro Life* (1927).
Vernon Loggins, *The Negro Author* (1931).
Howard W. Odum and Guy B. Johnson, *The Negro and His Songs* (1925).
Newbell N. Puckett, *Folk Beliefs of the Southern Negro* (1926).
Newman I. White and Walter C. Jackson, *An Anthology of Verse by American Negroes* (1924).

CHAPTER XXV

NEGRO LEADERSHIP AND THE GROWTH OF RACE PRIDE

Not a few books of short biographies of successful or eminent Negroes have been written in recent years both by white persons and by Negro authors. In the first case the purpose has been to give to white youth an appreciation and respect for Negro leadership,[1] and in the second case the purpose has usually been to develop a sense of pride of race in the minds of Negro youth. Both efforts are commendable. Progress cannot be made in interracial relations until each group knows something of the leadership of the other, and it cannot be hoped that any group will make much progress until it comes to believe in its own possibilities.

Long ago Benjamin Kidd called attention to consciousness of kind as the basis of coöperation. People who do not feel a common bond do not easily work together. This bond may be one of a common religion, a common race, or a common task; but in every case it must give rise to like-mindedness. Two men will not work harmoniously together whose ideals are completely disparate. An honest man will not long be compatible with a thief; a patriot will find little fellowship with a traitor. In producing a like-mindedness, common race or common religion is not, of course, necessary. Two men may belong to widely separated religious communions and yet have other common purposes. Likewise some of the strongest friendships have developed between persons of widely differing ethnic groups. But other things being at all equal, the bond of common race or religion, or common cause, does much to develop coöperation. It is on this basis perhaps that some of these books of biography have been written. The Negro as a handicapped competitor in modern life needs all the encouragement he can have. He therefore needs a united interest, and pride in his own group will help to bring that interest.

[1] Cf. Ralph W. Bullock, *In Spite of Handicaps;* Arthur H. Fauset, *For Freedom;* Elizabeth R. Haynes, *Unsung Heroes; et al.*

Race consciousness has many sinister implications; but these implications are not inevitable. If by race pride one implies discounting other races or, still more, hating other races, then race pride is a positive evil. But this is not necessary. One may be a good American, and proud of his country, without having any sense that a Britisher is inferior or that one need hate him. Indeed, the essence of true patriotism would be the appreciation of the worth of our institutions and our people, and ought to be the basis of a real appreciation of all the culture and development of other peoples, as well as a new respect for those who have achieved such progress. Appreciation of my own home and my own family ought to give me a higher sense of values for all home life, and a deeper respect for all families.

It seems sane, therefore, to hope that this movement to develop a sense of race pride and race consciousness is in the direction of progress. That such pride is growing is clear to anyone who observes the trends of social life among Negroes. If one goes into the rural Negro schools of the South he will be struck by the fact that nine out of ten of them will have pictures of Dr. Booker T. Washington and Frederick Douglass. They are much more apt to have such pictures than are our rural white schools to have the pictures of George Washington and Robert E. Lee. There is a sense of pride in the achievements of these two great American Negroes, and the Negro child is being trained in the appreciation of such leadership. It will be a great mistake if anyone attempts to cut the Negro child off from an appreciation of George Washington or even of Lee, just as it seems to be a short-sighted policy to deprive the white child of the inspiration which would come from knowing the struggles and achievements of Booker T. Washington, but there is every advantage in developing race pride among Negro children through fostering enthusiasm for Negro leaders. By race pride we do not mean race segregation — we should achieve the opposite, which is respect for and appreciation of all other peoples. One of the great services which Booker T. Washington has rendered the two races in America has been the inspiring of confidence of the Negro in himself, and the creation of deeper appreciation of the white man for the Negro. While a student at Hampton, Washington tells us, he kept wondering why he could not find some biographies of Negroes who had achieved great success. He says other students laughed at him and told him Negroes could not achieve greatness. They were without race pride —

and perhaps one of the largest contributions to the Negro youth of today is his story, *Up from Slavery*, which is proof that a Negro can achieve. So long as all the virtues and achievements are in the white race, the Negro will want to get away from his own race and slip over into the white race, if possible. Any race would do the same. "But build him up. Make him sufficient in himself, give him within his own race life that which will satisfy, and the social question will be solved. The trained Negro is less and less inclined to lose himself in the sea of another race." [1] I find among the better and more cultured Negroes a new sense of pride. They are no longer ashamed to be Negroes. Dr. Washington used to say he was happy he was a Negro — in spite of all the handicaps. "Indeed," said he, "adverse criticism has driven them [the Negroes] to think deeper than they otherwise would about the problems which confront them as a race — to cling closer than they otherwise would have done to their own people, to value more highly than they once did the songs and records of their past life in slavery. The effect has been to give them, in short, that sort of race pride and race consciousness which, it seems to me, they need, to bring out and develop the best that is in them." [2]

Another indication of a growing race pride on the part of the Negro is the new appreciation of the past history of the race. One can remember the time when the young Negro did not care to sing the old spirituals. He felt they were a badge of slavery. When I wrote my first book on the Negro, in 1909, a northern man who was the secretary of an important city Y.M.C.A. wrote me about a Negro quartette of his city which wanted to come South to sing. My friend, in commending them, said they were "real artists and had gotten completely away from the old slave music." One wonders what he would say now if he heard a concert at Fisk where the finest musical talent is used in developing not only the themes of the spirituals but of the work songs as well. Another indication of this growing pride is the use of Negro motifs in Negro art. The best illustration of this is the mural decorations of the Fisk library, done by Aaron Douglas. He has made these a work of rare beauty and interest, because he has given them a distinctively Negro flavor. The new interest in Negro history, literature, and art is one of the most marked characteristics of Negro thinking today. Dr. Schomberg has done

[1] Willis D. Weatherford, *Negro Life in the South*, p. 173.
[2] *The Story of the Negro*, Vol. I, p. 12 ff.

a notable thing in collecting all the records of the Negro which he could find and putting them at the disposal of the Negroes of Harlem, in the 135th Street public library. This spirit has percolated down to the lowliest child in the city streets. A white lady teaching a Sunday School class of Negro boys recently announced that she would tell them a story of a boy who had achieved; as quick as a flash one little Negro boy said: "Miss, if it's a Negro boy all right, but if it's a white boy we don't want to hear it." The boy was at least half right in wanting to hear of the achievements of his own race. In the early struggles of the slaves this principle of race pride was well recognized. In the chapter on Negro literature we have noted that one of the earliest forms of writing was the narratives of runaway slaves. They had a double purpose in mind: first, to excite the sympathy of the abolitionists; and second, to inspire confidence and race pride in the slaves and free Negroes themselves. William C. Nell, with the idea in mind of creating race pride, published in 1851 *Services of Colored Americans in the Wars of 1776 and 1812*, and in 1855 he brought out *The Colored Patriots of the American Revolution, with Sketches of Several Distinguished Colored Persons*, to which was added a *Brief Survey of the Conditions and Prospects of Colored Americans*. The most important of all these biographies was the *Narrative of the Life of Frederick Douglass*, which appeared in its first edition in 1845. This life was rewritten and enlarged almost every year during Douglass' lifetime, and a score of biographies have appeared since his death. Some have thought it the most influential single biography yet written in America. George L. Ruffin, in writing the introduction to the life of Douglass printed in 1881, declares that "Frederick Douglass is the most remarkable contribution this country has given to the world." It is still put side by side with Washington's *Up from Slavery*, and perhaps the two are the most common possessions of Negro homes. We referred to the volume by William Wells Brown called *The Rising Son*. In this, Brown, after a rather labored study of the origins and history of the Negro, appends brief biographies of sixty-seven Negroes which he thought would develop a sense of confidence on the part of his people.

The Negro, slave and free, did produce many notable leaders during the pre-Civil War days. The first notable group to arise were the Negro preachers. One of the earliest of these preachers was George Liehle, who was born in 1750 in Virginia, but was carried in the seventies by his master, Henry Sharpe, to a plantation near Savannah, Georgia. George attended the Baptist church in company with his master and on his conversion desired to preach. He was permitted to preach up and down the Savannah river. His master finally freed George in order that he might give his entire time to preaching. The earliest Negro Baptist church in America was established at Silver Bluff, where George Liehle often preached. During the Revolutionary War he went with a British officer, Colonel Kirkland, to Jamaica, but before leaving he baptized Andrew Bryan, who founded the first Baptist church in Savannah, in 1788. Andrew Bryan was born at Goose Creek, South Carolina, where the earliest missionary work for Negroes had been started. George Liehle wrote, about 1790, that "Brother Andrew Bryan, has two hundred members, and certificates from the owners of one hundred more, ready to be baptised." [1]

Contemporaneous with Andrew Bryan and George Liehle, working in the South, were two famous Methodist Negro preachers working in the North. Richard Allen came under Christian influence in 1779 and began his work as a minister in 1780. He was a slave, but, as in the case of Bryan, his master allowed him liberty to preach. Allen finally purchased his freedom, and from time to time accepted appointments from Bishop Asbury. Starting with a prayer meeting in Philadelphia, he soon developed a considerable congregation which he proposed to organize into a separate church. At first the white people in the church objected to the separate Negro church, but when the number of Negroes in attendance became large they were more than willing to accept the separation. The first church building was dedicated in 1794, and Allen was made deacon by Asbury in 1799. In 1816 a group of representative Methodist Negroes met in Philadelphia to organize the African Methodist Episcopal church. Daniel Coker, a preacher from Baltimore, was elected the first bishop, but on his refusal of the office, Allen was elected. This denomination had established a local church in Charleston, South Carolina, under the leadership of Reverend Morris Brown, which reported a thousand members in 1817. Reverend Mr. Brown's work was so successful in Charleston that the church membership in five years had reached three thousand. Then the Denmark Vesey plot disturbed all South Carolina, and Brown to save his life escaped to the North, by the help of General James Hamilton. His elo-

[1] *Rippon's Condensed Register*, p. 335.

quence and his native ability as a preacher ultimately won for him a bishopric in his church.

All these men and many others were preachers of rare power. The Negro has great native ability as an orator. He has enthusiasm and imagination, his language is picturesque, and he has a ready sympathy which quickly puts him in communication with his audience. All these qualities these early preachers possessed in high degree, while added to them were the qualities of deep earnestness and genuine interest in their people. Any attempt to catalog these preachers of great power would make too lengthy a list, for there were hundreds of them who had more than a local reputation. Those of the earlier period would necessarily include Reverend Lemuel Haynes, born in 1753, Lott Carey (1780), Bishop Daniel A. Payne (1811), John Jasper (1812), Leonard A. Grimes (1815), Samuel Ringold Wood (1817), Alexander Crummel (1820), and Henry M. Tanner (1833). The list could be extended to great length. These names, however, will indicate something of the early leadership of Negro ministers.

In order to set forth their place in the early life of the Negro in America it seems well to give a brief account of the work of two of these pioneer preachers, Henry Evans and John Jasper. Bishop Capers presents that of Henry Evans during the first quarter of the nineteenth century.

But the most remarkable man in Fayetteville when I went there, and who died during my stay, was a negro, by the name of Henry Evans. I say the most remarkable in view of his class; and I call him negro with unfeigned respect. He was a negro: that is, he was of that race, without any admixture of another. The name simply designates the race, and it is vulgar to regard it with opprobrium. I have known and loved and honored not a few negroes in my life, who were probably as pure of heart as Evans, or anybody else. Such were my old friends, Castile Selby and John Boquet, of Charleston, Will Campbell and Harry Myrick, of Wilmington, York Cohen, of Savannah, and others I might name. These I might call remarkable for their goodness. But I use the word in a broader sense for Henry Evans, who was confessedly the father of the Methodist Church, white and black, in Fayetteville, and the best preacher of his time in that quarter; and who was so remarkable, as to have become the greatest curiosity of the town; insomuch that distinguished visitors hardly felt that they might pass a Sunday in Fayetteville without hearing him preach. Evans was from Virginia; a shoemaker by trade, and, I think, was born free. He became a Christian and a Methodist quite young, and was licensed to preach in Virginia. While yet a young man, he determined to remove to Charleston, S. C., thinking he might succeed best there at his trade. But having reached Fayetteville on his way to Charleston, and something detaining him for a few days, his spirit was stirred at perceiving that the people of his race in that town were wholly given to profanity and lewdness, never hearing preaching of any denomination, and living emphatically without hope and without God in the world. This determined him to stop in Fayetteville; and he began to preach to the Negroes, with great effect. The town council interfered, and nothing in his power could prevail with them to permit him to preach. He then withdrew to the sand-hills, out of town, and held meetings in the woods, changing his appointments from place to place. No law was violated, while the council was effectually eluded; and so the opposition passed into the hands of the mob. These he worried out by changing his appointments, so that when they went to work their will upon him, he was preaching somewhere else. Meanwhile, whatever the most honest purpose of a simple heart could do to reconcile his enemies, was employed by him for that end. He eluded no one in private, but sought opportunities to explain himself; avowed the purity of his intentions; and even begged to be subjected to the scrutiny of any surveillance that might be thought proper to prove his inoffensiveness; any thing, so that he might but be allowed to preach. Happily for him and the cause of religion, his honest countenance and earnest pleadings were soon powerfully seconded by the fruits of his labors. One after another began to suspect their servants of attending his preaching, not because they were made worse, but wonderfully better. The effect on the public morals of the negroes, too, began to be seen, particularly as regarded their habits on Sunday, and drunkenness. And it was not long before the mob was called off by a change in the current of opinion, and Evans was allowed to preach in town. At that time there was not a single church edifice in town, and but one congregation, (Presbyterian), who worshipped in what was called the State-house, under which was the market; and it was plainly Evans or nobody to preach to the negroes. Now, too, of the mistresses there were not a few, and some masters, who were brought to think that the preaching which had proved so beneficial to their servants might be good for them also; and the famous negro preacher had some whites as well as blacks to hear him. Seats, distinctly separated, were at first appropriated to the whites, near the pulpit. But Evans had already become famous, and these seats were insufficient. Indeed, the negroes seemed likely to lose their preacher, negro though he was, while the whites, crowded out of their appropriate seats, took possession of those in the rear. Meanwhile Evans had represented to the preacher of Bladen Circuit how things were going, and induced him to take his meeting-house into the circuit, and constitute a church there. And now, there was no longer room for the negroes in the house when Evans preached; and for the accommodation of both classes, the weatherboards were knocked off and sheds were added to the house on either side; the whites occupying the whole of the original building, and the negroes those sheds as a part of the same house.[1]

The other picture of a slave preacher is that of John Jasper of Richmond, Virginia, who was born on a slave plantation in 1812. Working as a tobacco stemmer in a Richmond tobacco factory, converted after he was a mature man, never receiving any education more than mere ability to read and write, he yet became one of the most powerful voices in his day. Let a newspaper reporter tell you what he was like:

The man in question was a negro, and if you cannot appreciate greatness in a black skin you would do well to turn your thoughts into some other channel. Moreover, he was a negro covered over with ante bellum habits and ways of doing. He lived forty years before the war and for about forty years after it. He grew wonderfully as a freeman; but he never grew away from the tastes, dialects, and manners of the bondage times. He was a man left over from the old regime and never got infected with the new order. The air of the educated negro preacher didn't set well upon him. The raw scholarship of the new "ish," as he called it, was sounding brass to him. As a fact, the new generation of negro preachers sent out by the schools drew back from this man. They branded him as an anachronism, and felt that his presence in the pulpit was a shock to religion and an offense to the ministry; and yet not one of them ever attained the celebrity or achieved the results which came to this unlettered and grievously ungrammatical son of Africa.

But do not be afraid that you are to be fooled into the fanatical camp. This story comes from the pen of a Virginian who claims no exemption from Southern prejudices and feels no call to sound the praises of the negro race. Indeed, he never intended to write what is contained within the covers of this book. It grew up spontaneously and most of the contents were written before the book was thought of.

More than that, the writer of this never had any intention of bothering with this man when he first loomed up into notoriety. He got drawn in unexpectedly. He heard that there was a marvel of a man "over in Africa," a not too savoury portion of Richmond, Virginia, — and one Sunday afternoon in company with a Scot-Irishman, who was a scholar and a critic, with a strong leaning towards ridicule, he went to hear him preach. Shades of our Anglo-Saxon fathers! Did mortal lips ever gush with such torrents of horrible English! Hardly a word came out clothed and in its right mind. And gestures! He circled around the pulpit with his ankle in his hand; and laughed and sang and shouted and acted about a dozen characters within the space of three minutes. Meanwhile, in spite of these things, he was pouring out a gospel sermon, red hot, full of love, full of invective, full of tender-

[1] William M. Wightman, *Life of William Capers*, pp. 124–127.

ness, full of bitterness, full of tears, full of every passion that ever flamed in the human breast. He was a theatre within himself, with the stage crowded with actors. He was a battle-field; — himself the general, the staff, the officers, the common soldiery, the thundering artillery and the rattling musketry. He was the preacher; likewise the church and the choir and the deacons and the congregation. The Scot-Irishman surrendered in fifteen minutes after the affair commenced, but the other man was hard-hearted and stubborn and refused to commit himself. He preferred to wait until he got out of doors and let the wind blow on him and see what was left. He determined to go again; and he went and kept going, off and on, for twenty years. That was before the negro became a national figure. It was before he startled his race with his philosophy as to the rotation of the sun. It was before he became a lecturer and a sensation, sought after from all parts of the country. Then it was that he captured the Scot-Irish and the other man also. What is written here constitutes the gatherings of nearly a quarter of a century, and, frankly speaking, is a tribute to the brother in black, — the one unmatched, unapproached, and wonderful brother.[1]

These two statements indicate something of the power of the early Negro preachers. They were the leaders of their race. Perhaps more than any other influence they moulded the race. They were the forerunners of the present Negro preacher, who is still perhaps the most influential leader of his people.

"The Negro church is the only social institution which started in the forest [of Africa] and survived slavery. . . . The church preserved in itself the remnants of African tribal life, and became after emancipation the center of Negro social life." [2] In 1926 there were 42,585 Negro churches, valued at $205,782,628, with a membership of 5,203,487.[3] The 1926 census report does not give the number of Negro ministers, but the corresponding record for 1916 reports three Baptist organizations with 20,317 ministers, and five Methodist organizations with 15,607 ministers.[4] The census abstract for 1928 gives the total number of Negro ministers as 19,571, but this obviously is an error.[5] The total number of Negro ministers is therefore between 36,000 and 40,000. This group of churches and

---

[1] William E. Hatcher, *John Jasper, the Unmatched Negro Philosopher and Preacher*, pp. 7–10.

[2] *Efforts for Social Betterment among Negro Americans*, edited by William E. B. Du Bois. Atlanta University Publication No. 14, p. 16.

[3] Census Report. Religious Bodies, 1926, Vol. I, pp. 71 and 758.

[4] *Ibid.*, 1916, p. 66.

[5] *Statistical Abstract of the United States*, 1928, p. 56.

their ministers are the most potent influence for good or evil which the Negro race has. One says good or evil, for an ultra-conservative church led by an ultra-conservative, ignorant, and superstitious pastor may become a serious block, not only to progress but to simple morality. Carter Woodson, in his volume on the Negro church, puts great emphasis on the institution as the present hope of Negro life.[1] Since the Negro lodges have not on the whole developed social halls, the church has supplied that need for the race. It is also the educational center for the adults of the race. Here ideas are exchanged, and in former days the minister, being the best informed among them, became, as it were, their teacher. The church is gradually becoming the social service center for all Negro welfare work. This is a comparatively new feature of the church, but is probably destined to play a larger and larger part in the church's work in the future. The church is also the political center of the life of the Negro. It was not by accident that a large proportion of the political leaders of the race during reconstruction days were ordained ministers. They were the men who had led the people, and they had led the people because they were the ones who had discussed with them, in the church, the issues of the day. The political thinking of the Negro people today is largely moulded by the church. Unfortunately, the Negro church has not served the boys and girls of the race as well as it has the older people, and the growing gap between the educated youth and the influences of religion is in part due to this fact. In the survey of the Negro boy of Nashville, it was found that the Negro church made decidedly less appeal to the Negro boy after he passed the elementary grades in school. The average attendance at Sunday School of all the 3,063 day school boys reported was 52.4, but the average attendance at Sunday School of the Pearl High School boys was only 44.1. One would have expected the percentage to be higher here, for the high school undoubtedly represents the more privileged class of Negro families.[2] Many of the 126 Nashville Negro churches are doing very little for the Negro boy because their equipment is

[1] *The History of the Negro Church.* This volume has serious defects. It is not documented; thus there immediately arises the question of its thoroughness. Wherever it touches the relation of the Negro church to the white people it is bitter and prejudiced, a fact which robs it of the dispassionate spirit of history. It is often fulsome in its praise of the church. Nevertheless it has much valuable material.

[2] Willis D. Weatherford (Ed.), *A Survey of the Negro Boy in Nashville, Tennessee*, p. 126.

so inadequate, and their financial resources are so limited, that they can furnish neither opportunity nor leadership for a real boy's program. Data now being gathered indicate "that poor location, meager physical equipment, buildings in poor repair, little provision for religious education, low financial status, inadequate both in number and preparation, and small congregations, greatly handicap the majority of the Negro churches of Nashville." [1]

The weaknesses of the Negro church are numerous and glaring. But in spite of all its weaknesses, it is a great power. The 36,000 or more ministers are the heart and core of Negro leadership. It is here that one finds a sharp challenge. Many of these preachers are densely ignorant, and many are deeply superstitious. The picture which William A. Daniel gives of the training of Negro ministers is not altogether reassuring.[2] There are fifty-two schools which attempt to train ministers, but the majority of them are simply departments of a college with one or two or more theological teachers. The students accepted are often inadequately prepared, and frequently they are not of the highest grade of leadership. In view of the importance of the Negro minister in the leadership of the race, a most strategic move would be to lift this whole training process to a new level.

But of course there are notable exceptions. Many of the best Negro ministers have received excellent training from the best Negro seminaries, and others have graduated from the best white seminaries of the North. From place to place over the country an outstanding Negro minister is leading wisely and well. Such an example is that of Dr. W. M. De Berry, pastor of a Congregational church in Springfield, Massachusetts. "The church has a well equipped modern plant so beautifully located and managed as to attract large numbers. It has moreover a parish home for working girls, and a branch church at Amherst, Massachusetts. In the main plant are maintained a free employment bureau, a women's welfare league, a girls' and a boys' club, emphasizing the handicrafts, music and athletics. This church has solved the problem of supplying the needs of the people during the week, as well as their spiritual needs on Sunday." [3] I visited a church in Jacksonville, Florida, which

[1] Willis D. Weatherford (Ed.), *A Survey of the Negro Boy in Nashville, Tennessee*, p. 129.
[2] *The Education of Negro Ministers*.
[3] Carter G. Woodson, *The History of the Negro Church*, p. 277.

is doing equally good work. Atlanta, Nashville, and many other southern cities have individual churches which are serving as centers of life and influence. The number must be increased. More ministers of Dr. De Berry's type must be raised up, more well equipped churches must be erected, many inadequate ones must be abandoned, and the Negro preacher, who is still the most important leader of his race, must be given a more adequate opportunity. In many ways he is the one free voice among Negroes, and that voice must be made constructive and powerful.

Next to the Negro minister stands the Negro doctor in the leadership of the race. According to the census figures of 1928 there were 3,495 physicians and surgeons, and 1,109 dentists, among the Negro people.[1] In Africa the medicine man was perhaps the most influential member of society. He dispensed life and death with a high hand. Much of his activity was a pure practice of fetishism. But he did by experience come to know and use herbs and roots which were beneficial to human health. Naturally the prerogatives of this class of persons were taken up by certain slaves in America. The conjure doctors of the American slaves used their art more frequently for evil purposes than for good, but at times they showed real knowledge of curative art. As early as 1792 a Negro by the name of Cæsar had gained such distinction for his curative knowledge of roots and herbs that the Assembly of South Carolina purchased his freedom and gave him an annuity of one hundred pounds,[2] presumably that he might practice his art for the benefit of the slaves. Other Negroes who claimed to be herb doctors, who drew teeth, and who could bleed people, are referred to in early documents. Andrew Jackson's Negro body servant often bled him even after he entered the White House.[3] James Derham, born a slave in 1762, and finally owned by Dr. Robert Dove of New Orleans, was the first Negro to be recognized as a practicing physician. He learned his profession largely in the office of his master, though Dr. Benjamin Rush is said to have found him "perfectly acquainted" with his art.[4] The American Colonization Society, organized in Washington, D. C., in 1816, immediately faced the necessity of training leaders for those Negroes who were to be sent

---

[1] *Statistical Abstract of the United States, 1928*, p. 56.
[2] *Journal of Negro History*, April, 1916, pp. 101–102.
[3] James Parton, *Life of General Jackson*, Vol. III, p. 63.
[4] *Journal of Negro History*, April, 1916, p. 103.

to Liberia. The sixth annual report (1823) says: "The Board are well convinced that an institution which might receive under its patronage colored youths destined for the colony, impart to them a knowledge of agriculture and the useful arts, and educate them, in such manner as should best tend to insure their industry, economy, subordination and religion, would prove of incalculable advantage to this cause."[1] Ten years later, arrangements had been made to educate in New York three young men of color for the medical profession in Liberia. A Dr. Henderson had agreed to take these young men into his office and give them regular instruction.[2] It was thought that training men for medicine would not only insure the health of the colony but would induce more volunteers as emigrants, since it would open the door for them to these professions. In June of 1835 the *Jupiter* sailed from New York with a company of Liberian colonists aboard, and among the number was a Dr. Robert McDonall, a colored physician. Charles H. Webb, a colored man who was a medical student, was also listed, it being stated that he would continue his studies with the other physicians in Liberia.[3] This young man soon paid the price of heroism with his life, dying of fever on October 20.[4] That some of the young men who were helped to get a medical education by the Colonization Society did not wish to go to Liberia is proved by a complaint in the society's annual report of 1834. There the expenditure for medical education is called "unprofitable to a large extent," and the names of three students whom the society had educated, but who refused to fulfill their contracts, were given. Washington Davis, Page C. Dunlap and James H. Fleet were the three so named.[5] It is interesting to note that Davis is mentioned as still a student in the report of 1835.[6]

About the time that the Colonization Society began training colored physicians for Liberia, two important Negro physicians began to practice in America. James McCune Smith, a graduate of the University of Georgia, began practice in New York City in 1837. He attained some note as a physician and entered into the discussions of comparative anatomy on which were based certain claims as to the inferiority of the Negro.[7] The other early physician

---

[1] *Sixth Annual Report of the American Colonization Society*, p. 16.
[2] *African Repository*, November, 1832, p. 285. [3] *Ibid.*, February, 1835, p. 55.
[4] *Ibid.*, June, 1835, p. 177. [5] *Ibid.*, August, 1834, p. 165.
[6] *Ibid.*, August, 1835, p. 249. [7] *Journal of Negro History*, April, 1916, p. 104.

LEADERSHIP AND RACE PRIDE 501

who acquired considerable public notice was Martin R. Delany, born at Charlestown, Virginia, in 1812. He began the study of medicine in 1835. He was refused entrance into the Medical Department of the University of Pennsylvania, Jefferson Medical, and the Medical Colleges of Albany and Geneva, New York, but was received into the Harvard Medical School, where he graduated. He had a long and checkered career, being traveler, soldier, and physician. He served in the Civil War and was later made a major. He died in 1885.[1] He thus became the forerunner of the modern medical profession.

Most of the Negro physicians of the present day are graduates of either Meharry Medical College in Nashville, or of Howard Medical College in Washington. The Rosenwald investigator of Negro hospitals in 1931 sent out questionnaires to 1,035 Negro physicians who had graduated between 1918 and 1928. Of this number 630 replied. Of the 630, Meharry graduates numbered 286 or 45.41 per cent, Howard graduates numbered 259 or 41.18 per cent, and graduates of all other schools numbered 85 or 13.35 per cent. Only 34 per cent of these 630 physicians resided in the South, where the bulk of the Negro population is to be found.[2] Facts gathered by this Rosenwald investigator indicate that Negroes have considerable trouble in securing internships, and when ready for practice have difficulty in getting hospital facilities. It is well known also that Negroes experience more or less difficulty in gaining access to white medical colleges, as was the case with Martin Delany. Du Bois has set this forth in fiction in the story *Black Princess*. This is not so serious now as it was formerly, since both Meharry and Howard are well equipped. Meharry has just been removed from its old location in South Nashville, and is now located by the side of Fisk University, with a new equipment costing approximately $2,000,000, and with a first-class medical faculty. The leading physicians of the city, both colored and white, are among its teachers. The Negro physician is even more than his white brother a leader in his community. The inspiring story of Louis Thompkins Wright, now practicing in Harlem, can be read in Miss M. W. Ovington's *Portraits in Color*. Born in Georgia, educated at Clark in Atlanta, and at Howard Medical College, refused internship in Boston, winning

---

[1] William J. Simmons, *Men of Mark*, p. 1007 ff.

[2] *Negro Hospitals*, p. 42. This is a compilation of available statistics, issued by the Julius Rosenwald Fund.

some distinction during the World War, he has had a career full of interest. Or one can turn to a brilliant physician of Nashville, Tennessee, Dr. C. V. Roman. He is a practicing physician, a professor in Meharry Medical College, a brilliant speaker, an author of some note, and a citizen of rare insight and unselfish motives. No good movement of his city fails to elicit his interest and coöperation. Along with the ministers of Nashville the group of progressive Negro physicians are among the most influential citizens.

Medicine has offered to the colored woman an opportunity which the ministry has not afforded. As early as 1854 we hear of Dr. Emily Blackwell, a Negro woman physician, who had just graduated at Western Reserve Medical College, and who was a visiting interne at Bellevue Hospital. The Atlanta University Studies, No. 11, reported 160 women physicians among Negroes in 1900,[1] all of whom were perhaps not in practice. Dr. Sara W. Brown claims there were 65 colored women practicing medicine in 1920 and 35 practicing dentistry.[2] At least one of the women physicians served overseas during the World War and was decorated by the French government. In the *Crisis* for February, 1933, there is a thrilling article about the struggle of a colored girl to get a medical education, her victory, and her real contribution to the social life of a section of Philadelphia. In no other calling perhaps could this young woman, Dr. Alexander, make so large a contribution to her people.

It is not necessary to refer to the 35,442 school teachers who are making a contribution to the Negro race which is both inspiring and far-reaching. They are leaders *par excellence*. In 1928 there were 1,095 Negro actors, 259 artists, sculptors, and teachers of art, 5,902 musicians and teachers of music. Their contribution to the race is of first importance. Two or three brief records will show the place of leadership of these workers. Meta Warrick Fuller is one of the best known sculptors. She was born in Philadelphia and went through the School of Industrial Arts there. In 1899 she went to Paris to study. After three years of study there, her work was highly complimented by Rodin, who said: "Mademoiselle, you are a sculptor. You have the sense of form in your fingers."[3] She modeled the Negro group of figures at the Jamestown exposition in 1907. She was the sculptor of the "Spirit of Emancipation" which

---

[1] P. 96.
[2] "Colored Women Physicians," *Southern Workman*, December, 1923, p. 581.
[3] Mary W. Ovington, *Portraits in Color*, p. 221.

was the central piece in the fiftieth anniversary celebration of the Emancipation Proclamation. She has had exhibits at the Boston Public Library and, judged by any standard, would be considered one of the gifted sulptors in America.

Roland Hayes was born in Curryville, Georgia. When he was a young boy his parents moved to Chattanooga, where he worked in a sash weight factory or foundry. He sang in the church choir, and his choir leader, discovering that the boy had a remarkable voice, encouraged him to cultivate it. He studied four years at Fisk University, and later sang with the Fisk Jubilee Singers. Finally he went to Boston, where he studied under Arthur Hubbard. In May, 1915, he sang in Carnegie Hall, but got no real recognition. His first conspicuous success came at Symphony Hall in Boston in 1918. In 1920 he went to London. He was commanded to sing at Buckingham Palace by King George, and the whole of Europe was open to him. He was awarded the Spingarn Medal, 1924. He has one of the truest and most musical tenor voices on the concert platform today. His singing of the spirituals is profoundly affecting. He has lifted the thought of the Negro ability to a high level, and has become one of the leaders of the race who have inspired thousands of Negro youths.[1]

If one turns to the scientific world one immediately thinks of Dr. George Carver of Tuskegee, the wizard of chemistry, who was born just as the Civil War was closing (1864), in a one-room cabin in Missouri. With very slender physical strength and no money, he got his earliest education wandering through the woods and observing flowers and trees and buds. At twelve he entered an elementary school, and finally prepared himself to enter the University of Iowa. He was a student at that university when I first came to know him, at a Student Conference at Lake Geneva, Wisconsin. While in college he did almost every form of menial work, from washing to cooking, to pay his way. In college he studied science, music, and art. Competent judges say his paintings are of rare quality, though few know of his ability in this field. In 1896 he went to Tuskegee to teach, but really to become a research expert in chemistry. As one goes with him through his laboratory, one feels he is in the presence of real ability. Carver has followed Booker Washington's great injunction to "let down your bucket where you are." He has taken the common clays of Alabama and wrung from them beautiful and

[1] *Ibid.*, p. 227 ff.

lasting paints. He has taken the despised peanut and produced from it two hundred useful products. These include milk, cream, coffee, shoe polish, face lotions, breakfast foods, flour, and dozens of other articles of common use. From the sweet potato, which is one of Alabama's chief products, he has made more than a hundred articles of common use. From this he made hard rubber, tapioca, flour, crystallized ginger, and other things too numerous to mention. He, too, has become a leader inspiring Negro youth.

As our last illustration of Negro leadership let us turn to a young man, Paul Robeson, who was born at Princeton, New Jersey, in 1898. Unlike Dr. Carver he had ample opportunities. His father, though born a slave, was a college graduate, a minister of the gospel, a leader among his people. When Paul was quite young his mother died, and his aunt from North Carolina came to keep house for his father. In this manner the memories and customs of the old South were revived in his home. This had much to do with his sympathy and understanding of the southern Negro life from which the spirituals sprang, and out of the rich romance of which the Negro drama is developing.

Robeson went to Rutgers, where he became not only a leading football star — he was selected for an All American team — but also a member of Phi Beta Kappa. It is not usual for any student to be such an outstanding athlete and student combined. After his college career, he entered the law school of Columbia University, where he graduated. He then began the practice of law, but was not happy in this work. He knew Eugene O'Neill, and was by chance offered the opportunity to take the part of Jim Harris in O'Neill's play, *All God's Chillun Got Wings*. It was more than a success; so an earlier and more powerful play of O'Neill's was revived — *Emperor Jones* — and Robeson was given the leading part. He made a wonderful hit. The play was taken to London, where his success was immediate and brilliant. The critics reported him as the greatest dramatic find of decades. This was in 1924, when he was only twenty-six years of age. Returning to America, he was invited to work with Lawrence Brown in a concert at the Greenwich Village Theatre. Robeson was not a trained musician; he knew little or no music, but he had a wonderful voice; what was more, he had a sympathetic understanding of the Negro spirituals. The concert was a great success. At twenty-seven, therefore, Robeson was a recognized actor, and one of the most popular singers of Negro spirituals in New York.

He is a man of tremendous physical vigor, of deep culture, of artistic nature, and of high ambition.

As Micah in that wonderful sixth chapter of his prophecy was reminding the Hebrew people of Jehovah's goodness to them, he exclaimed: "He hath sent before thee, Moses, Aaron, and Miriam." Surely Jehovah could have done nothing greater for them than to send them great leaders. One could change a passage from Scripture and say that "where there are no leaders the people perish." The Negro people have been fortunate in having, even during slavery, men who were real leaders. As they have been advancing in education their leadership has multiplied. Ministers, doctors, lawyers, teachers, musicians, artists, literary men, and dramatic geniuses, all these are rising in sufficient numbers to set a new goal for the race. No Negro youth need any longer wonder whether his people can produce great leaders. Those who have watched the Negro actor, or who have followed the development of the Negro author, are led to believe that this race will make a great contribution to the culture of the modern world. They have a richness of emotion, a depth of sympathetic understanding, a passion of expression, which will lead them far in making this cultural contribution. Those white people who are most discerning are looking with great expectancy to what these leaders may do for the Negro race and for our common civilization. The growth of race consciousness and the development of a race pride due to such leadership are social phenomena which none of us can afford to pass over lightly or fail to recognize.

PROBLEMS FOR STUDY

1. If Carlyle's *Heroes and Hero Worship* is true to life, what bearing would his theories have on Negro leadership and the development of the Negro race?
2. Should Negroes be encouraged to depend on their own leaders (doctors, preachers, teachers, artists) only or should they look to the whites as well?
3. Why did the Negro preacher develop first among Negro leaders?
4. Why does the Negro preacher have such disproportionately large influence among his people?
5. Negro physicians may not practice even in the colored wards of hospitals in most cities. Why is this, and what should be done about it?
6. Is it wise to give Negro professional workers highly technical training?
7. Should the story of Negro leaders be placed in our school readers both for white and black pupils?

BIBLIOGRAPHY

Benjamin G. Brawley, *A Short History of the American Negro* (1931).
William W. Brown, *The Black Man, His Antecedents, His Genius and His Achievements* (1865).
William E. Hatcher, *John Jasper* (1908).
Robert R. Moton, *What the Negro Thinks* (1929).
Mary W. Ovington, *Portraits in Color* (1927).
Benjamin F. Riley, *The Life and Times of Booker T. Washington* (1916).
Charles V. Roman, *American Civilization and the Negro* (1916).
Booker T. Washington, *The Story of the Negro* (1924).
Booker T. Washington, *Up from Slavery* (1924).
George W. Williams, *History of the Negro Race in America, 1619–1880* (1885).

CHAPTER XXVI

CHANGING ATTITUDES OF WHITE PEOPLE

Attitudes are the outgrowth of long usage. Any society as it undertakes to meet the exigencies of life finds certain ways of acting more satisfactory and profitable than others. These ways may not be the best ways, by any means; but they are the best ways which that society has discovered. By long usage these particular ways harden into customs and dominate the thinking and attitudes of the people. When once an attitude has become stabilized, it becomes almost all-powerful. To go counter to it, to criticize it, or even to dare to discuss it, is rank heresy. The mores of a people have the authority of facts. To that people they are the supreme facts. They are not analyzed, they are simply accepted. Every child is born into these mores and never dares or even thinks to question them. It is for this reason that W. G. Sumner, in his monumental volume on folkways, claims that "it is not possible to change them by any artifice or devise, to a great extent, or suddenly, or in any essential element. It is possible to modify them by slow and long continued effort, if the ritual is changed by minute variation." [1] It is precisely this problem we face when we talk about changing attitudes in race relations.

We have seen something of the customs and ideals of the white people during slavery days. The sudden cataclysm of the Civil War did not wholly change these ideals. To be sure there was a different status of the Negro which called for a new set of actions on the part of the whites, but attitudes toward the Negro were not greatly changed. So true was this that the northern white man still wanted to treat him as his ward rather than treat him as a man who must stand on his own two feet, and the southern white man could not conceive of him as anything other than one who should obey orders. The conflict of northern and southern opinion brought on the bitter days of reconstruction, in which both extreme opinions tended to harden down into dogma. The way in which this

[1] P. 87.

southern attitude has developed into a dogma, accepted alike by white and black, is brought out in a recent novel by Welbourn Kelley, called *Inchin' Along*. Lige, who works for "Mist' Henry" wants to change his job, but in despair he exclaims to his friend: "But yo' know as good as me dat ef'n he say I cain' lef' 'im, — I cain' lef' 'im."

The dogma of the white man asserted that the Negro was inferior; that he was fit only for manual labor; that he really had no rights which were inherent; that anything done for him was a gratuity; that he must not associate with white people; and that any white person who associated with Negroes thereby put himself not on a plane with Negroes but far beneath them. Whenever a Negro seemed to show any tendency to leadership it was attributed to some white blood which had found its way into the Negro race. Sometimes the dogma went to the extent of declaring the Negro had no soul. In 1867, B. H. Payne, writing under the pseudonym of Ariel, published a pamphlet of forty-eight pages in which he attempted to prove by the Bible that the Negro was a beast and had no soul. The pamphlet, first written in 1840, ends with a flourish, in these words: "The finger of God is in this. Trust him. The Bible is true." [1] To this Dr. Robert A. Young published in Nashville, Tennessee (1867), a reply which closes with a malediction on the head of Ariel, and an admonition that he who takes away from the words of the book (Bible), God will take him out of the book of life.[2] This conception did not die with slavery, for as late as 1900 we find one Charles Carroll writing from St. Louis, Missouri, *The Negro a Beast*. The subscript to the author's name declares he spent fifteen years and $20,000 in compiling the book. To this book we have an answer by Dr. William G. Schell, "proving that the Negro is human, from biblical, scientific and historical standpoints." [3] Not satisfied with Schell's answer, Reverend W. S. Armistead published at Tifton, Georgia, in 1903, *The Negro Is a Man*, a scurrilous volume which quotes the Bible freely and seems to know all the facts—it even has a picture of Adam and Eve, coming straight out of heaven. The whole story and its actors would be ridiculous and laughable, were it not for the fact that it represents the tremendous power of mores to persist in spite of progress. Such illustrations almost convince one that Sumner is wholly right and mores cannot be changed. But when one

[1] "The Negro: What Is His Ethnological Status?" p. 48.
[2] "The Negro: A Reply to Ariel," p. 37.
[3] *Is the Negro a Beast?*

looks again, he cannot but see hope, and continue to work at the task.

In 1881 Atticus G. Haygood, then a professor at Emory College, Oxford, Georgia, later one of the most loved and influential bishops of the Methodist Episcopal Church South, wrote a book called *Our Brother in Black, His Freedom and His Future*. It was straightforward, honest, sympathetic. It faced the ugly facts of life among Negroes, but it saw also rays of hope. It told the southern people the Negroes were here to stay, they were free, and we must develop a new attitude toward them. He refused to discuss slavery, for he considered it a dead issue, and he said: "There are more living ones [issues] than we can manage."[1] He called upon both North and South to "cool off and recognize the truth of things."[2] His amazing foresight told him the relation of white and black was a "national race problem."[3] He saw and commended the white women who came from the North to teach colored children, although he deplored some of their mistakes. He took account of many deeds of kindness which he saw white people performing every day on behalf of Negroes. He insisted that the Negro was a neighbor and a member of the community.[4] In 1889 Haygood published another book, called *Pleas for Progress*. In it he threw his whole influence behind a program of education for the Negro. At the time these books appeared they were amazing for their sanity, their courage, and their vision. They were the beginning of a new attitude toward the Negro. They were read by thousands, especially among the Methodists, and undoubtedly did much to set new trends in thought and attitude.

In 1900 Edgar Gardiner Murphy, a native of Arkansas, a graduate of the University of the South and Yale, a rector of the Episcopal church, organized the Southern Society for the Consideration of Race Problems, which held its first conference in Montgomery, Alabama, in 1900. He published *The Present South* in 1904 and *The Basis of Ascendancy* in 1909. These volumes dealt with the underlying principles of social development, and in particular faced the complications in social thinking and planning which a bi-racial civilization entailed.

The same year that Murphy organized this southern society, Booker T. Washington brought out his volume, *Up from Slavery*, which was the first Negro biography to be widely read in the South. In 1909 the present writer published a book, *Negro Life in the South*,

[1] P. 40. [2] *Ibid.*, p. 100. [3] *Ibid.*, p. 118 ff. [4] *Ibid.*, p. 183.

which was a textbook for volunteer study classes in the student Y.M.C.A.'s of the country. Along with this volume there went a definite movement to induce college men and women to undertake activities for the welfare of Negroes. On many campuses the colored janitors and maids were organized into study clubs led by the white students. In one state university the students coöperated in organizing a City Welfare League for Negroes. In another the women of the campus fitted up a residence for a club house, where the white students conducted activities for Negro boys. In dozens of colleges the white students went out to Negro churches to teach Negro boys in Sunday School and to organize play and recreative activities. All this called for elemental information; hence the little study book was widely used. In a period of five years, some thirty thousand volumes were sold, and perhaps a much larger number of students studied it. In one state institution the entire student body of six hundred students attended lectures related to the various chapters for six successive Sunday nights. In some white colleges, groups of the students went to visit the Negro college in the same town or in a neighboring town. Churches began to organize study groups to consider southern problems, the Negro problem being one field of investigation. A new way of thinking and acting was gradually evolving. Meanwhile the educational forces of the South were pressing this question of race relations on the attention of the people. During the period from 1910 to 1930 a goodly number of books on the race problem appeared. Ray Stannard Baker wrote his *Following the Color Line*, Alfred H. Stone wrote *Studies in the American Race Problem*, Gilbert Stephenson wrote *Race Distinctions in American Law*, James E. Cutler wrote *Lynch Law*, Jerome Dowd wrote a series of three volumes on the Negro in Africa and America, and many other books appeared, of which we may mention Mary Helm's *The Upward Path*, William B. Smith's *The Color Line*, Theodore D. Bratton's *Wanted Leaders*, Alexander H. Shannon's *Racial Integrity*, Robert T. Kerlin's *The Voice of the Negro*, Frederick G. Detweiler's *The Negro Press in the United States*, and Robert E. Speer's *Of One Blood*. Colleges throughout the country began offering courses in Race Studies. At the present time probably seventy white colleges have fully developed courses of this kind, and several hundred students are annually enrolled in these courses.

As good an illustration of this general trend as one could find is the work in Nashville, Tennessee, where Vanderbilt University,

George Peabody College for Teachers, Scarritt College for Christian Workers, and Y.M.C.A. Graduate School, all located in the western section of the city, are coöperating in such studies. A mile away three outstanding Negro institutions are working: namely, Fisk University, Meharry Medical College, and A and I State Normal School. The Sociology Department at Vanderbilt has developed courses in Race Problems; the Vanderbilt School of Religion has a course under the leadership of Dr. Alva Taylor; Dr. Ullin W. Leavell at Peabody is giving courses in "bi-racial" education; Miss Louise Young at Scarritt gives a course with practice work at Bethlehem Center, of which she is the active head; and Y.M.C.A. Graduate School has courses under two professors which have an outreach into the community. Both Fisk and A and I Normal are giving courses on Negro History, Negro Culture, Negro Music, and Negro Art. Fisk has a Negro music and art week each year at which many white students are in attendance. In connection with all these studies Fisk is developing a library on the Negro in Africa, Europe, and the Islands, and Y.M.C.A. Graduate School is developing a full library of all material on the American Negro. The two combined have some eight thousand titles catalogued at the present time. This has given great impetus to research into the bearing of the race problem on modern American life. During the last five years, students in the Nashville white colleges alone have written fifty-five master's theses and six doctor's theses dealing with some phases of the racial question. Several research projects have been carried through and the results published, and a number of important research projects are under way. In addition Fisk professors and students have done valuable research work and have published a number of volumes. It would probably be well within the truth if one said that no other single topic of the day has received so much attention from the Nashville students as has the race question. The University of North Carolina is another center of interest in racial studies. Dr. Howard Odum and Mr. Paul Green have given an impulse to racial studies which has affected almost every educational institution in America. The work done there on Negro folk life, folk music, and Negro drama is quite distinctive. An article in *Social Science* hails all these facts as indicative of better "interracial adjustment." [1]

In 1918, when the Armistice was signed, the War Work Council

[1] W. Russell Tylor, "Some Factors of Interracial Adjustment," August-October, 1930, p. 508 ff.

of the Y.M.C.A. began at once to hold a series of ten-day conferences, both of white and colored men, for the study of readjusting the returned soldiers both white and colored into normal life. It was soon realized that the returning soldiers would not be the same men they were when they left America. They would have seen another world. They would be shaken out of their old traditions. In particular, many felt that a Negro boy good enough to fight for his country would feel good enough to demand a fair chance for life at home. If that fair chance was not given, many knew there would be hatred and hardship. The Commission on Interracial Coöperation was therefore called into being, and has exerted a wide influence on racial attitudes. The method of work of the Commission has been very simple. It has tried to bring together white and colored people in each local community, to think coöperatively about their particular problems. In one community they might study health problems. In another they might work at the school situation. In others they might face the practices which brought friction and aroused antagonism. No national program was evolved, save the one alone of getting leaders of the two races together to face their problems. The Commission has believed, and acted on the belief, that there is enough good sense and enough human interest in every community to solve questions of friction if only the leaders of the two races can come to know each other and associate their efforts around a common task. The results have amply justified this faith. In addition to the work of the local groups, the Commission on Interracial Coöperation has undertaken a number of significant studies. The latest of these is *Lynchings and What They Mean*, referred to in other chapters of this volume. The Commission has also undertaken certain studies of what other organizations are doing in this field.[1] Work has likewise been done in studying cases where justice seems to have gone awry, and in a number of instances courts have reversed their decisions. All of this has had definite effect on the racial attitudes of communities where action has been taken.

A very significant move of the Commission on Interracial Coöperation has been the holding of Institutes on Education and Racial Adjustment at Peabody College during the summer quarter, through which it is hoped the public school teachers of the country may be

---

[1] Cf. Willis D. Weatherford (Compiler), *Interracial Coöperation*, published by the Commission.

led to give attention to better relations between the races.¹ Notwithstanding Professor Sumner's careful argument, the folkways have been changing. Slowly to be sure, but surely changing.

The migration of Negroes from the South to the North during and just following the World War awakened the South from its short-sighted policy of economic injustice and awakened the North from its armchair attitude of coddling the Negro. Both realized that something was wrong. The South set about offering a fairer compensation for work, and the North waked up to the fact that an ignorant laborer was at times a handicap rather than an asset.

The growth of a skilled artisan class among Negroes has brought about a new attitude toward them on the part of the labor unions. Although the American Federation of Labor has always declared in favor of the Negro union, it has often refused the Negro entrance into the parent union; but as the number of skilled Negro workers has increased, many of the parent unions even in the South have admitted him.² However, admission has been so slow that a radical element in the ranks of unionism has arisen which is much more favorable to the Negro.³ Negro labor has become an important element in many industries such as the iron, lumber, tobacco, automobile, and now even the textile industries. The fear of the Negro as a strikebreaker has created a far more liberal attitude toward him in many fields. Thus, in Galveston, Texas, an agreement was reached among the stevedores that equal numbers of whites and blacks should be employed (1925). In New Orleans in the same year the white and colored longshoremen were amalgamated. In many of the recent coal miners' strikes Negroes and whites have walked out side by side. The State Federation of Labor in Virginia (1925) and Pennsylvania (1926) declared it was detrimental to the interest of labor to segregate white and colored; hence both were admitted to seats in the same convention. The Communist party has of late been very active in organizing and propagandizing Negro labor, a fact which has had the effect of liberalizing the attitude of old line unions toward the Negro. William Z. Foster, a director of the Com-

---

[1] The address of the Commission is "Commission on Interracial Coöperation, Standard Building, Atlanta, Georgia."

[2] Cf. James T. Hardwick, "The Economic Condition among Negroes of Nashville, Tennessee," an unpublished master's thesis, Y.M.C.A. Graduate School, Nashville, Tennessee.

[3] Cf. Sterling D. Spero and A. L. Harris, *The Black Worker*, chap. 14.

munist program, has declared in favor of the full economic, political, and social equality of the Negro. There can be no doubt that the Negro is coming into his own in the field of labor.[1] He is now being admitted freely into the United Mine Worker's Union, the Garment Worker's Union, and many others.[2]

Not only has the Negro begun to come into his own in the industrial field, but a new attitude is developing in the field of business. In 1900 Booker T. Washington organized the National Negro Business League, which has held annual meetings and has stimulated interest on the part of the most capable and enterprising Negroes. In 1928 this league made a survey of the Negro businesses in thirty-three cities, and found 2,757 individual businesses in these cities. They included grocery stores (19%), barber shops (14%), cleaning, pressing, and tailoring establishments (11.3%), restaurants (11%), drug stores (6%), automobile mechanics' shops (6%), contractors' businesses, hardware stores, and others.[3] In not a few of these establishments white people were employed, and in many cases white customers were the source of largest remuneration. While Negro barber shops and restaurants do not have as large a patronage from white people as they once had, other businesses are commanding more and more patronage from white people. This has a reflex in better attitudes, since it raises the Negro business man in the estimate of his white customer. This confidence is well earned, as anyone will believe who reads the list of outstanding businesses to be found in the *Negro Year Book, 1931–1932*.[4]

In 1918, the Southern Publicity Committee was organized by Dr. James H. Dillard. The purpose of this group was to send out to the press, particularly the weekly papers in small towns and rural districts, news stories of Negro achievements, and of instances of coöperation between white and colored people. It was a gesture of good will which has been taken up by the Commission on Interracial Coöperation and handled with conspicuous success by Mr. R. B. Eleazer, who is in charge of this department of work.

The women of the white churches of the South have made noteworthy progress in bringing about good will and coöperation. The

---

[1] For full discussion of the present union situation, see *Negro Year Book, 1931–1932*, Division 13.

[2] Cf. Lorenzo J. Greene and Carter G. Woodson, *The Negro Wage Earner*, chap. 17.

[3] *Negro Year Book, 1931–1932*, p. 133.　　　[4] P. 133.

women of the Methodist Episcopal Church South have established Wesley Houses, which not only serve the Negroes of the several cities where they are established, but also serve as centers where white women and colored women may meet face to face and discuss common problems of community welfare, community morals, religious life, and similar matters. The Southern Presbyterian women have for some years held an annual conference at Tuscaloosa, Alabama, where white and colored women work and plan together for a better religious and moral life in the South. Other church groups are carrying forward similar work. The Commission on Church and Race Relations, appointed by the Federal Council of Churches, has held certain notable conferences of white and colored people for promoting racial good will. The church has always been on the side of a more liberal attitude toward other races. Its very genius is that of brotherhood, but oddly enough it has been all too slow in asserting its convictions. So true is this that Dr. Du Bois in the *Christian Century*[1] boldly asserts that the church will not remove the color line. He thinks the church will follow an advancing liberalism, but it will not boldly assert the brotherhood of man in the face of opposing wealth and power.

The Y.W.C.A. and the Y.M.C.A., particularly in the student departments, have taken advanced ground in giving colored students equal rights with white students in conferences and conventions. They have really made Negro students integral parts of the movements without any form of discrimination. If the social atmosphere of the general community did not act as a restraining influence, the students would undoubtedly find little trouble in working out perfect harmony and good will.

In many ways the contacts between white and colored people have become more frequent and more extensive. There are many more opportunities for the best element in each race to know the corresponding group in the other race than there were twenty-five years ago. Not since the slave period have there been so many opportunities for personal contact. This has undoubtedly brought about a better understanding and greater respect. Some of these contacts are organized, such as those brought about by the Commission on Interracial Coöperation; others are normal or natural contacts growing out of business or political or educational relations.

[1] "Will the Church Remove the Color Line?" December 9, 1931, pp. 1554–1556.

Social contacts have not yet had much influence on understanding. A few more daring and more open-minded white people are willing to break custom and have a common meal with Negroes, but they do it always at the risk of loss of popularity or status, and sometimes at the risk of persecution. The widespread protest which went over the country when President Theodore Roosevelt served Dr. Booker T. Washington lunch in the White House found a recrudescence in the incident of Mrs. Hoover receiving Mrs. De Priest in the White House. A number of southern legislatures condemned this action unqualifiedly, and it cost President Hoover some popularity among the politicians of the South. The furor raised over this simple official act of the first lady of the land makes one wonder how much solid progress has been made in attitudes of good will. But it must be remembered that the large number of progressive leaders who saw in Mrs. Hoover's action nothing but an official act of courtesy did not exploit their ideas in the public press.

Taking a view of the whole situation, some writers believe that the social code of the slave days is tending to harden down into a modern etiquette of race relations, and that comparatively small progress has been made.[1]

The Negro has developed a reserve and a secretiveness which makes a widening gulf between the races. As Dunbar put it, Negroes "wear the mask." White people tend to accept an attitude of servility from Negroes, and hence we are just where we were at the close of the Civil War.

On the other hand there are many thoughtful people who would not agree with this interpretation of present social facts. Thomas J. Woofter, in an article in *Recent Social Trends*,[2] states that real progress in better understanding has been made, and a similar feeling is voiced by many other writers. Woofter points out elsewhere that the death of the Ku Klux Klan and the refusal of the Georgia courts to charter the American Fascisti, an anti-Negro organization, are indications of progress in public sentiment.[3] Arthus J. Klein believes that the action of the Southern Association of Colleges and Secondary Schools, in undertaking the rating of Negro schools within its territory, is a matter of "extreme educational importance and

---

[1] *Journal of Negro History*, January, 1933, pp. 30–32.

[2] *Recent Social Trends*. Report of the President's Research Committee on Social Trends, Vol. I, p. 600.

[3] "Race Relations," *American Journal of Sociology*, May, 1931, p. 1040.

of great "sociological interest."[1] Herskovits points to the increased liberalism of the white people in the matter of higher education, and to the fact that institutions like Fisk University, Meharry Medical College, and Howard University are getting a fairer share of funds as compared with former days. He points to a decrease in lynchings as an indication of better understanding. He thinks enlarged opportunities for making a living as well as making a life point to a growing attitude of friendliness.[2] But the Mrs. De Priest incident also gives him concern.

Perhaps one would sum up the situation by saying that great masses of American white people have not changed their attitudes from the attitudes held during slavery, but the leaders of the whites have undoubtedly adopted much more liberal attitudes; and since these leaders ultimately set patterns of thought, the social prejudice will gradually disappear and the relation between the races will slowly but surely become more friendly.

PROBLEMS FOR STUDY

1. List a number of dogmas of race relations, and account for the rise of these specific mores.
2. How are mores changed, if that is at all possible?
3. Will the church (with its auxiliaries, such as the Y.M.C.A. *et al.*) or the school (with its auxiliaries, such as the Adult Education Movement) be the more helpful agent in affecting the change of racial mores? Why?
4. What part can an organization like the Commission on Interracial Coöperation play in changing mores?
5. What influence will the larger mobility (migrations) of the Negro have in changing racial attitudes?
6. Was Booker T. Washington right in believing that Negro efficiency would develop respect for and friendliness toward him, or will his efficiency only sharpen competition?
7. Would the annulling of Jim Crow laws help or hinder racial understanding?
8. Does segregation in cities help or hinder racial understanding?
9. In certain northern cities the large increase of Negro population has radically changed the attitude of friendliness toward Negroes formerly held by the white people of those communities. Is this due to economic or other factors?

[1] "Education," *American Journal of Sociology*, May, 1930, p. 1068.
[2] "Race Relations," *American Journal of Sociology*, May, 1930, p. 1058 ff.

BIBLIOGRAPHY

Ray S. Baker, *Following the Color Line* (1908).
Emory S. Bogardus, *Immigration and Race Attitudes* (1928).
Edwin R. Embree, *Brown America* (1931).
Atticus G. Haygood, *Our Brother in Black, His Freedom and His Future* (1881).
Atticus G. Haygood, *Pleas for Progress* (1889).
Charles S. Johnson, *The Negro in American Civilization* (1930).
Robert R. Moton, *What the Negro Thinks* (1929).
Edgar G. Murphy, *The Basis of Ascendancy* (1909).
Edgar G. Murphy, *Problems of the Present South* (1910).
Howard W. Odum, *An American Epoch* (1930).
Arthur F. Raper, *The Tragedy of Lynching* (1933).
Recent Social Trends. Report of the President's Research Committee on Social Trends (1933).
Edward B. Reuter, *The American Race Problem* (1927).
William G. Sumner, *Folkways* (1906).
Willis D. Weatherford, *The Negro from Africa to America* (1924).
Willis D. Weatherford, *Negro Life in the South* (1915).

CHAPTER XXVII

PROGRAMS LOOKING TOWARD SOLUTION OR AMELIORATION OF RACE RELATIONS

The early colonists were most eager to get indentured servants and Negroes to supply the need for labor, but no sooner had the Negroes become numerous, and a class of free Negroes sprung up, than they began to fear lest the Negroes might become more numerous than the whites, and hence become powerful enough to give trouble. We have seen elsewhere that again and again the colonial legislatures passed laws prohibiting further imports, laws which were set at naught by the mother countries. After the Revolution, one of the most urgent questions was how to stop the importation of more slaves. It was Thomas Jefferson, a slave owner, who as President sent a message to Congress urging that a law prohibiting the slave trade should be passed, to take effect at the earliest moment the constitutional agreement would permit — namely, 1808.

Very early in the nineteenth century Virginia began looking about for a way to free itself of too large a number of colored people. In 1777 Jefferson, Pendleton, and Wythe were a committee of three to revise the laws of Virginia. The recommendations brought in about slavery were not satisfactory to Jefferson, since a plan of emancipation was not adopted. "Yet the day is not distant," he commented, "when it must bear and adopt it [emancipation] or worse will follow. Nothing is more certainly written in the book of fate, than that these people are to be free; nor is it less certain that the two races, equally free, cannot live in the same government. Nature, habit, opinion have drawn indelible lines of distinction between them. It is still in our power to direct the process of emancipation and deportation peaceably," [1] but if the state failed to do so he saw great trouble for the state. Jefferson's plan at this early date was to prepare the slaves by training for self-government, and then to colonize them, giving them implements, seeds, and domestic animals as needed to sustain themselves.[2] In 1801 Jefferson wrote

[1] Henry S. Randall, *Life of Thomas Jefferson*, Vol. I, p. 227.
[2] *Ibid.*, Vol. I, p. 227.

to Governor Monroe of Virginia that the West Indies, particularly St. Domingo, might be a suitable place for colonization.¹ As early as 1802 he wrote to Mr. King, the United States Minister in London, asking him "to negotiate with the Sierra Leone Company and induce them to receive such of these people [American Negroes] as might be colonized thither." ² The reports from Sierra Leone did not seem encouraging; so Jefferson undertook to secure a concession in South America from Portugal, which also proved abortive.³ In 1811 Jefferson wrote John Lynd that he would do anything in his power as a private citizen to secure such a concession from any other government, but expressed a belief that the United States should establish its own colony on the west coast of Africa.⁴ During the administration of President Jefferson, the Virginia legislature instructed Governor Monroe to correspond with the President to see if some asylum outside of the organized states might not be found to which the free people of color might be sent. This resolution was re-adopted by several successive legislatures; the one adopted December 21, 1816, read as follows:

RESOLVE: That the executive be requested to correspond with the President of the United States, for the purpose of obtaining a territory upon the coast of Africa, or at some other place, not within any of the states or territorial governments of the United States, to serve as an asylum for such persons of colour as are now free, and may desire the same; and for those who may be hereafter emancipated within this commonwealth, and that the Senators and Representatives of this state in the Congress of the United States, be requested to exert their best efforts, to aid the President of the United States, in the attainment of the above object.⁵

A similar resolution was adopted by Tennessee, and other states felt a similar urge. It was out of this general attitude that a group of men including such prominent citizens as Bushrod Washington, Henry Clay, and John Randolph, met on December 16, 1816, in Washington to discuss the question of colonization. Five days later they met again, and on January 1, 1817, a third meeting was held at which the "American Society for Colonizing the Free People of Color of the United States" was organized. William H. Crawford

---

¹ Henry S. Randall, *Life of Thomas Jefferson*, Vol. II, p. 674.
² *First Annual Report of the American Society for Colonizing the Free People of Color of the United States* (herein after called the American Colonization Society), p. 13.   ³ *Ibid.*, p. 14.   ⁴ *Ibid.*, p. 14.
⁵ *Second Annual Report of the American Colonization Society*, p. 80.

of Georgia, Henry Clay of Kentucky, Andrew Jackson of Tennessee, Richard Rush of Pennsylvania, John Taylor of Virginia, and four others were elected vice-presidents. Henry Clay, Daniel Webster, John Randolph, Samuel J. Mills, John Taylor, William Thornton, and Richard Lee were among the first contributors to the cause. The organization had ten planks in its constitution, which included colonizing (with their consent) of free people of color, and all the necessary steps to be taken thereto. Almost immediately a memorial was presented to both houses of Congress, calling attention to the condition of the free Negro, and also to the fact that slave states were passing laws to deter emancipation, in an effort to safeguard themselves against the danger of free Negroes, and praying that the United States would open negotiations with Great Britain or other powers, looking to establishing a colony in West Africa for free people of color. Again and again such a plea was made to Congress, and each time serious consideration was given to it, but nothing was ever done. Four legislatures petitioned the general government to assist in this work, but to no avail.[1] With the powerful persons who made up the officers and charter members it would seem that almost any action could have been secured, but evidently Congress did not see an adequate plan for carrying out the dream of the society. The society was forced, therefore, to rely on membership dues, on Fourth of July collections, on church contributions, and on contributions from certain state legislatures.[2] Reverend William Meade, later Bishop of the Episcopal church, was one of the earliest agents who helped in raising funds. The clergy in general were so interested that the third annual meeting of the society passed special resolutions of thanks for their aid.[3]

During the first year of its existence the Colonization Society engaged the services of Samuel J. Mills and Ebenezer Burgess to explore the west coast of Africa in search of a proper spot for a colony. These agents went to London and visited the Duke of Gloucester, who was patron and president of the African Institution, engaged in a similar task. The Duke received them most cordially, and later wrote to Bushrod Washington, the president of the society, assuring him of the hearty and cordial support of the "Institution."[4] The

---

[1] *Third Annual Report of the American Colonization Society*, p. 5.
[2] Early L. Fox, *The American Colonization Society, 1817–1840*, p. 57 ff.
[3] *Third Annual Report of the American Colonization Society*, p. 8.
[4] *Second Annual Report of the American Colonization Society*, p. 67.

reports of Mills and Burgess were thoroughly favorable, even though Mills did not live to deliver his in person. Liberia was the spot chosen for the colony. The society therefore began at once to send suitable persons out. Paul Cuffe had in 1815, and again in 1816, taken groups of colored people to Sierra Leone, paying the full expense of thirty-eight of these immigrants himself.[1] In 1817 the state of Georgia passed a law empowering the governor to appoint agents to receive contraband Negroes and sell them after sixty days' notice, but the third section of the law read:

> Be it further enacted, that if previous to any sale of any such persons of colour, the society for colonization of free persons of color within the United States, will undertake to transport them to Africa, or any other foreign place, which they may procure for free persons of colour, at the sole expense of said society, and shall likewise pay to his Excellency the Governor, all expenses incurred by the state, since they have been captured and condemned, his Excellency the Governor is authorized and requested to aid in promoting the benevolent views of said society, in such manner as he may deem expedient.[2]

Under this law, Reverend Mr. Meade was sent to Milledgeville, Georgia, to take over thirty-four native Africans who had been captured and were to be sold December 19, 1817. He received the Negroes, and reported to the society that they (the Negroes) were filled with joy at the prospect of return to Africa. Between 1820 and 1830 the society sent 1,420 Negroes back to Africa.[3]

In March, 1819, Congress empowered the President to appoint agents residing on the coast of Africa, who should receive Negroes captured by American vessels, and make proper disposition of such contraband slaves. This gave real impetus to the work of the Colonization Society.

Through the efforts of the Colonization Society a great many slaves were liberated on condition they would go to Africa. The funds of the society were always too scant to send all who were willing to go, so that the total effect on the number of Negroes in America was almost negligible. The society, however, did influence many planters to consider emancipation, and undoubtedly had considerable influence on the abolition of the slave trade.

Others besides the Colonization Society have advocated coloniza-

---

[1] *First Annual Report of the American Colonization Society*, p. 28.
[2] *Second Annual Report of the American Colonization Society*, p. 91.
[3] Early L. Fox, *The American Colonization Society, 1817–1840*, p. 89.

tion as the one way of solving the race problem in America. In 1864 one Reverend Hollis Read wrote a book of 418 pages which he called *The Negro Problem Solved*. The frontispiece shows a Negro stepping ashore in Africa, with the Bible coming down out of Heaven, and the lion and the lamb lying peacefully together at his feet. Colonization, Read says, is to be advocated "as a boon to the colored man, a privilege to every one who is fitted to profit by it, and the most suitable and hopeful agency by which to raise Africa from her present debasement and to assign her an honorable place among the Nations."[1] With astonishing self-assurance he showed how feasible it would be to send all the Negroes back to Africa, and he prophesied that the task would be accomplished in a reasonable length of time. In 1907 Dr. R. W. Shufeldt, a retired army surgeon and a member of numerous scientific societies, wrote a book called *The Negro a Menace to American Civilization*, in which with bitterness he demanded that all Negroes be sent back to Africa. He says: "I am so loyal to anything that will sustain the purity of the best of Indo-European blood, in the United States . . . that I would see every Negro in America at the bottom of the Pacific ocean, or howling in the Soudan, before I would allow them for any consideration whatever, to jeopardize by race intermixture the civilization it has taken us centuries to build up."[2] In 1914 Dr. Thomas P. Bailey, professor of psychology at the University of Mississippi, wrote *Race Orthodoxy in the South*, in which he advocated race segregation or colonization. In 1923, James D. Sayre wrote *Can the White Race Survive?*, in which he advocates a New League of Nations which shall be controlled completely by white men, where Esperanto shall be the common language, and no colored race shall have any share in control. In 1929, Earnest Sevier Cox wrote a book called *White America;* he would have us completely segregate the Negro. All of these later advocates fear contact with the Negro, lest that contact may mean amalgamation and that the white race shall sink its richer heritage in the sea of race mixture. The latest and most ardent advocates of Nordicism, or the separation of the most advanced type of white man from all contamination from other groups, are Madison Grant and Lothrop Stoddard. These writers assert as scientific fact what I am sure has not been proved: that specialized characteristics of advanced races are sure to be bred out first in any intermingling of blood with a less specialized group,

[1] *The Negro Problem Solved*, p. v.
[2] Pp. 161–162.

and that all mixed offspring, even of two superior stocks of dissimilar characteristics, is watered down, so to speak, to "generalized mediocrity."[1] This doctrine of superiority on the part of the Nordic peoples is the basis of the doctrine of exclusion of all alien races from America; it is the basis of the doctrine of strict caste in the matter of social relations between divergent groups; and unfortunately it is the basis of a brutal disregard of the value and worth of all other groups save the Nordics. All who express the belief that other peoples besides the Nordics may have real values are branded as sincere but misguided cosmopolitan enthusiasts.[2] This school of writers is to the race problem what Nietzsche and Bernhardi were to the problem of international relations before the World War. These war lords wrote down everybody except Germans as inferior, and they completely discredited any gospel of peace, good will, or love. Similarly the advocates of Nordicism discredit any gospel of the value and worth of all persons.

This then is the ultimate outcome of colonization or segregation as a solution of the race problem. It seems to have no possibility of ever being practicable, and if it were it would be based primarily on the idea of the inferiority of one race, which not only is not scientifically demonstrated as true, but furthermore is directly opposed to the spirit of good will among races.

Closely akin to this solution of colonization or segregation is another which one might call subordination. During the slave régime the Negro knew his place and usually kept it. By no stretch of his imagination could he think of himself as equal to the white master. He dared not even defend his life against the attack of "poor white trash." Politically, legally, socially the Negro was a nobody. The tradition of slavery survives to this day in the oft-repeated phrase that "we like a Negro who knows his place." His place evidently in this program is a hewer of wood and a drawer of water. When he comes into the presence of a white man he must stand hat in hand. He must have no real opinion of his own; he must never assert his rights when they seem to conflict with those of the white man. The good Negro is the humble, self-effacing, obedient, and servile Negro. Hence the younger Negro, the Negro with education, the Negro with independence of thought and action, is an "uppity" Negro.

[1] Lothrop Stoddard, *The Rising Tide of Color against White World-Supremacy*, p. 301.
[2] *Ibid.*, p. 226.

PROGRAMS FOR AMELIORATION

He wants to get out of his place. The fundamental philosophy behind this idea is precisely that of Stoddard and Grant; namely, that some races are inherently inferior and others are superior. The Negro is placed in the first class. This view is not confined to ignorant and isolated peoples of the South. Professor Charles C. Josey of Dartmouth wrote a book in 1923 in which he took precisely this position internationally. "Our culture and civilization are, in fact, built on domination,"[1] says Professor Josey, and by "our" he means the white man. To hold such a position one must deny flatly the doctrine of brotherhood; one must set aside as pure sentiment all ideas that other men have genuine values. This, Professor Josey coldly and brutally does.[2] He is entirely willing to hold our advantages economic and military in order that we may exploit all other races to add to the richness and colorfulness of our own culture.[3] This is precisely the point of view of the delta planter who sees to it that the Negroes on his place are in debt to him at the end of the year. If the Negro makes enough to pay out he may move away or seek a more advantageous contract. He must be kept subservient and dependent. If he cannot be kept so by charging him extra high prices for supplies, or by overcharging him for rentals, he must be kept so by false bookkeeping. A college student friend of mine kept books for a cotton planter in the Yazoo delta. A Negro came in with his first picking of cotton. After figuring his account, my college friend told the Negro he had a credit of $113. The planter stood near and said to the Negro, "You have enough more cotton to pay that, don't you?" "Yes, boss," was the reply. When the Negro had gone my college friend demanded his wages, telling the planter he would not work for any man who would cheat the ignorant and helpless. "But," said the planter, "it's the only way to keep a force on the land." This is Professor Josey's principle pure and simple — exploitation.

It is the solution long held by the less enlightened white man: exploit the Negro, keep him dependent, increase your culture and ease at his expense. Never let him suppose that he deserves wealth or culture or ease. There are plenty of white people who cannot with composure see a Negro or an Indian drive a good automobile or wear good clothes. It is hardly necessary to suggest that the Negro can

---

[1] *Race and National Solidarity*, p. 61.
[2] *Ibid.*, pp. 51–52.
[3] *Ibid.*, pp. 61, 87, 213, *passim*.

never become a self-respecting citizen so long as he receives or accepts such a station in life as these whites would set for him. It would seem that America would be too enlightened to continue to hold to this as a possible solution, but one who gets the opinion of the man of the street finds this a prevalent idea at the present time.

Closely akin to this solution, but going beyond it, is another more selfish, more brutal one — that of the extinction of the Negro. William Benjamin Smith, a very brilliant scholar and professor at Tulane University, published a book in 1905 entitled *The Color Line, A Brief in Behalf of the Unborn*. His main thesis is that the Negro is a distinctly inferior race, and he not only cannot but ought not to persist in the presence of the white man. Professor Smith undertakes to show in detail that the education of the Negro is impossible, and that even if it were possible, it would not in any sense affect his inheritance.[1] He even denies there is any place for the Negro to make a living save in the most menial tasks of life. Washington and his industrial education Smith calls magnificent but misguided.[2] The only sane procedure is to draw the color line tighter, and thereby starve or strangle the inferior race. The exodus to the cities he thinks will accomplish this, for there disease and death will do their deadly work.[3]

As generations pass on, the Negro will be hemmed every way within straighter and straighter limits, his numbers will decrease, his digit will move further to the right in the great sum of humanity, — slowly, silently, steadily he will be driven to the wall. . . .[4]

The vision then of a race vanishing before its superiors is not at all dispiriting, but inspiring rather. It is but a part of the increasing purpose of the ages, a forward creeping of the eternal dawn. . . .[5]

But may we not check or arrest them [these tendencies to death]? May not the strong Caucasian lend a helping hand to his weaker brother and lift him up, and the two walk along hand in hand through the centuries? This is a very idyllic picture. "Behold, how good and how pleasant for brethren to dwell together in unity." But a moment's reflection must show inadequate and unreal this dew of Hermon. It is not hard for altruism to run suicidally mad, if one let go the check reins of egotism. The first and highest, and unescapable duty of a race is to itself — to realize its own personality, to put forth its powers and potencies, to unfold the full flower of its own being. It must neither be unjust nor ungenerous in its treatment of others, but neither must it attempt self-immolation — especially as that sacrifice would be idle

[1] P. 165.   [2] *Ibid.*, p. 171.   [3] *Ibid.*, p. 175.
[4] *Ibid.*, p. 177.   [5] *Ibid.*, p. 187.

and unanswered. The most, the best that one race can effect for another, is merely some extra-organic amelioration of conditions. The organic destiny of that other, written in blood and bone and plasma, lies beyond the reach of the helping hand. We must dismiss, then, this vision of a higher race stooping down with arms of love and lifting up the lower to its altitude, as merely a pious imagination. The higher race may indeed stoop down; it has often done so; but never to rise again; instantly there falls upon it the Davidic curse: "Bow down their backs always." [1]

Professor Smith had predecessors and he has followers. There have not been wanting those who were entirely complacent in the presence of the fact that the Indian was dying out largely because of the white man's cruelty. There are many who feel that the white man should take what he wants at whatever cost to the less developed peoples of the world. But Professor Smith's prophecy has not proved true. The Negro is not dying out; education is proving a blessing; and the Negro is more and more coming into his own in industrial life. Thus Professor Smith's solution of the problem hardly finds any corroboration in facts.

Another solution to the race problem which has been offered is amalgamation. Half a century ago Friedrich Ratzel wrote: "Interbreeding is making rapid progress in all parts of the earth," [2] and commenting on this solution he argued that the half-breeds were in no sense inferior to the parent stocks. His contention was that since all the races had sprung from a common stock, in time all of them would be reunited into one whole.[3] In this process he felt there would be a leveling up and not down. Professor Edwin G. Conklin of Yale writes:

Even if we are horrified by the thought, we cannot hide the fact that all present signs point to an intimate commingling of all existing human types within the next five or ten thousand years at most. Unless we can reestablish geographical isolation of races, we cannot prevent their interbreeding. By rigid laws excluding immigrants of other races, such as they have at present in New Zealand and Australia, it may be possible for a time to maintain the purity of the white race in certain countries, but with the constantly increasing intercommunication between all lands and peoples such artificial barriers will probably prove in the long run as ineffectual as the Great Wall of China. The races of the world are not drawing apart but together and it needs only the vision that will look ahead a few thousand years to see the blending of all racial currents into a common stream.[4]

[1] *Ibid.*, pp. 188–189. [2] *The History of Mankind*, Vol. I, p. 12.
[3] *Ibid.*, Vol. I, p. 10. [4] *The Direction of Human Evolution*, p. 52.

Professor Franz Boas of Columbia University agrees with this general view of Professor Conklin, and he applies the principle to America and the race problem in the South. Assuming as proved fact that there are no superior or inferior races, and that what seem differences of faculty are only differences in stages of culture, Boas believes the sooner we forget race distinctions and encourage amalgamation the better. Professor Edward M. East of Harvard is not so sanguine. He thinks that crossing between relatively uniform types may be good, but between widely differing types may or may not be good. "In other words, though the variability opened up by race crosses is so great that if an all-knowing ruler were permitted to select and mate at will, a better type might be evolved; in the slow-going stumbling world of reality in which we live, it would be the height of folly to recommend it." [1]

Crossing of races has gone forward on a large scale in South America and there are those who think it proves crossbreeding to be good. On the other hand, Professor E. A. Ross of the University of Wisconsin quotes "the wisest sociologist of Bolivia" as saying that the Zambo, resulting from the union of Indian and Negro, is inferior to both parent races, and the Mestizo, resulting from the mating of white and Indian, is inferior to both parent races.[2] Whether this difference is due to biological or social inheritance we are not yet able to determine. Where there are two variable factors, neither of which can be completely eliminated, it is impossible fully to evaluate either factor. Both heredity and environment play upon every individual; hence how much each hybrid is influenced by one or the other cannot be determined. We do know that different races have developed different culture patterns, and some think they have developed some differences of psychic responses. If that be true, then racial characteristics built up over a period of thousands of years may render members of two very divergent races imcompatible in family relations. For the present at least, most races do not want to lose themselves in other races. The Jew does not want to lose himself in the Gentiles, the Negro does not want to lose himself in the white race. If the Negro writers properly interpret the thought and feeling of the Negro, he does not find satisfaction for his social nature in the white race. What ten thousand years may bring forth we do not know, but for the present, amalgamation does not seem to offer any satisfactory solution.

[1] *Mankind at the Crossroads*, p. 127.   [2] *South of Panama*, p. 41.

There is yet another solution which has been seriously offered for the problem of race relations in America; this might be called "parallel civilizations." The phrase was given currency by Edgar Gardiner Murphy some thirty years ago. By the phrase he meant that each race should be given the opportunity to develop itself to the fullest possible extent, finding within its own race lines opportunities for educational and social satisfaction. He believed that no race would live under oppression, and the oppressor would as surely lose its soul as the oppressed. "There is no place," he declared, "in our American system for a helot class. . . . We want no fixed and permanent populations of the inferior."[1] He further believed that the two races were so distinct in their developments that they would find a fuller satisfaction as separate races than as an amalgamated race. This would mean the fullest possible development of both races. Let Murphy's own words state the case:

> The perils involved in the progress of the negro are as nothing compared to the perils invited by his failure. And yet if any race is to live it must have something to live for. It will hardly cling with pride to its race integrity if its race world is a world wholly synonymous with deprivation, and if the world of the white man is the only generous and honorable world of which it knows. It will hardly hold with tenacity to its racial standpoint, it will hardly give any deep spiritual or conscious allegiance to its racial future if its race life is to be forever burdened with contempt, and denied the larger possibilities of thought and effort. The true hope, therefore, of race integrity for the Negro lies in establishing for him, within his own racial life, the possibilities of social differentiation.
>
> A race which must ever be tempted to go outside of itself for any share in the largeness and the freedom of experience will never be securely anchored in its racial self-respect, can never achieve any legitimate racial standpoint, and must be perpetually tempted — as its members rise — to desert its own distinctive life and its own distinctive service to the world. There is no hope for a race which begins by despising itself. The winning of generic confidence, of a legitimate racial pride, will come with the larger creation — for the capable — of opportunity within the race. The clew to racial integrity for the negro is thus to be found, as stated in an earlier chapter, not in race suppression but in race sufficiency. For the very reason that the race, in the apartness of its social life, is to work out its destiny as the separate member of a larger group, it must be accorded its own leaders and thinkers, its own scholars, artists, prophets; and while the development of the higher life may come slowly, even blunderingly, it is distinctly to be welcomed. As

[1] *The Basis of Ascendancy*, p. 233.

the race comes to have within itself, within its own social resources, a world that is worth living for, it will gain that individual foothold among the families of men which will check the despairing passion of its self-obliteration; and instead of the temptation to abandon its place among the races of the world it will begin to claim its own name and its own life. That is the only real, the only permanent security of race integrity for the negro. Its assumption is not degradation, but opportunity.[1]

This solution assumes that both races have values in themselves even though they differ widely in their special characteristics. It assumes that racial characteristics have been built up through long centuries of response to specialized environments, and these differences cannot be ignored. An Anglo-Saxon is not an Indian, and we need not try to delude ourselves into thinking he is. To ignore differences is to ignore facts, and that gets us nowhere. Why should we all be alike? Variety seems to be the very law of creation. The biologist has discovered and named 25,000 varieties of backboned animals, and no two varieties are alike. The botanist has discovered and named 100,000 varieties of flowering plants with no two identical. Why should we try to convince ourselves that all men are alike? The very glory of humanity is its variation with unity, or its unity in variety. We not only are not all alike, but we do not want to be so. This would be a world of dead monotony if all were built on the same psychic pattern. Variety enriches the culture of all. The contact of like and unlike brings new content to all life. This suggested solution assumes further that each race has a contribution to make to human culture which no other race can so well make. The long response to a particular environment has fitted each race to do some things exceptionally well. Conditions of life have developed the spirit of meditation and contemplation in the life of India, and the Hindus have a great message of quiet and meditation to give to the world. One who has read the wonderful literature of India can appreciate this contribution. Rabindranath Tagore found Americans too much in a hurry to live — he said we only existed. In similar manner the Chinese, the Japanese, the Negroes, have a contribution to make to our common civilization.

Writers of the Nordic school would have us believe that this group alone has made any contribution to the world's culture. But our Nordic culture is not our own creation. It is the synthesis of all the cultures of the earlier races and subraces. From the Phœnicians

[1] *Problems of the Present South*, pp. 273–274.

we got our alphabet; from the Arabs we got our numbers; from the Jews we got our religion. In fact, the Nordic civilization is a composite of all that the human race had discovered up to the time of its westward migration. This fact alone ought to keep us from boasting. How much richer will the culture of the world be when we are willing to accept the contribution of each of the races, white, yellow, and black, and blend these into a completer culture. If we could cease our silly Nordic boasting and recognize that we are simply one of many groups of mankind, our minds would be more open to receive the rich heritage of other cultures.

This solution holds a third assumption as true; namely, that all men are capable of progress. If all men are not capable of progress, it seems possible that none might be; for we are all too much alike to be different in this regard. The progress of the Negro in America since emancipation has forever laid at rest any doubt as to whether he is capable of progress.

This threefold assumption suggests certain practical steps toward a fuller solution of the race problem. The first of these suggestions is that the acid test of our civilization is our attitude toward "our brother in black," as Bishop Haygood so aptly called him. The test of our civilization is not how much money we have, or how much power we have, but how much of good will we have. Our religion will not be tested by the correctness of our creeds, but by our attitude toward our neighbor. The final test of righteousness is not correct intellectual interpretations but attitude toward human beings. The practical task of every good citizen, and of every educated person in particular, is to help develop a spirit of good will.

A second suggestion which these assumptions bring forward is that we as good citizens cannot be indifferent to the status and opportunity of the other man. Many of us are all too willing to condemn a whole race because some are lazy or criminal or dirty.

There is no more dangerous situation than that of a more cultured, more advanced, more privileged people living in the presence of a less privileged group. Such a situation is far more dangerous to the advanced than to the belated, for if it does not make good Samaritans of us, it is apt to make cruel tyrants. No people are therefore more sorely tested than those of us who live daily in the presence of a less advanced group. College students should take this into consideration as they face less advantaged groups. The fundamental social problem of our day is how to make the bottom-most man in our midst loom large enough and seem important enough that we shall cease to think of him as a means for our own aggrandizement — but rather think of him as a human being, and a brother, made in the image of a living God.

And this leads to a third practical suggestion looking to a fuller solution of this problem. How can we help build into the Negro race a larger appreciation of its own worth and dignity? No race can achieve which does not believe in its own possibilities. The treatment usually accorded the Negro has tended to make him think meanly of himself instead of seeing his own worth. The really great man is not one who makes others feel little in his presence, but one who arouses in others the sense of their own dignity. The function of those who would be social benefactors is therefore to open up to all men around them new avenues of self-appreciation. What most men need is more courage, more confidence, more self-respect. Respect from the white man for the Negro will do much to arouse this self-respect. To this solution of a developing life for both races we need to bring the fullest knowledge of facts, the fullest and deepest human understanding, and an attitude of unquenchable good will. He who is discouraged by the first failure of a fellow man need not hope to be of much service here. We are all too ignorant; we have too many weaknesses; our prejudices are too strong; unless we steadfastly set our faces to find the best there is in all men, we shall have small share in this or any other solution of racial problems.

PROBLEMS FOR STUDY

1. If the Negroes of the United States were willing to migrate to Africa, would it be practicable to transport ten or more millions and establish them in a new home?
2. Are those who advocate colonization interested in the Negro or interested in giving the white man complete freedom in America?
3. Is there any such thing as a "pure" Nordic race?
4. Is there any proof that mixture of races is either good or bad from the standpoint of civilization?
5. In the absence of such proof, would a program of race mixture be wise or unwise?
6. Can two races live side by side on terms of friendliness without amalgamation?
7. Can the doctrine of dominance of the Nordics be justified on the basis of either Christian principle, human attitude, or the principle of statesmanship?

8. Can there be parallel civilizations without both groups participating freely in civic and community life?
9. Would amalgamation between white and black destroy the contribution either or both could make to civilization?
10. Are there really such elements as racial characteristics? If so, how did they originate?

BIBLIOGRAPHY

Charles B. Davenport, *Heredity in Relation to Eugenics* (1911).
Charles B. Davenport and others, *Race Crossing in Jamaica* (1929).
Caroline B. Day, *A Study of Some Negro-White Families in the United States* (1932).
Edward M. East, *Mankind at the Crossroads* (1924).
Edward M. East and Donald F. Jones, *Inbreeding and Outbreeding; Their Genetic and Sociological Significance* (1919).
Alfred C. Haddon, *The Races of Man and Their Distinction* (1925).
Frank H. Hankins, *The Racial Basis of Civilization* (1926).
Ellsworth Huntington, *The Character of Races* (1924).
Charles C. Josey, *Race and National Solidarity* (1923).
Edgar G. Murphy, *The Basis of Ascendancy* (1909).
Joseph H. Oldham, *Christianity and the Race Problem* (1924).
Robert E. Speer, *Of One Blood* (1924).
Lothrop Stoddard, *The Rising Tide of Color against White World-Supremacy* (1922).

CHAPTER XXVIII

THE CHANGING ATTITUDE OF THE NEGRO

The racial attitudes of Negroes generally are not so readily to be obtained from their spoken opinions as from their actual behavior in racial situations. Since the days of the free Negro, there has always been an articulate group, and there has been a much larger inarticulate group whose chief symptom of disaffection, if any, has been that of various patterns of escape from the situation, by direct withdrawal or by dissimulation. It has not always been clear whether the articulate ones were expressing the attitudes of all Negroes, or only of themselves. Ordinarily it is assumed that they were articulating the dumb desires of the unlettered masses. In some cases they were; in others, there is some doubt. It is certain that all Negroes have not felt the same intensity of bitterness and resentment, and it is known that in the very nature of the primary relations existing in many slaveholding households there was neither resentment of status nor strong desire for freedom.

From the beginning, the articulate ones have been to a considerable degree "marginal men," freed from the full weight of an oppressive tradition, withal under enough pressure to be dismally uncomfortable.

The struggle for survival in an environment hostile to free Negroes tended to concentrate much attention upon the immediate problems of amelioration of free status. Not all free Negroes were abolitionists. This was primarily due less to lack of interest in abolition than to the pressure of their immediate and present discomforts. There seems never to have existed at the same time a single type of racial attitude. When, for example, the free Negro, David Walker, addressed his fiery appeal to the Negroes in 1829, he was expressing the conviction of most free Negroes about the inhumanity and disgrace of slavery, but by no means of all the slaves. Indeed, a great portion of the incendiary and infuriating "Walker's Appeal" was directed at the lethargy of the slaves themselves. The same general division in attitude has persisted since slavery was abolished. There has been the articulate group who denounce in bitter, biting language the social restrictions upon all Negroes. There have been those nearer the problem, realistic about the necessity for both internal and external improvement, and at the same time aware of a hostile racial opinion, backed by the prospect of ready violence. There have been the conciliators ready to gain small ground for the race, by conceding the unnecessariness of a great distance. There have been the sober or sullen ones, who get along by "attending to their own business" and who refrain from committing themselves to any but a noncommittal attitude. There are those who have lived so completely within the Negro world that their attitudes have seldom been challenged. And there are those who have abolished the problem for themselves by accepting in full the orthodoxy of the white race.

Such variety does not lend itself readily to a single pattern. It can be noted, however, that the extremes of this array are constantly in process of change. The articulate group, at one extreme, have been increasing in number, with the growth in literacy and the advancement of education and culture generally. There are "schools of thought" among them, and varying intensities in their attitudes. It is from this group that the racial leadership, for the most part, has come. On the other hand, the group of those who accepted fully the traditional race orthodoxy, being older and more closely related to the heavy conditioning of the institution of slavery, is becoming smaller. Moreover, the spread of literacy has exposed wider numbers of Negroes to the opinions of a variety of race spokesmen. These opinions have as often been communicated ready-made, as they have been spontaneously generated within these more naïve groups.

The Negro attitude toward the white race generally has been characterized by a defensive psychology. It is, indeed, doubtful if the racial attitude of a subject group can always be accurately described as prejudice. There may be sentiments of protest or revenge, scepticism or disillusionment. These reach the point of prejudice when hatred supplants fear, when anger overcomes caution, and when bitterness against wrongs overcomes the strength of authority. Prejudice carries with it a suggestion of authority and control.

It will be necessary to separate the articulate and the inarticulate groups, in the discussion of Negro attitudes. The aspirations and sentiments of the articulate ones have, apparently, always been considerably in advance of the latter. Only recently has there been any significant convergence of the attitudes of the two groups, and this has been due very largely to the development of communication and to the changing status of the whole mass of the Negro group.

The behavior index of attitudes for the period of slavery need only be suggested in slave crimes against whites, the attempts at insurrection, and in the fugitive slaves. Not all of these acts indicate racial attitudes quite as much as they indicate a simple desire for freedom. Such slave uprisings as Nat Turner's in Virginia, however, seem to have been inspired by a most intense racial feeling. The indiscriminate fury of this outbreak, though small, reflected a long and brooding hatred. Some of the fugitive slaves, from the security of their northern or Canadian retreats, manifested a distinct racial hatred. Some of the slave crimes were deliberate, diabolical, and consciously suicidal.

After the Civil War the attitudes of Negroes may be sought in the migrations and the boycotts for a period directed against the introduction of segregation in transportation and various public accommodations; and they may be observed in certain modified types of restricted production, as when apparently illiterate but not wholly ignorant tenant farmers were convinced that they were being cold-bloodedly exploited on their crops. Many of the crimes of desperation committed by irresponsible Negroes are at bottom motivated by an intense racial feeling. These examples are mentioned merely by way of suggesting the importance of the factor of racial feeling in certain social phenomena described more fully elsewhere in this volume.

The most important record of these racial attitudes, however, is in the expressions of those Negroes who have assumed more or less influential rôles as leaders of this race. The dominant attitudes expressed may be grouped by periods. The first period extends broadly from the first contact of the Negro with America to the Civil War; the second period extends through the reconstruction years to about 1880; the third from 1880 to 1916; and the fourth from 1916 onward.

The free Negroes were at first concerned chiefly with proving through argument and demonstrating through their own accomplishments the humanity of Negroes against the effective arguments of an abundant literature. They felt despised; they were little less uncomfortable in the North than in the South; they were in an uncomfortable dilemma about Christianity which tolerated slavery, although they never attacked it directly; they were almost childishly pleased, and boastful of the decency of white persons who treated them cordially; their utterances were full of outraged emotional expressions against "man-stealers," "thugs," "villains," "fiends," and vivid descriptions of the viciousness of the slave driver's lash. Frederick Douglass, one of the most brilliant of these fugitive Negroes, provides a good example of this general ground level of defense. In a satirical letter to a newspaper which had referred to him as a colored man rather than "a nigger," while accusing him of "unmitigated abuse of our country," he comments: "We have been laughed at and ridiculed so much that I am glad once in a while, to be able to turn the tables on our white brethren. . . . 'The colored *man* Douglass.' Well done! Not nigger Douglass — not black, but colored — not monkey, but man — the colored MAN Douglass. . . . In the brilliant light of the *Sun* [newspaper] I am no longer a monkey, but a Man — and henceforth, I may claim to be treated as a man by the *Sun*."

The closest approach to the white extremists who were actively engaged in documenting the defective physiology and mentality of Negroes were the Negro abolitionists. One intemperance called for another. These Negroes were not merely philanthropists; they had a vital stake in the outcome of this, the most dramatic contest of centuries. They could be vituperative on occasions. The reception of their message was by no means generally cordial. In the main, however, since theirs was an appeal to the sympathy of humanity, they trusted more to moral indignation to win support than to abuse. The most intemperate of these was, without doubt, David Walker, whose pamphlets, fuming with desperate indignation and hatred, advised slaves to rise up and throw off their bondage. It was one of the most disconcerting documents ever penned by a Negro. No other expressions of the free Negroes approached the "Appeal" in boldness and in the havoc of alarm which it provoked.

Such Negroes as James McCune Smith, Martin Delany, Henry Hyland Garnett, offered themselves as examples of ability, and counted upon the indignations to which gentlemen, "except in color," were submitted, to shame the nation into moral action. They argued well and phrased eloquently the logic of their human rights and aspirations. However, those who were interested in this cause did not need the arguments, and those who were not interested did not believe them.

Following the Civil War there developed several distinct racial stresses. At first the Negroes, taking too seriously the letter of the Emancipation Proclamation and the constitutional amendments, were interested in political expression. Vocal opinion, then largely centered in the South, was directed toward the awakening of the slumbering ex-slaves to their new status. Some of the Negro reconstruction characters were of sound and shrewd intelligence; others were men who had lacked education and experience in politics and government and demonstrated it. When, with the withdrawal of the military support of this arrangement, the various elements of the white population of the South combined to reassert dominance, the issues became realistically political. The sentiment of the Negroes, under such an overwhelming racial stress, became defensive again and on a different basis: it was no longer their major concern to reassert their humanity; they were under the necessity of asserting their right to survival.

This was a phase of the bitter contest with the white laboring class which was now rapidly gaining strength. The Negroes had inherited a contempt for this class from slavery. But it was a contempt which had effectiveness only so long as it related itself to the interests of the slave owners. Having lost this institutional support, this racial attitude was tragically meaningless. The rapid succession of segregation acts and the new restrictions in practice may have dammed up resentments and more hatreds of the "poor white" class, but it was increasingly inexpedient to voice them.

Occasional migrants from the South to the North could express themselves more freely. Many of these migrants had been forced North as a result of their indiscreet remarks. When, for example, Ida Wells Barnett of Memphis made a complaint about the frequency of lynching in the South, she was compelled to leave the city under threat of violence. There came a significant division between the northern and southern Negro attitudes on the question of race relations in the South. Most of the vocal Negroes in the North were expatriated southerners. They, together with some northern colleagues, became loud in the denunciation of lynchings, segregation, peonage, and the "general insults heaped upon the race in the South."

The small numbers of Negroes in the growing cities of the North had kept them from constituting a problem. Surviving abolitionist and unionist sentiment, though weak, generally, and more disposed to let the South settle its own Negro problem, gave them some small support in their verbal assaults upon the whites of the South. It will be observed that the speeches and articles of these Negroes were strongly and vividly emotional. They went so far as to condemn the Negroes living in the South for not speaking out; for their cowardice, and their policies of conciliation or capitulation.

The Negroes in the South, however, were too hard pressed for boastful speeches. With a hard-handed and meagerly educated white element coming to power, the odds were too strongly against them. They recognized that they needed more power and a firmer rooting in the soil. Their leaders had to employ conciliating devices to coax from the public chest their due in the matter of funds for education. One of these leaders, the principal of a state school for Negroes, characterized the then little known Booker T. Washington as a radical because he expressed the view that the Negro public schools should get more money. A few years later, when Booker T. Washington delivered his famous Atlanta address, a dangerous crisis in race relations had been reached. With extraordinary social insight he proposed a solution which checked the dread of social equality and created economic tolerance of Negroes in the South. He showed in a fortunate and simple figure of speech how the two races could live together separately; how they could have a common stake and interest in the prosperity of the South.

In proportion as this solution pleased the white South it infuriated northern Negroes. Washington was accused of "selling out the race"; of countenancing and rationalizing segregation; of being merely a polite "Uncle Tom." To most Negroes living in the South, however, the genius of this brilliant temporization was apparent. With the awakening interest of responsible southern white men, and the recognition of his ability and value by northern philanthropists, his influence spread to the North. As head of a Negro industrial school, a new contest of opinion arose over the merits of higher and industrial education. It was made an issue of profound racial significance, and it raged for fully two decades.

The World War marked a new period in the racial attitudes of Negroes. It was in some respects a revolt of the masses; it was an emancipation from the soil, and an introduction to the new life of free and impersonal competition in the industrial North; it lifted the living level of Negroes, and gave them a new outlook on life; it created a new sense of independence. Mere reference to events in this period should be sufficient to suggest the significance of this crisis: the war itself had carried thousands of Negroes to Europe and exposed millions to the spiritual disorganization of war. The riots that developed in northern cities around this period revealed in Negroes a modification of the traditional spirit of humility. There was evidence of the development of a nationalistic spirit in the widespread acceptance of the Garvey movement. There was the new race consciousness of younger Negroes as expressed in their literature.

The Negroes who remained in the South were not without a change in their racial attitudes. The concern over the numbers of Negroes leaving the section had stimulated some efforts to seek certain social improvements for them. There sprang up interracial bodies, sponsoring meetings in which the Negroes were allowed to say what was wrong. This invitation gave birth to a new articulation. These Negro spokesmen unburdened themselves of many grievances: inferior schools, poor wages, insanitary living areas, brutal police, injustice in the courts, incivility, insecurity of property and life. Many new Negro leaders were born in this emergency. Some of those who became overenthusiastic in their protests and demands found it expedient to join the migration. On the whole, however, it was the first important articulation of the southern Negro since slavery.

There are several fairly recent and somewhat related developments out of this period. The beginning of the industrialization of the Negro revealed the need for greater stress upon vocational training. In so far as this change of stress has softened the earlier contest between high and industrial education it may be said to have diminished the stress of the racial factor involved. Again, this same industrialization brought Negroes into contact with industrial workers. Such proximity, however, has not always softened racial attitudes, as the experience of Negroes with labor unions has, on the whole, revealed. But it has served to interest a few of these Negroes in the prospects of a new economic order. Although the numbers actually exposed to the economic doctrine of communism are not large, these Negro workers have been an excellent example of economic exploitation, and thus have been singled out for serious proselyting.

The results of this proselyting have been indirect and unexpedited. The projection of extremely radical economic and social programs has rendered more tolerable the less revolutionary campaigns for civil rights, which a few years ago were outlawed in the South.

The attitude of Negro college youth appears as yet to be one of scepticism about the possibility of improvement in race relations. As often as this attitude has found expression it has reflected a desire merely to "be let alone." This may be an indication of a disposition to resist further apology for race, and to assert a measure of self-reliance. It seems, however, never quite possible after college to be let alone, since there are still economic and other cultural necessities which relate themselves to the whole structure of slow changing race relations. Maturity comes, however, in a realistic world. The fact that many of them achieve a new adjustment as teachers and professional men, through becoming a part of the process of racial adjustment, suggests that the undergraduate attitude is but a subtle reappearance of defense psychology.

There have developed, over the past twenty years, two trends of policy which, in a measure, represent racial attitude, although they both have interracial participation. The point of view of the National Association for the Advancement of Colored People places stress upon the statutory rights of Negroes and aims both to insure more complete exercise of these rights, and to prevent further deprivation of them. It has learned to make advantageous coalitions with other groups in its programs. Its official organ, the *Crisis*, has been a stimulator to action. The other movement, headed by the National Urban League, has urged the necessity for an economic foothold in industry, and more complete integration of Negroes into urban life. Its programs have been carefully based upon studies, and in the attempt to be sound and scientific it has succeeded in making itself acceptably objective. The organ of this movement is *Opportunity*.

The influence of the Negro press cannot be ignored in the making and changing of Negro attitudes. These newspapers have wide circulation and are probably as influential in the selection, point of view, and stresses of the news articles as in the editorials. They are sensitive to every shade of racial discrimination and to manifestations of racial prejudice; they carry bold headlines about matters which a few years ago Negroes were most discreet about discussing in public. They are probably the most powerful sources of opinion within the Negro group, and undoubtedly the extent of their circulation offers some indication of their success in expressing the public opinion of the Negro group.

Reflected in most of these separate channels is what seems to be a broader and more significant change of attitude on race. It is the disposition to greater objectivity in the matter of race contact and relations, and about themselves. This can be noted when the expressions of most Negroes of influence are compared with those of two decades ago. There is a deliberate matter-of-factness about relations; a substitution of realism for emotional outburst; an effort, occasionally, to see the humor in situations which once could provoke only bitterness and despair. For those who are emancipating themselves to this extent, there is at least the relief from the embarrassing ritual of clanking their chains every time they arise to speak.

The change in Negro race attitudes over the years is by no means revolutionary; but the vanguard has unquestionably shifted forward.

PROBLEMS FOR STUDY

1. Since it has been more often the marginal Negro who has been the articulate one, what effect has this had upon present Negro-white relationships in America?
2. What evidences are there of the character of race relations existing between the non-articulate Negro group and the non-articulate white group?
3. To what extent may the migration of Negroes to the North be taken as an index to their attitudes?
4. What attitudes are implied in the terms "handkerchief-head Negro," "Uncle Tom," and "White folks' Negro"?
5. Compare the attitudes of the National Association for the Advancement of Colored People, the National Urban League, the Commission on Interracial Coöperation, and the American Communist party, as indicated in their programs.
6. What effect has increased education had upon Negro race attitudes?
7. Does the greater objectivity of certain Negroes, their increased measure of self-reliance and diminished apology for race, make possible greater or less interracial understanding, inasmuch as this attitude suggests increased confidence in their abilities?

CHAPTER XXIX

CAN THERE BE A SEPARATE NEGRO CULTURE?

The circumstances under which Negroes were introduced into the American culture obscured the serious problems ultimately to issue from this contact of widely different cultures. It could not have been anticipated in the beginning that such vast numbers would be introduced; and it is certain that there was no intention to attempt assimilation of these numbers. The requirements of the rôle for which Negroes were intended were relatively simple; their obvious physical differences were an advantage to identification, and their other social habits and wishes were reasonably controllable. There was no serious race problem under slavery. The problem arose with the sudden and complete destruction of the old social arrangement, and the necessity for making a new racial adjustment under the irreversible conditions of a tremendous Negro population growth, economic interdependence, and the partial acculturation of the Negro group. .

The most simple and agreeable solution of such a problem, as it first appears, would be the development of separate racial cultures, thus permitting each race, aided by human nature itself, to live its own life unhampered in its growth by the other. The Negro group in America is obviously different physically from the white group. The most natural organization of life is one that takes into account a group's unique physical characteristics. A race of short people would find itself adapting its cultural tools, its standards of beauty and acceptability, to itself in terms of its own dominant physical characteristics. The culture of the African is certainly different from that of the European. Religion, art, economic organization, concepts of morality, are all of another pattern. Moreover, with respect to æsthetic standards, where all people are black or brown, excellence and beauty are judged in terms of these values.

In evidence of the difference and mutual exclusiveness of these cultures, it has been noted by certain ethnologists that whiteness of skin, to certain African peoples who had never seen a white person before, suggested the unsightly discoloration of a person who had been dead long in the water. Another example of the color valuation is observed in the case cited of an African mother of a mixed blood baby, who tried to smoke it black over a fire, and, of course, unwittingly killed it. When native African girls of a west coast tribe apply for beauty's sake the equivalent of the American girl's cosmetics, they use a blue coloring for their lips and eyes. They thus achieve an accentuation of effect pleasing to the African male. A missionary, berating a Bongala man for filing his teeth, remarked that they were unbeautiful and looked like dog's teeth. The African, however, had his own standard and observed that the missionary's unfiled teeth were like bat's teeth. Among certain Mongolian peoples, with low nasal bones, the most beautiful woman is one who can balance a saucer on her cheeks. Similarly, among other groups, where obesity has a high æsthetic value, women have in extreme cases permitted themselves to become so helplessly obese as to require being fed by an attendant.

There are abundant evidences of the attempts among American Negroes, consciously and unconsciously, to approximate the physical standards of the American white culture. Sometimes these efforts become grotesque. Dr. Guy B. Johnson, of the University of North Carolina, has pointed out one of these adaptive traits in the popularity of hair straightening and skin whitening preparations. He asks, "Have hair straightening and skin lightening become permanent features of the Negro culture?" In five Negro newspapers he had noted that the largest amount of advertising carried was of these beauty preparations. The most race-conscious of all of these papers carried the largest proportion of space devoted to devices for obliterating the marks of difference. It may also be added that the most conspicuous wealth among individual American Negroes is that derived from the manufacture of certain of these preparations.

There is no such thing as an absolute standard of beauty, or form, or, indeed, of social morality. All is relative. It is when new concepts and standards of reference are introduced, and forced to supplant the original ones, that disorganization begins. The most disastrous effect of this disorganization is loss of self-respect, and of the essential security and poise which go with the feeling of physical and social adequacy.

For years Negroes have been urged to cease "imitating" the white man, and to use their own God-given qualities and graces to im-

CAN THERE BE A SEPARATE NEGRO CULTURE? 545

prove themselves. It has been commonly remarked that they are "happier in their own neighborhoods"; that they have their own churches and social sets; that they have their own newspapers, professional men, and their own Negro art and literature. Every city has its Negro quarter, its familiar hangouts and characters; the policy of official segregation has established special Negro compartments in trains, railway stations, amusement places, and special schools. Indeed, from this angle of view, the world of the Negro touches only slightly the world of the white man.

Some of the recognized cultural traits of the American Negro are his music, which includes spirituals, blues, and jazz; his sense of rhythm, as illustrated in the dance; his religion; and certain forms of art. The race pride of Negroes depends upon the development of some such distinctive background. Is not all of this culture? And for the greatest happiness of all, should not the wholesome extension of this type of bi-racialism be encouraged as the cultural objective of the Negroes? They would retain their self-respect and in addition have the aid of well-wishing white men.

There are, however, some formidable difficulties in establishing a separate culture in America. The first of these difficulties arises from the fact that the original African culture of the American Negro is very largely lost. Detached from the environment in which the culture evolved, it is not unnatural that the original culture drives should have weakened. An efficient integration of life presupposes the interfunctioning of innumerable elements of the complex structure of a society. African music and the dance, for example, are not mere amusement; they are almost invariably a phase of some ceremonial complex. "Music and the dance," as E. M. von Hornbostel observes, "serve neither as mere past times nor recreations. . . . Music is neither reproduction (of a 'piece of music' as an existing object) nor production (of a new object): it is the life of a living spirit working within those who dance and sing.[1] . . . Our [European] music cannot be a substitute for the Negro's own: not because it is so thoroughly different, or because it does not suit him, or because he is unable to understand it, but because it has not originated and grown within him."[2] The native African music and dance belong to Africa and the social organization of which it is a vital element.

The same is true of other phases of life. The difference in funda-

[1] "African Negro Music," *Africa*, January, 1928, p. 59.
[2] *Ibid.*, p. 60.

mental conceptions of law and justice between the African and the European offers another example. J. H. Driberg notes that the African conception of law is both more individual and more communal than the European. There are "many spheres of law — family, clan, association, and tribal, inter-related but independent, all subservient to the one tribal law, but individually self-sufficient." [1] There is no written code, but traditional observances. It is positive rather than negative, in that it directs the behavior of individuals and communities. A crime, thus, is a disturbance of individual or communal equilibrium, and the law seeks to restore this equilibrium. The penal theory familiar to the European does not enter African law except in acts regarded as subversive of the whole fabric of the society. Thus murder, theft, adultery, and slander are crimes against individuals, and restitution is usually sufficient; while witchcraft, incest, and sexual perversions are crimes against the whole body politic and merit expulsion from it.

These conceptions are parts of the intangible culture and are interrelated with the entire fabric of social life. When these conceptions are removed from the special social organization which is responsible for them, they no longer have purpose or utility. Indeed, it is because of the introduction of European conceptions of law into the administration of their colonial possessions that there has been such dismal disintegration of the social life of the natives. If such disintegration is possible in the African setting of the native, how much more thorough must be this disorganization when individuals are completely separated from their original setting and placed in a new culture. Reorganization of life is necessary for survival, and the only reorganization possible, in the midst of a dominant culture, is one based upon this culture's own postulates.

When attention is directed to American Negroes apart from the African culture, further difficulties appear. One of the firmest elements in any culture is that of its economic organization. There is not, and apparently cannot be, an exclusive Negro economy within the American culture, whether as a separate and distinct organization or one that is separate but the same. The work of Negroes is seriously proscribed, but all such work is within the American economic system. It must be evident how impossible any other arrangement would be. The excitement over the flurry of interest of an utterly inconsequential number of American Negroes interested in

[1] "Primitive Law in Eastern Africa," *Africa*, January, 1928, p. 63.

communism, as an economic system, indicates the opposition of the nation itself to such economic innovation on the part of Negroes. Interestingly enough, communism is the most common economic organization of African Negroes, and might be considered a logical economic basis for a separate American culture if one were possible. Equally futile is the prospect of a concentric capitalistic order, such as would provide Negro businesses supported by Negroes employing the entire Negro population, and at the same time supplying all their material needs. At present some 25,000 Negro businesses employ about 12,000 individuals other than the proprietors.

The standards of living are different, it is true, but the difference is not cultural; one is simply higher in the scale than the other. And all Negro standards of living are not low. The division is purely statistical. The code of morals by which Negroes live, however imperfectly, is European; the system of marriage is monogamy; the standards of justice and the law are American; vested property rights, the machine pattern of culture, are all Euro-American. Any American Negro who tried to live otherwise than by these codes and standards would quickly be crushed for his non-conformity. These are the basic elements of a culture, and conformity is the test of survival. There is not a Negro test of character, of capacity for self-maintenance, of intelligence, of law observance, of manners, of taste, or of æsthetic sense, that is not based upon this culture. When there is racial segregation it is not in terms of two cultures, but in terms of different planes of the same culture. The fact that there is discrimination is another way of indicating the identity of the culture, for the term has no meaning when they are different. There is a strong suggestion that what is really meant is that these different planes should constitute the separate cultures.

Few new unique cultures have been developed within man's knowledge of his own social life. The assumption that Negroes can develop a separate and different culture in America, however, carries with it the further flattery that they can resist the powerful influences of the culture with which they are already in complete contact.

Assuming that the minority Negro group were sufficiently powerful to resist surrounding influences to the point of creating even one or two strains that are culturally new, there is no certainty that they would be allowed to remain their own, by virtue of their creation. Stephen Foster has the official credit for the sentimental ballads which the slaves sang, and probably more Americans are familiar with the words and tunes of these ballads than can sing the American national anthem.

The extraordinary difficulty of living in the midst of a culture without absorbing it is illustrated in the fact of the immediate absorption by the American white race of every specialization developed by Negroes out of their unique American status. Jazz music offers one useful example. Negro music is one of the qualities which provide an argument for both the possibility and the desirability of a separate Negro culture. The origin of jazz music is the syncopation of the Negro ragtime melodies. The themes are Negro; the most effective instruments are those associated most commonly with Negro use; the improvisations which give to jazz themes a distinctive quality of syncopation are Negro.

Although jazz may have originated with American Negroes, it is, as everyone now knows, no longer a Negro specialization. Most of the popular American music is jazz, and most of the best-paid popular band and orchestra leaders are white. It no longer expresses the "native sense of rhythm" of the Negro, but "the complicated vigor of American life." It may be barbaric, but in Europe it has come to mean something typically American. As Gilbert Seldes, one of the æsthetes, reminds us most convincingly, there is in the words and music something "which underlies a great deal of America — our independence, our frankness, and gaiety. . . . If we give up jazz, we shall be sacrificing nearly all there is of gaiety and liveliness and rhythmic power in our lives." There is something terrifically ironic in this observation, which can be recognized as essentially sound.

What has happened in the case of jazz, however, has also happened in the case of other American Negro specializations. The complicated dances known as the "Charleston" and "Black Bottom" were creations of the folk Negro. These dances, as soon as they were introduced, swept sophisticated America and Europe, and in the end the champion performers who got into the papers were not Negroes, but white. Amos and Andy, the popular radio stars, achieved their popularity and sustained relations with the public, not merely because they are black-faced comedians, and are, presumably, representing Negroes, but because, in so representing them, they become basically and universally human.

It is scarcely less strange as a process to see a Negro "imitating" a white person than to observe Al Jolson blackening his face and floating to immense popularity singing "mammy songs," or to ob-

CAN THERE BE A SEPARATE NEGRO CULTURE? 549

serve a popular white stage star, unblackened, winning popular acclaim singing the Negro "blues." Even expressions of the Negro folk religion, such as are presented in *Green Pastures*, became a Broadway theatrical success; and the Negro religious services of Elder Micheaux of Washington, with their shouting, singing, and stamping of feet, are given a favorite hour on the radio. No national broadcasting company would, as yet, regard it as profitable to provide this special hour for the edification of Negroes of the culture level represented by these services. This mutual borrowing of specializations is not limited to non-material objects. While it may seem strange to observe Negroes straightening their curly hair and whitening their dark skins, the reverse process is the same when white women curl their straight hair and suntan their white skins. The Negroes never become wholly white by the artificial aid, nor do the whites become wholly brown, and both would deny that the objective was to be like the other; the whites, perhaps more indignantly than the Negroes. The physical process is similar whatever the conscious motivation.

Three important efforts have been made by Negroes in the direction of separate cultural development in America. The first of these to attract notice to itself was the so-called Garvey movement. Following the wave of nationalism in Europe, Marcus Garvey, a West Indian Negro in the United States, captured the imagination of American Negroes by promising a racial escape into a situation in which they could develop a life and culture of their own. His was a consistent philosophy, and a significant one. Along with the political slogan of "Africa for the Africans," and the commercial support to the idea of a steamship line by which this repatriation would be affected, he promised to salvage Negro self-respect. This was to be done by changing the connotation of "blackness"; it should have dignity, and a new and wholesome meaning. His steamship line would not be a "White Star Line" but a "Black Star Line"; there would be "Black Cross" nurses. No longer should Negroes pray to a white God; the God of the Negro must be visualized in the image of Negroes, as black. Although a dream impossible of achievement, it did offer a psychic relaxation for thousands of Negroes submerged in the American culture.

Though knowing full well that the whole fabric of the scheme was illusory and impossible, these Negroes supported it with an astonishing enthusiasm. At one time over 100,000 American Negroes were contributing from their small funds to purchase ships. They paraded as Black Cross nurses and Knights of the Order of the Nile in virtually every large city of the country. The difficulties encountered were the typical ones: Garvey violated some of the tenets of the dominant culture, in presuming to establish another one for Negroes, and he was promptly imprisoned in the Federal Penitentiary in Atlanta for six years. The movement could not survive this shock.

Another effort has been the milder one of inculcating race pride and respect by substituting Negro characters of history for white characters, or of supplementing history with the addition of these neglected names. The undoubted benefit of such supplementations, however, lacks an essential value of communicating this knowledge to white persons as well as Negroes. Race pride is not enough; there must also be respect for race. Status is determined not alone by what one group thinks of itself, but also by what others think of it.

Still another attempt has recently developed within the more sophisticated elements of the Negro population. Those of the younger generation of Negroes, who, by virtue of their competence in the general culture, have achieved a measure of cultural emancipation, have turned back frankly to discover the beauty and charm of the life of the folk Negro. The work of these writers is discussed at greater length in another chapter of this volume but deserves some attention here as an expression of a new race consciousness.

Commentators farther removed from this present phase of Negro expression will be able to define more clearly the influence of those social and economic forces shortly after the World War, moving beneath the new mind of Negroes, which burst forth with freshness and vigor in an artistic "awakening." The first startlingly authentic note was sounded by Claude McKay, a Jamaican Negro living in America. If his was a note of protest it came clear and unquivering. But it was more than a protest note; it was one of stoical defiance which held behind it a spirit magnificent and glowing. One poem, "If We Must Die," written at the most acute point of the industrialization of Negroes, when sudden mass contact in the northern states was flaming into riots, voiced for Negroes, where it did not itself create, a mood of stubborn defiance. It was reprinted in practically every Negro newspaper, and quoted wherever its audacious lines could be remembered. But McKay could also write lyrics utterly divorced from these singing daggers. "Spring in New Hampshire" is one of them. He discovered Harlem and found a language of beauty for his own world of color:

> Her voice was like the sound of blended flutes
> Blown by black players on a picnic day.

Jean Toomer flashed like a blazing meteor across the sky, then sank from view. But in the brilliant moment of his flight he illumined the forefield of this new Negro literature. *Cane*, a collection of verse and stories, appeared about two years ahead of its sustaining public mood. It was significantly a return of the son to the Southland, to the stark, natural beauties of its life and soil, a life deep and strong, and a virgin soil:

> O land and soil, red soil and sweet gum-tree,
> So scant of grass, so profligate of pines,
> Now just before an epoch's sun declines
> Thy son, in time, I have returned to thee,
> Thy son, I have in time returned to thee.

Here was, triumphantly, the Negro artist detached from propaganda, sensitive only to beauty. Where Dunbar gave to the unnamed Negro peasant a reassuring touch of humanity, Toomer gave to this peasant a passionate charm:

> Her skin is like dusk on the Eastern Horizon,
> O can't you see it, O can't you see it,
> Her skin is like dusk on the Eastern Horizon,
> — When the sun goes down.

More than artist, he was an experimentalist, and this last quality carried him away from what was, perhaps, the most astonishingly brilliant beginning of any Negro writer of this generation.

With Countee Cullen came a new generation of Negro singers. Claude McKay had brought a strange geographical background to the American scene which enabled him to escape a measure of the peculiar social heritage of the American Negro which similarly lacked the impedimenta of an inhibiting tradition. Cullen relied upon nothing but his own sure competence and art; one month found three literary magazines carrying his verse simultaneously, a distinction not to be spurned by any young poet. Then came his first volume, *Color*. He brought an uncannily sudden maturity and classic sweep, a swift grace and an inescapable beauty of style and meaning. The spirit of the transplanted African moved through his music to a new definition — relating itself boldly to its past and present:

> Lord, not for what I saw in flesh or bone
> Of fairer men; not raised on faith alone;
> Lord, I will live persuaded by mine own.
> I cannot play the recreant to these;
> My spirit has come home, that sailed the doubtful seas.

Thus he spoke, not for himself alone, but for the confident generation out of which he came. White gods were put aside and in their place arose the graces of a race he knew:

> Her walk is like the replica
> Of some barbaric dance
> Wherein the soul of Africa
> Is winged with arrogance.

and again:

> That brown girl's swagger gives a twitch
> To beauty like a queen.

No brief quotations can describe this power, this questioning of life and even God; the swift arrow thrusts of irony curiously mingled with admiration; the self-reliance and bold pride of race; the thorough repudiation of the double standard of literary judgment. He may have marveled "at this curious thing: to make a poet black and bid him sing," but in his *Heritage* he voiced the half-religious, half-challenging spirit of an awakened generation:

> Lord, I fashion dark gods too
> Daring even to give to You
> Dark, despairing features where
> Crowned with a dark rebellious hair,
> Patience wavers just so much as
> Mortal grief compels, while touches
> Faint and slow, of anger rise
> To sunken cheek and weary eyes.
>
> Lord, forgive me if my need
> Sometimes shapes a human creed.

"He will be remembered," says the *Manchester Guardian*, "as one who contributed to his age some of its loveliest lyric poetry."

Langston Hughes, at twenty-four, had published two volumes of verse. No Negro writer so completely symbolizes the new emanci-

CAN THERE BE A SEPARATE NEGRO CULTURE? 553

pation of the Negro mind. His is a poetry of gorgeous colors, of restless brooding, of melancholy, of disillusionment:

> We should have a land of sun
> Of gorgeous sun,
> And a land of fragrant water
>
> Where the twilight
> Is a soft bandana handkerchief
> Of rose and gold
> And not this land where life is cold.

Always there is, in his writing, a wistful undertone, a quiet sadness. That is why, perhaps, he could speak so tenderly of the broken lives of prostitutes, the inner weariness of painted "jazz-hounds" and the tragic emptiness beneath the glamour and noise of Harlem cabarets. His first volume, *The Weary Blues*, contained many moods; the second, *Fine Clothes to the Jew*, marked a final frank turning to the folk life of the Negro, a striving to catch and give back to the world the strange music of the unlettered Negro — his "blues." If Cullen has given a classic beauty to the emotions of his people, Hughes has given a warm glow of meaning to their lives.

The result of this emancipation, paradoxically enough, has been to enrich the general culture rather than to develop a distinctive Negro expression.

It is possible that the unique life of all Negroes in America, their physical differences, the naïveté of the unlettered, and any other discoverable qualities of the race, can give a dash of color to their contribution, but a separate culture seems, in the nature of things, an impossible dream. So long as they remain in contact with another and stronger culture they will be influenced by it and they will influence it.

Cultural contributions are, after all, individual rather than group contributions. As Dr. E. B. Reuter says of this possibility:

> Jews and Protestants and Republicans have made valuable culture contributions but they are the work of individuals; they are not group products.

The question in its application to Negroes draws from him an even more direct and explicit comment on the possibilities of racial art and culture:

> When it is asserted that Negroes have a peculiar aptitude for music, the statement can mean nothing more than that there are among the Negroes

more talented individuals per million of the population than among the whites. No one would assert that all Negroes have a talent for music nor deny that some white men are especially gifted in that respect. Musical composition is the work of individuals and not of groups. Quite irrespective of race, individuals will be attracted to and succeed in vocations along the line of their special abilities. It might conceivably be that Negro individuals in the future will write ten or a hundred musical compositions for one of equal rank produced by white men. But this would not make a Negro music: it would simply mean that Negro individuals contribute more than do white artists to the development of an art. The art itself is not racial.[1]

Cultures, after all, develop by constant borrowing and adaptation, rather than by the isolated evolution of some unique racial quality. The Christian religion came from the Semites, gunpowder and the printing press from ancient China; our symbols of number, the Arabic notation, decimal system, algebra, and trigonometry came from ancient India, our alphabet from the Phœnicians; iron smelting came from Africa, chemistry from the Hindus; and Greek civilization had its root in Egypt.

A race problem is scarcely ever settled within a generation. Despite the discomforts on the one side and the anxieties on the other, the mills of the gods grind exceedingly slow. Perhaps, no one living today will see the end of either the discomforts or the anxieties. As man has gained a large measure of control over physical forces it is hoped that he can gain at least an equal measure of control over social forces. It is possible for men to change their own attitudes toward themselves as well as toward others; it is possible even to change human nature. Meanwhile there is the clear obligation to find a basis of racial adjustment which yields the greatest measure of mutual tolerance and fullest expression of those principles which give purpose to civilization and meaning to life. "If you know well the beginning," says an old African proverb, "the end will not trouble you much."

PROBLEMS FOR STUDY

1. Slavery has been called an educative process for Negroes. Was it a mistake to destroy the African culture?
2. Park and Burgess describe assimilation as a process of "interpenetration and fusion in which persons and groups acquire the memories, senti-

[1] "The Possibility of a Distinctive Culture Contribution from the American Negro," in *Social Attitudes*, edited by Kimball Young, chap. 14, pp. 354–355.

ments, and attitudes of other persons or groups, and by sharing their experience and history are incorporated with them in a common cultural life." To what extent is this true of Negroes in America?
3. Alexander Pushkin, father of modern Russian literature; Alexander Dumas, French novelist; and Samuel Coleridge-Taylor, English composer, were of Negro descent, but their contributions were national rather than racial. Why did they not show a persistence of their African background?
4. Has the incorporation of the Negro personality in the American milieu placed him beyond hope of African repatriation?
5. It has been urged that whereas a separate culture is impossible, it would be desirable and possible for Negroes to develop a separate and satisfying social life within the American culture. What are the advantages and disadvantages of such an arrangement?
6. Are there any perceptible influences of Negro characteristics or behavior patterns upon the white population?
7. How may "acculturation" be distinguished from "imitation" in the process of group development within a given culture?

BIBLIOGRAPHY

Countee Cullen, *Color* (1925).
Countee Cullen, *Copper Sun* (1927).
Jack H. Driberg, "Primitive Law in Eastern Africa," *Africa*, January, 1928, pp. 63–72.
E. M. von Hornbostel, "African Negro Music," *Africa*, January, 1928, pp. 30–62.
Langston Hughes, *Fine Clothes to the Jew* (1927).
Langston Hughes, *The Weary Blues* (1929).
Claude McKay, *Harlem Shadows* (1922).
Claude McKay, *Spring in New Hampshire* (1921).
Edward B. Reuter, "The Possibility of a Distinctive Culture Contribution from the American Negro." Chap. 14 of *Social Attitudes*, edited by Kimball Young (1931).
Jean Toomer, *Cane* (1923).

BIBLIOGRAPHY

ADGER, JOHN B., *My Life and Times, 1810–1899.* Presbyterian Committee of Publication, Richmond, 1899.

African Repository. 68 vols. American Colonization Society, 1826–1892. See especially issues mentioned in the text.

ALLEN, FLOYD P., "Physical Impairment among One Thousand Negro Workers," *American Journal of Public Health*, June, 1932, pp. 579–586.

ALVORD, JOHN W., *Report on Schools and Finances of Freedmen.* Bureau of Refugees and Freedmen, Washington, January, 1866.

American Academy of Political and Social Science, *The Negro's Progress in Fifty Years.* American Academy of Political and Social Science, West Philadelphia, 1913.

American Colonization Society, *Annual Reports.* Washington, 1818–1910. See especially reports mentioned in the text.

American Freedman. American Freedmen's Union Commission, New York, 1866. See especially issues mentioned in the text.

Annals of Congress. Washington. See especially those mentioned in the text.

Anti-Slavery Record. American Anti-Slavery Society, New York, 1836. See especially issues mentioned in the text.

ARMISTEAD, W. S., *The Negro Is a Man.* Armistead and Vickers, Tifton, 1903.

ASBURY, FRANCIS, *The Journal of the Rev. Francis Asbury, Bishop of the Methodist Episcopal Church, from Aug. 7, 1771, to Dec. 7, 1815.* N. Bangs and T. Mason, New York, 1821.

Association for the Religious Instruction of the Negroes in Liberty County, Georgia, *Annual Reports.* Savannah. See especially the reports mentioned in the text.

AZURARA, GOMES E. DE, *The Chronicle of the Discovery and Conquest of Guinea* (tr. by C. Raymond Beazley and Edgar Prestage). Hakluyt Society, London, 1896–1897.

BACON, LEONARD W., *A History of American Christianity.* Charles Scribner's Sons, New York, 1901.

BAILEY, THOMAS P., *Race Orthodoxy in the South.* Neale Publishing Company, New York, 1914.

BAKER, RAY S., *Following the Color Line.* Doubleday, Page and Company, New York, 1908.

BALLAGH, JAMES C., *A History of Slavery in Virginia.* Johns Hopkins Press, Baltimore, 1902.

BALLAGH, JAMES C., *White Servitude in the Colony of Virginia.* Johns Hopkins Press, Baltimore, 1895.

BANCROFT, FREDERIC, *Slave-trading in the Old South*. J. H. Furst Company, Baltimore, 1931.
BANCROFT, GEORGE, *History of the United States from the Discovery of the Continent to the Establishment of the Constitution in 1789*. D. Appleton and Company, New York, 1839.
Baptist Church, *Minutes of the Charleston Baptist Association* (1835).
Baptist Church, *Minutes of the Southern Baptist Convention* (1845).
Baptist Church, *Minutes of the Welch Neck (S.C.) Baptist Association* (1841).
Baptist Church, *Proceedings of the Baptist General Convention in Richmond* (1835).
Baptist Church, *Proceedings of the Southern Baptist Convention* (1849, 1859).
BARNES, HARRY E., *History and Social Intelligence*. Alfred A. Knopf, New York, 1926.
BARTH, HENRY, *Travels and Discoveries in North and Central Africa*. Harper and Brothers, New York, 1857–1859.
BASSETT, JOHN S., *Slavery and Servitude in the Colony of North Carolina*. Johns Hopkins Press, Baltimore, 1896.
BASSETT, JOHN S., *Slavery in the State of North Carolina*. Johns Hopkins Press, Baltimore, 1899.
BEAN, ROBERT B., "Some Racial Peculiarities of the Negro Brain," *American Journal of Anatomy*, September, 1906, pp. 353–389.
BENEZET, ANTHONY, *Some Historical Account of Guinea . . . with an Inquiry into the Rise and Progress of the Slave Trade*. New Edition, J. Phillips, London, 1788.
BENTON, THOMAS H., *Historical and Legal Examination of That Part of the Decision of the Supreme Court of the United States in the Dred Scott Case, Which Declares the Unconstitutionality of the Missouri Compromise Act, and the Self-Extension of the Constitution to the Territories, Carrying Slavery along with It*. D. Appleton and Company, New York, 1857.
BLAKE, WILLIAM O., *The History of Slavery and the Slave Trade, Ancient and Modern*. J. and H. Miller, Columbus, 1858.
BOAS, FRANZ, *The Mind of Primitive Man*. The Macmillan Company, New York, 1911.
BOAS, FRANZ, *Anthropology and Modern Life*. W. W. Norton and Company, New York, 1932.
BOGARDUS, EMORY S., *Immigration and Race Attitudes*. D. C. Heath and Company, Boston, 1928.
BOWDEN, JAMES, *The History of the Society of Friends in America*. Charles Gilpin, London, 1850, 1854.
BOWDEN, ROBERT D., *In Defense of Tomorrow*. The Macmillan Company, New York, 1931.
BRACKETT, JEFFREY R., *The Negro in Maryland*. N. Murray, Baltimore, 1889.
BRADLEY, ROBERT N., *Racial Origins of English Character*. G. Allen and Unwin, Ltd., London, 1926.
BRAITHWAITE, WILLIAM S. B., *The House of Falling Leaves*. John W. Luce and Company, Boston, 1908.

BRAWLEY, BENJAMIN G., *The Negro in Literature and Art in the United States.* Duffield and Company, 1930.
BRAWLEY, BENJAMIN G., *A Short History of the American Negro.* The Macmillan Company, New York, 1931.
BRITTEN, R. H., "Some Tendencies Indicated by the New Life Tables," *Public Health Reports,* April 11, 1924, pp. 737–749.
BROWN, SARA W., "Colored Women Physicians," *Southern Workman,* December, 1923, pp. 580–593.
BROWN, WILLIAM G., *The Lower South in American History.* Peter Smith, New York, 1930.
BROWN, WILLIAM W., *The Anti-Slavery Harp.* Bela Marsh, Boston, 1848.
BROWN, WILLIAM W., *The Black Man, His Antecedents, His Genius, and His Achievements.* Robert F. Wallcut, Boston, 1865.
BROWN, WILLIAM W., *The Rising Son; or The Antecedents and Advancement of the Colored Race.* A. G. Brown and Company, Boston, 1874.
BROWNING, JAMES B., "The North Carolina Black Code," *Journal of Negro History,* October, 1930, pp. 461–473.
BRUCE, PHILIP A., *Economic History of Virginia in the Seventeenth Century.* The Macmillan Company, New York, 1895.
BRUCE, PHILIP A., *Institutional History of Virginia in the Seventeenth Century.* G. P. Putnam's Sons, New York, 1910.
BRUCE, PHILIP A., *Social Life in Virginia in the Seventeenth Century.* J. P. Bell Company, Lynchburg, 1927.
BULLOCK, RALPH W., *In Spite of Handicaps.* Association Press, New York, 1927.
BURKE, EDMUND, *On Conciliation with the Colonies.*
BURLIN, NATALIE C., *Negro Folk-Songs.* G. Schirmer, New York, 1918.
BURTON, RICHARD F., *The Lake Regions of Central Africa.* Harper and Brothers, New York, 1860.
BURTON, RICHARD F., *Wit and Wisdom from West Africa.* Tinsley Brothers, London, 1865.
BUXTON, THOMAS F., *The African Slave Trade and Its Remedy.* John Murray, London, 1840.

CABLE, GEORGE W., *The Silent South.* Charles Scribner's Sons, New York, 1885.
CAIRNES, JOHN E., *The Slave Power.* Carleton, New York, 1862.
The Call of the New South. Southern Sociological Congress, Nashville, 1912.
CAREY, HENRY C., *The Slave Trade, Domestic and Foreign.* Henry Carey Baird, Philadelphia, 1872.
CARPENTER, NILES, *The Sociology of City Life.* Longmans, Green and Company, New York, 1931.
CARROLL, CHARLES, *The Negro a Beast or in the Image of God.* American Book and Bible House, St. Louis, 1900.
CARTER, FRANKLIN, *General Armstrong's Life and Work.* Hampton Normal and Agricultural Institute, Hampton, 1911.
CATTERALL, HELEN T. (Ed.), *Judicial Cases concerning American Slavery and the Negro.* Carnegie Institution of Washington, Washington, 1927.

BIBLIOGRAPHY

CHAMBERLAIN, ALEXANDER F., "The Contribution of the Negro to Human Civilization," *Journal of Race Development*, April, 1911, pp. 482–502.

CHAMBERS, WILLIAM, *American Slavery and Colour*. W. and R. Chambers, New York, 1857.

CHASE, STUART, *Men and Machines*. The Macmillan Company, New York, 1929.

CHRISTIAN, JOHN T., *A History of the Baptists*. Baptist Sunday School Board (Southern Baptist Convention), Nashville, 1922.

CLARK, TALIAFERRO, *The Control of Syphilis in Southern Rural Areas*. Julius Rosenwald Fund, 1930.

COFFIN, JOSHUA, *An Account of Some of the Principal Slave Insurrections, and Others, Which Have Occurred, or Been Attempted, in the United States and Elsewhere, during the Last Two Centuries*. American Anti-Slavery Society, New York, 1860.

COKE, THOMAS, *A History of the West Indies*. Nuttall, Fisher and Dixon, Liverpool, 1808.

COLLINS, WINFIELD H., *The Truth about Lynching and the Negro in the South*. Neale Publishing Company, New York, 1918.

Congressional Record, Senate, 4th Congress, Vol. 10, Part 5. Washington, 1880.

CONKLIN, EDWIN G., *The Direction of Human Evolution*. Charles Scribner's Sons, New York, 1922.

COOKE, DENNIS H., *The White Superintendent and the Negro Schools in North Carolina*. George Peabody College for Teachers, Nashville, 1930.

COOLEY, HENRY S., *A Study of Slavery in New Jersey*. Johns Hopkins Press, Baltimore, 1896.

CRAWFORD, DANIEL, *Thinking Black*. Morgan and Scott, London, 1914.

CULLEN, COUNTEE, *Caroling Dusk*. Harper and Brothers, New York, 1927.

CULLEN, COUNTEE, *Color*. Harper and Brothers, New York, 1925.

CULLEN, COUNTEE, *Copper Sun*. Harper and Brothers, New York, 1927.

CUTLER, JAMES E., *Lynch Law*. Longmans, Green and Company, New York, 1905.

DANIEL, WILLIAM A., *The Education of Negro Ministers*. George H. Doran Company, New York, 1925.

DAVENPORT, CHARLES B., *Heredity in Relation to Eugenics*. Henry Holt and Company, New York, 1911.

DAVENPORT, CHARLES B., and others, *Race Crossing in Jamaica*. Carnegie Institution of Washington, Washington, 1929.

DAVIS, J. R., "Negro Servitude in the United States," *Journal of Negro History*, July, 1923, pp. 247–283.

DAY, CAROLINE B., *A Study of Some Negro-White Families in the United States*. Peabody Museum of Harvard University, Cambridge, 1932.

DE BOW, JAMES D. B., *The Industrial Resources, etc., of the Southern and Western States*. Published at the office of *De Bow's Review*, New Orleans, 1852–1853.

De Bow's Review . . . Agricultural, Commercial, Industrial. 43 vols. J. D. B. De Bow (etc.), New Orleans, 1846–1880.

DEEMS, CHARLES F., *Annals of Southern Methodism for 1855.* J. A. Gray's Printing Office, New York, 1856.
DEEMS, CHARLES F., *Annals of Southern Methodism for 1857.* J. B. M'Ferrin, Agent, for the Methodist Episcopal Church South, 1858.
DELAFOSSE, MAURICE, *Negroes of Africa.* Associated Publishers, Washington, 1931.
DENISON, JOHN H., *Emotion as the Basis of Civilization.* Charles Scribner's Sons, New York, 1928.
DETWEILER, FREDERICK G., *The Negro Press in the United States.* University of Chicago Press, Chicago, 1922.
DETWEILER, FREDERICK G., "The Rise of Modern Race Antagonisms," *American Journal of Sociology,* March, 1932, pp. 738–747.
DIXON, ROLAND B., *The Building of Cultures.* Charles Scribner's Sons, New York, 1928.
DODD, WILLIAM E., *The Cotton Kingdom.* Yale University Press, New Haven, 1920.
DONNAN, ELIZABETH (Ed.), *Documents Illustrative of the History of the Slave Trade to America.* Carnegie Institution of Washington, Washington, 1930–1933.
DOUGLAS, PAUL H., *American Apprenticeship and Industrial Education.* Columbia University Press, New York, 1921.
DOW, GEORGE F., *Slave Ships and Slaving.* Marine Research Society, Salem, 1927.
DOWD, JEROME, *The Negro in American Life.* The Century Company, New York, 1926.
DOWD, JEROME, *The Negro Races.* The Macmillan Company, New York, 1907.
DREW, SAMUEL, *The Life of the Rev. Thomas Coke.* Lane and Tippett, New York, 1847.
DREWRY, WILLIAM S., *Slave Insurrections in Virginia (1830–1865).* The Neale Company, Washington, 1900.
DRIBERG, JACK H., "Primitive Law in Eastern Africa," *Africa,* January, 1928, pp. 63–72.
DUBLIN, LOUIS I., *Health and Wealth.* Harper and Brothers, New York, 1928.
DUBLIN, LOUIS I., "Tuberculosis among Industrial Workers," *American Journal of Public Health,* March, 1932, pp. 281–291.
DU BOIS, WILLIAM E. B. (Ed.), *Efforts for Social Betterment among Negro Americans.* Atlanta University Press, Atlanta, 1909.
DU BOIS, WILLIAM E. B., *Some Notes on Negro Crime, Particularly in Georgia.* Atlanta University Press, Atlanta, 1904.
DU BOIS, WILLIAM E. B., *The Health and Physique of the Negro American.* Atlanta University Press, Atlanta, 1906.
DU BOIS, WILLIAM E. B. (Ed.), *The Negro American Family.* Atlanta University Press, Atlanta, 1908.
DU BOIS, WILLIAM E. B., *The Negro Church.* Atlanta University Press, Atlanta, 1928.
DU BOIS, WILLIAM E. B., *The Souls of Black Folk.* A. C. McClurg and Company, Chicago, 1903.

Du Bois, William E. B., *The Suppression of the African Slave-trade to the United States of America, 1638–1870.* Harvard University Press, Cambridge, 1896.
Du Bois, William E.B., "Will the Church Remove the Color Line?" *Christian Century,* December 9, 1931, pp. 1554–1556.
Du Bois, William E. B., and Dill, A. G. (Eds.), *The College-bred Negro American.* Atlanta University Press, Atlanta, 1910.
Du Bois, William E. B., and Dill, A. G. (Eds.), *The Common School and the Negro American.* Atlanta University Press, Atlanta, 1911.
Du Bois, William E. B., and Dill, A. G. (Eds.), *Morals and Manners among Negro Americans.* Atlanta University Press, Atlanta, 1914.
Duff, Charles, *This Human Nature.* Cosmopolitan Book Company, New York, 1930.
Dunbar, Paul L., *The Complete Poems of Paul Laurence Dunbar.* Dodd, Mead and Company, New York, 1913.
Dunning, William A., *Essays on the Civil War and Reconstruction and Related Topics.* The Macmillan Company, New York, 1904.
Dunning, William A., *Reconstruction, Political and Economic, 1865–1877.* Harper and Brothers, New York, 1907.

East, Edward M., *Mankind at the Crossroads.* Charles Scribner's Sons, New York, 1924.
East, Edward M., and Jones, Donald F., *Inbreeding and Outbreeding: Their Genetic and Sociological Significance.* J. B. Lippincott Company, Philadelphia, 1919.
Edge, Frederick M., *Slavery Doomed; or the Contest between Free and Slave Labour in the United States.* Smith Elder and Company, London, 1860.
Educational Commission for Freedmen, *First Annual Report.* Prentiss and Deland, Boston, 1863.
Elliott, E. N. (Ed.), *Cotton Is King and Pro-Slavery Arguments.* Pritchard, Abbott and Loomis, Augusta, 1860.
Embree, Edwin R., *Brown America.* The Viking Press, New York, 1931.
Eppes, Susan B., *The Negro of the Old South.* J. G. Branch Publishing Company, Chicago, 1925.
Eppes, Susan B., *Through Some Eventful Years.* J. W. Burke Company, Macon, 1926.
Epstein, Abraham, *The Negro Migrant in Pittsburgh.* University of Pittsburgh Press, Pittsburgh, 1918.
Eubank, Earle, "The Consequences of Unemployment in Cincinnati." (Unpublished study.)

Falk, Isidore S., Rorem, C. Rufus, and Ring, Martha D., *Costs of Medical Care.* University of Chicago Press, Chicago, 1933.
Faris, Ellsworth, "The Mental Capacity of Savages," *American Journal of Sociology,* March, 1918, pp. 603–609.

FARIS, ELLSWORTH, "The Natural History of Race Prejudice," in Charles S. Johnson (Ed.), *Ebony and Topaz*. National Negro Urban League, New York, 1926.

FARIS, ELLSWORTH, "Racial Attitudes and Sentiments," *Southwestern Political and Social Science Quarterly*, March, 1929, pp. 479–490.

FAUSET, ARTHUR H., *For Freedom*. Franklin Publishing and Supply Company, Philadelphia, 1927.

FAVROT, LEO M., *A Study of County Training Schools for Negroes in the South*. John F. Slater Fund, Charlottesville, 1923.

FELDMAN, HERMAN, *Racial Factors in American Industry*. Harper and Brothers, New York, 1931.

FINOT, JEAN, *Race Prejudice*. E. P. Dutton and Company, New York, 1907.

FISKE, AMOS K., *The West Indies*. G. P. Putnam's Sons, New York, 1899.

FISKE, JOHN, *Old Virginia and Her Neighbours*. Houghton Mifflin Company, Boston, 1897.

FITHIAN, PHILIP V., *Journal and Letters, 1767–1774*. Princeton University Press, Princeton, 1900.

FLEMING, WALTER L., *Documentary History of Reconstruction, Political, Military, Social, Religious, Educational, and Industrial, 1865 to the Present Time*. A. H. Clark Company, Cleveland, 1906–1907.

FORD, HENRY J., "The Anglo-Saxon Myth," in *Readings from the American Mercury*, edited by Grant C. Knight. Alfred A. Knopf, New York, 1926.

FOSS, A. T., and MATHEWS, E., *Facts for Baptist Churches*. American Baptist Free Mission Society, Utica, 1850.

FOX, EARLY L., *The American Colonization Society, 1817–1840*. Johns Hopkins Press, Baltimore, 1919.

FOX, GEORGE, *A Journal or Historical Account of the Life, Travels, Sufferings, etc., of George Fox*. T. C. Gould, Philadelphia, 1931.

FRAZIER, E. FRANKLIN, "An Analysis of Statistics on Negro Illegitimacy in the United States," *Social Forces*, December, 1932, pp. 249–257.

FRAZIER, E. FRANKLIN, *The Free Negro Family*. Fisk University Press, Nashville, 1932.

FRAZIER, E. FRANKLIN, *The Negro Family in Chicago*. University of Chicago Press, Chicago, 1932.

FROBENIUS, LEO, *The Origin of African Civilization*. Smithsonian Institution, Washington, 1898.

FROBENIUS, LEO, *The Voice of Africa*. Hutchinson and Company, London, 1913.

GALLOWAY, OSCAR F., *Higher Education for Negroes in Kentucky*. University of Kentucky, Lexington, 1932.

GARRISON, WILLIAM L., *Thoughts on African Colonization, or an Impartial Exhibition of the Doctrines, Principles, and Purposes of the American Colonization Society, together with the Resolutions, Addresses, and Remonstrances of the Free People of Color*. Garrison and Knapp, Boston, 1832.

GARTH, THOMAS R., *Race Psychology*. McGraw-Hill Book Company, New York, 1931.

BIBLIOGRAPHY

Acts of the State of Georgia (1845).
GERBER, A., "Uncle Remus Traced to the Old World," *Journal of American Folk-lore*, October-December, 1893.
GIDDINGS, FRANKLIN H., *Principles of Sociology*. The Macmillan Company, New York, 1911.
GOLDENWEISER, ALEXANDER A., *Early Civilization*. Alfred A. Knopf, New York, 1922.
GOODELL, WILLIAM, *The American Slave Code in Theory and Practice*. American and Foreign Anti-Slavery Society, New York, 1853.
GOODELL, WILLIAM, *Slavery and Anti-Slavery; a History of the Great Struggle in Both Hemispheres; with a View of the Slavery Question in the United States*. William Goodell, New York, 1855.
GOVER, MARY, and SYDENSTRICKER, EDGAR, "Mortality among Negroes in the United States." *United States Public Health Bulletin*. No. 174. 1928.
GREENE, LORENZO J., and WOODSON, CARTER G., *The Negro Wage Earner*. Association for the Study of Negro Life and History, Washington, 1930.
GRIMKE, ARCHIBALD H., "Why Disfranchisement Is Bad," *Atlantic Monthly*, July, 1904, pp. 72–81.

HAARDT, SARA, "The Etiquette of Slavery," *American Mercury*, May, 1929, pp. 34–42.
HADDON, ALFRED C., *The Races of Man and Their Distribution*. The Macmillan Company, New York, 1925.
HANKINS, FRANK H., *The Racial Basis of Civilization*. Alfred A. Knopf, New York, 1926.
HARDWICK, JAMES T., "The Economic Condition of the Negro in Nashville." Master's Thesis. Southern College of the Y.M.C.A., Nashville, 1922.
HARRIS, JOEL C., *Uncle Remus, His Songs and His Sayings*. D. Appleton and Company, New York, 1931.
HARRISON, W. P., *The Gospel among the Slaves*. Southern Methodist Publishing House, Nashville, 1893.
HART, ALBERT B., *Slavery and Abolition, 1831–1841*. Harper and Brothers, New York, 1906.
HATCHER, WILLIAM E., *John Jasper, the Unmatched Negro Philosopher and Preacher*. Fleming H. Revell and Company, New York, 1908.
HAWKINS, WILLIAM G., *Lunsford Lane, Another Helper from North Carolina*. Crosby and Nichols, Boston, 1863.
HAYGOOD, ATTICUS G., *Our Brother in Black, His Freedom and His Future*. Southern Methodist Publishing House, Nashville, 1881.
HAYGOOD, ATTICUS G., *Pleas for Progress*. Publishing House of the Methodist Episcopal Church South, Nashville, 1889.
HAYNES, ELIZABETH R., *Unsung Heroes*. Du Bois and Dill, New York, 1921.
HAZARD, SAMUEL, *Santo Domingo, Past and Present; with a Glance at Hayti*. Harper and Brothers, New York, 1873.
HELPER, HINTON R., *The Impending Crisis of the South*. A. B. Burdick, New York, 1860.
HENING, H. W., *Statutes at Large, Being a Collection of All the Laws of Vir-*

ginia, 1619–1792. 13 vols. Richmond and Philadelphia, 1809–1823. See especially volumes mentioned in the text.

HENRY, HOWELL M., "The Police Control of the Slave in South Carolina." Ph.D. Thesis. Vanderbilt University, 1914.

HENSON, JOSIAH, *Truth Is Stranger than Fiction.* B. B. Russell and Company, Boston, 1879.

HERBERT, HILARY A. *Why the Solid South?* R. H. Woodward and Company, Baltimore, 1890.

HERSKOVITS, MELVILLE J., "Race Relations," *American Journal of Sociology,* May, 1930, pp. 1052–1062.

HERSKOVITS, MELVILLE J., *The American Negro.* A. A. Knopf, New York, 1928.

HERSKOVITS, MELVILLE J., "The Negro in the New World," *American Anthropologist,* January–March, 1930, pp. 145–155.

HERTZ, FRIEDRICH O., *Race and Civilization.* The Macmillan Company, New York, 1928.

HILLER, FRANCIS H., *The Treatment of Juvenile Offenders in Nashville, Tennessee.* National Probation Association, New York, 1930.

HOFFMAN, FREDERICK L., *Race Traits and Tendencies of the American Negro.* The Macmillan Company, New York, 1896.

HORNBOSTEL, ERICH M. VON, "African Negro Music," *Africa,* January, 1928, pp. 30–62.

HOWARD, GEORGE E., "The Social Cost of Southern Race Prejudice," *American Journal of Sociology,* March, 1917, pp. 577–593.

HRDLIČKA, ALEŠ, "Anthropology of the American Negro," *American Journal of Physical Anthropology,* April–June, 1927, pp. 205–235.

HRDLIČKA, ALEŠ, "Human Races," in *Human Biology and Racial Welfare,* edited by Edmund V. Cowdry. Paul B. Hoeber, Inc., New York, 1930.

HUGHES, LANGSTON, *Fine Clothes to the Jew.* Alfred A. Knopf, New York, 1927.

HUGHES, LANGSTON, *The Weary Blues.* Alfred A. Knopf, New York, 1929.

HUNDLEY, DANIEL R., *Social Relations in Our Southern States.* Henry B. Price, New York, 1860.

HUNTINGTON, ELLSWORTH, *The Character of Races as Influenced by Physical Environment, Natural Selection, and Historical Development.* Charles Scribner's Sons, New York, 1924.

HUNTINGTON, ELLSWORTH, *Civilization and Climate.* Yale University Press, New Haven, 1924.

HUNTINGTON, ELLSWORTH, *The Pulse of Progress.* Charles Scribner's Sons, New York, 1926.

HURD, JOHN C., *The Law of Freedom and Bondage in the United States.* Little, Brown and Company, Boston, 1858–1862.

HUSSEY, L. M., "Homo Africanus," *American Mercury,* January, 1925, pp. 83–89.

INGRAHAM, JOSEPH H., *The Sunny South; or, The Southerner at Home.* G. G. Evans, Philadelphia, 1860.

IRBY, NOLEN M., *A Program for the Equalization of Educational Opportunities in the State of Arkansas.* George Peabody College for Teachers, Nashville, 1930.

JAMES, CHARLES T., *Practical Hints on the Comparative Cost and Productiveness of the Culture of Cotton, and the Cost and Productiveness of Its Manufacture*. Joseph Knowles, Providence, 1849.
JAMES, WILLIAM, *Psychology, Briefer Course*. Henry Holt and Company, New York, 1923.
JEFFERSON, THOMAS, *Notes on the State of Virginia with an Appendix Relative to the Murder of Logan's Family*. Wilson and Blackwell, Trenton, 1803.
JERNEGAN, MARCUS W., "A Forgotten Slavery of Colonial Days," *Harper's Magazine*, October, 1913, pp. 745–751.
JERNEGAN, MARCUS W., "Slavery and the Beginnings of Industrialism in the American Colonies," *American Historical Review*, January, 1920, pp. 220–240.
JOHNSON, CHARLES S., *The Negro in American Civilization*. Henry Holt and Company, New York, 1930.
JOHNSON, CHARLES S., "The Negro in Los Angeles Industries." Unpublished study, National Urban League, New York, 1926.
JOHNSON, CHARLES S., "One Thousand Negro Families in Nashville (Tennessee)." Unpublished study made by Department of Social Science, Fisk University.
JOHNSON, CHARLES S., "Report on the Migration from Mississippi." In Emmett J. Scott, *Negro Migration during the War*. Oxford University Press, New York (etc.), 1920.
JOHNSON, CHARLES S., *Shadow of the Plantation*. University of Chicago Press, Chicago, 1934.
JOHNSON, CHARLES S., Unpublished documents from a Study of Racial Attitudes being made by Charles S. Johnson, Fisk University, Nashville, Tennessee.
JOHNSON, GEORGIA D., *The Heart of a Woman*. Cornhill Publishing Company, Boston, 1918.
JOHNSON, JULIA M., "The Standard of Living of 100 Negro Families of Nashville." Master's Thesis in Sociology. Fisk University, 1933.
JOHNSON, JAMES W. (Ed.), *The Book of American Negro Poetry*. Harcourt, Brace and Company, New York, 1922.
JOHNSON, JAMES W. (Ed.), *The Book of American Negro Spirituals*. The Viking Press, New York, 1925.
JOHNSON, JAMES W., *Fifty Years and Other Poems*. Cornhill Publishing Company, Boston, 1917.
JOHNSON, JAMES W. (Ed.), *The Second Book of Negro Spirituals*. The Viking Press, New York, 1926.
JOHNSTON, HARRY HAMILTON, *A History of the Colonization of Africa by Alien Races*. Cambridge University Press, 1913.
JOHNSTON, HARRY HAMILTON, *The Opening Up of Africa*. Henry Holt and Company, New York, 1911.
JOHNSTON, HARRY HAMILTON, *The Negro in the New World*. Methuen and Company, London, 1910.
JOHNSTON, J. HUGO, "Documentary Evidence of the Relations of Negroes and Indians," *Journal of Negro History*, January, 1929, pp. 21–43.

Jones, Charles C., *The Religious Instruction of the Negroes in the United States.* Thomas Purse, Savannah, 1842.
Jones, Lance G. E., *Negro Schools in the Southern States.* Oxford University Press, New York, 1928.
Josey, Charles C., *Race and National Solidarity.* Charles Scribner's Sons, New York, 1923.
Journal of Negro History. Association for the Study of Negro Life and History, Washington, 1916–

Kantor, Jacob R., "Anthropology, Race, Psychology, and Culture," *American Anthropologist*, April, 1925, pp. 267–283.
Keane, Augustus H., *Man, Past and Present* (revised and largely rewritten by A. Hingston Quiggin and A. C. Haddon). The Macmillan Company, New York, 1920.
Kemble, Frances A. *Journal of a Residence on a Georgian Plantation in 1838–1839.* Harper and Brothers, New York, 1863.
Kennedy, Louise V., *The Negro Peasant Turns Cityward.* Columbia University Press, New York, 1930.
Kentucky Educational Commission, *Public Education in Kentucky.* General Education Board, New York, 1921.
Kerlin, Robert T., *Negro Poets and Their Poems.* Associated Publishers, Washington, 1923.
Kerlin, Robert T., *The Voice of the Negro, 1919.* E. P. Dutton and Company, New York, 1920.
King, Henry C., *The Laws of Friendship, Human and Divine.* The Macmillan Company, New York, 1914.
Kingsley, Mary H., *Travels in West Africa, Congo Français, Corisco, and Cameroons.* Macmillan and Company, London, 1897.
Klein, Arthur J., "Education," *American Journal of Sociology*, May, 1930, pp. 1063–1067.
Krapp, George P., "The English of the Negro," *American Mercury*, June, 1924, pp. 190–195.
Krehbiel, Henry E., *Afro-American Folksongs.* G. Schirmer, New York, 1914.
Kroeber, Alfred L., *Anthropology.* Harcourt, Brace and Company, New York, 1923.

Lasker, Bruno, *Race Attitudes in Children.* Henry Holt and Company, New York, 1929.
Leavell, R. H., "The Negro Migration from Mississippi," in *Negro Migration in 1916–1917.* United States Department of Labor, Washington, 1919.
Leavell, Ullin W., *Philanthropy in Negro Education.* George Peabody College for Teachers, Nashville, 1930.
Le Fevre, Louis, *Liberty and Restraint.* Alfred A. Knopf, New York, 1931.
Léger, Jacques N., *Haiti, son histoire et ses détracteurs.* Neale Publishing Company, New York, 1929.
Leiper, Henry S., *Blind Spots.* Friendship Press, New York, 1929.

LEONARD, ARTHUR G., *The Lower Niger and Its Tribes.* Macmillan and Company, London, 1906.
LEWINSON, PAUL, *Race, Class and Party.* Oxford University Press, New York, 1932.
LIGON, R., *True and Exact History of the Island of the Barbadoes.* H. Moseley, London, 1657.
LIPPMANN, WALTER, *Public Opinion.* The Macmillan Company, New York, 1927.
LIPPMANN, WALTER, "The Underworld, Our Secret Servant," *Forum,* January, 1931, pp. 1–4.
LOCKE, ALAIN LeR., and GREGORY, MONTGOMERY (Eds.), *Plays of Negro Life.* Harper and Brothers, New York, 1927.
LOGGINS, VERNON, *The Negro Author.* Columbia University Press, New York, 1931.
LONG, HOLLIS M., *Public Secondary Education for Negroes in North Carolina.* Teachers College, Columbia University, New York, 1932.
LOWIE, ROBERT H., *Primitive Society.* Boni and Liveright, New York, 1920.
Lynchings and What They Mean. Southern Commission on the Study of Lynching, Atlanta, 1931.

MALINOWSKI, BRONISLAW, *Sex and Repression in Savage Society.* Harcourt, Brace and Company, New York, 1927.
MALL, FRANKLIN P., "On Several Anatomical Characters of the Human Brain, Said to Vary according to Race and Sex, with Especial Reference to the Weight of the Frontal Lobe," *American Journal of Anatomy,* February, 1909, pp. 1–31.
Peter Martyr's Decades. Seville, 1511.
MASSIE, SUSANNE W., and CHRISTIAN, FRANCES A., *Homes and Gardens in Old Virginia.* J. W. Ferguson and Company, Richmond, 1930.
MATHEWS, BASIL J., *The Clash of Color.* George H. Doran Company, New York, 1924.
MATLACK, LUCIUS C., *The History of American Slavery and Methodism, from 1780 to 1849.* The Author, New York, 1849.
MAYO, MARION J., *The Mental Capacity of the American Negro.* Science Press, New York, 1913. (Also in *Archives of Psychology,* No. 28, 1913.)
MAZYCK, WALTER H., *George Washington and the Negro.* Associated Publishers, Washington, 1932.
McCORD, C. H., *The American Negro as a Dependent, Defective and Delinquent.* Press of Benson Printing Company, Nashville, 1914.
McCUISTION, FRED, *Financing Schools in the South, 1930.* Issued by State Directors of Educational Research in the Southern States as a Part of the Proceedings of the Conference Held at Peabody College, December 5 and 6, 1930.
McHENRY, GEORGE, *The Cotton Trade.* Saunders, Ottley and Company, London, 1863.
McKAY, CLAUDE, *Harlem Shadows.* Harcourt, Brace and Company, New York, 1922.
McKAY, CLAUDE, *Spring in New Hampshire.* Grant Richards, London, 1921.

McTyeire, Holland N., *A History of Methodism.* Southern Methodist Publishing House, Nashville, 1887.

Mencken, Henry L., and Nathan, George J., *The American Credo.* Alfred A. Knopf, New York, 1920.

Menzies, Allan, *History of Religion.* John Murray, London, 1910.

Miller, Kelly, *Race Adjustment.* Neale Publishing Company, New York, 1908.

Milligan, Robert H., *The Jungle Folk of Africa.* Fleming H. Revell and Company, New York, 1908.

Laws of the State of Mississippi (1859–1860).

Moton, Robert R., *Finding a Way Out.* Doubleday, Page and Company, New York, 1921.

Moton, Robert R., *What the Negro Thinks.* Doubleday, Doran and Company, New York, 1929.

Munford, Beverly B., *Virginia's Attitude toward Slavery and Secession.* L. H. Jenkins, Richmond, 1909.

Murphy, Edgar G., *The Basis of Ascendancy.* Longmans, Green and Company, New York, 1909.

Murphy, Edgar G., *Problems of the Present South.* Longmans, Green and Company, New York, 1910.

Nassau, Robert H., *Fetichism in West Africa.* Charles Scribner's Sons, New York, 1907.

National Conference on the Christian Way of Life, *And Who Is My Neighbor?* Association Press, New York, 1924.

Negro Hospitals. A compilation of available statistics. Julius Rosenwald Fund, Chicago, 1931.

Negro Housing. Report of the Committee on Negro Housing. Publication of President's Conference on Home Building and Home Ownership, Washington, 1931.

The Negro in Chicago. Report of the Chicago Commission on Race Relations. University of Chicago Press, Chicago, 1922.

The Negro in Richmond, Virginia. Report of the Negro Welfare Survey Committee, Richmond Council of Social Agencies, 1930.

Negro Year Book, an annual encyclopedia of the Negro. Edited by Monroe N. Work. Negro Year Book Publishing Company, Tuskegee Institute, Alabama, 1912– . See especially volumes mentioned in the text.

Niles' Weekly Register. 75 vols. Baltimore (etc.), 1811–1849.

North Carolina. Biennial Report of the Superintendent of Public Instruction of North Carolina for the Scholastic Years 1918–1919 and 1919–1920. Raleigh, 1921.

Norwood, John N., *The Schism in the Methodist Episcopal Church, 1844.* Alfred University, Alfred, 1923.

Nowlin, William F., *The Negro in American National Politics since 1868.* The Stratford Company, Boston, 1931.

Odum, Howard W., *An American Epoch.* Henry Holt and Company, New York, 1930.

ODUM, HOWARD W., and JOHNSON, GUY B., *The Negro and His Songs*. University of North Carolina Press, Chapel Hill, 1925.
OGBURN, WILLIAM F., *Social Change with Respect to Culture and Original Nature*. B. W. Huebsch, Inc., New York, 1922.
OLDHAM, JOSEPH H., *Christianity and the Race Problem*. Student Christian Movement, London, 1924.
OLIVEIRA MARTINS, JOAQUIM P., *The Golden Age of Prince Henry the Navigator* (tr. by James J. Abraham and William E. Reynolds). E. P. Dutton and Company, New York, 1914.
OLMSTED, FREDERICK L., *The Cotton Kingdom*. Mason Brothers, New York, 1862.
OLMSTED, FREDERICK L., *A Journey in the Back Country*. Mason Brothers, New York, 1860.
OLMSTED, FREDERICK L., *A Journey in the Seaboard Slave States*. Mason Brothers, New York, 1860.
OSBORN, HENRY F., *Men of the Old Stone Age*. Charles Scribner's Sons, New York, 1928.
OVINGTON, MARY W., *Portraits in Color*. Viking Press, New York, 1927.

PAGE, THOMAS N., *The Negro: The Southerner's Problem*. Charles Scribner's Sons, New York, 1904.
PAGE, THOMAS N., *Social Life in Old Virginia before the War*. Charles Scribner's Sons, New York, 1897.
PARK, ROBERT E., "The Bases of Race Prejudice," *Annals of the American Academy of Political and Social Science*, November, 1928, pp. 11-20.
PARK, ROBERT E., BURGESS, ERNEST W., and MCKENZIE, ROBERT D., *The City*. University of Chicago Press, Chicago, 1925.
PARTON, JAMES, *Life of General Jackson*. D. Appleton and Company, New York.
PASCOE, C. F. (Ed.), *Classified Digest of the Records of the Society for the Propagation of the Gospel in Foreign Parts*.
PAYNE, B. H., "The Negro: What Is His Ethnological Status?" The Proprietor, Cincinnati, 1867.
PHILLIPS, ULRICH B., *American Negro Slavery*. D. Appleton and Company, New York, 1918.
PHILLIPS, ULRICH B., *Documentary History of American Industrial Society*. A. H. Clark, Cleveland, 1909.
PHILLIPS, ULRICH B., *Life and Labor in the Old South*. Little, Brown and Company, Boston, 1929.
PHILLIPS, ULRICH B., *Plantation and Frontier Documents: 1649-1863, Illustrative of Industrial History in the Colonial and Ante-bellum South*. A. H. Clark, Cleveland, 1909.
PHILLIPS, ULRICH B., "The Origin and Growth of the Southern Black Belts," *American Historical Review*, July, 1906, pp. 798-816.
PINCHBECK, RAYMOND B., *The Virginia Negro Artisan and Tradesman*. University of Virginia, University, 1926.
PITMAN, FRANK W., *The Development of the British West Indies, 1700-1763*. Yale University Press, New Haven, 1917.

Presbyterian Church, *An Address to the Presbyterians of Kentucky Proposing a Plan for the Instruction and Emancipation of the Slaves.* Charles Whipple, Newburyport, 1836.

President's Research Committee on Social Trends, *Recent Social Trends in the United States.* McGraw-Hill Book Company, New York, 1933.

Princeton Review. Princeton, New York (etc.), 1825–1888. See especially issues mentioned in the text.

Protestant Episcopal Freedmen's Commission, *Occasional Papers.* George S. Rand and Avery, Boston, 1866.

PUCKETT, NEWBELL N., *Folk Beliefs of the Southern Negro.* University of North Carolina Press, Chapel Hill, 1926.

RANDALL, HENRY S., *Life of Thomas Jefferson.* Derby and Jackson, New York, 1858.

RAPER, ARTHUR, *The Tragedy of Lynching.* University of North Carolina Press, Chapel Hill, 1933.

RAPER, ARTHUR, Unpublished study made under the Commission on Interracial Coöperation, Atlanta, Georgia.

RATZEL, FRIEDRICH, *The History of Mankind.* Macmillan and Company, London, 1896–1898.

READ, HOLLIS, *The Negro Problem Solved, or Africa as She Was, and as She Is, and as She Shall Be. Her Curse and Her Cure.* A. A. Constantine, New York, 1864.

RECLUS, ÉLISÉE, *The Earth and Its Inhabitants.* 19 vols. D. Appleton and Company, New York, 1882–1894. See especially volumes mentioned in the text.

Report of the Board of Education for Freedmen. Department of the Gulf Office of the True Delta, New Orleans, 1865.

Report of the John L. Slater Fund (1931).

Report on the Economic Status of the Negro. Julius Rosenwald Fund, 1934.

REUTER, EDWARD B., *Race Mixture.* McGraw-Hill Book Company, New York, 1931.

REUTER, EDWARD B., "The Possibility of a Distinctive Culture Contribution from the American Negro," in *Social Attitudes,* edited by Kimball Young. Henry Holt and Company, New York, 1931.

REUTER, EDWARD B., *The American Race Problem.* Thomas Y. Crowell Company, New York, 1927.

RILEY, BENJAMIN F., *The Life and Times of Booker T. Washington.* Fleming H. Revell and Company, New York, 1916.

RIPPON, JOHN, *The Baptist Annual Register for 1790, 1791, 1792, and part of 1793.* London.

ROBINSON, GERALD T., "Racial Minorities," in *Civilization in the United States,* edited by Harold T. Stearns. Harcourt, Brace and Company, New York, 1922.

ROBINSON, JOHN, *The Testimony and Practice of the Presbyterian Church in Reference to American Slavery.* John D. Thorpe, Cincinnati, 1852.

ROMAN, CHARLES V., An Address to the National Medical Association in 1914.

ROMAN, CHARLES V., *American Civilization and the Negro*. F. A. Davis Company, Philadelphia, 1916.
ROSCOE, JOHN, *The Northern Bantu*. The Macmillan Company, New York, 1916.
ROSS, E. A., *South of Panama*. The Century Company, New York, 1915.
ROSS, FRANK A., *Urbanization and the Negro*. Publication of American Sociological Society. Vol. 26, No. 3. August, 1932.
RUGG, HAROLD O., *Culture and Education in America*. Harcourt, Brace and Company, New York, 1931.
RUSSELL, JOHN H., *The Free Negro in Virginia, 1619–1865*. Johns Hopkins Press, Baltimore, 1913.

SCHELL, WILLIAM G., *Is the Negro a Beast?* Gospel Trumpet Publishing Company, Moundsville, 1901.
Schools for Colored Preachers. Lange, Little and Hillman, New York.
SCOTT, EMMETT J., *Negro Migration during the War*. Oxford University Press, London, 1920.
SEMPLE, R. B., *History of the Rise and Progress of the Baptists in Virginia*. 1809. Revised and extended by G. W. Beale, Philadelphia, 1894.
SEWARD, T. F., *Jubilee Songs*. Biglow and Main, New York, 1872.
SHERMAN, CORINNE, "Racial Factors in Desertion," *The Family*, January, 1923, pp. 221–225.
SHUFELDT, ROBERT W., *The Negro a Menace to American Civilization*. Richard G. Badger, Boston, 1907.
SIMAR, THÉOPHILE, *Étude Critique sur la Formation de la Doctrine des Races, Au XVIIIe Siècle et Son Expansion Au XIXe Siècle*. Maurice Lamertin, Bruxelles, 1922. (This work has been translated by Alexander A. Goldenweiser as *Race Myth, A Study of the Notion of Race*.)
SIMMONS, WILLIAM J., *Men of Mark*. George M. Rewell and Company, Cleveland, 1887.
SIMPSON, B. L., *The Conflict of Colour*, by B. L. Putnam Weale (pseud.). The Macmillan Company, New York, 1910.
SMEDES, SUSAN D., *A Southern Planter*. James Pott and Company, New York, 1890.
SMITH, WILLIAM B., *The Color Line*. McClure, Phillips and Company, New York, 1905.
SNAVELY, TIPTON R., "The Exodus of Negroes from Southern States," in *Negro Migration in 1916–1917*. United States Department of Labor, Washington, 1919.
Society of Friends, *A Brief Statement of the Rise and Progress of the Testimony of the Religious Society of Friends, Against Slavery and the Slave Trade*. Joseph and William Kite, Philadelphia, 1843.
Society of Friends, *The Book of Discipline, Agreed on by the Yearly Meeting of Friends for New England, Containing Extracts of Minutes, Conclusions and Advices, of That Meeting; and of the Yearly Meeting of London, Pennsylvania and New Jersey, and New York, from Their First Institution*. John Carter, Providence, 1785.

The South in the Building of the Nation. 13 vols. Southern Historical Publication Society, Richmond, 1909–1913. See especially volumes mentioned in the text.

The Southern Literary Messenger. 38 vols. T. W. White (etc.), Richmond, 1834– . See especially volumes mentioned in the text.

The Southern Workman. Hampton Normal and Industrial Institute, Hampton, 1908– . See especially volumes mentioned in the text.

SOUTHEY, THOMAS, *Chronological History of the West Indies.* Longman, Rees, Orme, Brown and Green, London, 1827.

SPEER, ROBERT E., *Of One Blood.* Council of Women for Home Missions, and Missionary Educational Movement of the United States and Canada, New York, 1924.

SPERO, STERLING D., and HARRIS, A. L., *The Black Worker.* Columbia University Press, New York, 1931.

SPIVAK, JOHN L., *Georgia Nigger.* Harcourt, Brace and Company, New York, 1932.

SPRING, LINDLEY, *The Negro at Home.* Published by Author, New York, 1868.

STAFFORD, ALPHONSO O., *Animal Fables from the Dark Continent.* American Book Company, New York, 1906.

STEPHENSON, GILBERT T., *Race Distinctions in American Law.* D. Appleton and Company, New York, 1910.

STODDARD, LOTHROP, *The Rising Tide of Color against White World-Supremacy.* Charles Scribner's Sons, New York, 1922.

STONE, ALFRED H., "Some Problems of Southern Economic History," *American Historical Review,* July, 1908, pp. 779–797.

STOUGHTON, AMANDA L., and GOVER, MARY, "A Study of Negro Infant Mortality," *Public Health Reports,* November 8, 1929, pp. 2705–2733.

STOWE, HARRIET B., *Father Henson's Story of His Own Life.* John P. Jewett and Company, Boston, 1858.

STROUD, GEORGE M., *A Sketch of the Laws Relating to Slavery in the Several States of the United States of America.* Henry Longstreth, Philadelphia, 1856.

SUMNER, WILLIAM G., *Folkways.* Ginn and Company, Boston, 1906.

SYDNOR, CHARLES S., "The Free Negro in Mississippi before the Civil War," *American Historical Review,* July, 1927, pp. 769–788.

Thirty Years of Lynching in the United States, 1889–1918. National Association for the Advancement of Colored People, New York, 1919.

THOMAS, EDGAR G., *The First African Baptist Church of North America.* Privately printed, Savannah, 1925.

THOMPSON, ANNA J., "A Survey of Crime among Negroes in Philadelphia," *Opportunity,* August, 1926, pp. 251–254.

THOMPSON, EDGAR T., "The Plantation." Ph.D. Thesis. University of Chicago, 1932.

THOMPSON, R. E., *A History of the Presbyterian Churches in the United States.* Christian Literature Company, New York, 1895.

THORPE, FRANCIS N., *The Civil War: A Natural View.* C. Barrie and Sons, Philadelphia, 1906.

THURNWALD, RICHARD, "The Missionary's Concern in Sociology and Psychology," *Africa*, October, 1931, pp. 418–434.
TIFFANY, C. C., *A History of the Protestant Episcopal Church in the United States of America*. Christian Literature Company, New York, 1895.
TOCQUEVILLE, ALEXIS DE, *Democracy in America*. George Adlard, New York, 1838.
TODD, T. WINGATE, "An Anthropologist's Study of Negro Life," *Journal of Negro History*, January, 1931, pp. 36–42.
TOOMER, JEAN, *Cane*. Boni and Liveright, New York, 1923.
TOZZER, ALFRED M., *Social Origins and Social Continuities*. The Macmillan Company, New York, 1925.
TREXLER, HARRISON A., *Slavery in Missouri, 1804–1865*. Johns Hopkins Press, Baltimore, 1914.
TROLLOPE, FRANCES, *Domestic Manners of the Americans*. Whittaker, Treacher and Company, London, 1832.
TURNER, FREDERICK J., "The South, 1820–1830," *American Historical Review*, April, 1906, pp. 559–573.
TYLOR, EDWARD B., *Primitive Culture*. John Murray, London, 1903.

United States, *6th Census of the United States, 1840*.
United States, *7th Census of the United States, 1850*.
United States Bureau of the Census, *14th Census of the United States, 1920*. Government Printing Office, Washington,
United States Bureau of the Census, *Negro Population in the United States, 1790–1915*. Government Printing Office, Washington, 1918.
United States Bureau of Education, *Survey of the Negro Colleges and Universities of the South*. Government Printing Office, Washington, 1928.
United States Bureau of Education, *Biennial Survey of Education in the United States, 1916–1918*. Government Printing Office, Washington, 1921.
United States Bureau of Education, *Negro Education: A Study of the Private and Higher Schools for Colored People in the United States*. Government Printing Office, Washington, 1916.
United States Bureau of Labor Statistics, *Cost of Living in the United States*. Bulletin No. 357. Government Printing Office, Washington, 1924.
United States Department of Commerce, *Religious Bodies, 1916*. Vol. 1. Government Printing Office, Washington, 1919.
United States Department of Commerce, *Religious Bodies, 1926*. Vol. 1. Government Printing Office, Washington, 1930.
United States Department of Commerce, *Statistical Abstract of the United States, 1928*. Government Printing Office, Washington, 1928.
United States, *Medical Statistics of the Provost Marshal General's Bureau*. Vol. II. 1861–1865.
USELTON, LIDA J. *Prevalence of Venereal Disease in the United States*. United States Public Health Service, Venereal Disease Information. December 20, 1930.

VAN DEUSEN, JOHN G., *Economic Bases of Disunion in South Carolina*. Columbia University Press, New York, 1928.

WALLIS, WILSON D., "Some Phases of the Psychology of Prejudice," *Journal of Abnormal and Social Psychology*, January, 1930, pp. 418–429.

WARDEN, CARL J., *The Evolution of Human Behavior*. The Macmillan Company, New York, 1932.

WARNER, SAMUEL, *An Authentic and Impartial Narrative of the Tragical Scene Which Was Witnessed in Southampton County (Virginia) on Monday the 22nd of August*. Warner and West, New York, 1831.

WASHINGTON, BOOKER T., *The Story of the Negro*. Doubleday, Page and Company, New York, 1924.

WASHINGTON, BOOKER T., *Up from Slavery*. Doubleday, Page and Company, New York, 1924.

WASHINGTON, E. DAVIDSON (Ed.), *Selected Speeches of Booker T. Washington*. Doubleday, Doran and Company, New York, 1932.

WEALE, B. L. PUTNAM, see Simpson, B. L.

WEATHERFORD, WILLIS D., "The Attitude of the Churches toward the Negro during Slavery." (Unpublished study.)

WEATHERFORD, WILLIS D. (Compiler), *Interracial Coöperation*. Interracial Committee of the War Work Council of Y.M.C.A. (n.p.), 192–?

WEATHERFORD, WILLIS D. (Ed.), *Lawlessness or Civilization — Which?* Williams Printing Company, Nashville, 1917.

WEATHERFORD, WILLIS D., *The Negro from Africa to America*. George H. Doran Company, New York, 1924.

WEATHERFORD, WILLIS D., *Negro Life in the South*. Association Press, New York, 1915.

WEATHERFORD, WILLIS D. (Ed.), *A Survey of the Negro Boy in Nashville, Tennessee*. Association Press, New York, 1932.

WEEKS, JOHN H., *Congo Life and Jungle Stories*. Religious Tract Society, London.

WEEKS, STEPHEN B., "George Moses Horton: Slave Poet," *Southern Workman*, October, 1914, pp. 571–577.

WEEKS, STEPHEN B., *Southern Quakers and Slavery*. Johns Hopkins Press, Baltimore, 1896.

WEGELIN, OSCAR, *Jupiter Hammon, American Negro Poet*. Heartman, New York, 1915.

WERTENBAKER, THOMAS J., *The Planters of Colonial Virginia*. Princeton University Press, Princeton, 1922.

WESLEY, CHARLES H., *Negro Labor in the United States, 1850–1925*. Vanguard Press, New York, 1927.

WESLEY, CHARLES H., "A History of Negro Labor in the United States, 1850–1923." Thesis. Howard University, 1925.

WESLEY, JOHN, *Journal* (Everyman's Library). E. P. Dutton and Company, New York, 1907.

WESLEY, JOHN, *The Works of the Rev. John Wesley*. 7 vols. J. Emory and B. Waugh, New York, 1831.

WESTERGAARD, WALDEMAR C., *The Danish West Indies under Company*

Rules, 1671–1754; with a Supplementary Chapter, 1755–1917. The Macmillan Company, New York, 1917.
WESTON, GEORGE M., *The Progress of Slavery in the United States.* The Author, Washington, 1857.
WHEATLEY, PHILLIS, *Memoir and Poems of Phillis Wheatley, a Native African and a Slave, also Poems by a Slave.* Isaac Knapp, Boston, 1838.
WHEATLEY, PHILLIS, *Poems on Various Subjects, Religious and Moral.* Thomas and Thomas, Walpole, 1802.
WHIPPLE, CHARLES K., "The Family Relation, as Affected by Slavery." American Reform Tract and Book Society, Cincinnati, 1858.
WHITE, NEWMAN I., and JACKSON, WALTER C., *An Anthology of Verse by American Negroes.* Trinity College Press, Durham, 1924.
WIGHTMAN, WILLIAM M., *Life of William Capers.* Southern Methodist Publishing House, Nashville, 1858.
"Concerning the Origin of Wilberforce," *Journal of Negro History,* July, 1923, pp. 335–337.
WILBERFORCE, SAMUEL, *History of the Protestant Episcopal Church in America.* Stanford and Swords, New York, 1849.
WILDER, FRANCIS S., "Crime in the Superior Courts of North Carolina," *Social Forces,* March, 1927, pp. 423–427.
WILLIAMS, GEORGE W., *History of the Negro Race in America, 1619–1880.* G. P. Putnam's Sons, New York, 1885.
WILLIAMS, GOMER, *History of the Liverpool Privateers, with an Account of the Liverpool Slave Trade.* William Heinemann, London, 1897.
WILLITS, JOSEPH H., An Address before the Conference on the Economic Status of the Negro, Sponsored by the Julius Rosenwald Fund. Washington, 1933.
WILLOUGHBY, WILLIAM C., *The Soul of the Bantu.* Harper and Brothers, New York, 1928.
WILSON, HENRY, *History of the Rise and Fall of the Slave Power in America.* James R. Osgood and Company, 1875.
WILSON, J. L., *Southern Presbyterian Review,* March, 1848.
WILSON, JOHN L., *Western Africa: Its History, Condition, and Prospects.* Harper and Brothers, New York, 1856.
WILSON, WOODROW, *Division and Reunion, 1829–1889.* Longmans, Green and Company, New York, 1898.
WISSLER, CLARK, *Man and Culture.* Thomas Y. Crowell Company, New York, 1923.
WOODBURY, ROBERT M., *Infant Mortality and Its Causes.* Williams and Wilkins Company, Baltimore, 1926.
WOODSON, CARTER G., *A Century of Negro Migration.* Association for the Study of Negro Life and History, Washington, 1918.
WOODSON, CARTER G., *The Education of the Negro prior to 1861.* Association for the Study of Negro Life and History, Washington, 1919.
WOODSON, CARTER G., *Free Negro Heads of Families in the United States in 1830.* Association for the Study of Negro Life and History, Washington, 1925.
WOODSON, CARTER G., *The History of the Negro Church.* Associated Publishers, Washington, 1921.

WOODSON, CARTER G., *The Negro in Our History*. Associated Publishers, Washington, 1928.
WOOFTER, THOMAS J., "Race Relations," *American Journal of Sociology*, May, 1931, pp. 1033-1044.
WOOLMAN, JOHN, *The Journal of John Woolman*. James R. Osgood and Company, Boston, 1871.
WORK, MONROE N., see *Negro Year Book*.
WORK, MONROE N., and JOHNSON, CHARLES N., "Report on the Migration during the World War," in Emmett J. Scott, *Negro Migration during the War*. Oxford University Press, London, 1920.

YARBROUGH, WILLIAM A., *Economic Aspects of Slavery in Relation to Southern and Southwestern Migration*. George Peabody College for Teachers, Nashville, 1932.
YOUNG, DONALD R., *American Minority Peoples*. Harper and Brothers, New York, 1932.
YOUNG, ROBERT A., "The Negro: A Reply to Ariel." J. B. McFerrin and Company, Nashville, 1867.

INDEX

Abbott, Grace, 381.
Abolition papers, 193.
Abolitionists, 110–111, 118, 119, 131, 140, 161, 192, 204–205; Negro, 256–257, 534, 537. *See also* Church, the, and slavery.
Adams, Henry, 333.
Adams, John Q., 143.
Adger, John B., 270.
Adrian, Cardinal, 115.
Adventurers, 164, 298.
Africa, Europe in, 53; geography of, 22–25.
African art, 93, 95.
  civilization, 84, 85, 91.
  culture, 22, 27–49, 84, 86, 88, 91–93, 460, 543; and the American Negro, 83 ff., 231, 444, 545.
  customs, 39, 87–90, 91.
  dance, 545.
  folk lore, 72, 95, 459.
  language, 88, 94, 96, 459.
  law, 546.
  literature, 93.
  music, 460, 462, 545.
  "Negro problem," 54.
  philosophy, 93.
  political and social organization, 92.
  psychology, 89–90.
  traits, 86.
  types, 85.
African Methodist Episcopal Church, 202.
Agassiz, Louis J. R., 5.
Agricultural credit, 325.
  education, 356.
  products, 157.
Agriculture, 146–147, 152; Negroes in, 324 ff.
Alexander, J. E., 90.
Allen, Floyd P., 373, 379.

Allen, Maud, 473.
Allen, Richard, 202, 492.
Alvord, John W., 353.
Amalgamation as a solution of the race problem, 527–528.
Amendments, Thirteenth, Fourteenth, and Eighteenth, 62, 411, 414, 415.
American Expeditionary Forces, 60, 235.
American Indian, 52, 68, 72, 87, 99, 106, 108, 109, 242, 326, 427.
Anacaona, Queen, 115.
Andrew, James O., 205, 207.
Andrews, Isaac, 190.
Angell, James R., 90.
Anglo-Saxonism, 16–18.
Angola, 84, 117, 124.
Animism, 37.
Anne, Queen, of England, 126.
Anti-Semitism, of Wagner, 16.
Antislavery legislation, *see* Slave trade, attempts to suppress.
Antislavery Society, 204.
Apprenticeship, *see* Indenture.
Arawak Indians, 114.
Arkwright, Richard, 136, 150.
Armistead, W. S., 508.
Armstrong, Samuel C., 278, 356.
Aryanism, 14–16.
Asbury, Francis, 201, 203, 492.
Ashanti, 34.
Assiento, 116, 122.
Azurara, Gomes Eannes de, 83.

"Back to Africa" movement, 234.
Bacon, Izard, 246.
Bacon, Leonard, 197, 201, 210.
Bahio, *see* Haiti.
Bailey, Thomas P., 217, 523.
Baker, Ray S., 415, 510.
Ballagh, James C., 103, 104, 107, 108.

INDEX

Banks, General, 353.
Banneker, Benjamin, 241.
Bantu, 29 ff., 35; religion, 36 ff.
Baptist church and slavery, 74, 210–214.
Barbados, 117, 183.
Barnes, Harry E., 17.
Barnett, Ida Wells, 538.
Barth, Henry, 32, 33, 34.
Bascom, Henry B., 205.
Bassett, John S., 193, 267, 404, 407, 408.
Batuta, Ibn, 92.
Baxter, Richard, 184.
Bean, Robert B., 225.
Bede, 17.
Bell, James M., 470.
Bell, John, 142.
Bell, Philip A., 484.
Benezet, Anthony, 84, 115, 124, 189, 192, 351.
Benton, Thomas H., 138.
Berkley, Bishop, 187.
Bernhardi, 524.
Bibb, Henry, 465.
Birney, James G., 301.
Birth of a Nation, 62.
Black Codes, 73, 103, 111, 412, 414.
Blackwell, Emily, 502.
Blair, Francis P., 294.
Blake, William O., 123, 266.
Blease, Cole, 77, 416.
Blumenbach, Johann Friedrich, 4, 5.
Boas, Franz, 5, 7, 19, 70, 72, 90, 91, 93, 528.
Boehler, Peter, 188.
Boganda, 34.
Bogardus, Emory, 68, 69.
Bornu, 32 ff.
Bory St. Vincent, 5.
Boulainvilliers, Count de, 12, 15.
Bowden, Robert, 443.
Brackett, Jeffrey R., 403.
Brain measurement, 225.
Braithwaite, William S., 474, 475, 476.
Brawley, Benjamin, 482, 483.
Breckinridge, John C., 142.
Brown, Morris, 492.
Brown, Moses, 270.

Brown, Sara W., 502.
Brown, Sterling, 452.
Brown, William G., 303.
Brown, William W., 479–480, 481, 491.
Browning, James B., 414.
Bruce, Philip A., 101, 106, 166, 169, 175, 183, 185, 299.
Bryan, Andrew, 210, 213, 492.
Bryan, Samuel J., 202.
Bryce, Viscount, 50.
Buffon, Georges, 4, 5.
Burgess, Ebenezer, 521.
Burgess, Ernest W., 385.
Burial customs, African, 39.
Burke, Edmund, 127.
Burleigh, Henry T., 464.
Burlin, Natalie C., 460.
Burton, Sir Richard F., 89, 459.
Buttrick, Wallace, 363.
Buxton, Thomas F., 274.
Byrd, William, 125.

Caonabo, 115.
Cable, George W., 72, 433.
Caesar, 191, 499.
Cairnes, J. E., 294.
Calhoun, John C., 137, 140, 200, 224.
Capers, Bishop, 202, 208, 209–210, 493.
Carey, Henry C., 116, 117, 118.
Carey, Lott, 213, 250, 493.
Carlyle, Thomas, 13.
Carpenter, Niles, 341.
Carpetbagger, 410, 412, 413, 414, 415, 421.
Carroll, Charles, 224, 508.
Carrothers, James D., 473.
Cartwright, Edmund, 136.
Cartwright, Samuel, 373–374.
Carver, George, 503.
Casor, John, 105.
Catechisms·for slaves, 200, 202.
Cato, William, 481.
Catterall, Helen T., 242, 248, 249.
Cattle culture, 29–31.
Caucasoids, 6, 7, 10.
Chaka, 36.
Chamberlain, Alexander F., 91.
Chamberlain, Houston S., 16.

INDEX

Chambers, William, 294.
Chase, Stuart, 316.
Chestnut, Charles W., 482.
Chicago Commission on Race Relations, 230.
Children, race attitudes of, 60, 65–66. See also Negro children.
Chinese, American attitude toward, 52, 54–55, 69.
Christian, Frances A., 302.
Christian, J. T., 213.
Christianity, 63. See also Slaves, Christianizing of.
Church, the, and slavery, 74, 183 ff. See also Baptist church, etc.
Clapperton, 33.
Clark, Taliaferro, 378.
Class, 11–13.
Clay, C. C., 295.
Clay, Henry, 139, 140, 520, 521.
Coalter, Hannah, 246.
Cobb, Howell, 296.
Cobb, Irvin S., 232.
Coffin, Joshua, 193, 268, 270.
Cohen, Octavus R., 232.
Coke, Bishop, 202.
Coke, Thomas, 113, 114.
Colgan, Rev., 186.
Collins, Winfield H., 439.
Colonization, 256, 257, 519–524.
Colonization Society, 198, 204, 270, 499, 500, 520.
Columbus, Christopher, 113–114, 116, 165.
Comfort, Silas, 205.
Commission on Church and Race Relations, 515.
Commission on Interracial Coöperation, 440, 512, 515.
Communism, 540, 547.
Compromise of 1850, 140.
Cone, Spencer, 211, 212.
Conference for Education in the South, 358.
Conklin, Edwin G., 527.
Connelly, Marcus C., 484.
Consciousness of race, see Race consciousness.

Conyngham, Kate, 170, 171, 174, 179.
Cooke, Dennis H., 224.
Cooley, Henry S., 266, 269.
Cooper, Thomas, 158.
Cornish, Samuel E., 484.
Cotter, Joseph, 473.
Cotton, 110, 120, 121, 135–136, 146, 148, 150, 151, 152, 159, 160, 294, 298, 309; gin, 110, 124, 136, 150, 243.
Cox, Ernest S., 523.
Crandall, Prudence, 351.
Crawford, 5.
Crawford, William H., 520.
Crime, see Negro crime.
Crisis magazine, 541.
Crompton, Samuel, 150.
Crossing the color line, 234, 250.
Crummel, Alexander, 195, 481, 493.
Cuffe, Paul, 256, 464, 522.
Cullen, Countee, 473, 475, 478, 483, 551, 553.
Cultural contributions of the Negro, 553–554.
  development, 454; of the Negro, 442–457.
  distance, 445, 452.
  lag, 58, 443, 445.
  mobility, 452.
  patterns, 442–443.
  planes, 443, 444.
Culture, and evolution, 9, 93; and race, 8–9; definition of, 22, 442; differences in, 22; influence of environment on, 22, 26, 27, 28, 31, 36, 48; origin of, 25–26; primitive, 28; spread of, 25–26. See also African culture, Negro culture.
Custom, power of, 69 ff.
Cutler, J. E., 426, 510.
Cuvier, 5.

Dahomi, 34.
Dalcho, Rev., 194.
Dale, Sir Thomas, 299.
Daniel, William A., 498.
Davis, Daniel W., 473.
Davis, J. R., 102, 103.

580 INDEX

Davis, Jackson, 361, 363.
Davis, Samuel, 197.
Davis, Washington, 500.
De Berry, W. M., 498.
De Bow, James D. B., 111, 123, 124, 136, 159, 177, 261, 262, 263, 264, 292, 293, 294, 298, 302.
Deems, Charles, 209.
Dehan, Bishop, 194.
Delafosse, Maurice, 92.
Delany, Martin, 481, 501, 537.
Delinquency, Negro, see Negro delinquency.
De Priest incident, 516.
Derham, James, 499.
Dett, Robert N., 464.
Detweiler, Frederick G., 50, 484.
Dewey, John, 90.
Dickinson, Colonel, 171.
Dickinson, William, 193.
Differences, biological, 4; cultural, 53, 453; regional, 8; religious, 18; sex, 6, 18.
Dillard, James H., 364, 514.
Dinkins, Charles R., 473.
Dixon, Roland B., 31, 36.
Dixon, Thomas, 73.
Dodd, William E., 148, 153, 159.
Dogma, see Race dogma.
Donnan, Elizabeth, 83.
Douglas, Aaron, 490.
Douglas, Paul H., 100, 101, 103.
Douglas, Stephen A., 141.
Douglas, William, 481.
Douglass, Frederick, 257, 331, 334, 484, 489, 491, 537.
Dowd, Jerome, 35, 510.
Downing, Emanuel, 121, 290.
Drama, Negro, see Negro drama.
Dred Scott decision, 141–142.
Drew, Samuel, 202.
Drewry, William S., 272.
Driberg, Jack H., 546.
Drolet, Godias J., 370.
Du Bois, William E. B., 123, 134, 276, 279, 358, 418, 426, 434, 453, 483, 496, 501, 515.
Duff, Charles, 13.

Dunbar, Paul Laurence, 471–473, 482, 516, 551.
Dunlap, Page C., 500.
Dunning, William A., 414, 415.
Durkheim, Émile, 216.

East, Edward M., 528.
Economy, Negro, see Negro economy.
Edge, Frederick M., 157.
Education of Negroes, see Negro education.
Educational Commission for Freedmen, 352.
Edwards, Bryan, 120.
Eleazer, R. B., 514.
Elizabeth, Queen, of England, 117, 122.
Elliott, E. N., 301.
Elliott, Stephen, 195.
Embree, Elihu, 193.
Embury, Philip, 201.
Environment, influence on physical traits, 7, 8, 48. See also Culture, influence of environment on.
Episcopalian church and the Negro, 74, 194 ff.
Eppes, Susan B., 169, 173.
Epstein, Abraham, 336.
Eskimo culture, 22, 26, 28.
Established church and the Negro, 186 ff.
Etiquette of race relations, 216, 516.
Eubank, Earle, 318.
Eugenics, 61, 226, 275.
Evans, Henry, 493–494.
Evolution, 7, 9, 10; and culture, 9, 93.
Extermination as a solution of the race problem, 526.

Falk, Isidore S., 379.
Family life, African, 45 ff.; Negro, see Negro families.
Faris, Ellsworth, 52, 90, 96.
Fauset, Jessie, 473, 482.
Feldman, Herman, 320.
Fetish, 42–44.
Fetishism, 35, 37.

INDEX

Feudalism, 11, 50; and southern plantation, 147, 180.
Fichte, 14.
Finot, Jean, 4, 5.
Fisher, Rudolph, 483.
Fisk, Clinton B., 332.
Fiske, Amos K., 115.
Fiske, John, 164, 165, 175.
Fithian, Philip, 168.
Fleet, James H., 500.
Fleetwood, Bishop, 186.
Folk beliefs of Negroes, 95.
  lore, 71–72.
  stories, 459–461.
Ford, Henry J., 17, 18.
Forten, James, 256.
Fortune, Thomas, 473.
Foss, A. T., 212.
Foster, Stephen, 547.
Foster, William Z., 513.
Fox, George, 183–184, 188.
Franklin, Benjamin, 153.
Frazier, E. Franklin, 239, 240, 245, 276, 277, 345.
Free Negroes, *see* Negro, free.
Freedmen, 332, 409.
Freedmen's Bureau, 353, 410, 412, 454.
Freeman, E. A., 17.
French Revolution, 13.
Frobenius, Leo, 85, 91, 93.
Fugitive Slave Acts, 103, 111, 140.
Fuller, Meta Warrick, 502.
Furman, Richard, 211.

Gabriel's rebellion, 269, 351.
Galton, Francis, 225.
Garden, Alexander, 186.
Garnett, Henry H., 481, 537.
Garrison, William L., 204, 254.
Garth, Thomas R., 8.
Garvey, Marcus, 549.
Garvey movement, 540, 549.
General Education Board, 363.
Gens, 34, 46, 48.
George, David, 210.
Gerber, A., 459.
Ghana, 92.
Gibson, Bishop, 186.

Giddings, Franklin H., 65.
Giles, William B., 254.
Gliddon, George R., 5.
Gobineau, Count de, 14, 15, 16.
Gobinism, 15.
Goldenweiser, Alexander A., 27, 28, 48, 72.
Goncalvez, Antam, 83, 117.
Goodell, William, 263, 264, 267, 405, 407.
Gover, Mary, 369, 376.
Grant, Madison, 16, 523, 525.
Grant, Ulysses S., 410, 412.
Gratiolet, Louis P., 225, 226.
Green, Paul, 483, 511.
Greene, Lorenzo, 514.
Gregory, Montgomery, 484.
Griffith, David W., 62.
Grimes, Leonard A., 493.
Guacanagari, 114.
Guadalupe Hidalgo, Treaty of, 139.
Guinea, 84.

Haardt, Sara, 279.
Haeckel, 5.
Haiti, 114, 115, 119, 130.
Hall, G. Stanley, 225.
Halleck, General, 352.
Hammon, Jupiter, 466.
Hammond, Briton, 464, 466.
Hankins, Frank H., 18.
Hargreaves, James, 136.
Harper, Ellen W., 470.
Harris, Joel C., 254, 459, 460, 461.
Harrison, W. P., 195, 208, 301.
Hatcher, William E., 496.
Hausa kingdom, 33–34, 91.
Hauser, Otto, 18.
Hawkins, Sir John, 122, 123.
Hayes, Roland, 455, 503.
Haygood, Atticus G., 208, 509, 531.
Haynes, Lemuel, 493.
Hazard, Samuel, 116.
Headrights, 106, 164.
Hegel, 14, 18.
Helper, Hinton R., 157, 293, 296.
Henry, Howell M., 268, 269, 270, 425.
Henry, Patrick, 126, 150.

Henry, Prince, of Portugal, 83, 117.
Henry, Robert, 197.
Henson, Josiah, 465.
Herbert, Hilary A., 414.
Herder, 14.
Heredity, 7.
Herskovits, Melville J., 3, 84, 94, 95, 96, 242, 517.
Hertz, Friedrich O., 5, 12.
Heyward, Dubois, 72.
Higginson, Thomas W., 463.
Hiller, Francis H., 427.
Hispaniola, 114, 119, 123.
Hitler, Adolf, 18.
Hoffman, Frederick, 229, 312, 375, 376.
Home life of Negroes, see Negro home life.
Home ownership, Negro, see Negro home ownership.
Hoover, Herbert, 418, 516.
Hopkins, Bishop, 196.
Hornbostel, Erich M. von, 95, 545.
Horton, George M., 468, 472.
Hospitals, Negro, see Negro hospitals.
Housing, Negro, see Negro housing.
Howard, George E., 219.
Howard, O. O., 353, 354, 356.
Howells, William D., 471.
Hrdlička, Aleš, 6, 8.
Huger, Daniel, 200.
Hughes, Langston, 452, 475, 476, 483, 552-553.
Humor, Negro, see Negro humor.
Huntington, Ellsworth, 8, 48.
Hurd, John C., 262, 263, 267, 404, 408.
Hussey, L. M., 285.
Huxley, 18.

Illegitimacy, see Negro illegitimacy.
Illiteracy of non-slaveholding whites in the South, 154-155; Negro, see Negro illiteracy.
Immigration, 55, 155, 157, 291, 312; laws, 18, 340, 341.
Income of Negroes, 318, 319, 324, 372.
Indenture, 100 ff., 121; Indian, 106; Negro, 103 ff.

Indentured servants, 107, 165-166, 175, 241, 311.
Indians, see American Indians.
Indigo, 120, 121, 309.
Industry, 146-147, 314, 316. See also Negro industrial workers.
Infant mortality, 381; Negro, 279, 376, 381.
Inferiority complexes, 73.
Ingraham, Joseph H., 172, 174, 179.
Instinct, racial, 55.
Insurrections, Negro, 110, 119, 268-272, 536; effect of, on education, 351; fear of, 130, 131, 132, 162, 185, 186, 208, 244, 257, 264, 267-268, 272, 292, 351, 404, 405, 409, 519.
Intelligence, 226. See also Tests.
Interbreeding, see Race crossing.
Intermarriage, see Race crossing.
Irish immigrants, 251, 313.

Jackson, Andrew, 137, 171, 179, 298, 499, 521.
James, Charles T., 291-292, 293.
James, William, 76.
Japanese, American attitude toward, 52, 55, 321.
Jasper, John, 493, 495-496.
Jazz music, 548.
Jeanes Fund, 357, 361.
Jefferson, Thomas, 104, 109, 127, 128, 131, 137, 151, 224, 243, 303, 304, 351, 374, 479, 519.
Jernegan, Marcus W., 101, 311.
Jim Crowism, 58, 76, 401, 417.
Johnson, Andrew, 410, 411.
Johnson, Anthony, 104.
Johnson, Georgia D., 473-475.
Johnson, Guy B., 544.
Johnson, James W., 452, 460, 462, 473, 475, 478.
Johnson, Julia M., 449.
Johnson, Rosamund, 464.
Johnson-Jeffries prize fight, 59.
Johnston, Sir Harry H., 85, 117.
Johnston, J. Hugo, 242.
Jolson, Al, 548.
Jones, Charles C., 185, 186, 187, 194,

INDEX

195, 197, 199, 200, 202, 210, 214, 350.
Jones, Jesse T., 365.
Josey, Charles C., 525.
Juvenile delinquency among Negroes, 344, 345.

Kano, 33, 92.
Kansas-Nebraska bill, 137, 141.
Kant, Imanuel, 5, 14.
Kantor, Jacob R., 9.
Kayak culture, 26.
Keane, Augustus H., 29, 30, 31, 35, 36, 48, 225.
Keith, Sir Arthur, 10.
Keith, George, 185.
Kelley, Welbourn, 508.
Kemble, Fannie, 295.
Kennedy, Louise V., 343, 344.
Kerlin, Robert T., 485.
Kidd, Benjamin, 488.
King, Rufus, 129.
Kingsley, Mary, 37, 38, 46, 47.
Klein, Arthur J., 516.
Klein, Julius, 315.
Kosciusko, 351.
Krapp, George P., 94.
Krehbiel, Henry E., 462.
Kroeber, Alfred L., 3, 6, 11.
Ku Klux Klan, 18, 234, 416, 516.

Labor, free, 157; immigrant, 55, 155, 157, 312, 332, 335, 341; Negro, *see* Negro labor; skilled, 316; slave, 83, 109, 150, 153-154, 155, 157, 238; unskilled, 315, 335-336.
  agent, 336, 337, 338, 339.
  conflicts between whites and Negroes, 55-57, 61, 68, 153-154, 251, 310, 311, 312, 316, 328, 329, 332-333, 409, 416, 538.
  policy, 320-321, 326.
  unions, 316, 317, 321, 513.
Lafayette, 119, 254.
Laing, Major, 27.
Lamarck, 5.
Lane, Lunsford, 285.
Larsen, Nella, 482.

Las Casas, Bishop, 115.
Lasker, Bruno, 65, 66.
Law and justice, race antagonism and, 61, 421.
Lawrence, Abbott, 293.
Laws, bastardy, 107; fornication, 107; limiting franchise, 311.
Leavell, R. H., 336, 338.
Leavell, Ullin W., 511.
Lee, Richard, 521.
Lee, Robert E., 409, 412.
Le Fevre, Louis, 274, 275.
Léger, Jacques N., 114.
Leibnitz, 5.
Le Jeau, 185.
Leonard, Arthur G., 38, 39, 41.
Lewinson, Paul, 414, 418, 420.
Leys, Norman, 274.
Liehle, George, 210, 213, 491.
Ligon, R., 116.
"Lily white" movement in Republican party, 418-419.
Lincoln, Abraham, 142, 299, 410, 411, 138.
Linnæus, 5.
Lippmann, Walter, 61, 216, 232.
Literacy rate of free and slave states, 155.
Literature, stereotypes of Negroes in, 62. *See also* Negro literature.
Livingstone, David, 23, 87, 88.
Locke, Alain, 484.
Locke, John, 186.
London Company, 99, 100.
Long, Huey, 416.
Long, Jefferson, 333.
Louis XIV of France, 117.
Ludlam, 185.
Lundy, Benjamin, 193.
Luschan, von, 91.
Lynching, 57, 59, 61, 62, 231, 433-440, 538.

Macon County, Alabama, study of plantation community in, 445.
Madison, James, 137.
Makemie, Francis, 197.
Malinowski, Bronislaw, 91.

Mall, Franklin P., 225.
Mandingo empire, 92.
Manumission, 109, 150, 238, 239, 240, 241, 243 ff., 250. *See also* Church, the, and slavery.
Marginal man, 281, 534.
Maroons, 119.
Marshal, Samuel, 186.
Marshall, C. K., 302.
Martyr, Peter, 116.
Mason, George, 126, 293.
Massie, Susanne W., 303.
Mathews, E., 212.
Matlack, Lucius C., 203, 204, 465.
Matrilinearism, 91.
Mayo, M. J., 226.
McClelland, George M., 473.
McCord, C. H., 431.
McCuistion, Fred, 359.
McDonall, Robert, 500.
McDuffie, George, 160.
McHenry, George, 159.
McKay, Claude, 475, 477, 478, 482, 550-551.
McTyiere, Holland N., 208.
Meade, William, 195, 196, 521, 522.
Meharry Medical College, 501.
Mencken, Henry L., 231.
Menzies, Allan, 43.
Methodism and slavery, 74, 201 ff.
Methodist Episcopal Church South organized, 207; zeal for evangelizing Negroes, 208.
Mexican labor, 55-56, 314, 317, 320-321.
Micheaux, Elder, 549.
Migration, westward, 151, 174, 296, 312, 331. *See also* Negro migration.
Miles, N. R., 334.
Mill, John S., 218
Miller, Herbert A., 16, 19, 57.
Miller, Kelly, 435.
Milligan, R. H., 46.
Mills, Samuel J., 521.
Mirabeau, 119.
Mission boards and Negro education, 355.

Missouri Compromise, 138, 141, 253.
Mitchell, Broadus, 147, 152.
Momboddo, Lord, 90.
Mongloids, 6, 7, 10.
Montesquieu, 12, 13.
Montlosier, Count, 15.
Morandal, 119.
Moravian mission to the Negroes, 188.
Mores, 71-76.
Morton, 5.
Mulatto class, 106, 107, 227, 240-242, 403; superior advantages of, 250, 456.
Muller, 5.
Munford, Beverly B., 126.
Murphy, Edgar G., 509, 529.
Mutation, 10.
Myers, John L., 50.

Narratives, slave, 464.
Nassau, Robert H., 35, 37, 38, 39, 40, 42, 46, 47, 459.
National Association for the Advancement of Colored People, 439, 541.
National Geographic Magazine, 72.
National Recovery Act, 327.
National Urban League, 541.
"Native Problem," 54.
Neau, Elias, 186, 268, 350.
Negro artisans, 57, 96, 154, 277, 305, 310-311, 513.
  artists, 310, 502.
  businesses, 514.
  characteristics, 85 ff.
  children, 399-400; retardation of, 226, 345.
  church, 287, 496-499.
  crime, 61, 230, 231, 282, 344, 424 ff., 455.
  culture, 62, 442 ff., 543-555.
  dances, 548.
  death rate, 368.
  delinquency, 428 ff.
  dependence on white race, 277.
  drama, 483.
  economy, 546.
  education, 223-224, 228, 278, 279-280, 282, 349 ff., 454, 457, 539;

higher, 364; vocational, 323, 328, 356–357, 540; weaknesses of, 358 ff.
families, 276, 345, 398–399, 445–451; desertion among, 86; income of, 372. *See also* Negro home life.
farmers, 231, 323 ff.
folk lore, 95.
free, 238 ff.; descendants of, 451; population in 1860, 245; superior status of, 250, 456; status of, 251 ff., 312, 403–405, 409, 534.
health, 231, 368 ff.
history, 490, 550.
home life, 384 ff.
home ownership, 231.
hospitals, 380.
housing, 343–344, 384–386.
humor, 284.
illegitimacy, 229, 240, 249, 276–277.
illiteracy, 228, 358, 382, 432, 454.
immorality, 229–230.
industrial workers, 309–324, 432. *See also* Labor conflicts.
inferiority, 51, 219, 223–225, 228, 282, 508.
intelligence, 95, 225, 226.
juvenile delinquency, 344.
labor, 57, 309 ff., 331, 333, 336, 372, 513.
leaders, 420, 488 ff., 502–505; doctors, 499–502; preachers, 491–496; teachers, 502.
legal status, 403 ff.; present political status, 417–422.
literature, 459 ff., 550–553.
migration, 57, 234, 312–313, 324, 331 ff., 382, 456, 513; table showing character of, 342.
mortality, 231, 275, 368–370, 375–377, 380, 382, 455; from tuberculosis, 275, 279, 370–376; from venereal disease, 377–378; infant, 279, 376, 381.
music, 95, 452, 455, 460, 462–464, 545, 548.
occupations, 252, 314, 327, 328, 387–388.

population, 335, 341–343, 346, 366, 426.
press, 336, 338, 484, 541–544.
psychology, 58, 281, 535.
religion, 74, 96. *See also* Negro church.
residence areas, 384–386.
servants, 105, 225, 311.
slave owners, 250–251.
urbanization, 312, 343, 347.
women, under slavery, 446; workers, 316, 320, 321, 381.
Negroids, 6, 7, 10.
Nell, William C., 481, 491.
Newbold, N. C., 363.
Nicot, Jean, 165.
Nietzsche, 524.
Nixon, A. L., 419.
Nordicism, 16, 18, 26–27, 523–524, 530.
North Europeans, 6, 55, 340.
Northwest Ordinance, 129.
Norwood, John N., 203, 207.

Odegarde, Peter, 18.
Odum, Howard, 511.
Ogburn, William F., 443.
Ogden, Robert C., 357.
Oglethorpe, 188.
Oldham, J. H., 53.
Oliveira Martins, Joaquim P., 117.
Olivier, Sir Sidney, 50.
Olmsted, Frederick L., 151, 154, 156, 176, 177, 179, 294, 295, 304.
O'Neall, J. B., 261.
O'Neill, Eugene, 483, 504.
Opportunity magazine, 541.
Origin of man, 10, 14, 22, 69.
Origin of race, *see* Race.
Osborn, Henry F., 69.
Osborne, Charles, 193.
Osceola, 242.
Otey, Bishop, 196.
Othello, 464.
Overseers, 120, 152, 263, 278, 406–407.
Ovington, M. W., 501, 502.

Page, Thomas N., 168, 172, 180
Parallel civilizations as a solution of the race problem, 529 ff.

586   INDEX

Pareto, Vilfredo, 216.
Park, Mungo, 30, 88.
Park, Robert E., 217, 444.
Parton, James, 499.
Payne, B. H., 508.
Payne, Daniel A., 493.
Penn, William, 188.
Pennington, W. C., 481.
Peter Martyr, 116.
Peters, Jesse, 210.
Phi Beta Kappa, Negroes in, 455.
Phillips, Ulrich B., 109, 120, 122, 147, 148, 152, 156, 158, 253, 290, 425.
Pickering, 5.
Pierce, E. E., 352.
Pietro, Alonzo, 84.
Pigmentation, 6.
Pinchbeck, Raymond, 372.
Pinckney, Charles C., 129, 130, 194, 209.
Pitman, F. W., 117.
Pitt-Rivers, 54.
Plantation life, 164 ff., 324.
Planters in Virginia Colony, 164.
Pleasants, Robert, 192, 351.
Polk, James K., 139.
Polygamy, 46, 47, 87, 91.
Polygenesis, 10.
Poor whites, 56, 73, 151–152, 153–155, 157, 197, 293, 294, 304, 310, 311, 409, 410, 416, 420, 538.
Pope Urban VIII, 165.
Pouchet, Félix, 4.
Prejudice, race, *see* Race prejudice.
Presbyterian church and slavery, 74, 198 ff.
Prichard, James C., 4, 5.
Propaganda, 53, 60, 67, 235, 483.
Puckett, Newbell N., 95, 459.
Pygmies, 6, 11.

Quakers and slavery, 183, 188–194, 247, 351.

Race, classifications of, 5–7; definitions of, 4–5; meaning of, 3–5; origin of, 9–10.
adjustment, 65 ff., 400–401.
and culture, 8–9.
and religion, 3.
antagonisms, 19, 50 ff.; causes of, 52–59, 60, 67–69; results of, 60–63.
antipathy, 53, 67, 69.
attitudes, 53, 217, 507 ff.; of children, 60, 65–66; of Negroes, 534 ff.
behavior patterns in relation to, 3, 51.
conflict, *see* Race antagonisms.
consciousness, 19, 65, 66, 488 ff.
crossing, 11, 85, 87, 94, 217, 234, 242–243, 250, 456, 528.
culture and, 8–9.
differences, functional, 7–8; in immunity to diseases, 8; in mentality, 8, 9, 61, 224; in susceptibility to disease, 8; structural, 6–7; theories of, 10, 19.
dogma, 217 ff., 508; influence on the Negro, 233 ff., 535.
heredity, 7, 97.
mentality, 8, 9, 61, 90, 224.
myths, 12, 14, 17, 18.
prejudice, 18, 19, 65–71, 154.
pride, *see* Race consciousness.
relations, 4, 11, 19, 61; and racial dogma, 217, 218.
riots, 57, 59, 231, 233, 251.
social aspects of, 11.
theories, 11–18, 19, 224.
traits, 5, 7, 89.
types, 5.
variations, 7–8.
Races, inequality of, 14–16, 17, 51, 61, 219, 224, 524, 525, 528.
migration of, 10, 11.
physical traits of, 5, 7.
Raciation, 9–10.
Randolph, John, 137, 246, 520, 521.
Rape, 230, 425, 427, 434.
Raper, Arthur, 324.
Ratzel, Friedrich, 85, 527.
Read, Hollis, 523.
Reclus, Élisée, 24, 32, 33, 35, 117, 119.

INDEX 587

Reconstruction, 75, 332, 333, 410 ff., 497, 507, 538.
Reformation, the Protestant, and the slave trade, 13.
Religion, in Africa, 37–45; race and, 3. *See also* Negro religion.
Religious Instruction of Negroes, Association for the, 199.
Renaissance, 12.
Rents, high charge to Negroes, 344.
Reuter, Edward B., 19, 459, 553.
Rice, 121, 135, 294, 309.
Rice, David, 199.
Ring, Martha D., 379.
Rippon, *Annual Register*, 213.
Robeson, Paul, 455, 504.
Robinson, Gerald T., 56.
Robinson, James H., 218.
Robinson, John, 198, 199.
Rolfe, John, 100, 165.
Roman, C. V., 283, 502.
Roman Empire, 19.
Roosevelt, Franklin D., 327.
Roosevelt, Theodore, 516.
Rorem, C. Rufus, 379.
Roscoe, John, 38.
Rosenwald Fund, 319, 363, 378.
Ross, E. A., 528.
Ross, Frank A., 335.
Rousseau, 12, 13, 14.
Ruffin, Judge, 263, 406, 424.
Rugg, Harold, 457.
Rush, Benjamin, 499.
Rush, Richard, 521.
Russell, John H., 104, 105, 106, 240, 403.
Russworm, John, 484.

Saint-Hilaire, Geoffroy, 4, 5.
Samford, William H., 431.
Saxon, Rufus, 353.
Sayre, James D., 523.
Scalawag, 410, 413, 415, 421.
Scarborough, John, 190.
Schell, William G., 508.
Schlegel, Friedrich, 14.
Schomberg, Dr., 490.
Schopenhauer, 18.

Schulius, George, 188.
Scott, Emmett J., 337.
Scott, Orange, 204, 206.
Seashore music tests, 95.
Secession, arguments for, 143 ff.
Secker, Bishop, 350.
Seldes, Gilbert, 548.
Semitics, 15–16, 27, 29, 54, 326.
Semple, Robert B., 211, 213.
Servitude, *see* Indenture.
Sex, and race, 59–60; crimes, 230–231.
Shaw, Clifford, 345.
Sherman, Corinne, 86.
Shufeldt, Robert W., 523.
Sieyès, Abbé, 12.
Sikes, John, 190.
Simar, Théophile, 14.
Simmons, William J., 501.
Singleton, Benjamin, 333.
Slater Fund, 364.
Slave artisans, *see* Negro artisans.
  codes, 118–119, 260 ff.
  crime, 265–266, 425–426, 536.
  insurrections, *see* Insurrections.
  labor, 83, 109, 150, 153–154, 155, 157, 238, 278.
  laws, 260 ff.; fugitive, 103, 111, 140.
  occupations, 252.
  population, 153, 161, 239.
  quarters, 168.
  songs, 452, 490, 547.
  trade, 13, 83–84, 117 ff., 122 ff., 239, 274–275; attempts to suppress, 125–135.
Slaveholders, Negro, 251.
Slavery, in medieval Europe, 11–12, 108; in Roman Empire, 19; in United States, development of, 51, 99 ff., 121–125; in West Indies, 114 ff.; origin of, 83.
  economics of, 13, 109, 118, 120, 135–137, 146 ff., 291–296.
  effects of, on immigration, 155–157; on manufacturing, 152, 158–159, 166, 291–293; on Negroes, 75, 274 ff.; on whites, 157, 159, 162, 177, 201, 214, 290 ff.

INDEX

Slavery, justification of, 51, 63, 108, 110, 149, 161, 162, 214, 224, 298, 301.
political aspects of, 125–135, 137–144, 160–161, 296–299.
social aspects of, 153, 162, 168 ff.
Slaves, as property, 108, 263, 264, 406; Christianizing of, 74, 83, 108, 114–115, 121, 183 ff., 263, 285–287, 299, 349; education of, 150; effect of, on land values, 148–149; ignorance of, 150, 152; investment in, 148–149; legal status of, 260 ff., 406; life of, on plantation, 172; price of, 148; punishment of, 260 ff., 407, 425; religious life of, 173, 286–287.
Sloane, Sir Hans, 93.
Smith, Hoke, 416.
Smith, James, 246.
Smith, James McCune, 252, 257, 484, 500, 537.
Smith, Jaret, 481.
Smith, S. L., 363.
Smith, William, 246.
Smith. William B., 526–527.
Snavely, Tipton R., 336.
Social organization of the old South, 72–73, 175, 179, 180, 302–303; after the Civil War, 75–76, 408 ff.
Society for the Propagation of the Gospel in Foreign Parts, 185, 186, 187, 194, 349, 350.
Solid South, 416–422.
Solomon, Job, 93.
Songhoy, 92.
Soule, Joshua, 205.
South Europeans, 55, 326, 340.
Southern Baptist Convention, 212.
Southern Education Board, 357.
Southey, Thomas, 114, 116.
Soviet system of marriage, 60.
Spencer, Herbert, 90.
Spirits in African religion, 38–42.
Spirituals, *see* Negro music.
Spivak, John L., 433.
Spratt, L. W., 156.
Spring, Lindley, 89, 90.
Squatter sovereignty, 139, 140.
Stafford, A. O., 159.

Stanley, Henry M., 23.
Status and race, 58, 68, 73.
Stephenson, Gilbert, 510.
Stevens, Thaddeus, 412, 413.
Stiles, Joseph, 200.
Stoddard, Lothrop, 16, 523, 525.
Stone, Alfred H., 155, 157, 158, 510.
Stoughton, Amanda L., 376.
Stowe, Harriet B., 465.
Stroud, George M., 261, 262, 263, 264, 267, 407.
Stubbs, Bishop, 17.
Subordination of the Negro as a solution of the race problem, 524.
Sudanese, 29 ff.
Sugar, 116–117, 118, 120, 121, 135, 294, 298, 309.
Sumner, William G., 70, 507, 508, 513.
Sunderland, Le Roy, 204.
Superiority complexes, 73.
Sweinfurth, 85.
Sydenstricker, Edgar, 369.
Sydnor, Charles S., 246, 249, 256.
Syphilis, 378.

Taboos, 71, 90, 217.
Tagore, Rabindranath, 530.
Talbot, John, 185.
Tanner, Henry M., 493.
Tariff, 160–161, 298.
Tatom, Absolom, 248.
Taut, François, 4.
Taylor, Alva, 511.
Taylor, John, 521.
Taylor, John W., 137.
Teasdale, John, 135.
Tests, intelligence, 8, 55, 61, 95, 96, 227; Seashore music, 95.
Teutonism, 16.
Texas question, 138.
Thomas, Edgar G., 210.
Thomas, Samuel, 185, 349.
Thomas, W. I., 90.
Thomas, William H., 431.
Thompson, Anna J., 431.
Thompson, Charles L., 201.
Thompson, Clara, 473.
Thompson, Edgar T., 99, 105, 106, 146.

INDEX

Thornton, William, 521.
Thorpe, Francis N., 155.
Thurman, Howard W., 65.
Thurnwald, Richard, 91.
Tiffany, C. C., 186, 194.
Tillman, Ben, 77, 416.
Tobacco, 100, 106, 108, 109, 120, 121, 135, 146, 150, 165, 294, 298, 309, 310, 313.
Tocqueville, Alexis de, 164, 290, 304.
Todd, John, 197.
Todd, T. Wingate, 226.
Toomer, Jean, 551.
Topinard, Paul, 4, 5.
Toussaint L'Ouverture, 119.
Tozzer, Alfred M., 5.
Tredgold, A. F., 226.
Trexler, Harrison A., 161.
Trollope, Mrs., 178.
Tsetse fly, 25, 30, 31.
Tuberculosis among Negroes, 370–376.
Turner, Frederick J., 110.
Turner, Nat, 271, 272, 351, 403, 480, 536.
Tyler, E. B., 22, 225.
Tylor, W. Russell, 511.

Ukuku, 35.
Underground Railroad, 103, 193.
Unemployment, 317–320.
Urbanization, 314, 335; Negro, 312, 335, 343, 347.
Uselton, Lida J., 377.

Van Deusen, John G., 159.
Vardaman, 76, 416.
Vassa, Gustavus, 464.
Venereal disease, 229, 377–378.
Vesey, Denmark, 257, 268, 270, 351, 480, 492.
Vocational training for Negroes, *see* Negro education.
Vogt, Karl, 225.
Voltaire, 13.

Wagner, Richard, 15.
Waite, 85.
Walker, David, 464, 534, 537.

Wall, James, 256.
Wallis, Wilson D., 228.
Ward, Artemus, 236.
Ward, Herbert, 86.
Warden, Carl J., 6, 8, 10.
Washington, Booker T., 278, 356, 363, 426, 465, 489–490, 503, 509, 514, 516, 526, 539.
Washington, Bushrod, 520, 521.
Washington, George, 203, 467.
Watt, James, 150.
Wayland, Francis, 162, 211, 212.
Weale, Putnam, 69.
Webb, Charles H., 500.
Webster, Daniel, 521.
Weeks, John H., 41, 44, 459, 460.
Weeks, Stephen B., 192.
Wertenbaker, Thomas J., 100.
Wesley, Charles, 252, 255, 333, 334.
Wesley Houses, 515.
Wesley, John, Negro mission of, 187, 188, 201.
Wesleyan Methodist church, 206.
Weston, George M., 153.
Wheatley, Phillis, 467, 472.
White, Clarence C., 455.
White, George L., 463.
White, Walter F., 483.
"White Man's Burden," 54.
Whitfield, George, Negro mission of, 188, 201.
Whitman, Alberry A., 471.
Whitney, Eli, 135, 136, 150.
Whittier, John G., 465, 481.
Wightman, William M., 209, 210.
Wilberforce, Samuel, 194, 195.
Wilberforce University, 248.
Wilder, Francis S., 427.
Wiley, Hugh, 232.
Wilhelm II, of Germany, 16.
Williams, George W., 252, 334, 354, 405.
Williams, Roger, 210.
Williamson, Atkin, 186.
Willits, Joseph H., 318.
Willoughby, William C., 36.
Wilmer, R. H., 196.
Wilmot Proviso, 139.

Wilson, Henry, 126, 128, 130, 134, 138, 141, 412, 414.
Wilson, John L., 38, 88.
Wilson, Woodrow, 136, 137, 138, 142.
Winans, Dr., 208.
Winthrop, John, 121, 218, 290.
Wise, Henry A., 293.
Wissler, Clark, 9, 26, 72, 93.
Witch doctor, 44.
Woman, in Africa, 45–47; Negro, 446; subject sex, 18, 218.
Women workers, 314, 316, 321, 371, 381.
Wood, Samuel R., 493.
Woodbury, Robert M., 381.
Woodson, Carter, 241, 245, 252, 334, 352, 497, 498, 514.
Woofter, Thomas J., 516.
Woolman, John, 189.

Work, "made," 319.
Work, Monroe N., 338, 346, 426, 463.
Wren, Sir Christopher, 167.
Wright, Louis T., 501.
Wundt, Wilhelm, 216.
Wyman, Jeffries, 225.

Yancey, Charles, 304.
Yarbrough, William A., 148, 149, 152, 159, 160.
Yeomen, 175–176.
Y. M. C. A. and race, 76, 418, 512, 515.
Y. W. C. A. and race, 418, 515.
Young, Louise, 511.
Young, Robert A., 508.

Zinzendorf, Count, Negro mission of, 188.